Between the Black Box and the White Cube

EXPANDED CINEMA AND POSTWAR ART

Andrew V. Uroskie

UNIVERSITY OF CHICAGO PRESS Chicago and London

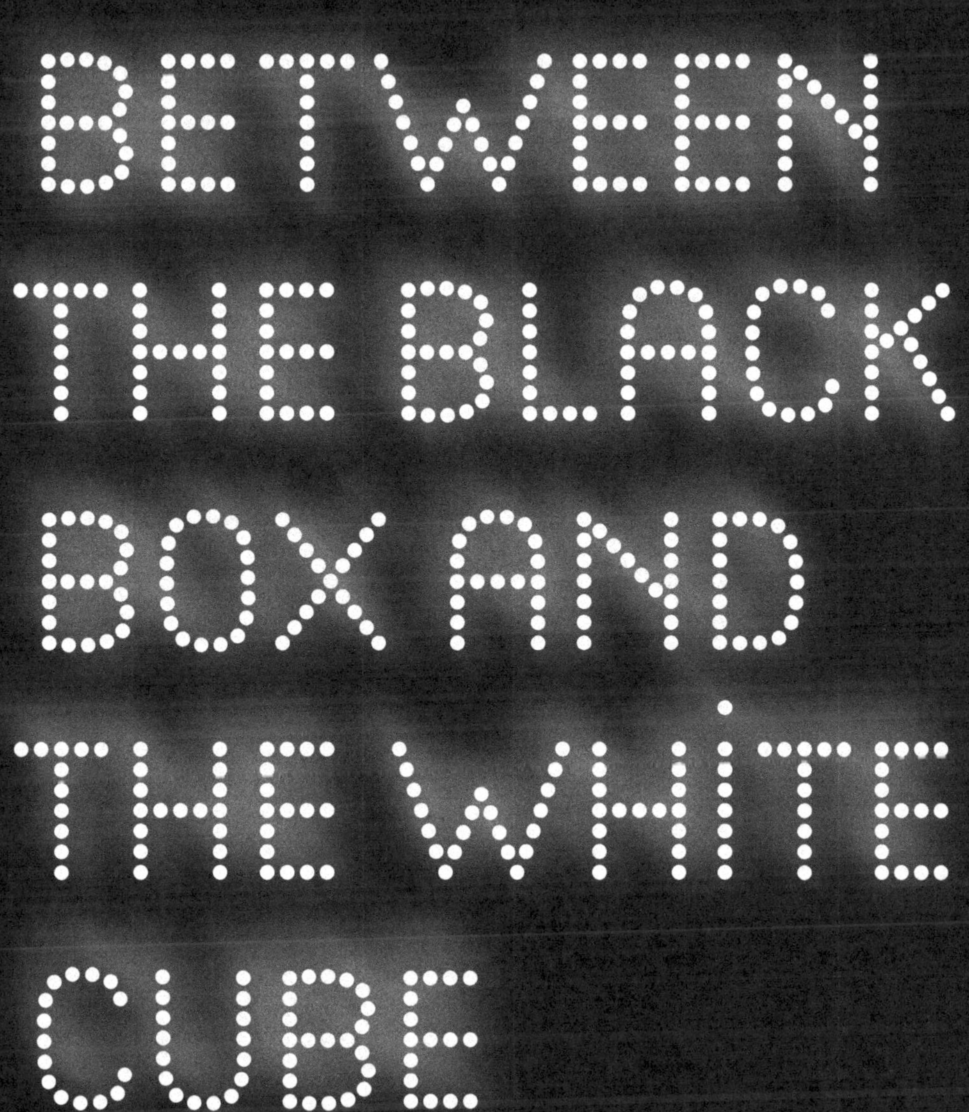
BETWEEN
THE BLACK
BOX AND
THE WHITE
CUBE

The University of Chicago Press, Chicago 60637
The University of Chicago Press, Ltd., London

23 3 4 5

ISBN-13: 978-0-226-84298-1 (cloth)
ISBN-13: 978-0-226-84299-8 (paper)
ISBN-13: 978-0-226-10902-2 (e-book)
DOI: 10.7208/9780226

Library of Congress Cataloging-in-Publication Data

Uroskie, Andrew V., author.
Between the black box and the white cube : expanded cinema and postwar art / Andrew V. Uroskie.
pages cm
Includes bibliographical references and index.
ISBN 978-0-226-84298-1 (cloth : alk. paper)—ISBN 978-0-226-84299-8 (pbk. : alk. paper)—ISBN (invalid) 978-0-226-10902-2 (e-book) 1. Art and motion pictures. 2. Art, Modern. 3. Art—20th century. I. Title.
N72.M6U76 2014
700.9'045—dc23

2013022931

TO ZABET

Contents

Acknowledgments

This project originated at UC Berkeley between 2002 and 2004 and was revised, rewritten, then revised again over the next half decade as I moved from San Francisco to Atlanta to New York City. When I began, exhibitions like *Seeing Time* (1999) at the SFMoMA and *Into the Light* (2001) at the Whitney were unprecedented, and the literature was only beginning to adapt to the new "cinematic aesthetic." In a decade's time, the moving image has become a ubiquitous dimension of contemporary art, if perhaps one too uncritically accepted.

I was greatly fortunate to be at Berkeley during the existence of an incredible interdisciplinary academic community across the Departments of Rhetoric, Art History, Film, and Performance. First and foremost, I owe an incalculable debt to Kaja Silverman—her engagement, support, and friendship have been sustaining, and she has continuously served as a model of both intellectual ambition and pedagogical refinement. I am also profoundly grateful to Anne Wagner and Anton Kaes for many years of wise counsel and genuine friendship throughout the writing process. Shannon Jackson, Linda Williams, Judith Butler, Hubert Dreyfus, Christina Kiaer, and T. J. Clark were all formative in shaping my thinking, as were my extraordinary graduate student colleagues Eve Meltzer, Huey Copeland, Josh Shannon, Julia Bryan-Wilson, Homay King, Domietta Torlasco, Scott Combs, Ara Osterweil, Kris Paulsen, John Muse, Julian Myers, Guo-Guin Hong, Michael Sicinski, Patrick Anderson, and Spyros Papapetros, among many others. Pam Lee and Jeffrey Schnapp at Stanford, Edith Kramer at the Pacific Film Archive, and Benjamin Weil at SFMoMA were all supportive interlocutors during my years in the Bay Area. Since then, Melissa Ragona, Frazer Ward, Judith Rodenbeck, Gloria Sutton, Mike Zyrd, Tess Takahashi, Liz Kotz, T. J. Demos, Federico Windhausen, Julia Robinson, Eivind Røssaak, Noam Elcott, and Tom McDonough have all provided valuable support and inspiration. Special recognition is due to Lawrence Douglas at Amherst College and to Slavoj Žižek, Mladen Dolar, and Alenka Zupancic in Ljubljana and Paris for their support during a crucial period before I began graduate study. My faculty colleagues in the Art Department at Stony Brook University have always been tremendously supportive, and my graduate there students have been a fount of intellectual sustenance and camaraderie—they continually amaze and inspire me and make teaching a genuine pleasure.

I am grateful to the critical audiences I have had as I presented this material over many years of annual conferences at the College Art Association and the Society for Cinema and Media Studies, as well as at the University of Chicago, NYU, Columbia University, the CUNY Graduate Center, the University of Pennsylvania, the University of Georgia, Georgia Tech, Simon Fraser, and UC Irvine. Tamara Trodd's symposium Screen/Space: The Projected Image in Contemporary Art in Edinburgh, the Nam June Paik symposium organized by the Institut National d'Histoire de l'Art in Paris, and the symposium on cinema and contemporary visual art organized by an international audiovisual studies group in Gorizia, Italy, were all especially valuable opportunities in which I was able to engage international scholars in the field.

I was fortunate to have my research supported by the Chancellor's Fellowship at Berkeley and a Humanities Center Fellowship at Stanford, as well as by faculty development grants at Georgia Tech and Stony Brook University. Early versions of this material have been published in the journals *October*, *Grey Room*, and *Animation* as well as in the anthologies *Art and the Moving Image: A Critical Reader* and *Screen/Space: The Projected Image in Contemporary Art*. I am grateful to the editors for their valuable feedback.

Susan Bielstein, my editor at the University of Chicago Press, has been a steadfast supporter from the beginning, and her encouragement and counsel have truly proven invaluable. Anthony Burton and Norma Sims Roche provided expert guidance with regard to image copyrights and copyediting, respectively, in the final stretch. A special thanks to my dedicated and tireless graduate assistant Jennie Goldstein, without whose editorial and logistical acumen I would have surely never escaped the black hole of image permissions.

None of this would have been possible without the unwavering support of my extended family.

This book is dedicated to Zabet Patterson: my toughest critic and closest friend.

INTRODUCTION: FROM MEDIUM TO SITE

Framing Exhibition

Approaching *The Paradise Institute,* a work by the Canadian artists Janet Cardiff and George Bures Miller, we find ourselves in a doubly enclosed space. Already within the "white cube" of the gallery, we encounter a large, two-level plywood box complete with stairs and doorways leading in and out. Looking inside from a distance, we can just make out the plush stadium seating commonly associated with the multiplex theater. Yet there is nothing slick or manufactured about the surrounding plywood construction—on the contrary, it seems to have been practically thrown together. Both the box and its interior seem out of place in a museum setting, albeit for different reasons.

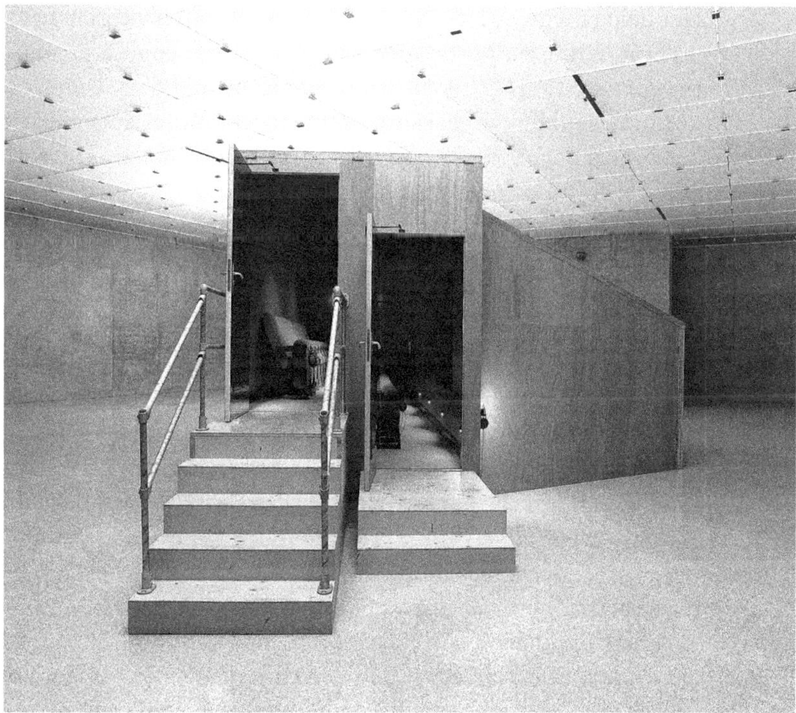

Figure I.1. Janet Cardiff and George Bures Miller, *The Paradise Institute*, 2001. Approach.

While the box is not without a certain minimalist aesthetic, it fails to hold our attention as form. Circumnavigating the work does not prompt us to reflect on its structure per se, so much as it heightens our anticipation to discover what lies within. The kind of theatricality invoked is not the phenomenological sense of the term with which Michael Fried designated the pull of minimalist sculpture, but more the prosaic feeling of suspense with which we might await a fairground attraction or a theatrical spectacle.[1] And as with such attractions, here one may not simply enter, but must first obtain a ticket and wait in line for the performance to commence. Even at a distance, *The Paradise Institute* evokes a social space whose conventions are distinct from those of the art gallery or museum.

Climbing the steps, we find headphones waiting on the seats. When we place them over our ears, the exterior sounds of the gallery are quickly muffled, and our immediate aural environment is swallowed up in the projected static of white noise. Darkness follows as the doors to the outside are closed. Simultaneously relaxed by the seating and made anxious by the claustrophobic enclosure (how would we leave if we needed to get out?), we wait for the show to begin. But as soon as the noise of our fellow audience members falls away, noise and conversation begin anew. Over to the left, and just behind us on the right, people are again talking—new people. Cardiff and Miller recorded the audio for the piece using binaural technology, which gives a powerful sense of spatial location to the sounds we hear. While aurally isolated from the actual people around us, we hear the conversations of people who seem to surround us. There is a sense of uncanny doubling as real and recorded sounds overlap and coalesce.

We hear people rustling in their seats, taking off items of clothing, and whispering to one another—all preparing for the movie, for the main attraction. A cell phone goes off and a woman quickly tells the caller, "I have to go, I'm in a movie." Occurring in an eerily precise stereo sound and at seemingly discrete spatial locations, the experience is quite realistic—which is not at all to say that it is simply taken for reality. Even those spectators who might have been momentarily fooled quickly recognize that they are listening to an illusion. But far from ruining the work, the spectator's double consciousness—her simultaneous experience of real and recorded sounds, and her ability to distinguish between them—is fundamental to the experience the work seeks to engender. For within *The Paradise Institute*, reality is not so much banished as redoubled, creating a spectatorial environment distinct from yet coexistent with the physical space of the theater.

As the screen lights up, its glow falls on a miniature diorama of seats, a proscenium, and a balcony, at the far edge of which we might understand ourselves to be seated. Cardiff and Miller have here constructed an alternate universe, a heterotopia in miniature. Gazing on this tiny diorama,

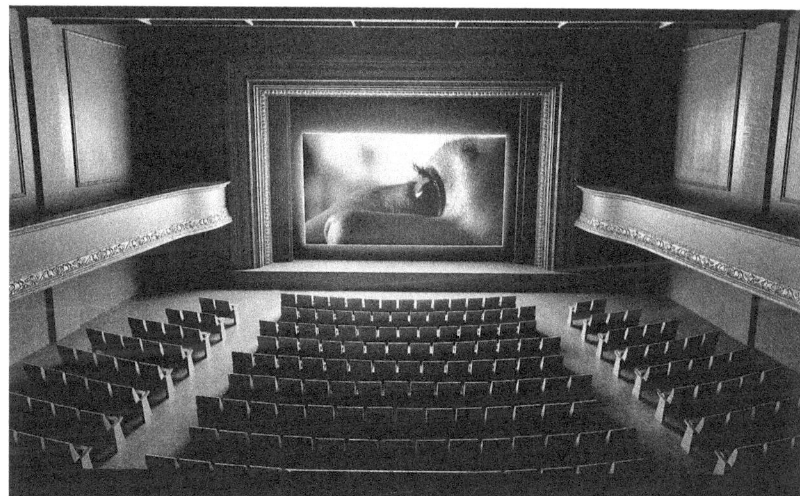

Figure I.2. Janet Cardiff and George Bures Miller, *The Paradise Institute*, 2001. Interior.

seated comfortably on our full-sized chairs, we can give ourselves over to the spectacle because we are secure in the knowledge that it *is* a spectacle and that we are situated on the outside of that spectacle, looking in. The headphones we are given to wear—like the diorama before us and the makeshift theater in which we sit—draw attention to the staged character of the illusion. Yet *The Paradise Institute* will not allow any secure boundary between reality and illusion to be maintained. If the apparatus is foregrounded, it is not for the purpose of dismissing illusion and maintaining a contravening reality, but rather so as to throw our demarcation of reality and illusion into doubt.

Suddenly, we are addressed by woman's voice just to our left: "Here's your drink ... have some of my popcorn." In between distracting bursts of crunching, she says that she has heard of the film we are about to see, that it was based on a real story, that the experiments carried out in it were done by Americans in World War II. But then again, she may be mistaken—that may be another movie. On the screen, the film begins. But with this voice beside us, it is as if we have already been placed in the center of the fiction, rather than simply before it. Dramatic elements are now erupting all around, and it is not clear they even belong to the same drama. Before us on the screen, we see a nurse approach a man strapped to a bed. His chest is bare. While he begs her to stop, she slowly bends down and presses her lips to his chest, kissing and then lightly biting him. The scene is emotionally charged, but like the voices, it solicits our attention without grounding it in a coherent narrative.

A voice from the audience behind us crudely interjects, "Now that's nursing!"—distracting us again, pulling our attention away from the characters on the screen and toward those seated in the audience. At several points, the woman's voice beside us asks whether "you might have accidentally left the stove on at home." As she does so, the film cuts to scenes of a burning house, which feel completely exterior to the narrative space of the film, despite the fact that that narrative space has not been fully established. This other scene strives to become "our" house, despite our conscious disavowal. And it is a house—as Freud once described the subject of the unconscious—of which we are an uncertain or absent master. "Do you want some more popcorn?" we are repeatedly asked, and it soon begins to feel as if we are *choosing* to answer with our silence. As repetition works performatively to assign ownership and responsibility, we cannot help but feel implicated in the conversation. We leave the comforts of our typical, distanced spectatorship and begin to occupy an awkward space inside the fiction.

As the story evolves, the uneasy distinction between the two sides of the screen begins to break down completely. A diabolical man merely evoked in the narrative seems to become detached from it, crossing over into our space on this side of the screen. A sense of vertigo overtakes us as we are constantly thrust into new and different locations. As the suspenseful music builds and the screen goes blank, we lose all ability to discern where the fiction is located. The diabolical man, now beside us in the audience, laughingly describes our predicament: "You thought you were pretty smart—playing both sides. How long did you think it could last?" We hear a crowd of people pounding on the plywood theater within which we are seated, demanding that we "get out!" As the crowd begins shouting a countdown, we see a burning house on the screen before the film abruptly ends, the doors to the outside open up, and we file out of the black box for the newly comforting light of the gallery.

Within *The Paradise Institute*, we do not really confuse fact and fiction because we know full well that everything taking place is a fiction. But it is not a coherent or delimited fiction. It is fractured, multiple—existing in too many places at once. Rather than remaining in its proper place on the far side of the screen, its fictional world seems to spill over into the space of the theater—crowding us out, leaving us with no escape. Tellingly, the work begins with an admonishment that the spectator will not be able to leave once the performance has begun, and unlike traditional theaters, it contains no brightly glowing exit sign reassuring us that its fictional world can be quickly and definitively left behind in the event of an emergency. In this, Cardiff and Miller's work seems not only to hyperbolize the enclosure of the cinematic situation, but to allegorize its egress into a more wide-ranging cinematization of society—a condition it presents as ambivalently pleasurable and nightmarish at the same time.

From Medium to Site

The word "paradise" derives from the Old Iranian *pari* (around) + *daiz* (build), used to designate an artificially constructed enclosure. The work's title refers not merely to an imagined world, but to the specific conditions of imaging and imagination made possible by the cinematic enclosure. *The Paradise Institute* itself is doubly enclosed: physically situated within the art gallery's white cube, it nevertheless stages a dramatic encounter with the cinema theater's black box and thus with a tradition of aesthetic exhibition and spectatorship quite antithetical to the space within which it is housed. The work plays out within a miniature theater that both is and is not a cinematheque. The seats are real, comfortable—we are encouraged to sit in them. Yet the diorama before the screen is miniaturized, the space compressed as if viewed at great distance through an enormous telephoto lens. The scene is eminently theatrical. The art gallery—and by extension, the art world—has become a place to stage the cinematic experience.

These two cultural sites—art gallery and cinema theater—have long been conceptualized in diametric opposition. Within the gallery's brightly illuminated container, the aesthetic spectator navigates a physical encounter with the space of the object-cum-installation in a temporality of her choosing. The cinema's black box, by contrast, intentionally negates both bodily mobility and environmental perception so as to transport the viewer *away* from her present time and local space, into the narrative space of the cinematic world on screen.[2] These two institutions, these two models of exhibition and spectatorship, would seem irreconcilable. Yet since the 1990s, artists and arts institutions around the world have embraced the idea of moving-image installation to such an extent that it has already become the norm rather than the exception within contemporary art galleries and museums.

The confusion of inner and outer space within *The Paradise Institute*, its ambivalent position between the traditions of the black box and the white cube, is metonymic of the ambivalent exhibitionary situation of contemporary moving-image art practice. Art institutions have responded by increasingly accommodating the traditional conditions of cinematic exhibition, creating de facto black boxes that exist uneasily alongside their familiar white cubes. But the creation of these spaces alone has done little to reconcile many of the vexing aesthetic and conceptual issues raised by the meteoric rise of the moving image in and as a contemporary art practice. How are we to understand the hybrid new institutional situation these works have entailed—this complex of exhibitionary and spectatorial models adopted from the traditional sites of the black box and the white cube?

The Paradise Institute's explicit staging of these disjunctive sites may be hyperbolic, but it is hardly idiosyncratic. In fact, such a staging can be seen to reflect a more generalized turn away from long-standing concerns with the specificity of a work's *medium* toward a newfound importance of thinking about the specificity of a work's *site*. Rooted in a response to 1960s minimalism and Maurice Merleau-Ponty's phenomenology of embodied experience, postwar art criticism first began to articulate a concern with site as a means of shifting attention away from the art object as a discrete, isolated, and autonomous entity toward a more encompassing concern with the situation or environment in which any aesthetic encounter inevitably takes place.[3] A popular interpretation of site specificity—one that reached its peak with the debates over Richard Serra's *Tilted Arc* (1981–1989)—held that an artwork and its physical site were indissociably linked. Serra contended that to move his sculpture was to destroy it, since its creation was utterly specific to the physical location where it was installed.[4] Yet this literal and material conception was only one of a number of ways of thinking about site. For if minimalism shifted attention from the self-contained object to the environmental conditions of its display, the postminimalist practice of institutional critique would explore those conditions in their social, cultural, and institutional parameters. As has been articulated in a broad and diverse literature, postminimalist works exchanged a phenomenology of individual perception for a cognitive and conceptual analysis of institutions and practices, making the artwork a function of its site, always already enfolded within a cultural frame that guides and prestructures the aesthetic encounter.[5]

Such a *situational* perspective is fundamental to any investigation of the moving image in contemporary art, in which the institutional and cultural dialectic of the black box and the white cube remains a perplexing quandary. Over the last decade, this renewed conception of site has been the focus of a wide-ranging literature attempting to think about the newfound installation of the moving image within contemporary art in terms of a more general theorization of place, site, and situation.[6] Our contemporary experience of place has itself become inextricably bound up with the technologies and institutions of mediation. Moving images never merely represent place, they must always also take place—they must be produced and exhibited within material spaces that are themselves structured through social, institutional, and discursive vectors. Furthermore, the moving image is itself radically nonlocalizable: it exists simultaneously in the spatiotemporal event of projection and in the realm of imaginative transport that the act of projection makes possible. Giuliana Bruno, for instance, has given particular emphasis to the kinds of displacement occurring within the body of the cinematic spectator as cognitive and affective linkages are formed through a logic of association. Stressing the bivalency of our common rhetoric of the moving image, she describes the "mobile dynamics involved in the act of viewing films, even if the spectator is seemingly static. The (im)mobile spectator moves across an imaginary path, traversing multiple sites and times. Her fictional navigation connects distant moments and far-apart places."[7] For Bruno, as for many contemporary theorists, the complex nature of cinema's movement belies any totalizing critique of cinematic illusionism—a critique itself born of early attempts to straitjacket film into the modernist paradigm of medium-specificity.[8]

Indeed, for roughly the first half century since its birth, cinema's relationship to artistic modernism had almost invariably been conceived as a question of ontology—as a search for cinema's singular essence. Through reflection on cinema's specificity as a medium, the idea went, this essential nature could be isolated and purified within a properly modernist art of cinema. Yet time and time again, cinema's complex ensemble of social and technological factors frustrated this mode of reduction.[9] Not only could cinema not be definitively confined to a singular material ontology, it could not even be definitively separated from the rival arts of painting, music, sculpture, and performance. But for artists and critics of the postwar era, the idea that cinema might never be able to be fashioned into a properly modernist art began to seem less of a problem with cinema than a problem with the medium-specific conception of artistic modernism.

For Rosalind Krauss, who has described this expansion in terms of a "post-medium condition," its historical origins were grounded in three fundamental events of the early 1970s.[10] First, she contends, a widespread critique of presence within poststructuralist philosophy had the effect of making the quest for singular essences within aesthetic modernism seem hopelessly quixotic. Second, the aesthetic implications of Marcel Duchamp's readymades were finally internalized within conceptual art and were understood to raise a problem of *art in general* that threatened to subsume the consideration of any given individual. But it is Krauss's third event—the historical arrival of video technology and its "instant success" within art practice—that touches most directly on the present investigation.

For despite the many attempts to locate the "specificity" of video as an artistic medium, Krauss argues, video could not be definitively separated from broadcast television, and thus it was necessarily implicated within "diverse forms, spaces, and temporalities for which no single instance seems to provide a formal unity for the whole."[11] Modernist theory "found itself defeated" by this "constitutive heterogeneity," which precipitated a larger shift away from both a critical paradigm of medium-specificity and those forms of artistic practice—such as the structural film—fundamentally grounded on that paradigm.[12] Krauss's argument here harks back a quarter century, to her 1976 essay for the inaugural issue of *October*. In "Video: An Aesthetics of Narcissism," Krauss had described video as raising a particular challenge to the modernist conception of medium-specificity. While the material technology of video is obvious enough, she wrote, "the ease of defining it in terms of its machinery does not seem to coincide with accuracy; and my own experience of video keeps urging me towards the psychological model." Against her own commitment to Clement Greenberg's formalist paradigm, she admitted that video art was oriented more by "the reception and projection of an image, and the human psyche used as a conduit" than by any interrogation of the material qualities of the apparatus itself.[13]

But what seemed a difficulty specific to video soon became, within Krauss's "Sculpture in the Expanded Field," a more general problem with the modernist conception of medium *tout court*. Leveraging the structural anthropology of Claude Levi-Strauss, she suggested that the organization of contemporary art was no longer "dictated by the conditions of a particular medium . . . on the grounds of material, or, for that matter, the perception of material," but rather around "terms that are felt to be in opposition within a cultural situation."[14] The shift she announced, from an analysis of a work's material medium to an analysis of a work's *situation* within a cultural field—was provocative in its time and enduring in its application.[15] Krauss's use of the term "expanded" is intriguing because the term was not particularly common within the art criticism of the period. It seems reasonable to assume that she appropriated it from one of her essay's key examples: Robert Morris, who had employed the term in his 1966 "Notes on Sculpture" thirteen years before. Morris uses the term three separate times in his conclusion to this canonical text on minimalism, first contending that the sculptural work is no longer the myopic focus of attention, but simply one component within a newly "expanded situation." He adds that recent works have "expanded the terms of sculpture by a more emphatic focusing on the very conditions under which certain kinds of objects are seen," and concludes by reiterating that the sculptural object must henceforth be understood within an aesthetic situation that has become both "more complex and expanded."[16]

Few would dispute the obvious aesthetic and conceptual lineage from "Notes on Sculpture" to Krauss's "Sculpture in the Expanded Field," in which Krauss would take Morris up on both his "complexity" and his "expansion" of the sculptural field. What has been insufficiently acknowledged is that the rhetoric that Morris employs so emphatically was decidedly not idiosyncratic at the time *he* was writing. Morris might have been the first to apply it to the sculptural situation. But he would have been well aware that the predominant reference point for aesthetic "expansion" in New York circa 1966 was to be found in a contemporary rhetoric of expanded cinema. Neither Morris nor Krauss has acknowledged this link. And to the extent that the expanded cinema would enter the retrospective art historical consciousness, it would do so through a text that—quite inadvertently—functioned to conceal the close historical association between these two correlative expansions.

Situating Expanded Cinema

As Anne Wagner has noted, the hyperbolically rigorous formulation of Krauss's diagrammatic structures in "Sculpture in the Expanded Field" suggests a palpable yearning for something like a scientific model of art criticism—one in which "the idiom of sculpture might thus be plotted and structured, schematized and categorized, so that what is new and relevant in ongoing practice could be cleanly and confidently intelligible, its proper place laid open to view."[17] Krauss describes her field as "logically expanded" yet contained by a "finite set of related positions." The continual movement from one to another of these positions is "entirely logical" and the "strongest work will reflect the condition of the logical space."[18] Humanism was in crisis in the 1970s, and its attempts to renew and reassert itself by means of the cultural credibility of science were suddenly everywhere in evidence. Yet beyond this more general context, there was a more specific discursive lineage from which Krauss would have wanted to distance herself: Gene Youngblood's *Expanded Cinema*.

The two texts, occurring at either end of the 1970s, occupied extreme points on the rhetorical spectrum. Far from the conspicuous rigor of structuralist equations, Youngblood's unapologetically funky, tie-dyed, star-child ethos announces itself at the outset with a particularly striking image: "a hairy, buckskinned, barefooted atomic physicist with a brain full of mescaline and logarithms, working out the heuristics of computer-generated holograms or krypton laser interferometry" heralding a new "Paleocybernetic Age" as the new Dawn of Man.[19] Crafted deep within the trenches of the late 1960s West Coast counterculture, this was a synergetic vision of artists using advanced technology to midwife an imminent sociopolitical revolution. At the book's center, science fiction author Arthur C. Clarke—whose six-channel, Super Panavision feature *2001: A Space Odyssey* (1968) with Stanley Kubrick had arguably become the first countercultural epic—concludes his interview declaring that "the goal of the future is total unemployment, so we can all play."[20]

Indebted to the sweeping world historical visions of Marshall McLuhan, Buckminster Fuller, and Norman O. Brown—all cited regularly within the book—*Expanded Cinema* was less art criticism than Weltanschauung. The domain circumscribed by Youngblood's "expanded cinema" is ultimately nothing less than life itself: "a process of becoming, man's ongoing historical drive to manifest his consciousness outside of his mind."[21] For art critics of Krauss's generation, engaged in an arduous struggle to shift profoundly conservative institutions of art and academe toward an engagement with the deeply suspect terrain of contemporary

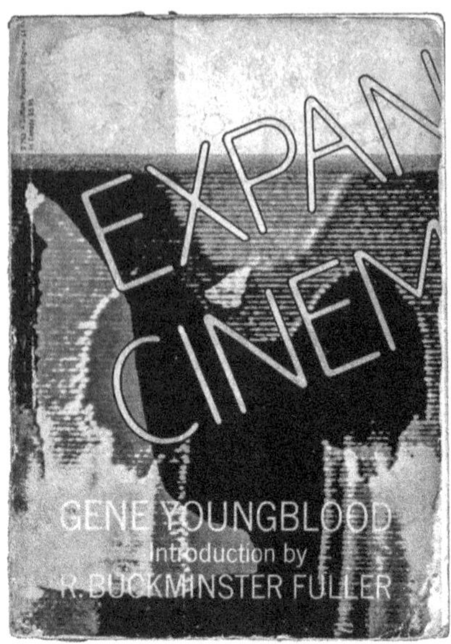

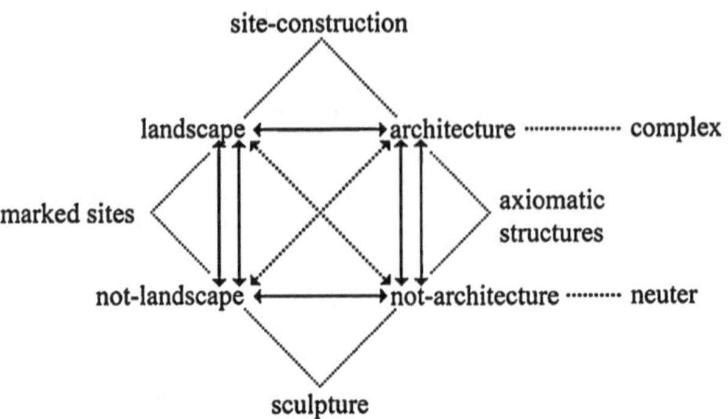

Figure I.3. Gene Youngblood, *Expanded Cinema* (New York: Dutton, 1970). Cover.

Figure I.4. Klein group diagram. From Rosalind Krauss, "Sculpture in the Expanded Field," *October* 8 (Spring 1979): 38.

art and Continental philosophy, Youngblood's subject matter alone made the book a difficult sell; the rhetorical style necessarily consigned it to oblivion. As the principal optic through which the idea of expanded cinema would be viewed, Youngblood's book ironically ensured that the idea was largely excised from the art historical record.[22]

Yet the history of the expanded cinema cannot be recovered simply through a recovery of *Expanded Cinema* because Youngblood, by his own account, was not much concerned with the prior history or development of the idea. His criticism, written largely for the *Los Angeles Free Press* in the late 1960s, is an invaluable account of the cultural zeitgeist and a tour de force of parascholarly speculation, but it is not particularly representative of the art or criticism that occasioned the term's emergence in mid-1960s New York. Within Youngblood's text, "expansion" is left ill defined—a generic synonym for a diffuse formal, technological, or conceptual novelty. This generality, combined with an outsized attention to the latest technologies of video, holography, and early computing, helped to cement a mistaken association between expanded cinema and technological innovation. To his credit, Youngblood occasionally tried to forestall such an association. Like Sheldon Renan, who had previously described the expanded cinema as "a spirit of inquiry," Youngblood began by describing it as a kind of "expanded consciousness."[23] But consciousness of what? And what kind of consciousness?

As this study will show, the idea of expanded cinema that emerged between 1964 and 1966 in New York was not primarily a "consciousness raising" about sociopolitical conditions, nor was it a meditative inquiry into the interior of one's own consciousness. Rather, it was an emerging consciousness of the paradoxical site specificity of cinematic practice: a growing awareness of the institutional conditions through which art's exhibition was structured, and the concomitant understanding that a reinvention of these institutions would run parallel to any possible rejuvenation of the avant-garde project.

For the artists and critics of this earlier New York scene, as well as for many of those who would follow in the next decade in Europe and America, the very complexity of the sociopolitical issues they faced required disembarking from the extravagant rhetoric of world historical revolution in order to bring a degree of analytic specificity to the particular social and cultural situations in which they were themselves embedded. It was a concern that developed in parallel with the ideas of John Cage and the aesthetics of sculptural minimalism, and one that would come to be more explicitly theorized under the rubrics of site specificity and institutional critique in the decades to come. Within the expanded cinema, it emerged not so much from an intentional effort of abstraction and conceptualization, but more as an almost inevitable consequence of the displaced condition of the moving image within the institutions of postwar art.

Minimalist painting and sculpture are typically seen as the fountainhead for a whole range of critical interrogations into material and ideological structures of exhibition that would become increasingly prevalent over the late 1960s and 1970s. Yet the expanded cinema anticipated many of these problematics in a more direct and tangible way than was possible within painting or sculpture, precisely because it was necessarily forced to reach outside the disciplinary conventions of the gallery's "white cube" altogether. While early works such as Robert Morris's Green Gallery exhibition (1963) and Hans Haacke's *Condensation Cube* (1963–1965) were crucial in helping to mitigate the autonomy of the sculptural object and focus attention on the terms of its institutional containment, artists quickly began to risk reinventing the wheel—specifically, Duchamp's *Bicycle Wheel* of 1913.

Consciously or unconsciously, spectators of painting, film, and performance have always understood the art gallery, the cinema hall, and the theatrical stage as being governed by their own particular conventions of production and reception. Calling attention to this fact, in and of itself, accomplished little. Well before the modern era, self-reflexivity had long been a staple of all manner of aesthetic production and, on its own, was neither especially innovative nor particularly critical. Absent some "outside" against which to constitute a figure/ground relationship, the early practitioners of "institutional critique" risked remaining trapped within a deadened reflexivity—forced to gesture vaguely toward a sphere of life naïvely supposed to exist outside the regulation of either institutions or media. By contrast, the most sophisticated projects moved beyond the cul-de-sac of mere self-referentiality toward a cunning juxtaposition of exhibitionary frames. Robert Smithson and Marcel Broodthaers invoked museums of natural history and galleries of ethnography because they functioned in some senses very much like museums and galleries of modern art, despite having radically distinct histories, audiences, purviews, and missions. By defamiliarizing accepted paradigms of exhibition and reception, these kinds of institutional dislocations allowed for generative new models of ambivalence and contradiction beyond the ritual lamentation of institutional "enclosure." In Krauss's terminology, they allowed the conventions of these different sites to become "layered" in new and unforeseen ways.[24]

The expanded cinema might be understood as precipitating an analogous change of venue for the motion picture experience. It was comparatively easy to make different kinds of films, but much more difficult to change the way in which films were seen. When artists of the early 1960s turned to the technology of cinema, they found an already existing cultural practice that could never have the aesthetic autonomy of painting or sculpture. However much they wanted to divorce themselves from Hollywood's model of industrial practice, its half-century dominion had established protocols for exhibition and spectatorship that had long since been internalized by layperson and connoisseur alike. Artists turning to cinema's material technology were necessarily implicated in these preexisting models of cinematic exhibition and spectatorship, as well as in shared assumptions about the legitimate nature and purpose of the moving image. These artists discovered the need to grapple not simply with the forms of commercial cinema, but with these accepted norms of cinematic exhibition and spectatorship. The expanded cinema recognized that it was no longer sufficient to change the form of cinema: one needed to change the total situation within which the moving image was exhibited and seen as well as the context within which it was understood.

In order to recover a sense of the difficulty and possibility that the moving image occasioned for artists of this period, we need to move beyond the account of medium-specificity so familiar from midcentury modernist criticism. Rather than asking how film was articulated as an artistic medium, we need to ask instead how the very idea of "medium" was being transformed by the essentially hybrid and diffuse nature of the moving image. Doing so requires taking seriously the metaphor of spatial dislocation that lies at the heart of the term "expanded cinema." It entails setting aside long-standing fixations on cinematic *ontology* in order to explore the aesthetic and conceptual consequences of cinema's curiously displaced cultural *situation* within the postwar era. Attending to this displacement, we might adapt André Bazin's famous inquiry to ask not *what* is cinema, but *where*?[25] For it is only by adopting such a situational or environmental perspective that we are able to grasp the significance of the moving image within postwar art practice as a force of material, perceptual, affective, and institutional *dislocation*.

Writing about the disruptive transformations wrought by the invention of photography and cinema upon the early twentieth-century conceptualization of art, Walter Benjamin described the manner in which technologies become uniquely visible in their birth and obsolescence—the way in which a technology's obsolescence can trigger remembrance of the utopian aspirations of its birth.[26] Americans in the 1960s were witnesses to a dramatic conjunction of birth *and* obsolescence within moving-image culture. As broadcast television surged forward, the film industry found itself in a precipitous decline. Despite a massive growth in drive-in theaters all over suburban America, overall ticket sales dropped by an astonishing 75 percent from 1946 to 1963.[27] B-movies and theatrical gimmicks signaled ever more desperate attempts to lure back a vanishing theater audience. The ornate movie palaces of Hollywood's golden age were quite literally falling apart in every major American city. Yet at the very moment that cinema's future looked most uncertain, the lost glamour of cinema's past was being newly presented to millions of people in their homes, between commercials, on television.

Isolated in his bed as a sickly child, Andy Warhol experienced classical cinema almost exclusively through the interlaced lines of the cathode ray tube. Rather than experiencing the collective space though which the cinema had long been understood, he came to know it as a private experience, one that reached him in the most intimate of spaces. Television prompted not only a radical disruption of space, but a newly asynchronic quality of time. Despite its technological novelty and its unique ability to broadcast live, much of early television actually consisted of Hollywood cinema. Broadcasters, suddenly faced with hundreds of hours to fill, turned to a dead stock of feature films often unseen for decades. In the days when it was nearly impossible to see films more than a few months old, television brought this previously neglected work to public consciousness with a newly historical distance. Even as it threatened its future, the television industry paradoxically helped establish an interest in cinema's forgotten past.

At the same time, and after decades of theoretical debates, the question of cinema's status as a modern art seemed to have finally been resolved. Following in the footsteps of Venice and Cannes, the New York Film Festival, founded in 1963, bestowed both critical recognition and cultural legitimacy on the European-centered "art cinema" of the time, granting it a prestigious institutional home alongside the city's symphony orchestra and opera company at the recently created Lincoln Center for the Performing Arts. Film was said to have finally "taken its place alongside the other arts."[28] But the vision of cinema developing at Lincoln Center was one that quite literally had no place for the radically divergent conjunction of art and the moving image that was then emerging. Working outside the framework of the European art cinema—but equally distant from the expressive, personal, and "visionary" experimental film—the artists of this expanded cinema were not interested in advancing the medium of cinema as an autonomous art so much as in utilizing the idea of the moving image to challenge the institutions and practices of postwar art as such.

The peripheral location of these practices within traditional histories of art and film was by no means accidental. The difficulty of situating expanded cinema within the discursive landscape of art or film history has been inextricably bound up with the difficulty of locating its practices definitively within a singular exhibitionary site. The discursive and institutional promiscuity of the moving image—its failure to establish itself solely within the institutions of the theater or the gallery, within the discourses of film studies or those of art criticism—has occasioned a critical blindness that cannot be remedied through the simple reintroduction of a few neglected artists or works. Yet the difficulty of definitively locating this work within the accepted historiographic and critical landscape of the period is a direct index of its contemporary relevance. For in their sustained effort to give birth to a radically new way of experiencing the moving image, these artists both necessitated and helped to forge a novel institutional and discursive location *between* the white cube of the art gallery and the black box of the cinematic theater whose implications have yet to be fully registered, let alone understood.

Just as minimalist sculpture's interrogation of the gallery space would lead to sculpture's expansion into the landscape, thus changing our ideas about the nature and possibilities of sculpture, the expanded cinema's interrogation of the cinema theater would lead to an expansion of the moving image into the art gallery and the performance stage, where it would transform our understanding of the nature and possibilities of the moving image. The movement of the moving image became something to be explicitly *staged*, drawing attention to the theatricality implicit in its presentation and spectatorship. In articulating this exhibitionary situation as such—foregrounding the often unconscious, implicit conditioning of aesthetic production and reception—the expanded cinema moved away from the autonomous, medium-specific practices that we associate with high modernism and toward the more environmental, mediated, and site-specific conceptual practices that would follow in its wake. Marshall McLuhan may have proclaimed that "the medium is the message," but the artists of the expanded cinema understood that the very nature of a moving-image *medium* was irrevocably bound up with the specificity of its exhibitionary *situation*. As both a conceptual inquiry and an aesthetic practice, the expanded cinema sought to break free of the norms of industrial exhibition and spectatorship by returning to forgotten models of early and precinematic history, locating the cinematic event somewhere between the immersive tradition of the movie theater's black box and the more distanced perception characteristic of the gallery's white cube, and employing the dislocating qualities of the moving image as a metaphor through which to consider the spatiotemporal character of art in a newly televisual age.

During the 1960s, the films of Jean-Luc Godard would introduce ideas from theater, literature, music, and painting to subvert established codes of cinematic representation. The expanded cinema might be understood as proposing a fundamentally analogous yet opposite strategy: asking how the moving image might be introduced as a subversive agent into the material and institutional spaces of the other arts. Not content to restrict cinema to an autonomous and isolated purity, these artists sought to mobilize the idea of cinema in order to intervene within a diverse array of exhibitionary situations. By destabilizing accepted conventions of exhibition and spectatorship, these artists did not seek to bolster a modern art of cinema, but rather to leverage the aesthetic, historical, and even ontological hybridity of cinema to initiate an interdisciplinary transformation of postwar art and its institutions.

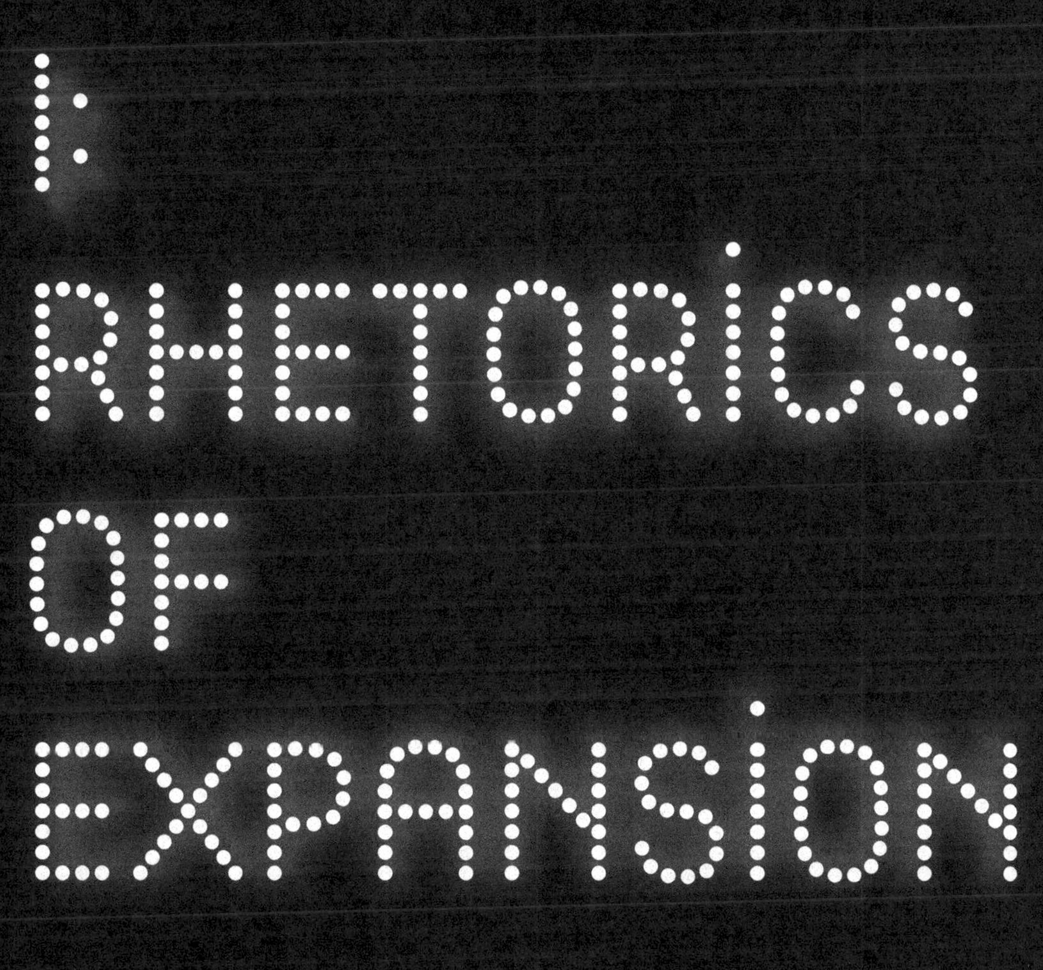

I: Rhetorics of Expansion

You know, this 3-D process isn't all that glamorous or new or exciting.

ANDY WARHOL

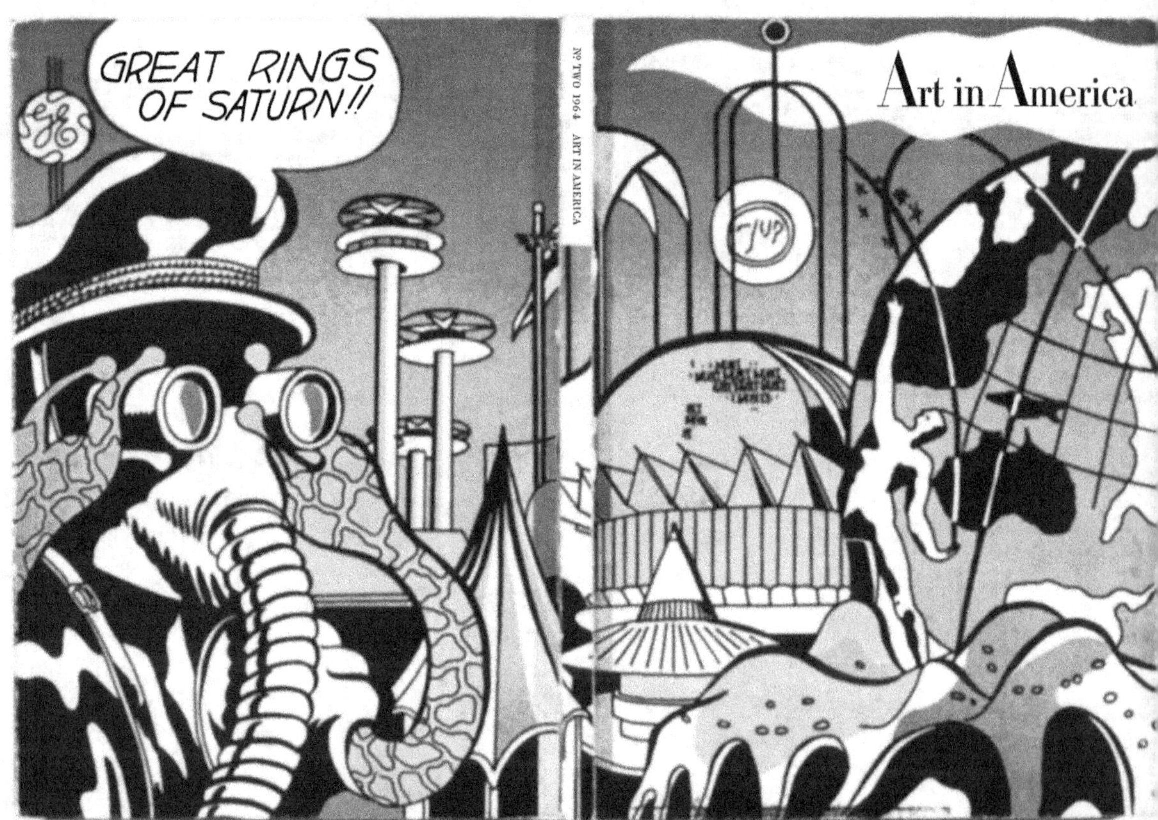

Multiscreen Cinema and the '64 World's Fair

Figure 1.1. Roy Lichtenstein, *New York World's Fair*, cover illustration for *Art in America*, April 1964. © Estate of Roy Lichtenstein.

In April 1964, the World's Fair came to New York. Reports of nightmarishly congested parking and two-hour-long exhibit lines were unable to dissuade millions of visitors from all over the world. Many locals attended the fair not once or twice but literally dozens of times during the two summers it was open.[1] Yet if the success of previous World's Fairs had rested on their ability to inhabit a futural temporality—to offer viewers spectacular yet convincing dreamworlds of tomorrow—the New York World's Fair managed to botch the job entirely. Despite its resolutely "space-age" theme, it was widely criticized as being neither forward-looking nor visionary. Largely planned and designed in the late 1950s, by the mid-1960s it had become a kind of living relic, a ready-made ruin. As America and the world had changed drastically, the fair seemed frozen in time. Rather than familiarizing viewers with a strange and exciting future yet to come, it managed to defamiliarize that which had seemed natural only a few years back.

On the same site a quarter century before, the 1939 World's Fair had been received with both popular and critical acclaim. General Motors' *Futurama* exhibit was a heady vision of the future metropolis featuring towering skyscrapers, elevated multilane highways, and cars for everyone. Coming at the end of the Great Depression, when many families didn't yet own cars and superhighways were cultural novelties, *Futurama* inspired millions. Yet for the baby-boomer generation coming of age in 1964, burgeoning suburbs and extended workaday commutes were beginning to provoke a reconsideration of the automotive romance. General Motors doubled down. Its updated *Futurama II* showcased a robotic "Jungle Road Builder" intended to delve deep into the last untrammeled jungles of the world, eviscerate everything in its path, and leave behind elevated asphalt superhighways. For the nascent youth culture of the 1960s, these kinds of technologies were a proverbial "road to nowhere"—a vision of the future better left in the past.

What did seem particularly new and exciting was the spectacular range of multiscreen cinema that was there on display. *Man in the 5th Dimension* at the Billy Graham's Christian Evangelical Association Pavilion, Saul Bass's *The Searching Eye* at the Kodak Pavilion, *American Journey* at the US Pavilion, *The Triumph of Man*—"an immersive panoramic journey through the ages"—at the Travelers Insurance Pavilion, *To the Moon and Beyond* at the Transportation and Travel Pavilion, and Charles and Ray Eames's *Think* at the IBM Pavilion were among the most popular exhibits of the fair. *To Be Alive!*, produced by Alexander Hammid and Francis Thompson for the Johnson Wax Pavillion, was perhaps the most popular and celebrated of them all. Hammid was principally known for his collaboration with Maya Deren on *Meshes of the Afternoon* twenty years before, and Thompson for his prismatic city symphony *NY, NY* of 1957. Their collaboration on *To Be Alive!* proved quite unlike these earlier works. A program presented the short film's message: "While millions of people are frustrated in this complex modern world of ours, there are millions of others who retain a sense of the underlying wonder of the world, who have a capacity for finding delight in normal, everyday experience, and who realize that there can be great joy in simply being alive!"[2]

While the fair would be roundly criticized for its aesthetic conservatism, Thompson and Hammid's panoramic triple-screen film was an instant standout. Combining images from Africa, Italy, and the United States, *To Be Alive!* was like an abridged, cinematic version of Edward Steichen's *The Family of Man* from the decade before, and it was similarly well received. According to the company magazine, "more than 300 members of the New York press corps gave the film a standing ovation" after the advance screening, and played to "capacity audiences every day of the fair."[3] Viewers were forced to wait "as long as two hours" to see the eighteen-minute film, and attendance over the twelve months of the fair reached more than five million within its single theater. "Tremendous success brought inquiries and requests to see the film from throughout the world. Celebrities came almost every day until our guest register read like an international Who's Who of entertainment, business and government leaders."[4] As with *The Family of Man*, the frenzied pitch of excitement was in no small part due to the particular conjunction of an innovative aesthetic form with a clear and uplifting social message.

To Be Alive! received a number of honors, including the 1965 Academy Award for Best Short Subject Documentary. More intriguingly, the film would also take pride of place within a special issue of the underground journal *Film Culture* devoted to expanded cinema the following year. "*To Be Alive!* and the Multi-Screen Film" began with the breathless declaration that now that *To Be Alive!* had been given an Academy Award, the multiscreen film, "once a freak of the film world ... was recognized as a new and effective motion picture form by the Industry."[5] One might reasonably ask why a publication devoted to experimental and avant-garde film would concern itself with what the industry considered "effective," but this declaration exemplifies the confusion surrounding the rhetoric of expanded cinema within the mainstream and alternative press. While the term often implied a broad range of activities beyond the industrial

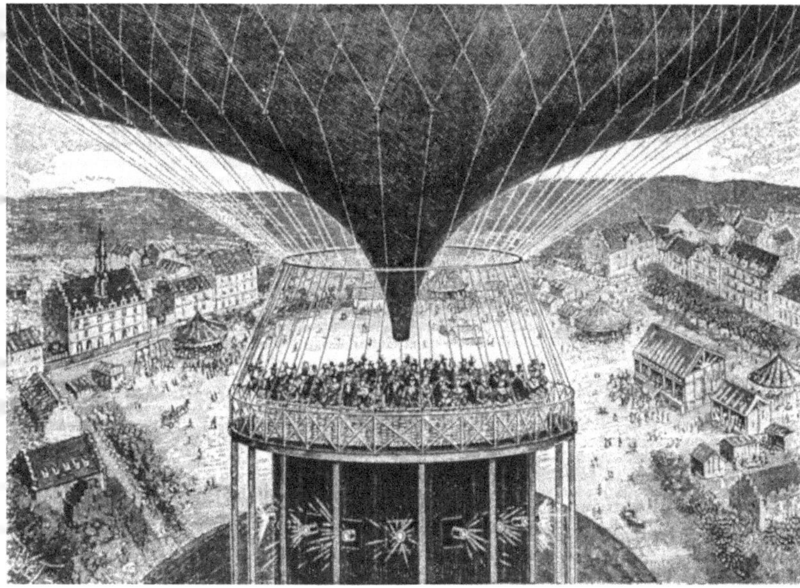

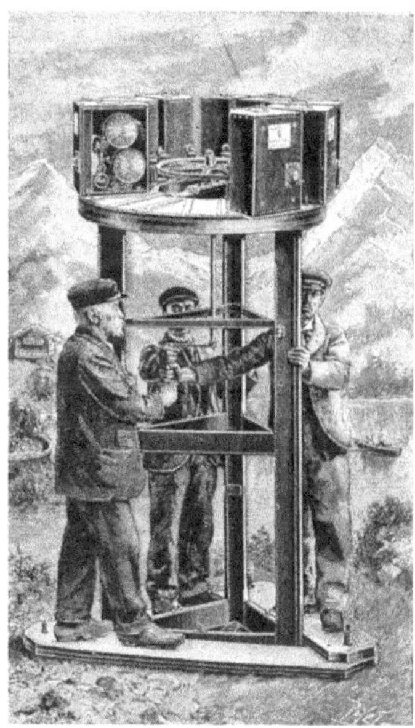

Figure 1.2. Raoul Grimoin-Sanson, illustration of Cinéorama at the 1900 Exposition Universelle in Paris. *Scientific American*, supplement, no. 1287, September 1, 1900. Interior of exhibition.

Figure 1.3. Raoul Grimoin-Sanson, illustration of Cinéorama at the 1900 Exhibition Universelle in Paris. *Scientific American*, Supplement, no. 1287, September 1, 1900. Multiple camera apparatus.

norms of cinematic presentation, the most obvious and persistent of these activities, and therefore the one most quickly and powerfully associated with it, was the use of multiple projection. Yet the widespread excitement over multiscreen cinema as new technology and a new form of cinematic practice was possible only due to a particularly acute form of historical amnesia, because the multiscreen cinema that emerged in the 1960s was neither particularly novel nor greatly innovative. Rather, it was merely the latest iteration of a technology that had been invented and reinvented compulsively, and almost continuously, since the late nineteenth-century birth of cinema itself.

Well before the emergence of classical Hollywood, even before the most rudimentary grammar of industrial cinema, Raoul Grimoin-Sanson provided the template for the monumental, immersive cinematic spectacle with his Cinéorama of 1897. Conjoining the nineteenth-century fascination with panoramic painting and the newly invented technology of cinematographic projection, this ciné-panorama employed ten synchronized, radially facing movie cameras in a hot air balloon to capture its ascent over the city of Paris. For its debut at the Paris Exposition Universelle of 1900, spectators were situated within a similar basket while ten synchronized projectors, located beneath them, projected the film in a 360-degree panorama some one hundred meters in circumference. Despite its unqualified popular success, Grimoin-Sanson's exhibit was prematurely shut down after being declared a fire hazard by the city police, and his company went bankrupt immediately thereafter. Its commercial failure would serve as a template for a range of beleaguered efforts over the next fifty years as a succession of artists and engineers again and again reinvented the ciné-panorama as a spectacle of overwhelming and immersive monumentality.[6]

The most famous of these attempts within film's silent era was undoubtedly Abel Gance's "invention" of his three-screen Polyvision cinema for his 1927 feature *Napoléon*. And during a few brief climactic moments at the end of that film's final reel, Gance would indeed use these three screens in a radical new way, presenting different images on each in a kind of simultaneous montage. Yet for most of the final reel, the multiple screens functioned just as they had for Grimoin-Sanson: augmenting the scale of the image with the creation of a single, continuous ciné-panorama. It was certainly this expanded scale, rather than any novel possibilities for juxtaposition, that captured the immediate attention of Hollywood. By the late 1920s, Fox was promoting its Grandeur process, Paramount its Natural Vision, and Warner Brothers its Vitascope—all expensive, large-format processes that magnified the size and quality of the cinematic image but failed spectacularly at the box office and were abandoned soon after their introduction.

After the Great Depression, the multiscreen panoramic cinema was again "invented" by Fred Waller for the 1939 World's Fair. His Vitarama used eleven linked cameras and projectors to display a greatly enlarged image inside a hemispheric screen, while his enormous domed "movie-mural" within the fair's Perisphere was even larger.[7] While generating considerable excitement at the time, his work was also quickly forgotten. In the 1950s, multiple projection would once again be rediscovered by Hollywood as it desperately sought ways of contesting the falling box office receipts that attended the rising popularity of television. Cinerama, like its distant namesake, used linked cameras and projectors to create a single panoramic image, while Todd-AO, VistaVision, CinemaScope, and Ultra Panavision achieved a similar scale by means of larger film (Todd-AO), anamorphic compression (VistaVision, CinemaScope), or both (Ultra Panavision).

Contemporary advertisements for all three processes regularly invoked a similar rhetoric of immersion: the viewer did not watch at a distance, but was brought "inside" the spectacle. Often coupled with this immersivity was the promise of a new kind of "active" cinematic subject: a Todd-AO advertisement from the 1950s describes "a quality so perfect that the audience become part of the action, not just passive spectators." This parody of the Brechtian imperative reveals the nature of this early industrial "expanded cinema." Beyond the minutiae of diverse technological inventions, beyond the breathless publicity campaigns proclaiming the utter novelty of each newly minted procedure, we can locate a single, almost unwavering aim from the multiscreen Cinéorama of 1900 to the multiscreen Cinerama of the 1950s: the enfolding of the spectator in an immersive, diegetic world through the overwhelming sensory con-

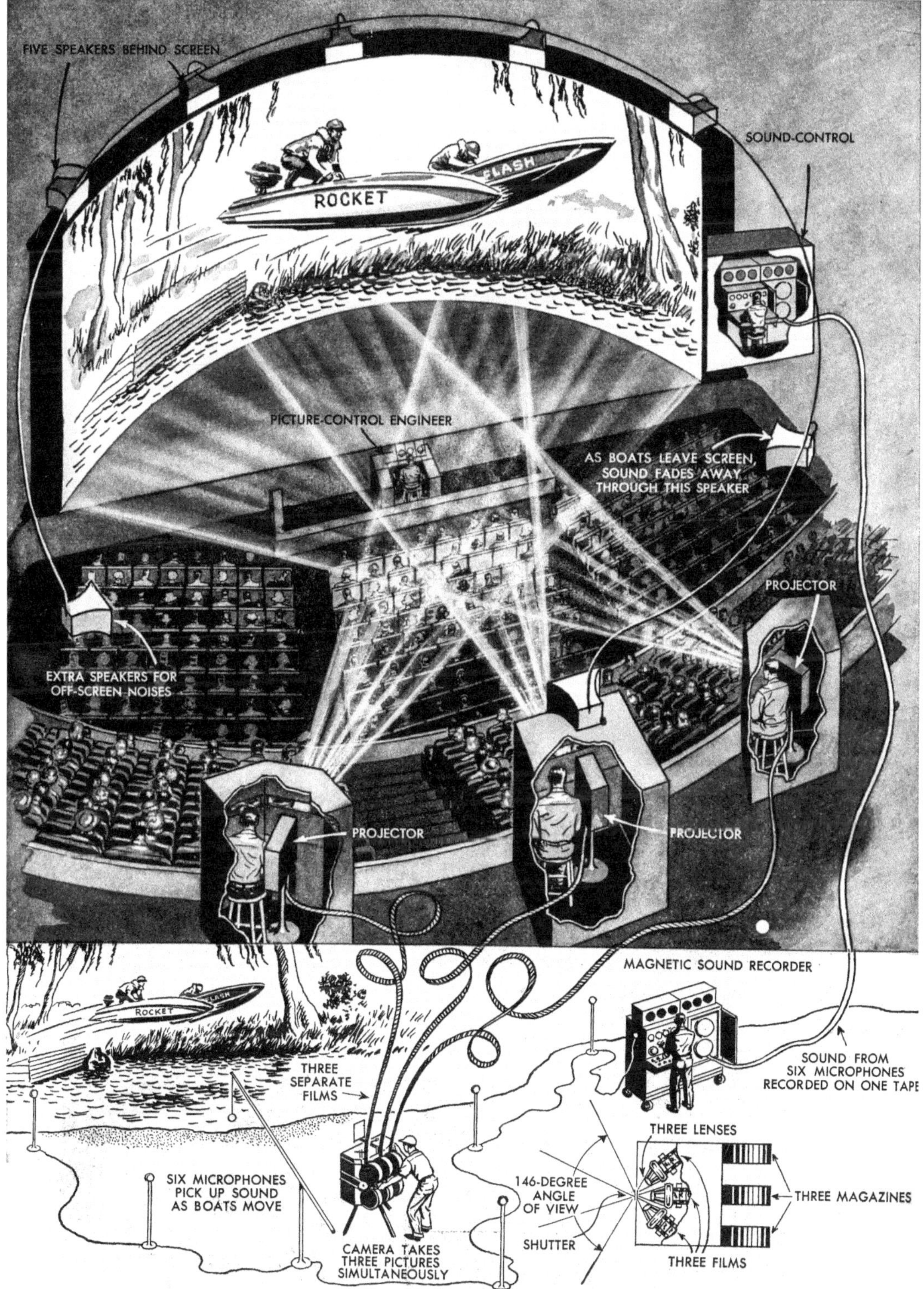

Figure 1.4. Schematic from *This Is Cinerama* souvenir book, 1951.

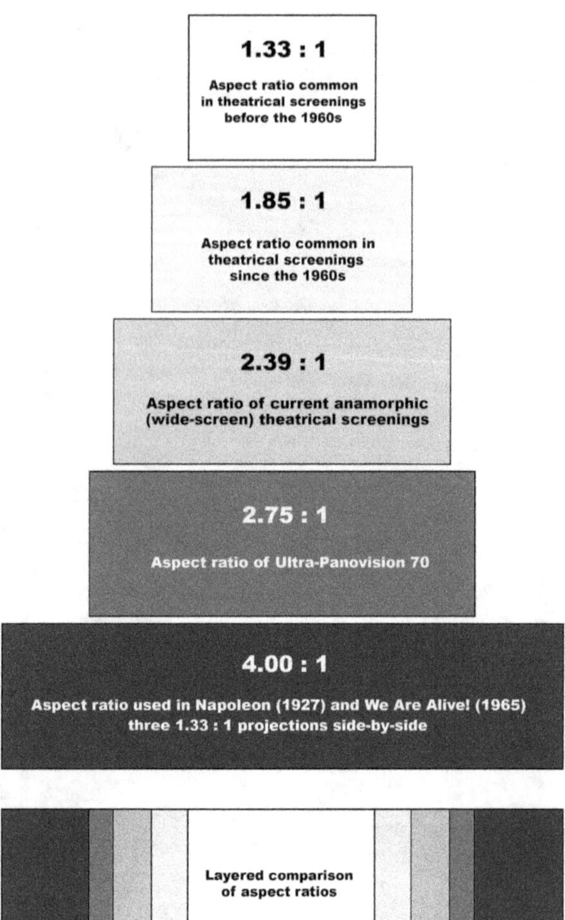

Figure 1.5. Comparison of widescreen processes.

ditions of display. These supposedly radical innovations in multiscreen projection were, on a fundamental level, structured by a surprisingly fixed understanding of the spectator-screen relationship. By immersing the subject within an overwhelming accumulation of visual data, they sought to produce a heightened experience of reality without too great a concern for realism. Within industrial practice, the history of multiscreen technology might reasonably be considered little more than a footnote in the history of widescreen technology.[8]

As such, it should come as no surprise that the industrial adoption of CinemaScope in the 1950s and early 1960s would signal the obsolescence of multiscreen experimentation within the industrial cinema. Of the various processes, CinemaScope was clearly the least impressive, containing only a fraction of the visual or auditory detail of the other alternatives. Nevertheless, because it required only minor modifications to existing processes of production and distribution, it was considered the only economically feasible option for mass distribution. Using only a single lens, CinemaScope adequately addressed the desire for a larger and more immersive spectacle without the complexity and risk that attended multiple projection formats like Cinerama.

Returning to the '64 World's Fair with this history in mind, it is difficult to understand what was so wildly innovative about Thompson and Hammid's piece. In his interview for *Film Culture*, Thompson claimed that *To Be Alive!* had not intended to subsume the multiple screens into a single, oversized image, yet all the evidence points to the film having precisely this effect. Maxine Haleff describes the width of the three screens as "enveloping" the viewer and producing an effect of "heightened reality."[9] The fair's guidebook was even more explicit, advertising "the Tri-Screen System that puts *you* in the picture."[10] Both mirrored the rhetorical tropes regularly employed to advertise Cinerama, Todd-AO, and CinemaScope throughout the previous decade. In fact, Hammid was quite forthright in his description of the triple camera setup he had designed for the film: "the purpose is to have the cameras aligned so that the images coincide precisely."[11] In discussing those few sequences making simultaneous use of different images, Thompson spoke not of montage or juxtaposition, but of *narrative efficiency*: "We love this method, because we can say a lot more using less viewing time ... in the pottery sequence, we show the beginning, middle and end of one process all at once, and it's done." Multiple images here do not disrupt or even complicate the narrative, they merely accelerate it. Thus, despite their implicitly disjunctive potential, multiple screens were understood principally as a means for creating a singular panoramic, introducing audiences to the "novel" experience of multiscreen spectatorship while keeping the resulting experience firmly within the comfortable conventions of industrial practice.[12]

Jonas Mekas—filmmaker, critic, and champion of the underground film community—was one of the few to dissent from the prevailing excitement over these new multiscreen spectacles. As the World's Fair was wrapping up in the summer of 1965, he wrote that the idea of "expansion" presented within these new multimedia shows was simply a quantitative rather than a qualitative change: "Expanded consciousness is being confused with the ability to see more color images, with the expanded eye, with the quickness of the eye."[13] Mekas's lament signals a prescient concern that, while shifting the formal vocabulary of cinematic representation, these works merely reiterated the same exhausted model of immersive spectacle that had characterized their historical predecessors for over half a century. The kind of "active" spectatorship these works proposed was not unlike those advertisements for Todd-AO and CinemaScope a decade before: it consisted in having to keep pace with the increased amount of visual data being generated through the encompassing size of the spectacle. Mekas's worry would prove well founded. Having already found success with three screens, Thompson and Hammid doubled the number of screens to six for their *We Are Young* (1967) at Expo 67 in Montreal. And not to be outdone, Roman Kroitor there developed a projector that handled 70mm film lengthwise, thus magnifying the image by a factor of four and setting the stage for the popularization of the now celebrated IMAX cinema. Within a decade, the legacy of these vivid demonstrations of the efficiency of sensory bombardment could be found everywhere, from multinational trade shows and corporate exhibitions to rock concerts and religious revivals.[14]

More fundamentally, the obsession with these supposedly new material technologies failed to represent any critical investigation of cinema itself as a *social technology*—as a set of historically contingent practices of exhibition and spectatorship. Yet the attention lavished on the supposedly revolutionary multiscreen spectacles of the World's Fair served to displace and conceal another vision of cinematic expansion that was then emerging. For just as the World's Fair was packing up at the end of August 1965, preparations were being made for an entirely different sort of festival at the Film-Makers' Cinematheque that winter. If the World's Fair effectively summarized the past and predicted the future of multimedia spectacle, the decidedly low-tech, artisanal, and critically unheralded Expanded Cinema Festival would serve both as its antipode and critical rejoinder. Minimalist rather than maximalist, the "expansion" in its name did not concern the size or number of screens, nor the speed or intensity of the imagery projected on them. A conceptual rather than a formal expansion, it did not concern the formal qualities of cinematic *image* so much as the institutional qualities of the cinematic *situation*. By actively embracing the heterogeneous conditions of exhibition and spectatorship within cinema's forgotten infancy, it sought to transform the discussion then taking place about the modern art of cinema. Rather than asking what kinds of cinema might be properly designated as "modern art," it asked how the very nature of modern art was being reconceptualized through its belated incorporation of the aesthetics and philosophy of the moving image.

The Cinematic Situation: Expanded Cinema and the Undisciplining of Spectatorship

Film is an art in evolution. It is the dark glass for the physical and visual change in motion about us. But now, the most revolutionary art form of our time is in the hands of entertainment merchants . . . Vistavisionaries of Hollywood, with their split-level features and Disney landscapes . . . what of the artists, poets, experimenters in America, who must work as if they were secret members of the underground?

STAN VANDERBEEK, "The Cinema Delimina," 1961

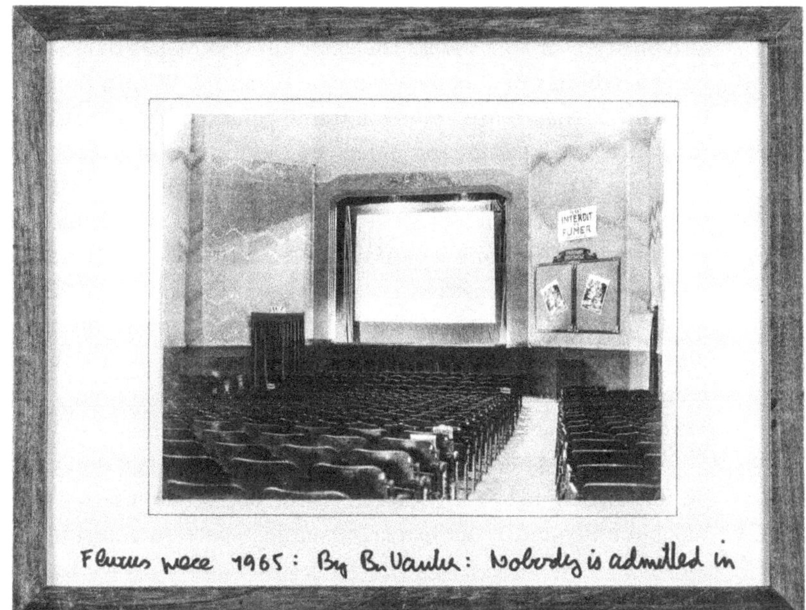

Figure 1.6. Ben Vautier, *Fluxus Piece 1965: Nobody Is Admitted In*. The Gilbert and Lila Silverman Fluxus Collection, gift, Museum of Modern Art, New York.

Writing in his movie column for the *Village Voice* in November 1965, Jonas Mekas was resolutely uncertain how to describe what was then taking place at the Expanded Cinema Festival, or how it should be understood in relation to the established norms of cinema: "Not all that's happening at the Film-Maker's Cinematheque this month can be called cinema," he wrote. "Some of it has no name of any kind." These new practices, he said, had "dissolved the edges of this art called cinema into a frontiersland mystery. Light is there; motion is there; the screen is there; and the filmed image, very often, is there; but it cannot be described or experienced in terms you describe or experience the Griffith cinema, the Godard cinema, or even Brakhage cinema."[15] Unbound by the narrative, exhibitionary, or spectatorial conventions of the Hollywood studio film (Griffith cinema), the European art film (Godard cinema), or the New American Underground (Brakhage cinema), this new work seemed to function at "the edges of this art called cinema"—working along the frames and boundaries of cinema—to affect a practice of dissolution. In his review, Mekas figures cinema both as an abstract idea and as a concrete experience, as an institutionalized model of perceptual relations and as an uncertain medium for artistic practice.

In contrast to the monumental, technology-driven spectacles of the recently concluded World's Fair, the most significant works of the Expanded Cinema Festival that winter were notable not for what they added to the commonplace experience of cinema, but for what they took away. A single work serves to reveal the vast aesthetic and conceptual chasm between these two contemporary visions of cinematic expansion: Nam

June Paik's *Zen for Film* (*Fluxfilm #1*). It was the "almost classical simplicity and purity"[16] of Paik's work that first allowed Mekas to grasp the underlying aesthetics of this new expanded cinema. Within the *Fluxus Codex*, the work is represented not by a frame enlargement or a still from a performance, but by a singular object: an old film spool and its case.[17] It is a strangely fitting image, capturing as it does the peculiarly bifurcated nature of Paik's cinematic practice: torn between aesthetic object and theatrical event. Paik's name is partially covered, which—accidental or not—is indicative of the collective, even anonymous Fluxus spirit in which the work was created. The reel is old, rusted and damaged with time, yet the film is perfectly clear and transparent. Laid against the heavy rusted metal of its container, it is barely visible. When discovered, it seems almost ethereal.

The celluloid itself seems to partake in a transformation as it is pulled off its containing spool—stacked on the reel, it looks heavy and substantial, but unwound, it dissipates into empty space, into nothingness. Yet it

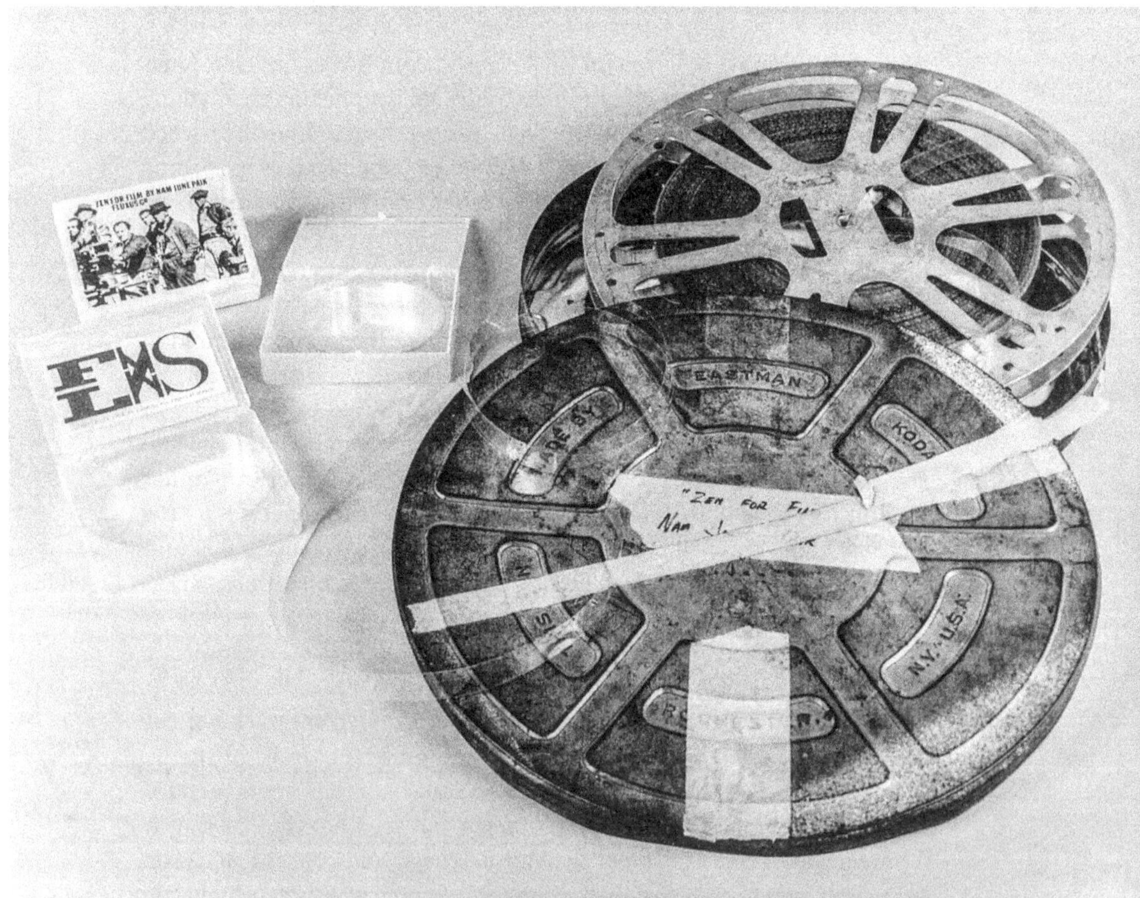

Figure 1.7. Nam June Paik, *Zen for Film*, 1964. Unique 16mm film. The Gilbert and Lila Silverman Fluxus Collection, gift, Museum of Modern Art, New York. *Zen for Film* exists in three versions: the original 16mm film (at right) exists as a unique print; it was later produced in a small version for handheld loop viewer (at left) with a cover designed by George Macunias; eventually, it was incorporated into the Fluxfilm theatrical compilation in the 1970s.

is a nothingness that *goes on and on* for hundreds of feet, like a pure index for time passing. For the spectator first experiencing the film, there is nothing: no image, no sound—nothing to see. There is no "film" there. But after time allows the shock to subside, there is a subtle but totalizing transformation within the spectator's frame of reference. Comparable to the reversal of a figure/ground relationship, Paik's film suddenly appears there where it previously was not. The experience of the bright screen illumination, faintly flickering, suddenly becomes visible as such. One has the experience of simply being present in a particular space, watching light being projected through a moving celluloid strip. It is an experience diametrically opposed to that of the narrative film, wherein all sense of local space and present time are meant to be definitively negated by the spatiotemporal conditions of the cinematic narrative into which we have become absorbed.

Zen for Film (*Fluxfilm #1*) was both an individual work and a more general manifesto for a new conception of cinematic practice. Bruce Jenkins has described Paik's work as being "unburdened by either the seriousness of the Godardian intervention or the shame of the Brakhagean attitude toward mainstream media," and thus able to offer up "an immaculate conception of the cinema that was at once child-like and cunning . . . a gesture that seems both infantile and recherché . . . a radical intervention to the nature of a medium that seemed no longer stable, fixed, finished."[18] As the title clearly indicates, this was only the first in a series of future Fluxfilms. Appropriately for an initial work, Paik used not film stock, but film leader—the introductory material used to feed the photographic material through the mechanical gates. His radical gesture consisted simply in using that leader as the final product, a "degree-zero" phenomenology of cinematic experience.

Despite all this simplicity, *Zen for Film* is a dynamic work whose content has continued to develop over the span of its existence. At its first exhibition, the print was relatively clean, and the normal accumulation of dust and scratches from the process of running through the projector was not yet visible. Of course, in normal films, these processes are almost never visible. Prints inevitably age—they accumulate dust, marks, scratches, blips in the soundtrack, even tears that have to be taped up. But even when these signs of aging are present, the spectators rarely notice them, caught up as they are instead in both the dense visual field of the photographic image and the unassailable progression of the cinematic narrative. We have the illusion that, excepting films from an entirely different era, films do not age. Or rather, that films do not even exist—the cinematic image simply appears, as if by magic, on the screen before us. But Paik reverses every element of this situation, point for point. We are trapped not in the progression of the narrative and the visual density of the photographic image, but in a temporality of the present—in a heightened experience of our phenomenological environment that, though perhaps familiar within the museum or gallery space, remains utterly foreign within the cinematic theater. For once, we are not there, in the dreamworld of the film, but here, within our own bodies, in present time and local space, resolutely sequestered on this side of the cinematic screen.

And on this side of the screen, we become acutely aware of the process of projection itself—the normally invisible and inaudible workings of the projector as the celluloid winds through its various cogs and sprockets to be pierced by the white-hot beam of concentrated light, illuminating both the dim cone of particulate dust above us and the bright rectangular plane across the room. The difference between the materiality of the process and the immateriality of the resulting image becomes newly evident. Who knew that projectors were so noisy, so laborious? The process suddenly seems so material, so tangible, so corrosive. Does the delicate celluloid—which typically contains such an extraordinary wealth of information—really have to be forced through all those mechanical gears, such that a single scratch becomes magnified a hundredfold? Heated to such an extent that a momentary catch or slippage of the early nitrate film stock carried a significant risk of fiery explosion? It becomes difficult to reconcile the ethereal cinematic image, so directly geared into the body of the viewer, with this clumsily mechanical process of screening, the churning gears, the friction, the light and the heat that together constitute the physical labor of projection.

On the screen, at first, we see nothing. In fact, the very brightness of the screen's unchecked reflectivity may cause us to squint or turn away. But as our eyes adjust and we become more attentive to the minimal surface, we begin to notice minor occurrences we have trained ourselves to overlook. The tiny marks of dust on the lens or the celluloid, the small scratches or indentations, are all blown up on the wall like an abstract canvas, illuminated, and endlessly progressing in subtle variation. But in contrast to the narrative feature, we are not invited across the barrier of the screen, and thus our eyes begin to wander. We notice the environment within which the screening is taking place, itself undergoing subtle modulations of light, yet stilled and silent under the auratic pressure of the film's presentation. We see the reactions of the other audience members illuminated by the screen in a curious reversal—has the film itself become a projector? Have we become the entertainment? While the ordinary rules of cinematic projection and spectatorship have obviously been suspended, one thing seems certain: the *exhibition* of the film has itself become the event. It makes no sense to talk of the content or even the form of *Zen for Film* without first acknowledging its more foundational aspect as an event, the screening as itself a kind of performance. Paik put the work of showing on display. By removing the depth of the photographic

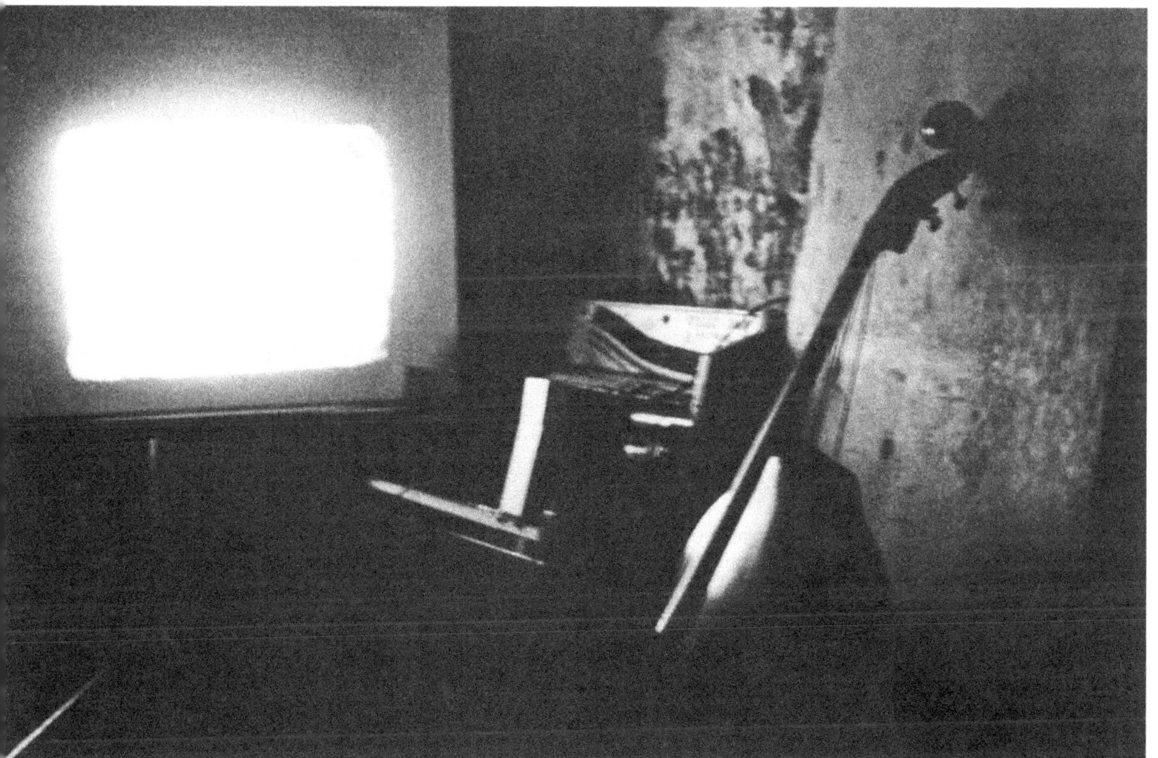

Figure 1.8. Nam June Paik, *Zen For Film*, documentation of 1964 premiere at Fluxhall. Photo by Peter Moore. © Estate of Peter Moore/VAGA, New York, NY.

image, by removing the narrative progression involved in even the most abstract film or soundtrack, Paik left the event-like character of the cinematic exhibition as the sole element on which his spectators could focus. By reducing the cinematic transaction to its barest essentials—projector, screen, audience, and environment—he articulated a positive field within which a new model could begin to take root.

Zen for Film had originally premiered, in Paik's absence, in May 1964 as part of the *12 Fluxus Concerts* series. The rhetoric of the concert, which was commonplace within artists' performances of this time, reveals the extent to which Paik, like so many students of John Cage, was indebted to the expanded conception of music the composer had developed in the 1950s. By the time *Zen for Film* was presented at the Expanded Cinema Festival the following year, it had already come to seem emblematic of a much larger reimagining of the cinematic experience that was then occurring.[19] Cage himself described Paik's film as forming a kind of conceptual trilogy with Robert Rauschenberg's *White Paintings* of 1951 and his own composition *4′33″* the following year. Cage had previously characterized the *White Paintings* as a kind of temporal event or performance, a kind of filmless cinema in which the canvas becomes a screen for the projection of lights, shadows, and particles. His description of *Zen for Film* placed it in similar conceptual terrain, but in an unmistakably different context. He began by invoking his oft-repeated story of a poetry contest to choose the Sixth Patriarch of Zen Buddhism. An elder monk had written what was assumed to be the winning entry: "The mind is a mirror; it collects dust; the problem is to remove the dust." Yet the contest was unexpectedly won when an illiterate kitchen hand, hearing these words, dictated his own entry in response: "Where is the mirror, where is the dust?"[20]

Cage continued, in reference to Paik's film, "In this case, the dust is on the lens of the projector and on the blank developed film itself. There is never nothing to see. Here, we are both together and separate. My *4′33″*, the silent piece, is Nam June's *Zen for Film*. The difference is that his silence was not sounds but something to see."[21] Cage saw that the absence in these works was conceived as an opening up to the outside, to a modality of perception fundamentally rooted in the experience of process. Dust—whose insignificant materiality was normally imperceptible—became the evidence of process, the figuration of an ongoing temporality within a form of spectatorship now conceptualized as an event. As complement and antipode to the human (ashes to ashes . . .), dust was like the high and low sounds Cage heard in the anechoic chamber: a perpetual background hum of life unframed and unframeable. By contrast, the aesthetic event is always framed, and what these three "silences" all produced was a consciousness of that framing as such. Cage described the three works in terms of a change in location:

> In [*4′33″*] the sounds of the environment remain, so to speak, where they are, whereas in the case of the Rauschenberg painting the dust and shadows . . . come to the painting. In the case of the Nam June Paik film . . . the focus is more intense. The nature of the environment is more on the film, different from the dust and shadows that are the environment falling on the painting, and thus less free.[22]

In each, the spectator is led to a manner of perceiving that initiates an understanding of the aesthetic environment and the degree to which our perceptual encounter is thoroughly disciplined and channeled prior to the event of spectatorship. Cage saw Paik's work as a kind of magnifying glass: "less free" in that it was a deliberate and focused intensification. While this can be understood as a kind of analytic reduction of the material of film to its limit or degree zero of articulation, Paik's *Zen for Film*, like Cage's *4′33″*, followed Rauschenberg's *White Paintings* in contending that "there is no zero to which returning applies."[23] Watching *Zen for Film*, one was "seeing something that won't exist again," Cage would later state, "but that also will exist again—in another form. In fact, it will never not exist. It's like the silent piece, which you can always hear."[24]

For Rauschenberg, Cage, and Paik, the point of these formal reductions was not a reflexive investigation of the essence of the material itself, but rather a foregrounding of the particular situation of spectatorship, the manner in which the aesthetic event must always take place within a given environment. Like Francis Picabia's audacious set design for the ballet *Relache* (1924), in which hundreds of lights on stage were trained on the audience rather than the dancers, *Zen for Film* effected a complete *reversal* of perspective.[25] While most often understood in terms of its magnification of dust and scratches and the insistent figuration of material entropy this implies, the brilliant light of Paik's projection must also be understood as the illumination of the spectatorial environment as an essential force in the production of cinematic meaning. And yet *Zen for Film* does not evoke precisely the same phenomenological consciousness that the work of sculptural minimalism sought to make explicit. For even as Paik abjures the construction of a distinct cinematic space-time, the title and mechanism of his work necessarily invoke the larger culture of cinema and cinematic exhibition. As such, *Zen for Film* causes an unresolved, and perhaps unresolvable, reorientation in our understanding of cinematic experience. We become newly aware of the ineluctable *hybridity* of cinema's environmental situation—of its curious existence *in between* the fictional time and space of the cinematic image and the literal time and space of the exhibitionary situation.

At the beginning of the 1950s, Rauschenberg's *White Paintings* and Cage's *4'33"* would together initiate an aesthetic revolution whose implications have long been considered central to the postwar development of the plastic and performing arts. In clarifying these implications for the moving image, Paik's *Zen for Film* extended this aesthetic revolution into the realm of cinema. Cage saw *Zen for Film*, like Rauschenberg's *White Paintings* or his own *4'33"*, not so much as an individual work of art, but rather as a fundamental gesture of reorientation, an invitation to a vast, uncharted domain of aesthetic and conceptual inquiry.

Sheldon Renan would succinctly register the implications of this reorientation in his 1966 essay for the "Expanded Cinema" issue of *Film Culture*.[26] He describes his experience watching movies in the Blue Mouse, an aging movie theater in Portland, Oregon:

> There is a slight stain across the screen in the Blue Mouse. And the pictures that play over it are scarred with a steady rain of scratches worn into the film. Age-cracks flash by like brittle lightning. Chemical deterioration turns moldy once gorgeous Technicolor. Crude splices make characters jerk, dialogue disappear. The framing slips and Kirk Douglas poses heroic in the sunset with his feet standing on his head. Critics do not go to the Blue Mouse. Critics assume that, unlike the performance of a play or the

dancing of a dance, a film is the same from seeing to seeing. Critics write of films as if each had a content fixed and immutable.[27]

In "The Work of Art in the Age of Its Mechanical Reproducibility," Walter Benjamin contended that the inherent reproducibility of the cinematic medium voided any necessary relation to physical site, the traditional foundation of art's unique "aura."[28] Yet Renan here explicitly contrasts his own heightened experience of the cinematic situation with this critical commonplace, describing the man in the Blue Mouse as being moved not by the movie alone, but by "the whole sensuous movie experience." What the crumbling, dilapidated condition of the Blue Mouse foregrounds are those ordinarily invisible environmental factors through which the cinematic event is inevitably yet unconsciously governed. The perceptual reversal elicited within Paik's *Zen for Film* has become a generalized condition of the cinematic experience as such.

For Renan, the Blue Mouse reveals that film "never exists purely by itself," but is a function of "quite variable conditions"—a whole range of "affective elements" substantialized within a "total cinematic experience."[29] The cinematic screening is not conceptualized here as a mechanistic repetition, but rather as a specific, ephemeral iteration—a temporal event structured by the variability of its performative conditions. In language quite obviously indebted to Cage and Rauschenberg, he concludes, "No movie ever looks quite the same. No movie IS quite the same. A movie is a thing alive, and it slowly dies. In that vulnerability, of film's materials and of our own awareness, is the richness of the movie experience."[30] Renan may have been inspired by the surrealist Robert Desnos, who wrote in 1927, "There are cinemas where it's irritating to watch even the most beautiful film, others where the atmosphere is seductive enough to make the silliest story bearable. Above all, cinema auditoriums must be afflicted with the same decay as the films they show."[31] More proximately, he had surely been provoked by Claes Oldenburg's performance of *Moveyhouse* for the Expanded Cinema Festival at the Forty-First Street Theater in December 1965.

While film screenings in the festival's small theater were rarely even half-full, Oldenburg's performance was unusually crowded. For the concluding days of this month-long festival, Robert Rauschenberg and Robert Whitman joined Oldenburg in a triple bill of theatrical premieres, so it was understandable that many would take this opportunity to see what all the talk was about.[32] But Oldenburg's *Moveyhouse* was claustrophobic not simply because of the crowds, but also because the artist had prohibited anyone from sitting in the theater's seats.[33] Like spectators late to a sold-out feature, the audience for *Moveyhouse* were forced to crowd the aisles to see whatever they could see. It had been billed as a "sculpture in light, time and space, etc., using actual material."[34] This actual material was, first and foremost, the theater itself. A single flashlight shone through the blades of a fan whose slow movement rhythmically punctured the light on its way across the room to faintly illuminate the screen. Absent a projected film image, light and screen did not melt away in the production of another, cinematic space, but remained resolutely here, in the space of the theater—obdurate, physical objects to be looked at rather than through.

Like the light of Paik's projector, Oldenburg's faintly flickering screen causes a reversal of perspective: rather than creating a window on another world, it simply illuminates the seats and the space of the theater itself. With such a change in perspective, Oldenburg here seems to want to invoke the nineteenth-century origins of cinema, in which the movement of the moving image was as startling and provocative as the questions it seemed to pose for the future of modern art. *Moveyhouse* recalls this earlier moment by displacing movement from the screen to the theater, estranging his spectators from their familiarity with the cinematic experience. In the seats where his spectators were specifically not allowed to sit, Oldenburg had placed a small audience of his own: exhibitionists, rather than voyeurs. Following index cards given out by uniformed ushers,

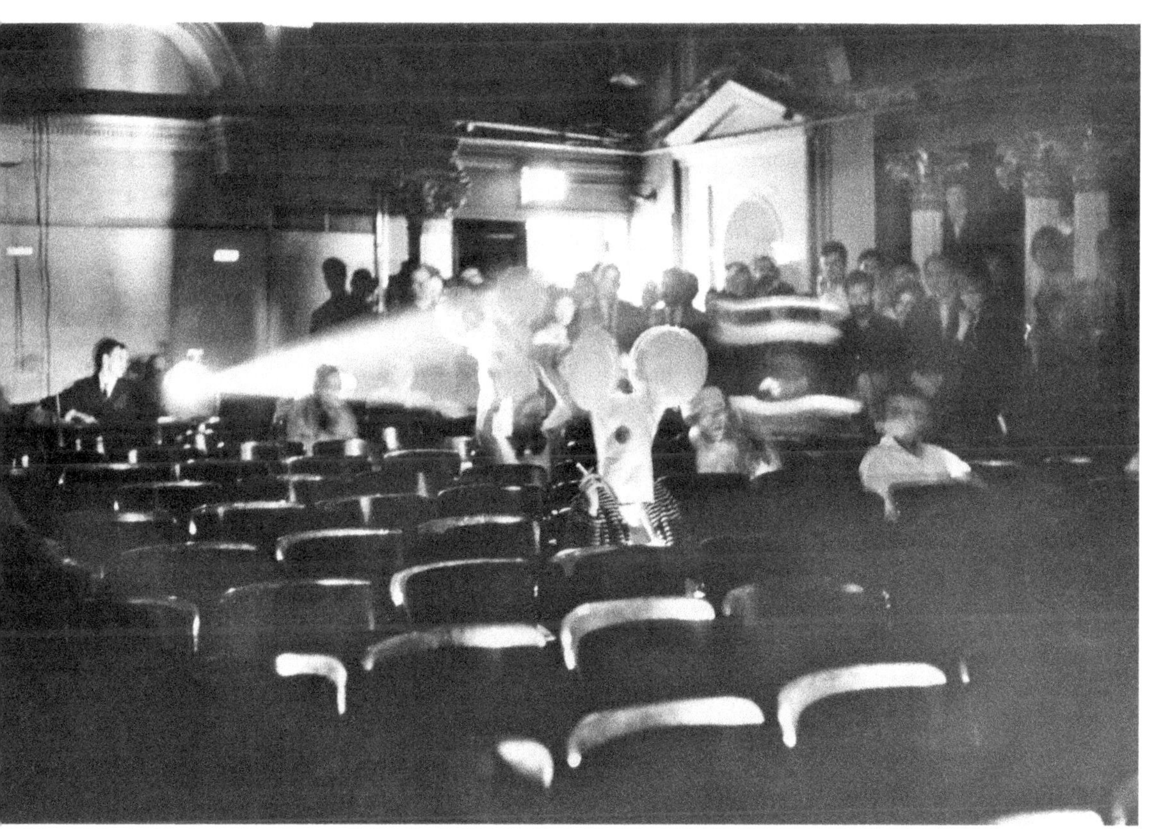

Figure 1.9. Claes Oldenburg, *Moveyhouse*, performance at Forty-First Street Theater, New York, December 1–3, 16–17, 1965. Photo © Estate of Robert R. McElroy / Licensed by VAGA, New York, NY.

these individuals would smoke, take off their coats or put them back on, snore loudly, tear out clippings from a newspaper, change their seats, cause a commotion, and generally act like an audience *not* transfixed or captivated by the movie they had paid to see. They were an audience, in other words, that would not seem out of place in the Blue Mouse that Renan describes. Collectively, these individuals did not define a distinct theatrical space any more than the flashlight created a distinct cinematic space. For while the demarcation between the chairs and the aisles might seem to form a barrier analogous to that of the proscenium stage, Oldenburg's actors were themselves oriented toward the blank screen. *Moveyhouse* thus invokes one of the great self-reflexive tropes from cinematic history—we watch an audience watching the movie, and so make a spectacle of a perception of spectacle that is ultimately our own.[35]

The purposeful dissolution of these boundaries between actor and audience, of the frame by which we understand the work of traditional theater, had emerged as central tenet of the Happenings—a mode of nontheatrical performance that, by the time of *Moveyhouse*, had become well known, if not well understood. Yet *Moveyhouse* was less an intervention against the theatrical stage than a particular staging of what might be called the theater of cinema. Echoing Renan, Oldenburg described how "sitting in a certified theater I find myself always watching what I am not supposed to; the peeling walls, the frayed rugs, the crossing and uncrossing legs of girls in the audience, etc. etc. and I see no reason for eliminating the power which place has over the audience."[36] In their admittedly perverse accounts of cinematic spectatorship, Oldenburg and Renan were remarkably close to what Roland Barthes would describe a decade later, in "Leaving the Movie Theater," as a "perverse" mode of cinematic spectatorship: "ready to fetishize not just the image but precisely what exceeds it: the texture of the sound, the hall, the darkness, the obscure mass of the other bodies, the rays of light, entering the theater, leaving the hall."[37]

Far from condemning this "perverse" model of spectatorship, Barthes presented it as a uniquely fluid and multifocal model of critical engagement. As was common in the film theory of the 1970s, Barthes described the captivating power of the cinema in terms of an imaginary identification—a process of interpellation that needed to be resisted through the imposition of a certain critical distance.[38] But Barthes himself resisted the idea that this critical distance should be imposed solely through cognitive means, such that the ideal spectator would arrive at the cinema "armed with the discourse of counter-ideology."[39] Such a purely intellectual resistance to cinema's fascinating power did not reveal the complexity of its inner workings so much as negate them entirely. As such, it had the paradoxical effect of leaving the unconscious, affective nature of this power wholly intact.

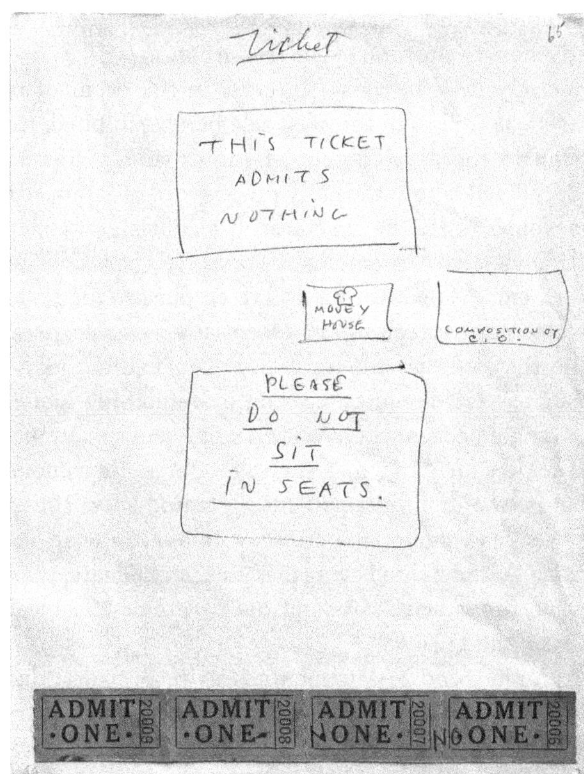

Figure 1.10. Claes Oldenburg, notebook page for *Moveyhouse* performance, "This Ticket Admits Nothing," 1965. Collection of Claes Oldenburg and Coosje van Bruggen.

Rather than withholding one's fascination with the image, Barthes proposed that one might allow oneself to be "hypnotized by a distance"—by all that "exceeds" the image within the total "cinematic situation." This distance "is not critical (intellectual); it is, one might say, an amorous distance … a *jouissance* of *discrétion*." Barthes asks that this last term be considered not only as "discretion" or "discernment," but in terms of its etymological roots as "separation" or "disjunction."[40] Comparing this split attention to the liminal state of emerging from a movie theater, groggy and bedazzled, he speaks of "being fascinated *twice over*, by the image and its surroundings."[41]

Such a hybrid form of attention would refuse the absorptive singularity of the dream, but no longer in the name of a simple material or ideological "reality" beyond all dreaming. Rather, it would work to replace the strict opposition between reality and dream with the structural ambivalence of fantasy. The world of the cinematic projection thus "remains concomitant to the consciousness of reality (that of the place where I am)" and the double consciousness thus precipitated within the spectator becomes a kind of "dislocation."[42] Within this newly hybrid mode of attention, the traditional, monological relationship between spectator and image would not be negated so much as "complicated" by a newfound attentiveness to the total cinematic situation.

It was precisely this "perverse" interest in the event of cinematic exhibition itself, as well as in the spectacle being exhibited, that would become central to the development of the expanded cinema in mid-1960s New York. Well before the early proponents of "apparatus theory" in the 1970s would locate the spectator in a consistent, coherent, and unified position vis-à-vis the cinematic spectacle, the artists and critics of expanded cinema had sought instead to emphasize the radical *contingency* of the cinematic screening, its essentially unstable, performative character, and the essential heterogeneity of its exhibitionary environment. For Renan, there could be no single overarching model of cinematic spectatorship because there was no single universalizable context of cinematic exhibition with which such a model would coincide. Where Walter Benjamin saw an infinitely identical, reproducible cinematic text overturning the place-bound aura of the work of art, Renan—under the influence of Cage—understood every instance of cinematic projection as a singular event, fundamentally conditioned by the malleable dynamics of its specific time and place.[43]

Oldenburg understood his Happenings as reconfigurations of very commonplace situations and experiences: "simply sitting and watching in an isolated way something that's *very familiar*."[44] The utterly unremarkable practice of going to the movies constituted a prime target. Yet Oldenburg's *Moveyhouse*, like Renan's Blue Mouse, actually served to highlight the radical transformations then taking place within this familiar institution. Oldenburg stressed that it was only *after* he had seen the Forty-First Street Theater that he agreed to do a work for the festival. His description situates it at the intersection of public and private histories: it is "the room in the Wurlitzer building where the Wurlitzers used to promote the sales of their violins and things by giving recitals. My friend Rudy Wurlitzer can remember having a recital in there. That's why its walls are all done up with scenes of Europe, pillars along the side, and all that kind of stuff gives it a certain identity . . . something like that late Paramount; there's enough to look at, if you don't want to look at the screen or the stage."[45]

The baroque embellishments of the Forty-First Street Theater, a miniature version of Hollywood's golden-age cinema palaces, provided a feast for the eyes independently of anything taking place on the screen. Its ornamentation provided it with "a certain identity" that gave Oldenburg "something to work with"—something that could not be reproduced in any "neutral" space.[46] The theater's name itself was part of this identity—not in its innocuous incarnation as the Forty-First Street Theater, but rather, as it was known to Oldenburg, as the "Wurlitzer auditorium." The

Wurlitzer family's organs were an iconic feature of many golden-age theaters in the 1920s and 1930s, including both the Paramount that Oldenburg references and the Blue Mouse described by Renan. These theater organs, typically used to introduce the evening's entertainment, embodied the tradition of live theatrical performance that maintained a direct continuity with the live piano accompaniment and sound effects within the so-called silent cinema and, going back even further, with cinema's ancestry in nineteenth-century vaudeville stage and variety shows.

By the 1940s, the Wurlitzer organs had mostly vanished from the theaters, and with them, the links to this historical tradition. The opulent décor of these theaters was not so easily removed, and thus often persevered despite decades of neglect, as in the case of the Blue Mouse. The Wurlitzer auditorium indexed not only a generic past, but a specific moment within cinema's early cultural history that had become newly relevant in the 1960s: cinema's uncertain status as a modern art and its proper place vis-à-vis established paradigms of fine art and culture. Faux colonnades and trompe-l'oeil murals—high camp by the 1960s—recalled cinema's early anxiety over its working-class roots in the nickelodeon and the traveling peep show as well as the tension that the proponents of this characteristically American art form felt in measuring up against the established cultural patrimony of Europe.

But these theaters did more than point toward the past: they spoke to the massive transformations taking place in cinematic exhibition in the present. New York's Paramount—only a few blocks from the Wurlitzer auditorium, off Forty-Third Street, and with a lobby modeled after the Paris Opera House—closed three months after *Moveyhouse* was performed.[47] At the very moment that the classical golden-age theater was experiencing a dramatic and irrevocable decline, the moving image was migrating to a heterogeneous range of new sites: from the grandiose new purpose-built Cinerama theaters to decaying, impoverished, working-class theaters like the Blue Mouse; from expansive twenty-five-hundred-car drive-in theaters in the suburbs to the intimately sized black-and-white television sets in the family living room. Last but not least, a range of new independent theaters—some converted from preexisting movie houses, others nothing more than a projector and some temporary seats—were dedicated to new forms of experimental and art cinema.

The Blue Mouse Renan describes was built in 1912, still in the industry's infancy. It was among the first theaters in the Pacific Northwest and had its heyday in the late 1910s and 1920s, when it premiered the first sound films in the region (introduced by its own Wurlitzer organ). By the 1930s, however, it was playing only second-run films. After the Blue Mouse was forced to relocate to a much poorer neighborhood, the organ was sold, and the theater became increasingly derelict, screening

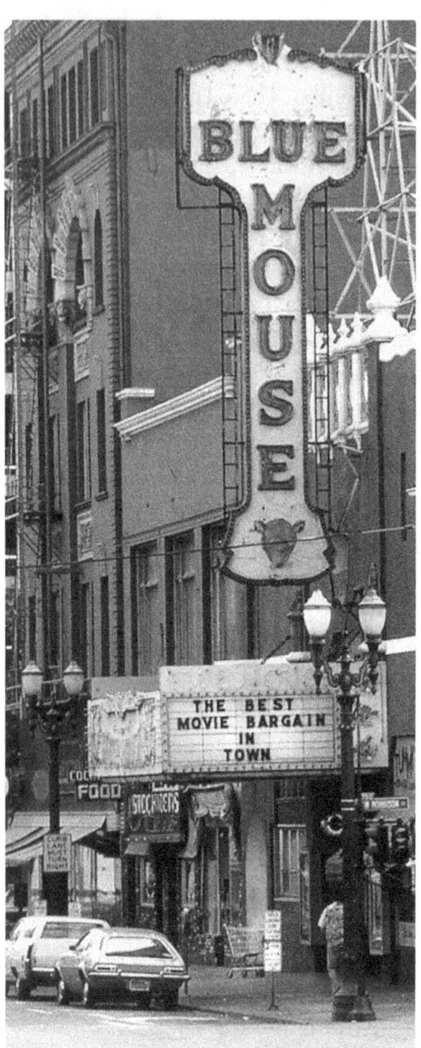

cartoons and serials on the weekends. Only the name and original signage remained of its noble origins. The Wurlitzer auditorium, while superficially resembling a golden-age theater, had actually begun its life as a musical recital hall before being converted into a stage for off-Broadway theater in the late 1950s. In December of 1965, at the conclusion of the Expanded Cinema Festival, it had become the latest venue for the quintessentially peripatetic Film-Makers' Cinematheque.[48] "All this moving around has got to stop," festival producer John Brockman had declared of an organization that had held six separate locations over the last two years, "I took this job to bring some sanity to the experimental film world."[49] Just two years later, the Film-Makers' Cinematheque would leave to circulate among several more temporary venues, while the Forty-First Street Theater would spend its final days as a porn theater, like so many others around Forty-Second Street.

The histories of both the Blue Mouse and the Wurlitzer auditorium highlight the degree to which these institutions are neither singular nor eternal, but constantly changing to accommodate new social functions. Just as "movie theater" is an abstraction that fails to account for the tremendous heterogeneity of screening sites across the twentieth century, "film" cannot be seen as a single thing from one era to the next. If critics did not visit the Blue Mouse, as Renan charged, it was because they felt obliged to ignore the idiosyncrasies of the theatrical context as extraneous to the film itself. Theaters like Blue Mouse and the Wurlitzer auditorium, by contrast, virtually insisted on their context. As such, they necessarily promoted the "diffuse" or "disjunctive" attention Barthes described.

Figure 1.11. Blue Mouse theater, Portland, Oregon, with original 1912 signboard, immediately prior to demolition, 1977.

Moveyhouse was not a work of film theory: it was impressionistic rather than didactic. Nevertheless, it conveyed a strong impression of the dynamic and unfixed character of cinematic exhibition: that cinema is not an eternal medium possessed of a singular essence, but a deeply historical form whose seven-decade trajectory had been one of almost constant transformation. On the one hand, there was the specificity of the cinematic situation *in general*—the particular bodily habitus promoted through its confluence of mechanical and architectural design. Within the cinematic screening, in contrast to spectators in a gallery or actors on a stage, the conjoined elements of projector, screen, and seated audience were all "fixed" in place, and this fixity was understood to engender certain perceptual and psychological consequences for the spectator. As initially developed by Jean-Louis Baudry and Christian Metz in the early 1970s, the theory of the cinematic apparatus, or *dispositif*, conceptualized the cinematic situation as a deep structure analogous to the Quattrocento system of perspectival representation, to which any cinematic spectator would be invariably subjected. Yet Renan and Oldenburg point toward another, less considered path, which involves not the psychoanalysis or phenomenology of an ahistorical structure, but an archeology of the variability and transformation of heterogeneous sites of exhibition and the differing models of spectatorship they engender.

John Cage had long been instrumental in articulating that a work's exhibitionary context constituted as significant an aspect of the work as anything internal to its material form. And Cage had attended Oldenburg's *Moveyhouse*, alongside Robert Rauschenberg, Robert Whitman, Merce Cunningham, Robert Morris, Yvonne Rainer, Andy Warhol, and Marcel Duchamp—an audience that attests not only to the work's perceived importance, but to the interdisciplinary milieu within which these ideas of art, film, and performance were being incubated. Yet Cage, for his part, was not enthralled so much as horrified. "It was a police situation," he later remarked to Richard Kostelanetz, "it was politically bad—telling people not to sit down. I refused, so I sat down, and so did Duchamp."[50] Duchamp, at seventy-eight, could certainly be excused for not wanting to stand for the length of the performance in a uncomfortably crowded aisle—he later apologized to Oldenburg for having to sit down—yet Cage felt something much larger was at stake.

> Kostelanetz: Were you uncomfortable standing up?
>
> Cage: No. I refuse to be told what to do.
>
> Kostelanetz: When you go to a conventional concert, do you sit in the seat?
>
> Cage: No one tells me that I can't get up and walk around. They do give me a ticket for a seat, and if I use it, that's my business.[51]

Cage's rejoinder is sincere and impassioned, yet seems profoundly odd—even petulant: "I refuse to be told what to do." Is Cage's difficulty with the prohibition itself or simply its explicit articulation? We do not normally think of the cinema as imposing uncomfortable restraints on our behavioral freedom any more than would a symphony concert, a dance performance, or an exhibition of paintings in a museum. In all these situations, the proper social conventions have become so natural and ingrained as to go unarticulated and unperceived. Yet it was precisely the unconscious disciplining of both art and its audience to which Cage and Oldenburg wished to call attention. For while Cage may have protested Oldenburg's measures, the strength of his objection illustrates the clarity of his understanding. As both artists knew, the black box of the cinematic theater was an institution guided, like any, by largely unwritten rules of behavioral conduct—rules that were aesthetically arbitrary and historically contingent. The necessity of taking one's seat, remaining quiet, and focusing one's attention on a single frame for an extended time within a darkened space was only a slightly more hyperbolic degree of control than that exhibited by the white cube of the museum or gallery space. Much as we might wish to touch the raised surface of a Pollock canvas, it would be quite rare to witness a patron insisting on this right as a result of having paid admission to the museum.[52]

Artists were increasingly coming to question the most basic paradigms of exhibition and spectatorship, and Cage himself had played a significant role in the inauguration of these inquiries. Since his infamous "silent piece" *4'33"*, Cage had sought to probe the conventional framing of the aesthetic experience and its habitualized modes of encounter. The invisible structures of order and discipline involved in going to a cinema, an art gallery, or a theatrical performance ran headlong into the anarchistic impulses of a younger generation who had begun to experience this bodily regulation as metonymic for a more general field of disciplinary control. While this larger field of disciplinary regulation was difficult even to comprehend, let alone transform, the concrete spaces of the gallery and theater emerged as suitable proxies—battlegrounds where this more diffuse cultural critique might be given particular form and substance.[53]

Cage's use of the term "police situation" may sound forced when describing the experience of Oldenburg's *Moveyhouse*, but his phrase ironically points to an episode that would be pivotal in a more general disciplining of cinematic spectatorship in this period—a project that the expanded cinema in general, and Andy Warhol's early work in particular, sought to contest. Linda Williams has described the early 1960s as ushering in an unprecedented disciplining of cinematic spectatorship through the adoption of new protocols of theatrical exhibition.[54] For Williams, no film better concretized this transformation than the landmark thriller that captured the imagination of audiences around the world: Alfred Hitchcock's *Psycho* (1960).

Because this film that came to define a new cinematic era, the internal dynamics of Hitchcock's *Psycho* have been subjected to nearly endless scrutiny by film historians and theorists. Less often considered—but of potentially equal importance—are the *external* dynamics of the work: to wit, Hitchcock's unprecedented concern for, and control over, what Renan termed "the total cinematic situation." As Stephen Rebello recounts in his book on the making of *Psycho*, a central part of Alfred Hitchcock's publicity campaign included strict rules that theater doors be locked after the screening commenced—and included warnings to this effect throughout the local papers, which declared, "No one ... BUT NO ONE ... will be admitted to the theatre after the start of each performance of *Psycho*."

> Hitchcock not only advised but also insisted that theatre owners follow his decree against admitting patrons once the picture began; finally he demanded the enforcing of his decree as a contractual prerequisite for any theatre exhibitor who booked the film ... Ticket buyers were accustomed to casually dropping in and out in the days when movie houses opened at 10:00 am and double-features, short subjects, and previews of coming attractions ran continuously through late evening. Owners of several major theatre chains feared that patrons would rebel at being told when and how they could view a movie—even by the mighty Hitchcock. Some chains rumbled about boycotts. Hitchcock stood fast ... Publicity kits included tips for hiring Pinkerton guards to enforce the admission policies. "This man of the law will not only handle lines and crowds admirably," advised Hitchcock, "but can also help your cashier explain our policy when doors are closed."[55]

Cage's "police situation" is here not only literally manifest, but contractually stipulated. The managing of the theater, the audience, and the screening procedures were all precisely delineated: "Close your house curtains over the screen after the end-titles of the picture, and keep the theatre dark for ½ minute," Hitchcock demanded of the theaters that would exhibit his film. "During these 30 seconds of stygian blackness, the suspense of *Psycho* is indelibly engraved in the mind of the audience ... Never, never, never will I permit *Psycho* to be followed immediately by a short subject or newsreel."[56] Latecoming spectators could dislocate the viewer—bringing her back to her physical body, located in a seat, among other viewers, in a physical space in which she is watching a film, rather than being wholly immersed in its world. Hitchcock insisted on nothing less than absolute autonomy for the "narrative space" of his cinematic creation and nothing less than absolutely immersive spectatorship from his audience.

One might reasonably object that this was a mere ruse for publicity, an echo of William Castle's legendary B-movie antics of the 1950s for a mainstream audience. Yet Williams makes it clear that Hitchcock is only a particularly visible instance within a much more general promotion of spectatorial discipline. Well into the 1950s, she reminds us, it was common practice to view multiple shorts and features in a single theatrical outing, and audiences often arrived partway into a feature without suffering either the guilt or social opprobrium that would later emerge. Yet for the auteurs and cinephiles of the day, in the midst of their struggle

Figure 1.12. The Invisible Cinema theater, designed by Peter Kubelka and built by Giorgio Cavaglieri for Anthology Film Archives at The Public Theater, 425 Lafayette Street, New York, 1970–1974.

to lift film from its lowly status among the rival arts, such informal, haphazard behavior could no longer be countenanced. Film would no longer be treated like a mere entertainment, a distraction to be picked up or left off as the spectator so desired. The seriousness of an art form was felt to be indissociable from the rigorous disciplining of its spectatorship. For cinema, this disciplining required the regulation of the spectatorial body within the theatrical space.

Williams's essay concerns the changes generally taking place within the mainstream industrial cinema of the 1960s. But perhaps the most hyperbolic literalization of this paradigm would take place within the cinematic avant-garde. The architecture of Peter Kubelka's theater for the Film-Makers' Cinematheque might seem a caricature of this idea of spectatorial discipline if it had not been intended in all seriousness. This so-called Invisible Cinema effectively cordoned off each patron within her own individual cell, isolated from any visual, auditory, or physical distraction by neighboring audience members. Here, the unruly possibilities of a collective gathering are conspicuously neutralized in favor of a repetition of what was considered the ideal theatrical environment—the private screening.[57]

It was precisely this model of spectatorial discipline that Andy Warhol's *Sleep* (1963) sought to upend. Warhol had an ambivalent relationship with Hollywood, and the feeling was decidedly mutual. Regardless of his burgeoning celebrity, not a single one of his *Elvis* paintings sold during his first Los Angeles exhibition in 1963, and what critical reviews he received were almost uniformly hostile. But Los Angeles being a movie town, there was real excitement when Warhol's debut film *Sleep* premiered at the Cinema Theatre in late June of the following year. A crowd of five hundred eagerly purchased tickets for a film billed only as "something strange, unusual, daring, that lasted six hours."[58]

"Six hours" was typical Hollywood exaggeration: *Sleep* ran only five hours and twenty-one minutes. Nor were films of such length entirely unprecedented. Erich von Stroheim's *Greed*, both silent-era adaptations of *Les Miserables*, and Abel Gance's *Napoléon* had all stretched over five hours. But these silent epics had gone to great lengths to ensure their audiences' attention, using everything from intricate plot twists and risqué costumes to rudimentary special effects. And like any other evening performance of theater, music, or dance, they had featured regularly scheduled intermissions, in which audience members were permitted to leave their seats. *Sleep* dispensed with all of this. At a time when the new Technicolor process was being lauded for its advancements over earlier, more primitive forms of color, Warhol's film lacked any color whatsoever. At a time when stereophonic and even four- and six-channel sound was being used to lure viewers away from the single-channel audio of the home television set, Warhol's film lacked any sound whatsoever.

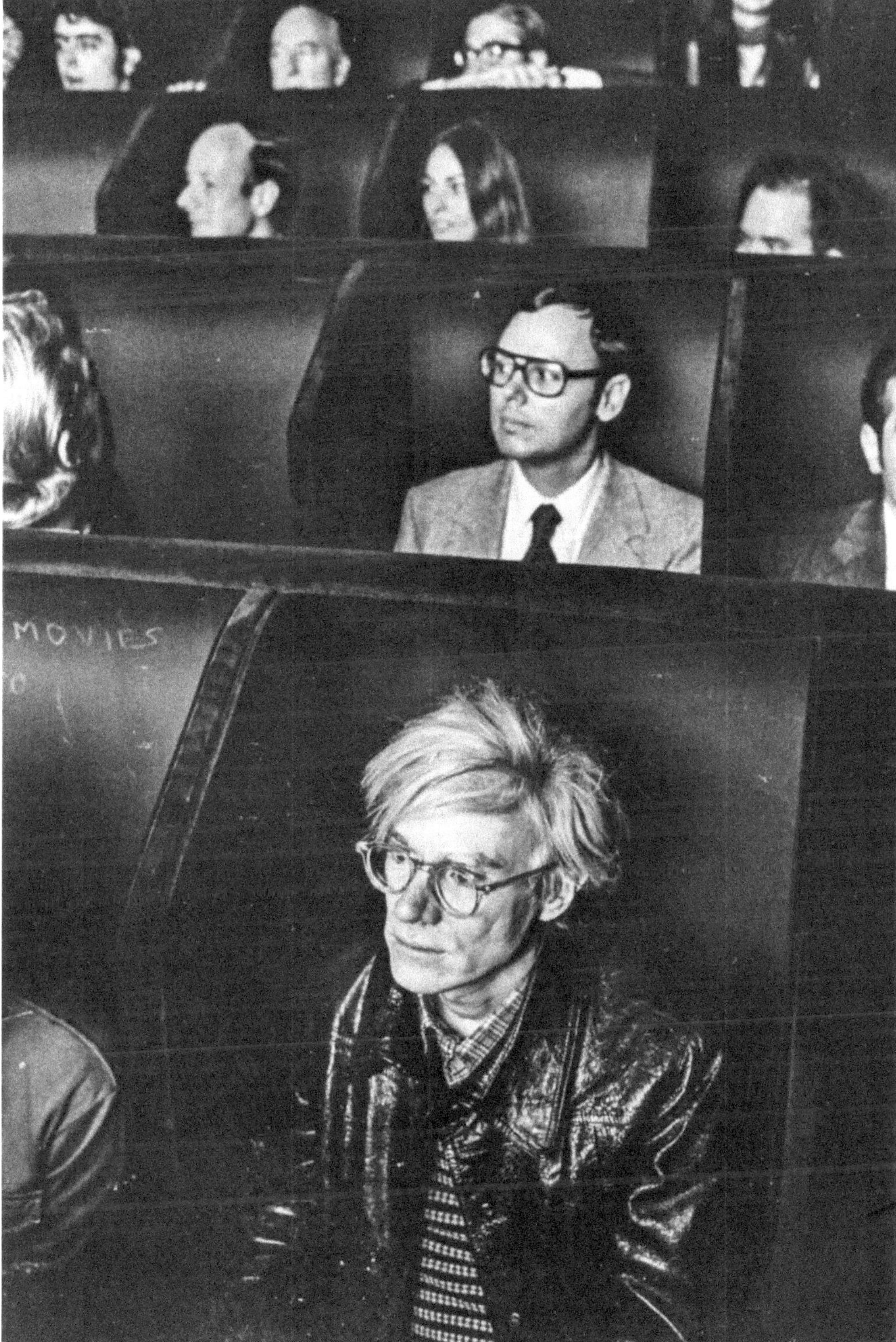
MOVIES

Stan Brakhage, the most important and critically lauded experimental filmmaker of the time, had also done away with sound, but the perceptual battery elicited by his signature rapid-fire editing and tightly structured formal compositions more than compensated for the loss. By contrast, Warhol's early films were so utterly lacking in perceptual stimulus that many came to question whether he had removed the "motion" from the motion picture altogether. Moreover, there were no intermissions—just a continuous three-hundred-twenty-one-minute silent, black-and-white feature. At a time of exploding studio budgets, narrative exuberance, star-studded casts ... *anything* that could lure an audience back to the theater—Warhol's *Sleep* seemed determined to drive them away. The results of this intervention were far from benign. The theater manager, Mike Getz, described the opening in a letter to Jonas Mekas:

> Amazing turnout. 500 people. *Sleep* started at 6:45 ... People started to walk out at 7, some complaining. People getting more and more restless. Show finally changes to close-up of man's head. Someone runs up to screen and shouts in sleeping man's ear, "WAKE UP!!" Audience getting bitter, strained ... Lobby full, one red-faced guy very agitated, says I have 30 seconds to give him his money back or he'll run into theatre and start a "lynch riot." "We'll all come out here and lynch you, buddy!!" Nobody stopped him when 30 seconds were up; he ran back toward screen ... thoughts of recent football riot in South America. People angry as hell, a mob on the verge of violence.[59]

Getz describes how he was forced to give out free passes, and how one woman later called to inform him that she had been forced to leave early, fearing imminent violence. Whence the incredible aggressiveness? The sense of "getting cheated" was clearly pervasive that evening, although the event seems to have generated an affective investment wholly out of proportion to the paltry ticket price. There was clearly some greater indignity that the Los Angeles audience felt it had been made to suffer, some more painful situation it had had to endure than the prosaic, commonplace affair of failing to be sufficiently entertained.

In both its minimal articulation and its radically expanded duration, Warhol's *Sleep* could not but provoke comparisons with Cage's historic first production, earlier that year, of Erik Satie's eighteen-hour-long *Vexations*.[60] In both works, an extreme reduction of incident, repeated over an extended duration, resulted in a phenomenologically charged perceptual situation. Minor variations struck with novel resonance; in the absence of variation, the viewer was thrown back on herself, on her own act of spectatorship. Within this temporal dialectic of stillness and movement, Warhol's early "portrait films" fail to provide anything like the kind of direct and immediate encounter one might expect from their literalism or lack of expressivity. Rather than simply presenting recorded reality, they present the reality of recording—the mediation and distance inherent in the cinematic situation.

Warhol's negation of the most commonly elaborated practices of commercial cinema would come to be widely understood as a method of systematic reduction toward film's *material* essence. The normally moving, transcendent camera is replaced by the fixity of the unblinking stare in order to call attention to the cinematic frame itself and its delimitation of the optical field. Malcolm Le Grice—a leading voice in the British "structuralist" appropriation of Warhol in the next decade—would characterize Warhol's discovery as the creation of what he termed a "shallow" time. Within the rhetoric of modernist aesthetics, the illusionary deep space of perspective characteristic of European painting since the Renaissance had been progressively abandoned in favor of what Clement Greenberg called "the integrity of the picture plane."[61] Le Grice viewed Warhol's presentation of this shallow time as an analogous effort to rid the medium of an unnecessary "illusionism" so as to permit "a credible relationship between the time of interior action and the physical experience of film as a material presentation."[62] In refusing the ubiquitous practice of montage, Warhol refused the construction of a cinematic time distinct and separate from the time of the spectator. This, in turn, was understood to enable a more direct consideration of the material stuff of film itself as a medium of artistic practice. Contrary to the absorptive qualities of Hollywood's narrative time, Le Grice understood Warhol's "direct" or unedited time to be anti-illusionistic, reflexive, and materialist.

Yet Warhol himself was no more invested in the strict modernist conception of medium-specificity than was Oldenburg or Paik. Perhaps even more shockingly, he didn't seem to care whether or not his films were fully viewed. This is not to repeat the oft-heard premise that these films were merely "conceptual" and were not to be literally experienced in the theater as such. Rather, it is to claim the opposite: that the radical purchase of Warhol's turn to film was as much a challenge to protocols of cinematic exhibition and spectatorship as it was the "innovation" he brought to formal composition and editing. These works, while taking place within the exhibitionary conditions of the movie theater, cannot be understood as "movies" in any conventional sense of the term, and this was the principal source of their power. These films were unrecognizable as such not simply to the average moviegoer, but also to the vast majority of new wave, experimental, or avant-garde filmmakers of the time. While such things were unconscionable to the aesthetically ambitious auteurs of the day, Warhol was apparently untroubled by viewers becoming distracted, talking, or even walking in and out of the theater during the screening of his films. And that is precisely what happened. Sympathetic audiences often lingered for a time, went into the lobby to "hang out," then went back into the theater after a time to continue the experience.[63] Warhol did not object to any of this. In fact, Warhol described his early films as efforts "to help the audiences get more acquainted with themselves" and specifically characterized this familiarization as social rather than introspective: "Usually, when you go to the movies, you sit in a fantasy world, but when you see something that disturbs you, you get more involved with the people next to you."[64]

Warhol's cinema did not bring new imagery or new themes into the language of cinema so much as it hijacked the institution of cinema, and the particular cultural space of the cinematic theater, for an entirely new form of aesthetic practice. *Sleep*'s radical duration, far from remaining a formal feature of the *work*, must rather be understood as a transformation of the theatrical *site*. Within a traditional theatrical screening, the film is understood to exist for our benefit. We always know that the film has concluded before we exit the theater and that there is nothing more to be seen. *Sleep* steadfastly inhibited this assimilatory conception of spectatorship, in which the visual field can be fully and definitively "taken in."[65] Like so many artists since the 1990s who have produced works of literally unwatchable durations (i.e., days or weeks), Warhol made the audience members who chose to leave *Sleep* fully conscious of their own decision to *abandon* the cinematic image in midstream. In so doing, Warhol subtly nodded to the artifice of the cinematic situation as well as to the spectatorial labor inevitably involved in the production of cinematic meaning.

Stripping the film of color, narrative, and montage can be understood as a way of stepping back from the teleological thrust of industrial practices—especially those of the 1950s, which, as we have seen, were increasingly devoted to the grandiosity of the immersive spectacle. Reversing the trajectory of increasing diegetic immersivity, in which the spectator was psychologically incorporated into the narrative world of the film, his practices would recall an earlier moment when the practices of cinematic exhibition and spectatorship were less specifically delimited. Asked once what movie era he most admired, Warhol did not choose either the glamorous Hollywood of the golden age or the silent masterpieces of the 1920s. Instead, rather precisely, he designated "the early 1910s"—the brief period immediately before D. W. Griffith's phenomenal success installed a basic paradigm and template for the industrial narrative drama.[66] Warhol's earliest films—silent, colorless, focused on a specific tableau or incident—superficially resemble the *actualitiés* of the earliest days of cinema. But more important than this formal similarity was a certain dream of "early cinema" and a kind of liberation it seemed to offer. In gesturing toward a kind of primal scene of cinematic production, Warhol's "early films" reminded his viewers of a moment before the formal conventions and societal expectations of the theatrical drama were so rigidly prescribed.

This preindustrial model of exhibition would come to be theorized as a "cinema of attractions" in the work of Tom Gunning and André Gaudreault in the mid-1980s and within an ever-expanding film historical literature since that time.[67] The term was taken from the Soviet filmmaker and theorist Sergei Eisenstein, who had taken the exhibitionistic "attractions" of the fairground and circus as a model for his efforts to theorize a revolutionary cinema that would counter the individualist worldview he felt was perpetrated by Hollywood's immersive, voyeuristic, character-driven narratives. Eisenstein had chosen the term "attraction"—popular in the late nineteenth century but then considered beneath the cultural aspirations of the day's cinephiles—to signal his interest in plumbing the fantastic heterogeneity of late nineteenth-century exhibitionary models. For Gunning, as for Eisenstein before him, the term embodied a refusal of the progressive, developmental model of history, a "liberation" of these first practices "from the teleological approach that classed them as 'primitive' attempts at later forms" in order to recover a "different configuration of spectatorial involvement, an address that can . . . interact in complex and varied ways with other forms of involvement."[68]

Within this past, as Gunning and others have shown, film was more akin to the "open" spectacles of a fairground or carnival than to the enclosed illusion of the narrative drama that industrial practice would come to enforce. Far from the immersive spectacle to which contemporary cinematic audiences would become accustomed, what fascinated early audiences—first and foremost—was the very spectacle of projection. To take but a single example, early audiences in Japan were often seated *perpendicular* to the projector and the screen. That this particular preindustrial arrangement would be precisely reconstituted within Oldenburg's *Moveyhouse* seems no mere coincidence. Artists who turned to the moving image over the course of the 1960s were generally invested in recovering these "different configurations of spectatorial involvement" within a prehistory of cinema that might serve as prologue to its future reinvention.[69] The formal aesthetics of early cinema were employed as an index of that cinema's social and cultural situation—the idea of reinventing the space of the theater itself and the possibilities of audiovisual exhibition and spectatorship that could take place therein. It was not some specific practice that these artists wanted to recapture, but rather a basic sense of wonder—the liberating incoherence and heterogeneity of a time before the formal conventions and societal expectations of cinematic technology became so myopically delimited.

Taken together, Paik's *Zen for Film*, Warhol's *Sleep*, and Oldenburg's *Moveyhouse* articulated a kind of "degree zero" of cinema—a desire to reinvent not merely the formal possibilities of the cinematic image, but the sediment of social conduct and expectation that maintained a larger conceptualization of "cinema" as such. Far from wanting to employ the latest and most sophisticated technologies of the moving image, a whole range of artists who would come to be grouped under the rubric of expanded cinema sought to return to the early and precinematic technologies of the previous century. Shadow plays, lantern slides, and mutoscopes were combined with a willful primitivism of technique—the unmoving camera, the silent image, the single extended shot—that reframed cinematic exhibition less as a medium for narrative than as a performance in its own right. Dwight MacDonald well expressed the critical exasperation with what was then termed the "New American Cinema" when he quipped, "I'm still hoping for something Cinematic, whether New or American."[70] His frustration was both apt and telling. For while they were fascinated with the technology and culture of cinema, most of these artists were uninterested in the established codes of either mainstream or experimental cinema. Most were not, and did not desire to become, "filmmakers."

One reason for this was cinema's recent institutional legitimation. Beginning in Venice and Cannes, a postwar boom in international film festivals, together with an increasingly broad range of critical literature had begun to establish the idea of the "European art film" as a distinct and autonomous form of modern art. With the establishment of the New York Film Festival in 1963 at the prestigious Lincoln Center for the Performing Arts, this incremental development had been given a concrete and poignant specificity. Having only recently emerged from the shadow of European cultural patrimony, postwar American artists were, unsurprisingly, reluctant to turn their gaze again toward Europe.[71] The critical consensus at the New York Film Festival—in thrall to the European cinema, and decidedly hostile to the experimental cinema of the New York underground—only exacerbated the division.[72]

Against the backdrop of the New York World's Fair on the one hand and the New York Film Festival on the other, a wide-ranging body of art practice and criticism would explore the new terrain of expanded cinema. During a particularly frenetic period in New York from 1964 to 1966, a fantastic range of artists from a variety of disciplinary traditions were involved: Andy Warhol, Stan VanDerBeek, Robert Whitman, Ken Dewey, Robert Breer, Nam June Paik, John Cage, Bruce Conner, USCO, Ken Jacobs, Tony Conrad, Paul Sharits, Yoko Ono, Takehisa Kosugi, Roberts Blossom, Elaine Summers, Trisha Brown, and Meredith Monk, among numerous others. Criticism quickly followed. Michael Kirby devoted an issue of the *Tulane Drama Review* to what he called "Film and the New Theatre." Jonas Mekas and Jill Johnson penned numerous reviews in their columns for the *Village Voice*, and screenings and public discussions on the topic took place at the fourth New York Film Festival and at the "Projected Art" exhibition at Finch College in the winter of 1966. Only a few months later, George Macunias would help produce the special issue of *Film Culture* devoted to the topic, and Sheldon Renan would complete his pathbreaking

Introduction to the American Underground Film, attempting to summarize what had recently transpired.

By 1967, the place of the moving image within late modern aesthetics had been radically thrown into question. Over the next decade, the moving image would not only grow in importance within contemporary art practice, it would become increasingly woven into the very nature of that practice. For writers such as John Gruen, Michael Kirby, Susan Sontag, and Sheldon Renan, Greenberg's critical delineation of a certain kind of modernism—one grounded in fidelity to a rigidly delineated and compartmentalized understanding of the artistic medium—no longer seemed the most fertile ground for aesthetic and conceptual inquiry. Refusing a rhetoric of medium-specificity that sought to dictate in advance what was essential and inessential, proper and improper, the artists working in expanded cinema sought instead to reconceptualize both cinema and contemporary art practice by means of their mutual imbrication. Refusing the bureaucratization of aesthetic experience into traditional disciplinary regimes, as well as the progressivist teleology on which it was premised, the artists and critics of this "Combine Generation" sought new models of interdisciplinary juxtaposition, wherein the institutional traditions of music, dance, theater, and film would be consciously brought to bear on one another.[73]

Ken Dewey, whose own exploration of the performance situation had long been driven by an interest in issues of context and situation, perhaps captured the idea most succinctly in his statement for the Expanded Cinema Symposium in 1966—a statement with which both Oldenburg and VanDerBeek appeared to concur:

> I think an easy way to understand what's going on in Expanded Cinema, a kind of justification for it is this—Hollywood has created contexts in which its films can be seen ... Loew's Sheridan, any one of these palaces. This was to put you in a certain context when you see the film. Well, now, as we move into new areas, some ... have been acutely aware of the problems of introducing their work into that kind of situation ... the context becomes overwhelmingly important, particularly where the whole tone, the whole material and everything else—is changed. In the so-called Expanded Cinema, what is emerging is a consciousness of that context. And little by little, methods are developing for dealing with it, for altering it.[74]

Despite their formal diversity, these artists shared a common desire to understand, articulate, and ultimately reimagine the institutional situation of cinema—the literal and figurative "place" of the motion picture—within the increasingly interdisciplinary spaces of contemporary art. Departing from the conventions of the black box screening, artists were beginning to incorporate the moving image across a multiplicity of exhibitionary sites: from prestigious music halls to abandoned television studios, from individual loft apartments to public churches, from auditorium lobbies to theatrical stages.

The works produced within these spaces were generally not "site-specific" in the way that term would later come to be understood. In the beginning, many locations were chosen simply out of necessity or convenience. But as it became increasingly commonplace to depart from the specific rules and conventions of the classical cinematic screening, there was a growing recognition that the very nature of a moving-image medium was irrevocably bound up with the particular conditions of its exhibition. As such, fundamental changes in the cinematic situation—not simply the physical architecture and mechanics of moving-image exhibition, but also the institutional and discursive context within which this exhibition was seen and understood—would necessitate a fundamental reconceptualization of the cinematic experience.

At the very historical moment in which cinema's specificity and autonomy as a modern art had finally been unambiguously legitimated, the expanded cinema sought to throw everything back into question. Not content to restrict cinema to an autonomous and isolated purity, these artists sought to harness and exploit cinema's historical and conceptual multiplicity in order to intervene within a diverse new range of situations and contexts. Unconcerned with the elevation of cinema to the level of a fine art, they sought instead to ask how the *idea* of cinema might function to subvert established codes of exhibition and spectatorship within the established arts more generally, thus precipitating a more fundamental transformation in the spaces and possibilities of "post-cinematic" art as such.

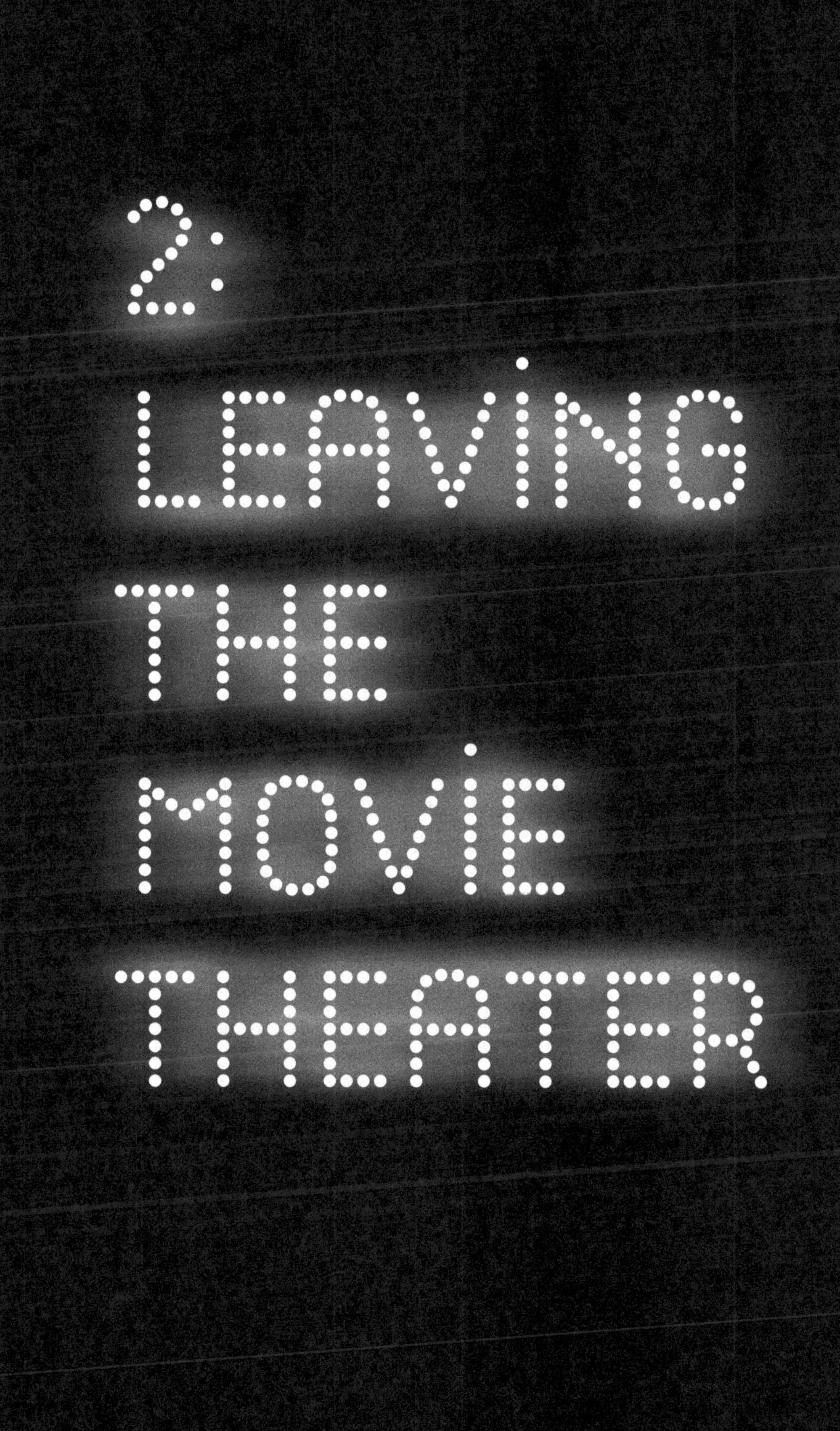
2:
LEAVING
THE
MOVIE
THEATER

I was not, in my youth, particularly affected by cinema's "Europeans" . . . perhaps because I, early on, developed an aversion to Surrealism—finding it an altogether inadequate (highly symbolic) envisionment of dreaming. What did rivet my attention (and must be particularly distinguished) was Jean-Isidore Isou's *Treatise*: as a creative polemic it has no peer in the history of cinema.

STAN BRAKHAGE

Isou's *Treatise* (1950) on Disjunctive Cinema

Though long neglected within both art and film history, the Parisian Lettrists must be considered the first theorists of the postwar expanded cinema. The cinematic manifestos of Isidore Isou (born Ioan-Isidor Goldstein) and Maurice Lemaître (born Moïse Maurice Bismuth) announced the postwar rehabilitation of the Dada legacy as distinct from the watered-down surrealism into which it had descended. Their works were not films in any traditional sense so much as self-conscious manifestos in film toward what was being called simply *une cinema d'aielleurs*.

These provocative early interventions posed questions regarding the nature and specificity of cinema, its institutions, and modes of spectatorial address that laid the aesthetic and conceptual foundations for the development of expanded cinema and intermedia performance in the years to come. Yet because these works self-consciously departed from aesthetic conventions then understood as "specific" to the cinematic medium, they were systematically neglected within official histories of midcentury art and film—even those exclusively concerned with the postwar avant-garde film.[1] Nevertheless, the influence of Lettrist cinema was both specific and direct. Stan Brakhage—doubtless the most significant figure in the emergence of the New American Cinema of the 1960s—attended the first screening of Isou's *Traité de Bave et d'Éternité* in San Francisco in 1953 and was profoundly affected by the event, describing it not only as a seminal moment for the development of his own aesthetic, but as a work he would regularly screen and analyze in his classes on experimental film history and practice over the next four decades.[2]

In her extended study of Clement Greenberg, Caroline Jones has detailed the extent to which midcentury aesthetics were dominated by a rhetoric of isolated and purified opticality.[3] A parallel, subterranean current would counter this ascendant visuality with the complexities of aurality. Simultaneously in France and America, in the development of *Musique Concrete* and in the work of John Cage, the 1950s began with a renewed interest in the possibilities of sound and its disjunctive relationship to both visual and spatial experience. It was this idea of a disjunctive or disunitary assemblage—in which sensory experiences are placed in open conflict, rather than synesthetic coherence—that best serves to characterize the cinematic manifestos of the Parisian Lettrists. Despite their name, the Lettrists' interest in language was neither an indication of its absolute value nor a straightforward denigration of the visual, but simply a recognition of the weak and haphazard development of what we would now term cinema's "intertextual" possibilities. Their audiovisual manifestos—some of the first "film essays" that deserve the title—sought to introduce a disjunctive textuality to the tightly integrated synthesis of industrial cinema. And they did so by bringing these ideas to the heart of the international cinema community in 1951 by means of a legendary provocation of the International Film Festival at Cannes.

We should recall that the Cannes festival, while initiated before World War II, had taken place only three times prior to 1951. While the festival was obviously a marker of prestige and renown for the directors in competition, it was just as much a place to debate and institutionalize the appropriate aesthetic trajectory for the growing consensus around the idea of cinema as a modern art. The two most popular and successful films that year, Vittorio De Sica's *Miracle in Milan* and Joseph Mankiewicz's *All About Eve,* were polar opposites in terms of form. *All About Eve* represented the height of the polished American studio picture, while *Miracle in Milan* deployed the gritty, naturalistic aesthetic of Italian neorealism. By screening these two films, the jury at Cannes probably thought itself quite catholic in its taste, not insisting on a particular formal program but able to celebrate heterogeneous forms and traditions within its conception of film art.

It was into this atmosphere of cultured sophistication that the young Jewish Romanian expatriate Isou brought a half-completed, rather incongruously titled work, *Traité de Bave et d'Éternité* (hereafter, *Treatise*), that entirely confounded this emphasis on cinematic realism.[4] Filled with an audacity and egotism rare even for a twenty-five-year-old, this self-proclaimed revolutionary went door to door, harassing the administrators of the festival until they agreed to grant him a small, peripheral exhibition. It would be a considerable understatement to say that the jury did not like what they saw. Almost immediately, the room was filled with boos and hisses, and after the first section was completed and the screen went completely blank, the audience became apoplectic and the screening was unable to continue.[5] Isou took their disdain as a badge of honor—and as copy for his future posters. He also took comfort in the fact that the one member of the jury aligned with the avant-garde, the seminal surrealist Jean Cocteau, bestowed on him a hastily concocted *Prix de spectateurs d'avant-garde* so that he would not go away empty-handed.

Although young, Isou was not unknown to the Parisian artistic milieu. Quitting Romania and traveling to post-*Libération* Paris at twenty years of age, Isou had quickly built a reputation for himself as a language poet in the tradition of his fellow countryman Tristan Tzara, the cofounder of Dada's legendary Cabaret Voltaire. Penning manifestos on everything from political economy and history to aesthetics and erotics, he created a small circle of devoted followers for himself and his self-proclaimed movement, *Lettrisme*. Isou had come to Paris with impeccable revolutionary credentials, having been the leader of a youth organization in Romania devoted to the Communist Party. Yet his youthful dedication to the party had soured, and upon arriving in Paris, he vocally distanced himself from the French Communist Party. Rather, Isou had become convinced of the rising power and importance of youth culture for the future transformation of society, and this idea would remain a defining feature of the Lettrist and, later, the Situationist program. The roots of Situationism date from this first screening of *Treatise* at Cannes, where a young philosophy student by the name of Guy-Ernest Debord had been impressed by Isou's ideas on social and political transformation and had taken up with the group upon their return to Paris.

Isou had laid out the basic tenets of his aesthetic in his 1947 volume *Introduction to a New Poetry and a New Music*.[6] Much of this early manifesto rests on a fundamental distinction between two successive phases in the development of the artistic medium. The *phase amplique*—the "amplifying" or "growth" phase of a medium—comes at the beginning, as the basic formal conventions and vocabularies are elaborated, and gives expressive form to various thematic concerns. The *phase ciselante*—the "chiseling" or "deconstructive" phase—occurs when exhaustion with the terms of this "expressivity" has set in and routine and formal stagnation are judged to have taken over. At this point, an advanced art practice ceases to employ the medium as a means to represent external subjects and themes, and instead takes up the very conventions and vocabularies of the medium itself as its subject.

In the abstract, Isou's theory seemed little more than an idiosyncratic articulation of some of the broader principles of aesthetic modernism. But his programmatic articulation of these principles to the field of film and cinematic culture would prove a revolutionary spark, establishing an avant-garde cinema in Paris practically ex nihilo and intuiting a range of formal and conceptual issues that would prove central to experimental film and media artists for decades to come. Isou's first contention was that cinema, precisely *because* it was already being considered, seen, and discussed in the ciné-clubs of Paris as an art, had already reached its first death. A superficial level of quality could be maintained simply through the mining of past innovations and the reshuffling of various forms and themes, but it was precisely the ease of such formulae that heralded the close of a certain era of wide-open possibility.

Describing Isou's motivation in a rare American review, Guy Coté writes, "The motion picture had, until this new movement appeared, been the only valid art form on which a concentrated destructive attack had not been launched within the last hundred years ... *Pour un cinéma ailleurs!* is today the message of St. Germain-des-Prés."[7] Lettrist films were indeed an attack and a provocation, but they have too often been understood as purely anarchic negations without structure or meaning. Deliberately enraging their audiences in a jejune allegory of political revolution, their message was: "As I rebel against cinematic decorum, so you should rebel against the decorum of an unjust society!" Hence the countless, and mainly apocryphal, stories of rioting audiences, police arriving with fire hoses, and the like. As Greil Marcus and others have noted, these "events" were almost all exaggerated—if not concocted—for the sake of publicity. The Lettrist cinema is best understood not as empty provocation, but as a series of complex constructions: admixtures of proposition and cancellation, recombinations of appropriated audiovisual material into new assemblages for thought and experience.

Isou had a profound respect for the history of cinema and its historical evolution. Unlike many future practitioners of experimental film and video, he clearly saw himself as the descendant of a half century of aesthetic development within the moving image. For Isou, this development had become stalled by the very success of the studio system. It had reached such a peak of technical competence—it had so mastered the seamless conjunction of cinematography, acting, dialogue, and sound—that the creation of perfectly autonomous cinematic worlds took place automatically, by rote. While he did not put it in these terms, Isou seemed to evoke the Wagnerian *Gesamtkunstwerk*, or "total work of art," in his condemnation, arguing that individual elements in the film, such as the soundtrack, were inevitably subordinated and thus invisible in the course of their synthesis. In his view, both studios and audiences had become resigned to this model of immersivity, whether in the sophisticated manner of a Bresson or Wyler or in the tawdry antics of the Cinerama or the 3D cinema. The art of cinema thus no longer questioned its basic structures of representation.

Against this synthetic vision, Isou argued for the independence of multiple textual or discursive levels that could move in and out of synthesis, generating a multiplicity or disruption within the heart of the work itself. Rejecting the realist aesthetics of André Bazin then dominant within film criticism, Isou's *cinéma discrepant* harked back to the proposals of Dziga Vertov and works like his *Enthusiasm, or the Symphony of the Dombas* (1930). The Latin verb *discrepare* (from *crepare*, "to make noise," and *dis*, "to split off") connoted not only the idea of atonality, but also the purposeful disjunction of different modalities. Reversing the traditional privileging of image over text, this disjunctive cinema would incorporate long passages of spoken literary and philosophical text into the space of the theatrical presentation, allowing cinematic spectators to become readers and listeners in addition to viewers. By deliberately unlinking the sound from the picture, Isou sought to create a textual level that could float free of the narrative cinema's diegetic world. Autonomous, yet constantly creating new kinds of association through its interaction with the image, this new textual level would transform the synthetic coherence of the immersive narrative film into an audiovisual constellation composed of multiple and divergent modalities of experience.

While Isou's principal *written* treatise would be articulated the next year in his book *Aesthetics of Cinema*, his first, and arguably most powerful, articulation of these ideas was presented through the very medium they set out to critique.[8] Audiences for *Treatise* in 1951 were right to question whether what they were seeing was even a film—it certainly bore no relationship to any known work, past or present. Even though Stan Brakhage described it as "one of the most powerful films I've ever seen," he tellingly added, "I am not sure it is a work of art so much as it is a powerful film essay."[9]

Treatise begins neither with language nor with image, but with sounds—an endlessly repeating, incomprehensible yet distinctly human chant. The darkness of the theater and the anticipation of the opening image obliges us to attend to the specificities of these sounds even more acutely than in a concert hall. Because we are unable to translate these sounds into language and hence signification, they obdurately remain sound, human sound—curiously physical and substantial for all its immateriality. For almost four minutes, we are left in the dark with this looped, two-second repetition. Absent any other stimuli, this chant acquires a mesmerizing rhythm and sonority. Thus anchored in our memory, this hybrid human-mechanical force seems to persist behind the imagery that follows, a kind of motor powering the film's forward movement.

The film's opening sequence shows a poster announcing Charlie Chaplin in "L'opinion Générale" (presumably a play on *L'opinion Publique*, originally *A Woman of Paris*, 1923). As the protagonist Daniel—played by Isou, but voiced by Albert LeGros—leaves the theater and his eyes strain against the midday sun, a voice-over tells us that Daniel feels as if his head has been used as a drinking vessel by savages. We are told that "the characters and setting of this story are—of course—imaginary," yet Daniel is clearly Isou, even if he is not voiced by Isou, and the lecture on film aesthetics we hear is quite evidently a lecture from Isou, even though the lips of the character on-screen never mouth a single word. This textual splitting and overlap—of actor and director, of fictional character and flesh-and-blood person, and of non-diegetic and quasi-diegetic monologue—is an element Godard would employ throughout the next decade.

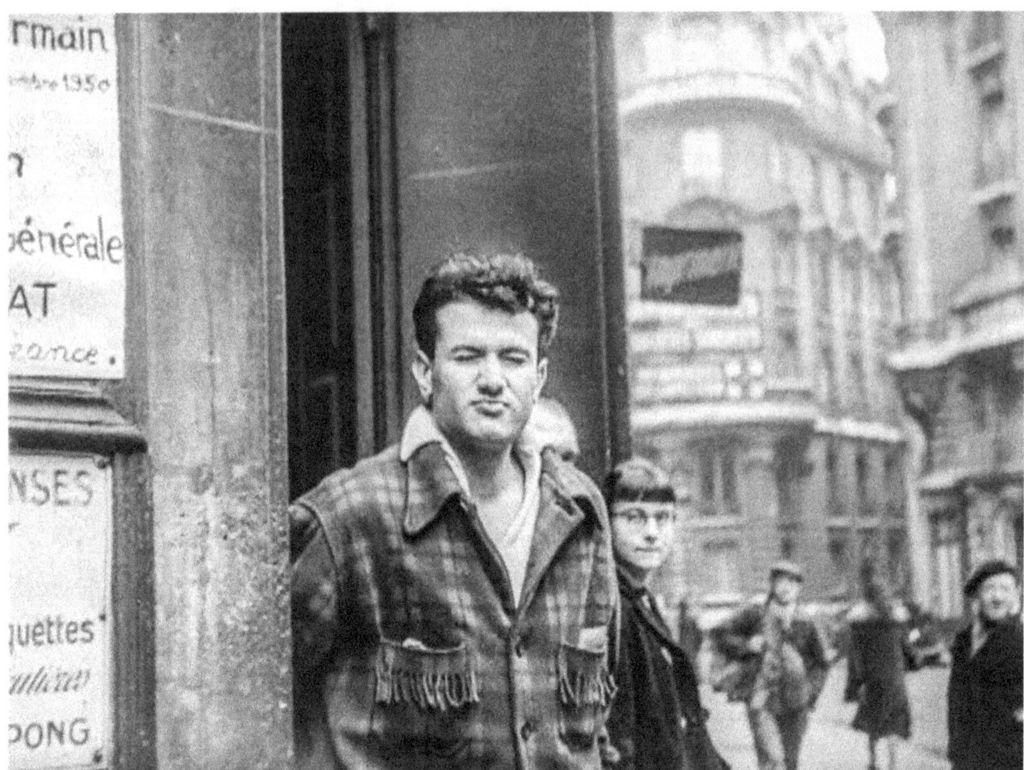

Figure 2.1. Jean-Isidore Isou, *Traité de Bave et d'Éternité*, 1951. Film still: Daniel (Isou) leaving the movie theater, squinting against the daylight.

Isou's complex narrator heralds for cinema what has by now become practically an axiom of modern art—that the world is already bloated with images and can suffer no more. True aesthetic innovation can come only from reworking and transforming preexisting imagery, ripping it from its original context and feeding it into new circuits of analogy. "The creators of old had an empty space in front of them in which they could move," the narrator would later state, "but we, the Epigones, the late-comers, all we have to work with for material are historical memories." Throughout the lecture, ostensibly given in a film screening and repeatedly interrupted by various boos, catcalls, and ridicule, we are given impossibly "blank" shots of Daniel wandering the streets of Paris. Like the kind of "stalled action" Gilles Deleuze described as the postwar "crisis of the movement-image,"[10] Daniel is presented in perpetual motion, seen from constantly changing perspectives. Yet all this movement, of the character and of the camera, is emphatically superfluous, for neither can be understood as purposeful or directive. Rather, both are self-consciously futile and incoherent—as disjunctive as the endlessly repetitive chants we hear. Their movement is not the movement of a diegetic narrative being developed so much as the barren, incidental movement of the film as it runs through the projector gate. Serving to mark the mere passing of time, they afford us no information through which we could "enter" the story. To the contrary, they are designed to keep us, like Daniel, outside the space of the cinema proper.

In his public defense of Isou after the debacle at Cannes, Cocteau contended that what the audience could not see was the very absence Isou had intended to show. His own *Orpheus* had begun on a strikingly similar note, with an image of the journal *Nudism* containing nothing but blank pages. "This is ridiculous," says Orpheus, and the head of the Poets' Café responds, "Less ridiculous than if those pages were covered with ridiculous texts." By forcing his audience to attend to these prosaic images—not without beauty so much as without coherence or purpose—Isou forces us to privilege the spoken text and the sounds we hear. He allows the sound—the younger and less developed of the sound/image pair—to become unchained from the image. For since the origin of the sound film, sound has principally served narrative continuity by smoothing over the juxtaposition of images. It was precisely the natural ease of this unification Isou sought to contest.

Against this ubiquitous unity of sound and image, with the sound always in thrall to the image, the narrator contends that "to conquer, one must divide," and goes on to offer a range of suggestive ways of conceptualizing this new endeavor. The text should not simply remain "internal and necessary to the image" but occasionally "come from completely outside, from beyond, a kind of prophecy." This sound would function as an extra dimension to the image, "as a *surplus*, unconnected with the organism." Finally, he contends that "words, through their shadings and definitions" can be strategically employed to "reveal the limitations of the image."

The disjunction of word and image was actually an early feature of cinema, but was chiefly understood as a mere technological limitation. Because the earliest cinematographs did not have the ability to record sound alongside their images, cinema was felt to be at a competitive disadvantage to theater. Using title cards to indicate those key moments of dialogue that could not be adequately expressed through pantomime, the "silent" cinema unintentionally offered a hybrid experience in which audiences were forced to shift from viewers of images to readers of text and back again. One way around this dilemma was to have a live announcer—such as the Japanese *benshi*—describe the unfolding of the narrative and the dialogue for the audience as the images flickered on the screen.[11] Together with the live music that was almost always a feature of "silent" films, these announcers added another dimension of hybridity to what was more of a "mixed-media practice" than what the industrial cinema would become.

Figure 2.2. Athanasius Kircher (1602–1680), *Ars Magna Lucis*, 1st edition: figures projected by sunlight, 1646. Division of Rare and Manuscript Collections, Cornell University Library.

Charles Musser has even argued that one of the oldest precursors of the cinema was made up of just such a hybrid conjunction of voice, text, and image.[12] In his 1646 treatise *Ars Magna*, the Jesuit polymath Athanasius Kircher had already established a multiple-screen projection device through which fictional and nonfictional works would be shown to spectators in a darkened room. A separate narration of these images would have constituted yet another textual element, necessitating that spectators, already in the seventeenth century, comprehend a range of perceptual information simultaneously conveyed not only through multiple signs, but through multiple orders of signification.

Musser does not describe these early practices as pre- or proto-cinematic—awkward moments before cinema could realize its full potential within the classical narrative form. Rather, he views the classical narrative cinema itself as but a single moment in a much larger and more diverse history of "screen practices." For once we begin to consider the diversity of early cinema, on the one hand, and the radical transformations of contemporary televisual practice on the other, the specific norms of the production and exhibition of the "classical cinema" appear less like a teleological end point in the development of the medium, and more like an idiosyncratic moment within a larger, continuously changing history of multimodal screen practices.

In *Treatise*, the narrator states, "if what I produce can be called 'cinema,' then I deserve no merit, for it already exists. We must find out how the cinema can go beyond itself. It's not only a matter of bringing something new into the cinema, but to open up a new road for the cinema as such." If Isou would subordinate the image to a complex and multivalent textuality, he would also transform the image through a vast range of formal innovations. In the second section of the film, Isou begins to incorporate a range of "found footage" that seems to diverge, quite inexplicably, from the love story he begins to tell, even as the romantic narrative seems increasingly to be diverging from itself. While framed by the encounter of a man and a woman at a bar and the complicated series of liaisons that transpire between them, it branches off for long periods to discuss filmmaking, religion, politics, and the narrator's childhood memories. The images often seem like they might correspond to the text, but only as illustrations, never as the basis for an immersive cinematic identification.[13] More spectacularly, images soon begin to appear upside down and backward, creating a dizzying vertigo as the camera moves up and down the mast of a fishing boat bobbing on the sea. But most significantly, the second part of the film reveals drawing, painting, and scratching into the very surface of the celluloid emulsion, a kind of cinematographic graffiti that feels quite unlike anything ever before in the history of painting or cinema.[14] These marks, which shudder and vibrate, instantly bring a flatness to the three-dimensional depth of the cinematic image, seeming to

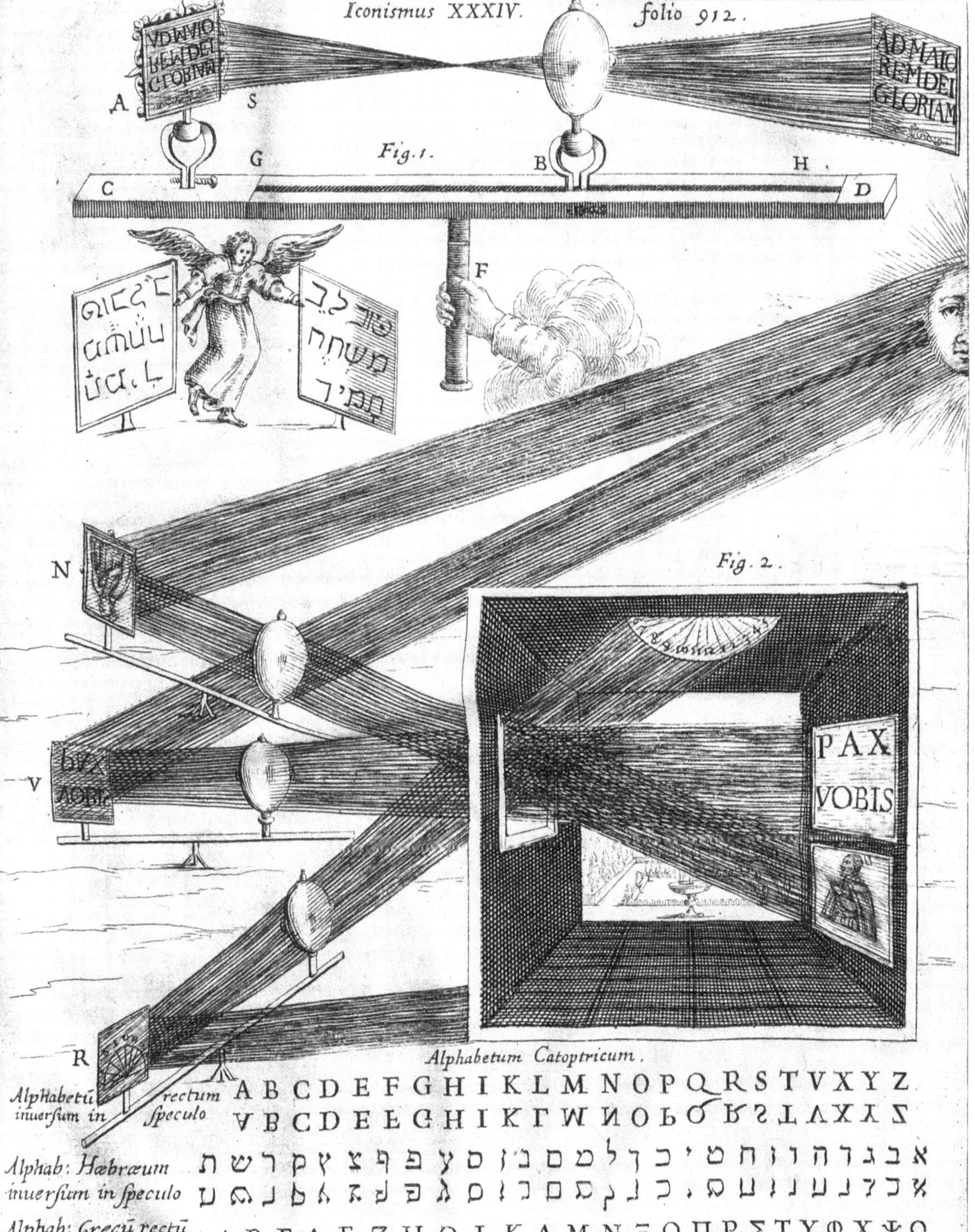
Iconismus XXXIV.
folio 912.
AD MAIO
REM DEI
GLORIAM
A
S
B
C
G
H
D
F
Fig. 1.
Fig. 2.
N
V
R
PAX
VOBIS
Alphabetum Catoptricum.
Alphabetũ rectum
inuersum in speculo
A B C D E F G H I K L M N O P Q R S T V X Y Z
Alphab: Hæbræum
inuersum in speculo
א ב ג ד ה ו ז ח ט י כ ך ל מ ם נ ן ס ע פ ף צ ץ ק ר ש ת
Alphab: Grecũ rectũ
inuersum in speculo
Α Β Γ Δ Ε Ζ Η Θ Ι Κ Λ Μ Ν Ξ Ο Π Ρ Σ Τ Υ Φ Χ Ψ Ω

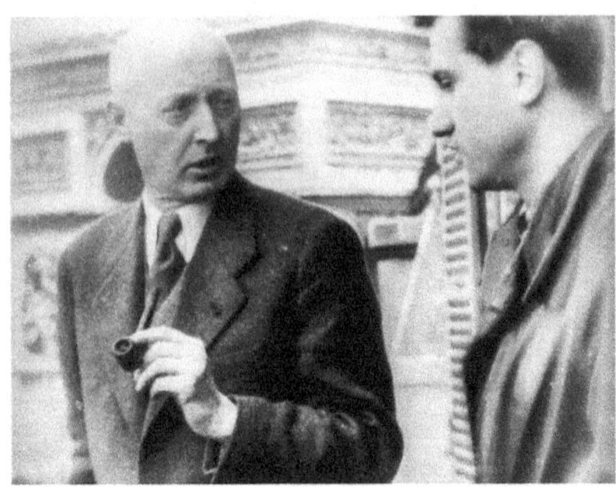

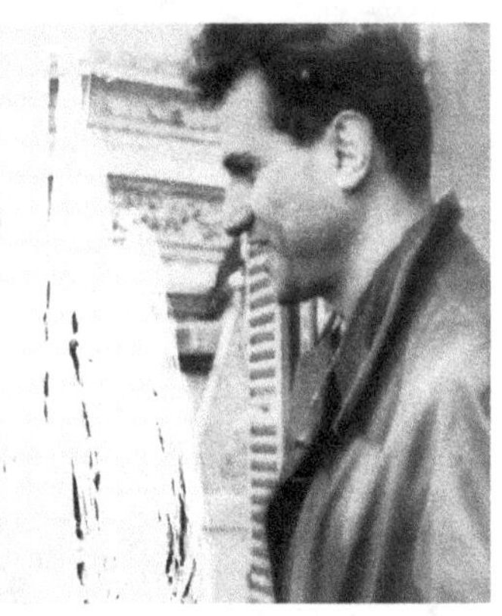

Figure 2.3. Jean-Isidore Isou, *Traité de Bave et d'Éternité*, 1951. Film stills. Daniel's companion is erased through the addition of white paint.

take place both *in* and *on* the image. They immediately counteract the persistence of vision by which cinematic technology operates, calling our attention to these moments as constructions made from a series of individual still images—bringing us back to the photogrammatic basis of the cinematographic movement.

If Isou's intervention seems more like graffiti than drawing, it is because his marks do not produce new and complete images so much as they deface or counteract the preexisting imagery. In a brief but poignant scene clearly inflected by Isou's early commitment to, but subsequent disillusionment with, the Hungarian Communist Party, the narrator recounts an adolescent's coming-of-age struggle with religion and politics. We see an image of three men working at a tooling machine. It has the absolutely generic, prototypical visual construction that has come to signify "worker" in all its class-based anonymity. We hear, "politics, perhaps because it lives upon a singular doctrine, always rehashes the same formulations as if it took men for new-born babies." As if to underline the violent reduction Isou finds in the image, he has painted over the men's faces individually and connected them with a single flickering strand. "Do I become bored more quickly than others?" we hear, as we see a brief image of students walking to school. But the scene quickly shifts to a Jewish temple, where we can barely make out an individual concealed by a dark metal gate. "When I was a kid, each night I'd invent a new prayer. I always wanted *other* prayers. Truths repeated too often cease to amuse me." Over the darkness of the gate, Isou has scrawled a brilliantly white Star of David. Because Isou has drawn the star differently in each frame, but has kept the form and placement similar, the effect is that of a hauntingly transitory yet bright and powerful icon, shimmering with an adolescent energy born of anger, frustration, and longing. The star frames the figure alternately like a halo or like a prison cage.

The voice continues, "And a truth that has stopped amusing me is a lie, because it has exhausted the warmth that made it new," while we now witness a French political ceremony with Bảo Đại, the last emperor of Vietnam, probably just after his abdication in favor of Hồ Chí Minh. With the country teetering between French control, Japanese control, and independence, between empire, Communist republic, and puppet regime,

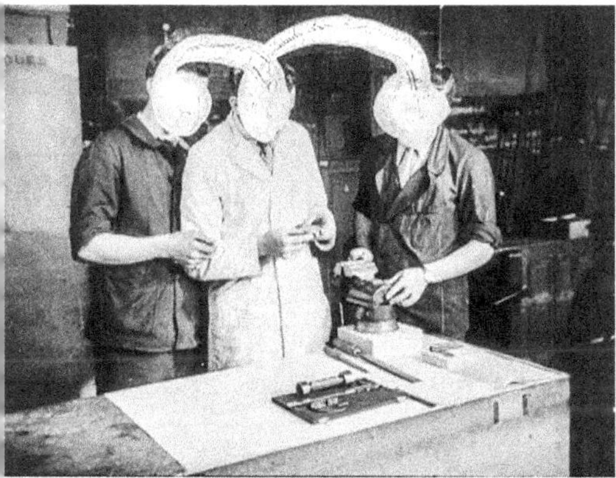

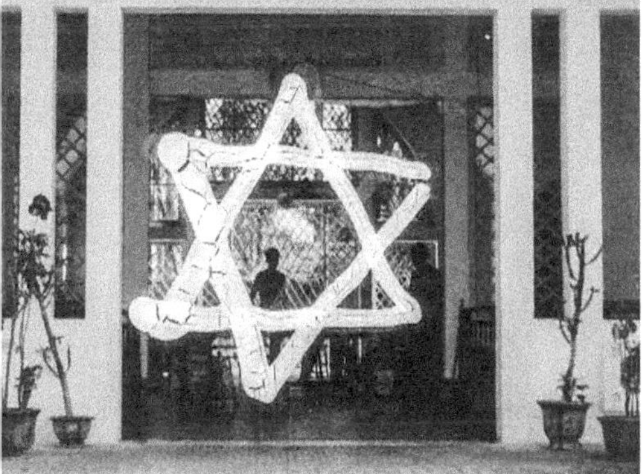

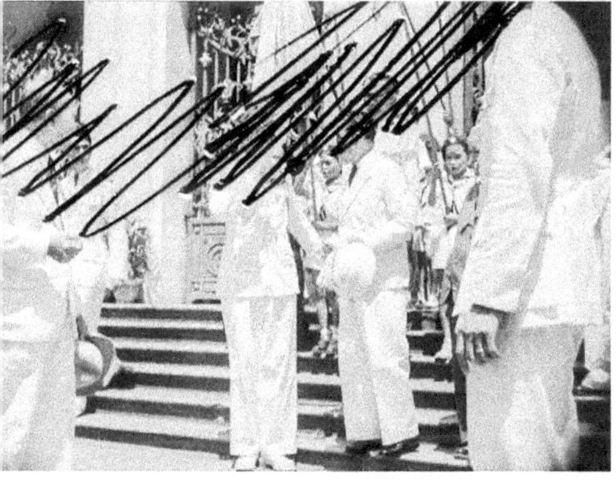

Figure 2.4. Jean-Isidore Isou, *Traité de Bave et d'Éternité*, 1951. Film stills.

the superficial dignity of such a ceremony must have seemed the very embodiment of political sophistry to Isou. Now in black, rather than white, Isou scribbles over the faces of the principal actors, leaving us to see only the universal *form* of the pageantry involved and the faces of the young children being made to stand at attention. Isou bookends his experience of religious intimacy and exclusion with the kinds of rehashed political spectacles produced for men taken "as new-born babies." He does not film his own story, but uses images already in circulation within the wider visual culture, surgically intervening in their operation at specific moments, for specific purposes. His "writing" over the image serves to conceal, distort, accent, or focus our attention, and in so doing, provides a model for an artistic practice based on intervention into a preexisting image repertoire, utilizing the affective charge from recognizable imagery as the basis for a creative and critical practice.[15]

The third section of the film, and perhaps the most incongruous, would bequeath an entirely different legacy to the emergence of the moving image in the art of the 1960s and 1970s: the documentation of performance. The Lettrists were then known, first and foremost, for a model of performance that reached back past the surrealists, still dominant in the Parisian aesthetic milieu, to the Dadaist poetics of Tristan Tzara and Richard Huelsenbeck. Like the artists Susan Sontag would describe in her essay "Against Interpretation" a decade later, the Lettrist poets sought to evacuate signification from their work in order to invent an aesthetics of pure sound. Following in the footsteps of Antonin Artaud, Lettrist poetics was grounded on the idea that art had become too tame and civilized, and that what was most urgently needed was to fashion the brute cry of the animal underlying man's refined exterior. In practice, this meant that while Lettrist poems could be given a kind of notation, they principally existed only for the duration of their performance. Rather than crafting his own vision, Isou effectively dedicated the final section of his film to a collective

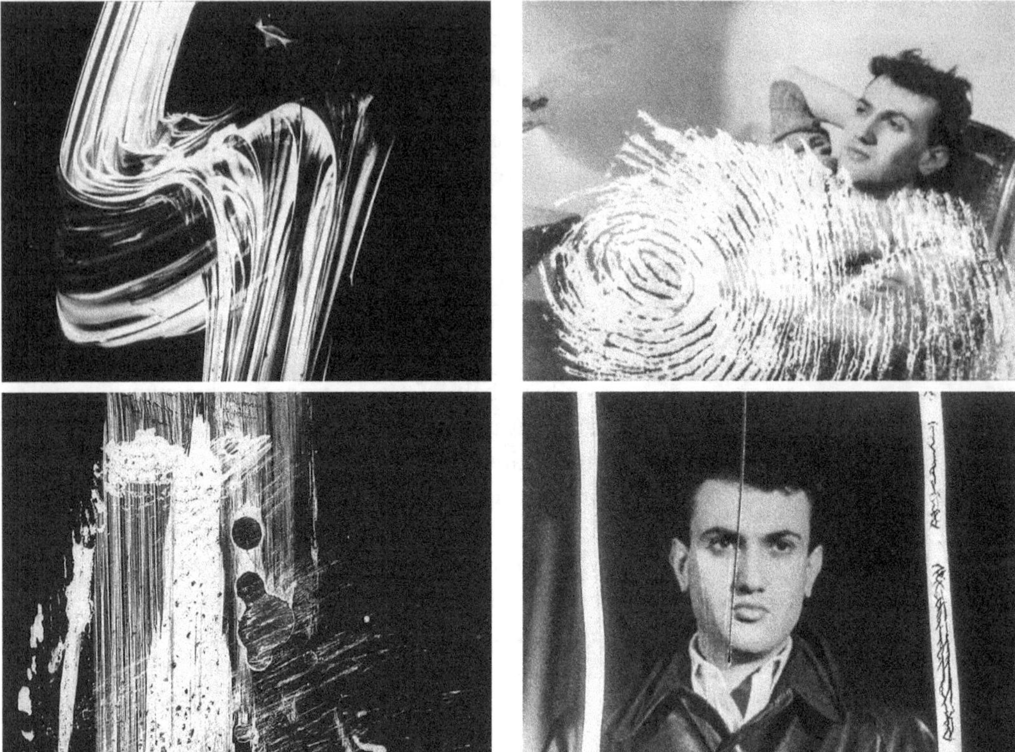

Figure 2.5. Jean-Isidore Isou, *Traité de Bave et d'Éternité*, 1951. Film stills. Abstract painting from final section accompanying Lettrist poetry.

Figure 2.6. Jean-Isidore Isou, *Traité de Bave et d'Éternité*, 1951. Film stills. Self-portraits of the author.

documentation of these sound performances. Each of the performers is announced in turn, shown standing against a blank wall, while a scrawl of paint crosses over them, symbolically cancelling their image while insisting on the materiality of the celluloid medium. As each poem begins, the screen goes black, while this material trace remains—its brilliant, chaotic variations marking a pure flow of time, coextensive yet distinct from the poetic noises to which we attend.

Near the film's conclusion, we are presented with a portrait of Daniel that effectively summarizes multiple dimensions of the work. Rather than a properly cinematic image, it is merely a repeated still frame: an unmoving moving image. And this very immobility is framed both inside and outside of the image. Outside, we hear the narrator's voice, continuing to speak. This narrator—who is and is not Daniel, just as Daniel is and is not Isou—highlights the lack of connection between sound and image, subject and voice. Within the frame, a disjunction between the forward march of time and the paradoxical stillness of this image is articulated by the continuous undulations of three thin lines. On either side of Daniel's face, a trail of paint rests above the photographic surface, while in the center, a furrow trawled into the emulsion cuts directly across. While these lines appear formally similar, we innately grasp their distinct materiality.

Raised simultaneously above and below the surface of the film, we are here granted a dimensionality wholly at odds with the "realistic" depth of the photographic image. Still and moving, material surface and photographic depth, Daniel is narratively presented in a moment of indecision and radical questioning, just as the spectator is presented with a radically unresolved and irresolvable portrait of the artist.

While generally despised by those few who saw it in Paris, *Treatise* would not remain an isolated work. Maurice Lemaître, Isou's disciple and collaborator, had already begun the process of expanding on the ideas in *Treatise* before the final version of the work had even been exhibited. This second Lettrist work, together with its accompanying theorization, would attempt to move beyond "film" entirely, and in so doing would provide the aesthetic and conceptual foundation for the heterogeneous practice of expanded cinema that would emerge over the next two decades.[16]

The Cinematic Situation: *Has the Film Begun?* (1951)

Lemaître's work of 1951, *Le film est Déjà Commencé?* (*Has the Film Begun?*), confronts its viewer with pyrotechnics of formalism. As Isou does in *Treatise*, Lemaître here paints, scratches, and draws over the surface of the film emulsion in ways that seem sometimes connected with the underlying photographic images and sometimes completely independent of them. Additionally, abstract and representational imagery has been multiply superimposed. Splashes of color have been selectively added to the black-and-white footage. Images are regularly under- or overexposed. They are wildly misregistered, reversed or upside down, deliberately scarred by light leaks, dust and debris, and holes punched through the surface of the celluloid. The film has been soaked in soapy water so that the gelatin structure of its base has begun to run and reticulate, disintegrating before our eyes. Old scraps of film taken from a processing laboratory, pieces of film leader, and unprocessed negative film have all been intercut into the work. There are sections that produce a stroboscopic or "flicker" effect through the alternation of pure black and white with pure color frames. Words, numbers, and other kinds of symbols are presented for such short durations that they strain the viewer's cognitive abilities. Finally, elements of text are split and recombined to create novel syntactic connections. During an audible discussion of Griffith's *Intolerance*, for instance, "IN TO LER" appears on the screen as if to suggest the emergence of a cinematic grammar on the model of a musical scale.[17]

The spectacular audacity of what Lemaître terms his "image-track" is worthy of a much more detailed investigation than I can provide here, prefiguring as it does much of the formal development of the "materialist" film practices of the later 1960s and 1970s. But it is important not to allow the formal experimentation *within* the film itself to distract us from

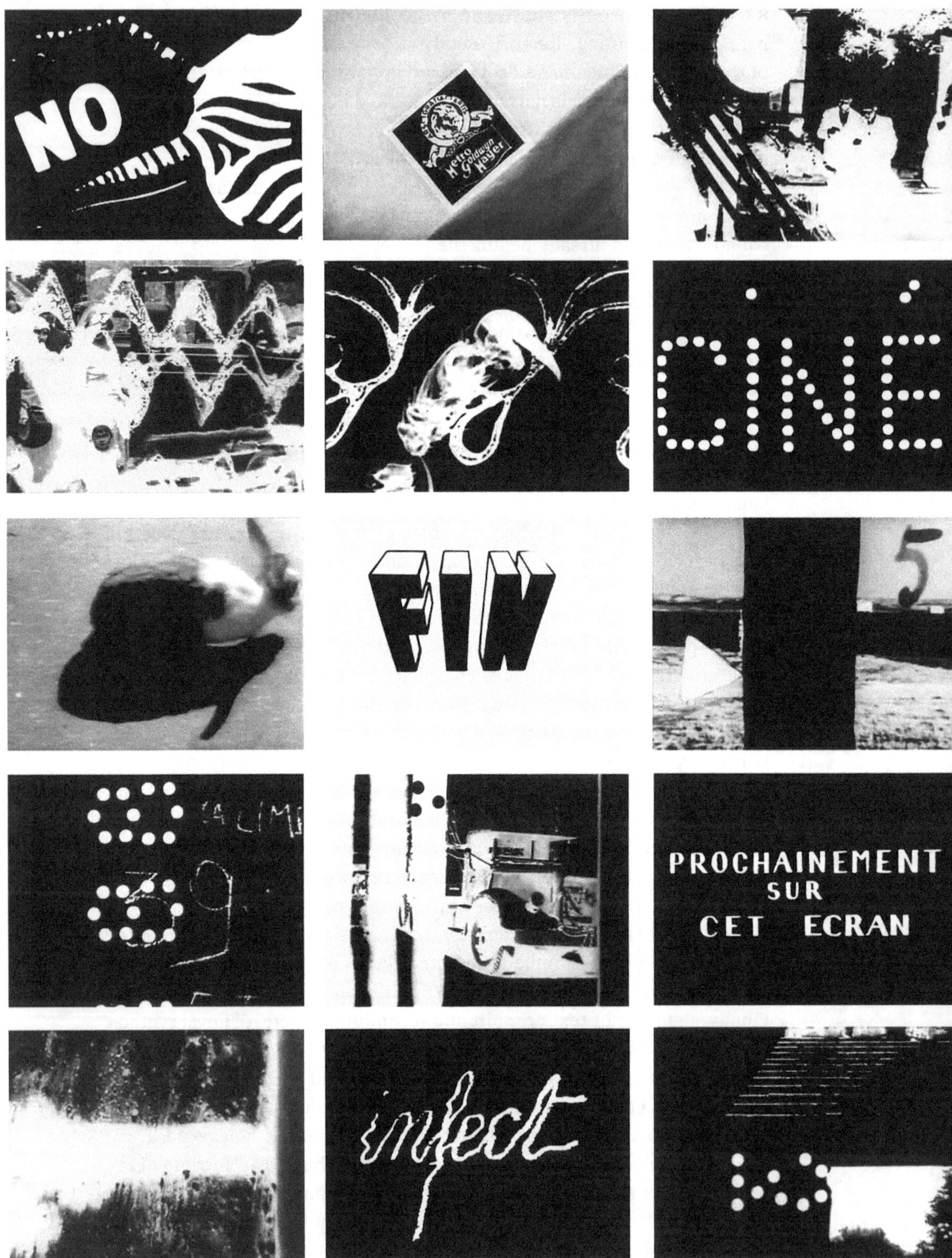

Figure 2.7. Maurice Lemaître, *Le Film est Déjà Commencé?*, 1951. Film stills.

Lemaître's more encompassing investigation into the event of cinema *outside of it*. For if Isou's cinematic *Treatise* exemplified the overt concern with textuality typically understood to characterize the Lettrist enterprise as such, Lemaître's *Has the Film Begun?* moves beyond this textual model toward what can only be described as a kind of cinematic "situationism" *avant la lettre*.

Lemaître was adamant that his work not be described as a "film," but rather as "*un séance du cinema*." He insists on juxtaposing *séance* with *cinéma*, stressing the difference between the two expressions rather than their complementarity. In so doing, he highlights something of the subterranean linguistic properties concealed within this commonplace term. In English, we speak of a film *screening*, or a film *exhibition*—spectacles that are produced *for*, and directed *toward*, an observing audience. Yet the French term *séance* is most commonly used to denote assemblies or meetings—activities in which a public is constituted and a variety of interactions take place. It is a term that carries with it the strong democratic connotations of the French Revolution. One speaks of the right of *séance*. Bridging these different meanings, one might describe the *séance* as a period of time consecrated to an activity during which the rules and conventions adopted by the assembled group are dictated by that activity. It is a delimited and demarcated space and time for a particular mode of being, a particular *habitus*, in Pierre Bourdieu's sense of the term.[18] For Lemaître, thinking of his production in terms of a *séance du cinéma* is meant to underline a radically new emphasis on the idea of *film as event*. Rather than a material object, each film is a performance that occupies a particular place over a particular time. Lemaître wants to focus our attention on this expanded cinematic situation, this performative, exhibitionary frame.[19]

The question of framing permeates every aspect of Lemaître's creation, and it confronts us even before we attempt to describe Lemaître's work. This work, itself titled in the interrogative, disperses even as we attempt to fix it in time and space. *Has the Film Begun?* was not simply the name of a film, but also of a film-performance, a score for this performance, and a lengthy treatise on the theory and aesthetics of Lemaître's ideas of film-performance in general with which the score for this individual performance concludes. Within this theoretical treatise, he describes his principal contribution as the delineation of four independent areas for experimental research in the domain of the film-performance: sound, image, projection screen, and projection environment. Each of the four is to be considered an independent site for inquiry, as well as in terms of its necessary and ongoing relationship to the other three.

What Lemaître seems to have understood from Isou is that the attack on the image—the act of chiseling inscriptions by hand into the smooth surface of the photomechanical reproduction—was not simply

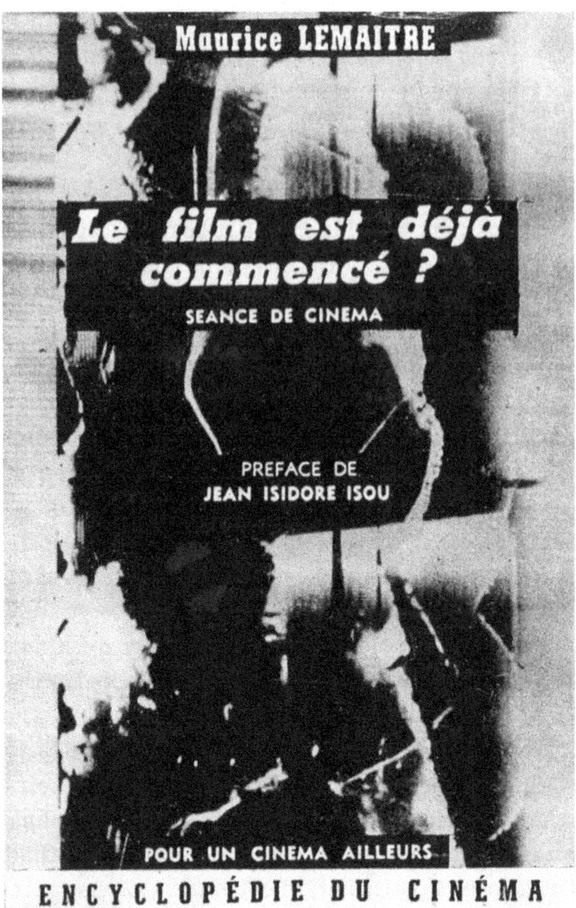

Figure 2.8. Maurice Lemaître, *Le Film est Déjà Commencé? Séance du Cinéma* (Paris: A Bonne, 1952). Cover.

a transformation of film's material surface but rather a transformation of the spectator's whole manner of relating to the film-as-event. If the film was both physically and metaphorically "chiseled," then the audience would no longer observe a putatively transparent depiction, but rather the exhibition of an audiovisual assemblage. By scratching the surface of cinema's metaphorical window, Isou was activating the larger institutional space of the cinematic encounter and the various spectatorial conventions heretofore taken for granted. If the screen was no longer simply a window, but also a canvas on which to draw, then it followed naturally for Lemaître that neither the physical surface of the projection screen nor any of the accepted conventions of the cinematic environment could be considered "transparent," but must instead be considered by the artist as active, fundamental elements in the construction of the total audiovisual environment. Within his score, we find not only the disjunctive organization of sound and image familiar from Isou, but an additional

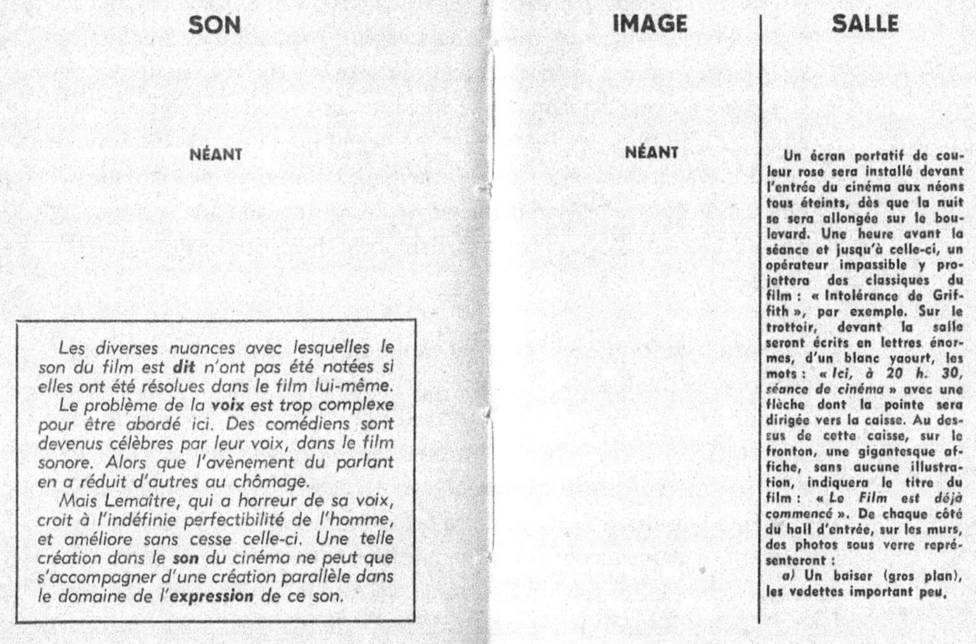

Le film est déjà commencé ?

Organisation d'une Séance de Cinéma

SON	IMAGE	SALLE
NÉANT	NÉANT	Un écran portatif de couleur rose sera installé devant l'entrée du cinéma aux néons tous éteints, dès que la nuit se sera allongée sur le boulevard. Une heure avant la séance et jusqu'à celle-ci, un opérateur impassible y projettera des classiques du film : « Intolérance de Griffith », par exemple. Sur le trottoir, devant la salle seront écrits en lettres énormes, d'un blanc yaourt, les mots : *« Ici, à 20 h. 30, séance de cinéma »* avec une flèche dont la pointe sera dirigée vers la caisse. Au dessus de cette caisse, sur le fronton, une gigantesque affiche, sans aucune illustration, indiquera le titre du film : *« Le Film est déjà commencé »*. De chaque côté du hall d'entrée, sur les murs, des photos sous verre représenteront : *a)* Un baiser (gros plan), les vedettes important peu,

*Les diverses nuances avec lesquelles le son du film est **dit** n'ont pas été notées si elles ont été résolues dans le film lui-même.*

*Le problème de la **voix** est trop complexe pour être abordé ici. Des comédiens sont devenus célèbres par leur voix, dans le film sonore. Alors que l'avènement du parlant en a réduit d'autres au chômage.*

*Mais Lemaître, qui a horreur de sa voix, croit à l'indéfinie perfectibilité de l'homme, et améliore sans cesse celle-ci. Une telle création dans le **son** du cinéma ne peut que s'accompagner d'une création parallèle dans le domaine de l'**expression** de ce son.*

Figure 2.9. Maurice Lemaître, *Le Film est Déjà Commencé? Séance du Cinéma* (Paris: A Bonne, 1952). Opening pages of performance score with distinct columns for "Sound," "Image," and "Room."

third column devoted to the environmental situation exterior to the filmic text, making clear that the chamber within which the film is being screened is not a nullity or empty void (whether dark or lit), but rather an active component of the work's disjunctive orchestration.

For Lemaître, the total environment he designated with the term "Syn-Cinéma" was not a coherent synthesis of diverse media elements in the mode of the historical *Gesamtkunstwerk*, but one entirely opposed to its audiovisual spectacle of seamless coherence. In fact, Lemaître's attention to the physical space of cinematic exhibition could be understood to *reverse* the convention of the theatrical "black box" through which Wagner had integrated the spectacle of the "total work of art." While technologies of the projected image from Kircher to Edison had necessitated a darkened space in which the faint light of the projection might be screened, the traditional theater was obviously under no such compulsion. Frederich Kittler describes the 1876 opening of Wagner's theater in Bayreuth:

Figure 2.10. Advertising poster for Maurice Lemaître, *Le Film est Déjà Commencé?*, 1951.

> Wagner did what no dramaturg before him had dared to do (simply because certain spectators insisted on the feudal privilege of being as visible as the actors themselves): during opening night, he began *The Ring of the Nibelung* in total darkness, before gradually turning on the (as yet novel) gaslights. Not even the presence of an emperor, Wilhelm I, prevented Wagner from reducing his audience to an invisible mass sociology and the bodies of actors (such as the Rhine maidens) to visual hallucinations or afterimages against the background of darkness. The cut separating theatre arts from media technologies could not be delineated more precisely. Which is why all movie theatres, at the beginning of their screenings, reproduce Wagner's cosmic sunrise emerging from primordial darkness. A 1913 movie theatre in Mannheim, as we know from the first sociology of cinema, used the slogan, "Come in, our movie theatre is the darkest in the whole city!"[20]

Lemaître's conception of the film *séance* within the SynCinéma can be understood as the first explicit attempt to theorize the nascent domain of expanded cinema in which the traditional delineation of film and performance is consciously undermined for the sake of an aesthetic and conceptual interrogation of film-as-event. According to Lemaître, the SynCinéma simultaneously undertakes two actions in a kind of pincer movement: it drags us out from the putative transparency of the screen-as-window metaphor toward the real social and material space of screening, while simultaneously theatricalizing this real social and material space as an event. Not unlike the title cards Bruce Conner would strategically deploy throughout *A Movie* (1958), Lemaître's work is constantly beginning and beginning again in medias res. Direct appropriations of Hollywood advertising messages and industrial logos constantly seem to be announcing coming attractions, suggesting that the film has already concluded, or alternatively, that it is just about to begin.

Wanda Strauven has remarked on how Tom Gunning's idea of the preindustrial "cinema of attractions" functions to reverse our accepted paradigm of cinematic "monstration," in which a spectacle is shown to the spectator, in favor of a more bidirectional encounter that acknowledges "the magnetism of the spectacle shown."[21] Rather than immediately conceptualizing Lemaître's work as a kind of theatrical spectacle, it seems more fitting to try to understand it within this model as a mode of *solicitation* toward its spectatorial audience. For Lemaître's title is quite obviously a question—a query for its spectator rather than the proffering of a message.

If Isou's interrogation confined itself principally to the way we understand the sound/image relations within the film as constructed object, Lemaître's "disjunctive cinema" expands out to incorporate the

le Film est déjà commencé?

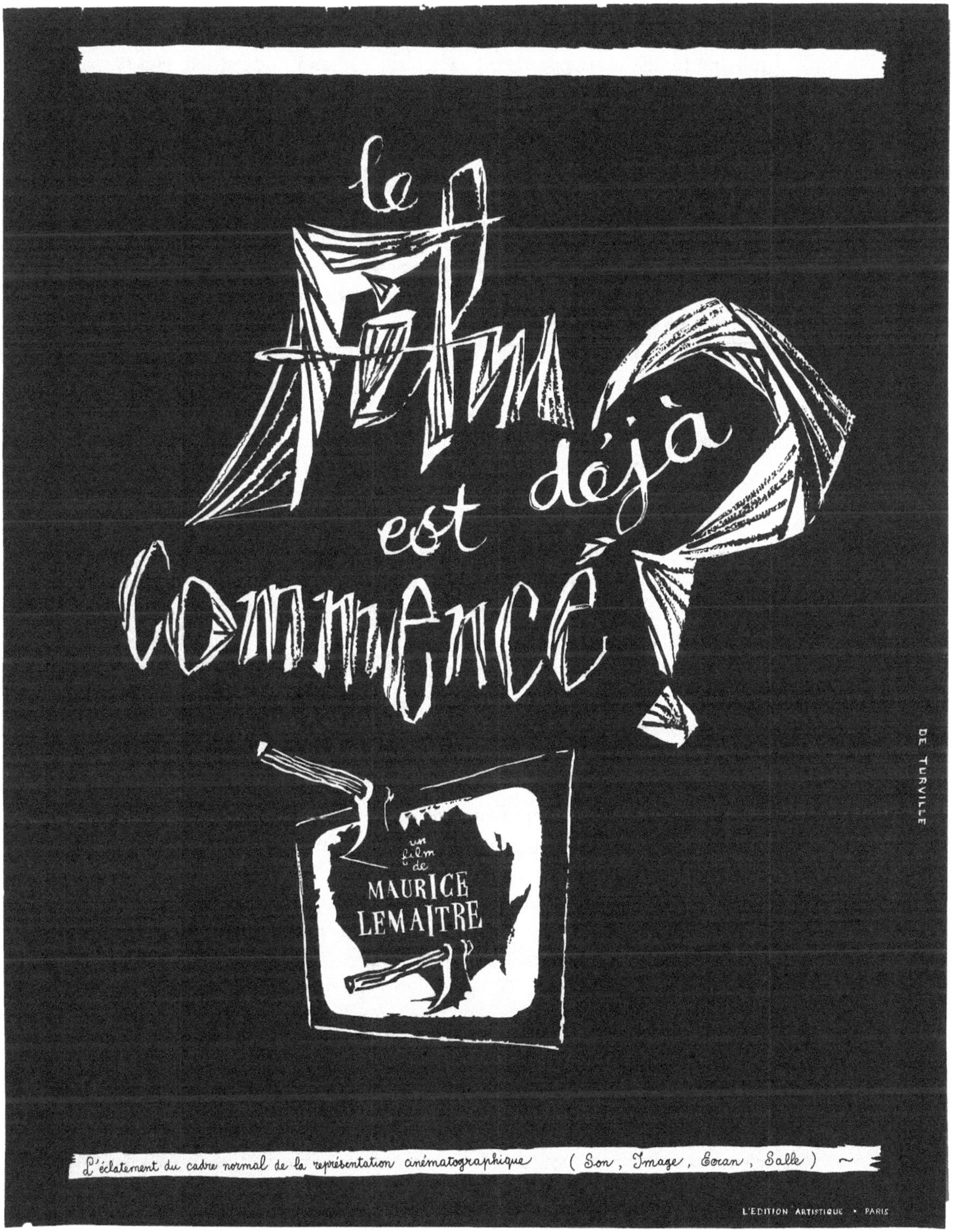

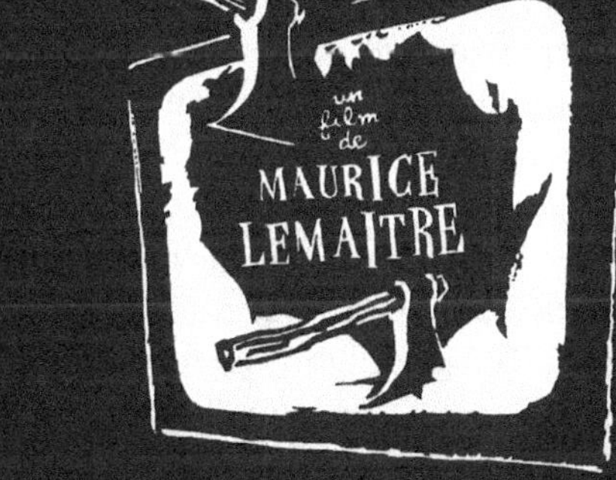

DE TURVILLE

L'éclatement du cadre normal de la représentation cinématographique (Son, Image, Écran, Salle) ~

L'EDITION ARTISTIQUE • PARIS

institutional framing of the cinematic situation itself. Simultaneously highlighting and disrupting our expectations of the ways in which the moving image is supposed to be encountered and understood, *Has the Film Begun?* consistently works to juxtapose the inner and outer space of the cinematic spectacle, ceaselessly modulating and confusing the very boundaries of the cinematic text.

> When the audience is let in, the screening room will be dark and there will be no attendants to help people with seating. They will take their seats in an indescribable confusion. The rectangular screen will be deformed by the addition of a number of colored pieces of drapery from which objects will be hung and placed in motion. While the spectators are still being seated, the concluding scene of a Western will be shown and the lights in the room will then be turned on. An announcer will tell the audience to leave the room. Maurice Lemaître will then begin to read a lengthy defense of his film, which will be interrupted by shouting. The projectionist, holding a bulk of celluloid film in his hands, will appear beside the director and, accusing him of making a film in contradiction to his own ideas, begin ripping the film stock apart. The "producer" of the film will intervene, attempting to save as much of the film as possible. He will chase the projectionist out of the theatre while shouting at him. A title card on the screen will indicate that the film is dedicated to Isidore Isou. The extras in the room will shout to turn out the lights. This occurs to a loud "ah . . ." of collective satisfaction. Footage from several random films is then projected upon the screen while the lights are again turned up. More collective shouting. After a few moments, the lights are definitively put out.[22]

There is certainly an effort here to *épater le bourgeois*. But this shock or outrage has a precise purpose and directionality: it is intended both to make visible and to denaturalize the conventionality of cinematic exhibition and spectatorship. Lemaître returns to this framing of the cinematic event again and again on every level, traversing the "inner" and "outer" space of the spectacle, constantly picking up and setting down the boundaries of the aesthetic experience itself. His work is not a simple dissolution of "art" into "life," but a highly organized and scripted series of experiential encounters wherein the boundary or barrier between the aesthetic and the everyday can be *seen* to have been situated. Seeing these boundaries, the audience begins to experience them as such.

The point is not that anything can be art, that there are no boundaries or rules—precisely the opposite. Lemaître's *Has the Film Begun?* makes it clear that, over and above any formal grammar of the image, cinema has developed as a particular kind of art through the establishment and perpetuation of certain concrete parameters of exhibition and spectatorship. For Lemaître, *une cinéma ailleurs*, an "other" cinema that breaks radically with the nature and purpose of industrial cinema, cannot rely merely on a transformation of the cinematic image. Nor can it be content to introduce a newly heterogeneous cinematic grammar through the juxtaposition of image and text. Ultimately, such a cinematic investigation must confront the institutional and exhibitionary frameworks within which the projection and spectatorship of the moving image *take place*: the ways in which our unconscious beliefs about the nature and purpose of cinema condition our reception of that encounter before we even enter the cinematic theater. As if to underline the point, Lemaître begins the work even before its "beginning," relocating it from the theater's interior to the street outside:

> A portable, rose-colored screen ringed with neon is installed before the entrance of the cinema and DW Griffith's *Intolerance* is projected for an hour before the film is to begin … Some actors who have infiltrated the waiting crowd will begin to insult others. To stop a scandal from beginning, the doors of the theatre will burst open and a group of all ages will rush *out* of the theatre. They will form an excited group in front loudly exclaiming their disgust for the film they are about to see. They will place themselves in front of the outdoor screen and interject their wild approval. The director will attempt to dissuade those waiting in line to see the film. He will begin to insult the couples, proposing to give them money to get a motel room instead.[23]

If the work, slated to commence at 8:30 p.m., begins too early—with both the screening of another film entirely and the play of actors in and around the audience of that film—it also begins too late, as the audience is let into the theater proper only after an hour of this preliminary spectacle has already transpired.[24] But even inside the theater, Lemaître continues to modulate our experience of the spectacle's boundaries, moving ceaselessly between the inner and outer space of the film. The whole theatrical preface described above is once again enumerated for the audience, while actors playing angry spectators loudly interject their disapproval of the film and exasperation with its director. As these events are being acted out in the theater, we simultaneously hear them being called out as stage directions to be acted on. When the house lights dim and the projection begins, the audience—now seated comfortably in their seats—*hears* an audience fumbling around in the dark trying to take their seats, while a voice-over describes this imaginary spectacle taking place. A title card prohibiting smoking in the theater appears on the screen, and we hear altercations breaking out in the audience—altercations that are, in fact, solely the province of the soundtrack. On the screen, the concluding scene of a Western begins and then begins again. A title card reads: "From Maurice Lemaître/*Has the Film Begin?*/Next week," after which the screen goes dark and the house lights come up while a voice simultaneously describes the screen going dark and the house lights coming up. While people are still complaining about finding their seats, we hear new ones complaining about the lights going up. The lights go back down, and while a series of title cards play up the excitement of Lemaître's film as a coming attraction, people in the audience now point out the rudeness of someone presumably smoking in defiance of the prohibition recently shown.

By this point, with at least part of the audience likely exasperated, it may very well have been impossible to determine what was part of the film and what was outside of it, what was staged and what was real. Superimposing multiple levels of representation, *Has the Film Begun?* elicits the experience of multiple temporalities running in parallel, coming together at specific moments before again breaking apart. For that potentially revolutionary audience Isou had described as *"le generation des ciné-clubs,"* Lemaître's *Has the Film Begun?* proposed a cinematization of life, as well as its redundant theatrical orchestration, in a *mise-en-abyme*.

Toward an Expanded Cinema

The film does not record the filmic process in this way without projecting a cerebral process. A flickering brain, which relinks or creates loops—this is cinema. *Lettrism* had already gone a long way in this direction, and, after the geometric epoch and the "engraving" epoch, proclaimed a cinema of expansion.

GILLES DELEUZE, *Cinema*

What Lemaître described as the "transformation of cinematographic representation into a theatrical combination" would come to have great currency over the next decade in the work of Robert Breer, Bruce Conner, and Stan VanDerBeek, among others.[25] This layered disjunction of space and spectatorship, of site and psyche, would emerge as a recurrent theme within the evolution of the moving image in contemporary art. It is an expanded conception of cinema that Lemaître's fellow Lettrist Marc'O (Marc-Gilbert Guillaumin) described as an exploration of the "three dimensional psychology" of the cinematic situation. In a 1952 treatise, he concluded that "what *acts*" within this new mode of aesthetic practice "is not so much the *transmitter* (producer of sensation), but the manner in which *reception* is prepared (the spectator brought to a particular state of receptivity)."[26] The idea that the modern artist should concern himself with the psychological states of "receptivity" was almost unprecedented within the discourse of the period, yet it obviously prefigured the later turn toward "reception aesthetics" within art and film theory decades later. In fact, it was precisely this shift of emphasis—from the brute materiality of artistic production toward the institutional framing of spectatorial reception—that would connect many of the diverse currents of expanded cinema and intermedia art over the next two decades.

Since the birth of cinema, Marc'O claims, we have seen a constant transformation of the spatial framing of cinematic projection.[27] But while cinema has always been dramatically affected by the diversity of its situations, these have been treated merely as technical problems to be mastered rather than artistic elements to be explored. That is why, for Marc'O, the most fundamental basis for a future art of the moving image lies in the investigation and development of these kinds of framings, both the manner in which they engender particular forms of spectatorial receptivity and the effects of the distortion and transformation they effect on the representation of things in the world. This new model of avant-garde practice is oriented not only toward the deconstruction of cinematic grammar, but also toward a much wider deconstruction and rearticulation of the total cinematic *situation*, understood in both material and psychological terms. Following Isou, Marc'O contends that traditional cinema—bloated and stalled due to its mastery of overfamiliar conventions—must be understood as raw material for the artist to hack apart and recombine into new configurations. Following Lemaître, he counsels that this "chiseling" or "deconstruction" of preexisting visual culture is but a waypoint toward the positive construction of new audiovisual situations, a new "amplification" making use of precisely those framing elements previously considered marginal to the cinematographic event.[28] In "Prolegomena to Any Future Cinema," his short contribution to a 1952 anthology on Lettrist cinema, the young Guy Debord celebrated the "situational cinema" articulated by Lemaître and Marc'O, writing, "Values related to artistic creation are being displaced by *a conditioning of the spectator*, with what I have called *three dimensional psychology* . . . a cinema that brings another phase of amplification. The arts of the future will be the complete overturning of *situations*, or nothing at all."[29]

Gil J. Wolman, who would coauthor the "User's Guide to *Détournement*" with Debord in 1956, provided a model of this in his exhibition of *The Anticoncept* at the Musée de l'Homme in Paris that year. The work's soundtrack consisted of a wildly heterogeneous array of sonic elements, organic and mechanical, as well as literary references and rhetorical wordplay. But against this sonic effusion, Wolman's film was rigorously minimal, devoid of photographic imagery, representational or nonrepresentational signs, or anything else that could possibly be, as we say, "read." It consisted merely of an alternation—not evenly spaced and monotonous, but irregularly syncopated in a complex rhythm—of white discs on a black ground. Significantly, the film was not projected on a traditional cinematic screen. Rather, the circular flashes of light were made to correspond to a three-dimensional object: a large, white, helium-filled

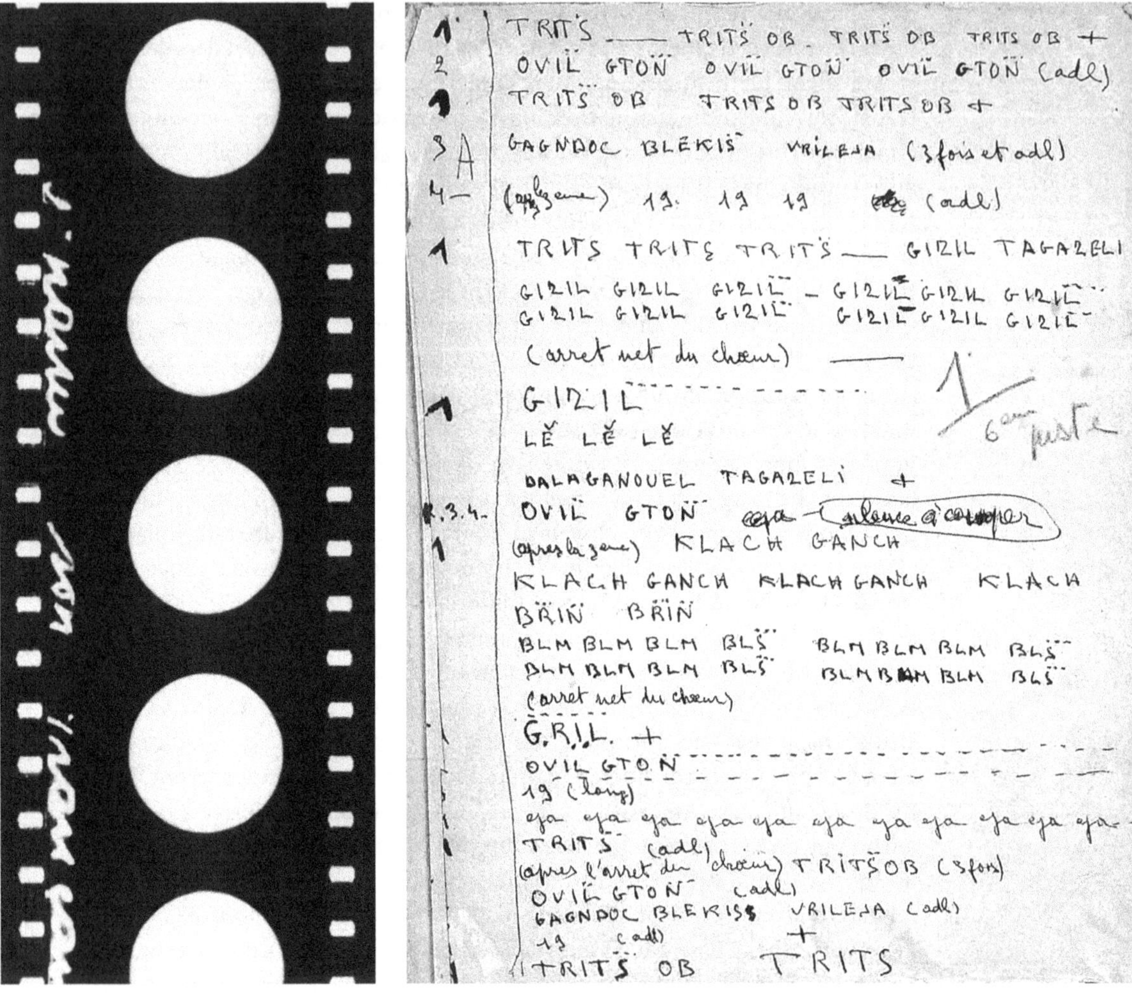

Figure 2.11. Gil J. Wolman, *L'anticoncept*, 1951. Filmstrip.

Figure 2.12. Gil J. Wolman, vocal score for *L'anticoncept*, 1951.

meteorological balloon lashed to the floor in the corner of the room. The film's stroboscopic visuality was, in a sense, "anchored" to this concrete, material, yet curiously weightless object. Since the projected disc conformed to the shape of the balloon on which it was projected, the balloon itself seemed to change in appearance, pulsing rhythmically with a brilliant luminosity. Like *Has the Film Begun?*, Wolman's *Anticoncept* creates an experience in which the total theatrical environment becomes integral to the cinematic event. But Wolman went much further than Isou or Lemaître in his efforts to gear directly into the spectator's body. Wolman describes the intensity of the light as such that "the spectators that closed their eyes perceived the movement through the eyelids. Even those that turned around could not escape: the movement became one with the space."[30]

Wolman's conception was doubtless revolutionary, but its substantial pedigree within avant-garde practice must also be recognized: Bruno Corra's "Chromatic Music" of 1912—arguably the very first treatise on "abstract cinema"—already describes a screening no longer delimited by the rectangular frame of the standard projection screen, but rather spilling out to encompass the totality of the exhibition space. To accommodate such a projection, the walls, ceiling, and floor would be painted white, rather than black, and spectators would be encouraged to wear white clothing so as to become fully integrated into the event of projection.[31] Even closer to Wolman's Artaudian aggressivity was Picabia's set design for the ballet *Relâche*, within which he exhibited his avant-garde film *Entr'acte* (1924): "A drop curtain constructed of 370 spotlights," as Rosalind Krauss memorably described it, "strikes out at the audience directly—absorbing it, focusing on it—by lighting it. So the audience is blinded even while it is illuminated."[32] Despite these important historical precedents, Wolman's aggressive reformulation of cinematic immersivity represented a crucial new direction for avant-garde practice within the postwar period. It led directly to Guy Debord's *Howls for Sade* (1952) later that year (explicitly dedicated to Wolman and itself beginning with Wolman's sound poetry). But more generally, and despite its sonic emphasis, *Anticoncept* would prove the prototype for the "flicker film" aesthetic that would emerge over the next decade in the varied work of Peter Kubelka, Tony Conrad, and Paul Sharits.

While lacking any obvious thematic content, Wolman's film was nevertheless banned by the French government on account of its "subversive" character, and concerted efforts to lift the restriction were to no avail. If the Lettrists were not welcome within traditional venues of plastic art, performance, and classical cinema, they found themselves no more welcome in the growing ranks of cinephiles and self-described proponents of "avant-garde" cinema. "The intellectual of the ciné-club judges without ever permitting a sensibility to trespass certain original boundaries, boundaries which have already been superseded by new contributions he has chosen to ignore," Marc'O wrote in his treatise for the Lettrist cinema anthology.[33] Furthermore, because "the avant-gardist will always be the first to believe in an immutable *essence* to cinema," an essence of which it has satisfied itself that it comprehends, "it is the worst reactionary when faced with a new avant-garde." Consequently, the Lettrists rejected the term itself, for in the context of cinema, "*avant-garde* has itself come close to signifying *classical*."

Incomprehensible at film festivals like Cannes, scorned by cinephiles of both conventional and independent cinema, and often censored on the few occasions when it was actually exhibited, the Lettrist cinema quite obviously lacked any institutional foundation. And Isou and Lemaître soon discovered that filmmaking was an expensive proposition. Even though they used recycled film, the paltry sums raised by their screenings were unable to cover even their initial expenses, and within a few years, they were forced to return to the more traditional, salable formats of the canvas and the written page. But despite its limited production and tenuous reception, this spectacular eruption of formal and conceptual innovation served to revitalize the historical project of radical interrogation that had started (and stopped) with the Dada and constructivist movements decades before.

Whether through rediscovery or invention, the Lettrists founded the postwar traditions of the flicker film, the essay film, and the film-performance that would develop over the next two decades. Directly, through the teaching of Stan Brakhage, or indirectly, through word-of-mouth reception of its scandalous early exhibitions, the Lettrist cinema would influence a younger generation of artists on both sides of the Atlantic by its questioning of the fundamental norms and protocols by which cinematic exhibition and spectatorship were imagined. In so doing, it provided a powerful alternative to the model of the European "art film" that was quickly becoming institutionalized within the film societies and international festivals as well as within the emerging critical and academic study of the medium.

The Lettrist cinema was not simply a new aesthetic of filmmaking, but rather a fundamentally different model of the cinematic situation, a rethinking of moving-image exhibition and spectatorship beyond the situation implied by the traditional cinematic theater. In retrospect, our first image of Lettrist cinema—that of Isou/Daniel leaving the theater—might stand as an apposite metaphor for the Lettrist imagination of cinema *tout court*. We have already observed that Barthes's short essay "Leaving the Theatre" is useful for characterizing the "situational" optic through which a variety of artists and critics—from Claes Oldenburg and Nam June Paik to Ken Dewey and Sheldon Renan—characterized the idea of expanded cinema as it had emerged in mid-1960s New York.[34] In their film essays and film-performances, the Parisian Lettrists of the early 1950s had already undertaken a reconceptualization of cinema that privileged precisely the disjunctive cinematic situation Barthes would later describe. Isou's *Treatise* pursued this project by means of a distanciation *interior* to the film: its detached voice-over and split subject in Daniel/Isou, the purposeful tedium of its endlessly repeating quasi-diegetic landscape and intentionally caricatured love story, its admixture of textual and iconic signs, etched into the celluloid so as to bring our attention "out" of the film to its material surface—all these elements would be taken up and elaborated in various forms of experimental cinema and avant-garde practice in the decades to come.

After Isou's *Treatise*, Lemaître took a different path, one more in keeping with the radical alternative Barthes would propose. No longer would he maintain the traditional "black box" within which the audience was made to disappear. No longer would the literal space of exhibition dissolve before the narrative space of the film. Instead, the site of exhibition would itself be remade, reconstructed, and incorporated into an experience that attempted to incorporate but exceed the contours of the traditional cinematic experience. Both the moving image *and* its exhibitionary situation would here vie for the audience's attention. Rather than *pushing the spectator out* of the picture, rejecting or refusing the spectatorial desire for immersive identification, Lemaître's film-performance *pulled the spectator in*—but it pulled in different directions simultaneously, and this disjunctive experience had the effect of strengthening and loosening the grip of each in turn. In contrast to the singularly *resistant* spectator Barthes opposed, armored "against the film with the discourse of counter-ideology," Lemaître's spectator was necessarily split from within, *dislocated* across multiple sites of investiture.

Insofar as we take the movie theater for what Barthes describes it as—a hypnotic lure, absorptive and immersive, that locates the viewer precisely and coherently within its cinematic world—the Lettrist films might be understood as animated by this project of "leaving the movie theatre." Not "having left," for they were not a simple negation, but "leaving"—an ambivalent, intermediary state; a process that needs be continuously maintained. More important than any of the Lettrist works individually was the inauguration of this collective project: the initiation of a radical inquiry into the site of cinema within postwar art practice, the overturning (Debord's "*bouleversement*") and reimagination of established situations of exhibition and spectatorship.

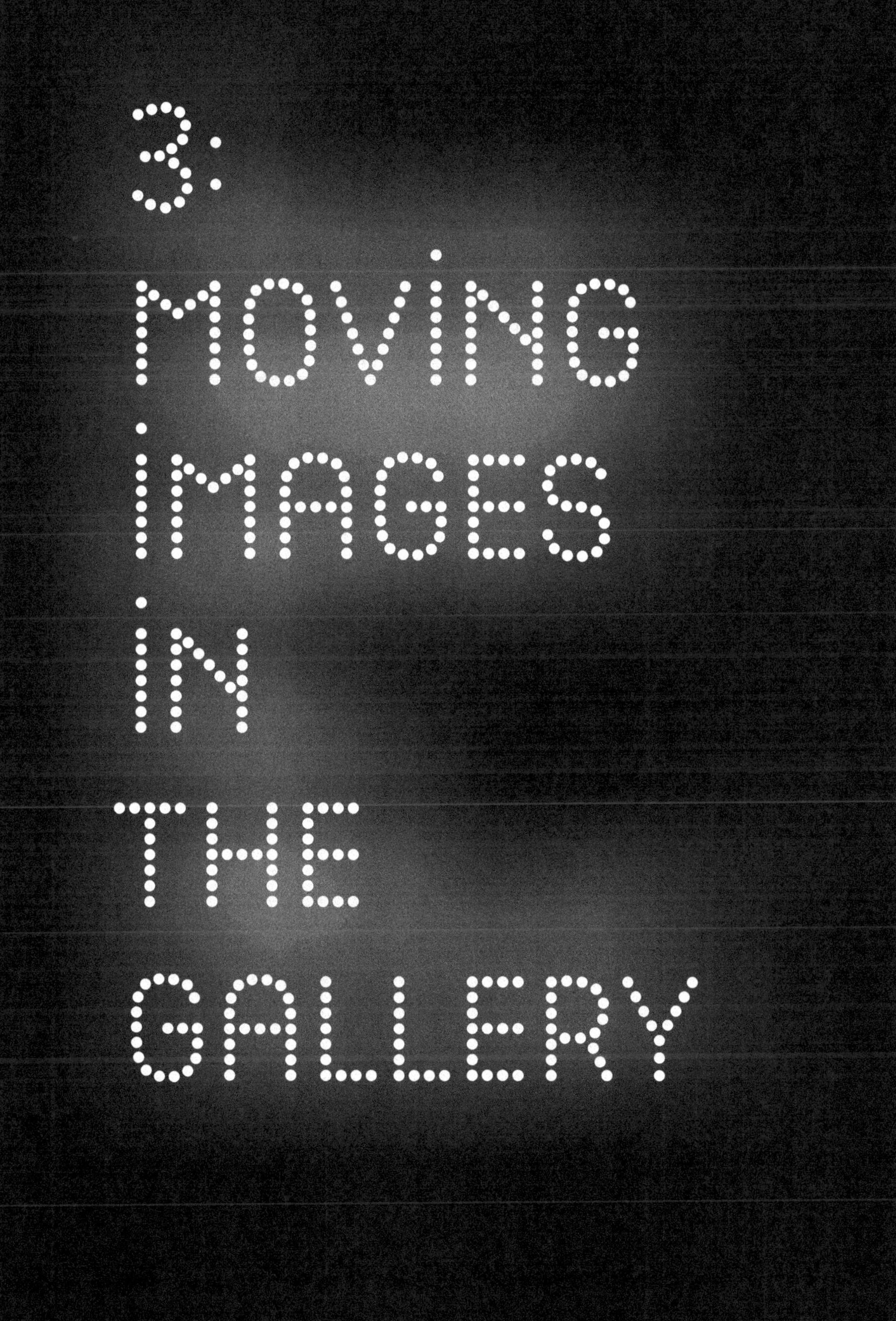

3: Moving Images in the Gallery

Movement art has this great quality: it gives us a new evaluation of art. It poses the problem whether art in our time is possible at all.

RICHARD HUELSENBECK, "Moved Movement," 1961

We are all compelled toward motion and change and moving pictures. This is the mechanical metaphysic of our time.

STAN VANDERBEEK, "The Cinema Delimina," 1961

Cinema and *Movement* (1955)

Through his idea of SynCinéma, Lemaître sought to reconfigure the very material conditions of cinematic exhibition and spectatorship. The Lettrists conceptualized the exhibitionary space of the theater not as a given and immutable backdrop against which a work would be presented, but as itself a living constellation of elements to be manipulated in the service of an overarching cinematic event. The idea of a new institutional situation for the moving image, one divorced from the exhibitionary and spectatorial premises of the narrative theatrical drama, had led Lemaître—like his Dada predecessor Francis Picabia—back to the multimedia situation of cinema's origins in the late nineteenth-century variety show.

But the Dada movement had uncovered a different model in the prehistory of industrial cinema that would influence another model of expanded cinema: one that took place not within the black box of the cinematic theater, but within the white cube of the gallery space. This model was not a matter of simply introducing cinema into the gallery—of dimming the lights and turning the white cube into a black box. Rather, it was a process of thinking about how the temporality and kinetics of the moving image might be introduced into dialogue with modernist painting and sculpture. It was a process significantly aided by the historical recovery, in the early 1950s, of the legacy of Marcel Duchamp—specifically, Duchamp's recovery of the Victorian "philosophical" toy as a tool of cinematic investigation. With their quasi-sculptural form, these optical devices allowed the idea of the cinematic to be displaced from the familiar darkness of the theater and situated within the bright light of the gallery. As the moving image was brought both literally and figuratively inside the gallery space, it would disrupt the established traditions of exhibition and spectatorship therein, ultimately contributing to a wide-ranging transformation of the idea of the gallery as such over the course of the 1960s.

This transformation might be traced to an exhibition whose brief duration and modest scale belies its significance as a turning point in the development of postwar modernism. *Movement* was held in the small Parisian gallery of Denise René in the spring of 1955. René's show effectively launched the careers of Victor Vasarely, Jesús Rafael Soto, and Jean

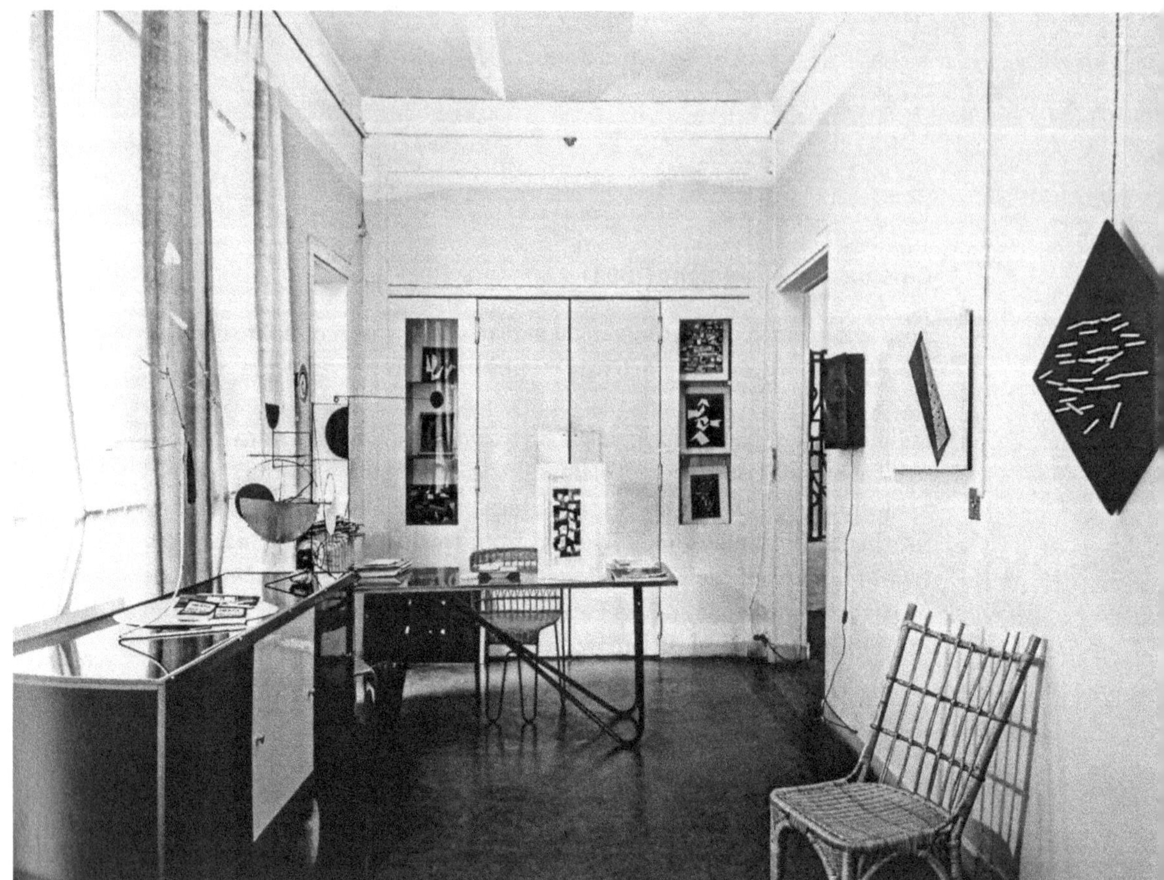

Figure 3.1. Installation view of the exhibition *Le Mouvement*, Galerie Denise René, Paris, 1955.

Tinguely, as well as playing an important role in the rehabilitation of Marcel Duchamp then under way. It prompted the 1959 exhibition *Vision in Motion*, as well as the larger 1961 traveling exhibition *Art in Motion*, and inspired the Op Art movement that would culminate in the Museum of Modern Art's 1966 exhibition *The Responsive Eye* in New York. Posing the question of movement within the historically static and timeless space of the art gallery, it had ramifications that would be felt over the next two decades in the physiology of perception, the association of art and engineering, and—most importantly for our purposes—the emergence of the moving image within the postwar gallery space.

Perhaps the most obvious category of works to be exhibited within *Movement* were those that involved the locomotion of sculptural form. With poignant delicacy, Alexander Calder's mobiles indexed the subtle shifts of atmosphere within their local environment, often responding indirectly to the spectator's movement about an indoor gallery space.[1] But this sculptural locomotion and physical displacement was also at issue in works powered by direct human intervention, such as Yaacov Agam's

Transformable Pictures (1955), as well as those completely independent of the spectator, such as Jean Tinguely's electrically powered *Metamatic Reliefs* (1955).[2]

A second category of movement was the purely optical conception exemplified by the wall-mounted reliefs of Victor Vasarely and Jesús Rafael Soto. This work had neither its own physical locomotion nor the potential for physical manipulation by the spectator, but was nevertheless "interactive" in the sense that it was highly dependent on the physical position and movement of the spectator for the creation of its optical effects. For both kinds of works, mobility was set over and against the presumed stasis and fixity of traditional painterly and sculptural form. An aesthetic ideal of timeless perfection—one that had increasingly come to inspire a critique of the museum as mausoleum in light of the dramatic postwar rebuilding of society—gave way to a newfound admiration for protean structure.

These two forms—which would be called Kinetic Art and Op Art in the years to come—have long been taken as the principal formal and conceptual innovations of the *Movement* exhibition. Yet beyond these two forms, *Movement* invoked a specific idea of the *moving image*—of cinema—whose aesthetic and conceptual significance within postwar art would grow in the years to come. Vasarely, then the dominant figure at Galerie Denise René and author of the exhibition's "Yellow Manifesto," made no secret of his profound interest in the idea of cinema. Channeling the enthusiasm of the historical avant-garde, he understood the kinetic nature of the works in the exhibition to have descended from cinematic ideas, and he proclaimed that the future would herald "a new era of cinematic abstraction" across the arts.[3] Roger Bordier similarly ended his important review of the exhibition by declaring that "one cannot speak of modern art and of movement without emphasizing the outstanding part that motion pictures can play in this realm." Despite his repeated proclamations about forthcoming films, Vasarely would never directly engage the domain he described, and Bordier's few lines on the subject quickly give way to prevarication.[4]

It is telling that the artist at Galerie Denise René most actively involved in pursuing this intersection of cinema and the plastic arts—a young, unknown American expatriate painter by the name of Robert Breer—would be almost entirely forgotten by the art historical literature. Despite this neglect, Breer's studied transition in this period between the still and the moving image, and his recasting of the problems of modern painting *within* cinema, were to prove a crucial pivot around which the question of cinema would emerge within the space of the postwar art gallery. Breer had come to Paris at the end of the 1940s, just as the city was beginning to rebound from Nazi occupation. He spent a great deal of time around Vasarely and his circle, and by 1952 he had become the only American among the group to exhibit regularly. He accepted what he would later describe as its "abstract, geometric, post-Cubist orthodoxy: a painting is an object and its illusions have to acknowledge its surface as a reality," yet he always retained a touch of the apostate. The group's rhetoric of absolute structure and fixed composition increasingly provoked in Breer an interest in movement and the ways in which painterly form might be elaborated as an ongoing process, rather than a closed finality.

In working through these painterly questions, Breer began to make his preparatory "thumbnail sketches" on small index cards. Producing a small stack of cards over the course of several days, he would rifle through them by hand, animating his painterly studies in various ways as an aid to composition. He soon began to consider this process of arriving at and departing from set forms more compelling than the attempt to fix them once and for all on his full-sized canvases. During a visit to his family home in Detroit, he overcame an "inherent hostility to the camera" and filmed, image by image, a series of transparencies that he had painted and then projected with a slide projector.[5] "Backing into cinema," as he describes it, Breer analytically decomposed one of his "rigid" painterly compositions into index cards, then slides, and finally single frames, or photograms, to produce his first animated film, *Form Phases I*, in 1952. Typically, animators work on large sheets to produce an illusion of precise detail with reduction, but Breer did the exact opposite: he worked in a deliberately small format so as to maintain the integrity of his individual lines and brushstrokes. It was merely the first of many ways in which he would come to develop a practice that, while legible within the rubric of "animation," deliberately rejected the formal and institutional codes by which the work of traditional animation had been conceived. Upon returning to Paris with the camera, Breer became more and more interested in the possibilities of cinematic abstraction, and he began working systematically on paper index cards and film to produce *Form Phases II* and *III* in 1953 and *Form Phases IV* in 1954. In Breer's view, these works were in dialogue with his painterly compositions, revealing "how forms became locked in each other" but enabling him to emphasize "the process of painting rather than any fixed composition."[6]

Beautiful and fluid, whimsical yet formally compelling, the *Form Phases* quickly attracted a level of critical and popular recognition that had eluded Breer's works on canvas. Their most significant early screening took place in 1955, in the context of the *Movement* exhibition. As a "supplement" to the official exhibition, Pontus Hultén had been asked to coordinate a parallel show of abstract moving-image works at the Cinémathèque Française. While the exhibition at Galerie Denise René ran over the course of three weeks, the film component took on a much more punctual temporality, with a program repeated three times over

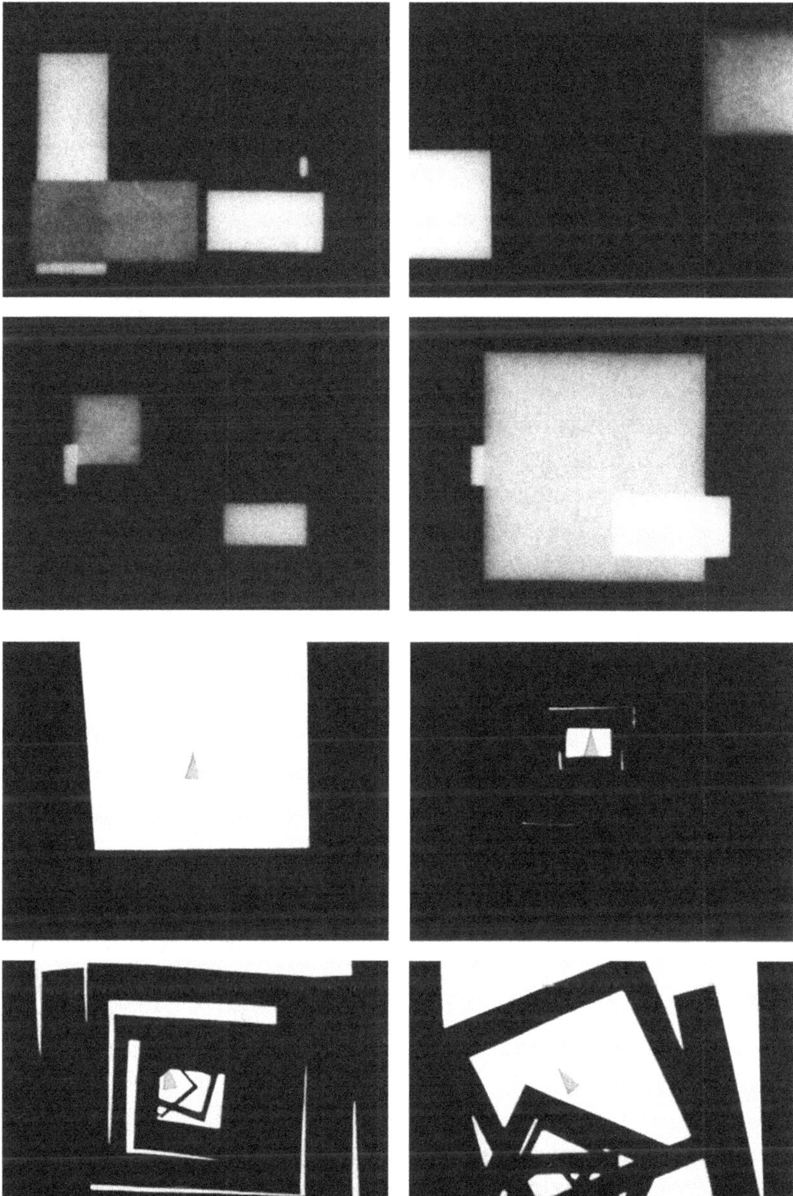

Figure 3.2. Hans Richter, *Rhythm 21*, 1921. Film stills.

Figure 3.3. Robert Breer, *Form Phases IV*, 1954. Film stills.

the course of a single evening. Breer describes enjoying the immediate feedback these films engendered. Yet he was less taken with the theatrical "black box" environment within which his films were projected. As a painter, trained to respect the material condition of the work as an object in space, he was decidedly uncomfortable in a situation in which a series of independent still images were imperceptibly transformed, by an unseen apparatus, into a seemingly fluid and immaterial field of movement. He was also uncomfortable with the idea that these works would take place in an exclusively cinematic context, for he understood the *Form Phases* as elaborations of his painterly practice: "I went from making paintings to animating paintings," Breer later explained; "for me, that was the whole point of making a film."[7]

While Hans Richter had declared that the problems of modern painting led toward cinema, even he had quickly come to regard his early works of "pure cinema," such as *Rhythm 21*, as unsatisfactory. Such an abstract "visual music" too easily bypassed the indexicality so foundational to the authority of the photomechanical document itself. Breer, too, came to despair of this problem, and already by the time of *Form Phases IV*, he had begun to find his painterly animations cartoonish.[8] Thus, while *Form Phases IV* was drawing acclaim during its screening for the *Movement* exhibition, Breer had already departed on a more radical path.

Breer's path was one that paradoxically presented a solution to the problem of "pure" abstraction, as well as the problematic "illusionism" of traditional animation, by means of a return to the still image. With his *Image by Images* of 1954, Breer conducted a simple experiment whose results would henceforth transform the entirety of his artistic practice. Breer had learned that "one could change the color of a given form from frame to frame to get a mixture, for instance, alternate yellow and blue and get green, but what interested me most was the very special vibration this produced. I decided to try a frame by frame mixture of contrasting *form*."[9] Using only six feet of film, he shot two hundred forty consecutive exposures, frame by frame, just like any other animator. Yet there was a single, crucial difference. Rather than attempting to make the frames as similar as possible in order to produce the smooth illusion of continuous motion that was the hallmark of professional animation, Breer set out to make every image "as unlike the preceding one as possible . . . the result was two hundred and forty distinctly different optical sensations packed into ten seconds of vision."[10]

While projecting the ten-second loop over long periods, he was "surprised to discover that the eye constantly discovered new images." The film offered a newly hybrid conjunction of the still and moving image. As a loop, it no longer had a definitive beginning or end; the duration of the piece had become unfixed, or fixed only by the wills of the projectionist and of the spectator. The image produced acquired, for all its frenetic movement, an usual degree of stillness, a kind of singular vibration, as when a series of objects move so quickly before us that differentiation becomes impossible and we begin to see the totality as a kind of continuous, undulating flow. The technique, as he wrote in one of his first published statements about the process, "tends to destroy dramatic development in

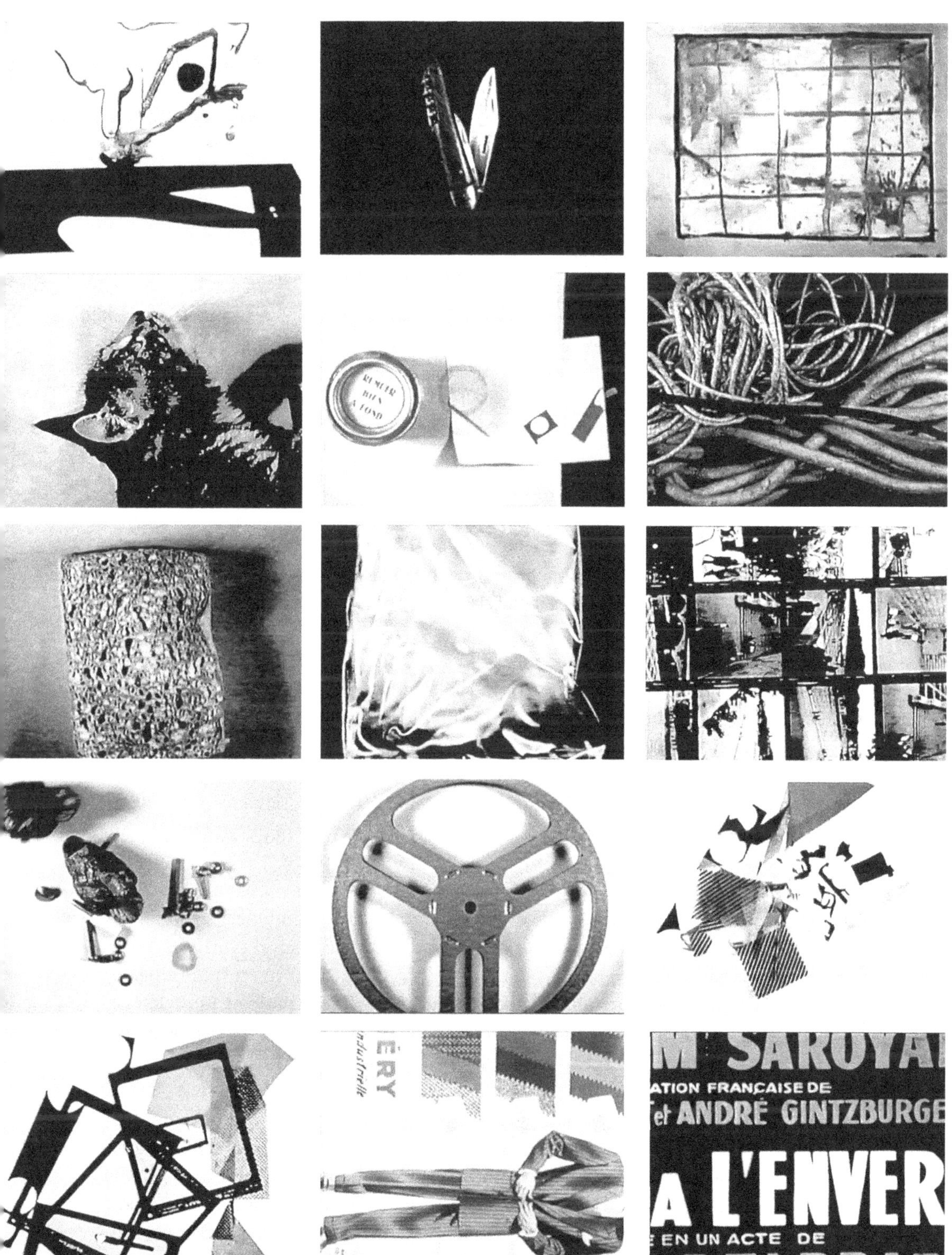

Figure 3.4. Robert Breer, *Recreation*, 1956 (Breer's re-creation of his 1955 loop film *Image by Images* for theatrical exhibition). Film stills.

the usual sense and a new continuity emerges in the form of a very dense and compact texture. When pushed to extremes the resulting vibration brings an almost static image on the screen."[11]

Thus, beginning with *Image by Images*, Breer repudiated not only the static "eternity" of the painted canvas but also the progressive temporality of the cinematic narrative (however abstractly conceived) for what he considered to be a juxtaposition of the models of both painting and cinema. Speaking with Guy Coté in 1962, Breer described his construction of film as a "space image" presented for a certain length of time:

> As with a painting, this image must submit to the subjective projection of the viewer and undergo a certain modification. Even a static painting has a certain time dimension, determined by the viewer to suit his needs and wishes. In [traditional] film, this period of looking is determined by the artist and imposed on the spectator, his captive audience. A painting can be "taken in" immediately, that is, it is present in its total self at all times. My own approach to film is that of a painter—that is, I try to present the total image right away, and the images following are merely other aspects of and equivalent to the first and final image. Thus the whole work is constantly presented from beginning to end and, though in constant transformation, is at all times its total self.[12]

The technology of film, once divorced from the constraining teleological conception of time inherent in the traditional narrative structure, could allow for a new way of thinking about the cinematic image as a kind of contingent assemblage. The process of framing by which this assemblage takes form does not take place simply at the moment of creation, in the hands of the artist, but during the event of spectatorial encounter. Breer would come to describe these films as "objects" as opposed to "continuities," as "blocks of time in which no time takes place."[13]

Cinematic assemblage, for Breer, could create a collision or conjugation of the moving image with the experience of modernist painting. With *Image by Images*, Breer created a dramatically novel synthesis out of his two most important reference points: Richter's abstract "pure cinema," on the one hand, and the decidedly "impure" aesthetic of Kurt Schwitters's *Merz* collage, on the other. Schwitters had not only introduced radically disparate forms of pre-formed material, but further dramatized their dislocation and juxtaposition by maintaining a "roughness" to the edges of the individual pieces. Similarly, Breer not only photographed the most disparate kinds of materials, but also consistently manipulated those fragments so as to further heighten their spatial and temporal incongruity. In so doing, he was able to advance on Richter's conception of a "pure cinema" through a juxtaposition of abstraction and referentiality.

Moreover, the very nature of Breer's process gestured beyond both film and painting, toward a quasi-sculptural situation. In cementing both ends of his film strip together to form a continuous loop, Breer embedded the projector within the film as an integral component. The work was not simply a projected image, but an entire apparatus of image production, simultaneously material and immaterial. Moreover, in creating an endless loop, Breer destroyed any sense of a distinct beginning or ending. The work would simply have to be set in motion and then stopped at a more or less arbitrary point. Or if it were left running, viewers would necessarily have to leave off viewing it—as they would any painting or sculpture. Yet unlike the viewer of any painting or sculpture, the viewer of Breer's work would constantly discover new images, making and remaking the work again and again in the process of viewing it. On a basic perceptual level, the work was literally different for each individual, and even for the same individual over time. Moreover, the rapidity of the image stream created something quite distinct from the usual narrativity of a motion picture. The images all seemed to fall into one another—not blending, precisely, but giving rise to a kind of singular image-in-motion.

Last but not least, Breer's *Image by Images* loop manifested its unusual qualities of temporality and materiality in a singularly dramatic way: it destroyed itself. At only six feet in length, the minor dust and scratches that inevitably scar any film print were magnified a thousandfold, and the work was subject to the ravages of accelerated material decomposition. Puncturing the illusion of film as an immaterial projection of light, the decay of the substrate reinforced Breer's conception of temporality as something exterior to the work, rather than contained within it.

Image by Images was to be the beginning of Breer's many attempts over the next decade to work on the threshold of the plastic and the temporal arts.[14] The looped work would not be part of the *Movement* show the following year. Even if it had not disintegrated, it was clear that the work did not "fit" within either the principal exhibition of painting and sculpture or the supplemental evening of screenings at the Cinémathèque Française. Almost by design, this sculptural-cinematic hybrid could not be accommodated within the traditional exhibitionary spaces of the time. Yet Breer was included in the exhibition, with a work that was characteristically neither painting nor sculpture nor film, but rather a curious combination of all three. It took a form so radically out of sync with everything else on display that it has customarily been left out of historical accounts of the exhibition altogether. This crucial work was the bridge by which Breer would join Marcel Duchamp, the most senior artist in the exhibition, in his recovery of the Victorian philosophical toy as a model for the exploration of cinema *within* the brightly lit space of the gallery's white cube.

Precision Optics and Philosophical Toys

Search nothing beyond the phenomena, they themselves are the theory.

GOETHE, *Theory of Colors*, 1810

One can look at seeing. MARCEL DUCHAMP, *The Green Box*, 1934

Just as important as Breer's confrontation with the formal conditions internal to painting and film was his stated dissatisfaction with the exhibitionary conditions of both the art gallery and the cinematic theater. For Breer, there could be no question of simply giving up one to join the other. Nor could the artist countenance any straightforward combination of the two within a generalized idea of synesthesia. While quite rigorous in maintaining the specificity of his material as a functional constraint, Breer began to introduce aspects of the singular image into the cinematic situation while simultaneously bringing a kind of cinematic movement into the stasis of the gallery environment. In so doing, he sought to question, destabilize, and potentially reinvent both of these institutional spaces through their mutual interaction.

Over the course of the late 1950s and early 1960s, Breer's work moved in two directions simultaneously. While introducing a form of stasis and singularity into the space of the cinematic theater though the frenetic "vibrating" images of his collage films, he would increasingly occupy the space of the gallery through a curious variation on kinetic sculpture whose quality of movement—true to Vasarely's term *Cinétisme*—was fundamentally cinematic. While Breer was generally interested in ideas of movement and duration, he criticized much kinetic sculpture as simply grafting an external quality of movement onto essentially static forms.[15] His unique solution to this dilemma took a form that was neither painting nor sculpture nor cinema, but a strange conjunction of all three. This strange multiple was a limited-edition artist's book produced on the occasion of the *Movement* exhibition. The book bore the title *Image by Images*, like the loop film Breer had produced the year before. It was neither an illustration nor a documentation of the previous work, but rather a translation of its principles to a novel situation: the space of the art gallery.

As we have seen, the title spoke to the process by which all of Breer's films had been constructed as well as to the self-reflexive emphasis on process to which Breer was becoming increasingly devoted. If the original *Image by Images* loop had sought to isolate and explore the potential of the photogram within the temporality of cinematic movement, his *Image by Images* book sought to isolate the very cognitive and perceptual workings of the persistence of vision on which the mechanical foundations of twentieth-century moving-image technology were based. As Breer later described it, "I wanted to simplify, I wanted to go back before the apparatus of cinema and get to the earliest exploitation of persistency ... I thought that the image could be changed into an object that would make a unity of the whole thing."[16] The childlike simplicity of this "image/object" contained within it a wealth of subterranean history.

Composed of scores of minimal, abstract ink drawings, each page differing only slightly from the ones following and preceding it, Breer's *Image by Images* was the first artist's book to employ the Victorian "kineograph" or "recorder of movement."[17] What the French call "pocket cinema" (*cinema à poche*), the Germans "thumb cinema" (*daumenkino*), and the British a "flicker book" was commonly known in America as a "flip book." Devised by John Barnes Linnett in 1868, it is a deceptively simple device by which the spectator-cum-projectionist animates a series of printed still images by rifling them between the thumb and forefinger. Perhaps the single most important aspect of the kineograph is that its temporality is not fixed, but remains utterly dependent on the spectator. Breer's kineograph was not precisely a loop, like his previous version of *Image by*

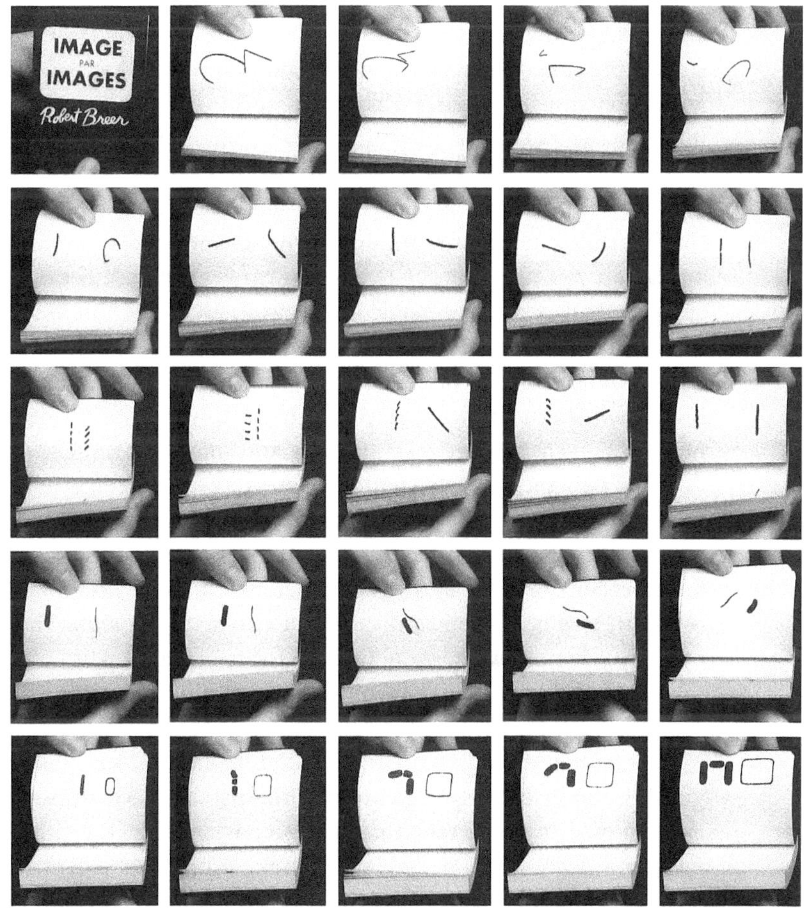

Figure 3.5. Robert Breer, *Image by Images*, 1955. Kineograph/flip book.

Images, but neither did it have the linear, progressive temporality we associate with the experience of theatrical cinema. With a manipulable temporality both literally and metaphorically at our fingertips, it begged to be stopped, started, slowed down, and sped up. Furthermore, the limited duration of the sequence practically ensured that it would be repeated through any number of these temporal iterations. It was almost impossible to view the work with the accustomed mechanical regularity. Try as one might, slight variations in speed would inevitably be introduced, foregrounding the sense that the "movement" of the images was being actively *created* by the spectator, rather than merely viewed.

Rather than merely grafting movement onto a static form, the human intervention necessary in animating this work created an encounter with an uncanny phenomenological hybrid: an obdurate physical object as well as an immaterial moving image. Viewable under ordinary light, the kineograph did not require the separate space of a darkened theater, but could be observed alongside other objects within the traditional space of the gallery. *Image by Images* would be the first of Breer's many attempts over the next decade "to make films concrete" by means of a cinematic-sculptural hybrid: "something you hold right in your hands, something that you are looking at in normal circumstances, under light, without sitting in a chair."[18] Taking on aspects of painting, sculpture, and film, these works "had some kind of development in time and yet could be looked at as concrete objects" in what Breer termed a "concrete situation." "I got disoriented by the theatrical situation of film," he explained, "by the fact that you have to turn out the lights and there is a fixed audience, and when you turn out the lights you turn on the projection light and you project this piece of magic on the wall. I felt that this very dramatic, theatrical situation, in some ways, just by the environment of the movie house, robbed some of the mystery of film from itself."[19] As viewers played Breer's work almost like an instrument, their perception would shift almost imperceptibly between stillness and movement, focusing on that delicate, ephemeral transition between the two. The simple mystery of this phenomenon—one fundamental to the cinematic experience—was precisely what Breer understood the "theatrical situation" of the movie house as conspiring to steal. The "concrete situation" Breer was trying to establish was not a demystification of cinematic illusion. The phenomenon in question was real enough. To focus on that reality was to move toward, rather than away from, the essentially mysterious perceptual, cognitive, and psychological phenomenon of the moving image.[20]

Despite being the first artist's book of its kind, Breer's abstract kineograph is almost entirely neglected within historical accounts of the *Movement* show.[21] To the extent that it was considered at the time, *Image by Images* probably struck most viewers as a marginal and eccentric addition

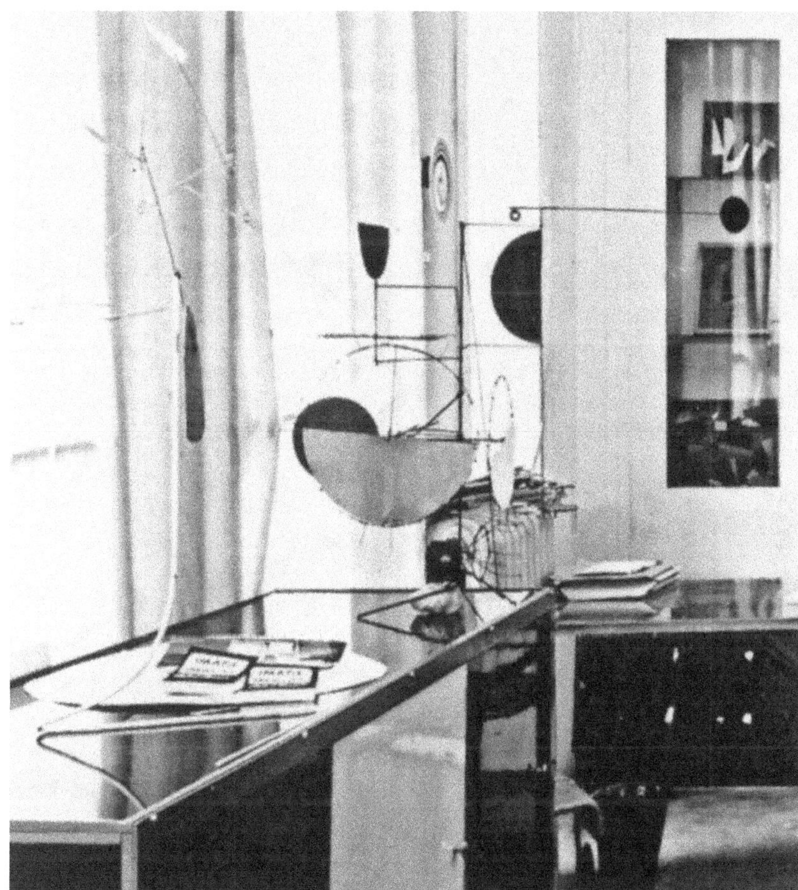

Figure 3.6. Installation view of the exhibition *Le Mouvement*, showing two copies of Breer's *Image by Images* kineograph on desk, Galerie Denise René, Paris, 1955 (detail of fig. 3.1).

to the show—a curiosity or souvenir rather than a significant work in its own right. After all, the technology Breer employed had long ago been rendered obsolete and survived only in the dusty collections of antique dealers. But Breer's neglected multiple was perfectly in keeping with the exhibition's most significant historical precedent as well as the oldest work there on display: Marcel Duchamp's *Rotary Demisphere (Precision Optics)* of 1925.

Like Calder's mobiles, Duchamp's work was intended to provide a pedigree from the historical avant-garde for the concerns of the younger, postwar generation. Its motor-driven apparatus seemed to lead to the kinetic vocabulary of Tinguely's *Méta-méchanique* constructions, while its hypnotic central spiral produced the powerful physiological effects that Vasarely's painting was beginning to explore. Yet these formal similarities were themselves by-products of the more substantive investigation Duchamp had inaugurated into what the artist termed "precision" or "psycho-physiological optics" around 1918. The historical recovery of this

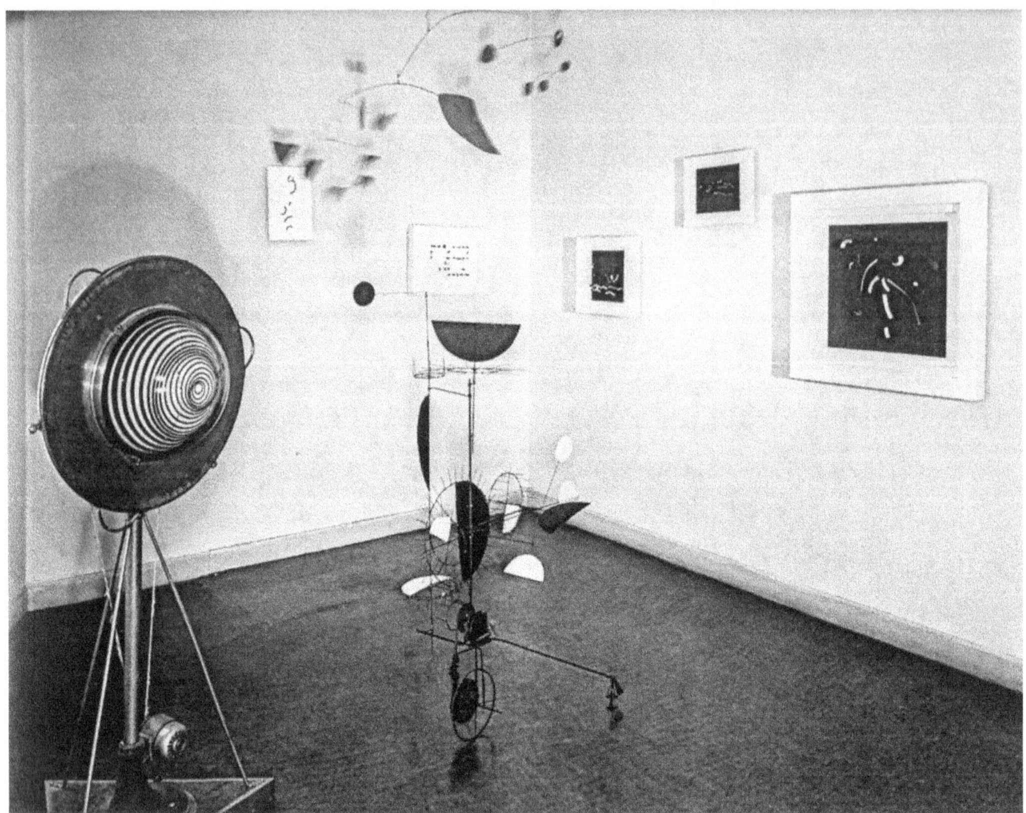

Figure 3.7. Installation view of the exhibition *Le Mouvement*, Galerie Denise René, Paris, 1955, featuring Duchamp's *Rotary Demisphere* (1925) at left.

work in the 1950s would provide the aesthetic and philosophical ground for the imbrication of art and cinema across a whole range of practices throughout the 1960s and 1970s.[22]

Paradoxically, Duchamp's influential critique of "retinal art" might best be understood through his study of optical phenomena. In his self-described profession as "ocularist," Duchamp sought to focus our attention on the act of seeing itself, rather than creating depictions to be seen. To advance this project, Duchamp would recover, in a series of assisted readymades, a variety of outmoded artifacts from the previous century often grouped under the Victorian term "philosophical toys." Developed and popularized in the mid-nineteenth century, these artifacts were themselves optical devices whose deceptive simplicity allowed them to achieve an unprecedented status as objects of leisurely entertainment, popular fascination, prolonged scientific investigation, and intense philosophical speculation.

Wheatstone's mirror stereoscope of 1832 can justifiably be described as the device that, perhaps more than any other, ushered in the modern scientific investigation of human vision.[23] The stereoscope was the first of many optical toys with a serious subtext. It did not precisely replicate our everyday three-dimensional experience of vision, but produced a new and different experience of three-dimensionality. As Jonathan Crary has explained, the philosophical toy served as an epistemological pivot around which previous conceptions of subjectivity were being thrown into question—implying a newly unconscious and corporeal basis for subjectivity that would nurture the early twentieth-century development of psychoanalytic and phenomenological thought.[24]

While histories of modern art have long given special attention to the nineteenth-century birth of photography, the contemporaneous invention of the philosophical toy—in the form of devices such as the thaumatrope, stereoscope, phenakistoscope, and stroboscopic disc—has been comparatively neglected.[25] Part of the rationale is obvious: the camera, as what C. S. Pierce would describe as a tool for indexical as well as iconic representation, was infinitely more useful. But from an epistemological perspective, the technology of the photographic camera was also infinitely more *familiar*, fitting seamlessly within the model of visual objectivity and referentiality descended from the camera obscura and the model of monocular perspective dominant since the sixteenth century. Philosophical toys were "philosophical" precisely insofar as they overthrew the earlier, decorporealized subject of vision on which a whole philosophical conception of subjectivity had been grounded. They conclusively demonstrated that visual perception could no longer be understood within a rhetoric of equivalence between interior and exterior reality, but instead concerned the conjunction of multiple *physiological* operations within the subjective mind. As the physicist Ernst Mach wrote,

> We are not yet fully conscious, or at least have not yet deemed it necessary to incorporate the fact into our ordinary language, *that the senses represent things neither wrongly nor correctly*. All that can be truly said of the sense organs is, that, *under different circumstances they produced different sensations and perceptions*. As these "circumstances," now, are extremely manifold in character, being partly external (inherent in the objects), partly internal (inherent in the sensory organs), and partly interior (having their seat in the central organs), it would naturally seem, especially when attention is paid only to external circumstances, as if the organs acted differently under the same conditions. And it is customary to call the unusual effects, deceptions or illusions.[26]

It was precisely this less studied tradition that Duchamp would make the explicit and sustained focus of philosophical attention within the series of optical toys he produced over the next fifty years, from his *Handmade Stereopticon Slide* of 1918 to his *Anaglyphic Chimney* of 1968, the year of his death. This psychophysiological interplay between surface and depth would become most prominent in his *Rotary Demisphere*.[27] Duchamp created *Rotary Demisphere* and *Discs Bearing Spirals* at roughly the same time, and both works made use of the curious effect of dimensionality obtained by rotation. Both works served as the basis for cinematographic projects: *Rotary Demisphere* for the artist's initial, failed attempt to construct an anaglyphic (three-dimensional) film, and *Discs Bearing Spirals* for the simplified, two-dimensional version he would create the next year, titled *Anemic Cinema*. Based on the image of the ocular demisphere, the abandoned anaglyphic film would have, in effect, provided two distinct experiences of perceptual depth on what the viewer would have rationally understood to be the perfect flatness of the cinematic screen. The first, static depth would be re-created through the red and blue offset images familiar from the various 3D cinema revivals that seem to recur every few years, while a second, mobile depth would be created through the rotation of the spiral pattern overlying the surface of the demisphere. When the film was accidentally destroyed in processing, Duchamp decided to substitute a linguistic form for the anaglyphic one in *Anemic Cinema*, alternating between the mobile depth created by *Discs Bearing Spirals*, in which our eyes come to rest at the vertiginous center, and the flat fields of spiraling words, whose punning wordplay demands our cognitive attention even as our eyes race to stabilize the linguistic field.[28]

For Duchamp, *Rotary Demisphere* was neither painting nor sculpture. In fact, the artist had expressly stated that he did not want it exhibited alongside works of painting and sculpture in a gallery context. But perhaps that was simply because its true context was not the white cube, but the black box. Like the works of so many of his time, Duchamp's "precision optics" were propelled by his fascination not with "the machine" in general, but with a particular machine—the most revolutionary and disruptive motor of twentieth-century aesthetics—the cinematographic apparatus. All of Duchamp's optical toys might be considered thinly veiled explorations, critiques, and transformations of this singular, insidious machine. *Rotary Demisphere* allowed Duchamp to approach the cinematic apparatus obliquely, to dissect its studied coherence into the strangeness of its otherwise invisible component parts.

Thus it becomes significant that the historical recovery of Duchamp's precision optics in the 1950s came at the very moment when the cinema, as a cultural institution, was itself undergoing a massive internal transformation. The industrial cinema was just then going into frenzied technological overdrive to ward off the incursion of domestic television. The linked oversized projections of Cinerama, with its vast landscapes of near-infinite detail, its eye-popping Technicolor palette, and its enclosing field of stereophonic sound, created an outsized model of industrial spectacle whose complex, expensive processes of manufacture were distant from the medium's primitive roots. The philosophical toy reached to the opposite extreme: its minimal internal mechanisms were all straightforwardly on display. Its effects were not built up, but stripped down. For many artists of the postwar era, it was this very simplicity and transparency that rendered what Breer called the fundamental "mysteries" of cinema all the more visible and compelling. The philosophical toy's ascetic mechanism geared uncannily into the phenomenological body's very capacities and limitations, softly but insistently overturning a vast philosophical architecture of authoritative intentionality—of the autonomous, rational, egoistic subject exemplified by the metaphor of immobile, single-point perspective.

It was Duchamp's recovery of the philosophical toy within these optical machines, and the model they presented for an investigation of cinema by means of a space historically and epistemologically *prior to* cinema, that was to influence the development of cinema's "expansion" into the institutions and discourses of late modern art over the next two decades. These deceptively simple machines were uniquely able to embody both the obdurate solidity of the sculptural object and the uncanny immateriality of a purely optical experience of movement and transformation. Navigating the uneasy, shifting constellation between these two poles, these devices allowed for an exploration of the aesthetic and conceptual foundations of the moving image in a space—that of the modern art gallery—where the synesthetic conjunction of the cinematic apparatus could be kept at a distance.

In what was to be an anomalous example, Tinguely produced his own philosophical toy for the *Movement* exhibition, titled *Virtual Volume, 2000 Revolutions per Second* (1955). Reiterating the Victorian *toupies caméléons*,

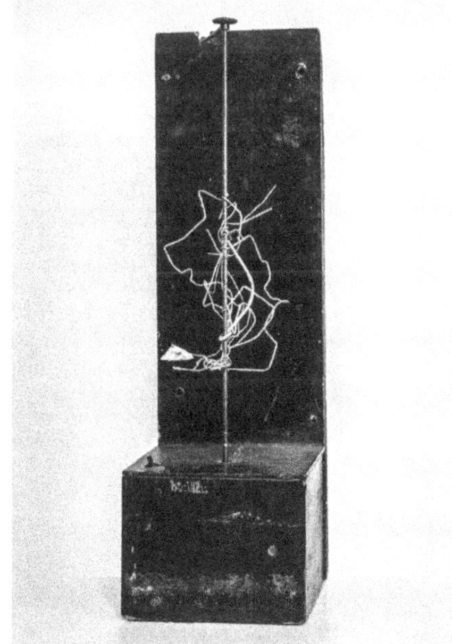

Figure 3.8. Jean Tinguely, *Virtual Volume, 2000 Revolutions per Second*, 1955 (at rest).

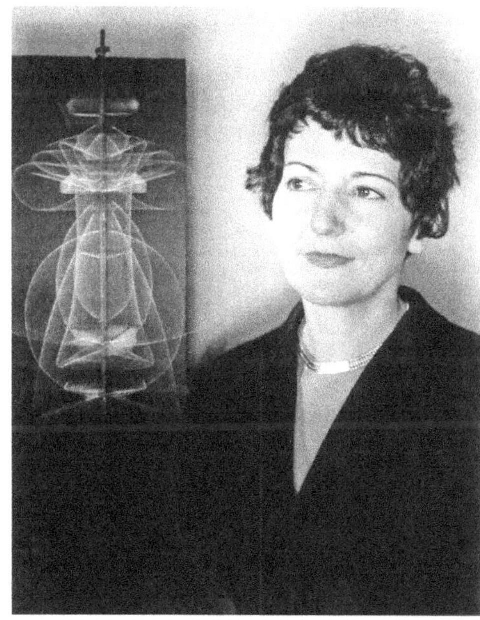

Figure 3.9. Denise René with Jean Tinguely's *Virtual Volume, 2000 Revolutions per Second*, 1955 (in motion).

or "spinning tops," Tinguely gathered a rather chaotic assemblage of wires around a single spinning pole that, once accelerated, would cause them to coalesce into a harmonic, symmetrical form. The effect was compelling—as it had been when Naum Gabo made his similar *Kinetic Construction* (*Standing Wave*) of 1919, and would be again within the popular kinetic sculptures of Len Lye throughout the next two decades. This singular image of motion was paradoxically too "static" for Tinguely's burgeoning interest in chance and process, and he abandoned his explorations in this vein.

Between Duchamp's *Rotary Demisphere* and Tinguely's *Virtual Volume* on the one hand and Breer's *Image by Images* kineograph on the other, there was an important difference—one that quite likely precipitated the exclusion of Breer's work from historical accounts of the *Movement* exhibition. By its nature, Breer's kineograph—like the original Victorian philosophical toy—was not bound either to the physical space of the art gallery or to the institutional context of an art world that regarded such spaces as necessary. In fact, this small multiple seemed decidedly out of place within a situation devoted to the physical installation of unique sculptural objects. However, Breer's kineograph was not as out of place as it might initially appear. For an important aspect of Duchamp's reappropriation of the philosophical toy lay precisely in what might be called its "domestic location." In the nineteenth century, the phonograph record both displaced and mass-produced the experience of live musical exhibition. Duchamp's Rotoreliefs were similarly mass-produced, works of art to be experienced not during a gallery or museum visit, but in the

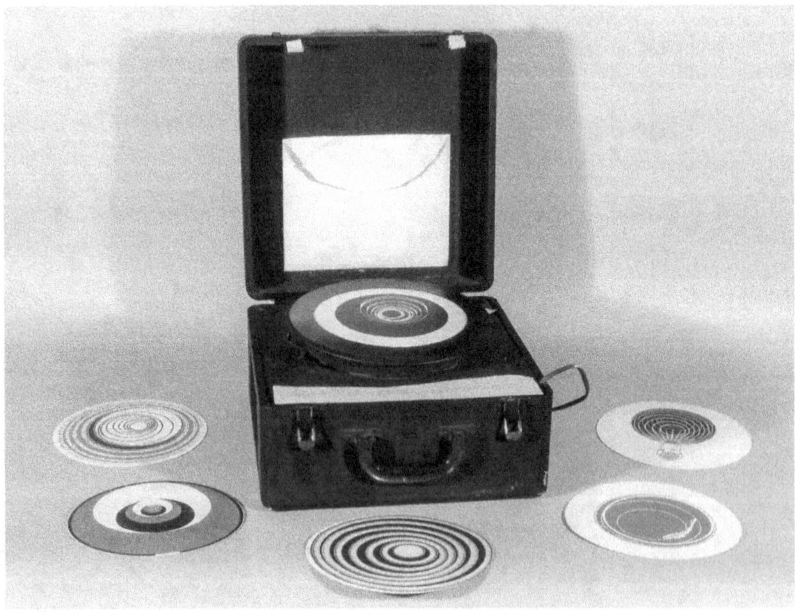

Figure 3.10. Marcel Duchamp, *Rotoreliefs (Optical Disks)*: *No. 1–12*, 1953. Color offset lithographs with commercial record player. Davis Museum and Cultural Center, Wellesley College.

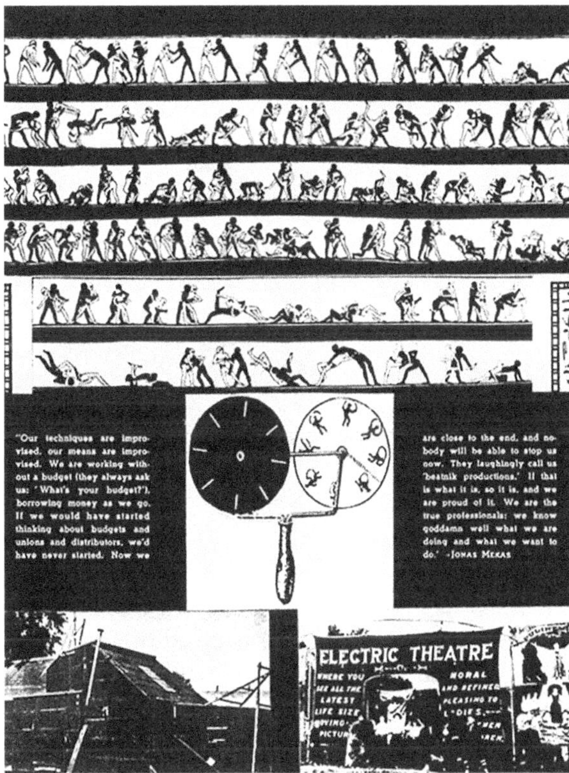

Figure 3.11. Stan Van-DerBeek, interior illustration for *Cinema Delimina* manifesto, *Film Quarterly* 14, no. 4 (Summer 1961).

intimate and everyday space of the private home. "Played" on the very living room phonographs that often constituted a focal point for domestic entertainment, these spinning discs produced their curious optical experience through a denaturing of that familiar apparatus. Duchamp went so far as to sell them at a commercial trade fair, where he sold only a few copies, but managed to take home an "honorable mention" in the industrial arts category.

Like Duchamp's Rotoreliefs twenty years before, Breer's *Image by Images* was produced in an edition of five hundred. It was put up for sale in a Parisian bookstore alongside the other paperbacks. Over the next decade, a wide range of artists would appropriate the primitive technology of the kineograph so as to operate outside the exhibitionary space of the art gallery, if not always the institutional structures of the art world. Only a year after the *Movement* exhibition, the Swiss-German artist Dieter Roth created a kineograph, *Design for Material 5* (1956), that formed its moving images not with ink, but by means of holes physically punched out of the pages. Stan VanDerBeek, Andy Warhol, Jack Smith, George Brecht, Yoko Ono, and Mieko Shiomi all made kineographs during the 1960s, which were distributed through early compendiums such as George Macunias's *Fluxus Anthologies* and *Aspen Magazine*. Hollis Frampton made cutout

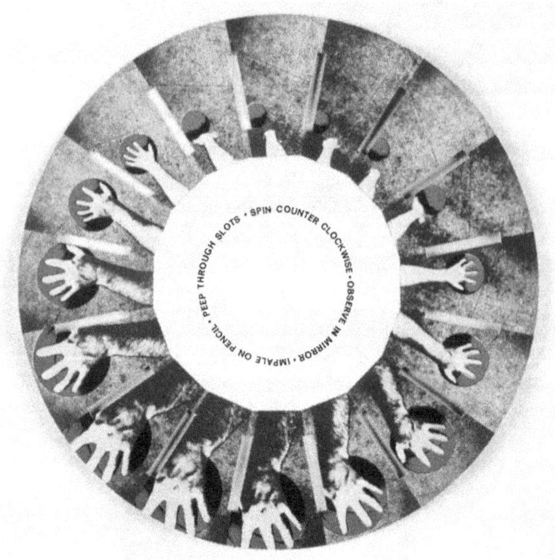

Figure 3.12. Hollis Frampton, *Phenakistoscope*, from the portfolio *S.M.S.* (*Shit Must Stop*), *No. 4*, August 1968. Davis Museum and Cultural Center, Wellesley College.

paper phenakistoscopes as well a paperback edition of his film *Poetic Justice* that might be understood as a conceptualist revision of the kineograph.

These and other works speak to an increasingly widespread interest in returning to the aesthetic and philosophical foundations of the moving image without the complications and constraints of industrial cinematic technology—that is, in returning to the *idea* of the moving image outside of its cultural elaboration within the industrial norms of the traditional cinematic theater. These works, which explore the underlying foundations of temporality and movement in the cinematic image, are probably best understood as different means of "escaping the white cube," as critics such as Lucy Lippard or Brian O'Doherty would have it, in order to recapture the particular conjunction of art, investigation, entertainment, and wonder that had been the original animating force in the popularization of the Victorian philosophical toy.

Concretizations of Movement: Breer's Mutoscopes (1958–1964)

Breer's abstract kineograph afforded him the freedom to exhibit outside the physical and institutional space of the art gallery—an opportunity whose revolutionary implications would be trumpeted repeatedly by artists and critics over the next decade. Yet Breer showed little interest in doing so. In fact, Breer disliked screening his films in cinema theaters specifically because he felt that they became divorced from the art gallery, for it was only within that context that he felt the relevance and significance of these works would be understood. Instead of simply abandoning the gallery space, Breer sought to engage it, to transform it from within. In order to advance a dialogue with the plastic forms of painting and sculpture as well as with the specific conventions of the gallery space, Breer proceeded to give his kineograph an even more sculptural form. Taking up the form of Hermann Casler's mutoscope of 1894, he transformed the spine of his book into a spool, and he added a crank and a stay for the momentary suspension of each image. The resulting device allowed a continuous moving image to be maintained indefinitely by the spectator-cum-operator.

Inexpensive to produce and simple to use, mutoscopes had remained a mainstay of popular entertainment decades after the emergence and industrialization of the motion picture. Part of the reason for their persistence was the private nature of the spectatorial experience they afforded: rather than the communal experience of the cinematographic projection, the mutoscope prompted a private encounter with an individual scene. A single individual placed his eyes to the viewer as he cranked

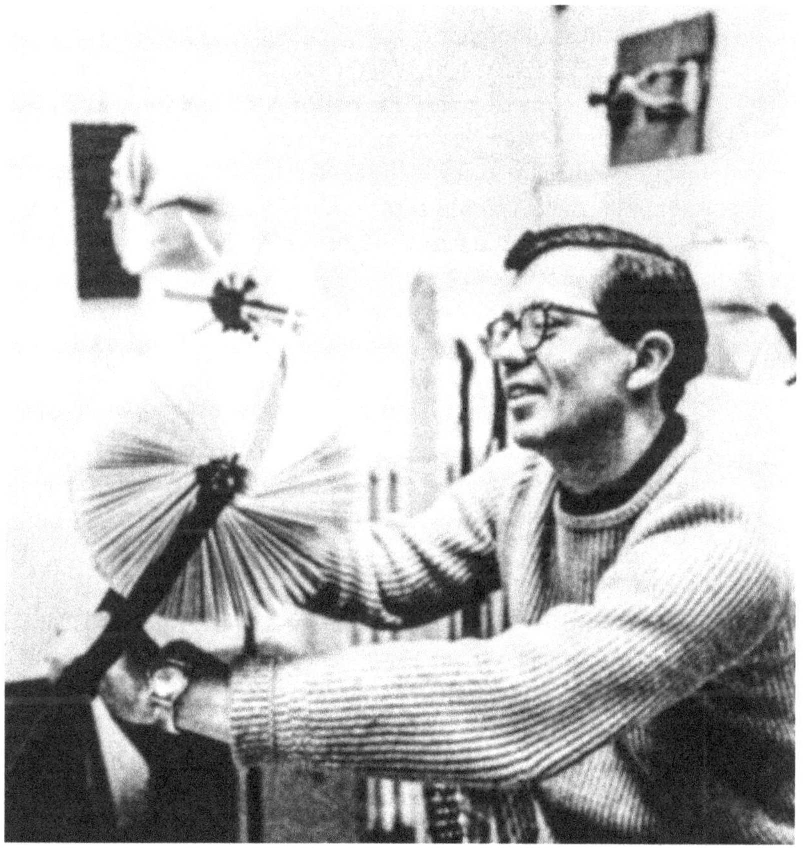

Figure 3.13. Photo of Robert Breer with freestanding and wall-mounted paper mutoscopes, 1958.

the wheel, which allowed him to view scenes that might prove embarrassing if viewed in mixed company. Furthermore, the action of cranking the wheel meant that, as with the kineograph, the temporality of the moving image was entirely under the control of the viewer. While tedious sequences could be quickly passed over, a particularly charged or favorite moment could be slowed to a crawl—or a single, poignant image frozen in time.

From roughly 1958 to 1964, Breer used the ready-made form of the mutoscope to explore the phenomenological basis of cinema at a remove from the established social and cultural imperatives of the cinematic theater.[29] Capable of negotiating between the material solidity of sculpture and the dematerialized cinematic image, the mutoscope allowed Breer to pose basic questions of cinema within the physical, institutional, and discursive space of the plastic arts. "The challenge was to make it continuous and endless," Breer said at the time, "a loop situation … composing something that had no beginning or end. You could stand there and crank all day long. Hopefully by turning it constantly it would reveal new things."[30] Set in motion only through the action of the viewer, the mutoscope thus exemplified precisely the kind of authorial divestment and fortuitous modulation then emerging as hallmarks of post-Cagean aesthetics. In fact, a gallery later exhibiting one of Breer's mutoscopes related the story of a peculiar visitor cranking the work in rapt fascination for the better part of an afternoon. When eventually approached about purchasing it, the man replied that he was "only a poor artist, and certainly couldn't afford such a thing." Only later did Breer discover the man's identity and retroactively dedicate the work to him with the title *Homage to John Cage* (1963).

During the first major exhibition of Breer's sculptural mutoscopes, at the 1959 *Vision in Motion* exhibition in Antwerp, Belgium, several were mounted directly to the walls of the gallery. Brushing up against the sides of their container, these wall-mounted works metaphorically addressed an experience that was and was not comprehensible from the perspective of modernist plastic abstraction.[31] Two years later, his mutoscopes and looped projections were exhibited as part of the traveling show *Art in Motion* (*Bewogen Beweging*) at the Moderna Museet in Stockholm, the Stedelijk Museum in Amsterdam, and elsewhere.[32]

The mutoscopes Breer made in Paris in the late 1950s had been composed out of paper index cards—the same paper cards used to construct his earliest painterly studies and subsequent *Form Phases*. In seeking more durable materials for his mutoscopes, he was led to begin working in translucent plastic. Breer used a metaphorics of transparency in describing his aesthetic investigations of the "limit condition" between materiality and immateriality, visibility and invisibility:

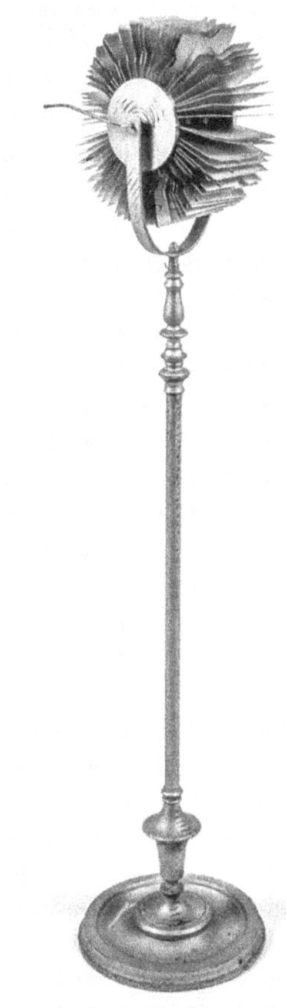

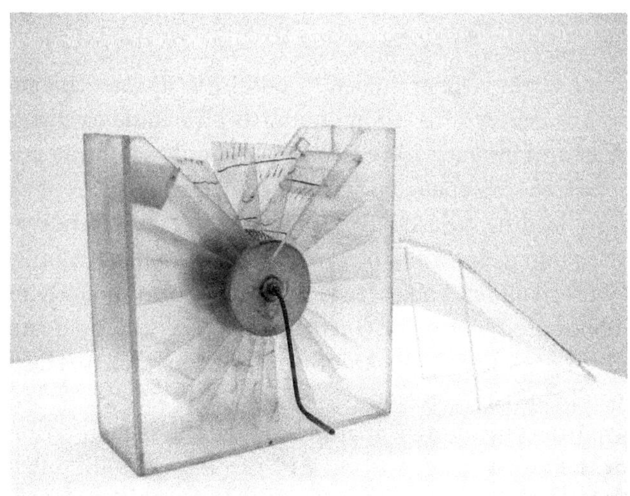

Figure 3.14. Robert Breer, *Homage to John Cage*, 1963.

Figure 3.15. Robert Breer, untitled mutoscope, 1964.

I thought that it would have more impact if you didn't turn out all the lights and turn on another light and all mystery, everything hidden. I wanted this to be in the open ... the fact of that rabbit sitting inside the magician's hat is the real mystery, not how it's dissimulated. The hat should be transparent and show the rabbit.[33]

Transparency is not presented here as a straightforward process of "demystification," because the basic cinematic processes are considered anything but straightforward. Breer understood the complexity and, indeed, the mystery of cinema's fundamental psychophysiological processes to have been obscured by the technological "evolution" of industrial cinema. An aesthetic of transparency, obtained by means of a deliberate formal reduction, was what could allow this fundamental mystery to again command center stage.

At rest, these transparent frames would appear as both image and object simultaneously. And in motion, the apparatus itself might be said to dissolve even as it remained in physical contact with the observer's hand. This transition—what Breer often referred to as a "threshold"—between work and frame, media and apparatus, becomes paradigmatically visible. In a work like *Homage to John Cage* (1963), the line between image and support is quite literally winnowed down:

I started sculpting them now, in a sense—the cards have been chopped away at the corners, progressively more and then diminishing again ... when you stop a card at a given point, there is a trigger mechanism that turns it into a cinematic machine—then the change of the shape of the card becomes part of a flowing change ... I began punching holes in them and treating them as a kind of sculptural object ... this kind of three dimensional movie ...

Breer's mutoscope works were grounded in a desire to *displace* cinema from the theater to the gallery so as to foreground its bifurcated nature as both tangible object and immaterial perception. Not only sculpture but also cinema, the mutoscopes opened a tiny window in the white cube's hermetic enclosure, leading to a qualitatively different experience of space and time. In so doing, Breer's recovery of the philosophical toy also transformed his Victorian found object into a critical optic, implicitly recalling a nearly obliterated history of cinema's emergence, an inchoate period of possibility when a multiplicity of exhibitionary and spectatorial models still competed for attention.

Thierry de Duve has compellingly articulated how the rehabilitation of Duchamp over the 1950s in France and America began to diminish Greenberg's critical stature among a younger generation of artists, and it

Figure 3.16. Robert Breer, *Mural Flip Book (Linear Mutoscope)*, 1964.

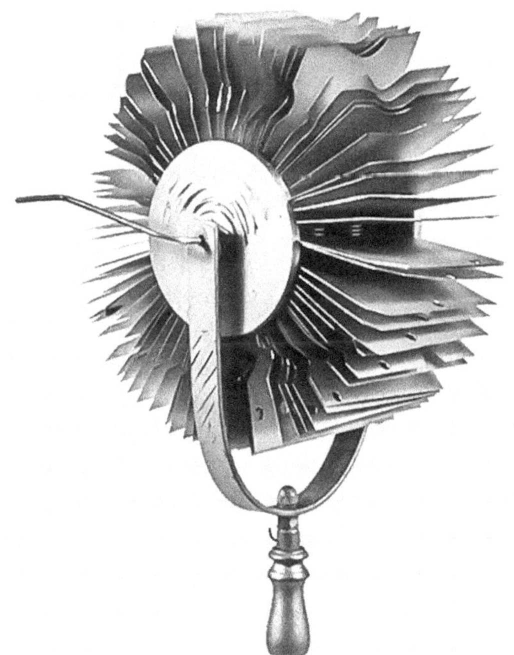

Figure 3.17. Robert Breer, *Homage to John Cage*, 1963 (detail of fig. 3.14).

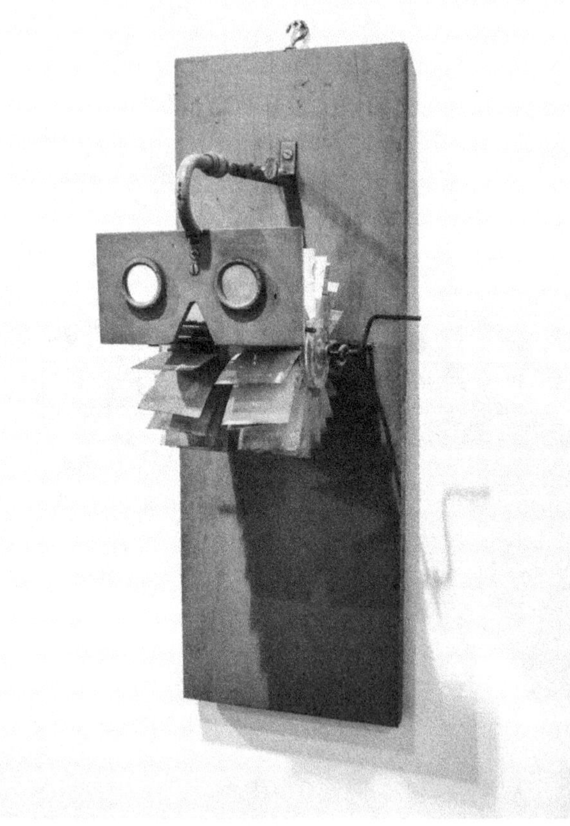

Figure 3.18. Robert Breer, *3D Mutoscope*, 1978 (a variation on his *Stereo Mutoscope* of 1964).

is doubtless correct that Duchamp came to authorize a newly conceptual emphasis less reliant on the articulation of medium-specificity.[34] More specifically, it was Duchamp's own recovery of the nineteenth-century philosophical toy in the form of his precision optics that was to serve several generations of younger artists as a model for analyzing the cultural force of cinema at a critical remove from the cinematic theater within which it had become naturalized. By breaking the synthetic coherence of the industrial cinema into its component parts, the model of the philosophical toy allowed artists a means to revisit the supposedly basic phenomena of cinematic projection and reception. Lying somewhere between image, object, and motion picture, and dislocated from the exhibitionary conventions of both the art gallery and the cinematic theater, the model of the philosophical toy allowed a postwar generation of artist/filmmakers to move back toward the future, just as it had done for Duchamp nearly a half century before.

Sculpture's Expanding Field (1961–1964)

Like *Art in Motion*, William Seitz's contemporaneous exhibition *The Art of Assemblage* (1961),at MoMA, prominently figured Duchamp as a wellspring for an emerging aesthetic. But while the European rhetoric of movement had allowed Breer an opening through which to bring the moving image into the traditionally static space of the white cube, no such opening was presented by the rhetoric of assemblage. Despite the fact that some of the most innovative work in assemblage was then taking place in experimental film—from the works of Robert Breer and Bruce Conner to those of Stan VanDerBeek and Harry Smith—none would figure in the exhibition, its catalog, or the symposia surrounding the show. On the whole, artists then attempting to work *between* art and cinema found little support for their work within the institutions of either art *or* cinema.

Coming to New York after a decade in Paris, Breer had been told to seek out Richard Griffith, the film curator at MoMA. A personal recommendation by Henri Langlois, curator of the Cinémathèque Française, described Breer's work as the most significant advance in experimental film since the 1920s. Nevertheless, MoMA was clearly not ready to embrace this kind of work: Breer found himself curtly dismissed by a secretary with the words, "Mr. Griffith really prefers Westerns."[35] And while Amos Vogel's Cinema 16 provided a venue for a great diversity of shocking and subversive material throughout the 1950s, it evidenced little concern for the domain of modern art as such.[36] Brian O'Doherty's review of Bruce Conner's assemblage exhibition at the Alan Gallery is indicative of the displaced situation of artists then attempting to work with the moving image. Within Seitz's MoMA exhibition, the idea of assemblage had been almost exclusively confined to the medium of sculpture. Yet, writing for the *New York Times*, O'Doherty claimed that assemblage "as a technique is permeating all of the arts with extraordinary vigor," and he devoted much of his interest to Connor's film with the curiously prosaic title, *A Movie* (1958):

> Some of the collage images are so well known ... that they send the mind pin wheeling out of the movie on a tangent while the next sequence is demanding attention ... the film clips of reality are used as objects—not as objects prompting Surrealist associations, but as objects from real life loudly claiming attention while being forced into a relationship to contribute to the movie. The movie is split open again and again by real life hurtling through it. This is remarkably like the effect Robert Rauschenberg gets in his latest paintings.[37]

While appreciating the publicity, the gallery soon found itself in the awkward situation of having to explain why the film O'Doherty's readers had

Figure 3.19. Installation view of the exhibition *The Art of Assemblage*, Joseph Cornell room, Museum of Modern Art, 1961. MoMA Archives, New York. Art © The Joseph Cornell Memorial Foundation / Licensed by VAGA, New York, NY.

come to see was not, in fact, on display. O'Doherty had been able to see the work only by convincing the gallery director to screen it privately in a back room.

Like Breer and Conner, many artists beginning to work with film understood their work within the context of contemporary developments in painting and sculpture and were thus largely illegible within a purely cinematic context. Only by encouraging "the private purchase and collection of films," VanDerBeek wrote at the time, could art institutions "plant film and film-makers firmly in the ranks of the other arts and artists" and "break the stranglehold that commercial cinema has on the eye and senses."[38] As we have seen, starting in 1955, Breer's kineographs and mutoscopes had attempted to open up just such a liminal exhibitionary situation between the black box and the white cube. In 1965, Robert Whitman's *Cinema Pieces* would engender the first published use of the term "Expanded Cinema" through their literal incorporation of cinematic projection into the space of sculptural installation. But several years before, the exhibition of Joseph Cornell's boxes—what the artist referred to as his "miniature theatres"—within *The Art of Assemblage* could be said to prefigure the hybrid nature of this later situation.

For the most part, the show presented the familiar "white cube" model for which MoMA had become internationally renowned since the 1930s. The large sculptural assemblages, made up of everyday "non-art" objects, were themselves readily legible as aesthetic structures, in large part due to the powerful framing effects such a neutral white container provides. Cornell's work was curiously set off from the rest of the show within its own exhibitionary space—a space dramatically opposed to the aesthetics of this white cube and the kind of experience of aesthetic spectatorship it provided. Within a relatively narrow passage in which both the ceiling and the walls had been painted a solid black, two rows of Cornell's boxes were carefully spotlit from above. The effect was such that these individually enclosed scenes seemed to glow from within.[39] The miniature scale of the works guaranteed that they could not be seen from a distance, but would necessarily engage each individual viewer closely in a quasi-private encounter. The gallery itself, as either a material or a social space, was made practically invisible.

This installation was certainly unusual for MoMA, but it was not entirely unprecedented. In her history of museological exhibition, Charlotte Klonk describes how Alfred Barr's exhibition strategy over the course of the 1930s and 1940s championed the plain white walls and uncluttered presentation that he had found in the "functional and flexible" interiors of Bauhaus design (albeit typically shorn of the political objectives such design had originally implied). Surrealism presented an inherent disruption to the order and functionalism of Barr's aesthetic—its fascination with the unconscious, the primal, and the irrational seemed to demand

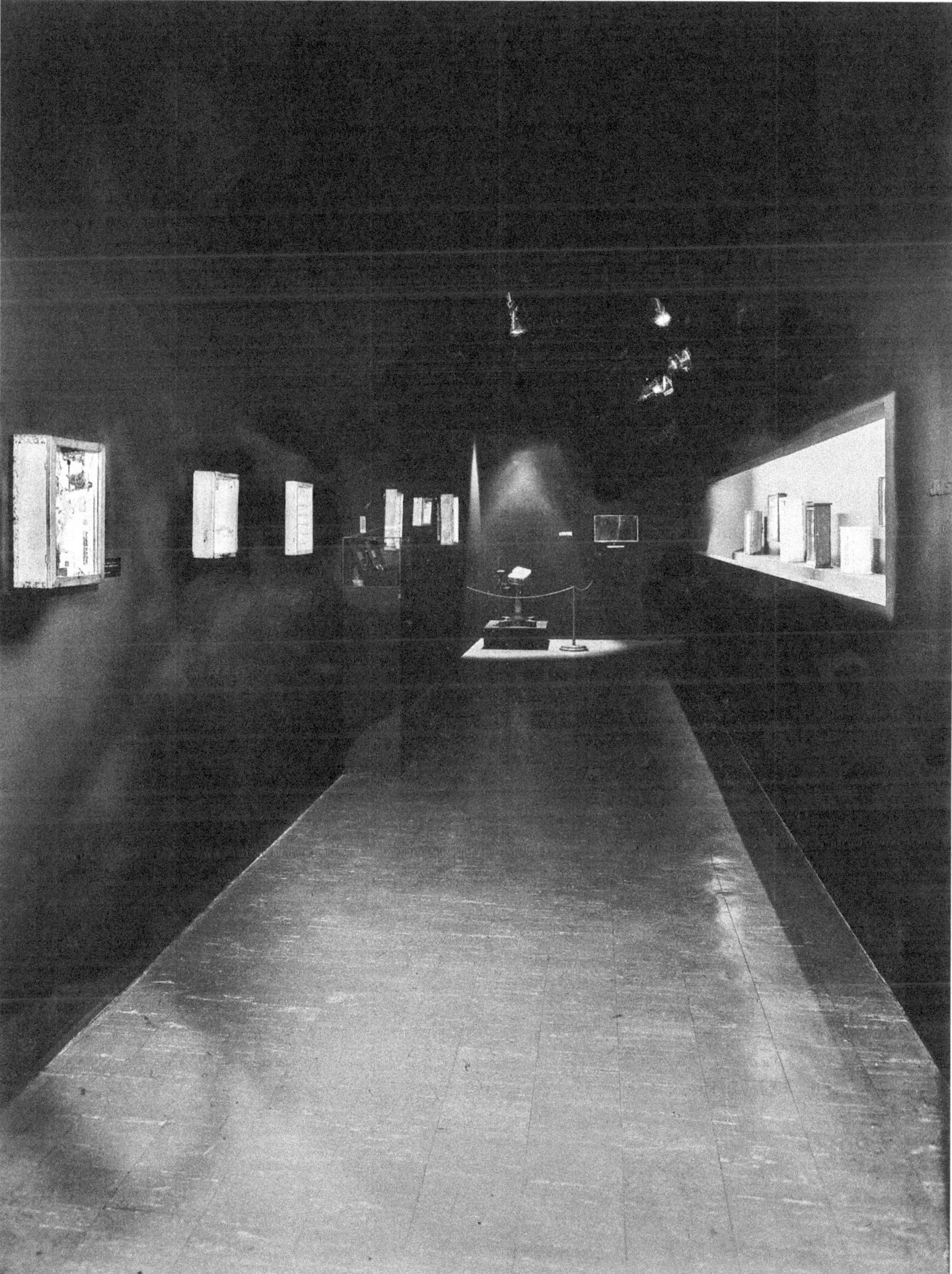

a different quality of display. The 1938 International Exhibition of Surrealism in Paris employed black walls and a radically darkened space as a metaphor for its plumbing of unconscious desire, and, Klonk contends, "the use of black as a conventional signifier for art that sprang from the depths of the psyche rather than the Apollonian mind" would become "one of Barr's most distinctive display innovations" over a series of scattered instances during the 1940s and 1950s.[40]

The pride of place given Cornell within *The Art of Assemblage*—in addition to his work being given this separate environment, there were more works by him than any artist save Kurt Schwitters—would be hard to justify on the basis of the artist's reputation at the time. But it is readily explained once we consider that Seitz's concept of assemblage as analogical juxtaposition is historically grounded in the early modern tradition of the *wunderkabinett*—a tradition of which Cornell's boxes are the foremost modern exemplar. Historically, the *wunderkabinett* functioned not only as a display of wealth, but as a tool of exploration, play, and discovery. As sources of both knowledge and entertainment, these cabinets were the direct precursors of the Victorian philosophical toy. Not unlike the motion picture, the *wunderkabinett* juxtaposed diverse materials from across time and space in order to propel its spectator on an imaginary voyage.

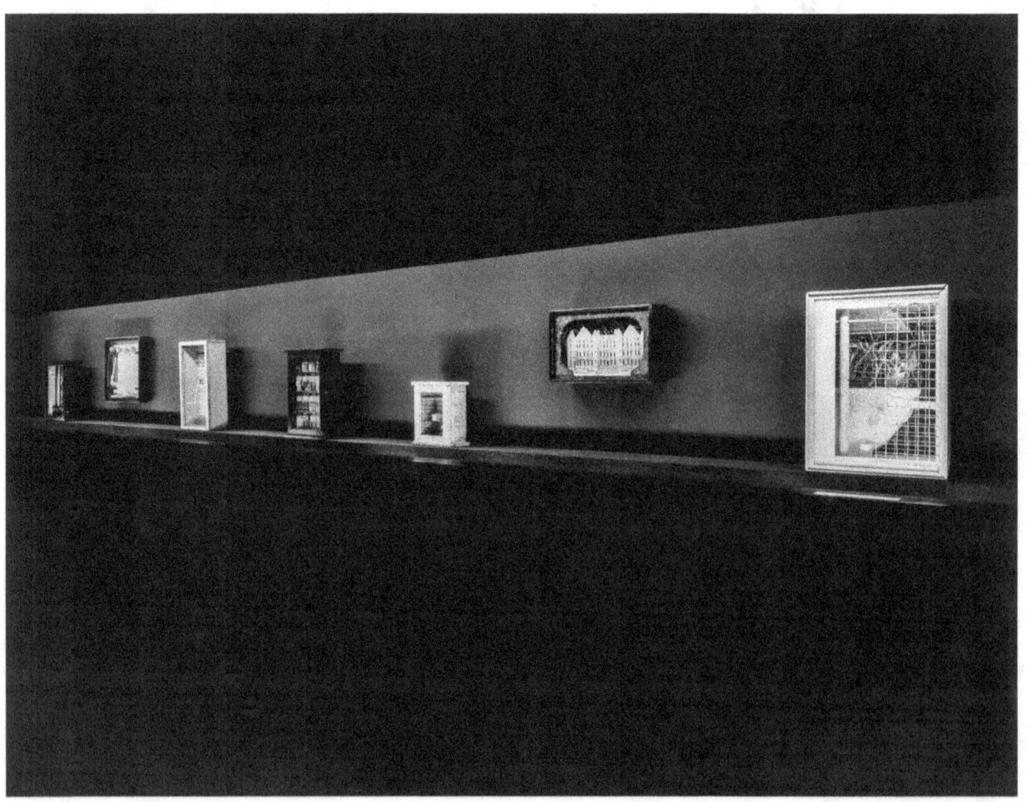

Figure 3.20. Installation view of the exhibition *The Art of Assemblage*, Joseph Cornell room, Museum of Modern Art, New York, 1961. Art © The Joseph and Robert Cornell Memorial Foundation / Licensed by VAGA, New York, NY. Detail.

Cornell has long been considered an "outsider" surrealist, having exhibited his first works in the 1932 Levy Gallery show in which the movement was first introduced to America. The installation and lighting within *The Art of Assemblage* was thus not intended to transform the experience of Cornell's boxes, but rather to dramatize a perceptual dynamic already implicit within them. For despite the obvious materiality of the items they contained, these "assemblages" functioned not through the literalism of the object but through the metaphor of the window. To view what Cornell called his "poetic theatres" was to be "carried away in the mind's eye," Cornell wrote in his diary about the exhibition. The viewer was taken away from the literal space of the gallery into an individual landscape of memory, association, and fantasy. Mary Anne Caws has described Cornell's boxes as the model of "seeing through" as a kind of spectatorial interpenetration, and within the literature on Cornell, one finds countless references to the ideas of projection, displacement, and spectatorial "travel" in the descriptions of these works. Just as the protagonist in Cocteau's surrealist film *The Blood of a Poet* (1930) literally traverses the mirror, the spectator becomes entranced and could be said to "enter into" Cornell's miniature worlds.[41]

A darkened environment within which a singular, glowing point of attention is marked by means of a piercing beam of light—here was the black box of the cinematic theater with which surrealism had long been associated. Born at the same time as psychoanalysis, the cinema was understood to unfold its stream of images like the mind itself, juxtaposing time and space to create its own reality out of the fragments of daily life. Like surrealism, the cinema had the unique, fantastic, and dangerously seductive ability to gear into the unconscious depths of desire—an ability that, in addition to provoking all manner of social panic among cultural critics, placed it at odds with the increasingly rationalized demands of modern social organization. According to André Breton, the surrealists appreciated "nothing so much as dropping into the cinema when whatever was playing was playing, at any point in the show, and leaving at the first hint of boredom—of surfeit—to rush off to another cinema where we behaved in the same way."[42] The cinema was not employed to flee reality, but to transform one's encounter with it through its radical juxtaposition with the cinematic.

Like Breer's philosophical toys, Cornell's boxes both were and were not cinema: situated in different contexts, and operating through different material logic, both were able to address fundamental aspects of the cinematic experience from their deliberately oblique perspective. Like Duchamp before him, Cornell had actually begun his exploration of the cinematic by means of the philosophical toy. His early works *The Traveler in the Mirrors* (1932) and *Surrealist Toy* (1932) were boxed sets of thaumatropic discs. These and similar devices were even advertised by his first

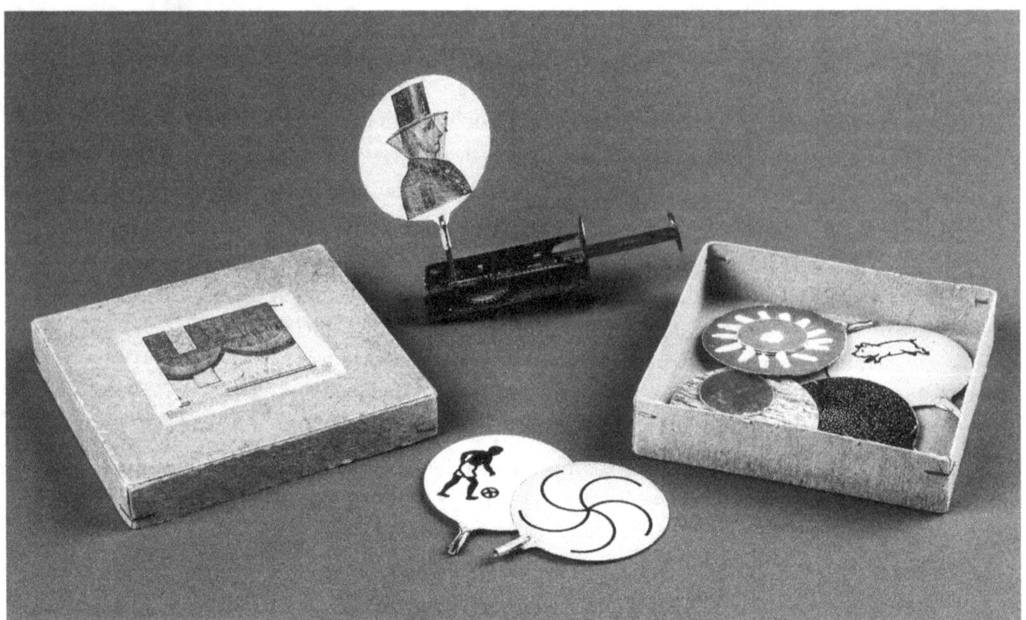

Figure 3.21. Joseph Cornell, *Jouet Surrealiste*, c. 1932. Smithsonian American Art Museum, gift of Mr. and Mrs. John A. Benton. Art © The Joseph and Robert Cornell Memorial Foundation / Licensed by VAGA, New York, NY.

dealer, Julian Levy, as "toys for adults," and the phrase—condescendingly appropriated by Cornell's critics—initially stuck to the artist's work as a pejorative. Like Duchamp, Cornell welcomed the oddly disjunctive context of the philosophical toy—the way in which it presented itself as more of a curiosity or experiment than a proper work of art.

The explicit theatricality of Cornell's installation at *The Art of Assemblage*, the "windows" it opened up within the modernist enclosure of the white cube, and the strangely theatrical darkened environment within which it was displayed—all of this seems deliberately out of step with the emerging ethos of the times. For it was just then that an aesthetic of minimalism, which deliberately repudiated any sense of illusionistic depth, any notion of the work of art as a window on another time or place, was beginning to take center stage. Minimalist painting and sculpture endeavored to foreground the phenomenology of the "here and now" of the gallery experience.

The work of Robert Morris—specifically, his first solo exhibition at Green Gallery in 1963—has regularly served as a reference point for this "literalist" conception of sculptural minimalism. In his 1966 "Notes on Sculpture," Morris would explain that these works are not "built up" according to the traditional logic of composition, but made intentionally "unitary" and "reductive" so as to strike the viewer immediately as "gestalt."[43] In so doing, they take "relationships out of the work and make them a function of space, light, and the viewer's field of vision." This idea of the "gallery-as-perceptual-laboratory" was to become the dominant model through which Morris's early work, and indeed, much of early minimalism, would be interpreted. Yet Morris's interest in the phenomenology of spectatorship was much more complicated than this literalist reading would suggest. For two years before, Morris had already employed a similarly reductive, minimal form to stage a vastly different kind of phenomenological encounter and a vastly different conception of the gallery as an exhibitionary space.

Box with the Sound of Its Own Making (1961) combined Dadaesque simplicity with an audacious technological gambit: no longer content to remain the silent object of interpretation, this work would speak loudly and continuously of its own process of manufacture.[44] The work was a self-consciously rudimentary structure—a simple walnut cube, eight and a half inches to a side. Yet accompanying the box, and hidden out of sight, Morris had situated a tape recorder that would play back a three-and-a-half-hour-long recording of the processes he had undertaken in crafting the box.

Annette Michelson was one of the first critics to take the work seriously, and in her essay "Aesthetics of Transgression" for the first Morris retrospective in 1969, she described Morris's elaboration of process within the work in terms of a seamless circularity: "the elaboration of formal modes of tautology."[45] *Anti-Illusion: Procedures/Materials*, the Whitney Museum of American Art's major exhibition of that year, provided the rhetorical trope that would continue to fuel much of the art and film criticism of

Figure 3.22. Installation view, Robert Morris exhibition at Green Gallery, New York, 1964.

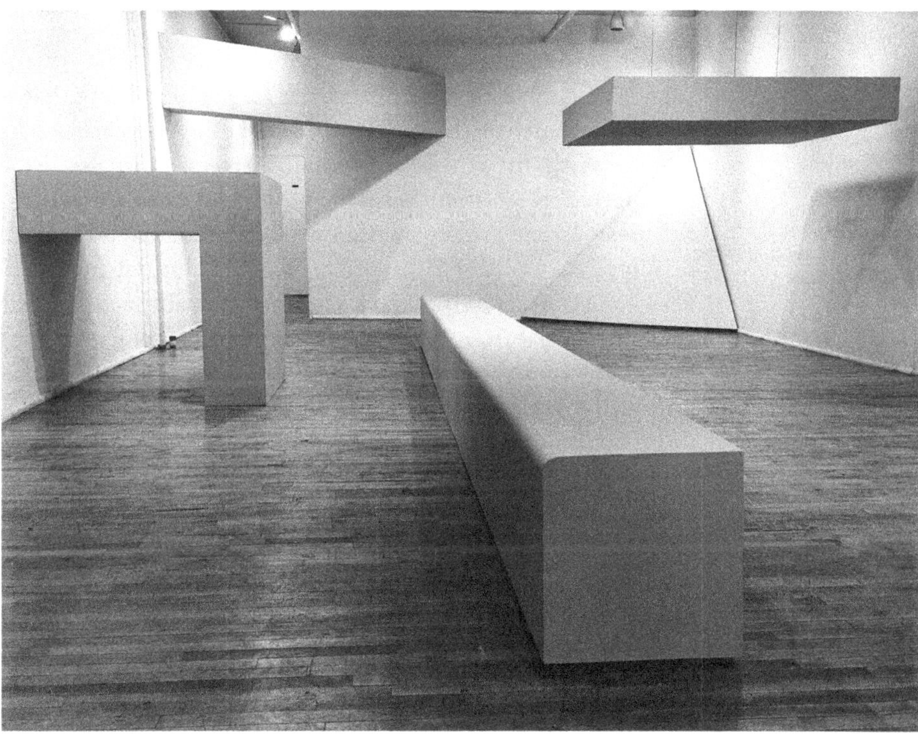

the next decade and beyond. Even in Morris's 1994 Guggenheim retrospective, it is confidently declared that the work "is meant to dispel the idea of secrecy, substituting instead the experience of an intelligible process and its duration."[46]

Yet the simplicity of Morris's *Box with the Sound of Its Own Making* is profoundly deceptive. Far from culminating in a literal, self-reflexive demonstration, the formal reduction inherent in Morris's *Box* was not unlike the "transparency" with which Breer understood his mutoscope works: a magnifying glass held up to a supposedly simple mechanism so as to reveal its inherent complexity. Morris's work—like Breer's, like Duchamp's—was never simply about physical forms *within* the museum, but also addressed the unspoken social conventions *of* the museum, its behavioral norms and spectatorial expectations. It bears noting that Morris's works of this period were deeply indebted to Duchamp, and that *Box with the Sound of Its Own Making* was itself quite explicitly a remaking of Duchamp's *With Hidden Noise* (1916)—a kind of a remake for the Age of Mechanical Reproducibility.[47] This early work of Duchamp's had consisted of a ball of twine, bounded by two square metal plates, into which an unknown object had been placed. As Duchamp well understood, the ball of twine—doubly enclosed within its immediate frame of metal and the institutional frame of the museum—was destined to remain untouched, let alone shaken. The title thus evokes the anticipation of a sound that will remain forever foreclosed—and thus all the more productive of desire.

By explicit contrast, the spectator of Morris's *Box with the Sound of Its Own Making* is immediately confronted with sound—the indelicate sounds of measuring, sawing, hammering, and sanding that pierce the pristine serenity of the gallery space, whether we choose to attend to them or not. Through this recording, viewers—now also listeners—are transported away from the here and now of the box in the gallery to the previous and remote locus of the box's manufacture. The recording disrupts the traditional situation of the sculptural form—its presentness—and indexes a time and a space that remain separate, distinct, and above all, *distant* from our local condition. In so doing, far from the usual temporal experience of presentness that could be said to characterize minimalist sculpture (especially in its more axiomatic forms), Morris's introduction of this mediating technology injected a kind of temporal feedback loop into the gallery space. We see the box in the present, yet we hear the construction of the box from its past—from before its birth as a concrete visual form. By bringing that past *into* the present, Morris makes past and present perpetually collide within our phenomenal experience of the supposedly singular piece. Our encounter with this "work"—both noun and verb, local object and distant process—remains bifurcated into a kind of spatiotemporal collage—the present-tense experience fused, confused, with an overlay of temporal and spatial coordinates.

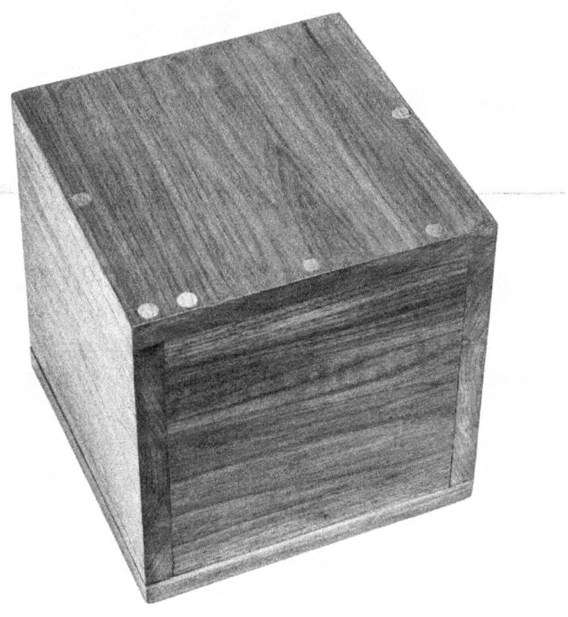

Figure 3.23. Robert Morris, *Box with the Sound of Its Own Making*, 1961. Seattle Art Museum.

Figure 3.24. Marcel Duchamp, *With Hidden Noise*, 1916/1964. Musée National d'Art Moderno, Centre Georges Pompidou, Paris.

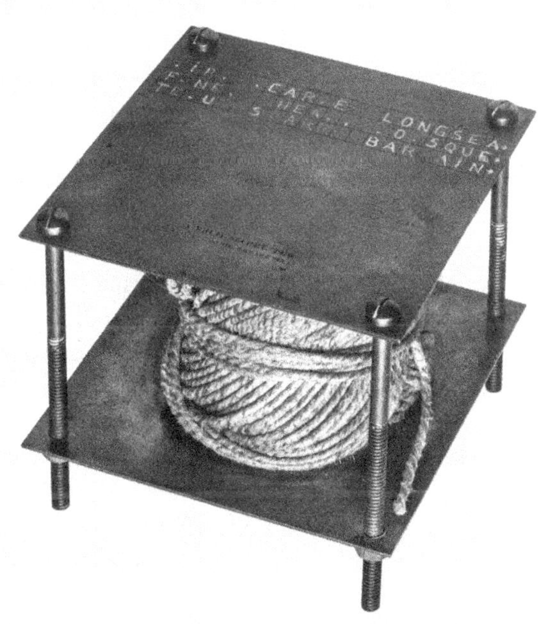

The early art historical representation of Morris's *Box* is important precisely because of the way it has often come to stand for the historical procedures and aspirations of artistic minimalism as such.[48] When a spectator encounters the specific sounds—the sounds of sawing, chopping, and planing that seemingly emanate from this small plywood box—something more is occurring than either the abstract demonstration of autoreferentiality or the work's *general* dependence on exterior structures of cultural signification. Rather, one of the primary conventions of the gallery space—that of silence—is being broken. With that broken silence comes a partial rupture of the frame, the enclosure, the invisibility of the gallery itself as a space of aesthetic experience. It is worth noting that in the photographic documentation of *Box*, the electrical cord is always cut off, even blurred and faded—as if somewhere along the line, this unsightly appendage was considered positively detrimental to the reproduction of the cube's basic unitary form. This was not simply a matter of critical misinterpretation, but a positive ambivalence stemming from the artist himself. After all, why would a work so seemingly devoted to a materialist and self-reflexive account of its own production deliberately choose to conceal the reproduction of the tape recorder? The mechanism was itself situated *hors champs*, outside the field of view. Perhaps we are closer to Duchamp's *With Hidden Noise* than initially suspected.[49]

In contrast to our experience in a movie theater, for instance, we do not simply surrender our experience of our immediate physical location to be within another, fictional world. Morris's work rather institutes a temporal layering—an enfolding of past and present, in which our attentive perception of the object can finally be located in neither a pure past nor a pure present, but exists only in some moving and uncertain space between the two. Only by shutting her eyes or ears can the spectator of Morris's *Box* inhabit a discrete spatiotemporal location. Thus, while retaining modernist sculpture's attention to the material object, Morris literally provides an "other" dimension to our experience. Self-reflexive facticity and "truth to materials" is here grounded not in a model of phenomenological enclosure, but rather in the perpetual displacement and dislocation of the subject-object dyad.

Like Morris, Nam June Paik was interested in utilizing the previously underdeveloped phenomenology of sound to convey the ways in which its interiority was being "breached" by the introduction of new technologies of recording and reperformance. Paik's "sculpture" *Random Access* (1963) consisted of prerecorded strips of magnetic audiotape, cut from their reels and glued directly to the wall of the exhibition space. These strips formed a series of overlapping stripes, radiating outward from an amorphous center. When visitors entered the exhibition space, they were invited to pick up a small magnetic tape head, attached through a wire to a speaker nearby, to physically read the sounds off the wall. In taking

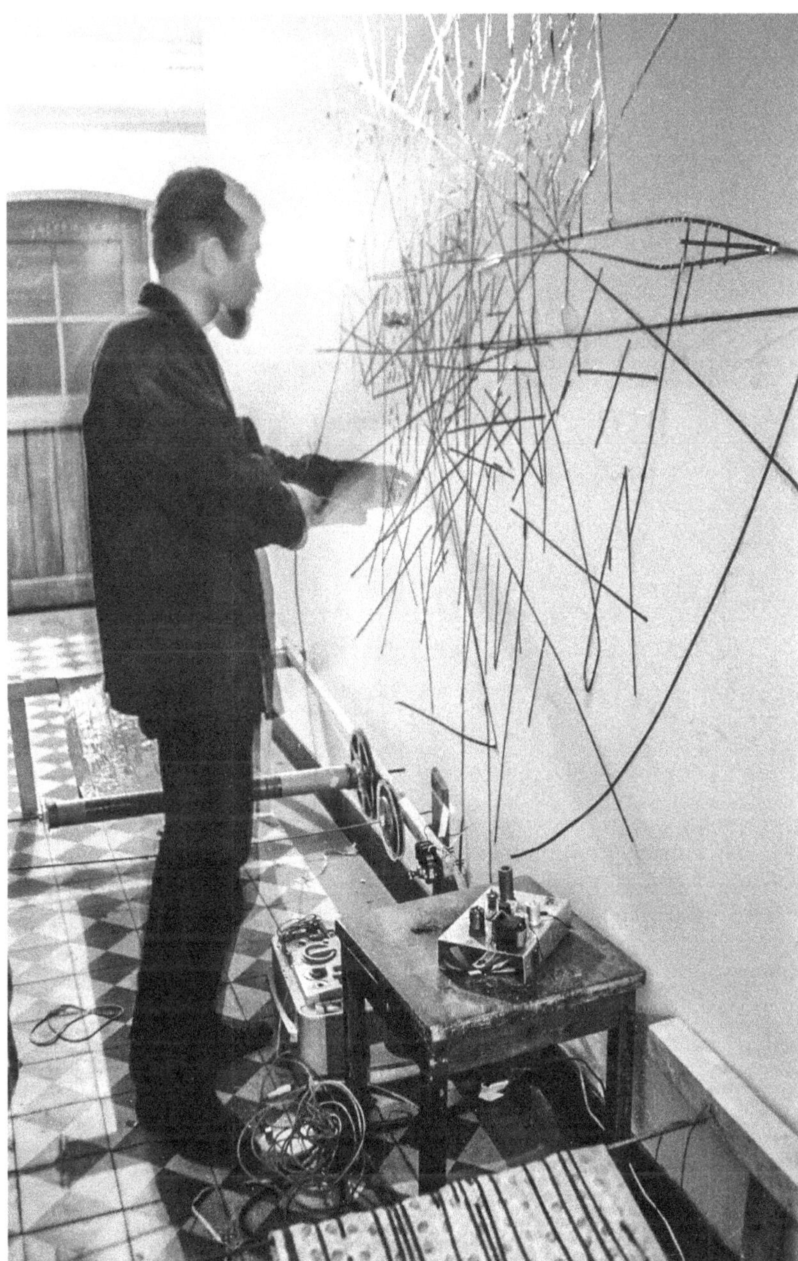

Figure 3.25. Nam June Paik, *Random Access*, 1963.

this tape head and wire in hand, the viewer-cum-operator became a kind of playback machine, substituting for the rotary mechanism that would ordinarily advance the tape. As with Breer's mutoscopes, the temporality of a commonplace mechanical experience became curiously "demechanized."[50] While film projector and tape recorder, as industrial technologies, must necessarily sync to a given speed, both Breer's mutoscopes and Paik's *Random Access* "demechanize" playback—render mechanical

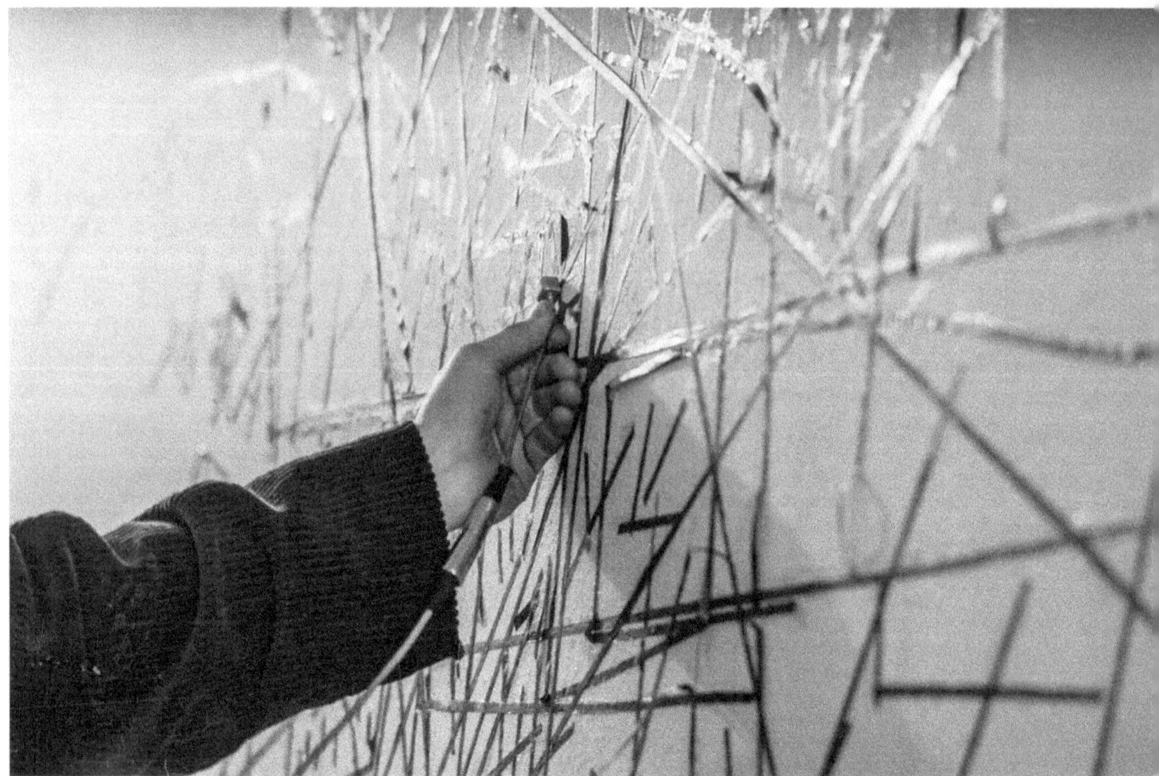

Figure 3.26. Nam June Paik, *Random Access*, 1963. Detail of spectator/participant "playing" the piece with the tape head.

consistency impossible through their dependence on human locomotion. Furthermore, in the case of Paik's *Random Access*, there exists no single, linear path on which to methodically advance. Paik thus succinctly defies the processional linearity of audio playback by extending the audiotape across a two-dimensional surface. The viewer is forced to choose—and choose again, every few inches—ever new pathways along this complex and intersecting web of connections. At each juncture, the decision produces its own feedback loop, as the viewer reacts to the soundtrack she herself is producing.

In this chapter, I have been discussing sculpture's desire to confront its physical and cultural territorialization within the white cube of the gallery space in this particular moment. In this context, it seems important to note that the collaborative act of creation to which Paik's work gives rise is not one that takes place just anywhere. Rather, it takes place on a wall—the wall of the white cube itself. To operate the piece, viewers must press their hands against the wall, which is to say, literally push against the barrier securing interior from exterior space. Paik made it so that *at the precise moment* a viewer's hand presses against that boundary, the phenomenal and ideological experience of the white cube is rent asunder. The contact induced between hand and wall immediately summons up a time and space disjunctive yet coextensive with that of the immediate environment. The time and space indexed by the magnetic recording may be separated from the present time by hours or months or from the present site by inches or miles. Yet this "other" space and time immediately comes crashing into our own, entering into our present phenomenal experience of the gallery site. Unlike Morris's *Box with the Sound of Its Own Making*, the passage Paik here effects is entirely voluntary and incumbent on the viewer. We are given an opportunity for exploration, but we are not forced to endure an ultimately untenable experience of spatial and temporal bifurcation. It is left entirely to the viewer whether to be a spectator or a participant, whether to remain wholly within the space of the white cube or to take an active role in its supersession.

Neither Cornell's miniature theaters, nor Morris's *Box*, nor Paik's *Random Access* directly used the material technology of the moving image. But all three addressed the gallery as newly hybrid space of exhibition and perception, transformed through the mediating effect of recording technologies. Neither a window on another world nor a mirror reflecting the literal space of the gallery, the work of art is imagined in these works as a kind of screen—both material and immaterial, local and distant. Combining the use of recording technology by Morris and Paik with the explicit interest in the quintessentially cinematic field of fantasy and identification in Cornell's miniature theaters, Robert Whitman's cinematic installations literally displaced the moving image from the black box to the white cube, challenging the accepted conventions of each, while giving rise to a conception of expanded cinema within the confines of the postwar art gallery.

Robert Whitman's *Cinema Pieces* (1963–1964)

Whitman's moving-image installations of 1963–1964, what he called his *Cinema Pieces*, bring us full circle to the question of movement within the gallery with which we began. In Galerie Denise René's 1955 exhibition, film may have served as the privileged point of reference, but within an institutional tradition of plastic display, the actual workings of cinema could only ever be marginal or implicit. Sculptural kineticism provided only a secondary animation of what was essentially a static medium. Nearly a decade after *Movement*, this situation had become ripe for a more literal transformation. The use of cinema within Whitman's *Window* installation at the Sidney Janis Gallery was explicit, albeit far from straightforward. Like the metaphorical articulation of cinema within Cornell's MoMA exhibition, *Window* (1963) simultaneously evoked both the literal space of the gallery and a fictional realm beyond, foregrounding the spectator's own imaginative labor as the reagent that allowed an almost magical process of translation to occur between the two.

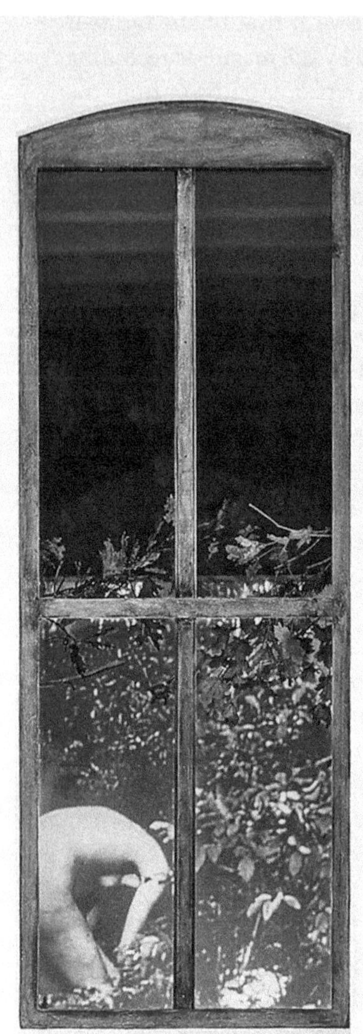

Whitman had been preoccupied with how the incorporation of everyday found materials, together with the novel spatiotemporal possibilities inherent in cinematic technology, might transform the traditional conceptions of theatrical performance and theatrical space. Encountering Cornell's film *Rose Hobart* (1936) in the midst of this inquiry, he was clearly smitten by Cornell's ability to generate such emotional power from physical and temporal assemblages of seemingly everyday objects and images. He prevailed on Cornell to lend his entire cinematic oeuvre for a series of screenings and events at an impromptu space Whitman was putting together with Walter de Maria. It seems far from coincidental that only months later, Whitman would combine Cornell's two major forms in a wholly novel manner of surrealistic assemblage.

As if ripped from a dream, *Window* presents us with the concretization of a metaphor. In it, a quaint-looking domestic window is rather incongruously set into the gallery wall. The very everydayness of this ordinary house window shifts our attention from the work qua sculpture toward the necessity of its physical situation within the gallery space. The work cannot be circumnavigated, as it no longer rests wholly and visibly within the gallery space. Rather, it is built directly into the gallery wall, its mechanism necessitating a separate and concealed location within which its scene can unfold. Rather than being framed by the ostensible neutrality of its architectural container, *Window* cuts across the borders of that container. Literally trespassing on the architectural boundary, it opens up a space beyond that is both physical and metaphorical. *Window* is not merely a hole, but an aperture.

Figure 3.27. Robert Whitman, *Window*, 1963.

While *Window* does not lead outside, it is nevertheless still possible to look *through* it, into a space beyond. There, we encounter an almost archetypal figure of the nude in the garden. But if the subject is as old as the picture window of painting itself, Whitman's sculpture provokes a spectatorial experience fundamentally different from that of the traditional painterly tableau. Perhaps the first thing we notice is that the material construction of the work is a deliberately heterogeneous mélange. The exterior window is a real, physical object: an ordinary wooden frame and window glass are physically set into the wall. Beyond this frame lies a darkened space—its physical dimensions uncertain—in which some real tree branches have been arranged. And beyond that crude diorama, perspectival space continues back, deep into a forest glen, where branches shift faintly in a gentle breeze, and a woman suddenly appears, remains for a moment, and then quickly vanishes. Of course, this final space is not "real," as we say, insofar it comes into being only on the illuminated surface of a rear-screen cinematic projection. Our phenomenal experience is thus split between two forms of "deep space": that which we could, in theory, navigate with our corporeal bodies and that which we inhabit only through a form of imaginative identification. The distinction between the real and the cinematic is obvious, and it initially seems inconsequential, even trite. Yet over time, as our attention becomes fixed on this doubly framed world on the other side of the glass and the flickering specter that inhabits it, it is rather our own act of looking that begins to feel strange and uncanny.

The garden beyond the window is a disjunctive, haunted space. Like an apparition, the woman appears only as a fleeting presence before quickly moving out of the frame, or simply vanishing before our eyes. When she is visible, she is not merely nude, but often engaged in the process of disrobing. In contrast to the putative wholeness of an aesthetic form we might safely admire from a distance, Whitman's nude throws us back on our own act of looking, on the affective conditions of a gaze caught up in a seemingly endless process of anticipation, delay, and deferral. For the majority of our time, we are simply watching an empty forest glen, waiting. And in those moments after the woman has walked out of the frame, or has simply vanished, our gaze moves into the "deep space" of the forest glen. Within this scene, the leaves and branches of the foliage alone remain constant, while the human figure is constantly moving in and out of the frame, appearing and then vanishing like an apparition. But even the trees appear haunted. For alongside these branches, swaying gently in the wind, our gaze inevitably falls on the other, "real" branches that intervene within the foreground. In this way, *Window* establishes a curiously intermediary space *beyond* the window but *before* the cinematic screen, in what seems like an obvious metaphor for the ontological duality of cinema itself. These "real" branches make an awkward incision in our cinematic tableau, drawing our uneasy attention out of the cinematic world and back into the physical, material space of the gallery—at least for a moment, before the screen's flickering movement, the subtle action within the cinematic tableau, grabs our attention, beckoning us back inside again, across the portal and into the space of the film.

With this constant back-and-forth movement, we are asked, in effect, to look *at* the screen at the same time that we are being conjured away by a spectacle transpiring *on* the screen. In *Window*, this materialization of the screen and the quality of mediation it effects are troped by the materiality of the real wooden window frame and the real foliage of the diorama beyond. "Reflexivity" seems too blunt a concept to describe this delicate interplay of materiality and immateriality, this triadic relationship of projection, spectator, and screen. For it is not simply a matter of the cinematic apparatus calling attention to the fact of its own materiality or to its own mechanical operation. Rather, the fetishistic transport of the cinematic screen—and the phantasmal registers on which this transport depends—are invoked while being simultaneously laid open to view. We are accustomed to viewing the modernist work as a material object forthrightly presented before us, just as we view the cinematic image as a world unto itself, cordoned off by the impermeable frame of the darkened theater. *Window* simultaneously presents us with both and with neither, producing a new kind of phenomenological hybrid that prompts a reconsideration of our own spectatorial habits and expectations.

One of the conditions of this travel, which the work foregrounds, is the conscious involvement, even complicity, of the spectator. Over time, the ostensibly transparent window comes to assume the reflective properties of a mirror. *Window* does not provide a view so much as frame our act of looking. This liminal visibility keeps us focused on the woman as spectacle, undercutting the stability and coherence of the cinematic space. Thus, even as we are pulled toward this other, cinematic space, we are denied the fiction that it is a coherent world we might occupy. It is a form of spectatorship that suggests not so much the high art of the classical nude as the low genre of the striptease. Yet the desire awakened by *Window* is ultimately not for more flesh, but for more presence—more continuity, more immersivity. We long to be drawn more fully, more convincingly, across the threshold. In constructing such a space, Whitman focuses our attention not on the here of the gallery space or the there of the cinematic world, but on our own desire and our complicity with the mechanism of transport itself. Whitman's field of operation is the subject's own desire for illusion, for transport—the fetishistic disavowal, "I know very well, but all the same . . ." that subtends the entire history of the moving image.[51] Deliberately staging the work of technological mediation, *Window* similarly foregrounds the historical association of erotic voyeurism with the development of moving-image technology. Like a striptease, Whitman's work both conceals and reveals its illusionistic operation.

Whitman's *Shower* (1964) updated the venerable motif of the nude bather for an audience of the televisual age. Across a darkened space, we see a shower stall built into the far wall. There is a woman inside, and the water is on, spraying out of the showerhead and splashing onto the vinyl curtain, forming droplets and running down in streaks. The woman

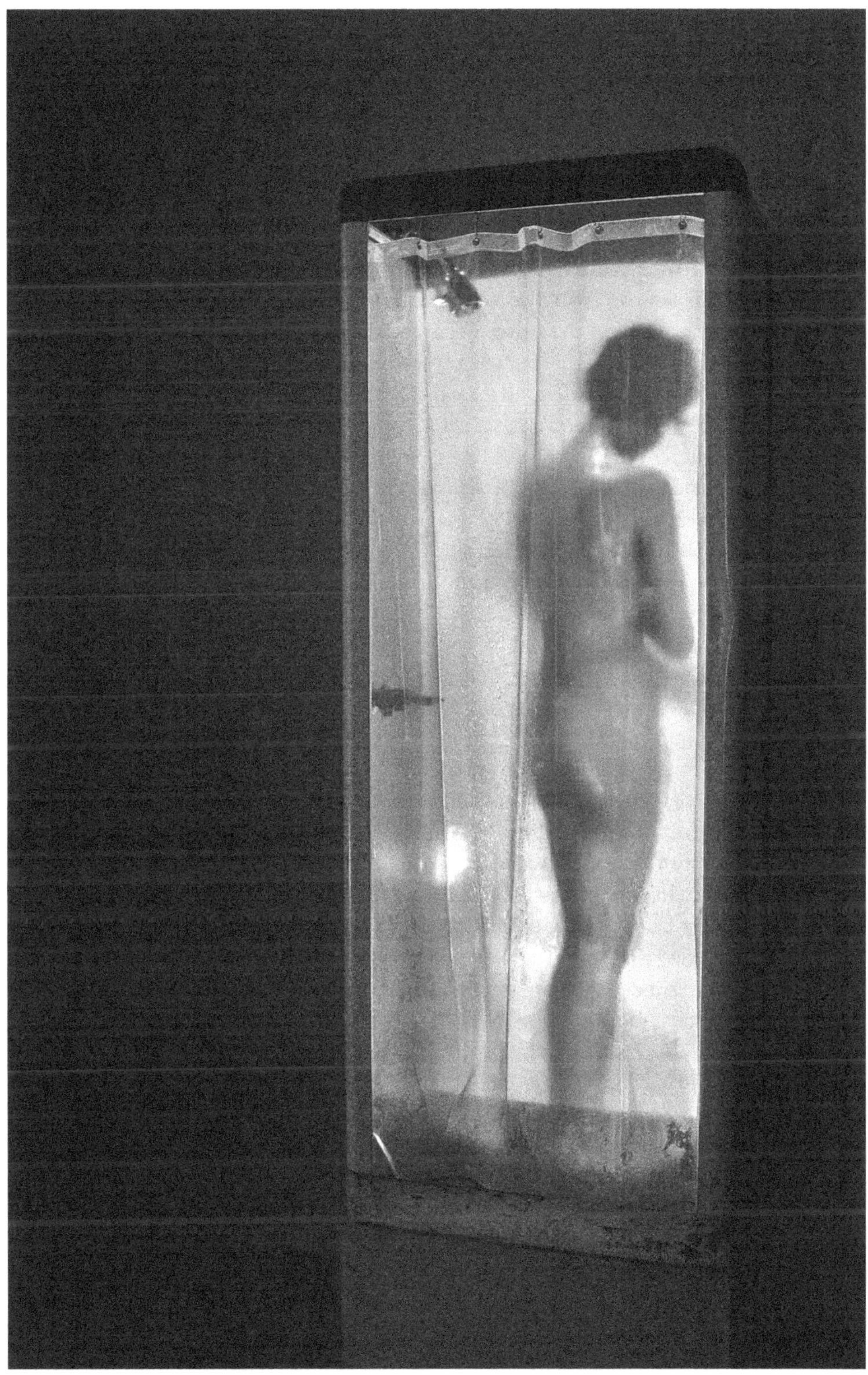

Figure 3.28. Robert Whitman, *Shower*, 1963.

turns, washing herself, unfazed by our presence. She is blurred by both the shower's steam and the precipitation that covers the vinyl curtain. In the tableau Whitman has devised, this woman is a cinematic projection, but everything else is, as we say, "real." The distinction comes so naturally to us, it feels so comfortable to separate out the real and the illusory. After a moment, we begin to understand: The sound we hear—real water splashing against real vinyl—is quite evidently real. There before us is a real shower stall, a real shower curtain, real running water. The woman seemingly immersed within that water, however, is a projected image. The woman is an illusion, a phantasm that issues forth from a concealed space behind the frosted glass of the shower's rear wall. As in the classical cinematic theater, the projector is hidden, out of sight behind a glass wall—though here, it remains concealed despite the fact that we stare at it quite directly. It seems an appropriate metaphor for the work as a whole. Whether or not one is initially fooled by the trompe l'oeil, the illusion is quickly dispatched. But in contrast to the theme park spectacle the work superficially resembles, the maintenance of the illusion is neither required nor expected—the work continues to fascinate long after we have seen *through* its mechanism. Even once we understand that the cinematic projection is forming on the rear wall of the shower, it is *as if* the initial vinyl curtain persists as a kind of screen, its rushing streams of real water serving not only to mark the passage of time but also to mark a barrier between the place where we stand and the fantasy image hiding coyly behind. This seems the only way to explain an oft-repeated erroneous description of the work, in which the film is said to be projected onto the vinyl curtain at the front, rather than onto a frosted-glass screen located behind.[52] While in *Window*, the "materialization" of the screen is troped by the presence of the wooden window frame and the real foliage of the diorama beyond, in *Shower*, it is instantiated by the physical structure of the shower itself and the translucent quality of the folded curtain through which we have to peer. Filtered through the vinyl curtain as through a second screen, the cinematic image comes to seem almost tactile.

Whitman's expanded field of sculptural practice includes not only the material technology of cinema, but also the identificatory relations that have dominated the cultural history of that technology. In *Window*, real objects are presented as interacting with realistic images, and vice versa, the illusory as existing alongside the actual in a natural pairing. Whitman writes, "Fantasy exists as an object, as a central physical entity, and as part of the story that you tell about other objects," and clearly his sculptural practice is one in which the notion of object must be expanded to include a whole range of phenomena outside the purely material.[53] Whitman's *Cinema Pieces* were certainly "one of the earliest examples of the projected image's shift away from the cinema screen into the medium of sculpture."[54] But perhaps more importantly, they also presented the reverse. For Whitman, the tactile, material space of the sculptural installation—and by its minimalist extension, the whole physical space of the white cube—becomes imbricated with the dematerialized dreamspace of the cinematic. In these works, the simple, almost axiomatic figures of window and mirror seem to signal that the representational space of Western painting, and the spectatorial conventions on which that tradition was based, were in the midst of a radical reconceptualization in the age of moving-image technologies. Rather than aiming to annihilate illusion in the name of a fully transparent and self-conscious reality, these works sought to address the increasing importance of the imaginary, the phantasmal realm of recognition and identification, within a newly televisual age. Revealing and concealing the "illusionary" operations of the media technology they employ, the *Cinema Pieces* rejected the contemporary ideology of the self-contained object. Like the phantasmally suffused objects of his contemporary Claes Oldenburg, Whitman's *Cinema Pieces* located an affective and imaginary dimension within otherwise prosaic spaces and materials.

There is a palpable sense that the *Cinema Pieces* work *through* us—that their images and our imagination become chiasmatically intertwined. Rather than attempting to fool the spectator, like the traditional fairground spectacle, they mirror the viewer's own desire for illusion, for belief. An active suspension of disbelief is manifested not only in the historical descriptions of *Shower*'s supposed "efficacy," but in the photographic documentation that has accompanied the work's exhibition.[55] Who would guess, from the photographic evidence, that the showering woman so essential to the trompe l'oeil is repeatedly displaced by close-ups of body parts being washed, or of a gigantic showerhead, displaced horizontally, spraying water dyed yellow, red, purple, blue, and black, like colors of paint? Consistently alternating with the nude bather, these images definitively void any sense of illusionism within the work, yet remain curiously absent from the work's photographic documentation.

Within early, teleological conceptions of cinema's history, the philosophical toy was regarded merely as a nascent, imperfect form of the industrial cinema to come. Jonathan Crary long ago proposed that their connection might more appropriately be understood as "a dialectical relation of inversion and opposition, in which features of these earlier devices were negated or concealed."[56] Like Breer's mutoscopes, Whitman's *Cinema Pieces* grew out of an attempt to interrogate fundamental aspects of the cinematic experience by setting up the postwar art gallery as a kind of laboratory for its analysis. By divorcing the spectatorial experience of the moving image from the established terrain of the cinematic theater, the phenomenological condition of the gallery space allowed these artists to isolate, distinguish, and foreground particular components of the cinematic experience—parts of that complex apparatus of cinematic exhibition normally subsumed within the seamless coherence of the cinematic spectacle.

Despite their curious resemblance to Duchamp's contemporaneous yet unknown diorama *Étant Donnés* (1948–1968), which would not emerge until the end of the decade, the formal characteristics of Whitman's *Cinema Pieces* would seem to place them at a far remove from Breer's mutoscope works and the return to the Duchampian topos of the philosophical toy that they heralded. Yet the two artists' works were conjoined in their attempt to envision the familiar white cube of the gallery as a newly hybrid space of materiality and immateriality, spectatorial distance and immersivity—one that invited its viewer to negotiate that which was simultaneously a material apparatus and a projective space. Legible neither as sculpture nor as cinema, these works gestured toward a transformation of the gallery under the pressure of the moving image even as they intentionally sought to alienate the moving image from its customary home within the cinematic theater.

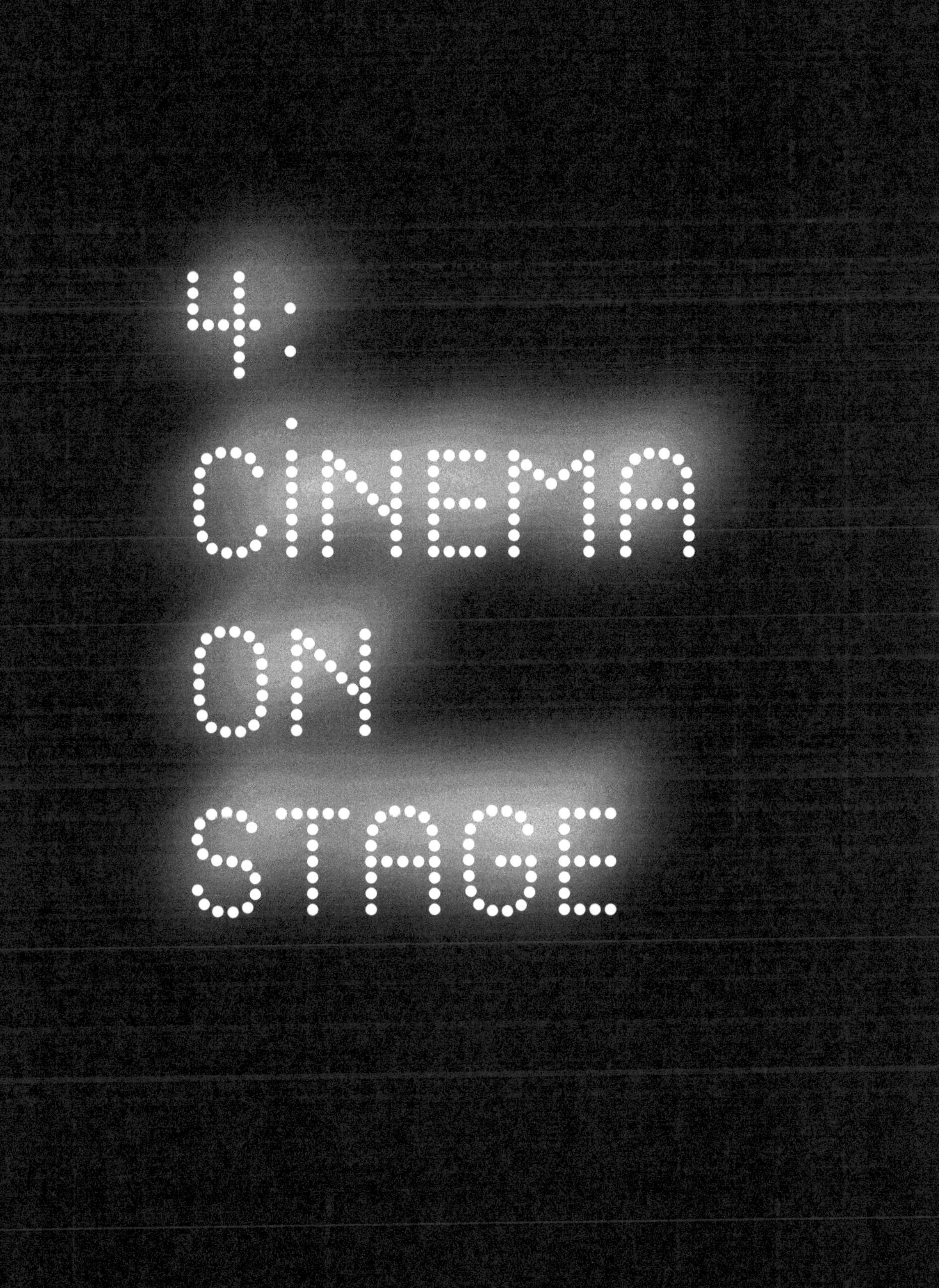
4:
CINEMA
ON
STAGE

We are told that the explanation is simple: *all* explanations are.

HOLLIS FRAMPTON, *A Lecture*, 1968

Staging Cinema: Robert Whitman's *Prune.Flat.* (1965)

Robert Whitman's *Prune.Flat.* begins with a *mise-en-abyme* of cinematic projection. On a screen before us, we see nothing but an image of a film projector (see fig. 4.3, top left). It is presented in profile, so we cannot see what it projects—only the projector itself as an image. Rather than drawing us "through the window" into a distinct cinematic world, the flatness of the image renders it palpably irreal, despite its prosaic reality. This image is not precisely a still; nevertheless, its movement is barely evident. Like Warhol's early cinema portraits, it offers us something like a moving still. A small spinning gear reveals the projector to be in motion, yet this motion is centripetal, and the cinematic frame itself is fixed. As an almost hypnotic stillness holds this ostensibly "moving image" before us for thirty long seconds, our attention begins to wander. We notice the bright light shooting overhead and the steady noise of the projector behind us, both of which are proximate indices of the image we see before us. Perhaps we are hearing the same projector we are seeing? Projection seems to be both in front of us and behind us—surrounding us, as it were. If so, a singular object would now be split into image and sound, the image taken in a distant space and a previous time and the sound taking place right here in the present. Moreover, the image would be a mere representation and the sound that representation's "reality."[1]

This meditation is abruptly punctured when the film suddenly appears to "skip" or "jump the gate." It is a movement that takes place not in the projector before us, but in its unseen twin behind. The very immobility of the cinematic frame highlights this literal movement of the celluloid through the projector. As this movement occurs within the cinematic frame, but not within the cinematic space, its self-reflexivity calls our attention not simply to the material condition of the image, but additionally to the exhibition space, the theater within which the projection takes place. For in seeing this briefest of disruptions—a mere transient flash—Whitman's audience would have had to wonder whether this movement was within the frame or exterior to it. In this underground theater, no one would have been expecting state-of-the-art projection, and such mechanical accidents were hardly uncommon to screenings in which a single worn print was repeatedly cycled through secondhand projectors by occasionally untrained projectionists. In other words, was this the kind of cinematic mishap—like dust or scratches or a minor misregistration—that we deliberately train ourselves to overlook, or something deliberately sown into the very surface of the film being projected?

Whitman's initial image succinctly poses a range of questions, ontological and experiential, with which *Prune.Flat.* will be concerned—all the more so because this initial "image" is not wholly one of cinematic projection. For at the bottom right corner, the absence of traditional cinematic imagery illuminates that which would otherwise remain invisible. A simple, obdurate, physical object—a chair—stands apart from the screen of projection at what, from the perspective of the seated audience, seems the most shallow of distances. Carving out its shape in the form of a silhouette, it refers us back to the chairs on which we are ourselves seated, thus acquiring a palpable solidity and weight compared with the projected background it obstructs. But most importantly, it rests on—and thus serves to index—a shallow proscenium stage that lies just to "this side" of the projected image. This stage, like the audience, rests in the medium between the two projectors. Our awareness of this space causes the complexity of this cinematic situation—this chiasmatic intertwining of real and cinematic—to be staged before us.

Whitman referred to his works as "theater-pieces," but they have tended to be situated within the category of "Happenings" popularized by Allan Kaprow. In his 1966 book *Assemblage, Environments & Happenings*, Kaprow sought to provide an account of modern art's engagement with its space of exhibition. He claimed that the foundational condition for the modern tradition of painting and sculpture had been its setting within the rectilinear confines of the museum space. Pointing to the storm of criticism that erupted from artists and critics when works were first installed within the curved walls of Frank Lloyd Wright's spiraling Solomon R. Guggenheim Museum, Kaprow contended that Wright's building not only served as a harrowing disruption of an ossified rectilinear tradition, but also represented a limit point for a field that had failed to keep pace with the rival arts. The museum was an old container within which contemporary art increasingly felt constrained. The new art must either abandon the museum space entirely or actively reconstruct its space of exhibition in ways the architectural imagination had not yet dared.

Yet Kaprow was not particularly interested in the reinvention of art's institutional spaces, and he tended to ignore the attempts to do so by so many of his contemporaries. His impatience not only with the art gallery, but also with the disciplinary traditions of music, theater, dance, and film, led him to reject what he termed the "enclosure" of art within institutions as such. He was consequently quite frustrated, during his 1968 interview with Robert Smithson, when Smithson refused his call to abandon the museum, describing art's institutional framing not as a hindrance, but rather its very condition of possibility.[2]

Kaprow was emblematic of a generation of critics whose basic conception of art was so inextricably bound up with the plastic forms of painting and sculpture that the widespread turn away from both could be understood only as "the death of art." Ignoring the important developments taking place across the traditions of music, theater, dance, and film, these critics failed to grasp how specific disciplinary conjunctions might leverage historical tradition to stage an intervention into fossilized aesthetic establishments. For throughout this period, neither art nor its institutions were in the process of dying so much as they were in the process of being reinvented. One of the most important sites of this reinvention was within the theatrical space, on that age-old site: the proscenium stage.

Michael Kirby's book *Happenings*, published a year before Kaprow's *Assemblage, Environments & Happenings*, had retained the term established in 1959 by Kaprow's *18 Happenings in 6 Parts*. Yet Kirby, like Whitman, rejected the ostensible neutrality of the happening in order to engage more precisely with the larger history and theory of twentieth-century performance. If Kaprow's philosophical background in aesthetics led him to the ontological question of "art-in-general," Kirby's interest in the historical coevolution of avant-garde theater, dance, and music led him to reflect more precisely on the traditions and codes that structured different models of exhibition and spectatorship.

At a time in which "American-style painting" was still very much the focus of the international art world, Kirby instead sought to articulate the importance of a "new theatre" emerging not out of the theatrical world, but rather from the musical practices of John Cage. By using what were ostensibly nonmusical elements, Cage's work had led to a new model of performance based around an intersection of music and theater. "Acting can be defined as the creation of character and/or place," Kirby wrote in 1965, and the musician, while performing, "attempts to be no one other than himself, nor does he function in a place other than that which physically contains him and the audience."[3] For Kirby, this model of "non-matrixed" performance—which would not establish character or place, but function exclusively within the present space and local time of the spectatorial audience—opened up an exciting new interdisciplinary inquiry across the traditional domains of music, dance, and theater. While Kaprow's anti-institutional stance and his dialectic of "art and un-art" would become much more widely known, it is Kirby's model of disciplinary juxtaposition that best allows us to understand Whitman's project in bringing together cinema and theater, as well as the association of performance and cinema more generally within the expanded cinema of this time.

Citing Kirby's work in her essay for the 1974 exhibition *Projected Images*, Barbara Rose distinguished Whitman from the other "Happenings Boys"

Figure 4.1. Robert Whitman, *American Moon*, 1960. Photo of 1976 performance by Babette Mangolte

Figure 4.2. Robert Whitman, *American Moon*, 1960. Performance at Reuben Gallery, New York, 1960. Photo © Estate of Robert R. McElroy/Licensed by VAGA, New York, NY.

on account of his predilection for the time-based forms of music and dance rather than the plastic forms of painting and sculpture, citing his affiliation with Anna Halprin and the Judson Dance Theater as well as with the composers La Monte Young and Terry Riley. Significantly, Rose also distinguished Whitman's persistent emphasis on "mechanical devices, constructed rather than 'found' environments, and of media such as slides and film."[4] She concluded that "Whitman's first essays in theater were his initial experiments with projected images as well." We might go further and understand Whitman's conjunction of theater and the projected image as a theater *of* the projected image: a deliberate *staging* of cinematic exhibition and spectatorship, the "acting out" of metaphors for the cinematic situation.

Already in 1960, Whitman had shot an 8mm color film and incorporated it into his theater piece *American Moon* at the Reuben Gallery. But more important than his literal incorporation of the cinematic image was the particular image of cinema that he had sought to create. Within the interior of the gallery, Whitman had constructed, in effect, a kind of movie theater. Six "tunnels," within which small groups of spectators were seated, radiated outward from a central point. Rather than orienting the spectators toward a single projected image, his enclosure within an enclosure served to dramatize the event of spectatorship itself. Each of these miniature theaters was covered by a set of translucent but partially obstructed screens. Since half of the audience would have been situated within the other's field of vision, the consciousness of seeing others would invariably be linked to the consciousness of being oneself seen, "on stage":

> Sheets of plastic partly covered with rows of paper rectangles were lowered over each opening, and projectors at the rear of each tunnel beamed the same film onto these mosaic screens. When the lights were out in the central space, the spectators could see through the transparent plastic that separated the pieces of paper and watch, from the rear, the film being projected in the opposite tunnel.[5]

Simone Forti, a dancer and choreographer who performed in both *American Moon* and *Prune.Flat.*, described these screens as "membranes."[6] It is a striking and highly apposite rhetoric for Whitman's investigation. As a semipermeable boundary, a membrane guarantees selective passage between two distinct spaces. Rather than thinking of the screen as merely a surface for projection, Forti helps us to recall the term's early meaning as a fire guard for the domestic hearth: a semipermeable boundary that combined the regulation of beneficial heat with protection against dangerous embers. Forti's metaphor emphasizes Whitman's interest in this essential duality of the screen as a device of both protection

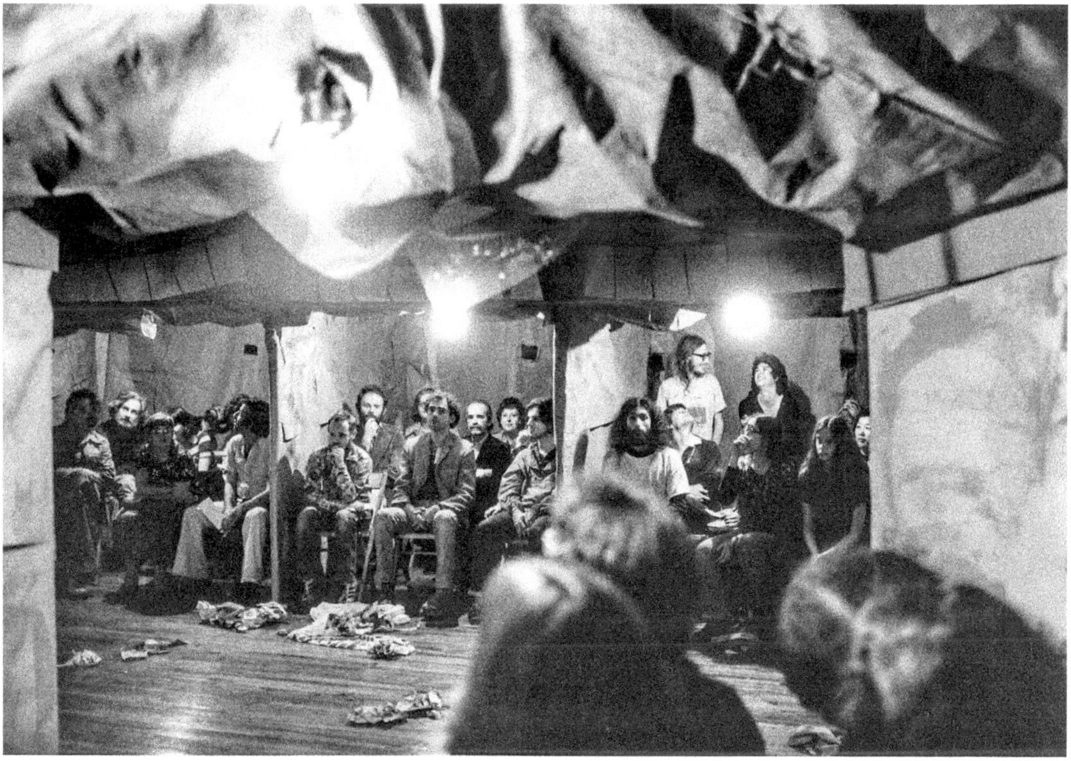

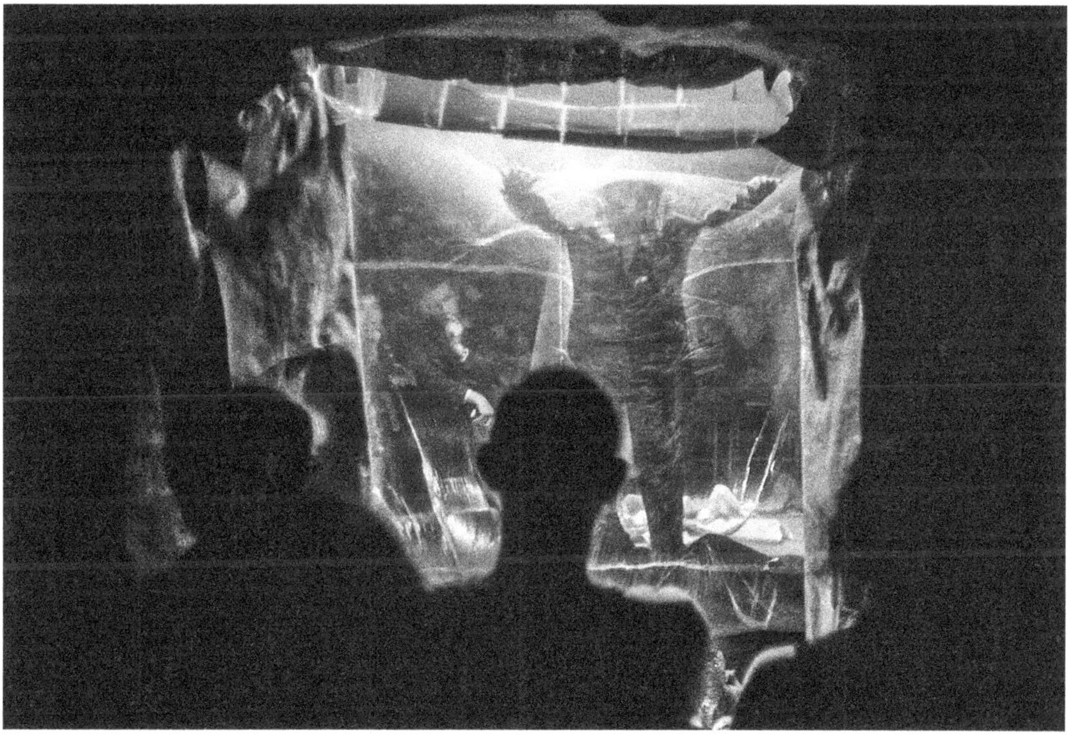

and projection, reminding us of the uncanny ways in which it can bring things close while simultaneously keeping them at a distance.

Whitman employed the metaphor of the screen to address the quasi-public, quasi-private nature of the spectatorial experience: bodies sheltered together in a communal act of spectatorship, but also bodies made visible to one another *as* spectacle. Whitman's interest in the metaphor of the screen tended to be concretized through the transactional space of screening: the conditions of enclosure and the directedness of perception within a darkened theatrical space. In one of the first essays on Whitman, Toby Mussman called attention to this "tendency to build an interior, womb-like space" within which to provocatively situate his audience in the works that followed: *Mouth* (1961), *Flower* (1963), *Water* (1963), and *The Night Time Sky* (1965).[7] This concern with the architecture of projection and spectatorship shifted the valence of Whitman's works from the expressivity of his early "happenings" toward the self-reflexive engagement with the cinematic event that would characterize the mid-1960s expanded cinema.

Whitman's heretofore implicit engagement with models of cinematic exhibition and spectatorship would become the explicit focus of his piece for the Expanded Cinema Festival in the winter of 1965. Paradoxically, it was the proscenium stage—that most traditional element of theatrical architecture—that encouraged Whitman to focus on the specificity of the *cinematic* situation. *Prune.Flat.* was the first of Whitman's "theater-pieces" to be performed on a proscenium stage. He had intended to create a work based around the general theme of cinema, but upon visiting the specific space at the Forty-First Street Theater, he became fascinated by the particularity of its compressed space:

> I went to the space. I got interested in the idea of a proscenium stage because of its very particular arbitrary nature ... It's a block, usually in the shape of a cube in space. That particular case was shaped like a cube cut in half so that it wasn't as deep as it was wide and high ... so I got involved with certain flatnesses—with certain movie ideas, in the way that I think about movies. Movies are fantasies. They do things to the space. They flatten it out. When you project on people, you flatten them out.[8]

Allowing only a limited space for performers in front of the large cinema screen behind it, the stage functioned to "flatten out" the live action. This ambivalent "shallow depth" seemed to register simultaneously both the phenomenological depth of the photographic image and the persistent flatness of the screen on which we see it projected. The curious amalgamation of theatrical and cinematic space provided Whitman with an apt metaphor with which to consider the idea of "projection" in cinema more generally, in its structural ambivalence between fantasy and materiality, place and placelessness. Leveraging the spatial dynamics of this particular theater, *Prune.Flat.* would reflect on what we might call film's "theatre" as such.

The work's title initially seems to employ "prune" as a verb signifying reduction or condensation. Significantly, this reduction is not an end in itself, but a scaling back for the explicit purpose of encouraging further growth and development. As such, *Prune.Flat.* could be placed in a lineage with those works, from Cage's *4'33"* and Paik's *Zen for Film* to the sculptural minimalism of Robert Morris or Donald Judd, that placed aesthetic *reduction* in the service of perceptual *expansion*. To "cut back content," as Sontag put it in her 1964 essay "Against Interpretation," allows us to "recover our senses ... to *see* more, to *hear* more, to *feel* more."[9] Yet such a purely formalist reading would have to confront Whitman's own explicit interest in referencing the small, fleshy fruit—one not uncommonly associated with the digestive tract.[10] Such associations would seem consistent with an artist whose earlier theater-piece *Flower* (1963), as David Joselit has argued, was devoted to an exploration of the relationship between the inner and outer spaces of bodies, their surfaces and their depths.[11] For Whitman, the two inquiries were not unrelated. The work of cinema—its inherent powers of absorption and transport—was understood to be crucially dependent on bodies: the thick bodies in the theatrical audience as well as the insubstantial bodies on the screen, those flickering images the audience both sees and sees through.[12]

While the initial image of a projector seems part and parcel of a modernist, self-reflexive aesthetic, *Prune.Flat.* quickly veers onto more complex and less familiar ground. Cinematic space is again flattened out as we look down onto a table on which an apple is being cut open (see fig. 4.3, top right). But Whitman has introduced a redoubling of this flatness with the introduction of two live dancers on either side of the stage. Moving slowly toward the center, bodies pressed up against the surface of the screen, they enter our field of vision almost as specters, both illuminated and concealed by the bright light of the projector. The contrast in scale brings us "out" of the close-up, and the apple is made to seem gigantic, as if suddenly magnified a thousandfold through this subtle change in perspective. Almost immediately, the formal juxtaposition of immaterial image and this new material reality is suspended: as the apple is cut open, a shimmering ooze of metallic glitter spills out over the actors, submerging them entirely in the cinematic image (see fig. 4.3, middle right). Initially visible only by the light of the projector, they have now, in turn, become camouflaged by it.

This play between illumination and concealment will be perpetually reenacted throughout *Prune.Flat.* as the projected image is shown to

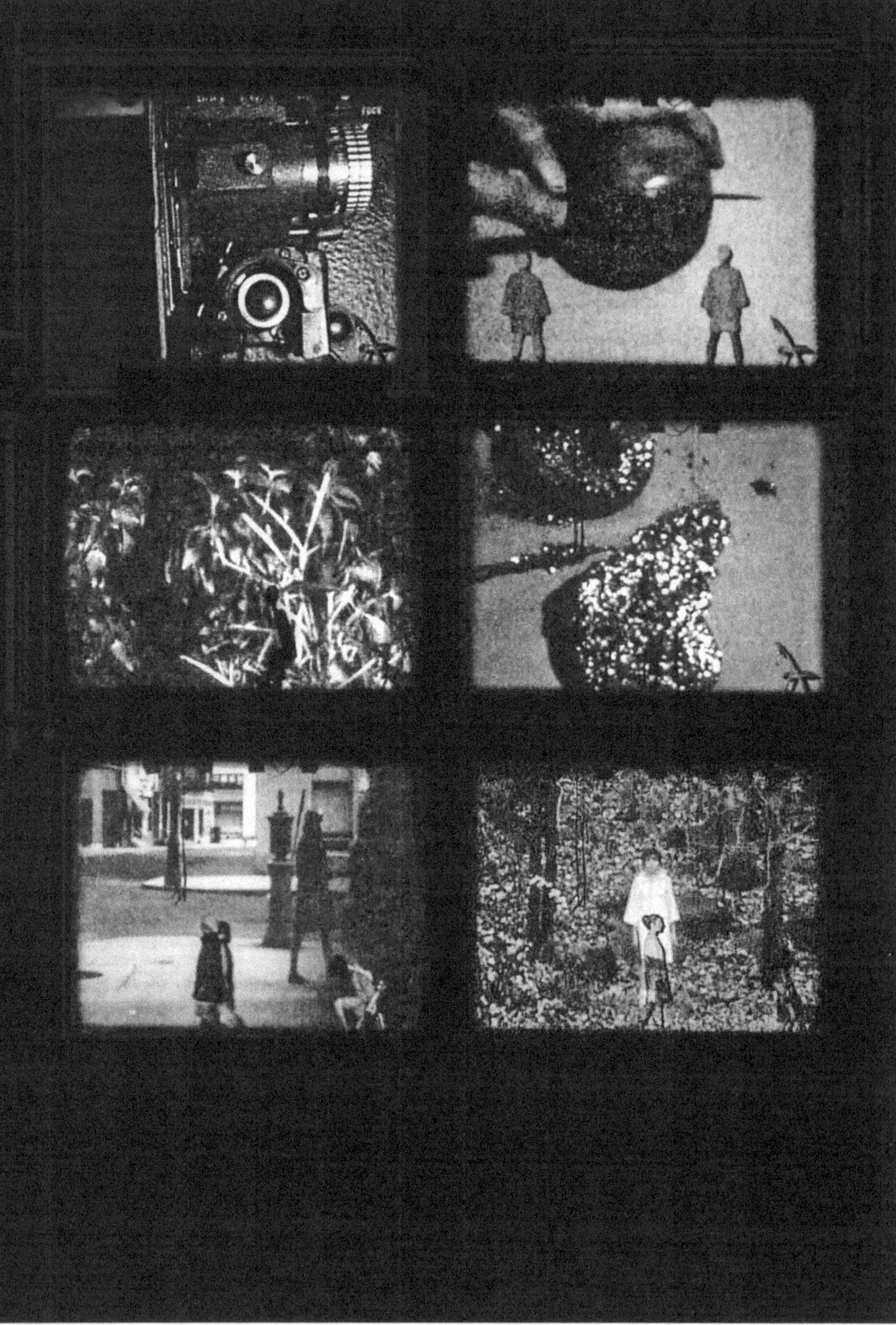

Figure 4.3. Robert Whitman, *Prune.Flat.*, 1965. Stills from video documentation of 2001 performance in *Robert Whitman: Performances of the 1960s*, DVD (Houston: Artpix Notebooks, 2003). Clockwise from top left: projection of projector, chair on stage visible at lower right; projection of apple being sliced open, two women on stage in white; apple opens to reveal glitter, concealing both dancers; projection of forest scene with live woman center stage illuminated by woman in projection; projection of street scene with women moving stage right, live woman similarly dressed moving stage left, secondary projection of woman in chair over live woman in chair on stage; projection of dense foliage conceals woman on stage, woman steps toward audience and becomes visible via shadow cut out from background image.

"close down" the perception of the material space of the theatrical stage while simultaneously "opening up" the phantasmal depths of the cinematic *mise-en-scene*. It is never so simple as having "real" space give way to "illusory" space, with a systematic effort to privilege the former at the expense of the latter. The didactic, moralistic idea of "cinematic illusionism," as the later rhetoric of "materialist" film criticism would have it, is simply not present within Whitman's work. In its place, there is a complex and ever-changing relationship of figure to ground. The positive articulation of presence within the real space of the theater is sometimes possible only through its illumination by the cinematic image, sometimes possible only by and through the manner in which the living body carves a space out of the background image through which it can be recognized (see fig. 4.3, middle left). Whitman does not lecture his spectators on the deceptions of the cinematic apparatus or infantilize them as passive dupes of cinematographic illusion. Rather, his layered images entail a complex imbrication of exhibition and spectatorship—a layering of the real and the phantasmal—that continually returns the audience to an understanding of, and an appreciation for, their own active role in the construction of the image.

In another sequence, we see two women dressed in white. One, shining brightly within a forest, exists only within the cinematic frame. A second woman crosses the stage, flush with the screen (see fig. 4.3, bottom right). Two spatial registers collide: suddenly the forest exists ambivalently as a deep space holding the first woman and as a non-space, a flat screen suffused with light that is starkly interrupted by the second woman's passage. Moreover, the second woman, despite existing before us in real space, is quite difficult to see. Her loose white clothes take on the projection of the forest, and she dissolves into the background, distinguishable only by the disruption of her movement. But when she passes in front of the image of the woman on-screen, she is dramatically bathed in the white light of her garment and appears "live" in front of us, canceling the illusory space of the background completely. Seconds later, this is all erased with a dark cloud, and two women have become one, or rather, the image has passed over into the space of the real, vying for our acknowledgment *as* the real. Out of the dark shadow, we see that a single woman in brilliant white has taken the place, and the attributes, of both. A hybrid image, both material and immaterial—both real and illusory, both literal and dreamlike—is created through the use of a second projector and film to project clothing onto the stage woman's loose-fitting white clothes. Her clothing becomes a screen for the "other space" of the projected image, even while her body remains on our side of the cinematic window, there before us on stage.

This hybrid construction of literal human presence and dreamlike cinematic projection will remain at the heart of the rest of the performance as

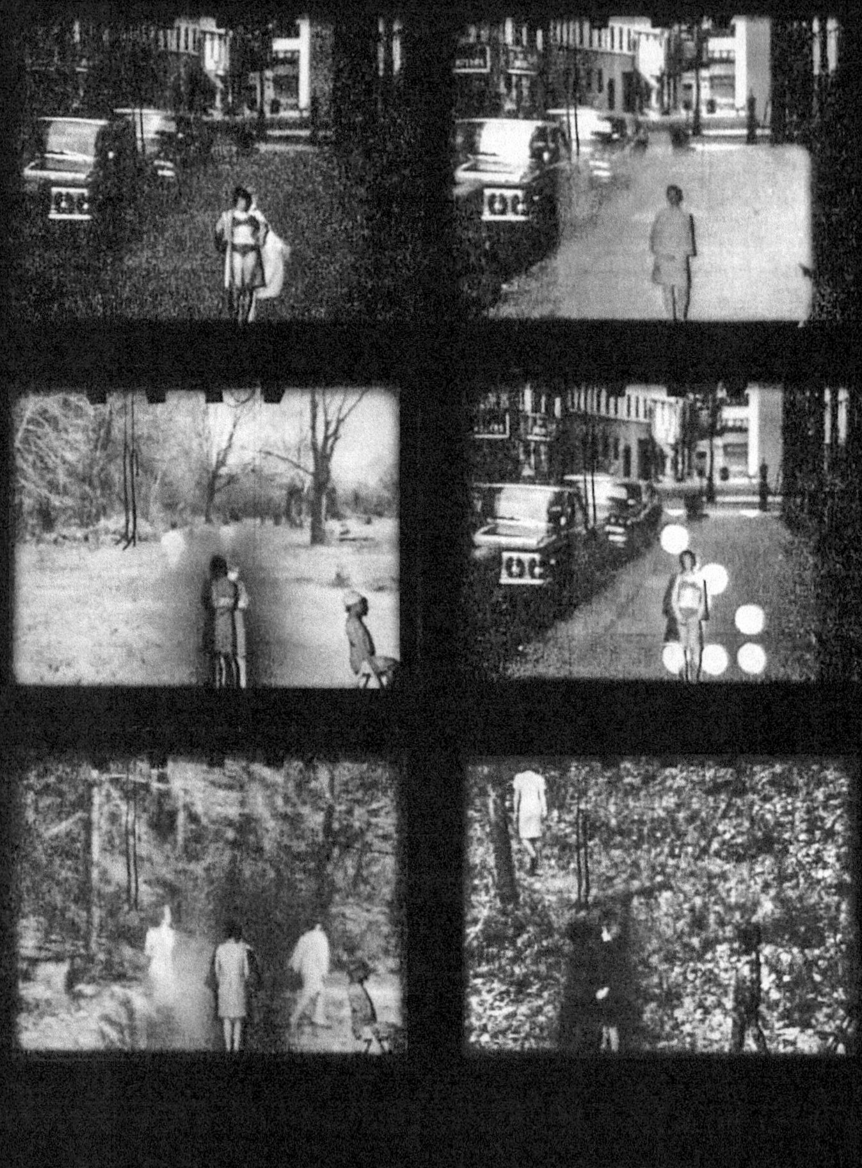

Figure 4.4. Robert Whitman, *Prune.Flat.*, 1965. Stills from video documentation of 2001 performance in *Robert Whitman: Performances of the 1960s*, DVD (Houston: Artpix Notebooks, 2003). Clockwise from top left: projection of street scene with secondary projection of disrobing woman covering live woman on stage; projection of street scene with blank secondary projection illuminating dancer; projection of street scene with secondary projection showing cut dots from splice; woman in projection walks away from camera while three live women walk across stage, left and right concealed by projection, center is covered by secondary projection; projection of two women running to the right while live women and secondary projections remain stationary at center and at right; same scene a moment later, as live women run "away" from the audience.

the woman's bright white costume is cinematically transformed through a spectrum of different hues. The most dramatic instance occurs later in the film, in which the "addition" of the projected image becomes an uneasy "subtraction." As we see a woman taking off her clothing, revealing first her undergarments, and then nothing at all, we encounter this sequence through a screen that remains clearly visible in the foreground: the loose white clothing of the actress before us on stage (see fig. 4.4, top left, top right, and middle right). This leads to an uncanny doubling of real and phantasmal projection in which the affective nature of the spectator's investment is foregrounded. The woman's body is here staged both as material, lit by the beam of the second projector, and as phantasmal, insofar as the audience is faced with a condition in which they "know very well" that this is all a relatively straightforward illusion, "yet all the same" that there is something magical about it, something haunting and impossible to ignore—the classical operation of the fetishism of vision as described by Freud.[13] That Whitman's display should self-consciously evoke the striptease should come as no surprise: erotic voyeurism probably played as formative a role in the evolution of early cinematic culture at the close of the nineteenth century as it would in the development of video and web-based moving-image technologies at the close of the twentieth. It is not for nothing that the first theorists of the cinematic apparatus would consistently turn to the psychoanalytic study of voyeurism in attempting to elaborate the essence of cinematic spectatorship.

In another scene, the woman who might be said to have originally "crossed over" the screen to the physical space of the theater has a black dress projected on her, while the woman in white reappears in the projected forest scene "behind" her (see fig. 4.4, bottom right). The woman in white then proceeds to walk "up" a path that takes her "deeper" into the forest, while the woman in black crosses the stage. Halfway across, she is followed by a second woman, who is barely visible as she blends into the forest background at the lower right of the screen. At this moment, the woman in black seems to split in two: while the actress continues across the stage, the projection of a woman in black—previously in nearly perfect sync with her—remains stationary. As the actress stops and turns back, she is barely visible as a dark shadow at the lower left of the screen against the bright light of her "lost" image. The result is a condensed vision of spatial and temporal dislocation, of movement into and out of the cinematic image, into and out of the imaginary "spotlight" through which visibility is granted.

In an interview with Whitman, Kostelanetz queried, "Something haunts me about that sequence in *Prune.Flat.* in which the filmed image of a nude figure is projected on a white-smocked girl. Is this image supposed to match the dimensions of her body precisely? In the several times I've seen it, sometimes it fits precisely, and other times it doesn't." Whitman replied, "No, only occasionally precisely."[14] Indeed, in his original notes, Kostelanetz had written, "On the second time round, I found myself less stunned by it. First of all, this time the performance itself was rather sloppily done; for whereas the projected figure of Mimi Stark is supposed to match her physical shape as precisely as possible, this time the image was quite often off center."[15] Later in the interview, he persisted: "The first time I saw *Prune.Flat.*, at its second performance at the Cinematheque, the nude image fit so precisely on the real girl that the illusion of her nakedness became persuasive. When the image flashed off the audience gasped. I thought this was a marvelous sign of the effectiveness of your deception." Whitman again demurred, "I don't think that's what the piece is about."[16]

Whitman rarely interfered with the interpretation of his work, so his admonition here acquires all the more significance. In describing the construction of his "special effects," Whitman repeatedly said that he was careful to keep things below a certain level so that there could be no question of how the effects were being achieved. If the woman on stage had worn a fitted leotard, she might have more easily meshed, in a convincing deception, with her naked projection. But instead, she was clothed in the billowing costume of a nineteenth-century mime, ensuring that the costume would always protrude from beneath the projected image it served to screen. In later performances, the image was even deliberately misregistered. Far from attempting to create the kind of perfect, seamless, immersive illusion Kostelanetz both suspected and desired, Whitman's work offered only fleeting moments of coherence, all the more dramatic for their ephemerality. It was precisely this liminality that served to foreground the viewers' *desire* for coherence, their readiness to surrender to what is obviously an illusion. The flickering, spectral bodies within *Prune.Flat.* served not so much as images but as screens for the spectator's phantasmal projection.

Whitman had no interest in unequivocally transporting the spectator into the world of the image—"I don't want the audience mindlessly to be part of the piece and swept along with it"—but instead sought out instances of "separation between the audience and the stage," which he "tried to keep and make even stronger."[17] The intentional inclusion of sprocket holes, flashes of white and colored film leader, and other crude marks of facture all served to foreground the materiality of the cinematic apparatus and to distance the audience from the spectacle. Unlike the more militant avant-garde filmmakers of the next decade, however, Whitman was not interested in aggressively withholding the pleasures of identification, immersion, or even voyeurism. Rather, he actively solicited and played on these desires in order to foreground their centrality within the work of spectatorship. Whitman encouraged his audience to invest itself in the creation of images, rather than simply confronting them with his own. The operative model of spectatorship was thus neither purely absorptive nor purely detached. As he stated, "I want objective rational distance as well as emotional participation. Let them come up on the stage, remembering that the work is an image to be perceived."[18]

The delicacy of this critical operation—its complicity with the techniques of cinematic spectacle, rather than the wholesale repudiation of them—proved too subtle for many critics either to understand or to accept. Still, the popularity of Whitman's production helped to make "expanded cinema" a commonplace term by 1966, and in so doing, it cemented an association of that term with a conjunction of stage and screen, an interaction of live performance with projected imagery. Unfortunately, it also helped to cement the very spectacular, synesthetic readings of the term that Whitman had himself attempted to forestall. Most pivotal among these readings was a lecture for the fourth New York Film Festival that fall given by the distinguished film scholar and critic Annette Michelson. "Film and the Radical Aspiration" was delivered just days before the first major critical symposium on expanded cinema—a symposium that had been organized in response to the growing interest in works like *Prune.Flat.* and in which Whitman himself would take part. Preempting that presentation, Michelson's spirited broadside inveighed against the emerging idea of intermedia practice, and against Whitman's practice in particular, on what she contended were both aesthetic and political grounds.

Michelson was not entirely opposed to film's "stimulus or nourishment from other, developing arts," and she singled out the films of Robert Breer, in their "intransigent autonomy," as an example of "a situation in which film and painting may converge within a tradition of radical formalism." She even allowed that "the extraordinary advantage of American cinema does lie partly in the possibilities of these convergences and cross-fertilizations ... a multiplicity of vital efforts unprecedented since the immediate post-Revolutionary situation in Russia. One thinks of its already established, though still embryonic, contacts with a new music, dance, theatre, painting and sculpture." Yet Michelson equated Whitman's "intermedia" practice with "the old dream of synesthesia": the discredited model of the Wagnerian *Gesamtkunstwerk* that was not only antithetical to the medium-specificity of artistic modernism, but also thoroughly debased through its imbrication with Fascist aesthetics. The timing of this initial critical salvo proved damning. In addition to preempting the Expanded Cinema Symposium, her talk was published several months later in an issue of *Film Culture* immediately prior to the journal's special issue on expanded cinema—the first, and last, collective publication on the movement.

The force of Michelson's rhetoric, together with her stature within the academic film community, undoubtedly led many to oppose this nascent exploration of intermedia and to view it as operating in opposition to the new intertextual strategies being developed in cinema at a moment when they might have been more productively aligned.[20] With the memory of the slick multimedia spectacles of the New York World's Fair still fresh, and with immersive sound and light shows suddenly de rigueur at all the fashionable dance halls and rock concerts, Michelson gave voice to a widespread suspicion that serious art practice was giving way to populist, technophilic kitsch.

In retrospect, however, the error of these early synesthetic interpretations has become clearer. Whitman's association with the "Happenings Boys" had been grounded in Kaprow's understanding of these performances as sui generis—individual expressions of what was commonly termed "painter's theater," descended from the "action painting" of Jackson Pollock. Yet in taking our cue from Kirby, rather than Kaprow, we are led beyond this painterly genealogy toward a more interdisciplinary framing of aesthetic exhibition and spectatorship under the sign of Cage. And it was highly apposite that Michelson's rethinking of this disciplinary "cross-fertilization" would ultimately be inspired by Yvonne Rainer, for it was the intersection of music, dance, theater, and film initiated by Cage's association with the Cunningham Dance Company in the 1950s, and extended by Rainer in the Judson Dance Theater in the 1960s—that would provide a fertile space in which to explore this new *staging* of cinematographic projection.[21]

Cinema, an abbreviation of the original "cinematograph," shared with choreography the desire for a registration of movement in time, and the projected image was welcomed into performance in this period not because of its ability to create a seamless, totalizing environment, but precisely on account of its heterogeneous, disjunctive nature. The projection of the cinematographic image itself inevitably entailed a live performance, yet the projected image could additionally serve as the medium for crystallizing the "liveness" of a performance in time—embalming a duration in amber, frozen, to be endlessly reprojected as an always new temporal hybrid of past-present performance. The duality of this performative condition fascinated a new generation of choreographers then seeking to challenge the traditional representation of performance on stage.

Forti, who had been integral to developing the choreography of *Prune. Flat.*, had been a member of Robert Dunn's choreography class at the Cunningham studio since the beginning of the decade. Dunn, a student of Cage's at the New School from 1956 to 1960, had introduced Cage's time structures and aleatory frameworks in an effort toward "constantly extending perceptive boundaries and contexts."[22] From his very first class performance at the Judson Church in 1962, Dunn had sought to make use of the *dislocating* qualities of the cinematographic image as part and parcel of this contextual expansion. Not unlike the audience of Lemaître's *Has the Film Begun?* a decade before, the audience of Dunn's first "Concert of Dance" entered the space to find a film already in progress. As Sally Banes describes, "Dance number one was actually a film, and it was billed under the musical term: *Overture*. So from the moment the concert started, the irreverent trespassing of artistic boundaries was present."[23] Dunn had juxtaposed footage shot by dancers John McDowell and Elaine Summers with W. C. Fields's comedy *The Bank Dick* (1940), sometimes orienting his cinematic "dancers" upside down or backward, displacing the idea of movement from the literal space of the stage to the mediated space of the screen. Furthermore, the film's presentation itself served to upend the usual situation of the dance performance by making a physical intervention into the space. "In order to get to their seats they had to walk across a movie that was going on. It was embarrassing, and Bob's whole point was to discombobulate them, to quash their expectations."[24] Just as this audiovisual environment lacked a specific moment of commencement, it also lacked a definitive conclusion, forming a continuous whole even as the concert shifted into physical, proximate space: "There was a marvelous segue between the unexpected film and the dance ... as the movie was just about to go off, the six or so people involved came out, the movie sort of dissolved into the dance, and as the stage lights came up the dancers were already on stage and the dance had already started."[25]

In his review of the work, Allen Hughes referred to powerful juxtapositions within the film as "perhaps, the key to the success of the evening" and tellingly referred to it as a "moving picture 'assemblage.'"[26] The "assemblage" here was not simply the juxtaposition of imagery *within* the cinematic frame, but the redoubling of that internal juxtaposition with a second, external juxtaposition of the physical movement on stage and the projected movement on the screen. What stands out is that, from the beginning, Dunn's Cagean emphasis on multiplicity placed the integration of film and performance under the sign of an *audiovisual assemblage* whose emphasis on juxtaposition was quite obviously antithetical to the totalizing, synesthetic experience of the Wagnerian *Gesamtkunstwerk*. Over the next decade, Dunn's students—from Rainer and Forti to Elaine Summers, Trisha Brown, and Meredith Monk—would be some of the first artists to make cinematographic projection an integral component of choreography, staging movement and cinema so as to denaturalize, and hence reimagine, the possibilities of both in turn.

VanDerBeek's *Movie-Mural* and the Cagean Origins of Expanded Cinema

Disorder is simply the order we are not looking for. HENRI BERGSON, 1920

Stan VanDerBeek was not a dancer, but he maintained a lifelong fascination with dance and, more generally, with the art of movement. Like so many artists of the period, VanDerBeek understood the moving image not simply as a technology, but as an idea—one that signaled a definitive break in the history of aesthetics and which offered up a fundamental challenge to static forms of thought and experience. To this day, VanDerBeek is probably best known as an "animator." But to make sense of VanDerBeek's fascination with this larger field of movement, and its importance for the art of the 1960s, we might begin by considering the idea of animation less as a technique of cinematic practice than as an essentially premodern idea involving the granting of life through movement.

Traditionally, these two terms—life and movement—are often conflated. Life requires movement; movement implies life. Yet with the invention of cinema, the relationship between these two terms was newly thrown into question. In his 1907 volume *Moving Pictures*, one of the first studies of the medium, Frederick A. Talbot declared, "What we describe as animated photography is not animation at all. All that happens is that a long string of snap-shot photographs ... are passed at rapid speed before the eye."[27] Talbot's use of the term "animation" was not unfamiliar, and neither was his critique of cinema. The French philosopher Henri Bergson—arguably the foremost thinker on temporality and movement during cinema's first decades—had popularized this critique, originally in relation to the chronophotography of Étienne-Jules Marey and Eadweard Muybridge and later to the cinematographic projections of the Lumière brothers. In *Creative Evolution*, Bergson reasoned that change and movement must—in deliberate contrast to Zeno's ancient paradox—be *in*divisible. He thus deliberately contrasted the regularized mechanism of cinematographic animation with the dynamic and essentially creative process of human intuition: "Such is the contrivance of the cinematograph. And such is also that of our knowledge. Instead of attaching ourselves to the inner becoming of things, we place ourselves outside them in order to recompose their becoming artificially. We take snapshots, as it were, of the passing reality."[28]

In addition to this rhetoric of originality and creation, the idea of animation continues to bear the traces of its older, theological origins. A creator (originally, the Creator) imbues inorganic material with life. But in Bergson's view, the mechanical animation of cinema certainly did not give life. Insofar as he understood life as endless modulation, transformation, and becoming, cinematographic animation seemed to him to reinforce the positivistic fallacy that time and movement were best understood as regular and uniform: the nature of temporal experience reduced to an imperious ordering of clock time, the experience of movement to a logic of the assembly line. For Bergson, the making and experience of art—through its seeming incongruity of imaginative leaps and starts—was alone capable of intuiting the nature of creative evolution irreducible to the positivistic worldview. For the motion picture to accomplish this, it would need to work *against* the very source of its initial fascination: the automatic reproduction of reality seemingly engendered by its *mechanical* linkage of movement and time.

Bergson's critique of cinematographic animation helps us to understand how VanDerBeek could be so fascinated by animation yet reject traditional methods of cinematography and animated film. Any attempt to understand VanDerBeek *as* an animator is fraught with difficulty, for his interest in film's animating movement was precisely in its movement *away* from the balkanizing tendencies of medium-specificity. From the very beginning, VanDerBeek refused to call himself a filmmaker, devising various neologisms for his works, such as "Flims" or "Visibles." But the playful distanciation in these terms possessed a serious undercurrent. For at that moment, a wide range of artists were turning toward the technology of the moving image, yet lacked "proper" cinematic training and, moreover, had no real desire to become "filmmakers" per se. Film, by the early 1960s, was already an established field, with complex forms of regulation, both implicit and explicit, governing the production and reception of the medium. And while it rejected many of the norms governing Hollywood's industrial practice, the postwar European art film movement—centered around festivals like Cannes and Venice throughout the 1950s and newly present in New York through the founding of the New York Film Festival in 1963—was itself increasingly seeking to define and delimit how film should be understood as a form of modern art.

In his first manifesto, "The Cinema Delimina—Films from the Underground," VanDerBeek had inveighed against the dangers inherent in this growing cultural legitimation. Written for the academic journal *Film Quarterly*, the artist's collage of text and image did more than disrupt the journal's staid scholarly conventions—it directed a challenge to those specifically implicated in the burgeoning cultural and academic institutionalization of cinema as an art form. VanDerBeek correctly foresaw a growing gulf between the legitimation of film art through organizations like the New York Film Festival and the Museum of Modern Art's film lending library and his own belief in a moving-image practice that could break with established protocols of theatrical exhibition and spectatorship so as to intervene more broadly in contemporary art and culture. What was at issue was not simply the material form of exhibition and the ways in which this form structured the spectatorial experience, but

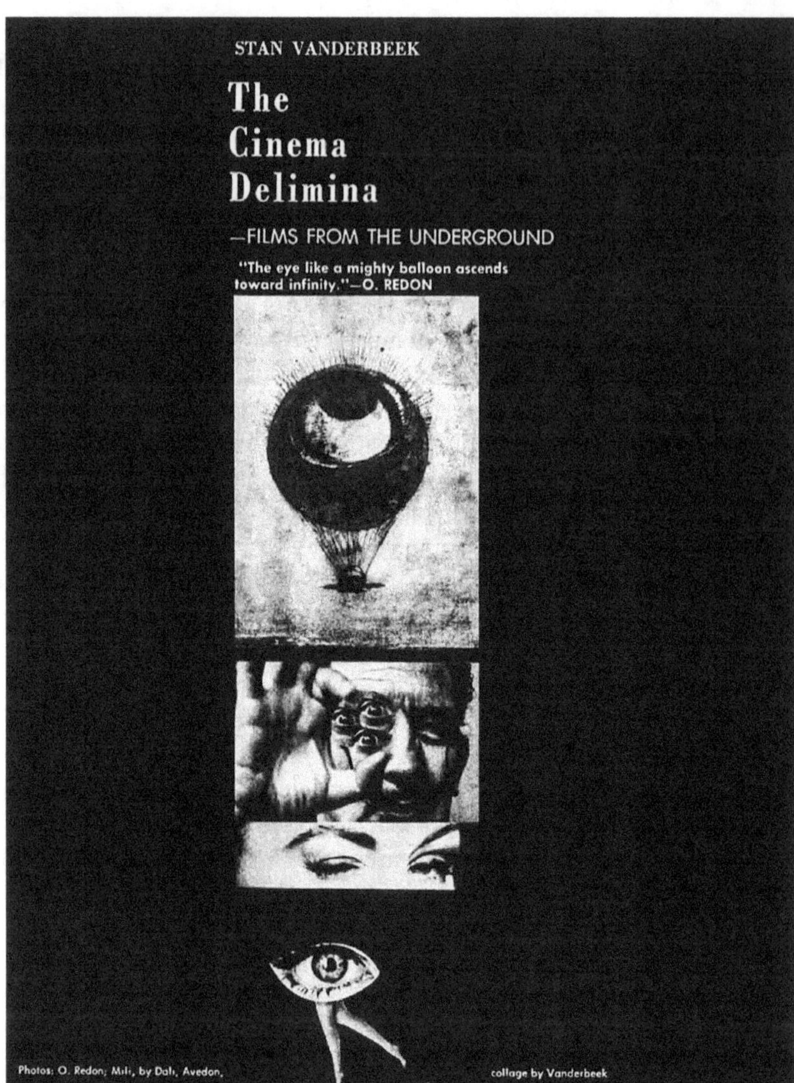

Figure 4.5. Stan VanDerBeek, cover illustration for the "Cinema Delimina" manifesto, *Film Quarterly* 14, no. 4 (Summer 1961).

the cultural and financial implications of these different exhibitionary models. VanDerBeek's playful neologisms implicitly reflected a more tumultuous confrontation then taking place between the "underground" film art of the New American Cinema and the decidedly "above ground" conception of the European art film then being championed at Lincoln Center.

In the summer of 1965, VanDerBeek would bring a glimpse of an entirely new vision to audiences at Lincoln Center, and perhaps fittingly, it was not screened during that year's New York Film Festival. In fact, it was not part of any kind of traditional cinema program, but rather part of a curiously hybrid production of musical composition and dance choreography organized for Lincoln Center's Philharmonic Hall. It was a marquee performance for the artist who, only a few years before, had had to sneak into his former employer's animation studio after hours to work and then screen his creations at his own storefront theater in the East Village. Within those few years, VanDerBeek's dozens of short, satirical collage animations had proved remarkably successful with the audiences of New York's independent cinematheques as well as with international juries screening experimental and animated films. Through his writings, public lectures, and interviews with news media, VanDerBeek had emerged as something of a spokesman for the "underground film"—a term many at the time credited him with inventing. His film *Breathdeath* (1964) had proved a high-water mark, winning awards internationally and helping him to secure both the financial lifeline of a Ford Foundation grant and a teaching position at Columbia University. Yet despite, or perhaps because of, what he had already achieved within this field of collage animation, VanDerBeek instituted an abrupt change of direction. His interest in collage would remain, as would his interest in the idea of animation. But his primary medium would no longer be the animated film. Instead, he began to *spatialize* the idea of animation through an interdisciplinary collage of film and performance. It was a practice for which he would become an early and steadfast proponent across his art, his writing, and his teaching—a practice he termed "expanded cinema."

While VanDerBeek was drawn to the movement of cinematic animation, he had also long been drawn to the art of movement in a broader, more interdisciplinary sense. VanDerBeek had first met Cage, Cunningham, and Rauschenberg when he was a student at Black Mountain College in 1951, and he had closely followed their groundbreaking collaborations in dance, music, and visual art over the next decade as he began his own practice. Their lives would become much more tightly intertwined in 1963, when VanDerBeek's Manhattan brownstone was condemned by the city, and he accepted an invitation from Cage and Cunningham to join them at The Land, a small artist's community in Stony Point, New York, where former Black Mountain colleagues M.C. Richards and David Tudor also lived. While building a house and beginning work on a domed theater he would call the Movie-Drome, VanDerBeek became newly fascinated by the idea of live performance and the opportunities it afforded him for rethinking his ideas about collage and animation. But his breakthrough would come when he was invited by Cage and Cunningham to occupy what had been Rauschenberg's place as the Cunningham Dance Company's resident visual artist, set designer, and "muralist" in what was arguably the company's most ambitious work to date: the production of *Variations V* for the New York Philharmonic's "French-American Festival" at Lincoln Center.

The interdisciplinary conjunction of art and technology within *Variations V* was unprecedented in its scale and complexity. Max Matthews of

Bell Laboratories built a fifty-channel mixer specifically for the performance, which was operated by Tudor and Cage. The composers Fredric Lieberman, James Tenney, and Malcolm Goldstein together operated two dozen tape recorders and radios that provided live audio signals to the mixer. These signals were themselves mediated by two sets of electronic relays distributed across the performance stage. The first set, created by Billy Klüver, the Swedish engineer who had helped Jean Tinguely build his *Homage to New York* in 1960, consisted of a series of photoelectric cells oriented toward the stage lights, which would be triggered as the dancers interrupted the beams. The second set, designed by the pioneering inventor of the music synthesizer, Robert Moog, consisted of a dozen five-foot capacitance antennae that reacted to the proximity of the dancers. This "sparse forest of electronic spears," as the *New York Times* reviewer Allen Hughes wrote at the time, suffused the stage with an invisible electromagnetic field.[29]

During the 1950s, Cage and Cunningham had established a collaborative relationship based on an idea of autonomous complementarity: "the belief that neither dance nor music need function as a dependent of the other."[30] In so doing, the pair sought to shift modern dance away from a ubiquitous model within which the music would enhance, but also *govern*, the movement of the dancers. Within this "propulsive" conception, choreography was almost a kind of musical interpretation, judged on its ability to form a singular synesthetic coherence. Cage and Cunningham intentionally segregated the creation of the sound from the creation of the movement until the performance, asserting their mutual independence as coequal elements, neither placed in a relationship of subordination to each other nor both subsumed within a preordained totality. For Cage, the necessarily public or social occasion implicit in the musical performance served as a metaphor for social relations more generally: "Though we are not living in a society which we consider good, we could make a piece of music in which we would be willing to live ... a representation of society."[31] This society did not involve leaders and groups, but rather an anarchic collaboration of individuals: according to Joan Retallack, Cage, "envisioned, and wrote music for, an ensemble or orchestra without a conductor, without a soloist, without a hierarchy of musicians: an orchestra in which each musician is, in the Buddhist manner, a unique center in interpenetrating and nonobstructive harmony with every other musician."[32]

Variations V marked a major shift for Cage and Cunningham in that it replaced their previous model of anarchic *autonomy* with a new paradigm of anarchic *interdependence*. Cage described wanting to push into a more interactive space, "to implement an environment in which the active elements interpenetrate ... so that distinction between dance and music may be somewhat less clear than usual."[33] Under the "propulsive" model, dancers might justifiably be considered human antennae, able to receive and instantaneously translate sonic variation into human movement. *Variations V* was an almost programmatic rejection of this paradigm: Cunningham's dancers were not antennae, but rather *transmitters* of sound through movement. Yet if the music had simply been *controlled* by the movement, one model of subordination would have merely been exchanged for another. Instead, the relationship between the two was intentionally complicated through a range of mediating technologies that themselves introduced new dimensions of authorial input.

According to Cunningham, the proximity sensors and photocells were not used "to produce a sound which you then heard, but [one] which was made available, like a library."[34] While the dancers' movements were not themselves directed by sound, as in a traditional performance, neither did their movements serve to direct the final soundscape the audience would hear. Rather, the movements on stage set a certain train of sonic events in motion. These events, in turn, were influenced by the choices made by Tenney, Goldstein, and Lieberman as they operated an orchestra of tape recorders and AM/FM radios. Due to the structural parameters established through these various mediating technologies, the relationship of sound and movement was kept indirect rather than determinate. Suggestive rather than prescriptive, it oscillated between independence and interdependence.

The movements of the dancers taking place on the stage were set against another field of movements occurring in the space above and behind it. There, in the space for which Robert Rauschenberg had long designed murals for the company's performances, was something entirely unprecedented: an immense variety of imagery, both still and moving, generated from a dozen different projectors organized around the space. VanDerBeek called it his *Movie-Mural*, and despite its almost total elision from the existing scholarly literature on *Variations V*, it was described in many of the initial reviews as the single most striking and unconventional aspect of the entire performance. Carolyn Brown, in her memoir of the twenty years she spent dancing with the Cunningham company, goes so far as to claim that VanDerBeek's *Movie-Mural* "stole the show."[35] While Rauschenberg's murals had established a precedent for competing centers of visual attention, the visual environment VanDerBeek created for *Variations V* was on a wholly different order. Moving from the background to the foreground, it competed directly for the audience's attention, provoking complaints that it did not know its place as décor. The reviewer for the *New York Herald Tribune* complained that the films were so large, so surprising, and so amusing that they distracted one's attention from the dancers.[36]

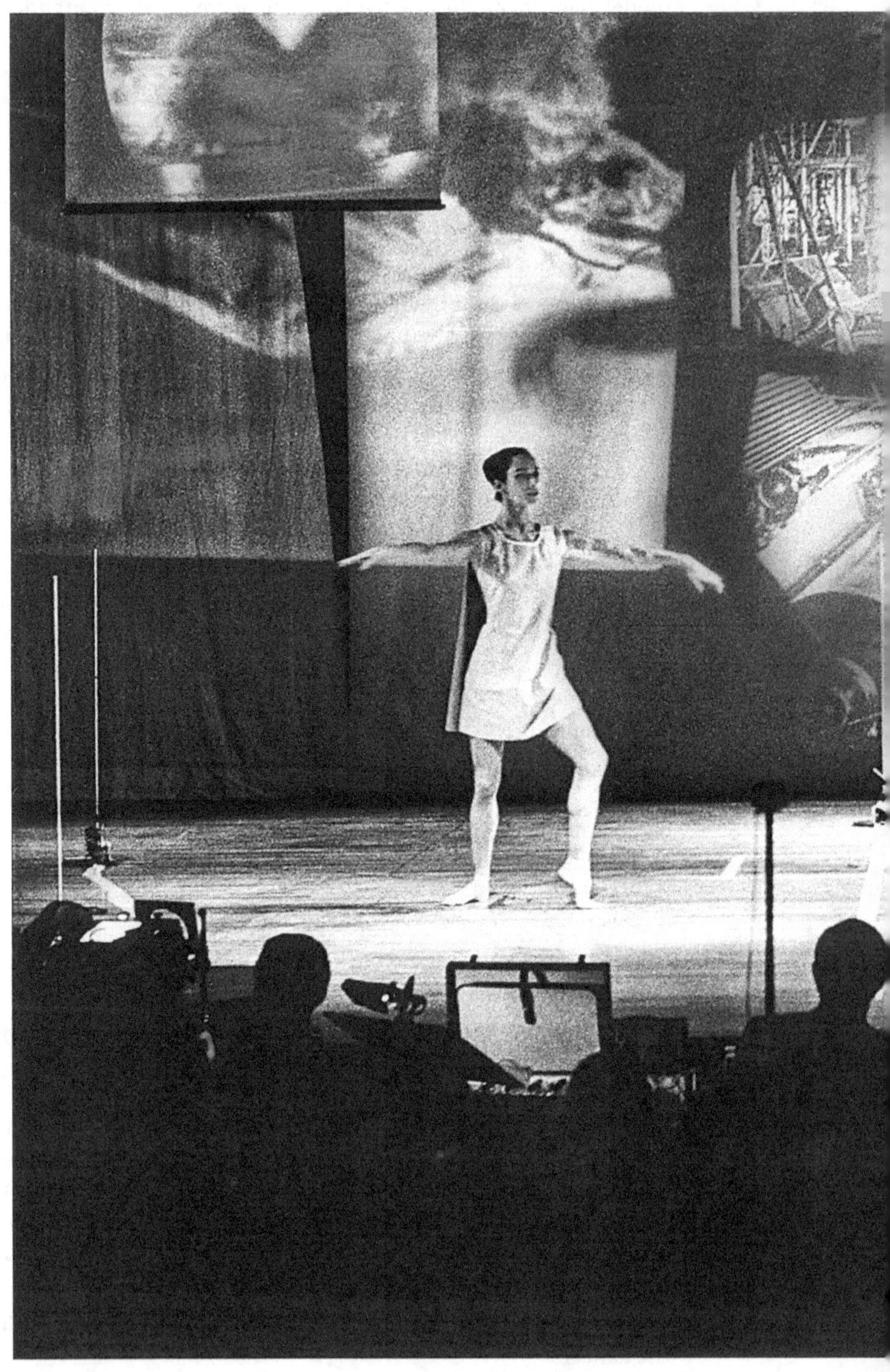

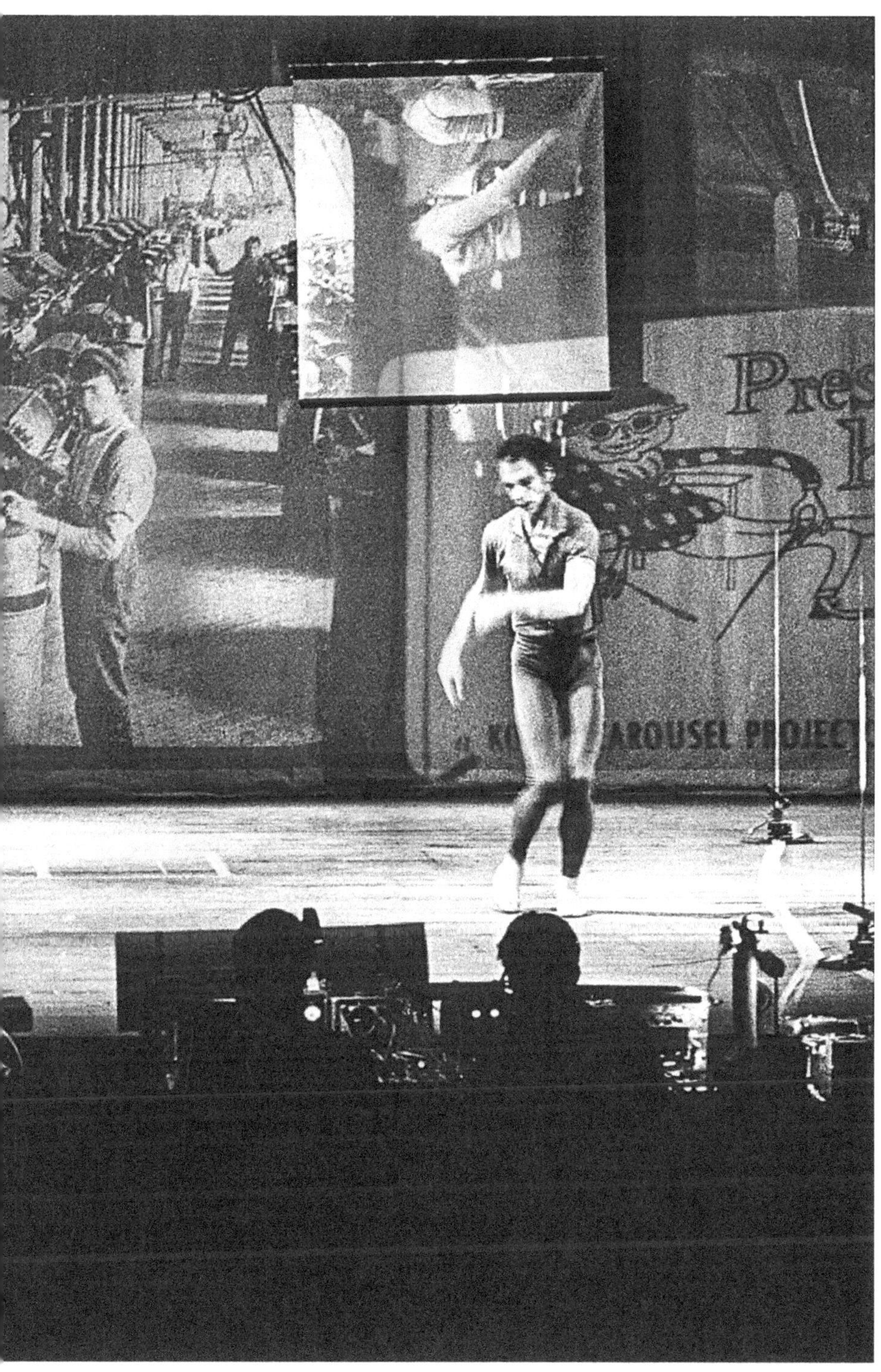

Figure 4.6. Carolyn Brown and Merce Cunningham in front of Stan VanDerBeek's *Movie-Mural* in the Merce Cunningham Dance Company production of *Variations V*, 1965. The shadow of Cunningham's hand is visible on the projection screen above Brown.

Figure 4.7. Film stills from the television production of *Variations V* directed by Arne Arnbom and filmed at Studio Hamburg, West Germany, 1966. Clockwise from top left: opening credits; film projection of dancer and his shadow overlapping screen; dancers on stage and screen; manual deframing of slides in background; shadows cast against projection screens and wall; dancers on stage and screen.

This would have been precisely the point. Through the use of multiple slide and film projections, and through the active transformation of these multiple projections during the course of the event, VanDerBeek's images would move with no less variation and complexity than the dancers. As such, the *Movie-Mural* would itself become part of the dance—an active collaboration with the other "living" movements on stage. Neither an autonomous spectacle nor a mere stage decoration, it invoked a movement of the so-called moving image outside the fixity of the cinematic frame, profoundly destabilizing our familiar experience of the moving image.

This quality of fracture can be most clearly observed in perhaps the most curious formal property of the *Movie-Mural* as a whole: the images are constantly breaking their frames. VanDerBeek deliberately mismatched the sizes of his projected images with the physical screens meant to receive them, so that there was a large degree of spillage or overlap between the various images. In so doing, he took up Cage's stated desire to "accept leakage" as a formal and conceptual principle, orchestrating a continuous movement of framing and deframing. Eliminating the conventional correspondence between the projected image and the receiving screen, these deframed images seem to invoke both a spatial and a psychological dynamics of projection. To cultivate such "leakage," he placed an array of small screens toward the rear of the stage. When projected, his larger images would become split, diffracted, or splayed out across multiple surfaces. Images, though still recognizable, became internally divided. Slide and movie projectors were deliberately positioned so that their beams would cross the paths of the dancers, like the active photocells of the work's soundscape. As this happened, the projected images would constantly be interrupted, the deep space of the photographic cut apart by the dark voids of the dancers' indexical silhouettes (see fig. 4.7, bottom left).

Cage had described his aim within the work as seeking "to implement an environment in which the active elements interpenetrate." Like the proximity sensors and photocells, the *Movie-Mural* actively promoted an interpenetration of live and mediated activity.[37] VanDerBeek began by shooting footage of the dancers during their rehearsals in the days leading up to the performance. During the live performance, these images were then projected beside the live dancers on stage. Various close-ups of dancers' feet and hands in subtle movement were shot, and certain sections of the larger movements of the body were slowed to quarter speed. The audience was thus witness to a curious overlapping of past and present performance as well as a separate and distinct perspective on many of the very actions then taking place on stage. Feet gathered together and then suddenly sprang outward; a hand gracefully twisted and arced as it traced a line of movement through the air. Movements seemed to take

MUSIC
JOHN CAGE

FILM
STAN
VAN DER BEEK

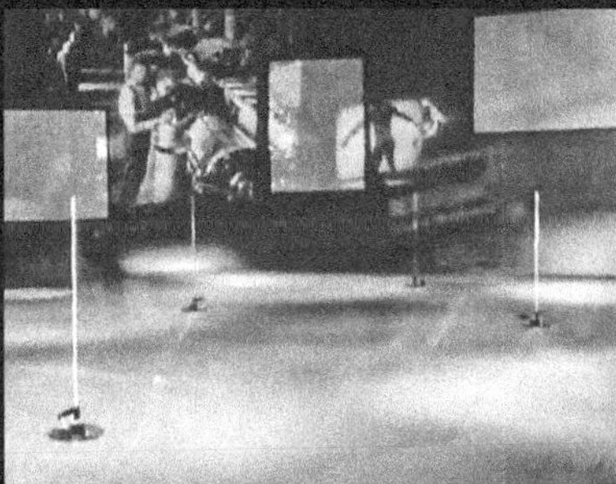

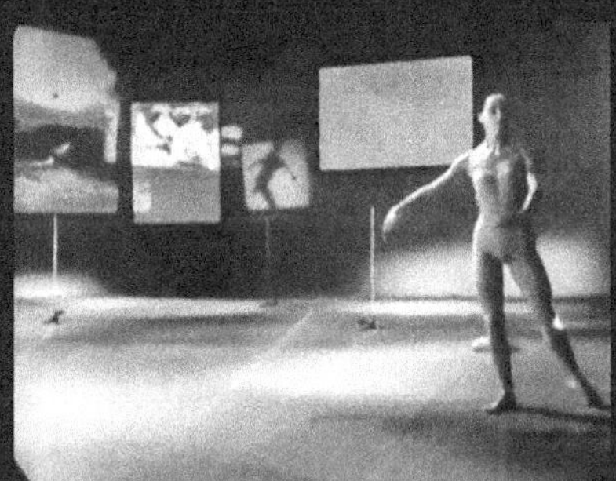

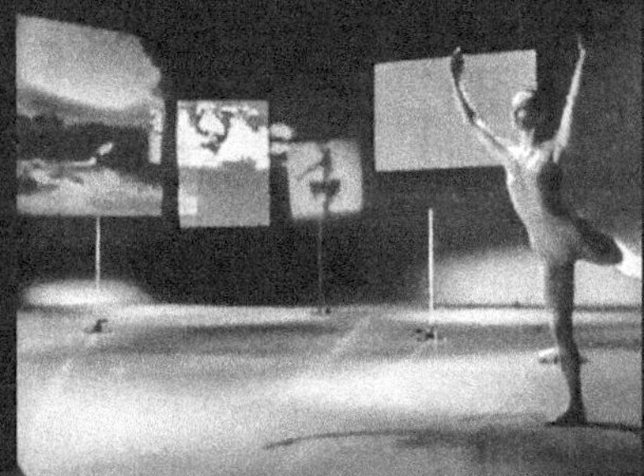

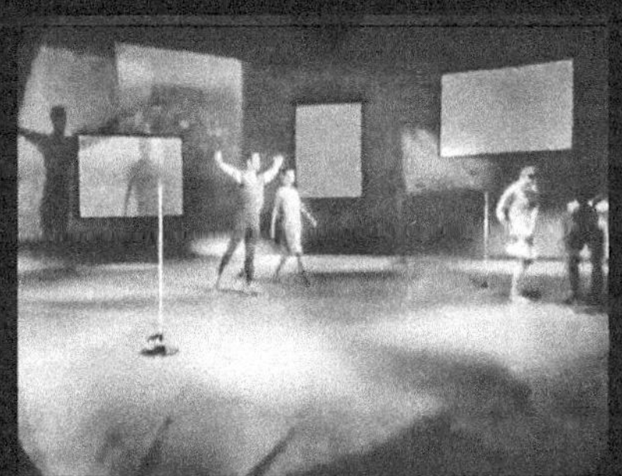

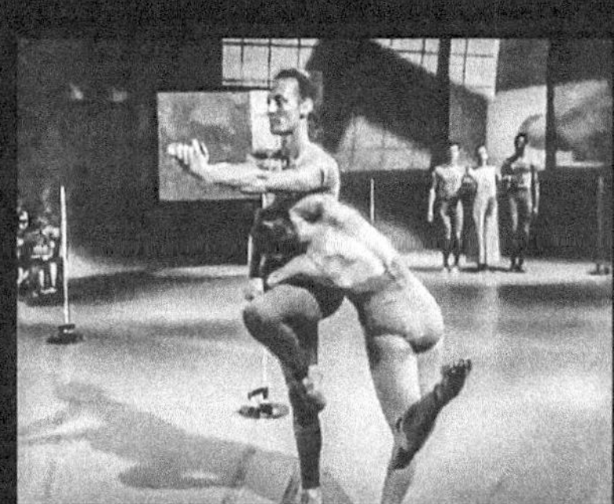

Figure 4.8. Film stills from the television production of *Variations V* directed by Arne Arnbom and filmed at Studio Hamburg, West Germany, 1966. Clockwise from top left: deframed projections in background; projectionist on stage; Cunningham in black, stage left, set against film of Cunningham in white, stage right; Gordon Mumma and David Tudor manipulating the electronic sound controls; dramatic changes in scale as Cunningham's hand appears in a film stage right; popular Hollywood film scenes, stage right.

place on stage and in the images, and occasionally to cross over from the one to the other. Like the sound triggers, VanDerBeek's images did not supplement, enhance, or reflect the dance choreography in a direct way, but rather acted with it in a relationship of relative autonomy. Motivated, but not strictly conditioned, by the other aspects of the work, they provided what was, in effect, a different layer of movements against which the dancers' movements would be juxtaposed. These images did not provide an intentional complementarity for the audience to grasp, but rather a series of largely unanticipated and unintentional correspondences between the movements on the screen, the movements on stage, and the movements in sound.

For the images of the *Movie-Mural* not only moved *like* the dancers, but from the perspective of the audience, moved *in and among* the dancers. In addition to the redoubling of live and prerecorded dance previously mentioned, the light from the film and slide projectors was constantly being interrupted by the movements of the dancers as they crossed the stage. Just as Billy Klüver's photocells made a sonic impression of the movement every time a dancer "tripped" the light beams crisscrossing the stage, VanDerBeek's moving images were overlaid with the shadows carved out by the dancers as they crossed in front of the multiple beams of projection. Images became actors on stage, not in such a way as to make the audience mistake the images for the actors, but so as to set up a range of correspondences, duplications, or reflections between the different dimensions of spatiality and movement.

In their duet, Cunningham and Brown specifically draw our attention as they cross the stage and seem to circle two 16mm projectors being operated on the left. Those projectors throw their beams back across the stage to the right, striking a far wall, where one imparts the image of a dancer—Cunningham himself—in a circling series of movements. In contrast to their traditional position behind or even parallel with our gaze, the perpendicular orientation of these projectors foregrounds the circling movements of their film reels, a movement itself redoubled by the circle Cunningham and Brown create around them through their dance. Cinematic projection is itself presented as theater, as another series of movements orchestrated and on display. Our gaze traces lines and circles that are reduplicated across the stage in real bodies and projected images, in past and present tense, all in motion.

These various movements are neither deliberately aligned nor deliberately juxtaposed, but in their intentionally imprecise alignment, function solely to pose the question of relationship for the spectator. VanDerBeek's *Movie-Mural* maintains the relative autonomy of these distinct media elements even as it places them in a "living" relationship of partial correspondence and occasional harmony. For whatever relationships could be seen would have to be picked from a vast sea of visual stimuli.

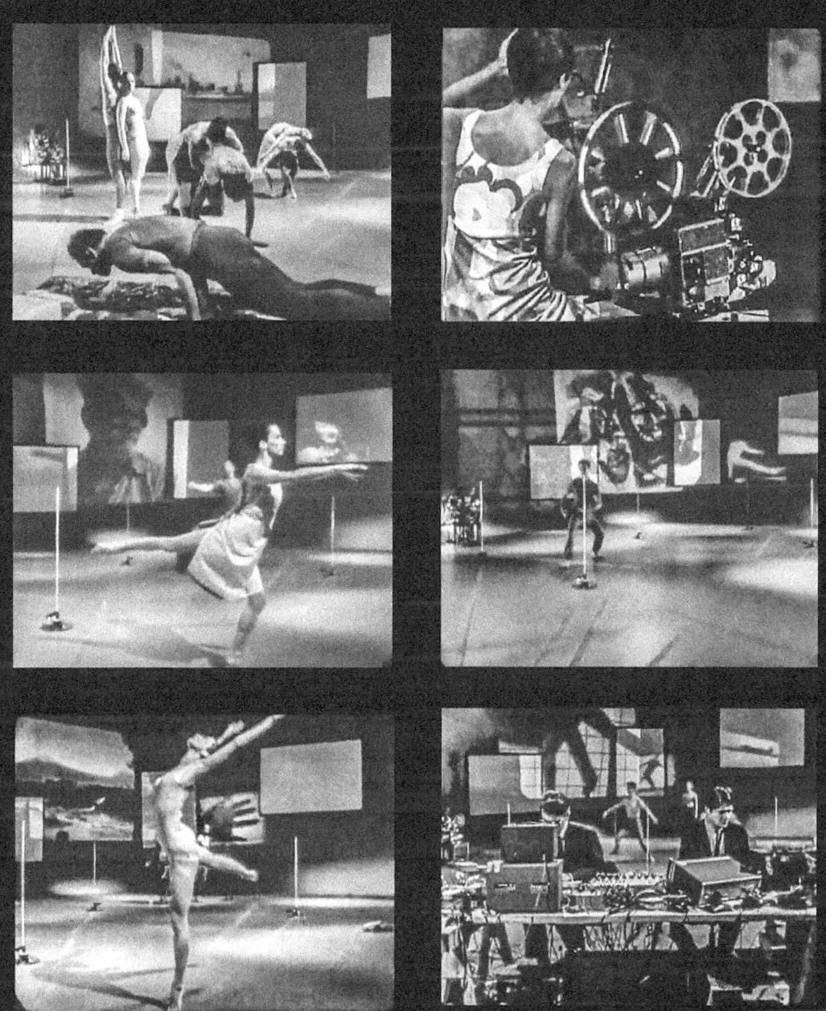

Alongside the images of rehearsal, VanDerBeek shows drawings, paintings, diagrams, classic photographs, television commercials, animated shorts, and Hollywood movies—a virtual cacophony of heterogeneous visual material through which the audience is invited to wander. In the diversity of images, we catch a glimpse of a commercial for Pan Am Airways, a TV cartoon called *The King and Odie*, and George Cukor's popular romantic comedy *Born Yesterday* (1950). These are not only different moving images, but different *kinds* of moving images—each of which implies a distinct modality of spectatorship. *Born Yesterday* would have been a familiar reference to many in the audience. VanDerBeek had probably refilmed a short sequence of it as it was being rebroadcast on TV. Perhaps he had simply stumbled on the old stock and decided to include it. Regardless, it was most likely employed for the associative significance of the title alone, rather than for any profound meaning to be discerned within the work's formulaic narrative. As such, the audience confronted a short clip whose title would have led to certain vague, likely idiosyncratic recollections. Presented here, deliberately ripped out of context, it was forced into strange new associations.

The diversity and heterogeneity of the images VanDerBeek employed within the *Movie-Mural* would have naturally led to its being understood, within the rhetoric of the time, as a kind of "assemblage" or "combine." These terms characterized a variety of artistic practices in the 1950s and early 1960s, from the "cut-up" writings of William Burroughs to the frenetic animations of Bruce Conner and Robert Breer. But the single most influential reference point within the New York art world of that period was incontestably the work of Robert Rauschenberg. Given that VanDerBeek quite knowingly took over Rauschenberg's role in designing the visual environment for *Variations V*, it seems important to understand how Rauschenberg had reconceptualized the idea of painting, helping to contest the postwar ascendancy of abstract expressionism and prepare the way for a diverse range of artists that John Gruen memorably termed "the Combine Generation."[38]

While there was an obvious formal similarity between the collage aesthetics of Rauschenberg and VanDerBeek, a much more important connection between them lay in their understanding of the idea of assemblage as a new paradigm for exhibition and spectatorship in the postwar era. Rauschenberg's "combines" of the 1950s existed somewhere between painting and sculpture, expressivity and nonintentionality. Their definitive acceptance into the canon of postwar art occurred with William Seitz's 1961 exhibition *The Art of Assemblage* at MoMA. In his catalog essay for that exhibition, Seitz sought to break the term's common conflation with collage as the mere incorporation of heterogeneous material within the singular pictorial frame of the canvas. Seitz understood the "radical juxtaposition" of assemblage not simply as a formal combination internal to a given structure or field, but rather as a kind of bridge between the inner and outer space of the aesthetic frame—a setting of the work's internal frame over and against the institutional frames within which that work was exhibited and seen. While tracing premonitions of this idea within the work of Picasso, Duchamp, and Cornell, it was clear that the combines of Rauschenberg served as Seitz's privileged example for the postwar development of the form.

In Leo Steinberg's interpretation, Rauschenberg's work upended a centuries-old representational doxa—unbroken even at the height of abstraction—that took the canvas as a figurative window on the world. This reorientation—which Steinberg described not as a literal configuration of the image, but rather of what he called its "mode of imaginative confrontation"—exchanged the vertical metaphor of the "picture window" for a newly horizontal metaphor of the drafting table or shop room floor. Here the canvas was analogous to a "receptor surface on which objects are scattered, on which data is entered, on which information may be received, printed, impressed—whether coherently or in confusion."[39] No longer referring to a perceptual encounter with the world, the work of art now seemed to implicate the "operational processes" of information management. As such, this kind of work was not "pre-formulated" *for* the viewer, but came about only through an idiosyncratic performance of information management *by* the viewer. The idea of Rauschenberg's canvases as "receptive" rather than "expressive" goes all the way back to the artist's first *White Paintings* of 1951, which he showed to Cage at Black Mountain College. While many saw the young painter's work as an unseemly combination of "passive" and "aggressive," Cage tellingly understood them as "hypersensitive." Like the proximity sensors Cage would increasingly come to employ, Rauschenberg's canvases served as a conduit for information. "One could look at them and almost see how many people were in the room by the shadows cast, or what time of day it was," Cage would say; "they became airports for the lights, shadows, and particles."[40]

The first live performance of the *Movie-Mural* at Lincoln Center in the summer of 1965 adopted Cage's metaphor of the white canvas as a receptive surface quite literally. A thirty-foot white canvas was set up behind the stage, and VanDerBeek's moving images and slides were actually projected on it. In taking Rauschenberg's place as the Cunningham company's "muralist," VanDerBeek both adopted Rauschenberg's conception of the "combine" and translated it into a manner of cinematic assemblage. Instead of the paint and cloth and assorted material objects that made up Rauschenberg's canvases, VanDerBeek would employ Hollywood dramas, television commercials, and animated cartoons, alongside graphic patterns, historical works of art, and recently shot close-ups of the dancers on stage, to create a kaleidoscopic visual field of past and present, local and distant, high art and popular culture—a dumping ground through which the audience would be forced to sift. The point is not that Rauschenberg and VanDerBeek shared a formal aesthetics of collage. Rather, it is that VanDerBeek's *Movie-Mural* was a deliberate attempt to reconceptualize the paradigm of cinematic spectatorship according to the principles of nonintentionality and anti-immersivity to which Rauschenberg, Cage, and Cunningham had long been devoted.

As the only non-filmmaker invited to the 1967 Cinema Now symposium, Cage praised VanDerBeek's *Movie-Mural* as perhaps the furthest cinema had yet gone toward an aesthetic of nonintentionality. Significantly, Cage did not describe the work as a form of audiovisual communication, but as an abdication of the speaker's place altogether: "a renunciation of intention which is effected by the multiplication of images. In this multiplicity, intention becomes silent, as it were, in the eyes of the observer."[41] "Multiplicity" was a term Cage often used to describe Rauschenberg's combine paintings. As such, it can be understood to link

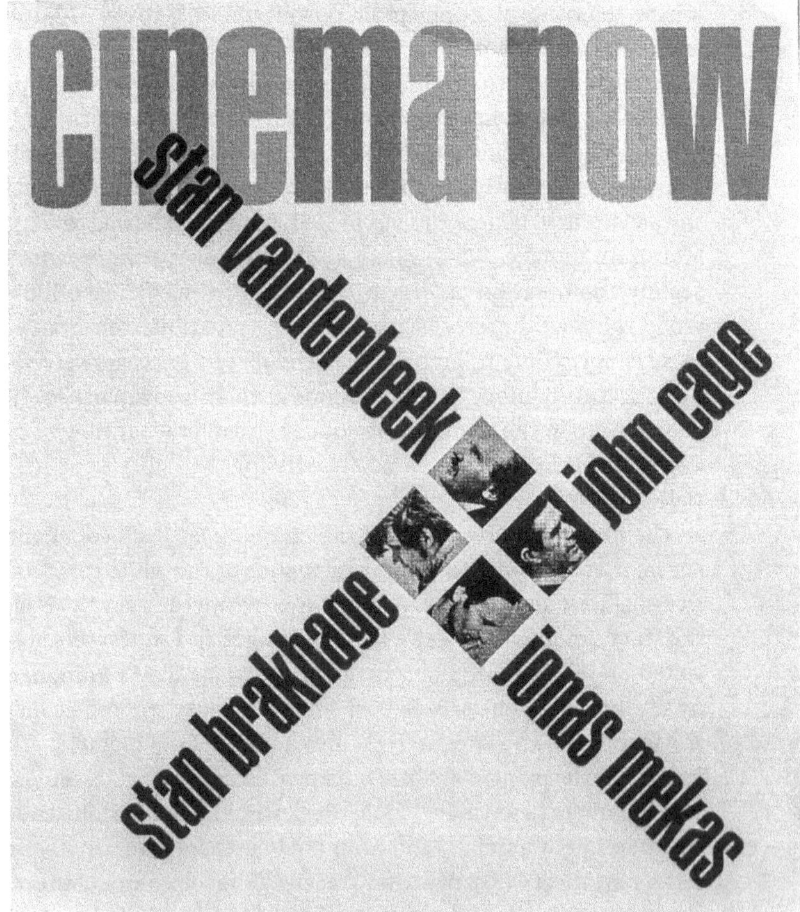

Figure 4.9. Cover of *Cinema Now: Stan Brakhage, John Cage, Jonas Mekas, Stan VanDerBeek*, Perspectives on Underground Film, no. 1 (Cincinnati: University of Cincinnati Press, 1968).

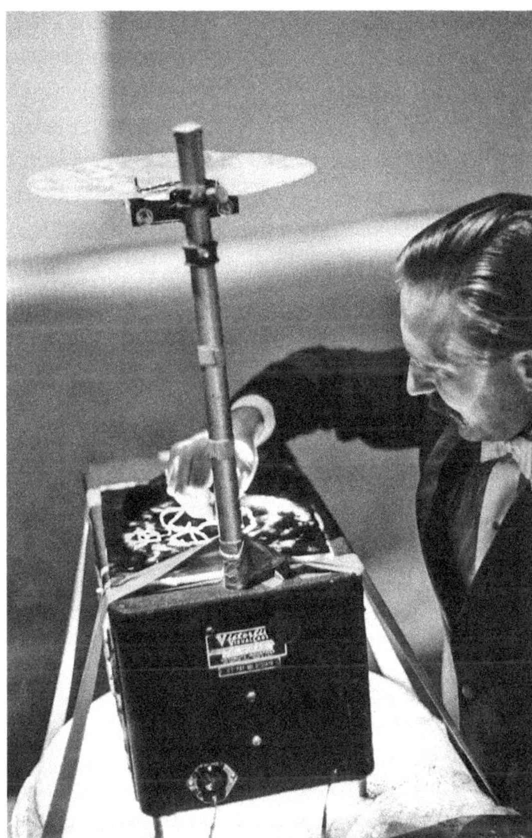

Figure 4.10. Stan VanDer-Beek painting on a transparency for projection as part of his *Panels for the Walls of the World* performance, School of Visual Arts, New York, 1965.

VanDerBeek's *Movie-Mural* to this distinctly new nonintentional, nonexpressive tradition, not through an aesthetic of formal reduction—as in Rauschenberg's *White Paintings*, Cage's own *4'33"* (1951), or Paik's *Zen for Film* (1964)—but through a surfeit of visual information. Since within these works, "a person can't look in all directions at once," Cage explained, "one's observation is no longer focused; rather, it's given some freedom ... individuality that can enter into the state of observing in contrast to the observer being given what someone else has already pre-digested."[42]

VanDerBeek's performance, true to the expanded conception of assemblage Seitz had articulated a few years before, signaled a shift of emphasis from the interior construction of the image to the exterior conditions of its encounter. The *Movie-Mural* gestured away from the moving image as self-contained entity and toward its new mobilization as but a single component of a larger intermedia assemblage, one whose complexity necessarily precluded singular authoritative control. Alongside this conceptual coherence, there was nonetheless a dramatic formal divergence between Rauschenberg's combines and VanDerBeek's *Movie-Mural*, and this divergence took on added weight in the context of a live performance. While

Rauschenberg's works would have competed for attention with the dancers on stage, they necessarily remained static, plastic constructions, quite easily contrasted with the dancers' living movements around the stage. By contrast, VanDerBeek's *Movie-Mural* would "animate" this background on multiple levels, erasing the traditional distinction between actor and set. Moving images of the dancers on-screen competed with the images of movement provided by those same dancers on stage. Additionally, this slippage between on-screen and off-screen movements could be found in the moving images of "non-dancing" bodies—in *Born Yesterday*, for instance—such that the movement of Judy Holliday on the screen would be placed in relation to the movement occurring in proximity on stage.

The animation VanDerBeek sought within the *Movie-Mural* did not simply place still images in motion, but rather animated the cinematic apparatus itself—mobilizing our idea of how cinema functions. The images not only surpass the boundaries of the screens—spilling out onto the walls of the space and interacting with the dancers on stage—but are constantly being manipulated, in real time, by projectionists who now function as dancers in their own right. In the 1966 performance recording, we can see the two film projectors on stage being stopped and started, reloaded and reoriented, across from the images being projected. But even the still images have been placed in motion: no slide projection remains constant for any length of time before it is shifted out for another. We could easily imagine these shifts being mechanized, either with a straight mechanical advance or with the kind of A-to-B dissolve that would become commonplace in trade presentations. But VanDerBeek has done neither. The slides' movements are clearly performed by hand—their artisanal quality is evident in their irregular movement within the context of the performance. The spectator is consistently brought back to the origin of their movement in the movements of the human animator—VanDerBeek, or one of his collaborators—as an active participant in the movement on display.

In the terms of Bergson's critique with which we began, VanDerBeek might here be understood as reversing the traditional technique of cinematic animation. Rather than still images placed in effortless motion, projection is itself exhibited through a display of effortful activity. VanDerBeek's slides shift and change through a sometimes clumsy mechanical labor that leaves no doubt as to its cause. As if to underline the point, the animator's hand itself makes an appearance toward the end of the performance, silhouetted on stage and screen by an overhead projector in a series of rhythmic gestures. In so doing, it models a transference between the human and the mechanical that takes place throughout the performance. The dancers on stage take on "mechanical" poses, but those poses only serve to convey the great human effort required to achieve them. Like the arduous performances of mechanization beneath it, the

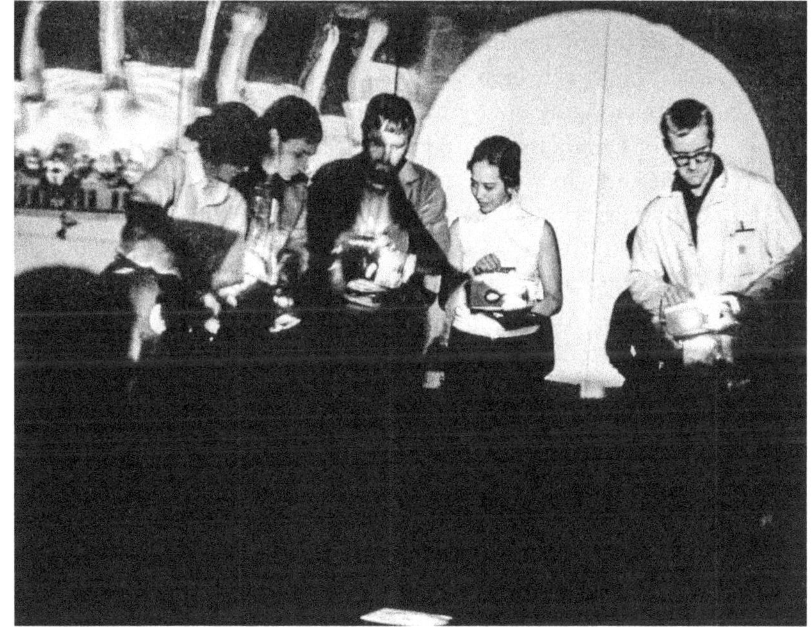

Figure 4.11. Stan VanDerBeek and assistants performing *Move-Movies* at the New Cinema Festival I/Expanded Cinema Festival, winter 1965. Photo by Peter Moore © Estate of Peter Moore/VAGA, New York, NY.

spatialization of VanDerBeek's *Movie-Mural* images—their constant ceaseless movement outside of their frames—depicts an act of human animation that is modeled on, but ultimately stands opposed to, the mechanical animation of the projectors.

VanDerBeek's *Movie-Mural* modeled a new paradigm of animation in which it was not the still image that was placed in motion, but the moving image that became newly animated through techniques of displacement and correspondence. By animating the cinematic apparatus itself, he dislocated the idea of projection from the fixity of the theatrical paradigm. Displacing the moving image into the institutional situation of the dance performance allowed for new ways to conceptualize movement across bodies and images. For Stan Brakhage and Jonas Mekas, the camera had become an extension of the body and thus an embodiment of their vision of the world around them. VanDerBeek, by contrast, followed Rauschenberg and Cage in exchanging a model of expression for one of appropriation. In his *Move-Movies: A Choreography for Projectors* (1965), presented at the Expanded Cinema Festival that winter, VanDerBeek and his associates employed handheld 8mm *projectors* in a new vision of cinematic choreography, recycling found footage in a real-time collaborative performance.[43] In this "ballet of handheld projectors," the movement of projection was conjoined with the movement of the human body. It was a performance that would inspire Trisha Brown's own iconic pas de deux, titled *Overture*, the following year, in which the dancer performed with an 8mm projector strapped to her back, projecting a prerecorded film of the same dance, which had been shot by Robert Whitman.

Uprooted from Cage and Cunningham's model of authorial divestment, the social and institutional dimensions of VanDerBeek's practice might easily be lost in the flurry of excitement over multiscreen cinema that was then taking hold. And it is just such a misleading formal homology that one finds in the first published accounts of the expanded cinema in 1967, in which VanDerBeek's work is associated with the superficially similar practice of Charles and Ray Eames. Within the *Film Culture* issue devoted to the expanded cinema, for instance, an image of the Eameses' *Glimpses of the USA* (1959) is curiously placed, without explanation, in the section devoted to VanDerBeek's work. The image seems to imply a historical precedent, or even stand in for an absent image of the interior of the artist's Movie-Drome, whose exterior is pictured immediately beside it. Similarly, the important chapter on expanded cinema within Sheldon Renan's *An Introduction to the American Underground Film* begins with this same image of *Glimpses of the USA*, and a similar association is directly implied between VanDerBeek and the Eameses, based on their shared interest in multiple projection and geodesic domes.[44]

Such superficial parallels tended to reinforce a misconception of VanDerBeek's practice as a poorly funded and less well rehearsed version of the spectacular multimedia environments at the World's Fair, when in fact their aims were diametrically opposed. *Glimpses of the USA*, commissioned by the US Information Agency for the American National Exhi-

Figure 4.12. Charles and Ray Eames, *Glimpses of the USA*, 1959

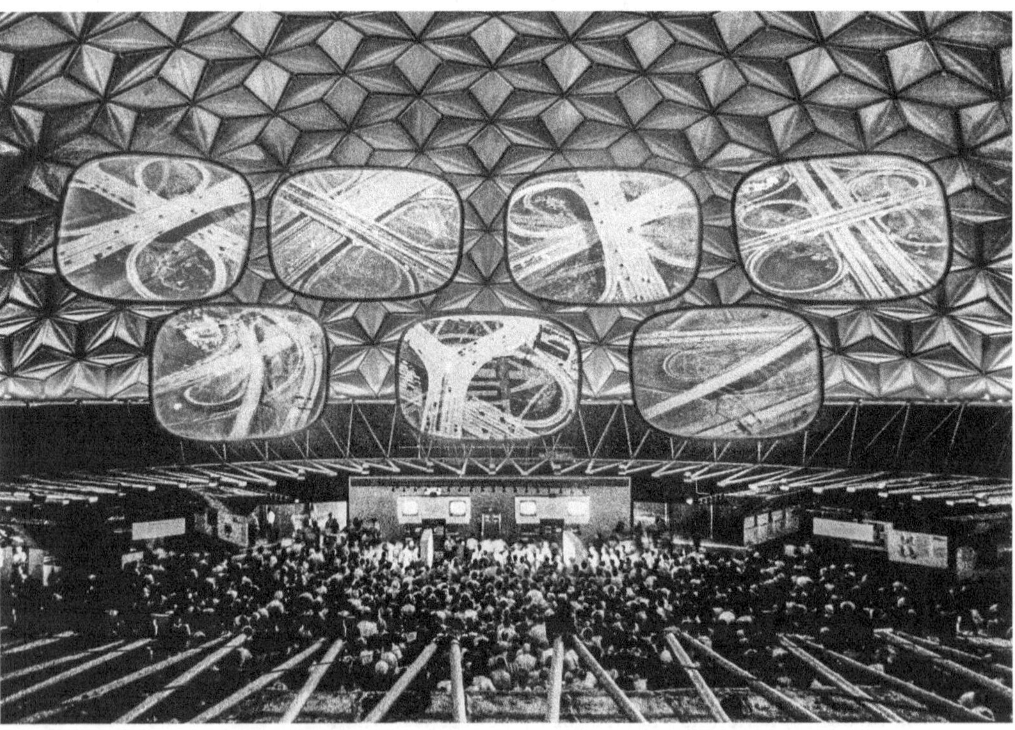

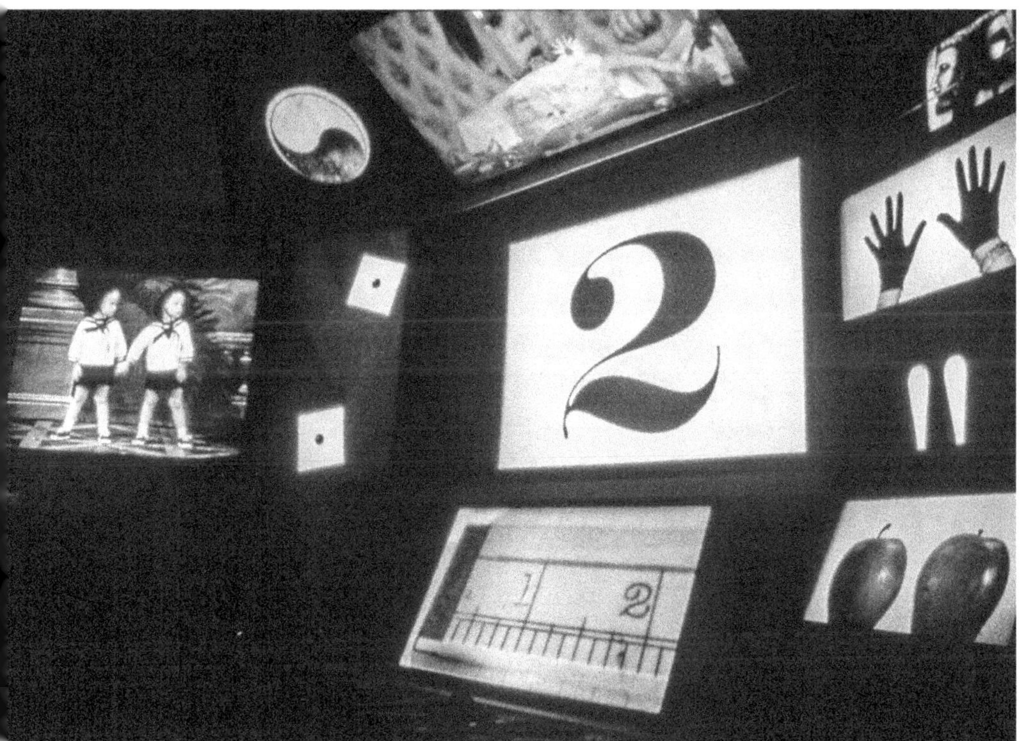

Figure 4.13. Charles and Ray Eames, *Think*, 1964

bition in Moscow, was an overtly didactic and monumentalizing work of Cold War propaganda intended to amaze and overwhelm its Soviet audience. The images spread across its seven massive screens were intentionally *cohesive*, rather than disjunctive, reinforcing one another to communicate a single, unmistakable message of limitless abundance and prosperity—a theme unsubtly echoed by the enormous golden dome within which it took place.[45] The Eameses' later *Think* presentation for the 1964 World's Fair may have been less overtly propagandistic, but it was no less didactic. Fuller's domed theater was there replaced with a massive elevated sphere into which the audience was lifted en masse. The number of screens was doubled, and these screens—like VanDerBeek's—were of various shapes and sizes. Yet the work's rapid-fire presentation was specifically organized to facilitate absorption and comprehension of the intended message—thus serving as a fundamental continuation of the very authorial and communicative models VanDerBeek was attempting to challenge.

As for the domed theater, Fred Waller had already completed two domed Cinerama theaters in 1963 for Hollywood's Sunset Boulevard and the Las Vegas strip. Even the monumentality of the spherical theater at the '64 World's Fair was but a pale shadow of the truly gigantic Perisphere built on those same grounds for the '39 World's Fair. There, a quarter century before, Waller had projected a "movie-mural" on the structure's

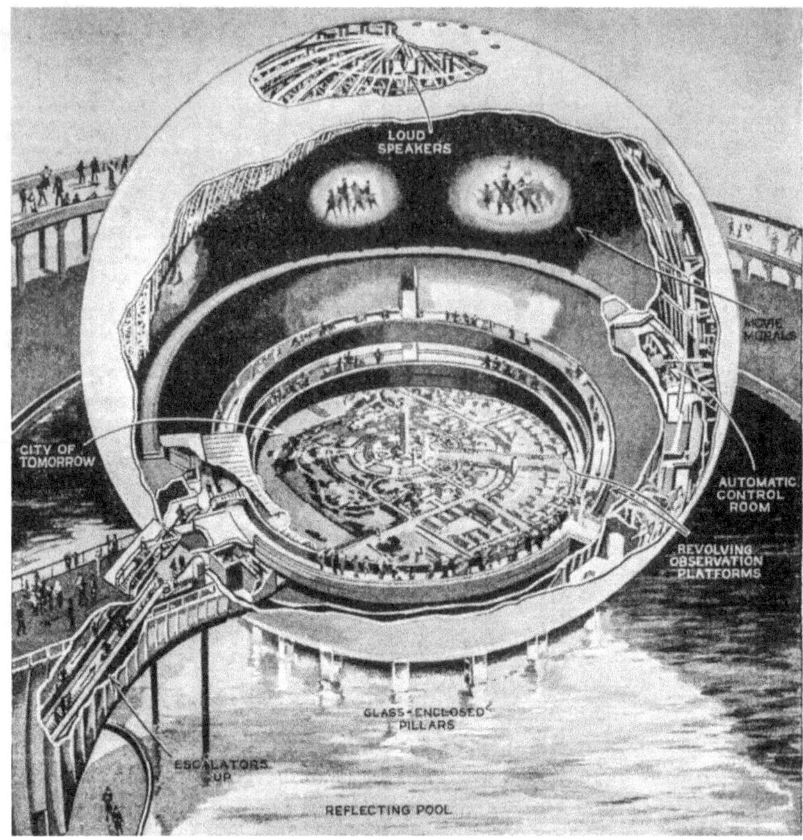

Figure 4.14. Illustration from "The City of Tomorrow" by Henry Dreyfuss, *Popular Mechanics*, March 1939.

enormous domed ceiling. A hundred times the size of VanDerBeek's Movie-Drome, the Perisphere was the site of the popular *Democracity* exhibit, an immense diorama depicting a future city of 2039. Audiences looked down from a rotating circular balcony, while the top of the sphere was bathed in blue light to suggest the sky. For the dramatic conclusion, this sky was turned into a vast cinematic mural: "a battery of ten four-fold projectors" and "a hundred of the largest long-focus f1.6 lenses ever made" were required to project these moving images on a screen over an acre in size.[46] But like so much from the history of world's fairs and industrial expositions, Waller's domed "movie-mural" was a great technical achievement hampered by its utter lack of aesthetic or conceptual innovation. For all its phenomenal size and expense, the ninety-second work seems to have depicted utterly generic scenes of "happy workers" going about their affairs, albeit at an intentionally overpowering, monumental scale.

If this image of VanDerBeek's *Movie-Mural* is admittedly spectacular, it is nevertheless fundamentally misread as an image of spectacle. At the very moment when so many cinematic spectacles at the New York World's Fair were generating acclaim—largely unmerited—on account of their formal novelty, the modesty of VanDerBeek's own project belied the

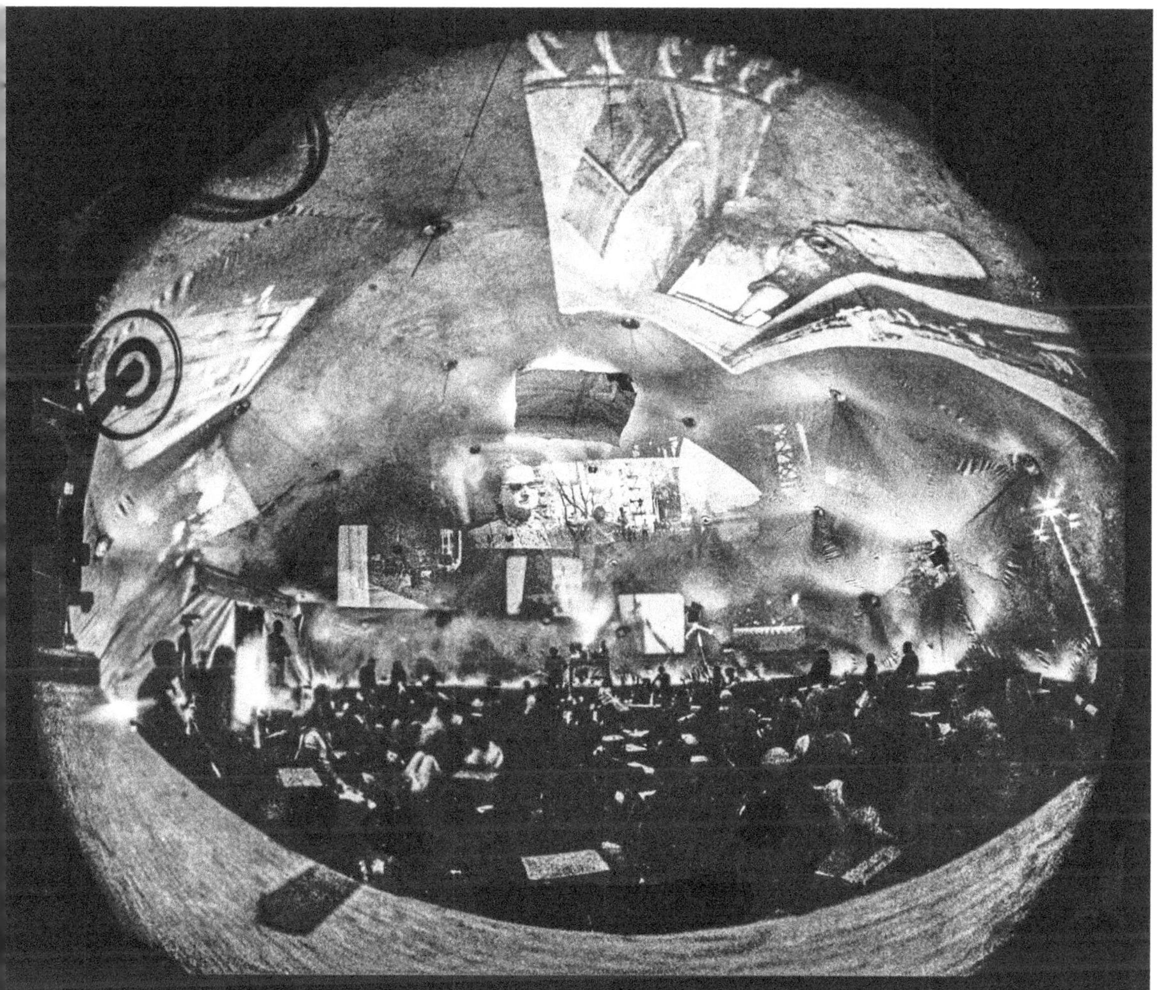

Figure 4.15. Interior of Stan VanDerBeek's Movie-Drome during unknown performance, Stony Point, NY.

radicality of its aesthetic and conceptual innovation. Conducted at an intentional remove from the established spaces of both art and entertainment, and grounded in his longtime association with Cage and Cunningham, VanDerBeek's *Movie-Mural* was an attempt at a new model of visual communication diametrically opposed to the didactic singularity of the authorial message. The living murals that appeared within *Variations V*, or on the heavens of VanDerBeek's Movie-Drome, were moving pictures in a radically different sense. Seeking to recast the idea of "movement" within the moving image, VanDerBeek's *Movie-Mural* brilliantly congealed a metaphorics of experience in the televisual age—simultaneously live and mediated, chaotic and predigested, focused and diffuse. The spatialization of cinematic projection and its real-time manipulation in performance were both attempts by VanDerBeek to recast our understanding of spectatorship beyond the traditional model of communicative *reception*—to extend Duchamp's idea that the mediation of aesthetic spectatorship itself invariably constitutes a complex act of *creation*.[47] Freed from an obligatory point of focus, spectators were given the responsibility of creating what sense and significance they would. This unstable field of correspondence was newly vulnerable—open to and dependent on the spectatorial motivation of audiences as never before. Rather than broadcasting content for their audiences to receive, VanDerBeek, Cage, and Cunningham together sought to orchestrate an environmental situation within which unanticipated forms of communicability and correspondence might spontaneously erupt.

The intermedia assemblage that was *Variations V* can be seen as a collage made of discontinuous elements and disjunctive media. But the important point is that, in its self-understanding as assemblage, it is only ever provisionally "made" at all, for the temporality of assemblage persistently belies the finality of a construction. The work of assemblage, we might say, is always only a work *to-be-constructed* through an act of collaboration, with its spectator actively solicited to rework light, movement, sound, and image. If animation historically connoted a singular act of "bringing to life," the kind of "life" granted by VanDerBeek's *Movie-Mural* was a flickering, contingent one. It offered an anarchic conception of the social, based on an irreducible respect for the singularity of the individual over and against all forms of collective interpellation. True to their creators' memories of Black Mountain and their contemporary efforts at The Land, these performances functioned as a transient microcosm of utopian freedom, a glimpse of a society within which "you would be willing to live." They did not do so through the seemingly chaotic profusion of imagery, sound, and movement alone, but through the complex and fleeting relationships of complementarity and correspondence that arose between those elements—relationships uncovered through the spectators' own work of construction, their own participation in the performance.

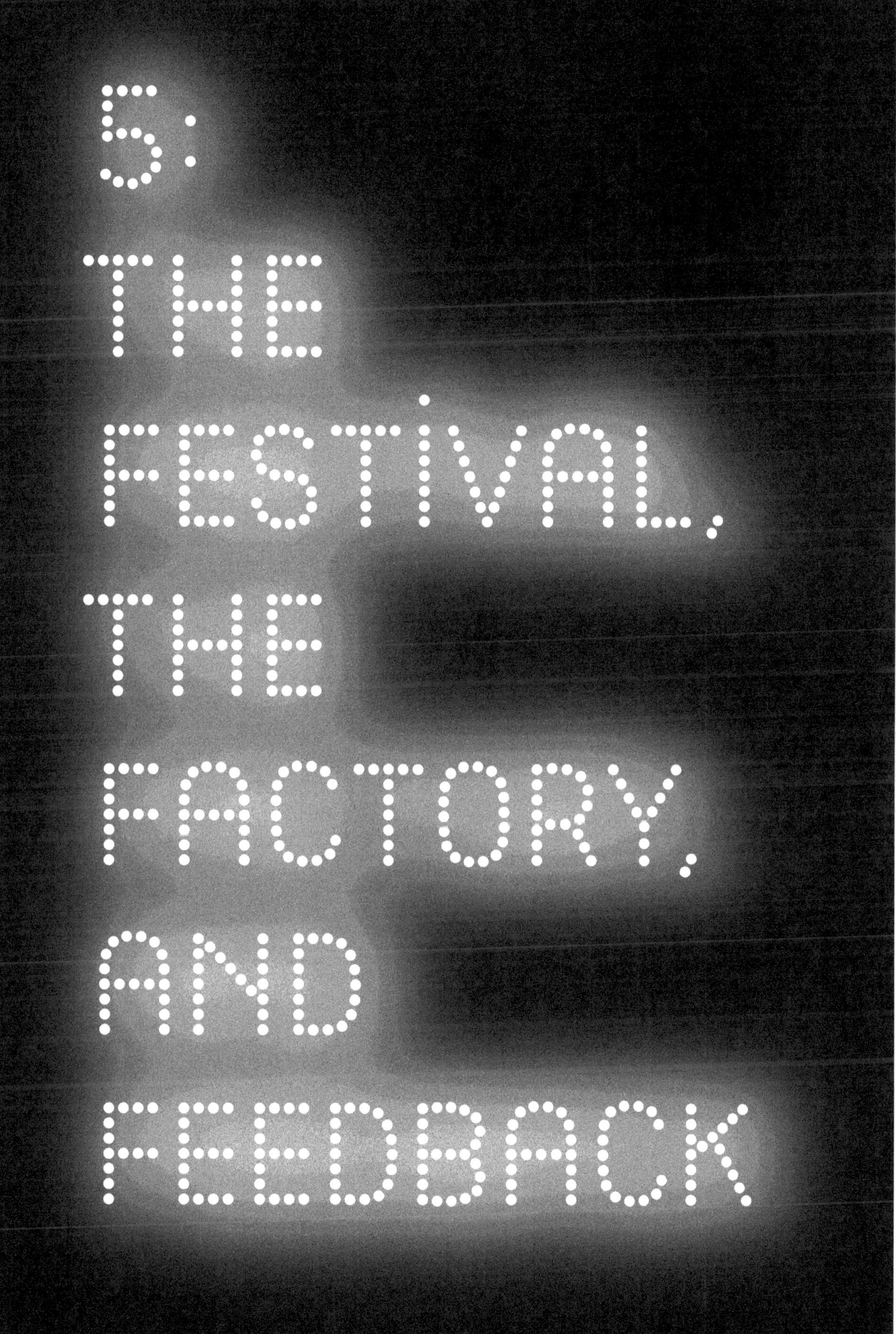
5:
THE
FESTIVAL,
THE
FACTORY,
AND
FEEDBACK

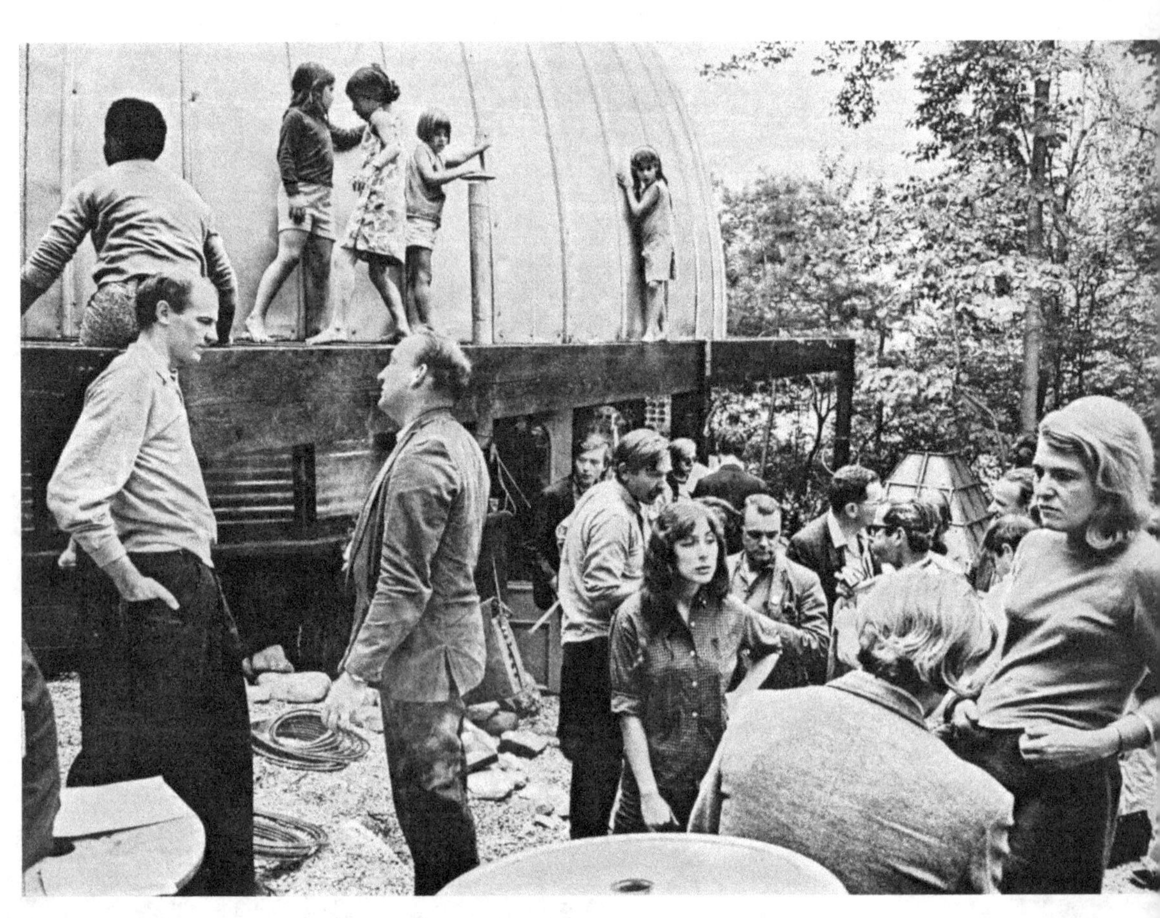

Artists against the Art Film

Figure 5.1. Outside Stan VanDerBeek's Movie-Drome, Stony Point, New York, 1966, during the fourth New York Film Festival. Photo © Elliott Landy.

A photograph taken during the Fourth New York Film Festival provides an index of the radical dislocation the idea of expanded cinema had engendered by 1966. It shows a mix of artists, filmmakers, critics, and other spectators who had been bused out that day to Stan VanDerBeek's home at The Land, about an hour north of Manhattan. Several small children are playing on an elevated platform supporting the apex of an aluminum grain silo. We can make out Andy Warhol in the distant background, talking perhaps to Paul Morrissey, while VanDerBeek himself appears in the center of the frame. The artist Ken Dewey, hands in pockets, stands at the far left talking to the art critic Fred Wellington, in a suit jacket. Annette Michelson, also with hands in pockets, seems lost in thought at the extreme right. We are far indeed from New York's Lincoln Center—the New York Film Festival's institutional home.

The films screened at Lincoln Center were presented as the apex of cinematic distinction: these were the greatest works of the world's greatest filmmakers. They were certainly finished products. Yet VanDerBeek had brought three dozen influential critics, filmmakers, and fellow artists from Lincoln Center to experience *Feedback*, a live multimedia performance requiring the manipulation of a dozen film, slide, and overhead projectors, alongside a barrage of audio equipment—which had never been rehearsed. The equipment was ready only two hours before the actual performance, and the theater within which it was taking place, VanDerBeek's Movie-Drome, was itself not completely finished. From what we know of that first performance, it went off pretty much as one might expect. There was reportedly some snickering during VanDerBeek's preliminary exposition, which concerned the urgent social and political necessity for an "international picture-language," and a general kind of noncommittal acquiescence during the performance that followed.[1] Suffice it to say that by the standards of the New York Film Festival, the event was not a success. By the fall of 1966, it had become clear that VanDerBeek was not interested in the critical standards by which works at the festival were being judged.

As we have seen, during the early 1960s, VanDerBeek had emerged as both an exemplar of and a spokesman for the "underground film." Now, in 1966, he had finally been asked to exhibit his work at the New York Film

Festival. Ironically, it was VanDerBeek's experience at Lincoln Center the year before that reinforced his decision to abandon both the traditional film-theatrical situation and even, to some extent, the medium of film itself. As we have seen, VanDerBeek's *Movie-Mural* had been an integral component of Cage and Cunningham's multimedia production *Variations V* for the French-American Festival at Lincoln Center in the summer of 1965. Both literally and metaphorically, VanDerBeek had traveled a long way in the intervening year.

Already in December of 1965, he had taken a version of his *Movie-Mural* performance—which he had taken to calling *Feedback*—to packed auditoriums in Berlin, Vienna, and Copenhagen, with the Berlin performance even being rebroadcast over German television. VanDerBeek's *Movie-Mural* would receive even greater attention when *Variations V* went on an extended international tour in 1966, with two separate trips across Europe and twenty-nine performances across the United States and Canada, including a special performance filmed for a German/Swedish television coproduction. Exhibited in a dozen countries and rebroadcast on television numerous times, VanDerBeek's *Movie-Mural* would become one of the key works through which the New York expanded cinema would become internationally known.

At home, VanDerBeek had been the subject of two short television features, and he was increasingly being given opportunities to lecture and perform at university campuses across America.[2] While continuing his long-standing interest in dance through collaborations with Elaine Summers and the Judson Dance Theater, he was becoming increasingly involved with computational media through a collaboration with Ken Knowlton at Bell Labs. In short, VanDerBeek—in only a year's time—had managed to reach a vast array of new audiences beyond the traditional confines of film culture. If the Movie-Drome remained unfinished at the time of the 1966 film festival, it was because the structure was, by its very nature, unfinishable. VanDerBeek's theater was less a physical environment than a conceptual model, one devoted to a larger process of questioning the exhibition and spectatorship of visual culture in the televisual age.[3] *Feedback* revealed the palpable disjunction between the open-ended experimentation of the expanded cinema and the new institutionalization of film art at Lincoln Center. A mirror held up to the New York Film Festival, *Feedback* asked both what it had become and what it had aspired to be.

Since its founding in 1963, the New York Film Festival had presided over an increasing recognition of the importance of cinema as a modern art, even as it precipitated a growing dispute as to the specificity of the cinematic medium within the broader topology of contemporary art practice. The Festival, co-organized by Amos Vogel, was founded as

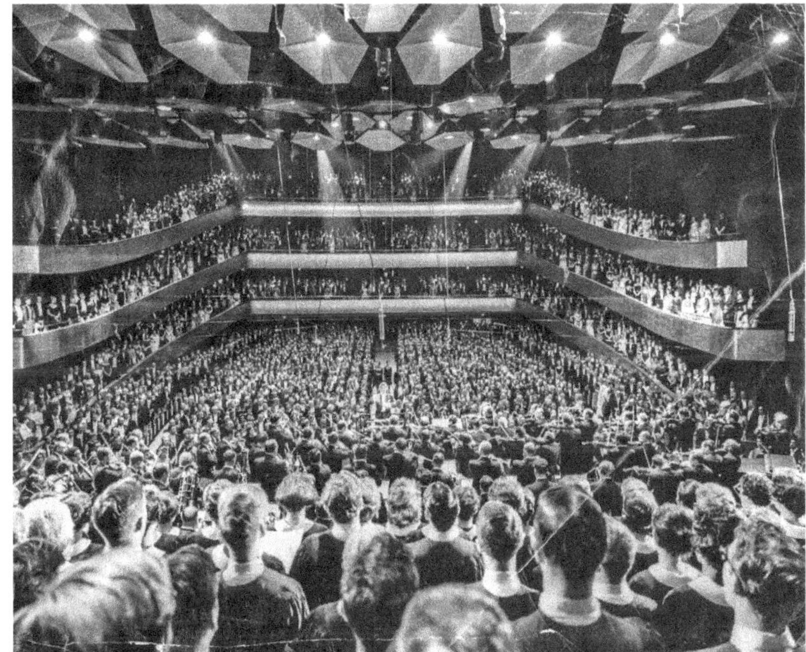

igure 5.2. Interior of .incoln Center's Phil-armonic Hall, open-ng night, September 3, 1962.

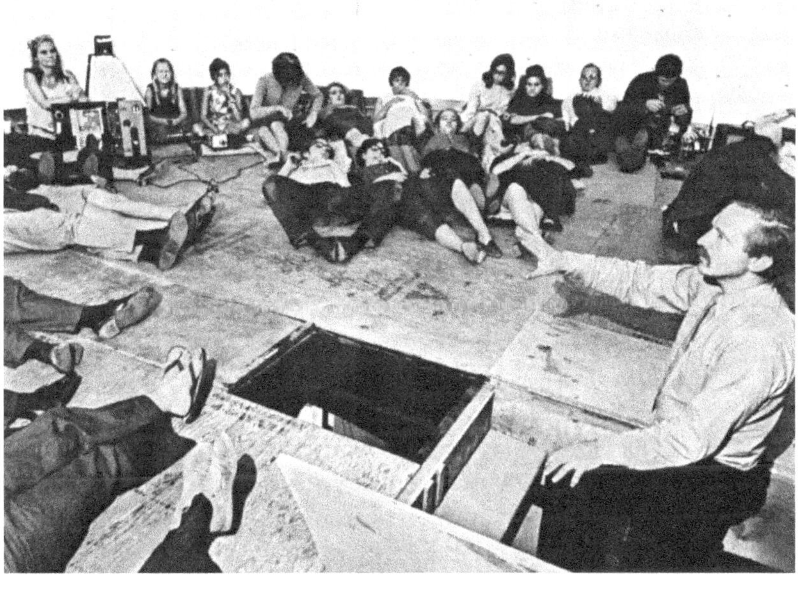

igure 5.3. Stan Van-)erBeek lecturing in-ide the Movie-Drome, tony Point, New York, 966. Photo © Elliott andy.

an institution devoted to the contemporary art of cinema. Like Vogel's legendary Cinema 16 before it, the festival had always intended to cast a wide net in its selection of films. Yet Cinema 16, unburdened by the mantle of Lincoln Center or the obligation to showcase the very best of world cinema, had screened a fantastically heterogeneous range of work, combining ethnographic documentaries, scientific films, and avant-garde experiments with more traditional narrative works. The festival, by contrast, was designed to be a forum for the art of cinema at a time when there was little critical or popular consensus about what that nomination might entail.

In the 1966 festival program, director Richard Roud lamented that the "low status of films in the so-called intellectual community" and "the way in which films are seen—and judged—more as illustrated literature than as anything else" had caused most critics to reject films that strayed from established practices of the industrial narrative. "The notion that film can come as close to painting as to literature or the theater never seems to have occurred to most of our intellectual critics," Roud concluded. Vogel would agree, but with a markedly different emphasis. It was not simply that cinema had finally caught up with the rival arts, but rather that cinema was increasingly enmeshed with a larger aesthetic transformation then taking place *across* the arts: "The cinema is changing . . . thematically, stylistically, philosophically, aesthetically . . . It was always a bit silly to imagine that film (insofar as it is art) could remain exempt from what is happening in other arts."[4]

Despite these public affirmations, that winter's program would paradoxically mark the zenith and conclusion of the festival's flirtation with those forms of quasi-theatrical film practice that had recently emerged precisely at the intersection of film and the plastic arts. Even as the 1966 program boasted "all new, state-of-the-art 16mm projection equipment" purchased to accommodate the ever-increasing number of international submissions, the split between experimental film and international art cinema had grown into a chasm. As Jonas Mekas wrote in the *Village Voice*, "For the last three years, the excuse given for not showing *The Art of Vision*, *Scorpio Rising*, or other films which we felt were superior to the usual festival fare was that there was no 16mm projection. And we thought that was true."[5] In attempting to understand this state of affairs, Mekas evoked the institutional situation of the festival at Lincoln Center: "There are good people working for the festival. Their intentions are good. But they are split between their own tastes and what Lincoln Center stands for."

Just as MoMA had come to be understood not simply as an institution of modern art, but as the very arbiter and bellwether of artistic modernism, the festival's prestigious location signaled the long-desired cultural legitimation of cinema as a modern art. The question of "what Lincoln Center stands for" had become particularly important in regard to cinema, for it seemed to stand in for a whole host of questions raised by cinema's newfound status. For the cultural recognition of film was not simply reflected in the programming of a few select urban theaters, but in the founding of a new academic discipline and the production of knowledge therein.[6] Over the next two decades, hundreds of new courses and millions of new students would be educated within this new academic field of film studies. What was at stake in these early debates about legitimation was the critical paradigm by which film would be incorporated into the discursive field of modern aesthetics at the very moment when the foundation of modernist medium-specificity was itself breaking down.

In his column, Mekas refers to Stan Brakhage not as a filmmaker, but as an artist. The shift is symptomatic. At a time when Clement Greenberg's model of medium-specificity was increasingly being questioned across a broad array of contemporary artistic practices, filmmakers and film critics were still pounding on the gates, insisting that an art of cinema be acknowledged precisely in its exclusive autonomy and independence. Perhaps the sole figure to repeatedly and effectively straddle the discursive gulf between "art" and "cinema" was the French new wave auteur Jean-Luc Godard. Conjoining sophisticated literary and philosophical allusions with a playful Brechtianism, creating a frisson of difficulty while employing young, stylish actors within the comfortable framework of the theatrical drama, and ceaselessly referencing Hollywood classics at the very moment when cinephiles were seeking to secure an aesthetic canon, Godard seemed predestined to become the paragon of the international "film artist." Between 1963 and 1968, the festival would screen almost twenty hours of Godard's films while refusing to run so much as a short by artists as diverse as Stan Brakhage, Kenneth Anger, Andy Warhol, Michael Snow, Paul Sharits, or Hollis Frampton.[7]

These artists were and were not "filmmakers." Like so many artists turning toward the moving image in this period, they were fascinated by the forms, the ideas, and the technologies of cinema, but their artistic practice could not be understood or appreciated within the increasingly hegemonic and normative model of international "art film" then becoming institutionalized. In chapter 1, I described the importance of Warhol's *Sleep* in its attempt to renegotiate the entrenched norms of cinematic exhibition and spectatorship. Yet when Warhol received an invitation to screen his work at Second New York Film Festival in 1964, it was in such a guise as to effectively neutralize any challenge the work presented to these traditional structures. Rather than being asked to present his works on the main screen with the rest of the festival works, Warhol was merely offered a space in the Lincoln Center lobby to display short excerpts of his films on 8mm loop viewers. Exhibited on these small, backlit projection devices, a work like *Sleep* was transformed both in scale—from more than twenty feet to less than twenty inches—and in duration—from over five hours to under three minutes. Lest this prove too long for the crowds on their way to the next feature, *Sleep*, *Eat*, *Kiss*, and *Hair-Cut* were all presented simultaneously, side by side, so that viewers might literally take them in stride. Even more than transforming the works in scale and duration, the installation unequivocally transformed the theatrical situation for which the works had been created—a situation in no way marginal or ancillary to the work, but rather of paramount importance to its very conception and functioning.

Marketed within the official promotional literature as an "extra added attraction," a literal sideshow to the serious works being exhibited in the theater, the festival's backhanded acceptance of Warhol's work seems, in retrospect, a clever form of inoculation. Presented within this liminal space—under the aegis of the festival, but kept well "within their place" vis-à-vis the actual films in competition—Warhol's works were denuded of their aura and stripped of their seductive inaccessibility. Warhol's desire to "open up" the theatrical situation raised the possibility of confusion, anger, and even resentment, but it also raised the possibility of a more radical critique of the traditional spectatorial paradigm. In their exhibition at the New York Film Festival, that possibility was effectively neutralized through the works' reduction to mere visual signs; the event of spectatorship was reduced to a mere recognition and confirmation of what was supposedly already known. Fifteen years later, Warhol still resented the treatment of his films. In *Popism,* he describes traveling to the Cannes Film Festival in 1967 with his *Chelsea Girls*, only to find that "the guy supposedly arranging everything hadn't even set up one showing." He compared the situation to "when the Lincoln Center Film Festival had so graciously shown our movies—on little crank up machines in the *lobby*!"[8]

Frustrated by his initial experience with the New York Film Festival, and with its subsequent lack of interest in any of the dozens of films he had made, Warhol soon abandoned any attempt to find favor with the emerging institutions and discourses of the modern art cinema. Instead, he became increasingly interested in both making and exhibiting his work in a private space that lay entirely within his own control. Nevertheless, he set up the Factory in such a way that it was rarely private and almost never under his control. In the institutional dialectic between the art gallery and the cinematic theater that we have observed, Warhol's Factory seemed to exist simultaneously as both and neither. It was a hybrid, variegated space of production and consumption, exhibition and spectatorship, in which these different aspects were not so much conjoined as confused through their mutual imbrication. As the site Warhol ambivalently ran and occupied ("I don't feel these people hang around me so much as I hang around them"), the Factory was itself structured by a dynamic oscillation of outer and inner space, an environment in which the traditional distinction between theatrical performance and interior identity was dissolved through the ubiquity of recording, registration, and reproduction—a (barely) controlled experiment in social and technological feedback.

Outer and Inner Space (1965): Feedback at the Factory

The Factory was quite unlike the steel mills for which Warhol's native Pittsburgh was known. Even before Warhol arrived, it had produced "the frivolous stuff of fashion," according to Caroline Jones, rather than "the serious matter of which tanks and destroyers were made."[9] Of course, fashion was anything but frivolous to someone so conscious of the power of the image and its constitutive role in the formation of subjectivity. While Warhol's Factory no longer produced clothing, it was organized around that intimate association of the inner subject and the outer image that fashion seeks to address. Warhol's taking over the space in January 1964 coincided with the high-water mark of his early career as a painter and the beginning of his almost fanatical devotion to film. Immediately, Warhol set about converting this space into something like a permanent theatrical stage: the large, bright windows were painted black, and everything else was covered in reflective aluminum foil or silver spray paint. Michelson has described its décor as bestowing "the minimal reflective potential upon surfaces, which could transform the Factory into a dim Hall of Mirrors, redoubling in its confusion of actor and audience the narcissistic dynamic of the site's theatrical economy."[10] Decades before reality television or social networking, lives in the Factory were lived on camera, and personal conversations and private phone calls were taped for the record. More than fifty thousand feet of celluloid and quite literally miles of audiotape were employed from 1964 to 1966 alone.

While Warhol's turn to film began in 1963, his engagement with tape recording would begin in August 1965, when he was given two very different tape recorders within the space of a few weeks. In conjunction with the Norelco Corporation, *Tape Recording* magazine loaned Warhol a brand-new high-end videotape recording system for a month in exchange for an interview about his experience. Television studios had been using videotape systems for over a decade, but it was only then that a number of companies were preparing to bring "consumer-level" equipment to the market. It is important to note that videotape recording, while obviously new and exciting, was here presented not as a new medium in and of itself, but rather as an "enhanced" version of an already familiar technology. Within *Tape Recording*, video was presented as simply a new kind of tape recording that additionally allowed images to be recorded alongside sound.[11] Reversing the historical evolution of cinematic technologies in the 1920s, in which sound was added to the "silent" image, the magazine's editors here imagined an audience of audiophiles—or eavesdroppers; the magazine explicitly catered to both—who might begin to incorporate *visuals* into their *audio* recordings.

Warhol was actually quite an appropriate choice for *Tape Recording*'s new promotion because he had become something of a tape-recording

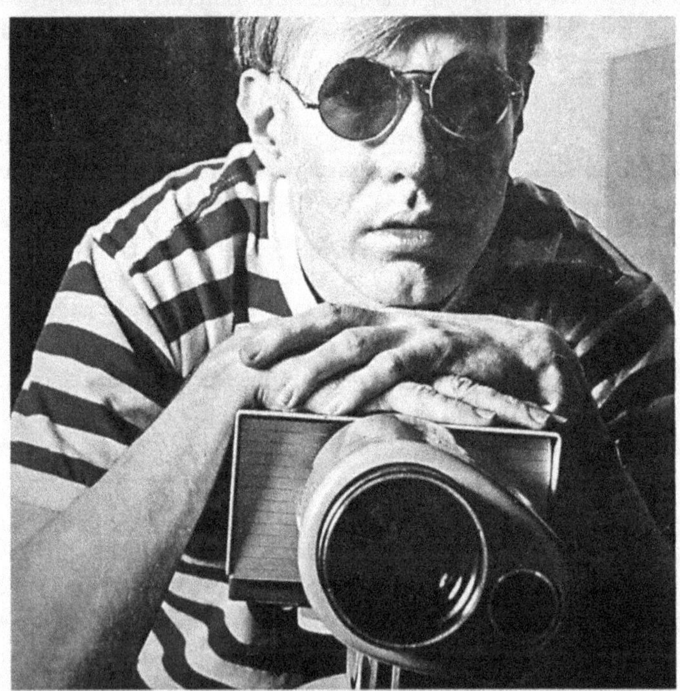

Figure 5.4. Cover of *Tape Recording*, October 1965.

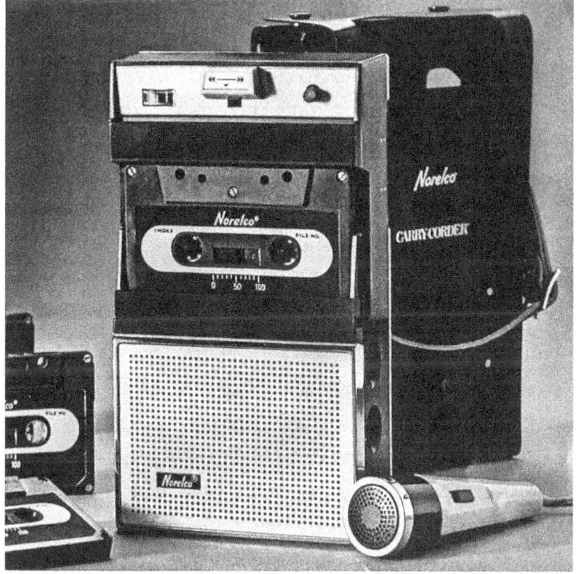

Figure 5.5. Norelco advertisement, *Tape Recording*, October 1965.

fanatic. Weeks before, Warhol had been sent a portable tape recorder by the Philips Recording Company and told that he could keep the machine as long as he did something to publicize it. He was immediately enthralled and began taking it everywhere, ultimately recording thousands of hours of encounters and conversations. As he would memorably describe it in his *Philosophy*:

> The acquisition of a tape recorder really finished whatever emotional life I might have had, but I was glad to see it go. Nothing was ever a problem again, because a problem meant a good tape, and when a problem transforms itself into a good tape it's not a problem anymore. An interesting problem was an interesting tape. You couldn't tell which problems were real, and which problems were exaggerated for the tape. Better yet, the people telling you problems couldn't decide any more if they were really having problems or if they were just performing.[12]

Warhol's first major endeavor upon obtaining his audiotape recorder was to instigate a book titled *a: a novel*, which would record a complete and unedited day in the life of his Factory "superstar" Ondine (Robert Olivo).[13] For the project, Warhol intended to accompany his subject over a twenty-four-hour period and record everything that transpired. Neither the idea of a "day in the life" novel nor the use of a tape recorder for journalistic reportage was in any way unconventional. The project's uniqueness lay in Warhol's unabashed literalism: his "day in the life" would actually chronicle every single second of a solitary day. His recordings were not notes out of which to cull and shape a compelling narrative, but rather the very material and form of the narrative itself. Furthermore, Warhol refused to manage the translation from audiotape to page, paying a pair of neighborhood girls to transcribe the continuous undulations of the audio signal without any understanding of its original context. The resulting "novel" lacked standard punctuation, confounded diegetic form, and often failed to distinguish individual subjects. It reads not as a series of discrete dialogic episodes, but as a swirling, ungrounded collage of voices—a largely indecipherable mass of language.

Taking its place in the history of modernist poetics, *a* gave textual form to the situational character of communication, offering a powerful object lesson in the problems of mediation within the documentary form. Developed under the aleatory practices of John Cage rather than the crafted expressionism of Stan Brakhage, Warhol's general conception of recording lay in harboring these very accidents of performance and production, allowing a space for the random, chance encounter to enter in. Works like *a* make a mockery of the documentary pretenses of the "reality" genres they foreshadowed. For while contemporary reality television is as heavily edited as any Hollywood drama, it is the very refusal to edit that allows *a* to capture the extraordinary heterogeneity of reality. A poignant example occurs near the beginning of the novel, when Ondine's amphetamine-driven tales of his sexual exploits are suddenly and inexplicably interrupted by the delivery of a strange new device to the Factory: a videotape recorder. Everyone is afraid to open the package until Paul Morrissey arrives and begins to explain how it works.

> Hello Paul
>
> PAUL—Hello. How are you?
>
> Fine, how are you? Are you excited about the new camera?
>
> P—Yeah, I wanna see it.
>
> You got, you gotta, you got, sit down here on the xx couch and tell me about it please.
>
> (P) The tape recorder, right? You set a aim at, the microphone at people. You aim the, the lens at the people.
>
> Oh.
>
> P—And the microphone.
>
> Oh.
>
> P—And the picture goes onto the tape and then you push the tape . . .
>
> Oh, do you hear this Lucky? Do you hear how this thing works?
>
> And you push the tape just like you play back your tape recorder and the

tape plays back through a television set.

Oh man, and you get a picture too.

(P) Yes, immediately.

Oh wow.

(P) So the sound . . .

This, its in films?

(P) Right. The sound . . . adequate or the lighting is not good . . .

You could fix it immediately.

(P) You stop it, you look at it and you say "Okay, let's do it again." Or "Let's continue with this light."

Is this a new product?

(P) Yeah. You remember Hamlet in Richard Burton Electronovision?

No, I never. I don't know anything about it.

(P) They had Richard Burton in "Hamlet" in the movie theatres.

Oh, og yeah, yeah.

(P) Electronovision, this is electronovision. You see they make it very cheaply but then they transfer the tape to movie film.

You got . . .

(P) To movie theatres.[14]

This brief scene offers us a privileged window into the initial reception of this technology and its curious intersection with the changing role and character of art institutions in its time. Warhol initially calls it a "camera," while Morrissey refers to it as a "tape recorder." Both its use and its relation to cinema are explained by invoking something called "Electronovision," which is assumed to be self-evident.

Short-lived and soon forgotten, Electronovision was an industrial process developed to enable the immediate and inexpensive recording of live performances on videotape for distribution to conventional cinemas. *Hamlet* (1964) was a "theatrofilm" made from the wildly successful Broadway run starring Richard Burton. For the recording, more than a dozen video cameras were placed around the stage at various angles, a single performance was captured live by constantly switching between them, and the resulting video was filmed directly from the television monitor to create the celluloid master. As one might expect, the result—a relatively washed-out black-and-white image with little visual detail and mediocre sound—proved distinctly underwhelming to audiences now conditioned to expect the glamour of Cinemascope, Technicolor, and stereophonic sound. These, after all, were the very advances the industry had developed

Figure 5.6. Advertisement for *Richard Burton's Hamlet* in Electronovision, a "Theatrofilm" exhibition that took place in over a thousand theaters on the weekend of September 23–24, 1964, before all prints were immediately destroyed.

to differentiate the cinematic experience and maintain its cultural relevance in the era of free and unlimited televisual content. Electronovision effectively combined the worst aspects of both worlds: its audiovisual quality was as poor as television's, yet it was neither free nor available in the comfort of one's own home.

Nevertheless, these formal qualities were understood to be secondary to the radical new model of exhibition and spectatorship the format proposed. For after the celluloid master was created from the video, a thousand celluloid copies were printed and shipped simultaneously to theaters across the country for a single two-night engagement. Although the film was shown in traditional cinema theaters, tickets were sold in advance for what was advertised as a unique theatrical event: four performances (screenings) would take place before all copies of the film were destroyed and the possibility of any future theatrical run or television screening deliberately foreclosed.[15] Paradoxically, the Theatrofilm process sought to maintain the aura and the exclusivity of Burton's Broadway performance while broadening its geographic reach.

Advertisements described the process as a deliberate conjunction of television, stage, and screen: "Theatrofilm's 'Hamlet' combines the dramatic excitement of the stage technique with the immediacy of television and big-screen effect of motion pictures."[16] This curious fusion of televisual, cinematic, and theatrical models of exhibition is symptomatic of the conflicted relationship between art and the moving image within the new televisual culture of the 1960s. In an era of free and ubiquitous television programming, cinema could no longer hold onto its claim as the most popular and democratic of the arts. Yet if the classical understanding of cinema—with its studio system of production and its opulent theatrical exhibition—was increasingly obsolete, no one was yet sure what might emerge in its place. Could the basic cinematic experience simply be enhanced, or would it have to be fundamentally transformed? Could the cinema compete with television for a mass viewership, or should it follow the lead of film's growing festival culture in catering to a more exclusive and specialized audience? Would changes primarily take place in the mode of production or in the structure of exhibition? Questions like these weighed on the industry and the public alike, and it was within this uncertain institutional climate that the artists of the 1960s first took up the technologies of film, and later, video.

Theatrofilm's ill-fated mixture of theatrical, cinematic, and televisual exhibition might seem little more than a historical curiosity—a transitional artifact from a period of cultural adjustment to new technologies. The process was largely a critical and commercial failure and would soon disappear. But the fundamental issues it raised about the fate of live performance in the televisual age have been surprisingly resilient. In fact, since 2007, the New York Metropolitan Opera has effectively resuscitated

TWO DAYS ONLY—SEPT. 23 & 24—AND NEVER AGAIN! AN UNPRECEDENTED ENTERTAINMENT EVENT!*

An ELECTRONOVISION Production ALEXANDER H. COHEN Presents

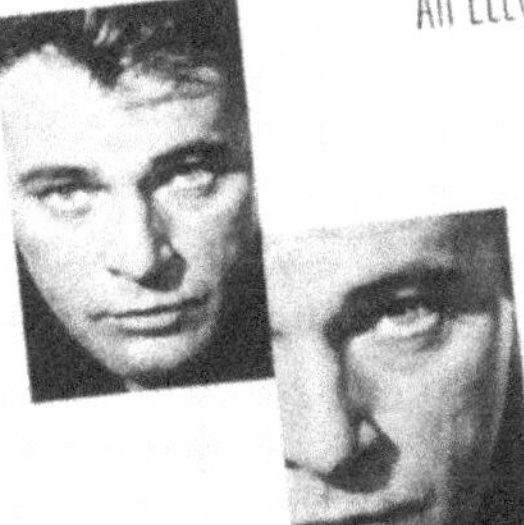

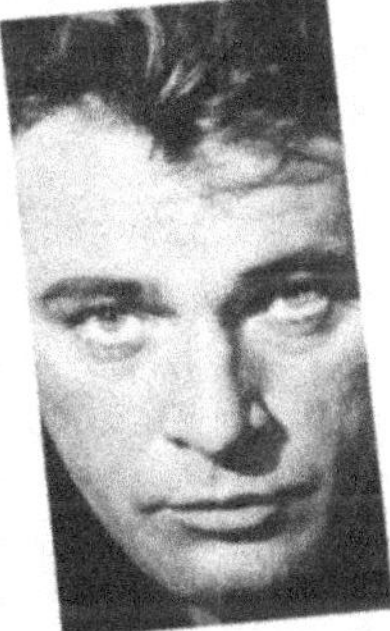

RICHARD BURTON

in JOHN GIELGUD'S Production of

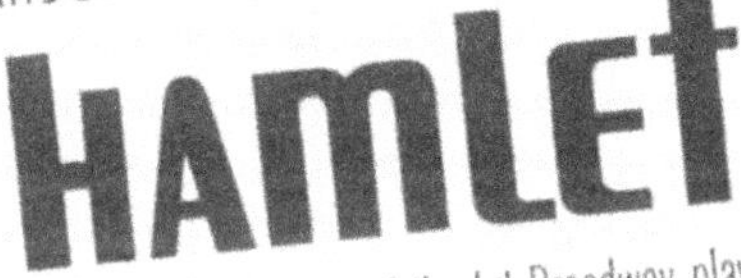

with the all star cast of the hit Broadway play!

TYPICAL CHEERS FOR THE PLAY: "...An astonishing triumph...the audience is not likely ever to see a better Hamlet than Burton's... Overwhelming, a revelation of what Shakespeare can be like..." —Newsweek "...The production... takes fire from Burton's own brilliance..."—Life "...A performance of electrical power and sweeping virility..."—N. Y. Times "...A notable theatre event."—N.Y. Post

An actual Broadway Performance brought simultaneously to 1000 theatres coast-to-coast through the miracle of ELECTRONOVISION.

* Tickets are on sale at a theatre near you for the two matinee and two evening performances. There will be no further showings of Richard Burton's Hamlet.

Directed by BILL COLLERAN · Produced by WILLIAM SARGENT, JR. and ALFRED W. CROWN
Executive Producer ALEXANDER H. COHEN · A THEATROFILM · Distributed by WARNER BROS. WB

Figure 5.7. Andy Warhol, *$199 Television*, 1961, Whitney Museum of American Art, New York.

the Theatrofilm model under its more contemporary-sounding "Live in HD" moniker, broadcasting live theatrical performances to over 850 movie theaters in 30 countries, and these broadcasts have emerged as a key source of much-needed revenue. But the very streaming technology that makes this new Theatrofilm possible has already threatened to replace these theater-based events with "on-demand" broadcasts to the individual home subscriber.

In the transcript from Warhol's *a,* Paul Morrissey does not seem particularly interested in these social and cultural dimensions of the Theatrofilm model of distribution. Rather, he sees video technology as a means to replicate the traditional cinematic production with greater efficiency. Most important, as he sees it, is video's ability to foreclose all manner of interruption and accident. As he says, "You stop it, you look at it and you say 'Okay, let's do it again.'" Ironically, this was precisely the model of industrial production that both Warhol *and* the Theatrofilm were seeking to overthrow. Both were committed to the particular character of performance prompted by the uncompromising record of an unedited single take. But there the similarity would end, for the master of the serigraphed soup can was certainly not interested in simulating an aura of singularity, uniqueness, and authenticity through the deliberate attenuation of copies. Rather, the video recorder provided Warhol with a new means to explore the social and psychological dynamics of feedback—an inquiry in which he had been engaged since the creation of the Factory through his nearly ubiquitous practice of recording.

To his arsenal of recording technologies, the videotape recorder added more than a new formal aesthetic—it brought with it a profound association with television and televisual culture, which had been nothing less than a lifelong obsession for the artist. Even if he did not have the ability to engage in broadcasting, much less the *live* broadcasting still in its cultural infancy, the videotape recorder allowed Warhol to take up the idea—ambivalently a fantasy and a nightmare—of seeing, and being forced to respond to seeing, one's own image on TV.

Yet precisely because of its technological novelty, it is crucial to distinguish what was truly new and innovative about Warhol's use of video technology. While the introduction of the Sony Portapak in 1967 is rightly considered a seminal moment for artists' engagement with the moving image, myth and legend have tended to inflate the relative significance of its early uses. While video technology's real-time feedback loop would be a subject of great aesthetic and philosophical inquiry in the early 1970s, the formal dynamics of this technology would have been well known to anyone in the New York area since 1964.

For as we have seen, the New York World's Fair had opened that summer to countless millions, and at the very entrance to the fairgrounds—given deliberate pride of place—stood the pavilion of the electronics

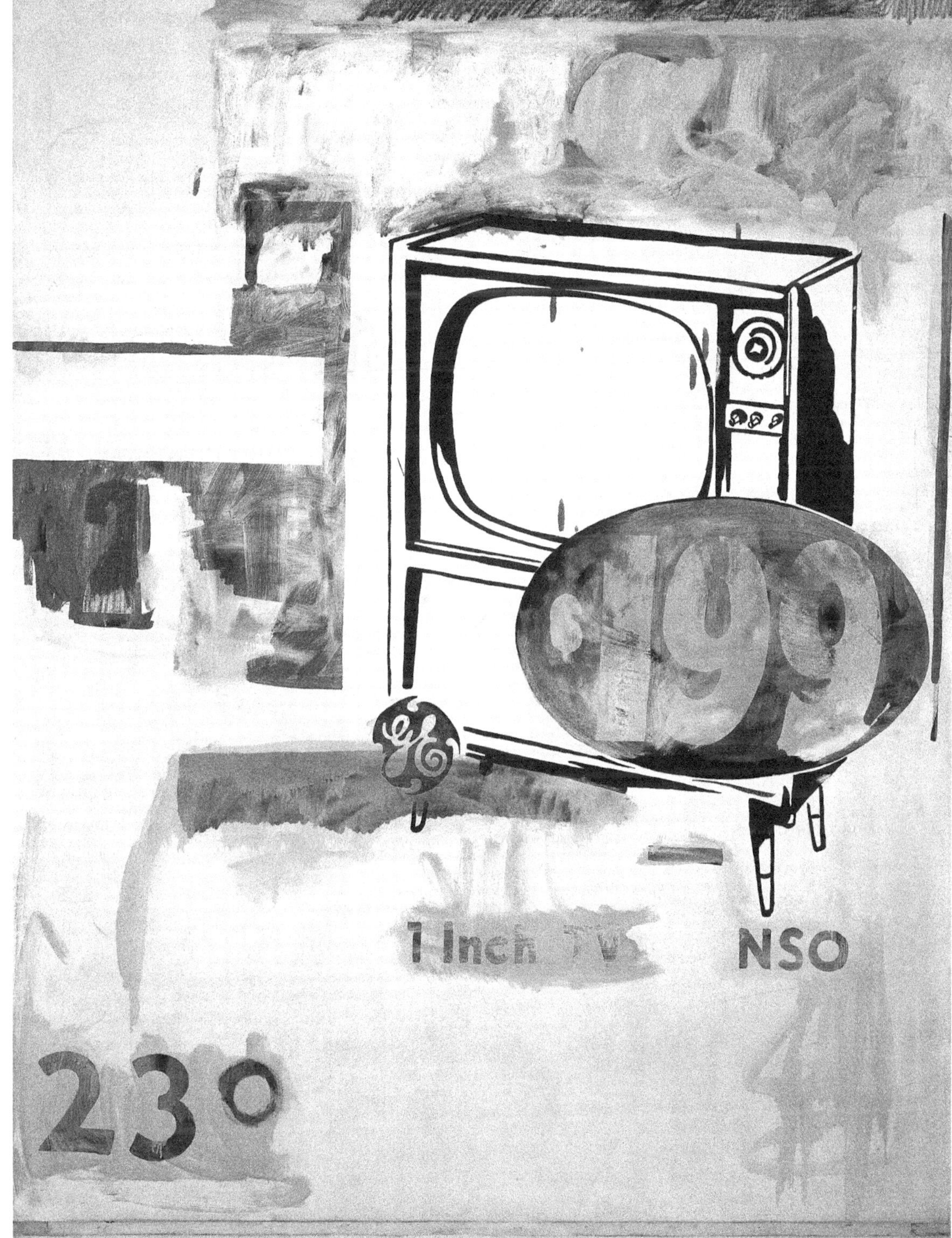
199
1 Inch TV
NSO
230

Figure 5.8. *See Yourself!* exhibit at the RCA Pavilion, 1964–1965 New York World's Fair. © *New York Daily News* Archive / Getty Images.

Figures 5.9. Young man photographing himself appearing live in color (top), in tape delay in black and white (center), and in tape delay in color (bottom), at the *See Yourself!* exhibit at the RCA Pavilion, 1964–1965 New York World's Fair.

corporation RCA. The company had been granted this location in honor of its history with the fair, for it had been on these same grounds that RCA had first introduced the futuristic new technology of television to the public in 1939. The intervening years had promoted television from a curious but marginal technological innovation to perhaps the predominant cultural force within postwar American life. For the '64 World's Fair, RCA's technological innovations were decidedly less spectacular—it showcased the wonders of its new color televisions and predicted that soon everyone would have one of their own. But this technological innovation was less important than the company's attempt to foreground a wider-ranging cultural dynamic that television could be said to have introduced: the idea of universal celebrity.

Within the RCA Pavilion's *See Yourself!* exhibit, visitors would enter a curved central area and step onto a turntable that slowly wound them past several gigantic video cameras weighing hundreds of pounds. Encountering their first television set, they would there see themselves live and in color as a camera directed at them played back their image in a real-time closed-circuit loop. Next, they would then encounter a second television on which they would see themselves in black and white as they were just

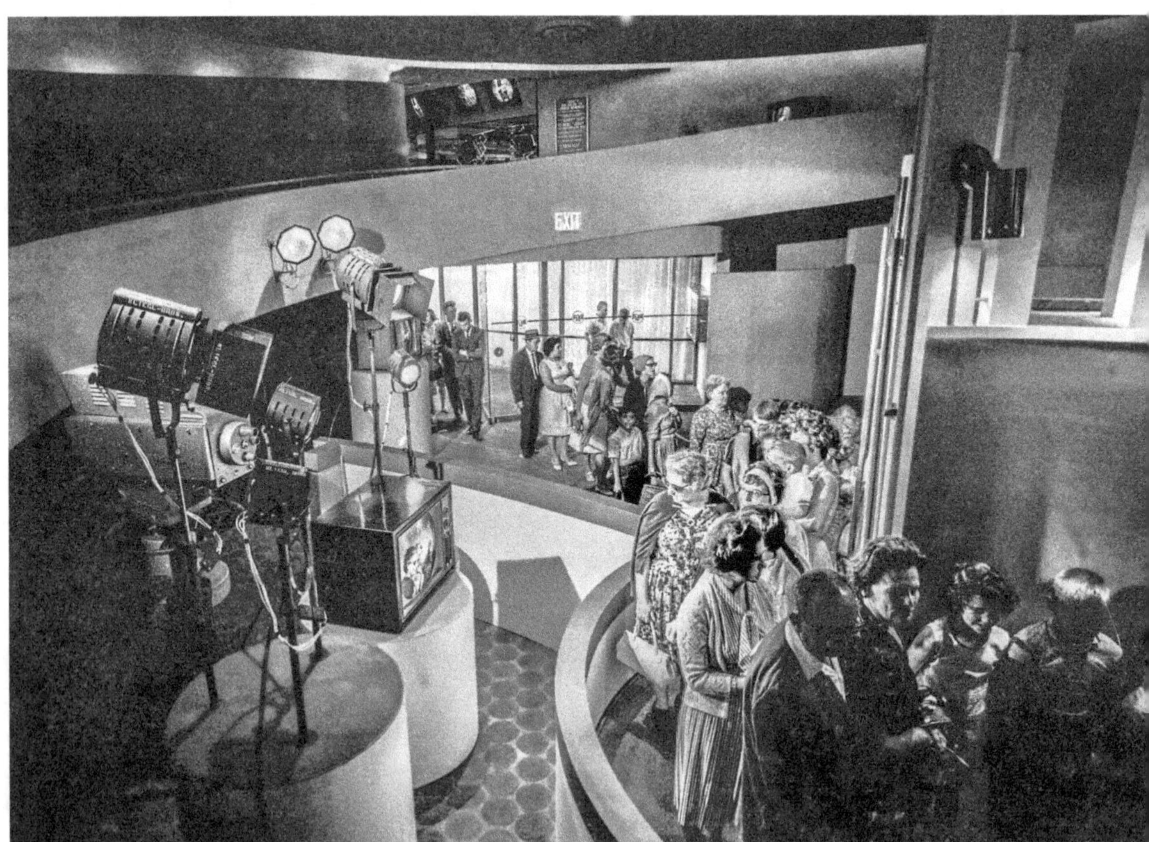

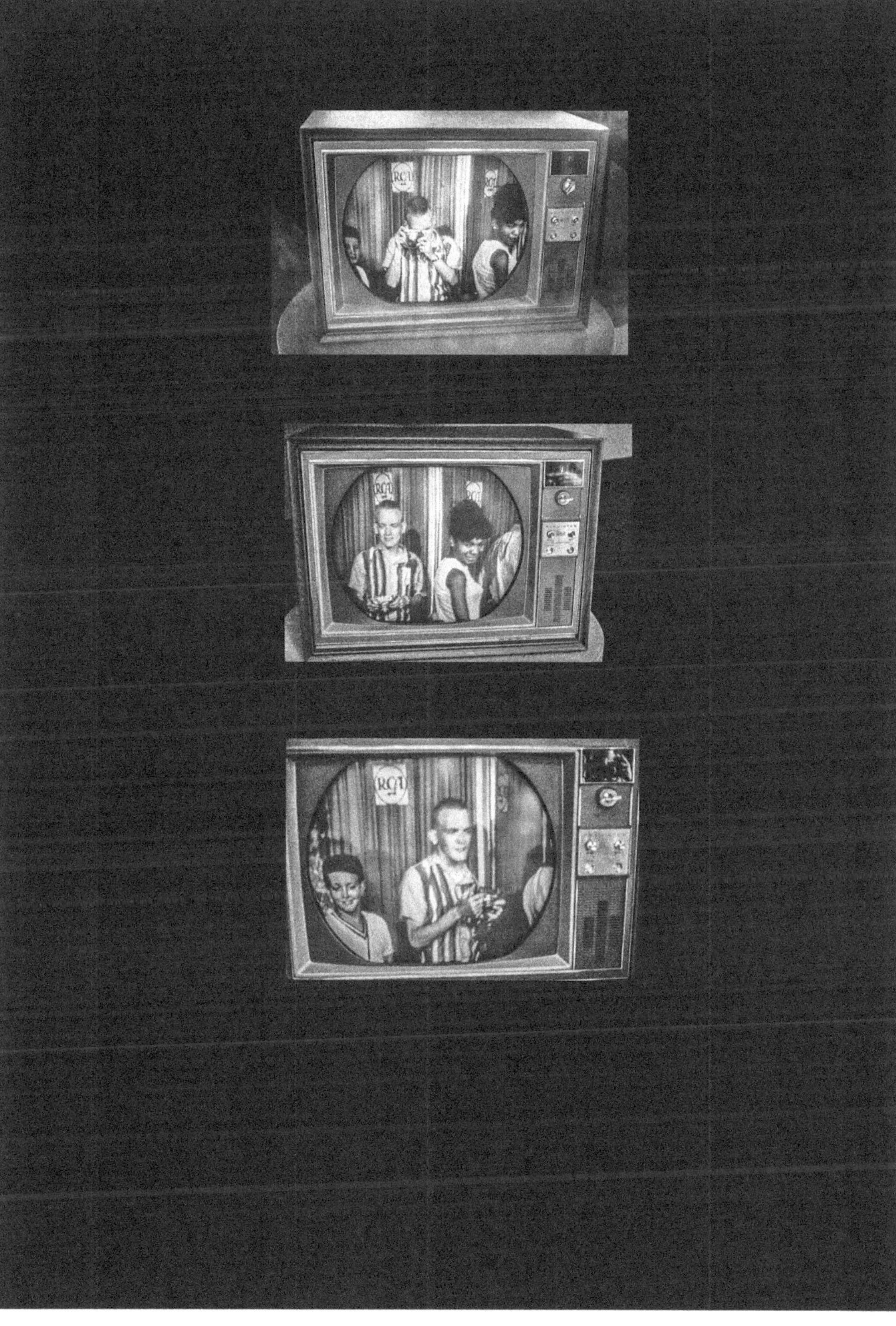

moments before, as a second camera, having captured them unawares, now presented them with that image through a tape-delay mechanism. Finally, they encountered a third television monitor that again showed them caught unawares through a second delayed video image in color.

The *See Yourself!* exhibit concluded at a glass-walled production center linked via closed circuit to two hundred fifty television monitors located around the fairgrounds. Throughout the six months of the fair, mobile crews were constantly interviewing fairgoers and shooting "news" programs about their experiences with the various exhibits. Lost children also became part of the exhibit when they were brought by the fair's security to the RCA studio, where they were televised and broadcast to tens of thousands of visitors in the hope of locating their parents. Since viewers at the RCA exhibit could literally watch these episodes being produced, the company had in effect created another gigantic feedback loop. The public no longer simply came to the fair to view the exhibits, but was itself made part of a show about the fair and the exhibits that was, in turn, exhibited to them as another part of the fair. Advertisements for the exhibit went so far as to claim that, given the great number of exhibits at the fair and the long lines at each exhibit, spectators would do well simply to watch the exhibits on TV rather than trying to see everything in person!

RCA's corporate video installation would demonstrate the purely formal dynamics of video feedback and tape delay to more people over the course of its six months than video artists the world over would manage within the next six years. But to say this is simply to register the changing criteria for advanced art within this period. Dissatisfied with the purely formal investigations of high modernism, artists turning to film, video, and performance in this period were increasingly exploring the wider social and cultural implications of these forms.

Outer and Inner Space may very well have germinated from Warhol's experience at the 1964 New York World's Fair. We know that Warhol attended the fair, since he specifically describes his excitement over Ford's "Magic Skyway" ride in a period interview.[17] It is impossible to imagine Warhol, given his fascination with television, missing a pavilion at the entrance to the fairgrounds from the company that had first introduced the technology of television twenty-five years before—especially one that lured its viewers with the quintessentially Warholian tagline "See Yourself on TV!"

The importance of the RCA Pavilion lay not simply in its demonstration of the peculiar phenomenological experience of seeing one's image both live and on tape delay, but also in its intuition of a more general economy of media feedback; it would exhibit the live production of television programs about the fairgoers' experiences, which were themselves exhibited throughout the duration of the fair to the fair's visitors.

Unintentionally, RCA had created a prescient vision of televisual society caught in a feedback loop of surveillance, voyeurism, and exhibitionism. Within *Outer and Inner Space* (1965), Warhol would explore this emergent dynamic of the media feedback loop, focusing in on the specific forms of subjective dislocation it had begun to entail.[18]

The work had begun as but another of Warhol's *Screen Tests*—three-minute-long films Warhol had shot of hundreds of visitors to the Factory since 1964—and had originally borne the simple title *Edie*.[19] Edie Sedgwick was Warhol's complex fascination throughout 1965. Warhol's constant companion and sartorial mimic, she was the "it girl" of the moment, the "Femme Fatale" Lou Reed sang about—at Warhol's request—on the Velvet Underground's debut album.[20] If Ondine had been subject to ubiquitous audio recording, Edie was perpetually situated in front of the camera. To complement his twenty-four-hour-long audiotape of Ondine, he had undertaken a twenty-four-hour-long film of Edie. While the film was never completed, enough material was generated to produce half a dozen lengthy character studies, from *Beauty #2* and *Poor Little Rich Girl* to *Face*, *Restaurant*, and *Afternoon*, among others. Edie was an ideal subject for Warhol in that she deposed herself—seemingly effortlessly and automatically—into a blank screen for projection. "She had a poignantly vacant, vulnerable quality that made her a reflection of everybody's private fantasies," Warhol wrote, "she could be anything you wanted her to be—a little girl, a woman, intelligent, dumb, rich, poor—anything. She was a wonderful, beautiful blank."[21]

By means of a novel technology, the videotape recorder, and a novel technique, the split-screen projection, *Outer and Inner Space* incorporated an unprecedented degree of aesthetic complexity while retaining the artist's trademark formal austerity. Using the video recorder, Warhol recorded two thirty-minute tapes of Edie unselfconsciously seeking to en-

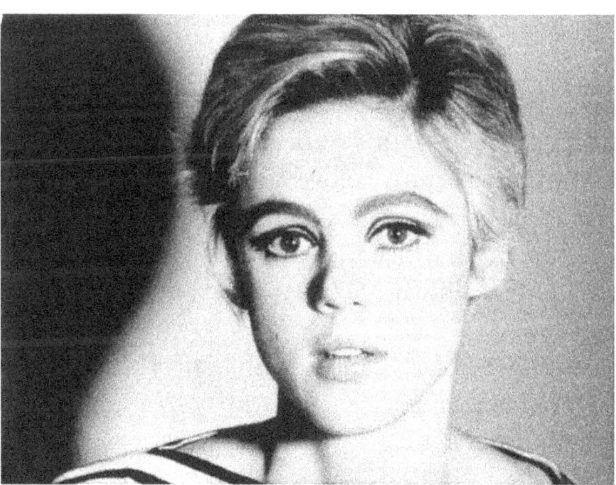

Figure 5.10. Andy Warhol, *Screen Test: Edie Sedgwick (ST 308)*, 1965. Film still © 2012 The Andy Warhol Museum, Pittsburgh, PA, a museum of Carnegie Institute. All rights reserved.

gage with a variety of weighty themes. For the duration of both tapes, she appears in close-up and in profile, the bright, high-contrast image of her face almost completely filling up the frame. What remains is completely black. Her face does not appear in space so much as seem cut out from it—without depth, the image is as flat as a screen print. Throughout the hour of video recordings, her face barely moves, and she never faces the camera. Rather, she gazes off to screen right—toward the empty black expanse at the edge of the frame. Warhol then played back this video on a television set as he filmed Edie, who was situated between the television and his film camera, where she seems to settle into the dark area beside her prerecorded video image. While the video is persistently fixed on a close-up of Edie in profile, the film presents her in a dimensional three-quarter view facing the camera. Due to this imbalance, at many moments, the video Edie seems to be speaking directly into her ear. Throughout the course of the film, this metaphor will become actualized—the video recording becoming the voice in the back of her head she struggles not to hear.

For the spectator, the film and video images are conjoined in a complex alternation of flatness and depth. Film has a tendency to flatten objects, and given the long lens Warhol here employs, we would expect this effect to be exaggerated. Yet the opposite is the case. The lighting under which Edie is placed, her three-quarter pose, and the unusually distant camera position conspire to grant her filmic image a sense of fullness and depth when compared with the exaggerated flatness of the video image, its cutout profile floating in an empty black void. Psychological depth cues also undergo a subtle manipulation. For identical objects, a change in size is often read as a change in distance. Since the "live" Edie's face is slightly smaller than her image on the video monitor, we might unconsciously want to read the video image as closer, but we know this is not the case: the television monitor is quite evidently situated behind the live figure, and thus farther away. Combined with the differences in resolution—the video image almost completely burned out, the film image full of nuanced detail—these depth cues present us with a kind of figure/ground relationship that initially highlights the vast formal difference between the two images. It is precisely this stark initial distinction that will allow us to perceive the film's narrative movement, a movement that occurs unconsciously, on a formal level, quite independently of the stories Edie will relate. It is a movement in which the two Edies—film and video, past and present—slowly but steadily move toward a relationship of convergence or accommodation.

The reels of Warhol's film camera were thirty-three minutes long, while those of his video camera were only thirty. While he could have easily edited them to sync, Warhol intentionally left them disjointed such that each film reel momentarily begins and concludes in the absence of its video counterpart. These brief interludes are crucial in revealing Edie's relationship to her prerecorded video image. As the sole protagonist of a sixty-six-minute film, required to keep up a steady monologue without the benefit of interruptions or retakes, one might reasonably expect her to be unnerved by the camera she is facing. Yet Edie, having been the subject of a half a dozen similar films over the preceding few months, begins the film like a confident professional: animated and relaxed, fully comfortable with the camera's attentive gaze. It is only with the onset of the video image that she suddenly shrieks in palpable horror and disgust. Quickly turning back to face the camera, she regains her composure and plays down her initial reaction, attempting to shrug off the strange mirror speaking beside her.

The sound of the video is barely discernible . . . to the spectator. It was not the best initial recording, but rather than editing it separately to ensure appropriately matched sound levels, Warhol simply rerecorded the distant television's playback on his film camera's already low-fidelity optical soundtrack. The resulting audio is indistinct, muddied, and muffled—emerging only in fits and starts. But it becomes obvious that our spectatorial experience is quite different from Edie's: she seems to hear her prerecorded voice loud and clear. In fact, since the video image is more or less behind her, she experiences her double more often as sound than as image. Her reactions to it are not so much reactions to the image we can see as they are to a voice we cannot hear. As such, the splitting of Edie across film and video is not only a split between present and past,

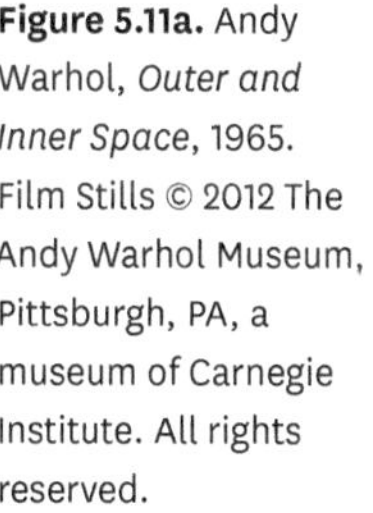

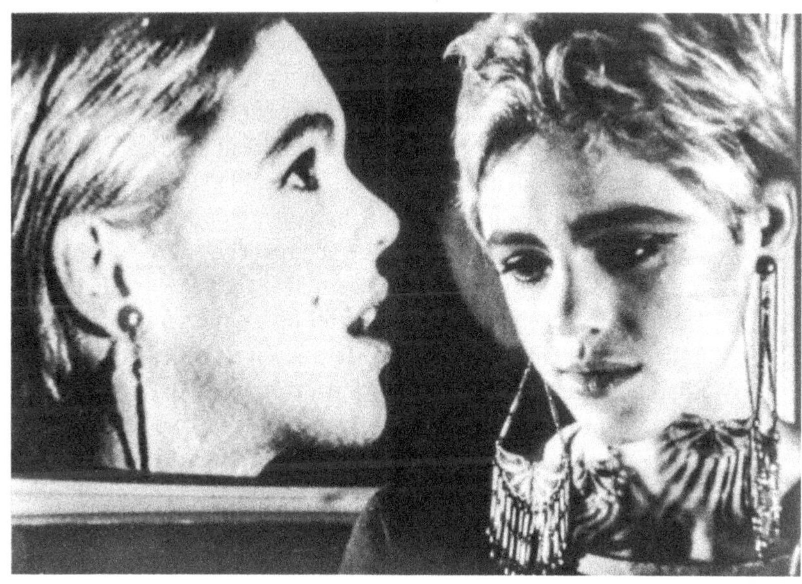

Figure 5.11a. Andy Warhol, *Outer and Inner Space*, 1965. Film Stills © 2012 The Andy Warhol Museum, Pittsburgh, PA, a museum of Carnegie Institute. All rights reserved.

but also a split between public and private—between the "outer space" of the public image and the "inner space" of the private monologue.

What can be heard of Edie's speech on the video monitor is vague and rambling—its tone steady and uniform, sedate and unselfconscious. In contrast, the "live" Edie before the camera is both hyperactive and hyper-self-conscious—conscious both of her own self-presentation before the camera and of this second, video self that has suddenly appeared and started to speak outside her conscious control. As the recorded image continues to speak unselfconsciously in the past, the live Edie becomes ever more desperate to divert attention from it, to reclaim her image in the present. About half the time, she's smiling and giggling, drawing attention to herself with exaggerated facial expressions and gestures. The rest of the time, she seems unable to cope with the competition from the video double, increasingly outraged at having to share the screen with that... *thing*: "I can't stand it—really, I can't stand it!" She is completely in control of herself in the present, but her prerecorded image—the one she can no longer control—begins to unnerve her: "How can I think about anything else when I have to listen to that nonsense?!" She continues to laugh and joke, yet despite her best efforts, she cannot keep from returning to this uncanny double—becoming amused, annoyed, angered, and finally saddened by this disjunction between her embodied self and its exteriorization. "Why should I listen to it?" she implores, while referring to herself in the third person, "I *hate* it!" As she is placed in the impossible position of being both speaker and listener, her self quite literally becomes an other, as in those anxiety-ridden moments when we become too aware of our own speech-as-performance and become paralyzed by this excess of self-consciousness. Even if she chooses to be silent, her recorded self will continue to speak for her.

"I'm out of my mind ... It's terrible ... horrid voice whisper in my ear," Edie exclaims. "I get absolutely abstracted. I get—I could just—I find the voice very disturbing!"[22] In his philosophical study of the voice, Mladen Dolar has argued that the Western metaphysical tradition was able to disavow this radical alterity of the voice, this trace of the Other within ourselves, only by privileging the voice as the source of an originary self-presence. Following Freud, he postulates that the divide between "inner and outer space"—the model of all other metaphysical divides—originally derives from the inner voice of consciousness and the narcissistic illusion of self-presence we acquire through a deliberate *mis*hearing of the otherness of our own voice: "The auto-affective voice of self-presence and self-mastery was constantly opposed by its reverse side, the intractable voice of the other, the voice one could not control."[23] Following this scenario, Dolar situates the voice as the *ur*-form of self-recognition. Just as the gaze haunts the field of vision from a place exterior to it, the voice functions as its aural analogue. Narcissus and Echo thus emerge as the two fundamental objects of psychoanalysis insofar as they represent the two forms of self-estrangement constitutive of subjectification.[24]

This self-estrangement forms the dramatic kernel of *Outer and Inner Space*. Edie treats her image like a dummy or a doll—a specter or hollow shell. Yet that very apparition is what threatens to overwhelm the flesh-and-blood Edie and unsubstantiate her in the here and now. For as the second reel begins, Edie appears noticeably worn down. The game has lost its charm and has become an ordeal to be completed. Most surprisingly, she no longer seems either concerned about or attentive to the video image that previously so disturbed her. Her own manner becomes less and less animated, her speech more and more akin to the droning monologue of the videotape. By the end of the second reel, the film and video images, while still formally discernible, have taken on a peculiar emotional equivalence. It is as if the "live" Edie has come to mimic, with neither overt intention nor desire, her prerecorded image.

Structurally, the film proceeds according to an almost classical A-B-A narrative form: we begin with a formal arrangement that then changes before ultimately returning to the way it began. At the beginning of the first reel, Edie and her video image are both presented in close-up, and the formal and psychological disparity between the two images is especially marked. Halfway through the first reel, the camera pulls back to bring Edie's whole torso into view. While Edie's video image and her "live" image have become less differentiated formally, the latter's animation and speech continue to differentiate the images psychologically. By the time we reach the second reel, this psychological differentiation has also become muddied—the real Edie has lost her former energy and spirit and has begun to adopt the endless monologue of her video image. For the first third of the second reel, the two images seem to reach their utmost similarity, both formally and psychologically. After this, the camera zooms in again to return to a close-up of the video image and the live Edie's face, side by side. Now, as in the opening moments of the film, their formal differences have again become pronounced. Yet, the formal similarity that has returned only serves to highlight the dramatic psychological change that has come over the live Edie—how undifferentiated from the video image her demeanor and performance have become.

So far, I have described the film as it was recorded in August of 1965. It is unclear whether or how often Warhol showed it in this form at the Factory that fall. When the work was first publicly exhibited at the Film-Makers' Cinematheque five months later, Warhol made a final, crucial transformation: the two reels were projected simultaneously, side by side. The resulting work was entirely transformed in that it not only documents but in effect re-creates this experience of temporal splitting for

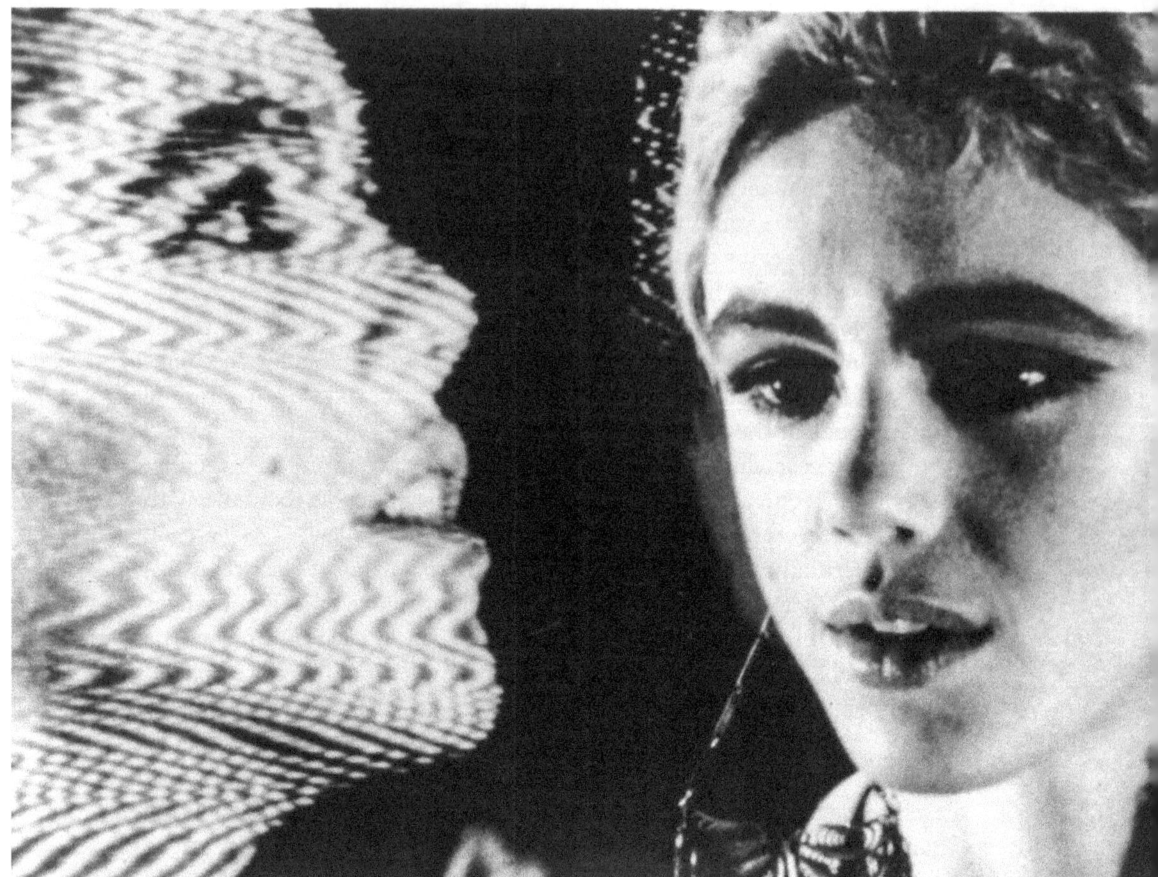

Figure 5.11b. Andy Warhol, *Outer and Inner Space*, 1965. Film Stills © 2012 The Andy Warhol Museum, Pittsburgh, PA, a museum of Carnegie Institute.

the theatrical spectator. Even more than before, Edie appears snared in a confrontation with the past as it forces its way into the present—trapped between the image she projects in the present and the video image from the past that both literally and metaphorically lies behind her. The film's double projection re-creates something of this temporal chiasm for the theatrical spectator, our perceptual situation unfolding as almost the mirror image of Edie's. Rather than being forced to confront an uncomfortable past from which we have been delivered, we view Edie's present confrontation with that past with knowledge of her future. We view the egoic shell she confidently projects the distance she establishes between herself and that *other* image from a future in which that shell has been broken, and that distance shot through.

The double-screen presentation preserves Warhol's reductive formal aesthetic while provoking an unprecedented degree of spectatorial activity. Our eyes immediately turn to the left screen, as that is where the visual action is taking place. The two large images of Edie's face—film and

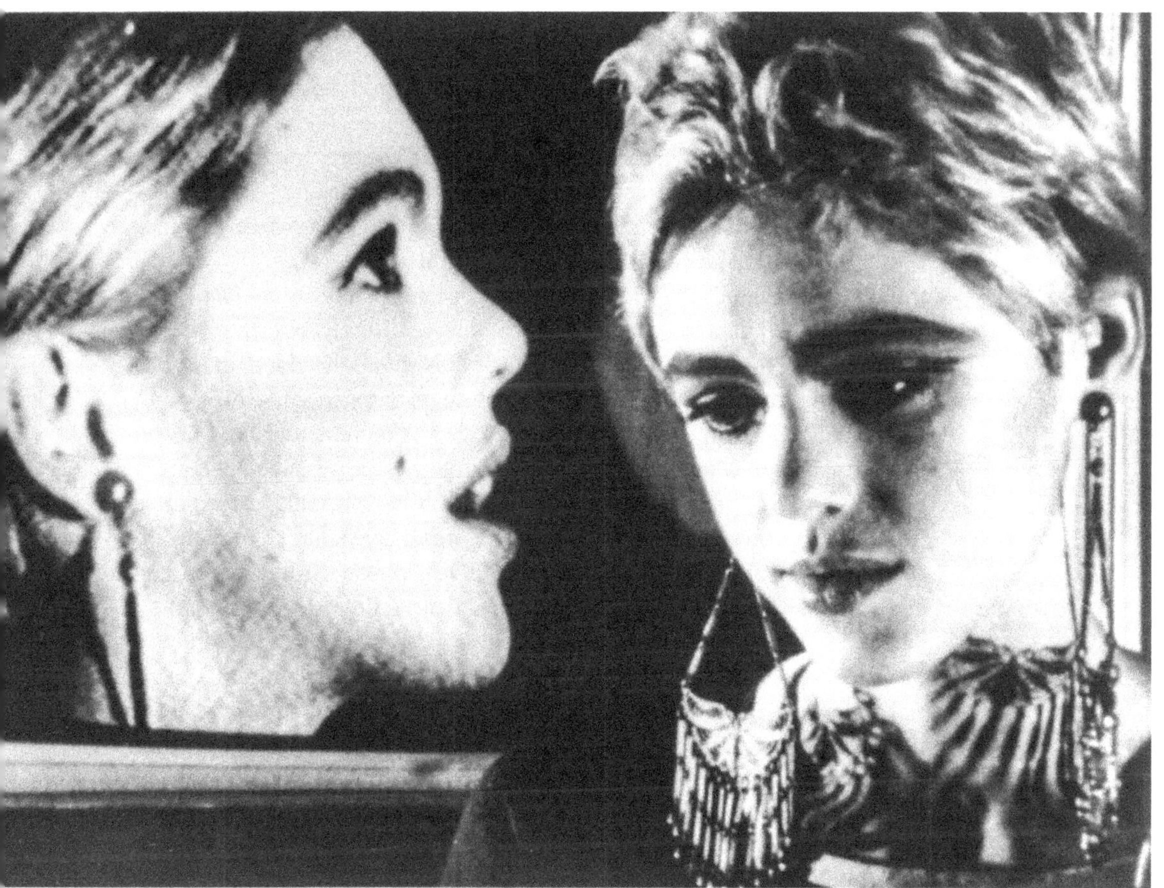

video—dominate the screen. The "live" Edie is animated and expressive. But just as we are trying to make sense of it, we hear the first distinct sound from the right reel, and our eye unconsciously follows. Here the scene is the same, but different. Still two Edies, a "live" and a video image, but they are smaller, farther from the camera. They are at a spatial remove, but we quickly come to understand that this distance is not merely spatial but also temporal. Accustomed to reading from left to right, we might automatically intuit a progression from present to future, but even if not, we are given many immediate clues. The video image, for instance, is already present on the right, but only just appears—to an excited and quite obviously initial response—on the left. Furthermore, in one of the first phrases we can distinctly make out—on the right—Edie tells us, "I can't remember what I *did* say . . ." her voice trailing off in an insubstantial attempt at recollection. These temporal signifiers mark what has by now already become apparent: that we are dealing with a "before and after" sequence. Not a singular moment, but two discrete blocks of time presented in juxtaposition, together evidencing a temporal ordeal that has clearly taken a psychological toll.

And this experience is not something merely given us to view, but something instantiated in the spectator's experience. Like Edie, the spectator is split within time: the present as past and the present as future. We are also split between perceptual registers—the visible and the audible—just as Edie is split between her own self-image and the voice at the back of her head that she cannot manage to dismiss. The two are, of course, importantly related. The video image is, for Edie, primarily *audible*. Since it is behind her, she rarely perceives the image directly, but its insistent monologue forces its way into her ear. For Edie, then, the video image has the qualities of an *echo*—it is primarily audible, but also something of an unwanted reflection. Edie herself—the "live" Edie, here and now in the present—this is what she desperately wants her inquisitive spectators to focus on. But her past keeps impinging on her present performance, undermining the stable identity that performance wishes to instantiate.

Despite the animated theatrics of the "live" Edie on the left screen, the spectator is inevitably drawn back toward the Edie of the right screen, where a subtle but perceptible change has already occurred. And if the distance we sensed on the right screen was originally understood in spatial and then in chronological terms, we are finally given to understand it in psychological terms. Here, after an extended period of confrontation with that other image, that other voice, her defenses have been lowered, her animated performance slowed to a crawl. From outright dismissal or anger, a complex psychological interplay has developed between the "two" Edies, between the Edie of the past and the Edie of the present. Her speech, like that of the video image, has come to assume the character of a monologue. "Pinned by the camera against a wall of time," she begins to free-associate, as if submitting to the psychoanalytic scenario. In so doing, she seems to lose her grip on the present moment and enter the time of the video image.[25]

As she does so, the metaphor of exchange, of crossing over, begins to emerge by way of the film's formal structure. A third of the way into the film, a slow zoom literally transforms the distanced image on the right screen into an uneasy reflection of the left. They are similar, but not identical: in this, the formal register mirrors that of the temporal and psychological. The two images—those of the left and right screens—take on a formal similarity, but only now that we have fully understood them in their temporal and psychological disjunction. After a few brief minutes, the image on the left screen pulls back to reveal the tableau that began the film on the right, completing the "chiasmatic" movement.

For the spectator, this gives rise to a schizoid experience of time. If we were to dissect the film formally, the structure appears quite simple:

a close-up pulls back to an establishing shot, then zooms again to a close-up. Yet our perceptual experience of the film is much more complex. Because the second reel was begun halfway through the establishing shot, and both reels are running simultaneously, we view the same shot later in the past of the left reel that we have already seen earlier in the future of the right. As the left screen zooms out toward the establishing shot that will begin the second reel—which we have already seen—we feel that we are catching up to the future, though it is a future that has already passed. And when we look at the right screen, we see the close-up of Edie that seems so similar to that shot on the left with which we began—but this formal similarity only underscores our knowledge that the two scenes are nothing alike.

A symphony of temporal exchange, this perpetual imbrication is as exhausting as it is exhilarating. Edie struggles to keep the viewer focused on a present that she can control and away from a past that she cannot. Warhol prevents the spectator from occupying any simple present. We are constantly being reminded of a present just past or a present yet to come. The split Edie experiences between her inner self and its exteriorization is thereby replicated in the spectator's own experience. The inner space of the film and the outer space of the theater converge in a present endlessly trapped between anticipation and recollection. The essential duality of Edie's role in *Outer and Inner Space*—her ambivalent position as both spectator and subject of the drama—exemplifies the more general situation Warhol created within the Factory.

The idea that broadcast television precipitated a widespread challenge not simply to our understanding of proximity and distance, but to our very conception of temporality was one that would draw many artists to the use of video feedback in the coming years. In the shrinking televisual world, as scenes of John F. Kennedy's assassination, of confrontations over civil rights, and of the escalating war in Vietnam took place inside one's home, the effects of these violent intrusions were being felt in new and unpredictable ways. As the ubiquitous televisual image brought that which was spatially distant into a precarious proximity, psychological borders became less distinct, more permeable. The inner space of the psyche and the outer space of the world seemed increasingly, frighteningly interwoven. One's relation to others—even one's basic sense of self—seemed newly in flux. Implicitly responding to this emerging culture of televisual feedback, *Outer and Inner Space* emblematized Warhol's Factory as itself a kind of feedback loop wherein subject, work, and environment were effectively collapsed, and it spoke to the ambivalent social and cultural ramifications of such a collapse.

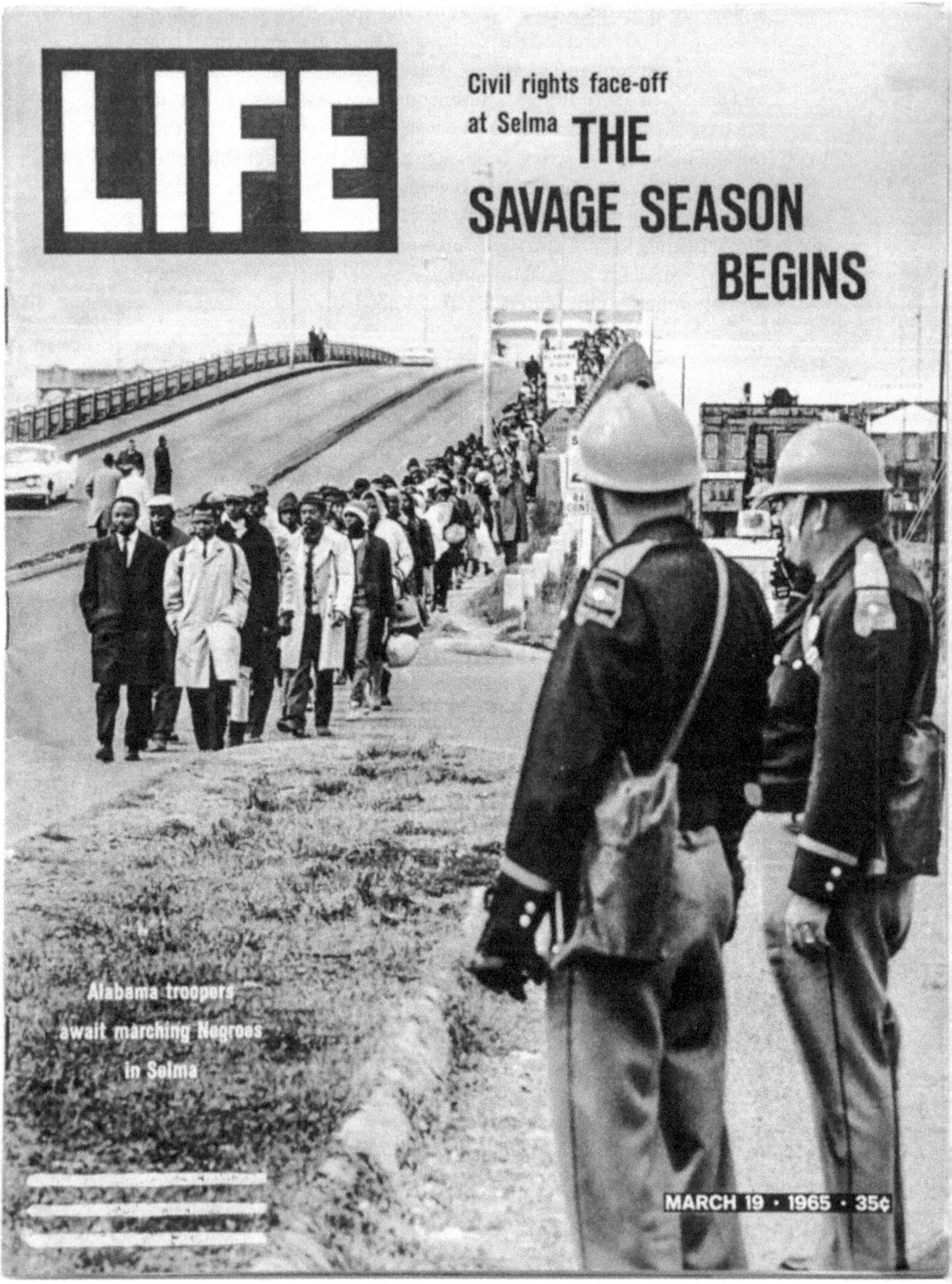

LIFE

Civil rights face-off at Selma

THE SAVAGE SEASON BEGINS

Alabama troopers await marching Negroes in Selma

MARCH 19 · 1965 · 35¢

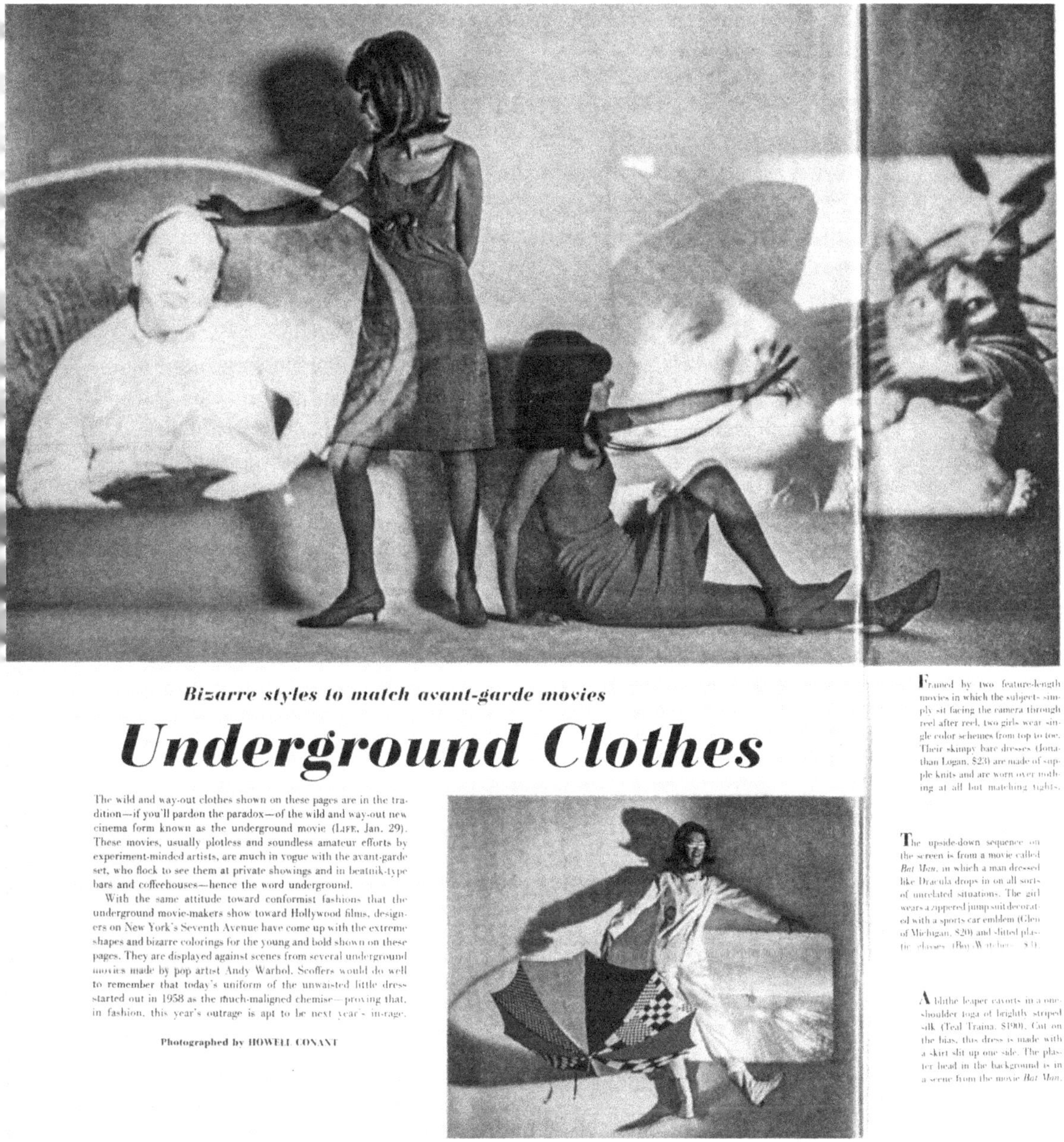

Bizarre styles to match avant-garde movies

Underground Clothes

The wild and way-out clothes shown on these pages are in the tradition—if you'll pardon the paradox—of the wild and way-out new cinema form known as the underground movie (LIFE, Jan. 29). These movies, usually plotless and soundless amateur efforts by experiment-minded artists, are much in vogue with the avant-garde set, who flock to see them at private showings and in beatnik-type bars and coffeehouses—hence the word underground.

With the same attitude toward conformist fashions that the underground movie-makers show toward Hollywood films, designers on New York's Seventh Avenue have come up with the extreme shapes and bizarre colorings for the young and bold shown on these pages. They are displayed against scenes from several underground movies made by pop artist Andy Warhol. Scoffers would do well to remember that today's uniform of the unwaisted little dress started out in 1958 as the much-maligned chemise—proving that, in fashion, this year's outrage is apt to be next year's in-rage.

Photographed by HOWELL CONANT

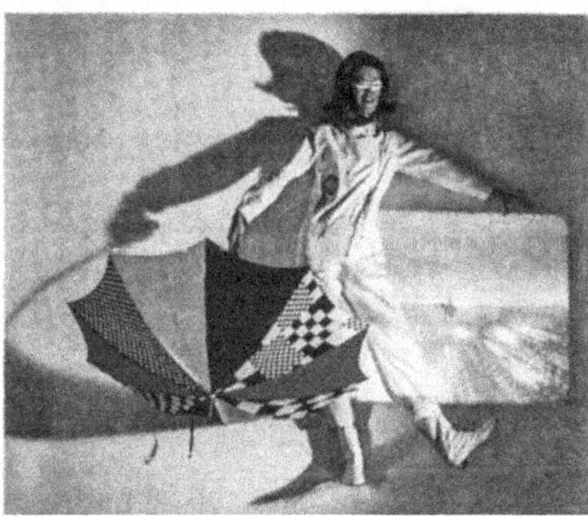

Framed by two feature-length movies in which the subjects simply sit facing the camera through reel after reel, two girls wear single color schemes from top to toe. Their skimpy bare dresses (Jonathan Logan, $23) are made of supple knits and are worn over nothing at all but matching tights.

The upside-down sequence on the screen is from a movie called *Bat Man*, in which a man dressed like Dracula drops in on all sorts of unrelated situations. The girl wears a zippered jump suit decorated with a sports car emblem (Glen of Michigan, $20) and slitted plastic glasses (Boy-Watchers, [illegible]).

A blithe leaper cavorts in a one-shoulder toga of brightly striped silk (Teal Traina, $190). Cut on the bias, this dress is made with a skirt slit up one side. The plaster head in the background is in a scene from the movie *Bat Man*.

Figure 5.12. Cover of *Life*, March 19, 1965.

Figure 5.13. "Underground Clothes: Bizarre Styles to Match Avant-Garde Movies," from *Life*, March 19, 1965.

The Past inside the Present: *Selma Last Year* (1966) at Lincoln Center

"The Savage Season Begins: Civil Rights Face-Off at Selma," declares the cover of *Life* magazine's March 19, 1965 issue. Inside, the cover story juxtaposes a photo of Martin Luther King Jr. with one of a young African-American marcher whose skull has just been cracked open by a baseball bat. Dramatic images of brutal police repression of a civil rights march in Selma, Alabama, will constitute the focus of the issue, as well as the balance of this chapter. But first a brief interruption—even before the first article, an editorial note announces that Howell Conant, "a crack photographer who runs a big New York Studio," will conclude the issue by showing "what some pretty girls look like in 'underground movies' fashions." To its credit, *Life* here captures the schizophrenic blend of politics and fashion that constituted the new media reality of the mid-1960s.

Already in early 1965, the underground cinema—or Warhol's version of it, at least—had become fashionable enough to bring before mainstream America. As at Lincoln Center the year before, Warhol's films were once again displaced from the theatrical setting, denuded of the durational experience that marked their raison d'être, and reduced to the fashionable photographic icons for which the artist was popularly known. But Conant's images were also prescient, for they mobilized the moving image in a way that looks forward to Warhol's own use of his early films as projected backdrops for the Velvet Underground during the "Exploding Plastic Inevitable" national tour over the course of the following year.[26]

Indeed, by the end of 1966, the idea of expanded cinema had served to deracinate the moving image for a whole generation of contemporary artists. Far from being confined to the movie theater, it was now showing up in art galleries and concert halls, theatrical performances and dance exhibitions. During the Expanded Cinema Symposium that fall, Ken Dewey would describe this new ubiquity of presentation as necessitating a new sensitivity to context: "We're suddenly thrown into this realm where the audience has got to know more, they've got to know, they've got to be able to evaluate what they are seeing and the conditions under which they're seeing a work."[27] The moving image was also beginning, slowly but surely, to become detached from its traditional celluloid medium. If the Norelco video system Warhol employed was still a prohibitively expensive industrial technology, the Sony Corporation's new Videocorders were being marketed directly to the middle-class consumer, giving rise to a newly televisual context wholly distinct from that of the traditional cinematic theater.

Questions of context had long been central to Dewey's thought and practice, and his installation for the New York Film Festival in the fall of 1966 would confront this new placelessness of the moving image with an unprecedented focus on the specificity of the institutional site of exhibition. The piece, titled *Selma Last Year*, was arguably one of the most formally and conceptually revolutionary works of its time, yet it is one that has been unjustly neglected within the art and film historical literature. Dewey's collaboration with minimalist composer Terry Riley and civil rights photographer Bruce Davidson resulted in an audiovisual installation of unprecedented ambition and complexity. Quite unlike the "old dream of synesthesia" Annette Michelson would denounce in her Festival lecture, "Film and the Radical Aspiration," that month, *Selma Last Year* exemplified the critic's call for an aesthetic of subversion equal to the period's entrenched "social and economic hierarchies."[28]

Unlike so many of the multimedia shows then emerging—whose multiple media tended to promote a unified, immersive amalgamation—*Selma Last Year* leveraged formal disjunction as a metaphor through which to confront the social disjunction then widening perilously within the social body. At issue were questions of identification and misidentification, exteriority and interiority, and the ability of art—through technologies of reproduction and representation—to provide an experience of alterity no longer comfortably distant, but disconcertingly proximate.

Like Allan Kaprow and the so-called painter's theater of the early 1960s, Dewey was less interested in the creation of objects than in the production of situations. But there was an important difference. While Kaprow's background was in painting and the plastic arts, Dewey's background had been in conventional theater and performance, and it was from these models of structure and exhibition that he was trying to break free:

> the whole thing that Allan Kaprow talks about—off the wall and into the room, add people. My adventure was a completely different one from that. I was trapped, literally, in the notion of all the formalities of theatre—the script, the rehearsal process and the architecture. The script defining what you were going to do, the rehearsal process defining how you were going to do it, and the stage defining where you were going to do it. My problem was to break myself loose from those dependencies—develop new methods in each of the three areas.[29]

Like those of Yvonne Rainer and Robert Morris, Dewey's "adventure" began to take form within Anna Halprin's dance company in San Francisco. It was through Halprin that he met Riley, who had written his early tape loop composition *Mescaline Mix* (1960–1961) for Halprin's production of *The Three-Legged Stool*. Unsatisfied with the rigorous structure of academic serialism, Riley had become interested in combining the new aleatory techniques promoted by John Cage and Karlheinz Stockhausen with what he called the "shamanistic" improvisation of John Coltrane. He had already begun working with tape-looped composition in the 1950s, and

Figure 5.14. Action Theater Presentation of *Sames* by Ken Dewey, 1965. Photo by Peter Moore © Estate of Peter Moore/VAGA, New York, NY.

he helped to found the San Francisco Tape Music Center in 1962 before moving to Paris. Dewey accompanied him as the production manager for the Halprin company, and the two lived among a number of expatriate artists—Riley playing gigs to entertain American soldiers stationed there, and Dewey collaborating with the members of the Living Theatre, themselves recently arrived from New York.[30] They would all collaborate on Dewey's 1963 production of *The Gift* for the Theatre of Nations. The Chet Baker Quartet was asked to perform Miles Davis's "So What" from his enormously popular 1959 album *Kind of Blue*. Riley recorded each of the soloists individually in isolation, then cut up, redoubled, modified, and recombined the recordings using a rudimentary tape-delay system that he referred to as his "Time-Lag Accumulator."[31] The hauntingly beautiful yet almost completely unrecognizable transformation was a breakthrough for Riley, securing his movement away from an earlier interest in serialism and *musique concrète* and toward the qualities of repetition and phase delay as a musical form. As Riley described his experience, "I was noticing that things didn't sound the same when you heard them more than once. And the more you heard them, the more different they did sound."[32]

Dewey himself was taken with this field of difference and repetition that Riley had opened up, and after the two returned to America in 1965, Dewey began to transpose these audio investigations into the field of performance and the moving image. For the Expanded Cinema Festival that winter at the Film-Makers' Cinematheque, the two continued their collaboration with an audiovisual performance titled *Sames* (1965), the first of Dewey's works to incorporate film projection within the context of a staged performance. Dewey had performed in Robert Whitman's West Coast production of *Water* (1963), in which film was projected directly onto the bodies of performers. But he considered Whitman's use of film mostly extraneous and supplemental within that work, a kind of decoration or prop. Dewey was more interested in Whitman's earlier *American Moon* (1960), in which the cinematic metaphor implied a more general reconfiguration of the theatrical situation. He was particularly interested in the possibilities of projecting films onto nearby buildings in order to invoke a radically disjunctive experience of scale and space.[33]

Dewey's interest in destabilizing the spectatorial conventions of theatrical performance led to a curious inversion. Perhaps playing off Warhol's own inversion of stillness and the moving image in his portrait films and *Screen Tests* the year before, and clearly rooted in the minimalist musical aesthetics with which he was well acquainted, Dewey's first use of film did not expand the action on stage so much as displace it. For *Sames*, his contribution to the Expanded Cinema Festival of 1965, five women dressed in bridal gowns were instructed to form a loose circle on stage and then stand absolutely still for the length of the hour-long piece. As Jonas Mekas wrote in the *Village Voice*,

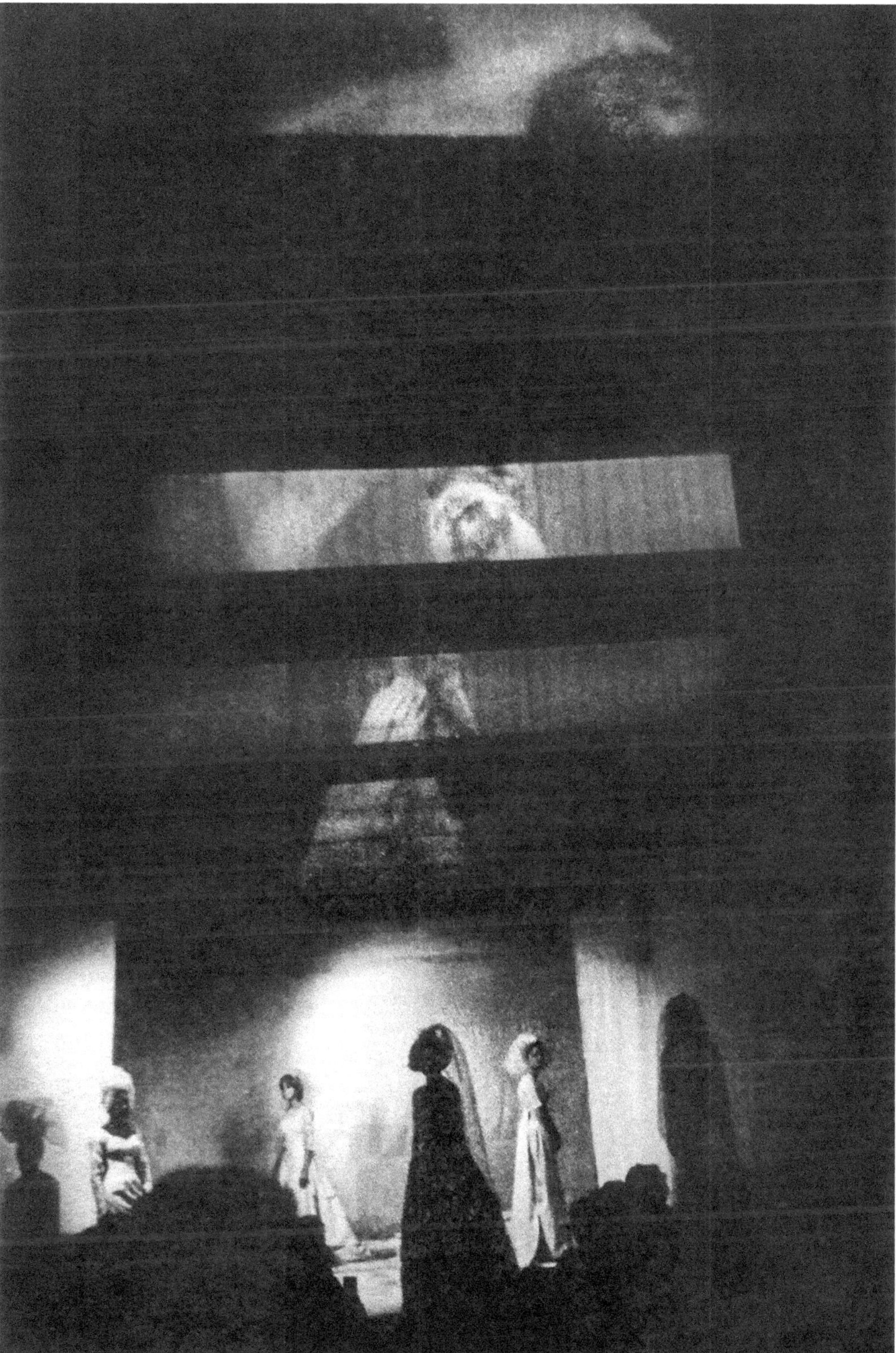

> Dewey's piece wasn't a shadow play, but it was shadowy from somewhere deep, or far, repeating, repeating, and overlapping themselves, and there was light going on and off, and when it was on, you could see four or five women standing on the white stage, white like milk, five women in milk and in wedding gowns, like in a store window on a misty morning, with streets still empty, in Williamsburg, Brooklyn.[34]

Sames staged a performance of enduring stillness, a theater of the frozen pose. The lack of obvious movement only caused the audience to look closer, where they would begin to discern traces of time's entropic forward march. Like Cage's night-long performance of *Vexations* two years before and the Warholian cinema of stillness that followed it, Dewey's work presented its audience with a simple image that became increasingly less simple over time—a dialectic of movement and stasis, fixity and transformation. As if to highlight this dialectic, the "brides" were spotlit in ways that would occasionally shift, transforming a set of live yet motionless bodies into a kind of moving image.

But if the collected women were turned into an image, with the proscenium stage that image's frame, that image was counterbalanced by the literal projection of a moving image *hors-champ*, or "outside the frame," on the rafters and ceiling of the exhibition space. There, a film depicted these same women as they traveled about the city, undertaking various typical actions, yet decked out in the very bridal regalia they were wearing on stage. Just as their costumes caused these women to seem displaced

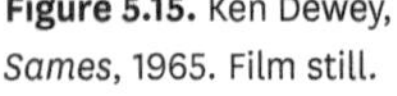
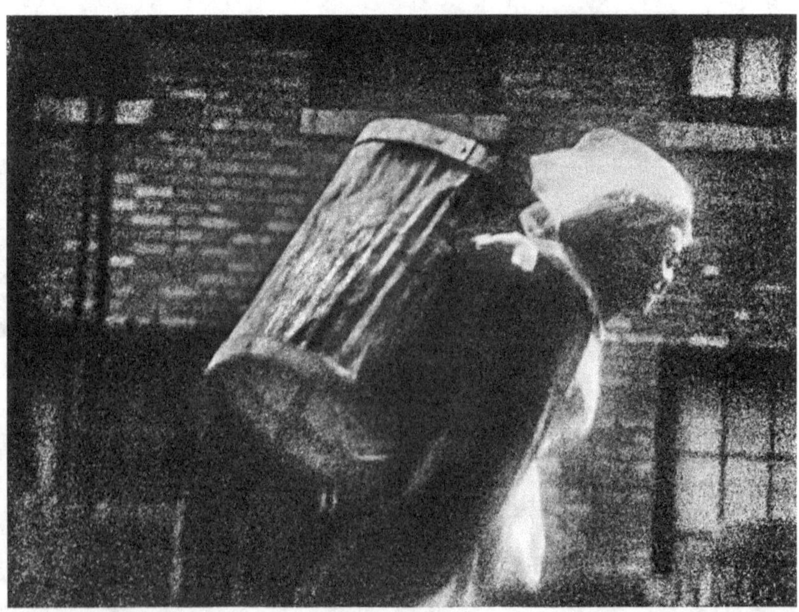

Figure 5.15. Ken Dewey, *Sames*, 1965. Film still.

from their normal everyday activity into the particular event of the wedding ceremony, the audience's attention was displaced from the stage to the ceiling. Yet the projected image in *Sames* was not intended to be the center of attention. Rather, the moving-image projection *actively competed* for attention with the live performers on stage in a manner much closer to the way in which VanDerBeek's *Movie-Mural* had interacted with the Cunningham company dancers in the production of *Variations V* just months before. Using "the ceiling beams as screens, breaking the image into four or five depth levels," Dewey's multiply decentered film was simultaneously more and less real than the bodies it represented.[35]

The bridal dress is both ordinary and extraordinary, as it marks both a common custom and a highly singular, ritualized occasion: there is one and only one situation or context within which it is justified, expected, and normalized. As such, the garment serves as an appropriate synecdoche for the illocutionary or performative condition that, according to Michael Kirby, characterized the "new theatre" more generally throughout this period. And it was precisely this illocutionary dimension that was heightened by the addition of a soundtrack Riley produced to accompany the work. The soundscape was made up of three independent works. *I*, from 1964, consisted solely of the dancer John Graham changing the signification of that pronoun through a wide range of vocal inflections, reflecting different contexts or situations.[36] Graham's voice was then subjected to the "Time-Lag Accumulator" to further transform the word through feedback and time delay into something that eventually came to approach a continuous drone. This work was then conjoined with two other pieces following a similar structure: *It's Me*—spoken by Riley himself—and *That's Not You*—spoken by his daughter. A cacophony of reference, Riley's score served to audibly redouble the experience of perceptual dislocation that Dewey produced through his inversion of the still and moving image, the profilmic "real" and its cinematic reproduction.

The various forms of spectatorial destabilization Dewey and Riley elicited within *Sames* remained principally on a formal level. Questions of gender, while obviously invoked, were not explored in any sustained way. Yet the formal strategies Dewey and Riley initiated within *Sames* would be given a more incisive social and political edge in their next collaboration, *Selma Last Year*. Immediately upon his return from Paris, Dewey had become involved in the American civil rights movement, traveling to Selma, Alabama, to participate in the march to Montgomery. Fascinated by the novel possibilities of sound recording and editing he had witnessed through his collaborations with Riley in Europe, Dewey secured a commission, and equipment, from a Finnish broadcasting company to produce high-quality audio recordings of the march. Dewey set about recording the answers he received to intentionally blank questions such as "What do you think about what's going on here?" to produce what he would later describe as audio portraits—of individual marchers, protestors, onlookers, and children who were only partially cognizant of what was taking place. Rather than standard interview equipment, Dewey employed an omnidirectional microphone to capture the texture of ambient sound in the speaker's immediate environment, so that a speaker's voice might be suddenly concealed behind the tumult of a helicopter passing overhead. The recordings were not so much interviews, as one would hear them on the radio or television, as attempts to capture the aural "atmosphere" of a given place and event. Working from Dewey's extensive audio documentation, Riley set about remixing the hours of audiotape—individuals within the march and those protesting it from the roadside, singular interviews and group chants, cars, whistles, army trucks, and police sirens—together into a twenty-minute audio collage.

While Steve Reich has acknowledged the importance of Riley's early work in sparking his own interest in "process" composition and tape phasing, Riley's interest in editing Dewey's documentary recordings of the Selma march would have been affected by Reich's own incorporation of such "found sound" into his composition *It's Gonna Rain* the previous year. First presented at the San Francisco Tape Music Center in January 1965, Reich's work captured the flip side of the 1960s counterculture then ensconced in the apotheosis of the civil rights movement. In distinction to the early tape compositions of Cage, Stockhausen, Pierre Schaeffer, or Reich explicitly chose fragments charged with social and cultural history and presented those clips initially without manipulation, ensuring that his resulting formal transformation of the material maintained an emotional, even theatrical, connection with its indexical, worldly referent.

Using a borrowed shotgun mic, Reich recorded the sermon of a young black preacher named Brother Walter "prophesying apocalypse in quasi-musical declamation" in San Francisco's central Union Square.[37] In *It's Gonna Rain*, Reich preserved the expressivity of the source material by keeping his own manipulation to a minimum, looping selected fragments and phase-shifting them so that the repetition of the preacher's voice multiplied and fragmented into an ecstatic cacophony befitting the sermon's apocalyptic theme. Soon after moving to New York, Reich was asked by the civil rights activist Trumer Nelson to edit down a series of tapes to create a documentary sound collage in support of a retrial for the "Harlem Six," a group of African American boys widely believed to have been wrongly convicted for the murder of a white woman during the 1964 Harlem riots. Reich agreed to do the editing work for the defense on the condition that he be allowed to use a section of the tapes in the creation of a musical piece.

For *Come Out*, Reich selected a brief passage that itself foregrounded questions of documentary representation. Daniel Hamm's testimony describes his purposely reopening one of the bruises he had sustained in order to have "the bruise blood come out to show them" the degree to which he had been beaten by the police. Reich repeated only that phrase—"come out to show them"—progressively decomposing it into a field of syllables, consonants, and pitched vowels so as to produce an effect of abstract intensification: "By not altering its pitch or timbre, one keeps the original emotional power that speech has while intensifying its melody and meaning through repetition and rhythm."[38] Premiering in April 1966 in New York City, *Come Out* extenuated the racial dynamics Reich had inaugurated the previous year in *It's Gonna Rain*, explicitly aligning the emerging interest in the possibilities of looped recording and feedback with the explosive social and cultural dynamics of the civil rights movement.

But if Reich considered *Come Out* to be a "musical piece" distinct from the more prosaic documentary sound collage he produced for the legal defense, Riley's audiotape for *Selma Last Year* foreswore such musical techniques in order to extenuate the very indexical, documentary nature of the recordings themselves.[39] There was no pitch shifting or phase manipulation, nothing "musical" at all about the resulting composition. Redoubling the spatial schism between the direct interview and the larger expanse of environmental sound playing against it in the background, Riley's soundscape cut across temporal registers, mixing up signals and cues to create a sonic collage in which time and space were consistently being fractured. But Riley's work had never been intended to stand independently. Rather, it functioned as an integral component of a larger audiovisual environment Dewey and Riley created together with their new collaborator, Davidson.

It would be almost impossible to overstate the importance of photo journalism to the success of the civil rights campaign.[40] While the ostensible goal of the march from Selma to Montgomery had been to present Alabama governor George Wallace with a petition to remove obstacles to black voter registration, no one seriously believed that the man whose mantra was "segregation now, segregation tomorrow, segregation forever" was likely to be persuaded. The real target of the march was the cameras of the network media and the national audience to whom those cameras gave privileged access. By 1965, there was a strong national consensus in favor of voting rights, but despite great efforts at voter registration, a mix of bureaucratic restraints and overt intimidation had kept 98 percent of the black population in Selma from being able to vote. By creating a media spectacle, Martin Luther King Jr. and the Southern Christian Leadership Conference (SCLC) would use photo and television journalism to bring the nation's attention to this situation, spurring Congress to pass a new

Voting Rights Act. Selma mayor Joseph Smitherman would later claim that "they picked Selma just like a movie producer would pick a set."[41]

Dewey was one of the many white Northerners who joined the march at Selma after "Bloody Sunday"—the first attempt on March 7, 1965. Police had been lying in wait that day as the marchers tried to cross out of Selma over the Edmund Pettus Bridge, and they brutally set on the marchers with whips, clubs, and tear gas. The national media were present, and the scenes were recorded on film and quickly broadcast on prime-time national television, where they broke into ABC's feature presentation of a Nazi war crimes documentary, *Judgment at Nuremberg*. The scene outside Selma that viewers saw on their TV screens looked like a war, and it brought people from around the nation to Selma to join the subsequent march to Montgomery. After another failed attempt and the death of a white clergyman, President Johnson personally intervened, and hundreds of armed FBI agents and National Guardsmen were deployed to protect the marchers. Dewey understood the final, successful march from Selma to Montgomery on March 21 as representing a momentous, yet precarious, racial alliance:

> The event had an extremely curious position in the civil rights movement. It was a fleeting moment. The March on Washington had been essentially a white march. The Jackson March, which followed, was a black march. For a complex number of reasons, Selma, which followed Jackson, seems to stand out as a moment at which there was a real contact. It was a fifty-fifty march. People on it recall the innocent—a kind of mutual affection which surrounded it. Perhaps it was illusory and even shallow—but it did grip the entire country and it was almost classical in its development and ultimate tragedy.[42]

The "classical" frame Dewey invokes was one he found represented in Davidson's photography. On the basis of his 1959 series of a Brooklyn street gang, Davidson had been invited into the Magnum group of documentary photographers and, in 1962, awarded a Guggenheim Fellowship to document "Youth in America." But his experience covering the 1961 Freedom Rides for the *New York Times* had been transformative, and he henceforth dedicated himself to covering the changing civil rights landscape. In considering Davidson's documentary practice, it is useful to recall how Anne Wagner has described the earlier work of Davidson's contemporary, Charles Moore. Writing about the ambivalent role of Moore's images of Birmingham, Alabama, in Andy Warhol's *Race Riot* series, she claimed that these images—which are tellingly *not* depictions of race riots, despite Warhol's title—tended to reproduce the familiar news spectacle of what she calls the "rioting black body" dehumanized under the "sovereign white gaze."[43] Davidson explicitly refused to portray his subjects as abject, suffering bodies—subjects that might elicit pity, but only at the cost of a profound disidentification. Unlike the press photojournalists during the Selma march, who rode on flatbed trucks and depicted either the leaders of the march or masses of faceless subjects, Davidson walked the fifty miles with the marchers, taking images of ordinary individuals or small groups. Dewey was taken by the pictures' unusually empathic perspective. He described them as simple "human portraits—almost classic in their composition."[44]

At the time that Dewey proposed their collaboration, Davidson was already engaged in planning for a show of his work at the Museum of Modern Art. The formal qualities of the two resulting exhibitions—which would take place simultaneously a short distance from each other—could not be have been more dramatically opposed.[45] We should recall that the exhibition of photography at MoMA in the postwar period had been a confused, even schizophrenic affair. Over the course of the 1940s and 1950s, beginning with *The Road to Victory* (1942) and most emblematically in *The Family of Man* (1955), MoMA adopted Edward Steichen's "informational" model of photographic exhibition, in which images were often uncredited, exhibited without frames or mats, and enlarged to the size of murals and plastered directly onto walls or plinths, only to be disposed of after the show had concluded.[46] Yet the early 1960s saw a dramatic, 180-degree change of direction when John Szarkowski, succeeding Steichen, reinstituted the "fine art" paradigm of minute, superbly crafted prints, well spaced on a blank white wall, mounted identically with archival white mats behind unobtrusive frames, and protected behind sheets of expensive, nonreflective plate glass.

While Davidson's MoMA exhibition would proceed along the lines of this "fine art" model, *Selma Last Year*, his collaboration with Dewey and Riley for the New York Film Festival at Lincoln Center, would evince a radically different model of exhibition and spectatorship. The project was initially titled *Faces and Voices* and was described as a deliberate conjunction of "two sets of portraits—the seen and the heard—two separate reflections on an event which drew together people from all across America."[47] Dewey conceived of the work not as a single multimedia spectacle, but as the bringing together of three distinct "atmospheres"—the image of the past, the sound of the past, and the work's situation in the present—in a nonsynchronous, nonsynthetic way. Working in the space between performance and installation, and subsuming their individual identities under the collective nomination "Action Theatre," Dewey, Riley, and Davidson would together produce a new kind of "continuous environment" that would have its basis not in a static form, but in a "process situation": "the living change of people and time."[48] Sensitive as he was to

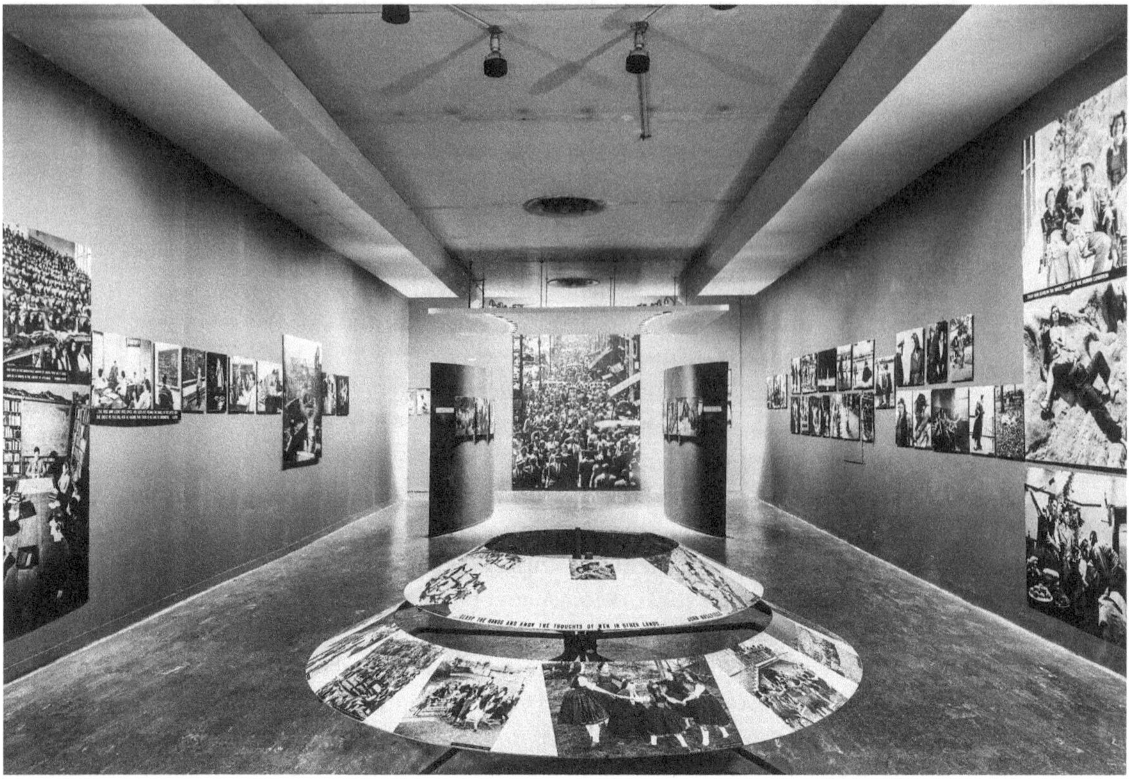

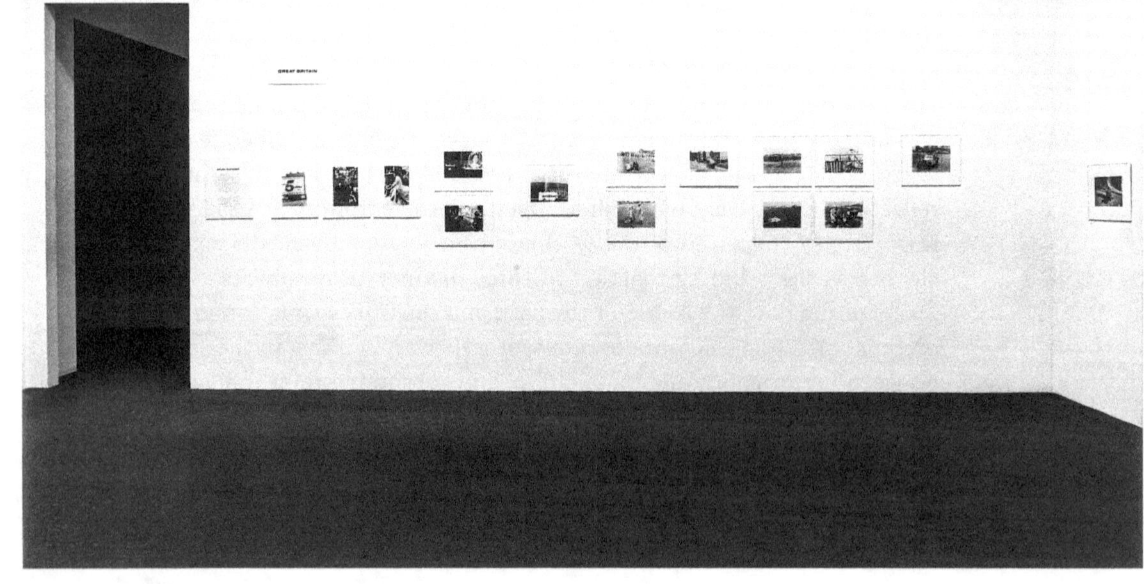
GREAT BRITAIN

Figure 5.16. Installation view of the exhibition *The Family of Man*, Museum of Modern Art, New York, January 24–May 8, 1955. MoMA Archives.

Figure 5.17. Installation view of the exhibition *Bruce Davidson—Photographs*, Museum of Modern Art, New York, July 7–October 2, 1966. MoMA Archives.

the specificity of context, Dewey would allow the third atmosphere—the physical and historical situation of the work itself—to change quite dramatically over the course of 1966.

The first of these situations was the First Unitarian Church of Chicago, just outside the University of Chicago in the Hyde Park neighborhood, from March 20 to 25—on the one-year anniversary of the Selma march. Dewey clearly understood the massive role religion had played in promoting national engagement with the civil rights movement in general and with the Selma march in particular. The news coverage of white clergy beaten by police in Montgomery and the death of the white Unitarian minister James Reeb in Selma was arguably a major factor in securing both juridical permission and federal protection for the final march. President Johnson specifically invoked Reeb's death in his speech to Congress. First Unitarian, for its part, was an institution specifically devoted to social and cultural diversity, with a long history of outreach in the racially and socioeconomically mixed neighborhood of Hyde Park.

Davidson's images were shown in two formats, both unframed. Medium-sized, fiberboard-mounted prints were affixed directly to long horizontal wooden beams hung across a church wall, while a series of slides were projected at a much larger scale onto a sealed arch across the lower nave. Displaced from the fine art museum, Davidson's photographs here lost their aura of precious commodity, but only to take on an entirely new and different kind of aura in its place. In the quiet and relatively confined space of the church, Riley's soundtrack would have been clearly

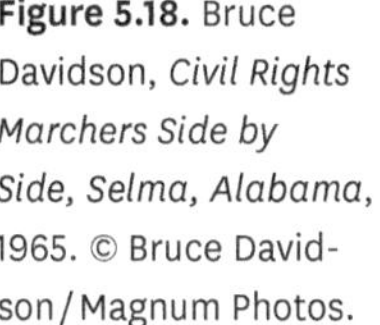

Figure 5.18. Bruce Davidson, *Civil Rights Marchers Side by Side, Selma, Alabama*, 1965. © Bruce Davidson/Magnum Photos.

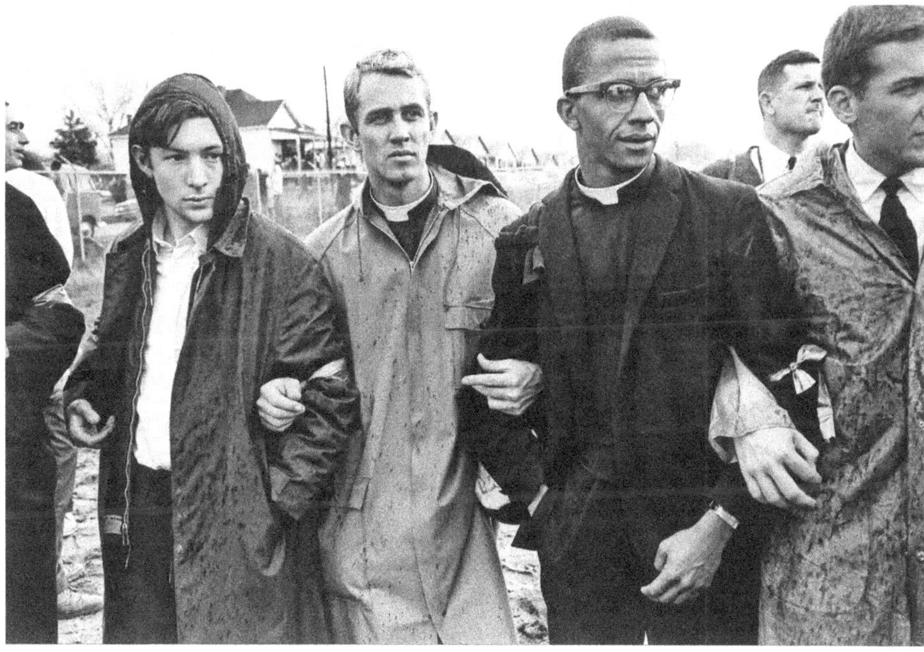

Figure 5.19. Projection of Bruce Davidson photograph on interior church wall, *Selma Last Year* installation, First Unitarian Church of Chicago, 1966. New York Public Library.

Figure 5.20. Visitor viewing Bruce Davidson photographs mounted within *Selma Last Year* installation, First Unitarian Church of Chicago, 1966. New York Public Library.

audible throughout. Dewey's press release advertises the work under the title *Selma Commemoration* and describes it as taking place "within the main sanctuary of the church" as a kind of reverential memorial. Davidson's prints, straightforwardly situated at eye level, were neither large enough to appear monumental nor small enough to feel precious. His projected images, appearing for fifteen seconds apiece, took on the location—and the scale—of a traditional religious painting. Like the simple wooden beams on which his prints were affixed, these images put unmistakable religious allusions into play. But just as significant would have been their ephemerality. For what might otherwise have seemed a conventional slide show took on, in this specific context, a palpable sense of haunting, of loss, of mourning. Such a sense would have been extenuated by Riley's omnipresent soundscape, in which the insubstantial voices of jaded old folk and naïve children, determined marchers and equally determined hecklers, echoed among the darkened stone walls.

Yet if the march being commemorated was unambiguously victorious—having overcome violence and impediment to reach both its proximate destination in Montgomery and its ultimate destination in the Voting Rights Act of 1965—why was the tone of the work less exuberant than melancholic? One answer lies in the work's immediate situation and context. For while it was timed to commemorate the anniversary of the Selma march, the specificity of the work's placement in Chicago—and more precisely, in the mixed-race neighborhood of Hyde Park—had everything to do with the inauguration of the "Chicago Freedom Movement" just two months before. This movement resulted from a bold decision by King and the SCLC to pivot from the overt civil rights violations in the South toward what would prove the much more intractable problem of substantive inequality in housing and employment throughout the cities of the North. Its ostensible goal was to pressure city governments to end housing segregation the way they had ended school segregation—through a mix of political persuasion, legal regulation, and—if necessary—armed intervention. Affordable housing would no longer be constructed exclusively in outlying, poor, black neighborhoods, but in the very heart of existing all-white neighborhoods. At least, that was the plan. But white Northerners, who had embraced the abstract ideals of the civil rights movement when it was far away in the Deep South, suddenly found themselves divided on the question of integration when it came to their own schools and neighborhoods. As the year wore on, such questioning—for many—turned to outright resistance.[49]

Dewey had always fixated on social psychology, but since returning from Europe, he had become increasingly preoccupied with questions of distance and intimacy—specifically, the paradoxical conjunction of distance *and* intimacy afforded though contemporary print and television photojournalism. *Selma Last Year* was fundamentally oriented around

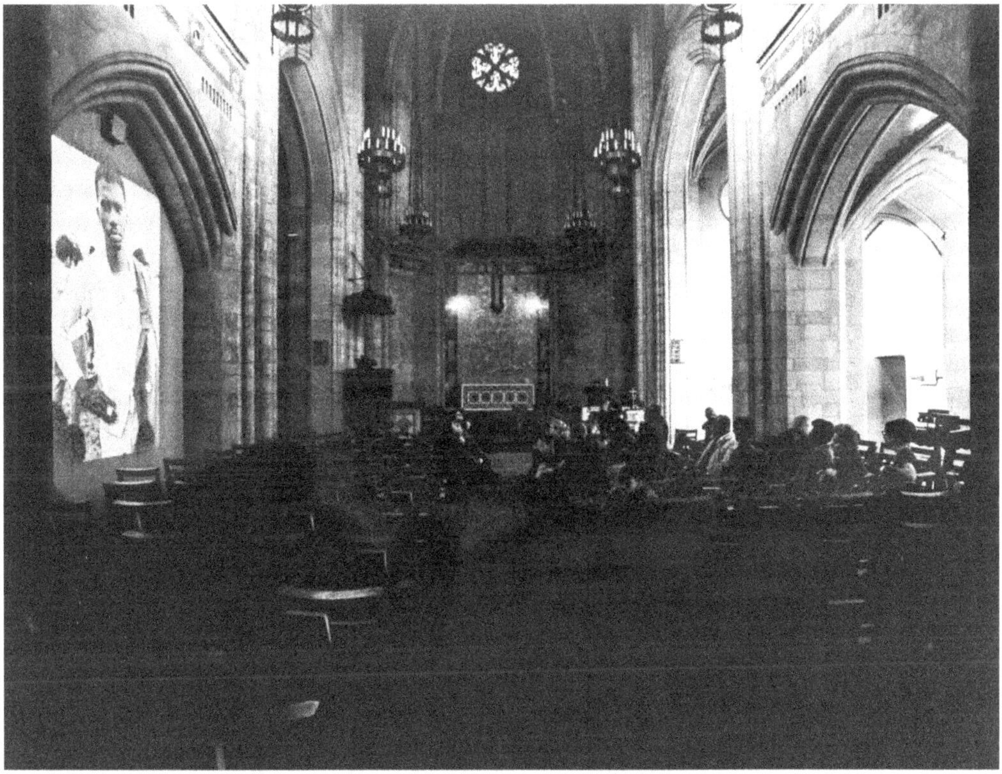

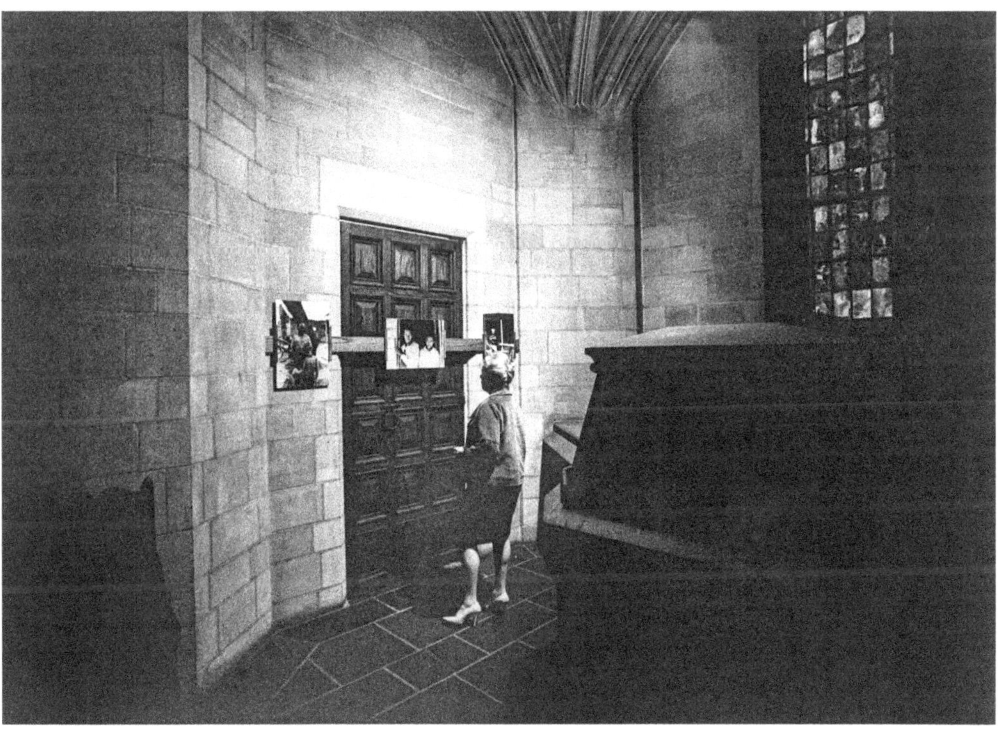

Figure 5.21. Entrance to *Selma Last Year* installation in Harper Court, Chicago, 1966. New York Public Library.

Figure 5.22. Visitor viewing Bruce Davidson photographs mounted within *Selma Last Year* installation, Harper Court, Chicago, 1966. New York Public Library.

such questions, in their temporal, spatial, and ultimately, psychological dimensions. The soundscape Dewey and Riley crafted for *Selma Last Year* was neither polemical nor manichean, but evidenced a range of emotional and psychological complexity.

Dewey was a Chicago native, and his decision to stage *Selma Last Year* in Chicago's Hyde Park was based in his understanding of the area's complex racial history. The University of Chicago, its anchor employer, had integrated in the nineteenth century, and by the 1950s it had graduated more black PhDs than any other school in the country. Nevertheless, its faculty and students were overwhelmingly white men of privileged backgrounds, and it remained an elite, affluent institution quite literally encircled by the poorer, predominately black neighborhood of Hyde Park. Rising crime had led the school to campaign for one of the largest urban renewal plans ever undertaken, and over the course of the late 1950s and early 1960s, whole city blocks were razed. Crime shrank and the average income soared, but the redevelopment drove out nearly 40 percent of the black residents and a vast number of small local businesses.[50]

Dewey's initial commemoration at the First Unitarian Church treated this local situation only obliquely, yet the work's subsequent installation endowed it with a decidedly more polemical edge. Harper Court was an outdoor shopping plaza constructed with the intention of allowing a number of small, predominately black-owned businesses to remain in Hyde Park through subsidized rents, thus helping to maintain something of the neighborhood's history and character in spite of its rapid gentrification. By installing the work after the plaza's construction in an NAACP-sponsored tribute, Dewey saw himself intervening directly in support of King's Chicago Freedom Movement, attempting to draw a broad connection between the specific and geographically delimited issue of voting discrimination in the South and the more widespread issue of housing discrimination across the nation. Now given the title *Selma Last Year: Its Faces and Voices*, Dewey's installation maintained the wooden support beams from the First Unitarian Church installation, but now situated them outside, in a precariously open space.[51] Their situation was precarious not simply because of their potential exposure to inclement weather, but in that the future of this space—Harper Court in particular, but also Hyde Park more generally—seemed delicately poised on a fulcrum. Poetically, Dewey's plans situated the slide projector in the interior of an as yet unoccupied shop space, so that Davidson's images would be projected against the exterior window in a strange kind of advertisement. Much rested on whether the public would view equal housing legislation—a government intervention into private, rather than public, space—as a necessary continuation of the civil rights struggle or as a dangerous new experiment in state-mandated social engineering.

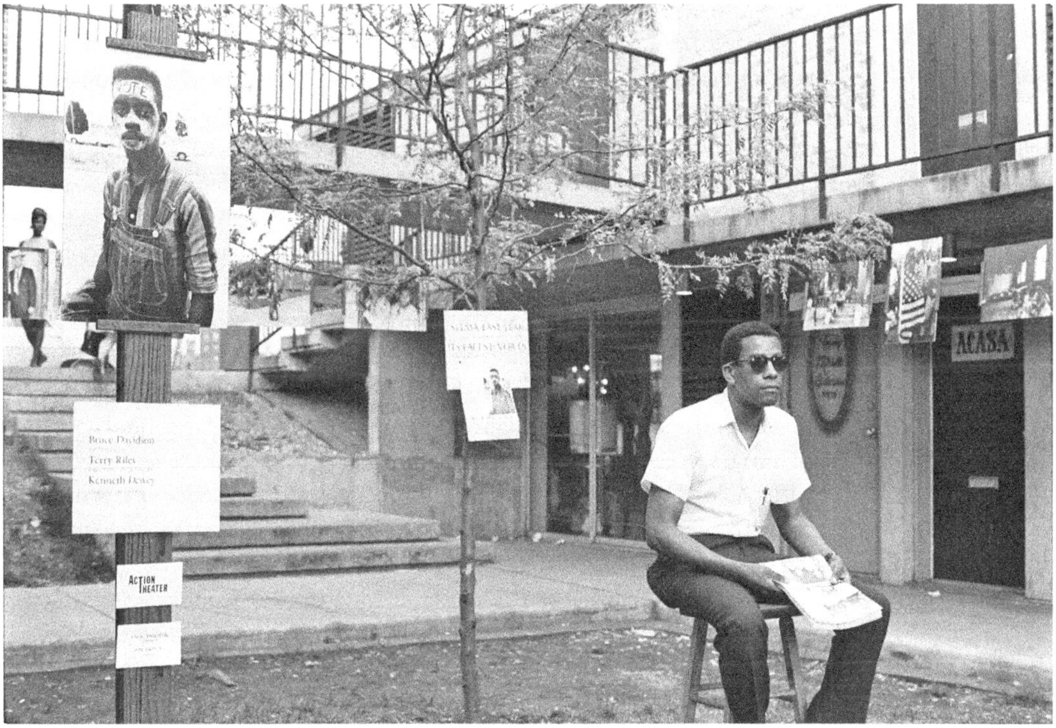

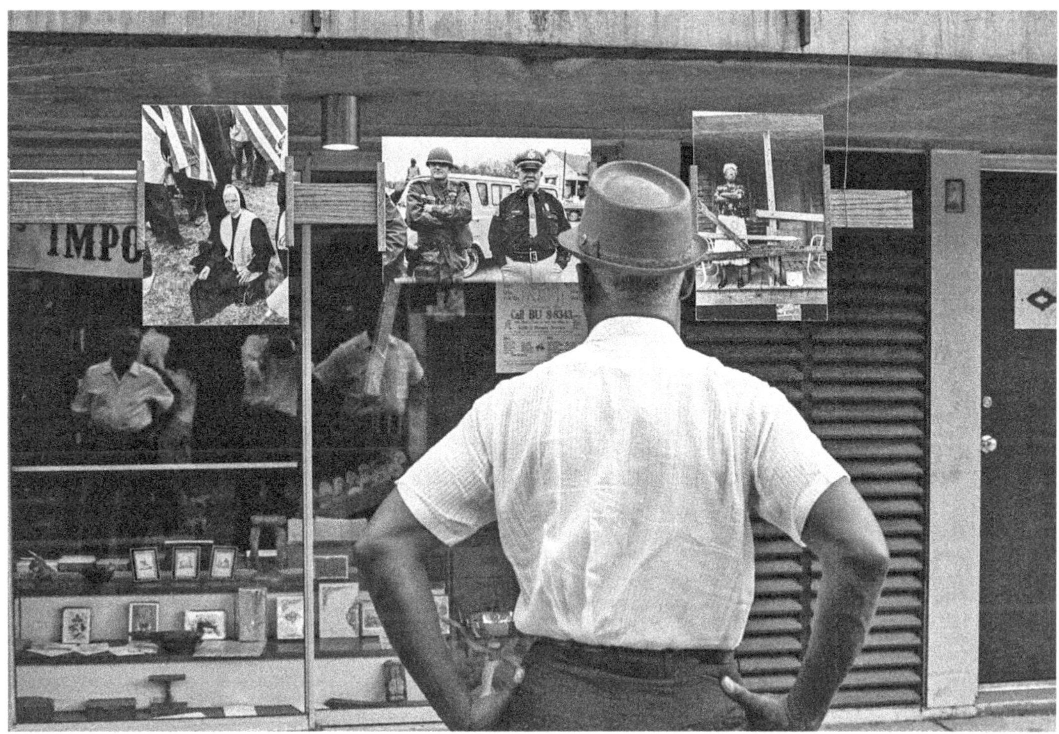
IMPO

Despite King's efforts, the latter narrative would prove the more persuasive for large numbers of whites, who felt their communities were under seige. That summer, whites violently attacked anti-housing discrimination marchers in Gage Park and Marquette Park. King was hit in the head by a brick during the latter march, and he was quoted the next day in the *Chicago Tribune* as saying, "I have seen many demonstrations in the South, but I have never seen anything so hostile and so hateful as I've seen here today."[52] The Chicago Freedom Movement was an unmitigated disaster. Not only had King failed to win additional public support for the movement, but the marches in Chicago had severely harmed its standing in the public eye. That August, a housing discrimination lawsuit was filed, which would result in the court finding that 99 percent of public housing was both black-occupied and in predominately black neighborhoods. But rather than comply with a court order requiring that the next 700 units be constructed in white neighborhoods, along with 75 percent of the new construction thereafter, the city simply stopped new construction of public housing altogether.[53] Similarly, a presidential commission inquiring into the causes of the Detroit riots in 1967 would declare that the country was "divided into two separate and unequal societies, one white and one black," but would conclude that neither the courts nor the federal government had the power to change this situation.[54]

In other words, far from being resolved, the civil rights struggle after Selma actually seemed to be threatening to tip over into mass violence. Only five days after the 1965 Voting Rights Act had been passed, riots in Los Angeles had given the national news media a disturbing new vision of mass mobilization—one that would only grow in power as riots spread to major cities around the country. The formation of the Black Panther Party that October would introduce a new image of the civil rights struggle—one in which King's commitment to nonviolence was replaced with a conspicuous display of loaded shotguns. In the few months since Dewey had presented his work at the First Unitarian Church of Chicago, the fragile coalition of racial, geographic, and socioeconomic communities that materialized briefly during the Selma march was in danger of unraveling completely.

Selma Last Year would be shown at New York's Philharmonic Hall at Lincoln Center from September 12 to 22, 1966, as one of the "expanded cinema" works organized in association with the New York Film Festival that year. Dewey felt that the stakes for the work had been raised tremendously. Just days before the Lincoln Center opening, a march on Cicero (near Chicago) had gone ahead without King's blessing and had quickly degenerated into open violence on both sides. Like VanDerBeek, Dewey invoked a global perspective in his description of recent events, expressing his concern that unless a majority of mankind learns to willingly balance their particular needs and wants and the particular aspirations of the groups of which they are a part (national, religious) with the needs and wants of the world as a whole, that we will gradually slip backward. The changes we make will be fearful, tightening retreats from the promise which exists. I can't tell you how strongly I feel that theatre within itself reflects, *is* these very problems.[55]

At Lincoln Center, *Selma Last Year* had the potential to reach many more viewers than ever before, but it would also reach a different kind of viewer, and Dewey was very conscious of the change. In contrast to the relatively diverse early audiences in Chicago, the audience at Lincoln Center would be disproportionately white and affluent. Dewey describes wanting to "break through" the "self-satisfied nature" of those largely insulated from the harsh reality of the civil rights struggle and rapidly becoming inured to its images of suffering: "Our problem was to introduce this into the Philharmonic Hall situation in such a way that it could function as a reference point for people's current backlash thoughts."[56]

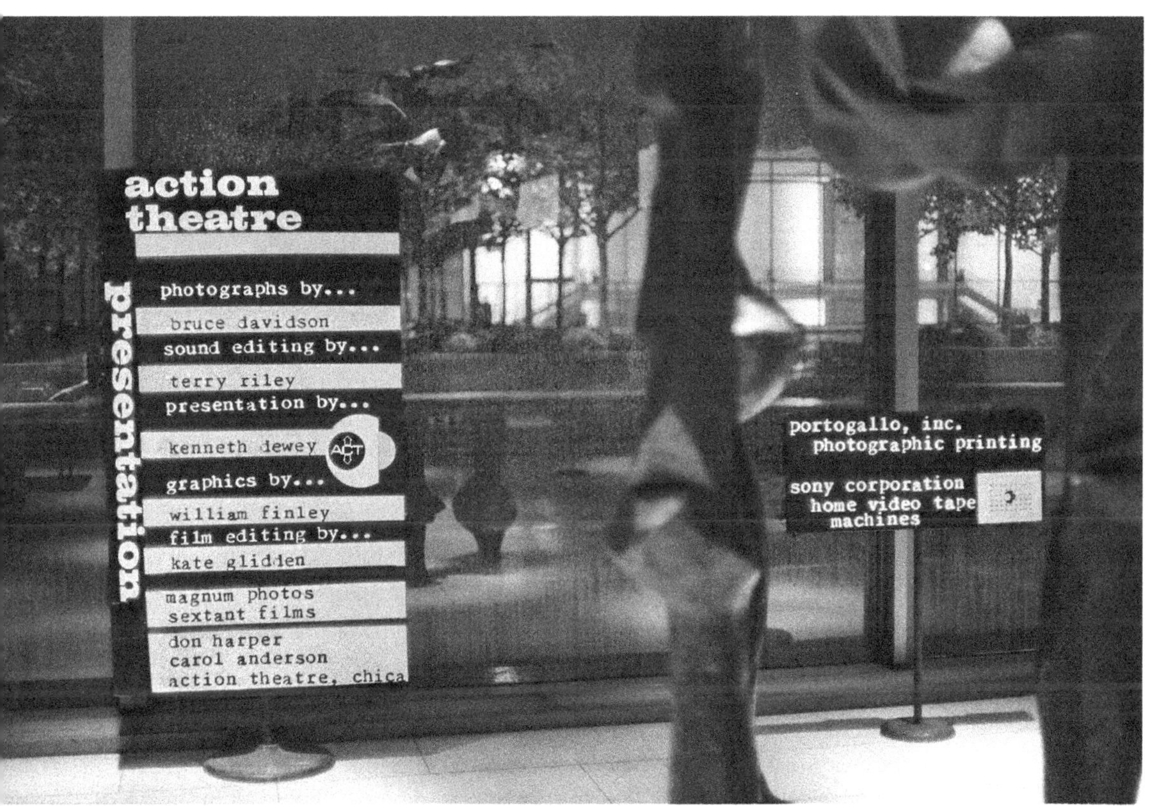

Figure 5.23. Credit signboards from the Lincoln Center installation of *Selma Last Year*, New York Film Festival, 1966. New York Public Library.

Selma Last Year would reflect the larger reality of the civil rights movement as it sought to sustain a precarious new balance. On the one hand, increased agitation was necessary if the movement was to maintain its momentum—the public might otherwise come to view the Voting Rights Act as the culmination of the struggle. On the other hand, the intensity and, more importantly, the proximity of this new agitation was engendering an exhaustion among those it most had to convince. For his part, Dewey sought to "break through" to his audience by creating an installation that confronted them while retaining its basis in emotional communication:

> The problem that we've had so much of in this country is that we get the logic of the situation, we get the logic of what should be done, but the emotional necessity is something we are unable to communicate until somebody goes out and kills somebody, until there's a riot. *We only take action on the basis of our emotional communication* . . . for me this whole thing—[is about] attempting to bring these two things into the same place.[57]

At Lincoln Center, Dewey would dramatically transform previous elements of the work while adding several others, which resulted in a qualitatively new experience. Rather than placing Davidson's images at eye level, where they had always been installed previously, he placed them near the ground, mounted to small, irregularly inclined plinths near the viewers' feet and scattered near the periphery of the mezzanine floor. They were in dramatic juxtaposition to the centrality, regularity, and uniformity of Davidson's MoMA exhibition then under way and the ostensible neutrality it afforded. Dewey described the verticality of the installation as a response to the "terrific weight" of Lincoln Center's institutional history "pressing downward." He also described the plinths as tombstones. But they functioned less in the sense of a memorial—as at the First Unitarian Church in Chicago—than as an exhuming of the dead. By September 1966, Selma was old news. Everyone had seen its dramatic imagery in countless newspapers, glossy magazines, and television programs. "The notion [at the New York Film Festival] was that this was a dead subject," Dewey would later state.[58] The doubly peripheral location of these images—small, out of the way, almost huddling together near the edges of the Philharmonic Hall lobby—conveyed a palpable awkwardness, a feeling that the images did not belong here, that they were out of place.

This feeling was reiterated in the images that *were* hung near eye level on the columns and banisters: documentary photographs of the works' previous installation at Harper Court and the First Unitarian Church in Chicago. The images Davidson captured at Selma were intentionally dramatic and absorbing. Dewey sought not to negate, but to complicate

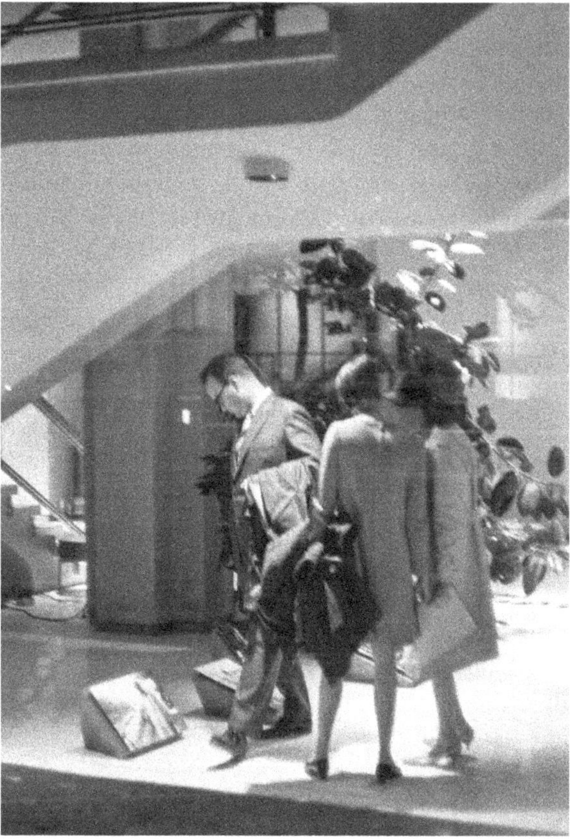

Figure 5.24. Visitor viewing Bruce Davidson photographs mounted near the floor in the Lincoln Center installation of *Selma Last Year*, New York Film Festival, 1966. New York Public Library.

this absorptive quality by means of his installation. The strange and peripheral placement of the Selma images necessitated a degree of physical adaptation in the viewer, making one aware, even self-conscious, of the act of viewing them. Encountering those same images in the dramatically different contexts of Harper Court and the First Unitarian Church only reinforced the singularity of this act of looking *in the present* and the ways in which it was necessarily, and unconsciously, being conditioned by the particularities of its time and place. Dewey spoke of the goal of his photographic juxtapositions in terms of a "mnemic layering" through which he intended to stage an incursion into the Lincoln Center site itself: "taking a familiar situation and putting pictures in such a way that they would burn in ... so that later, when people came back again ... and they were gone, they would still be there."[59]

A third part of the installation took place in a separate, darkened space downstairs. Spectators who entered this area were engulfed within a projected horizontal image approximately eight by ten feet in size. Two other projections of approximately four by five feet were visible on additional walls, while three projectors and a series of benches crowded the space. The three projectors, all showing slides of Davidson's photos, slowly progressed through a series of timed dissolves, each changing every fifteen seconds with a different rhythm of images. In addition, the space was completely suffused with sound—the ambient sounds of demonstrators and protestors, interviews, helicopters, trucks, and children. As visitors sat down, they became cut off from the rest of the festival upstairs. Dewey thought of the space as analogous to the march itself: "you had to go down and be involved."[60]

Dewey's conception of this "involvement" was immersive. Yet this immersivity was not a matter of suturing the spectator into a single representational perspective, as in the traditional feature film. Nor was it simply a matter of overwhelming the spectator through a barrage of audiovisual data. Rather, the spectator was subjected to an intentionally disjunctive environment, a representational cacophony in which sound and image were left purposely unaligned, competing for attention. The spectator's attention was then further split among the three large projections, each transitioning through a syncopated dissolve every fifteen seconds. Davidson's images were themselves already somewhat disjunctive: passive innocents and antagonistic dyads, broad surveys of groups as well as individuals in close focus. The three projectors were nestled among the few benches in a relatively small space, so the atmosphere probably would have felt more akin to a conventional slide show than the kind of slick multimedia spectacle many viewers would have previously experienced. Furthermore, the relationship of sound and image was deliberately kept asynchronous, "out of phase." While the sound collage cycled every twenty minutes, the slide projections cycled every twenty-one, ensuring that the relationship of the images to the sounds remained unfixed and perpetually changing—two people coming in at different times would not see the same piece. Dewey mentions a final aspect that was crucial to his imagination of the environment: with only one staircase in and out, spectators had no choice but to walk in front of an immense horizontal projection when entering or leaving the space, before having sufficient distance to view it. For those already within the environment, seated on the benches in the center of the room, every incoming or outgoing spectator would necessarily carve out a silhouette within the photographic scene—entering the representational space of Selma, but only as a kind of ghostly shadow or negative presence. It was an image that could not but provoke an uneasy identification, as those just entering the space enacted the seated participants' recent past, while those leaving it enacted their imminent future. The projected photograph was not only a spectacle to be seen, but a stage on which the spectator would appear to others.

This public staging of spectatorship echoed what was perhaps the most innovative aspect of the Lincoln Center installation. On the mezzanine

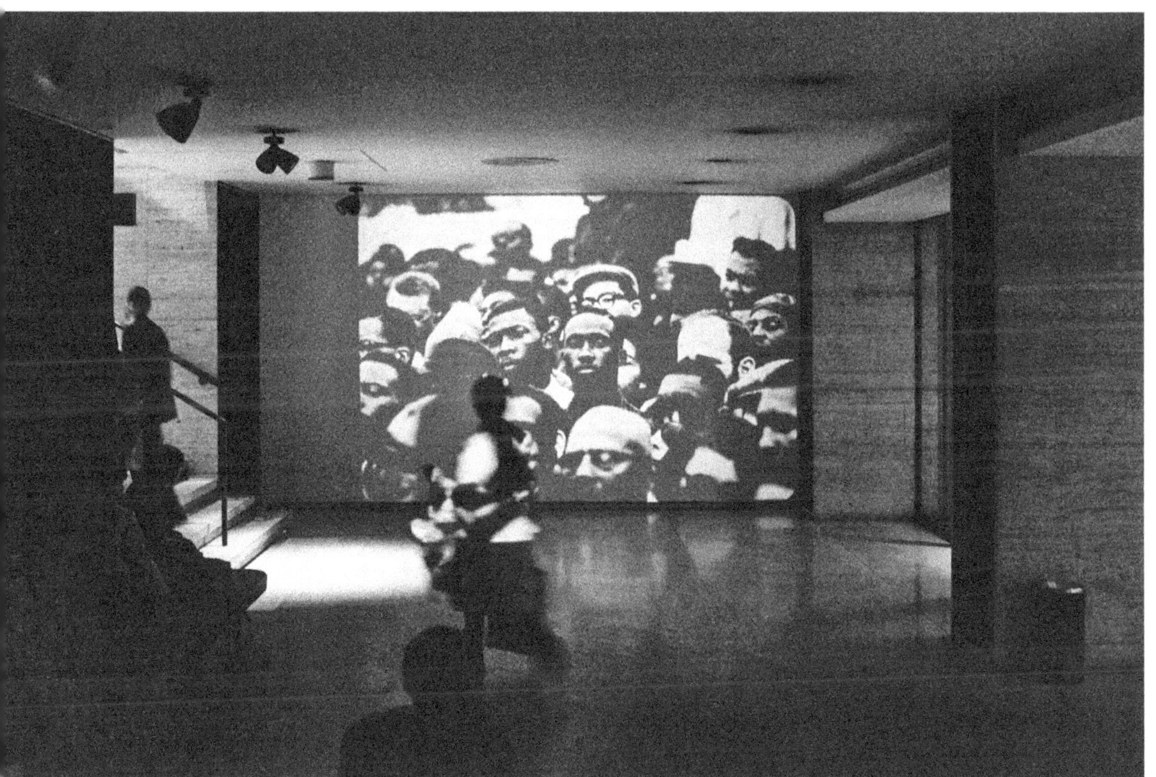

Figure 5.25. Large-scale projection of Bruce Davidson photographs within the darkened, lower-level audiovisual environment in the Lincoln Center installation of *Selma Last Year*, New York Film Festival, 1966. New York Public Library.

floor, opposite the stairwell leading downstairs, two unpainted plywood boxes stood side by side, elevated to eye level on plain white stands. On the left, an 8mm rear-screen film projector showed footage of the iconic confrontation on the Edmund Pettus Bridge, as it had been broadcast on ABC News. As opposed to the fleeting but noble Davidson portraits projected downstairs, the film footage came on like a traumatic nightmare constantly reenacted—the two-minute scene looped endlessly without pause. This film footage of "Bloody Sunday" was one of the most pivotal sequences to be broadcast during the civil rights struggles of the time. Comparable to the Zapruder film of Kennedy's assassination less than two years before, it galvanized national support for civil rights in undeniably visceral terms. Doubtless the reason this particular footage was so effective is that it inverted the stereotypical representation of the "angry black mob" so prevalent in media representations of the time. Even the comparably restrained initial coverage of the Selma march in the *New York Times* was framed in terms of a failure to maintain law and order: marchers were "fighting with bricks and bottles," and a "handful of volunteer possemen were pushed back by flying debris when they tried to herd the angry Negroes into the church where the march had begun."[61] The film footage, broadcast by television stations around the nation, showed

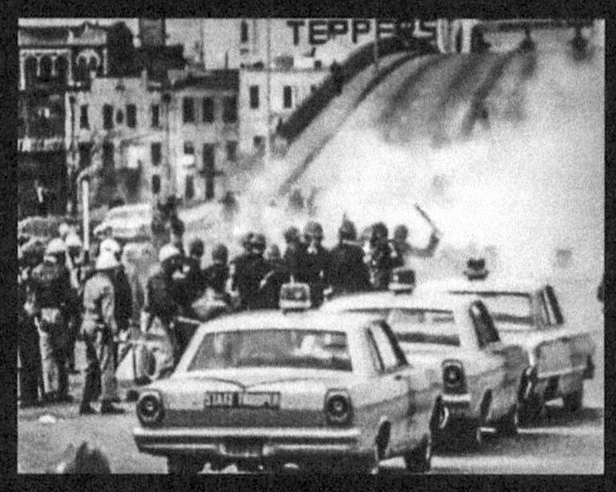
TEPPERS
STATE TROOPER

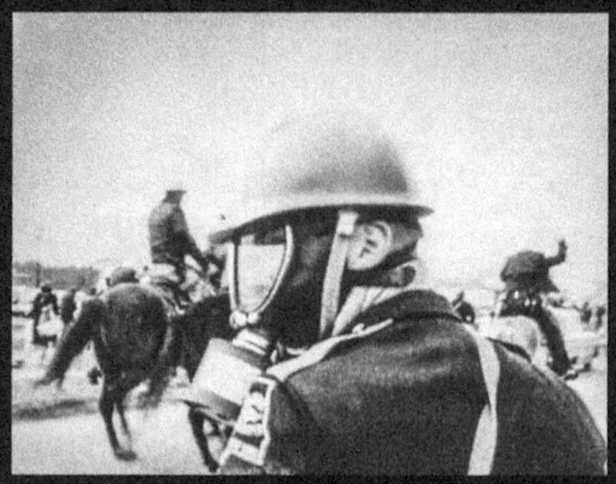

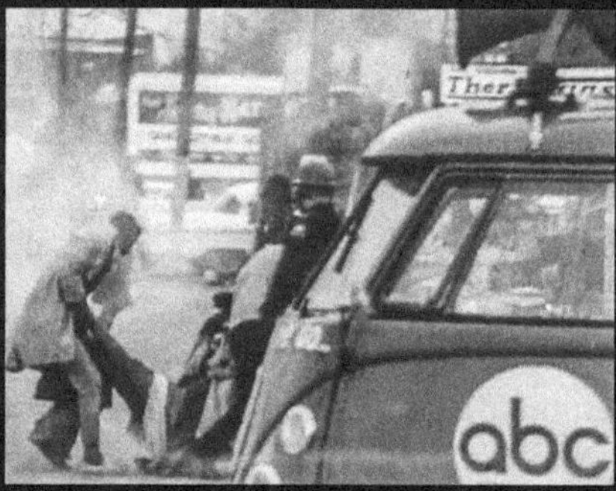
abc

Figure 5.26. ABC News footage from the Edmund Pettus Bridge confrontation on March 7, 1965, as used within the film loop viewer at the Lincoln Center installation of *Selma Last Year*, New York Film Festival, 1966.

something very different. In it, a mixed group of white and black men and women, young and old, stood on an embankment while an ominous line of dark-clothed men, their identities hidden under full-face gas masks, initiated a brutal attack using nightsticks, whips, and tear gas and continued to beat those who had fallen and were not fighting back.

At Lincoln Center, the traumatic scene was not quickly subsumed into some greater narrative, as in a traditional documentary film or television broadcast, but simply repeated again and again, looped continuously. While gruesome and difficult to watch, the footage must have also been difficult *not* to watch—the violence and chaos evoking a certain morbid fascination with the event as spectacle. Reflecting this ambivalence, Dewey chose to make the Selma footage difficult to watch in a wholly new way. Adjacent to the plywood box on the left, containing the rear-screen film projector, he had placed another box containing a television monitor. The image on that monitor, to a visitor just arriving, would probably have been unrecognizable. A black-and-white image of relatively low resolution and dynamic range, it depicted a mostly empty space, perhaps with some indiscernible movement in the background. As such, it would have been passed over in favor of the dramatic scenes unfolding on the film projector beside it. This temporal construction was essential to the drama of recognition Dewey sought to enact. For after a few seconds, spectators would surely have recognized something familiar out of the corner of the eye and turned back to the television monitor. There, they would have seen something shocking in both its familiarity and its unfamiliarity: themselves, but themselves as they had been eight seconds before, transfixed by the events at Selma unfolding on the other screen.

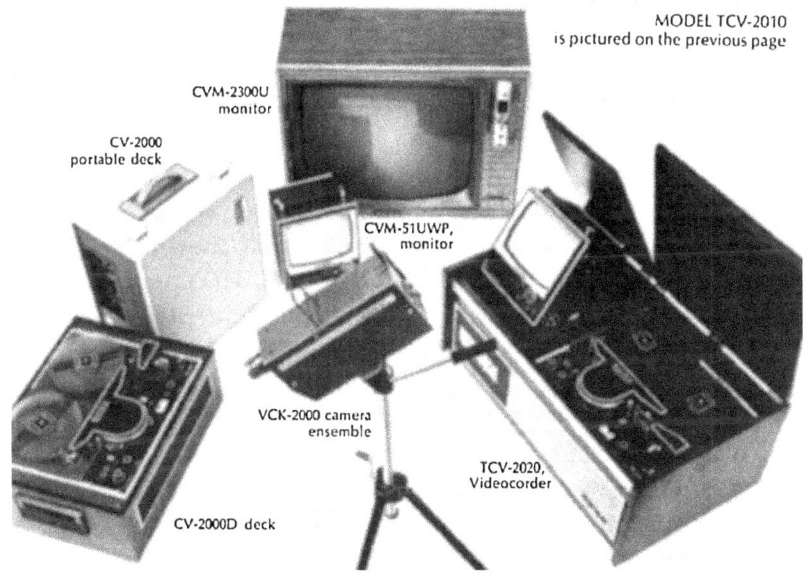

Figure 5.27. Videocorder advertising material from Sony Corporation illustrating the video equipment loaned to Dewey for use in the Lincoln Center installation of *Selma Last Year*, New York Film Festival, 1966.

Figure 5.28. View of the back of the film (right) and video (left) cabinets used in the Lincoln Center installation of *Selma Last Year*, 1966. New York Public Library.

Figure 5.29. Viewer observing the film (left) and video (right) setup used in the Lincoln Center installation of *Selma Last Year*, 1966. New York Public Library. The telltale sign of a video cathode ray tube display can be seen in the dark banding across the image that occurs at higher shutter speeds, probably necessitated by high-speed film.

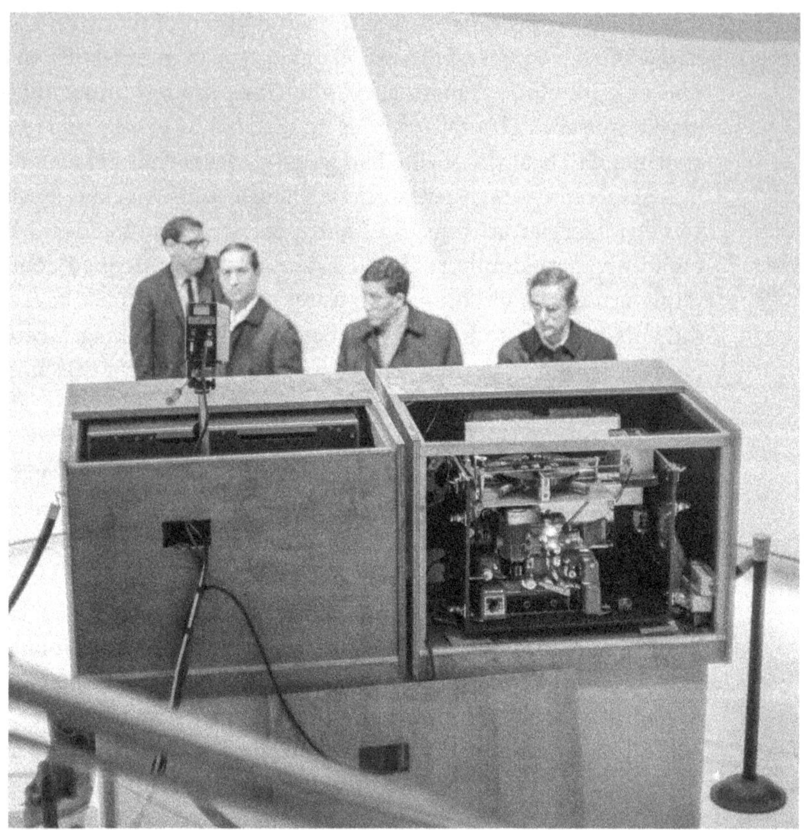

Capitalizing on the publicity to be gained through association with the prestigious and well-attended New York Film Festival, the Sony Corporation agreed to loan Dewey its new Videocorder equipment for the installation.[62] Quite obviously inspired by Riley's experiments in tape delay, but probably finding additional motivation in the industrial practice of delaying live broadcasts so as to censor unwanted content, Dewey set up the tape to run through two Videocorder units, delaying the live video playback by eight seconds. In so doing, he created a spectatorial juxtaposition whose aesthetic and technical economy was as great as its effect was profound. For spectators looking at themselves looking, it was not merely the event, but that act of spectatorship, that was itself being staged. Spectators were transformed into unwitting actors in an experience as familiar and pleasurable as it was disorienting and disturbing.

In a 1967 interview, Fred Wellington would essentially accuse the artist of trafficking in the technophilic spectacle of the World's Fair to the neglect of his earlier interests in social interaction.[63] Yet Dewey felt that the particular conjunction of film and video feedback in *Selma Last Year* was an extension of his previous work in "social theatre"—one specifically relevant to the situation of the New York Film Festival at Lincoln Center.

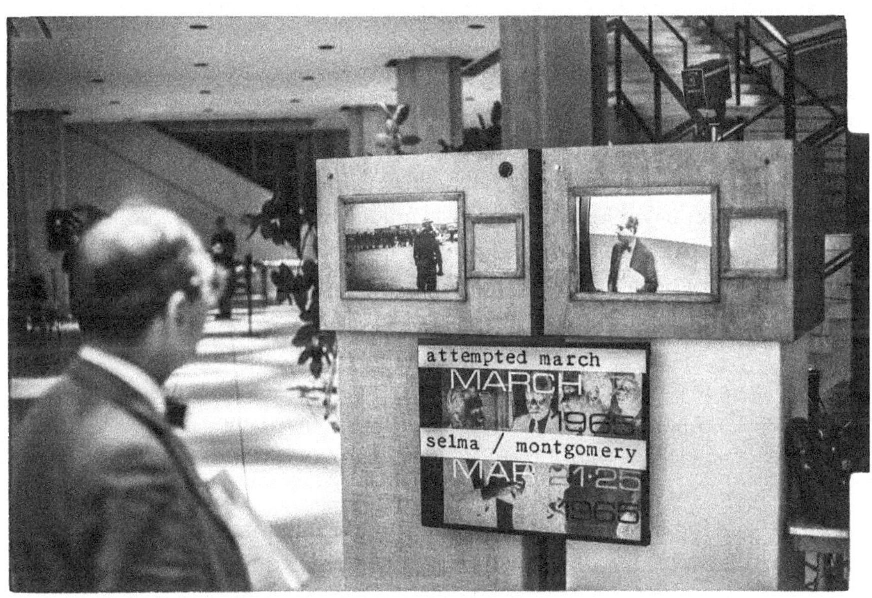
attempted march
MARCH
1965
selma / montgomery
MAR 21·25
1965

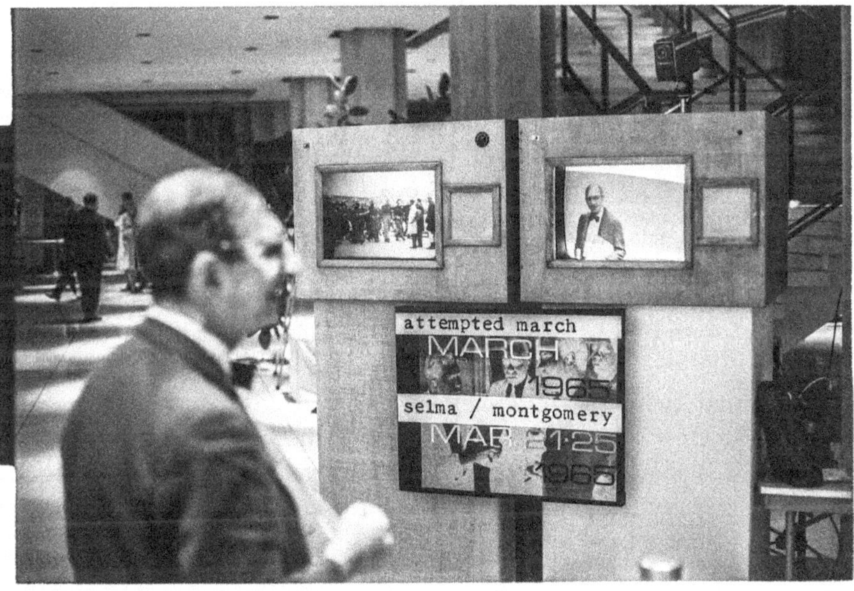
attempted march
MARCH
1965
selma / montgomery
MAR 21·25
1965

Indeed, while Dewey's use of video feedback might have been almost identical to its use at the RCA Pavilion in formal terms, the effects of this feedback within the overall context of the installation were almost diametrically opposed. At the World's Fair, the video feedback loop was detached from any conception of its increasingly powerful social role. Presented as a mere curiosity, this ostensibly neutral display played to the very narcissistic and exhibitionary tendencies that network television was just then discovering how to profitably exploit. *Selma Last Year*, rather than mirroring viewers back to themselves in a regressive fantasy of integrity and self-sufficiency, sought to disrupt this basic narcissistic circuit.

No term had yet arisen to classify what Dewey, Riley, and Davidson had created. A brief mention in the *New York Times* described it as a "static happening." A press release, of unknown authorship, described it as a "sight and sound visual happening portrait."[64] Today, we would place it under the generic rubric of "installation." Dewey, however, specifically referred to the work as a "continuous environment." Marshall McLuhan's idea that every new technology creates a new environment, with new forms of human association and perception, was fast becoming a cultural commonplace. Yet McLuhan's ideas were often far less sanguine than their popular reception would suggest. In a short piece titled "Art as Anti-Environment," written for *Arts News* in 1965, he ominously proclaimed that "such new environments that all of us react to with the precision of marionettes turn whole populations into servo-mechanisms."[65] Since the given environment always remains imperceptible as such, it is adopted at the time "without any difficulty or awareness of change. It is later that the psychic and social realignments baffle societies." McLuhan believed that contemporary art, having rejected its traditional role as personal expression, was now able to act as an "early warning system" for the "psychic and social consequences of the new environment" through its "training of our perception and judgment." Assuming that they can provide sufficient "contrapuntal stress" to avoid a mere mimetic repetition or intensification of their environment, the arts can effectively constitute a temporary autonomous zone or "anti-environment" from whose distance and vantage point the ordinary environment can be experienced.

Selma Last Year did not seek to represent the events of Selma, because those events had already been represented countless times. Indeed, while their widespread dissemination had been part of the original, successful strategy of the civil rights movement, the very familiarity of these images had since come to constitute a significant problem. As such, Dewey did not attempt to represent the events of Selma through yet another reiteration of its imagery so much as he sought to present the complexity of his viewers' own encounter with this imagery—with all the recognition and misrecognition that would inevitably entail. Dewey speaks of "a capacity of the piece to adjust itself to each person who comes in there, you know, to recognize them in a certain sense so it is constantly changing."[66] Within *Selma Last Year*, Dewey frames this event of spectatorship quite literally for the spectator, showing her own act of watching the moving image. The video monitor was not a simple mirror: his viewers did not see themselves seeing themselves. Rather, they saw themselves from outside, as another might see them.

Dewey had feared an almost unbridgeable chasm between the easy security of his largely white, privileged audience at Lincoln Center and the utter vulnerability of the civil rights marchers in Alabama. His solution was profound in its economy: to truly see these images of Selma, the audience at Lincoln Center were asked to look beyond themselves. It was a metaphorical demand made literal. Dewey understood how compelling the narcissistic lure of his video mirror would prove—how it would tear people away from the Selma footage in spite of themselves. Yet in foregrounding their own status as viewers, he invariably turned his audience toward the events at Selma and against their own narcissistic identification. Caught between conflicting imperatives, Dewey's audience was left without the possibility of an easy resolution, and their reaction was not hard to predict. "It got people very angry with themselves and angry with us," Dewey later recalled, "but I don't think it was unfair because Lincoln Center is so pleased with itself and the people who were going to it were so pleased with themselves that to be able to whip that around them a bit was good for them."[67]

While *Selma Last Year* did bring together photography, slide projection, sound, film projection, and video, these components in no way functioned holistically in the manner of a coherent, unified spectacle. Rather, both in their theoretical conception and in their practical execution, the multiple "environments" of *Selma Last Year* functioned according to a principle of *disjunction*. It may seem an obvious point, but it is one that would be historically significant. For in her influential polemic "Film and the Radical Aspiration" at the festival's critical symposium, Michelson would single out Dewey's work, alongside Whitman's, as a mere "revival of that old dream of synesthesia," the term with which she disparaged the idea of expanded cinema more generally. Given the specifically Brechtian flavor of advanced art and film criticism throughout the late 1960s and 1970s, one would readily expect that such a "synesthetic" project would arouse little interest, and it is thus lamentably explicable that Dewey's groundbreaking collaboration would be almost entirely forgotten within art and film history for almost fifty years.[68] This is doubly ironic in that Dewey's background and interest in social theater made him more of a natural heir to Bertolt Brecht's dramatic ideas than most of his contemporaries. He described his emphasis as specifically seeking to bring together the intellectual reflexivity of Brecht with the emotional force of Artaud, claiming that such a knitting together of rational analysis and emotional identification was necessary for any effective critique of contemporary media society.[69] Dewey found the projected image a uniquely powerful tool for accessing this essential register of affective identification. Yet *Selma Last Year* was certainly no simple return to the synesthetic ideal. Rather, it was a self-consciously disjunctive articulation of multiple atmospheres: one in which film and video would not enhance one another, but quite specifically struggle for attention. Through this disjunction, *Selma Last Year* staged a political problem of image and identification that would become decisive for the development of film theory over the next decade.

In practical terms, *Selma Last Year* was an abject failure. Whether out of deliberate censorship, malice, or merely administrative incompetence, the Lincoln Center staff refused to allow audiences near any of Dewey's complex, multi-part installation until just before the feature film was about to commence. As such, thousands of potential spectators literally rushed past the work—catching at best a glimpse of some imagery, a brief passage of the soundscape—on their way to secure a good seat for the night's festival program. This audience was obviously never given the chance to experience the different parts of the work, much less consider how those parts were aesthetically and conceptually conjoined. Dewey's complex work was thus reduced to a curiosity and quite understandably overlooked by most of the day's prominent critics of art, film, and performance. Like Warhol's installation in the lobby in 1964 and Bruce Conner's *10 Second Film* trailer of 1965, *Selma Last Year* would join the catalog of works foiled in their attempt to work within but against the parameters of the New York Film Festival at Lincoln Center.

Nevertheless, in its juxtaposition of documentary film and video feedback, sonic collage, and oversized photographic projection, *Selma Last Year* was formally and conceptually unprecedented. By placing his delayed televisual mirror immediately adjacent to a documentary newsreel clip—one that had itself played a major role in a broadcast news event just a year before—Dewey's installation succinctly indexed the challenge posed by televisual feedback to the postwar art cinema's long-standing concern for a "new realism." Like Warhol, Dewey seemed to intuit that long-standing debates over documentary *authenticity* were being displaced by a new set of questions around the complexities of audiovisual *temporality*. By working in this liminal space between art and cinema, Dewey had attempted to shift the festival's critical emphasis away from its exclusive focus on film as an autonomous and independent medium and toward an interrogation of the institutional situation of audiovisual spectatorship more broadly understood. Finally, by disrupting what he understood to be the conventional spectatorial dynamic, *Selma Last Year* sought to create a fissure in the isolating armor of the coherent, self-contained subject "seeing itself seeing"—to enable the possibility of an affective bridge between the self and the other through a fleeting, yet insistent, foregrounding of the self *as* other.

Both *Outer and Inner Space* and *Selma Last Year* brought film projection together with video feedback in ways that deliberately resisted formal synthesis and cohesion. The splitting both works occasioned—between multiple screens, multiple temporalities, and multiple registers of sensory experience—was left purposely unreconciled. Rather than producing a singular multimedia amalgamation, these works were intentionally, dramatically fractured. Their deliberately disjunctive use of media sought to express the social and psychological disjunction these media were then provoking within the culture more generally. Yet for all these similarities, *Outer and Inner Space* and *Selma Last Year* took place in manifestly different situations, which represented very different alternatives for future practice. Dewey's interest in the social force of institutions had led him to stage a site-specific intervention within the space of Lincoln Center and within the cultural politics of the New York Film Festival. Warhol's Factory, like VanDerBeek's Movie-Drome, was not an intervention so much as a wholly new manner of institution: a temporary, semi-autonomous space distinct from existing organizations of art, film, or theatrical practice.

Intervention or reinvention—by 1966, these were the two models that had emerged for maintaining the relevance of art and its institutions within a newly televisual age. In either case, the focus had decisively shifted from the material medium of a given individual work to the more encompassing situation within which that work took place, and to the traditions of exhibition and spectatorship embodied therein. This transformation was the legacy not only of Cage and minimalism, but of a nascent idea and practice of expanded cinema.

We do not say "experimental painting": painting is a repaired medium, constantly patched and reworked through the centuries, accepted through endless growth. Is the label "experimental film" to say that we cannot deny the cinema is still an unknown, only hinted at by hindsight, fantasy, dreams, hallucinations, comedy?

STAN VANDERBEEK, "The Cinema Delimina," 1961

It is because the aesthetic regime blurred the borders between what is art and what is mechanical, between what is poetic and what is prosaic, that the "mechanical" arts (photography, cinema, video) have been able to assume a place in art. We must therefore cast doubt on the idea that new technologies have the power to introduce breaks in the paradigms of art. If you take video and its derived forms, you will notice that its apparatus lends itself to any number of possible identifications.

JACQUES RANCIÈRE

EPILOGUE: THE HOMELESSNESS OF THE MOVING IMAGE

In her *Passages in Modern Sculpture,* Rosalind Krauss famously described the emergence of modernist sculpture in terms of a new condition of homelessness as the traditional monumental vocation of site marking gave way before the newly peripatetic condition of objecthood.[1] Cinema, while never originally site-specific in the same way, was nevertheless culturally bound to the cinematic theater as its proper exhibitionary site. A whole complex of social, cultural, and economic conventions would adhere to this particular model of exhibition. The postwar expanded cinema divorced the idea of cinema from the historical contingency of this exhibitionary model, creating a new and provocative condition of homelessness for the moving image within the institutions and discourses of contemporary art.

In introducing this study, I had recourse to Krauss's succinct yet ambitious genealogy of our contemporary "post-medium condition," in which she claimed that the "constitutive heterogeneity" of video marked the definitive collapse of the modernist conception of medium-specificity as an ontological investigation. No doubt, video's constitutive heterogeneity played an important role in this historical process. Yet as I have tried to demonstrate, it was the heterogeneity of *cinema*—its complex of mechanical, chemical, optical, cognitive, affective, and mnemonic processes—that the artists and theorists of the mid-1960s expanded cinema had already sought to reveal. Krauss chooses to begin her story at this later point because the structural film of the late 1960s and early 1970s was often understood within Clement Greenberg's high modernist conception of medium-specificity, and by overlooking the expanded cinema, she is able to construct an orderly progression whereby the postmodern heterogeneity of video comes to replace the modernist specificity of film. It allows her to leave these discrete historical categories intact. Yet as Krauss herself makes clear, the structural film intentionally deemphasized film's differential condition so as to help it accede to the coveted stature of modern art: "Structuralist film's self-definition, as I have said, was modernist," Krauss writes, "the impulse was to try to sublate the internal differences within the filmic apparatus into a single, indivisible, experiential unit that would serve as an ontological metaphor, a figure—like the 45-minute zoom—for the essence of the whole."[2] Yet the proliferation of these "internal differences" in the widespread adoption of video over the next decade would foreground what had already been inherent in film—its fundamental instability as a medium and the challenge its constitutive heterogeneity held for the modernist conception of medium-specificity as such.

I risk belaboring Krauss's account because the rhetorical construction of the moving image at this early moment—when its history and theory were only just beginning to be institutionalized within academic research and pedagogy—would frame much of the subsequent discourse around the place of the moving image within contemporary art. The heterogeneous, situationally oriented model of expanded cinema that emerged in the early to mid-1960s was not without its theorists, but it would prove too diffuse and inchoate to upset the dominant high modernist paradigm established by Greenberg. Within the academy, medium-specificity dictated that a body of practice called experimental film be made the exclusive province of a new discipline of film studies—partitioning off an aesthetic and conceptual domain whose practitioners had rarely understood themselves as far removed from the other arts. It dictated an autonomous study of the history, theory, and practice of film, rather than pursuit of its intersections with adjacent domains, such as photography, video, or performance. The effects of expanded cinema's displacement by the more traditional medium-specific aspirations of structural film and video art meant that when those medium-specific aspirations became untenable—as they quickly would—a large and diverse range of artists were left without critical support. Historians, theorists, and practitioners of experimental film within the academy were thus isolated and ill-equipped to contest the discipline's inexorable shift toward the study of popular culture. For if the modernist conception of medium-specificity was the only model for artistic specificity on offer, then these works could only be seen as *un*popular forms of cultural production—lacking even the socially diagnostic power of which the rising field of cultural studies would make use.

As this study has endeavored to show, the idea of expanded cinema that emerged in the 1960s was not a straightforward repudiation of medium: its artists and critics were almost single-mindedly concerned with the specific ways in which cinema functioned to destabilize existing art institutions and practices. It was rather that the cinema *had no specificity* in Greenberg's strict ontological sense. The material of projection was multiple—consisting of the celluloid strip, projector, and screen, to say nothing of the original camera and processing. Varying across space and time, the celluloid frame indexed a reality both past and distant while its projection constituted an event both present and local. The complexity of the cinematic *dispositif* included not simply the material conditions of production, but also the psychological conditions of spectatorship:

conditions both innate in human biology and born of the disciplinary codes of spectatorship formed over a half century of industrial exhibition. For the artists and critics of the expanded cinema, what specificity cinema possessed seemed less the timeless ontology of a material form than the contingent historicity of that form's cultural elaboration.

As D. N. Rodowick, one of the foremost chroniclers of the history of film theory, has described, the lack of consensus about the nature of the cinematic medium resulted in a kind of "aesthetic inferiority complex" vis-à-vis the traditional arts in the first half of the twentieth century.[3] In the postwar era, the precipitous decline in theatrical attendance that accompanied the proliferation of television threatened a questionable future for the institution of cinema. Yet by the mid-1960s, the success of the New York Film Festival—situated as it was amid the spectacular pomp of the Lincoln Center for the Performing Arts—seemed to signal the long-sought institutional legitimation of cinematic art. For Annette Michelson, writing in 1966, cinema was "on the verge of winning the battle for the recognition of its specificity": a battle that "every major film-maker and critic [over] the last half-century has fought."[4] Given the recently proclaimed "death of cinema," such institutional recognition was especially vital, and she praised the "intransigent autonomy" of those filmmakers committed to the cause, even as she castigated the "intermedia" as a symptom of its decline.

Much of the historical and conceptual significance of the expanded cinema arises from its rejection of the legitimating models of both the European art film and the avant-garde structural film—both attempts to stabilize a singular conception of cinema as a proper modern art. The failure of the historical expanded cinema to establish itself within postwar discourses of film studies or art history should thus in no way be understood as a simple historical oversight or accidental case of benign neglect. Its omission was rather structurally requisite insofar as it constituted a direct challenge to medium-specificity and even disciplinary specificity as a regulatory ideal. The discursive and institutional *promiscuity* of the expanded cinema—its interstitial location between physical, institutional, or discursive sites—would necessarily relegate it to a netherworld between art history and film studies insofar as those disciplines remained grounded on this ideal. Despite photography's challenge to the romantic conceptions of authorship and originality, Rodowick speculates that film was the first art form to fully confound Gotthold Lessing's division of the spatial and the temporal arts and thus "to challenge fundamentally the concepts on which the idea of the aesthetic were founded."[5]

French philosopher Jacques Rancière would agree with the importance Rodowick gives to cinema as a force of destabilization, but would contest the accepted narrative of aesthetic modernism Rodowick still takes for granted. Over nearly a dozen books, Rancière has sought to establish that the very idea of aesthetics has been misunderstood as a particular domain of philosophical reflection when it is more appropriately conceptualized as a historical regime of experience.[6] For Rancière, our modern aesthetic regime is that which bestows a particular mode of visibility and intelligibility by allowing certain objects and events to be perceived and conceptualized as art. This modern aesthetic regime is historically unprecedented in that it is no longer defined by positive rules about the proper nature and limits of art, but rather by the precise suspension or "disordering" [*dérèglement*] of customary relations between the various arts and the implicit hierarchical organization by which they were structured. Within this revolutionary sensibility—one that corresponds precisely to the emergence of social and political egalitarianism in the late eighteenth century—we can no longer know in advance what will qualify as art and by what criteria. Art will continuously challenge whatever criteria become established in the name of a kind of perpetual undoing of the distinction between art and non-art.

Rancière's genealogy of the aesthetic regime helps to explain how the institutional legitimation afforded the European art film, or in a different way, the avant-garde structural film, would precipitate a radical heterogeneity of artists' film and video over the course of the next decade. Simply put, the legitimation of certain forms of cinema as "high art" was antithetical to the hierarchical disruption that properly characterizes the work of art within the aesthetic regime. In the case of cinema, it was a disruption that had been historically predicated not on the medium's purity, autonomy, and specificity, but rather a paradoxically essential impurity, hybridity, and implication. The openness of the expanded cinema was correctly seen as a damning liability for film's legitimation as an autonomous sphere of modernist art. Yet, it was this very openness to other traditions, other institutional spaces, other visions of aesthetic practice and spectatorship that led it beyond the solipsistic cul-de-sac of high modernist theory. The expanded cinema prods us to reconsider the aesthetic and conceptual validity of our disciplinary frameworks insofar as they derive, consciously or unconsciously, from this medium-specific paradigm. For Rancière, a discipline "is not first of all the definition of a set of methods appropriate to a certain domain or a certain type of object. It is first the very constitution of this object as an object of thought ... a way of defining an idea of the thinkable, an idea of what the objects of knowledge themselves can think and know. It is therefore always a certain regulation of dissensus."[7] By implication, Rodowick's narrative about film theory's historical failure is thereby recast as a theoretical advance: the constitutive heterogeneity of cinema establishes a model for the reevaluation of the modernist conception of medium as well as the disciplinary fortifications that would be deployed in its name. The study of film—that debased field originally determined to mimic art history—ends up serving as a model for the reinvention of a contemporary art history, one that has turned away from the essentializing, ahistorical rhetorics of medium-specificity toward an archeology of media forms and culturally specific histories of audiovisuality across a range of discursive and institutional sites.

In situating the expanded cinema both historically and conceptually prior to the medium-specific rhetorics of both video art and structural film, we are spurred to reconsider the diverse investigations traditionally grouped under those rubrics as well as the substantive range of work that terminology rendered "out of place." To do so is to understand the moving image as a destabilizing force within the aesthetic and conceptual framework of medium-specificity itself, disorganizing institutional conventions of production and exhibition as well as those of spectatorship and criticism. For this reason, this book has not aimed to institutionalize the expanded cinema as a movement that might be neatly slotted into existing historical narratives so much as to articulate the motive, conceptual force of the expanded cinema as an unresolved disruption within the spaces, institutions, and discourses of late modern art. In so doing, it aspires to contribute to the more encompassing effort under way to reframe overarching narratives of twentieth-century art around movement rather than stasis, event rather than object.

Since the turn of the millennium, the moving image has reemerged within the contemporary art world with such overwhelming force and speed that it threatens to overcome the very strangeness of the questions it reignites. This is where the institutional challenge posed by the historical model of the expanded cinema acquires a renewed importance. Before the moving image becomes completely naturalized within the practices, spaces, and discourses of contemporary art, it is imperative that we attend to the strangeness it still carries within it, and thus its potential for a far-reaching reimagination of these very institutions. By displacing the conceptual orientation from one of the specificity of medium—in which individual forms are constantly demarcated, separated out, and even policed—this book has sought to bring a forgotten conceptual framework of site and situation to the story of the emergence of the moving image in contemporary art. This rhetoric—and the aesthetic and conceptual issues it implies—better allow us to critically engage the proliferation and the transformation of the moving image across the diversity of contemporary art practice.

The fundamental question of the cinematic situation—the conceptual tension between the essentially peripatetic nature of cinema's material exhibition and its ability to so powerfully evoke an experience of cognitive and psychological displacement—has evoked a whole matrix of questions and possibilities for artists working after the eclipse of the modernist paradigm. Contemporary moving-image installation takes place within this liminal or hybridized situation existing between the black box and the white cube: a situation whose liminality is both physical—embedded within the material structures of spectatorial institutions—and psychological—bound up with the problem of interiority and exteriority foundational to human subjectivity. The strongest work to date has tended to work on this dynamic, integrating both the material and the psychological components of the exhibitionary situation into the aesthetic and conceptual structure of the work itself.

As both the formal codes and the narrative structures of Hollywood have spread across the globe, they have created an international language within which contemporary artists have defamiliarized these codes and structures in rich and sophisticated ways, challenging our ideas of center and periphery just as the cinematic serves to challenge our ideas of interiority and exteriority. These artists no longer recoil reflexively from cinema's illusionistic power or from the lingering ambiguity of its institutional situation between high art and mass culture. Rather, they employ cinema's powers of spectatorial dislocation to address the dislocated qualities of contemporary subjectivity, just as they utilize cinema's ambiguous cultural and institutional location as a means to intervene within the palpably ambiguous landscapes of our new media ecology.

While not beholden to a material or even strictly geographic conception of site specificity, the particular placelessness invoked by the cinematic form does not float ungrounded, for it is necessarily situated within an iterative history of social and institutional conventions. At its most ambitious, "post-cinematic" art might be understood as a stratigraphic engagement with this history—making long-sedimented conventions immediate, tangible, and sensuous through a polyphony of spectatorial dislocation. As such, the original promise of the historical expanded cinema is reawakened for a new era.

Notes

Introduction

1. Michael Fried, *Art and Objecthood* (Chicago: University of Chicago Press, 1998).
2. The classic account is presented in Stephan Heath, "Narrative Space," in *Questions of Cinema* (Bloomington: Indiana University Press, 1981), 19–75.
3. Maurice Merleau-Ponty, *The Phenomenology of Perception*, trans. Donald A. Landes (New York: Routledge 2012).
4. Clara Weyergraf-Serra and Martha Buskirk, eds., *The Destruction of* Tilted Arc: *Documents* (Cambridge, MA: MIT Press, 1990).
5. Already in his articulation of the "Site/Non-Site Dialectic," Robert Smithson had sought to complicate this literalist conception by implicating the role of personal, institutional, and cultural memory that becomes stratigraphically sedimented within particular sites. Smithson, *The Collected Writings of Robert Smithson*, ed. Jack Flam (Berkeley: University of California Press, 1996). Douglas Crimp's 1986 essay on the Serra controversy, "Redefining Site Specificity," forged an important link between the earlier generation of postminimalist practices and the newly emergent cultural politics of the 1980s. Reprinted in his 1993 collection *On the Museum's Ruins* (Cambridge, MA: MIT Press), 150–86, it inspired a range of studies, from the "Roundtable on Site Specificity," *Documents* 4/5 (Spring 1994): 11–22, and James Meyer, "The Functional Site," *Documents* 7 (Fall 1996): 20–29, to Hal Foster, "The Siting of Contemporary Art," in *The Return of the Real* (Cambridge, MA: MIT Press, 1996), 184–99, and Miwon Kwon, *One Place after Another: Site-Specific Art and Locational Identity* (Cambridge, MA: MIT Press, 2002).
6. Some of the more significant examples over the past decade would include Nick Kaye, *Site-Specific Art: Performance, Place and Documentation* (New York: Routledge, 2000); Erika Suderburg, ed., *Space, Site, Intervention: Situating Installation Art* (Minneapolis: University of Minnesota Press, 2000); Scott MacDonald, *The Garden in the Machine: A Field Guide to Independent Films about Place* (Berkeley: University of California Press, 2001); Edward Casey, *Representing Place: Landscape Painting and Maps* (Minneapolis: University of Minnesota Press, 2002); Giuliana Bruno, *Atlas of Emotion: Journeys in Art, Architecture, and Film* (New York: Verso, 2002); Kwon, *One Place after Another*; Tacita Dean and Jeremy Miller, *Artworks: Place* (New York: Thames & Hudson, 2005); Jean-Christophe Royoux and Melik Ohanian, eds., *Cosmograms* (New York: Lukas & Sternberg, 2005); Jeffrey Skoller, *Shadows, Specters, Shards: Making History in Avant-Garde Film* (Minneapolis: University of Minnesota Press, 2005); Tom Conley, *Cartographic Cinema* (Minneapolis: University of Minnesota Press, 2007); Giuliana Bruno, *Public Intimacy: Architecture and the Visual Arts* (Cambridge, MA: MIT Press, 2007); Ina Blom, *On the Style Site: Art, Sociality and Media Culture* (New York: Sternberg Press, 2007); Claire Doherty, ed., *Situation* (Cambridge, MA: MIT Press, 2009); Maeve Connolly, *The Place of Artists' Cinema: Space, Site and Screen* (Bristol: Intellect Press, 2009); Tamara Trodd, ed., *Screen/Space: The Projected Image in Contemporary Art* (Manchester: University of Manchester Press, 2011);

and John David Rhodes and Elena Gorfinkel, eds., *Taking Place: Location and the Moving Image* (Minneapolis: University of Minnesota Press, 2012).

7. Bruno, *Atlas of Emotion*, 55–56.
8. For a historical overview of these debates, see D. N. Rodowick, *The Crisis of Political Modernism: Criticism and Ideology in Contemporary Film Theory* (Berkeley: University of California Press, 1995).
9. There is a rich and diverse literature devoted to this singular topic, but D. N. Rodowick provides a succinct overview in "Dr. Strange Media: Or, How I Learned to Stop Worrying and Love Film Theory," *PMLA* 116, no. 5 (October 2001): 1396–1404, as well as in the first chapter of his *Reading the Figural, or, Philosophy after the New Media* (Durham, NC: Duke University Press, 2001). He has undertaken a fuller study in *The Virtual Life of Film* (Cambridge, MA: Harvard University Press, 2007) and in his forthcoming volume *An Elegy for Theory*.
10. Rosalind Krauss, *A Voyage on the North Sea: Art in the Age of the Post-Medium Condition* (New York: Thames & Hudson, 1999); "'And Then Turn Away?' An Essay on James Coleman," *October* 81 (Summer 1997): 5–33; and "Reinventing the Medium," *Critical Inquiry* 25 (Winter 1999): 289–305. As Krauss begins her *Voyage* by acknowledging, her thoughts about "reinventing the medium" were inspired by Stanley Cavell's *The World Viewed: Reflections on the Ontology of Film* (New York: Viking, 1971). It is interesting to note that Barbara Rose uses the exact same phrase in the concluding sentence of her 1970 catalog *Claes Oldenburg* (New York: Museum of Modern Art), 187.
11. Krauss, *Voyage on the North Sea*, 31.
12. Krauss takes the term "constitutive heterogeneity" from Samuel Weber's important essay "Television, Set, and Screen," in *Mass Mediauras: Form, Technics, Media* (Stanford, CA: Stanford University Press, 1996), 110.
13. Rosalind Krauss, "Video: An Aesthetics of Narcissism," *October* 1 (Spring 1976): 50–52.
14. Rosalind Krauss, "Sculpture in the Expanded Field," *October* 8 (Spring 1979): 43.
15. See Eric de Bruyn, "The Expanded Field of Cinema, or Exercise on the Perimeter of the Square," in *X-Screen: Film Installations and Actions in the 1960s and 1970s* (Köln: Walter Konig, 2004), 152–76, and George Baker, "Photography's Expanded Field," *October* 114 (Fall 2005): 120–40.
16. Robert Morris, "Notes on Sculpture, Part 2," *Artforum* 5, no. 2 (October 1966): 20–23. In distinction to Krauss, Morris's original notion of site is more phenomenological than semiotic, though he would come to integrate the semiotic in his "Notes on Sculpture, Part 4: Beyond Objects," *Artforum* 7.8 (April 1969): 50–54, and in "The Present Tense of Space," *Art in America* 66, no. 1 (January–February 1978): 70–81.
17. "This is not the kind of expansion that Krauss's work foregrounds. She does not speak of consciousness or viewers or experiences. She never mentions wombs. For her there are only logics, makers, and forms. This is because her conceptual field is structural, categorical." Anne Wagner, "Splitting and Doubling: Architecture and the Body of Sculpture," *Grey Room* 14 (Winter 2004): 26–45.
18. Krauss, "Sculpture in the Expanded Field," 42–43.
19. Gene Youngblood, *Expanded Cinema* (New York: Dutton, 1970), 41.
20. Ibid., 150.
21. Ibid., 41.
22. Over the last decade, both Youngblood and the 1960s counterculture have been increasingly subject to reconsideration outside these early constraining binaries. Here, I am less interested in establishing the truth of the period than in historicizing the art

critical discourse vis-à-vis the aesthetic and academic institutionalization of the moving image.

23. Sheldon Renan, "Expanded Cinema," in *An Introduction to the American Underground Film* (New York: Dutton, 1967), 227; Youngblood, *Expanded Cinema*, 41.
24. Krauss, *Voyage on the North Sea*, 44.
25. André Bazin, *What Is Cinema?*, essays selected and translated by Hugh Gray (2 vols.) (Berkeley: University of California Press, 1967), originally published in French in 4 volumes between 1958 and 1965. The specific reformulation of Bazin's title seems to have been first used in a short review by Chris Dercon titled "Gleaning the Future—From the Gallery Floor," *Vertigo* 2, no. 2 (2002): 3–5.
26. Benjamin's idea was itself indebted to the work of the Hungarian Bauhaus artist Lazlo Moholy-Nagy, and it was most prominently articulated in relation to the present context in "A Little History of Photography," in *The Work of Art in the Age of its Technological Reproducibility, and Other Writings on Media*, eds. Michael Jennings, Brigid Doherty, and Thomas Levin (Cambridge, MA: Harvard University Press, 2008), 274–98. Krauss cites Benjamin's idea in *Voyage on the North Sea*, 41.
27. The motion picture industry was severely disrupted by the Supreme Court's landmark antitrust decision *United States v. Paramount Pictures, Inc.*, 334 US 131 (1948), which broke up the model of vertical integration on which the major studios depended throughout the "golden age."
28. Amos Vogel, "Witness and Catalyst," *Philharmonic Hall Program* (New York: *Saturday Review* 1965), 12.

Chapter 1

1. Robert Caro, *The Power Broker: Robert Moses and the Fall of New York* (New York: Knopf, 1974).
2. Ibid.
3. *Johnson Wax Company Magazine*, available on the 1964 World's Fair Online, accessed 2007, http://nywf64.com/johwax07.shtml.
4. Ibid.
5. Maxine Haleff, "*To Be Alive!* and the Multi-Screen Film," *Film Culture* 43 (1966): 4. This was the special "Expanded Cinema/Expanded Arts" issue of *Film Culture* designed by George Macunias as a oversized newspaper for the winter of 1966. "This issue started as an index to the artists working in the area of the Expanded Cinema," Jonas Mekas wrote in the introduction, "only as we went, our original conception changed and we decided to include all the other arts" (1). While the published title was *Film Culture—Expanded Arts*, there was obvious tension over how a journal titularly devoted to film would handle such a disciplinary expansion. "We intend to come out with other issues," Mekas continued; "next edition should include more Expanded Dance, more Expanded Music, more Happenings people," yet this intention was largely unfulfilled.
6. The history sketched here is explored in much greater detail in John Belton, *Widescreen Cinema* (Cambridge, MA: Harvard University Press, 1992); Alison Griffiths, *Shivers Down Your Spine: Cinema, Museums, and the Immersive View* (New York: Columbia University Press, 2008); and John Belton, Sheldon Hall, and Steve Neale, eds., *Widescreen Worldwide* (Bloomington: Indiana University Press, 2010).
7. While several sources claim that Waller's Vitarama film for the Petroleum Industry Pavilion was well received, Richard Koszarski states that it was rejected at the last minute

as being "too radical." See Richard Koszarski, *Hollywood on the Hudson: Film and Television in New York from Griffith to Sarnoff* (New Brunswick, NJ: Rutgers University Press, 2008), 391. I discuss Waller's "movie-mural" for the Perisphere exhibit in chapter 4.

8. Outside of industrial cinema, Disney's Circle-Vision attractions in the 1950s and 1960s employed nine cameras and projectors to project a 360-degree panorama in a process virtually identical to the original nineteenth-century Cinéorama.
9. Haleff, *To Be Alive!*, 4.
10. *Official Guide to the New York World's Fair* (New York: Time, 1964).
11. Hammid articulates the principal difference in saying, "Unlike Cinerama, which always uses the same focal length lens, we can photograph with the full range, from telephoto to wide angle." Haleff, "*To Be Alive!*" 4. These contentions were borne out in their later practice, for after initial experiments in three- and later six-screen projection, Thompson and Hammid focused on developing super-70mm or IMAX cinema in the 1970s and 1980s.
12. The monumental, spectacular, and profoundly immersive *Think* presentation by Charles and Ray Eames for the IBM Pavilion was doubtless the most formally audacious of the fair, lifting its audience into the air and enclosing them within its elevated, egg-shaped theater before bombarding them with the imagery of fifteen still- and moving-image projectors. But while the imagery was visually heterogeneous, it was not in the least disjunctive. To the contrary, like the Eameses' similarly monumental *Glimpses of the USA* (1959), it had been explicitly crafted for the purpose of effective communication. See Beatriz Colomina, "Enclosed by Images: The Eameses' Multimedia Architecture," *Grey Room* 02 (Winter 2001): 6–29.
13. Jonas Mekas, *Movie Journal: The Rise of a New American Cinema, 1959–1971* (New York: Macmillan, 1972), 199.
14. "So this is what's happening—the Expanded Cinema. Even the Lincoln Center for Performing Arts library has a multi-screen film wall. Even NBC has tried split-screen video for the Gemini launch/football game. And just wait until Montreal's Expo '68. Francis Thompson of the Johnson's Wax film, Disney, the National Film Board of Canada, etc., are busy preparing cinema dreams." Howard Junker, "The Underground Renaissance," *Nation*, December 27, 1965.
15. Mekas, *Movie Journal*, 208. The series was originally titled New Cinema Festival I, but became widely known as the Expanded Cinema Festival.
16. Ibid.
17. Jon Hendricks and the Gilbert and Lisa Silverman Fluxus Collection, eds., *Fluxus Codex* (New York: Abrams, 1988), 161 and 437–38. The Fluxus Codex is an encyclopedic compendium of works from the Gilbert and Lila Silverman Collection bequeathed to MoMA.
18. Bruce Jenkins, "Fluxfilms in Three False Starts," in *In the Spirit of Fluxus* (Minneapolis: Walker Art Center, 1993), 136.
19. Paik claimed to have conceived of the work years before, and given the work's integral relationship with the aesthetics of John Cage—whose influence Paik would have felt strongly when he was studying music in Germany in the late 1950s—such a chronology seems entirely plausible.
20. John Cage, *Silence: Lectures and Writings* (Middletown, CT: Wesleyan University Press, 1961), 272.
21. John Cage, "On Nam June Paik's *Zen for Film*," in *John Cage: Writer: Selected Texts*, 2nd ed., ed. Richard Kostelanetz (New York: Cooper Square Press, 2000).

22. Ibid.

23. Robert Rauschenberg, as quoted in "The Art of Assemblage: A Symposium," a panel discussion moderated by William C. Seitz at the Museum of Modern Art, New York, October 1961, in conjunction with the exhibition *The Art of Assemblage*. Reprinted in *Essays on Assemblage*, ed. John Elderfield, Studies in Modern Art, no. 2 (New York: Museum of Modern Art, 1992), 137–38.

24. Joan Retallack, ed., *Musicage: Cage Muses on Words, Art, Music* (Hanover, NH: Wesleyan University Press, 1996), 135–36.

25. On Picabia's set design, see Rosalind Krauss, *Passages in Modern Sculpture* (Cambridge, MA: MIT Press, 1996), 207–13, and George Baker, "Intermission: Dada Cinema," in *The Artwork Caught by the Tail: Francis Picabia and Dada in Paris* (Cambridge, MA: MIT Press, 2007), 289–337.

26. Sheldon Renan, "The Blue Mouse and the Movie Experience," *Film Culture* 43 (1966): 4.

27. Ibid.

28. Walter Benjamin, "The Work of Art in the Age of Its Technological Reproducibility: Second Version," in Jennings et al., *Work of Art*, 19–55 (see introduction, n. 26).

29. Renan, "Blue Mouse," 4.

30. Ibid.

31. Robert Desnos, "Picture Palaces," *Le Soir* 28 (May 1927). Reprinted in *The Shadow and Its Shadow: Surrealist Writings on Cinema*, 3rd ed., ed. Paul Hammond (San Francisco: City Lights, 2000), 78–79.

32. Branden Joseph has a detailed discussion of Rauschenberg's *Map Room II* (1965) in chapter 5 of *Random Order: Robert Rauschenberg and the Neo-Avant-Garde* (Cambridge, MA: MIT Press, 1999). I discuss Whitman's piece *Prune.Flat.* (1965) in chapter 4 of this book.

33. Richard Kostelanetz's original notes from the performance were published in "The Discovery of Alternative Theatre: Notes on Art Performances in New York City in the 1960s and 1970s," *Perspectives of New Music* 27, no. 1 (Winter 1989): 128–72.

34. Richard Kostelanetz, *The Theatre of Mixed Means: An Introduction to Happenings, Kinetic Environments, and Other Mixed-Means Performances* (New York: Dial Press, 1968), 150–52. Importantly, Oldenburg had already stressed the "supersensitiveness to place and to circumstance . . . the place itself doing the work" of his 1963 *Autobodys*, situated in an empty Los Angeles parking lot near a drive-in movie theater. See Claes Oldenburg, *Raw Notes: Documents and Scripts of the Performances: Stars, Moveyhouse, Massage, The Typewriter* (Halifax: The Press of Nova Scotia College of Art and Design, 1973), 80.

35. Such a staging of spectatorship has been used, with varying degrees of critical awareness, since the origins of cinema. Two of the most poignant and enduring examples from the age of silent cinema are Buster Keaton's *Sherlock, Jr.* (MGM, 1924) and Dziga Vertov's *Man with a Movie-Camera* (VUFKU, 1929).

36. Cited in Henry Geldzahler, "Happenings: Theatre by Painters," *Hudson Review* 18, no. 4 (Winter 1965–1966): 585, and in Roger Copeland, "Sense and Sensibility in Contemporary Dance," *Theatre* 4 (Summer 1973): 140.

37. Roland Barthes, "En sortant du cinéma," *Communications* 23 (1975), 104–7. Translation mine.

38. For an overview of the early debates over "apparatus theory," see Rodowick, *Crisis of Political Modernism* (see introduction, n. 8). Barthes was clear that Bertolt Brecht never advocated eliminating all manner of pleasure or identification from the theater, only counterbalancing them through modes of distanciation or estrangement. See John

Willett, ed., *Brecht on Theatre: The Development of an Aesthetic* (New York: Hill & Wang, 1964).

39. Barthes, "En sortant du cinéma," 106.
40. Ibid., 106–7.
41. Ibid., 106.
42. *Roland Barthes by Roland Barthes*, 90, as cited by Victor Burgin in his insightful commentary "Barthes's Discretion," in *In/Different Spaces: Place and Memory in Visual Culture* (Berkeley: University of California Press, 1996), 161–78.
43. Boris Groys recently described this idea of site specificity in surprisingly similar terms: "Because the distinction between original and copy is solely topological and situative, this means that all of the objects placed into a museum are actually originals—also and especially when they otherwise circulate as copies. The installation makes copying reversible: it transforms a copy into an original ... each new contextualization of the image is its originalization, its reinvention." See Boris Groys, "From the Image to the Image-File, and Back," in *40 Years Video Art.de: Digital Heritage: Video Art in Germany from 1963 to the Present*, ed. Rudolf Frieling and Wulf Herzogenrath (Ostfildern, Germany: Hatje Cantz, 2006), 50–57.
44. Quoted in Rose, *Claes Oldenburg*, 184 (see introduction, n. 10).
45. Kostelanetz, "Discovery of Alternative Theatre," 143.
46. "I didn't accept an invitation to do *Moveyhouse* in Hartford, because I knew the auditorium there was so neutral that it would have lost all its effect." Kostelanetz, *Theatre of Mixed Means*, 143–44.
47. The much larger Roxy Theatre had been razed in 1961, and the Capitol Theatre would soon fall in 1968, leaving only Radio City Music Hall as a symbol of New York's theatrical golden age.
48. On the Cinematheque's peripatetic existence, see Vincent Camby, "Underground Movies Find Showcase on 41st St," *New York Times*, January 7, 1966.
49. "Talk of the Town," *New Yorker*, December 4, 1965: 52–54. Fresh from a Columbia MBA and a stint a Bloomingdale's, the twenty-four-year-old Brockman—"I'm not a businessman, I'm a process"—helped produce the expanded cinema programs for the Film-Makers' Cinematheque and the New York Film Festival, before trademarking the term "Intermedia" and starting a business producing and marketing multimedia shows in the late 1960s and 1970s—interweaving the worlds of art and industrial spectacle this chapter has been attempting to pry apart.
50. Kostelanetz, *Theatre of Mixed Means*, 56.
51. Ibid.
52. But must an artist acquiesce to this prohibition? This question raises the larger question of *willed impermanence* as it comes into conflict with the preservative instincts of institutions, whether museal or academic.
53. This idea forms the principal structure of Branden Joseph's *Beyond the Dream Syndicate: Tony Conrad and the Arts after Cage* (New York: Zone, 2008).
54. Linda Williams, "Discipline and Fun: *Psycho* and Postmodern Cinema," in *Reinventing Film Studies*, ed. Christine Gledhill and Lucinda Williams (New York: Oxford University Press, 2000), 351–78.
55. Stephen Rebello, *Alfred Hitchcock and the Making of Psycho* (New York: St. Martin's Griffin, 1998), 149–52. See also William Castle's autobiography, *Step Right Up! I'm Gonna Scare the Pants off America* (New York: Putnam, 1976).
56. Rebello, *Alfred Hitchcock*, 151.

57. See Peter Kubelka, "The Invisible Cinema," *Design Quarterly* 93 (1974): 32–35; Sky Sitney, "The Search for the Invisible Cinema," *Grey Room* 19 (2005): 102–13.

58. The film's length has become a matter of not inconsiderable variation. Jonas Mekas reported that Warhol was making "an eight-hour-long movie that shows nothing but a man sleeping" in the *Village Voice*, September 19, 1963. Long after the film was released, that time would be repeated—for instance, critic Thomas Meehan writes of "Andy Warhol's eight-hour long film, 'Sleep'" in "Not Good Taste, Not Bad Taste—It's Camp," *New York Times*, March 21, 1965. The film's actual length is five hours and twenty-one minutes when it is properly screened at sixteen frames per second. In 1970, the industry standard for silent speed was increased from sixteen to eighteen frames per second to eliminate perceptible flicker, and projectors since then rarely accommodate sixteen frames per second. For this reason, Warhol's films have often been projected at eighteen or even twenty-four frames per second (sound speed), thus reducing or even eliminating their subtle slow-motion effect.

59. Mekas, *Movie Journal*, 146–47. Curiously enough, Getz ends by noting, "Fifty were still left at the end. Some people really digging the movie."

60. The premiere of Satie's *Vexations* was organized by John Cage in 1963, seventy years after it was first composed. See Branden Joseph's careful analysis of the film's formal structure in "The Play of Repetition: Andy Warhol's *Sleep*," *Grey Room* 19 (2005): 22–53.

61. Clement Greenberg, "Modernist Painting," *Arts Yearbook* 4 (1961): 102–8.

62. Malcolm Le Grice, *Abstract Film and Beyond* (Cambridge, MA: MIT Press, 1977), 95.

63. Callie Angel, *The Films of Andy Warhol: An Introduction* (New York: Whitney Museum of American Art, 1988).

64. Andy Warhol, interview by Gretchen Berg, in *I'll Be Your Mirror: The Selected Andy Warhol Interviews*, ed. Kenneth Goldsmith (New York: Carroll & Graf, 2004), 92. Asked about the "boredom" of his early films, Warhol would later describe them as attempting to "make comedy in the audience. People always have a better time, have more fun together than watching what is on the screen." Andy Warhol, interview by Bess Winakor, in Goldsmith, *I'll Be Your Mirror*, 225.

65. See Leo Bersani and Ulysse Dutoit, *Arts of Impoverishment: Beckett, Rothko, Resnais* (Cambridge, MA: Harvard University Press, 1993).

66. Steven Watson, *Factory Made: Warhol and the Sixties* (New York: Pantheon Books, 2003), 133.

67. For an overview of the concept and its evolution within film studies, see Wanda Strauven, ed., *The Cinema of Attractions Reloaded* (Amsterdam: Amsterdam University Press, 2006).

68. Tom Gunning, "How Attractions Came into the World," in Strauven, *Cinema of Attractions Reloaded*, 34; Thomas Elsaesser and Adam Barker, eds., *Early Film: Space, Frame, Narrative* (London: British Film Institute, 1990).

69. Gunning, "How Attractions Came into the World."

70. Dwight MacDonald, "Objections to the New American Cinema," in *The New American Cinema: A Critical Anthology*, ed. Gregory Battcock (New York: E. P. Dutton, 1967), 198.

71. Furthermore, regardless of their ambitions, American artists could not afford to compete with the heavily subsidized production budgets of many of Europe's "national cinemas."

72. On the New York Film Festival's relationship to the New American Cinema, see chapter 5.

73. John Gruen coined the term "The Combine Generation" in his essay "The New Bohemia"

in *New York, the Herald Tribune Magazine,* November 29, 1964, 8–9, 11–13, 17, 22, 24, later expanded into a short book titled *The New Bohemia: The Combine Generation. Art, Music, Drama, Sex, Film Dance in New York's East Village* (New York: Grosset and Dunlap, 1966).

74. "Expanded Cinema Symposium," *Film Culture* 43 (1966): 1.

Chapter 2

1. Incredibly, there is no discussion of either Isou or Lemaître in any of the canonical histories of experimental film: Renan, *Introduction* (see introduction, n. 23); Parker Tyler, *Underground Film* (New York: Grove Press, 1969); Youngblood, *Expanded Cinema* (see introduction, n. 19); David Curtis, *Experimental Cinema* (New York: Dell, 1971); P. Adams Sitney, *Visionary Film: The American Avant-Garde* (New York: Oxford University Press, 1974); Amos Vogel, *Film as a Subversive Art* (New York: Random House, 1974); Stephen Dwoskin, *Film Is ... The International Free Cinema* (London: Peter Owen, 1975); Le Grice, *Abstract Film and Beyond* (see chap. 1, n. 57); or Peter Gidal, *Materialist Film* (New York: Routledge 1989). One finally finds a passing reference to both in A. L. Rees, *A History of Experimental Film and Video: From the Canonical Avant Garde to Contemporary British Practice* (London: British Film Institute, 2000), which cites them as an indication of the postwar resurgence of the avant-garde in Europe and as a source for the American underground cinema (pp. 56, 63).
2. *Traité de Bave et d'Éternité* was screened on October 23, 1953, at the San Francisco Museum of Modern Art's "Art in Cinema" series under the heading "The Avant-Garde in France Today" and was introduced by Alan Watts. Scott MacDonald reproduces an announcement for the series in his *Art in Cinema: Documents Toward a History of the Film Society* (Philadelphia: Temple University Press, 2006), 253. Isou's *Treatise* was the subject of a 1993 letter Brakhage wrote to Frédérique Devaux on the occasion of her research for *Traité de bave et d'éternité de Isidore Isou* (Paris: Editions Yellow Now, 1994). The letter is unpublished in English, but held at the Brakhage archive at the University of Colorado, Boulder. The iconic "moving" signature Brakhage appended to his films clearly seems to have originated from his early encounter with Isou's *Treatise*.
3. Caroline Jones, *Eyesight Alone: Clement Greenberg's Modernism and the Bureaucratization of the Senses* (Chicago: University of Chicago Press, 2005).
4. I refer to the film as *Treatise* both in the interest of economy and to counter a series of mistranslations to which the title has been subjected. The French word *bavé* frequently refers to the liquid dripping from the mouth of an infant or a dog, hence "slobber." Yet Isou expressly draws on its connection with the material body of human speech, perhaps making "drool" or "saliva" a more appropriate choice. When Raymond Rohauer imported the film to America, it was given the unfortunate title *Venom and Eternity*, which removed all connection to human speech and omitted the crucial word "Treatise" entirely.
5. See Frédérique Devaux, *Le Cinéma Lettriste* (Paris: Editions Paris Experimental, 1992), 55–61.
6. Jean-Isidore Isou, *Introduction à une Nouvelle Poésie et à une Nouvelle Musique* (Paris: Gallimard, 1947).
7. Guy Coté, "Cinema Sans Sense," *Quarterly of Film, Radio, and Television* 7, no. 4 (Summer 1953), 335–36.
8. Jean-Isidore Isou, *Esthétique du cinéma*, in "Numéro Spécial sur Cinema," ed. Marc-

Gilbert Guillaumin, special issue, *Ion* 1 (April 1952): 7–154, reprinted in *Revue d'histoire du cinéma* 14 (Winter 1983).

9. Stan Brakhage, *Film at Wit's End: Eight Avant-Garde Filmmakers* (Kingston, New York: Documentext, 1989), 115.
10. Gilles Deleuze, *Cinema 2: The Time-Image* (Minneapolis: University of Minnesota Press, 1989).
11. The history of *benshi* reveals an amazingly regionalized and performative practice whereby particular "voice actors" would become much more popular and celebrated than the movies for which they performed. Some of these *benshi* took great liberties with the film text, turning a drama into comedy, for instance, or even adding pornographic scenes to a classic romance. This history compels us to rethink the cultural inflections of a subgenre of deliberate mistranslation in films such as Woody Allen's *What's Up, Tiger Lily?* (1966) or René Viénet's *Can Dialectics Break Bricks?* (1973).
12. Charles Musser, "Before Cinema: Towards a History of Screen Practice," in *The Emergence of Cinema: The American Screen to 1907* (Berkeley: University of California Press, 1994).
13. Jean-Luc Godard, in particular, owes an obvious and significant debt to the formal strategies devised by Isou and Lemaître.
14. Many of these marks were made not by Isou himself, but by the film's editor, Maurice Lemaître.
15. Isou's narrator claims to want to "make a film that hurts your eyes, like during the projection of those very old films in which you can see the numbers flashing by—1, 3, 5, 7—so quickly! I've always loved these flashing numbers. Perhaps because I always connected them with the beautiful classic films of old and my taste transposed itself from what I had loved to what went with that love." Here, as elsewhere, we see an obvious premonition of the issues that will be taken up in the so-called structuralist filmmaking of the late 1960s and 1970s.
16. Lemaître had joined the Lettrist group in 1950, and like Isou, he was taken with the idea of youth as a revolutionary cultural and political force. Starting two journals at that time, Lemaître used *Youth Front* as a vehicle for social and political thought while developing *Ur* as a more literary, visual, and philosophical vehicle for the movement.
17. A decade later, Godard would employ a similarly disjunctive wordplay within films such as *Contempt* (1963) and *Weekend* (1967).
18. Pierre Bordieu, *Distinction: A Social Critique of the Judgement of Taste* (Cambridge, MA: Harvard University Press, 1984).
19. Clips containing logos of various movie companies, or those employing language of cinematic advertising, not only disrupt the integrity of that frame, but reveal the complex ways in which experience might be multiply or even contradictorily framed.
20. Frederich Kittler, *Gramophone, Film, Typewriter*, trans. Geoffrey Winthrop-Young and Michael Wutz (Stanford, CA: Stanford University Press, 1999), 121.
21. Strauven, *Cinema of Attractions Reloaded*, 17 (see chap. 1, n. 62).
22. Maurice Lemaître, *Le Film est Déjà Commencé? Séance de cinéma*, preface by Jean-Isidore Isou (Paris: A. Bonne, 1952). Part of the Encyclopédie du Cinéma collection edited by André Bonne. One edition contained a paper band with the words "Un Pirandello du Cinéma."
23. Ibid.
24. Lemaître also transposes our expectations for historical punctuality: at a time when repertory film theaters were still uncommon and many of the early masterworks of the

medium unable to be seen, Lemaître substitutes the experience of an old-fashioned classic for the anticipated experience of the latest thing.

25. Maurice Lemaître, *Qu'est-ce que le lettrisme?* (Paris: Éditions Fischbacher, 1954).
26. Marc'O (Marc-Gilbert Guillaumin), "Introduction au Cinéma Nucléaire," in *Documents relatifs á la fondation de l'Internationale Situationniste*, ed. Gérard Berréby (Paris: Allia, 1985), 245. Translation and italics mine.
27. Ibid., 250–51.
28. Ibid.
29. Guy Debord, "Prolégomènes à tout cinema futur," in Berréby, *Documents*, 109.
30. Gil Wolman, "Le Cinématochrone—Nouvelle amplitude," *Ur* 2 (1952), cited in Kaira Cabañas, "How to Do Things Without Words: Gil Wolman's Lettrist Film *L'anticoncept*," *Grey Room* 42 (Winter 2011). Cabañas provides the most sophisticated reading of Wolman's work I have read to date, and I am here indebted to her groundbreaking archival research.
31. See Bruno Corra, "Abstract Cinema—Chromatic Music," in *Futurist Manifestos*, ed. Umbro Appollonio (Boston: MFA Publications, 2001), 66–69. Corra's conception of a white-clad audience was almost certainly indebted to the synesthetic ideas of the Russian composer Alexander Scriabin.
32. Krauss, *Passages in Modern Sculpture*, 207–12 (see chap. 1, n. 22).
33. Marc'O, "Introduction au Cinéma Nucléaire," 242. Italics mine.
34. Barthes, "En sortant du cinéma," 105 (see chap. 1, n. 34). Rather than Isou's *discrepant*, Barthes chooses *décolle* as his key term, thus linking this expanded conception of cinema to the postwar tradition of *Décollage*, not only in the well-known posters of Raymond Hains and Jacques Villeglé, but in the cinema collage/performances of Wolf Vostell.

Chapter 3

1. Significantly, none of Calder's early motorized sculptures were included.
2. Besides the great range of abstract sculpture to which Calder's work gave rise, a less sanguine strain might be traced through Jean Tinguely's auto-destructive sculpture *Homage to New York* at MoMA in 1960 to Nam June Paik's early robotic works of the mid-1960s.
3. Victor Vasarely, "Yellow Manifesto," reprinted in *Le Mouvement, Vom Kino Zur Kinetik* (Museum Jean Tinguely Basel; Heidelberg, Germany: Kehrer Verlag, 2010), 32.
4. Roger Bordier, "New Proposals: The Movement, The Transformable Work," reprinted in *Le Mouvement*, 33–41.
5. "At first I was scared of the camera. I had an aversion to photography, partly, I suppose, because of my father's fondness for it." "Robert Breer," interview by Scott MacDonald, January and February 1985, in *A Critical Cinema 2: Interviews with Independent Filmmakers* (Berkeley: University of California Press, 1992), 19. Breer's father was an engineer and inventor who had made his own 3D home movies in the 1940s.
6. Ibid.
7. On film as an "elaboration" of Breer's painterly practice, see MacDonald, "Robert Breer," 18. On "animating painting," see Robert Breer, "An Interview with Robert Breer Conducted by Jonas Mekas and P. Adams Sitney on May 13, 1971—in New York City," *Film Culture* 56–57 (1973): 39–55.

8. "I have an aversion to just purely abstract films. That's why I have trouble with Fischinger. I admire him in some ways and find him something of an abomination in others." MacDonald, "Robert Breer," 19.
9. Robert Breer, Ford Foundation grant proposal, October 29, 1963, Anthology Film Archives.
10. Robert Breer, interview by Lois Mendelson, August 9, 1977, in Lois Mendelson, *Robert Breer: A Study of His Work in the Context of the Modernist Tradition* (Ann Arbor, MI: UMI Research Press, 1981), 73, n. 72.
11. Robert Breer, "A Statement," April 1959, *Film Culture* 29 (1963).
12. Robert Breer, "Interview by Guy Coté," *Film Culture* 27 (1962), 17–20.
13. Breer, "Interview with Robert Breer Conducted by Jonas Mekas and P. Adams Sitney."
14. Hans Namuth's *Pollock 51* (1951) and Henri-Georges Clouzot's *Mystery of Picasso* (1956) might be viewed as parallel attempts to explore this "threshold" within the documentary film.
15. Robert Breer, "An Interview with Robert Breer Conducted by Charles Levine at Breer's Home, Palisades, N.Y. Approximate date July 1970," *Film Culture* 56–57 (1973): 65.
16. Robert Breer, interview by Hans Ulrich Obrist, December 18, 2001, in *Hans-Ulrich Obrist: Interviews* (Milan: Charta/Fondazione Pitti Immagine Discovery, 2003).
17. Johanna Drucker curiously does not mention Breer's book in her influential survey of twentieth-century artists' books. Johanna Drucker, *The Century of Artists' Books*, 2nd ed. (New York: Granary Books, 2004).
18. Robert Breer, "Interview with Robert Breer Conducted by Jonas Mekas and P. Adams Sitney," 59–70.
19. Ibid.
20. Contemporary neuroscience and psychophysics have called into question any simple distinction between the kind of movement we perceive within the cinematographic projection and that which we perceive regularly, thus complicating the traditional film-theoretical description of the status of cinematographic movement as "illusory."
21. Not only does Breer's *Image by Images* book go unmentioned in the literature, but one struggles to find Breer's name even mentioned among the artists in the *Movement* exhibition.
22. See Hans Richter, *dada: art and anti-art*, trans. David Britt (New York: Thames & Hudson, 1964), 89.
23. See the extensive bibliography in Nicholas Wade, "Philosophical Instruments and Toys: Optical Devices Extending the Art of Seeing," *Journal of the History of the Neurosciences* 13, no. 1 (2004): 102–24.
24. See Jonathan Crary, *Techniques of the Observer: On Vision and Modernity in the 19th Century* (Cambridge, MA: MIT Press, 1992), and Kittler, *Gramophone, Film, Typewriter* (see chap. 2, n. 18).
25. Jonathan Crary's work is here the exception that proves the rule. As might be expected, the philosophical toy has been subject to much greater attention within the discipline of film studies.
26. Ernst Mach, *Contributions to the Analysis of Sensations*, trans. C. M. Williams (Chicago: Open Court, 1897), 9. Cited by Mary Ann Doane in *The Emergence of Cinematic Time: Modernity, Contingency, the Archive* (Cambridge, MA: Harvard University Press, 2002), 80. Italics in original.
27. The various "discs bearing spirals" through which Duchamp explored the phenomenon

of depth perception were tied to the stroboscopic disc developed in different forms by Simon Stampfer and Joseph Plateau around 1833 and make use of the "persistence of vision" phenomenon discussed below.

28. P. Adams Sitney has described *Anemic Cinema* as highlighting the difference in the "automatic apprehension" of optical and verbal images. P. Adams Sitney, *Modernist Montage: The Obscurity of Vision in Cinema and Literature* (New York: Columbia University Press, 1990), 25.
29. The catalog for Pontus Hultén's *Paris-New York* exhibition at the Centre Pompidou in 1977 lists four items titled "Mutoscope," dated "1958–1964."
30. Breer, "Interview with Robert Breer Conducted by Charles Levine," 58–59.
31. The catalog for *Motion in Vision/Vision in Motion* lists Breer alongside Bury, Klein, Mack, Mari, Munari, Necker, Rot, Soto, Spoerri, Tinguely, and Van Hoeydonck. Curated by Marc Cammewaert, the exhibition took place at the Hessenhuis in Antwerp, Belgium, March 21—May 3, 1959.
32. *Bewogen Beweging*, literally, "Moved Movement," is commonly and hereafter translated "Art in Motion."
33. Breer, "Interview with Robert Breer Conducted by Charles Levine," 58–59.
34. Thierry de Duve, *Kant after Duchamp* (Cambridge, MA: MIT Press, 1996), 322.
35. MacDonald, "Robert Breer," 31.
36. The assessment of Vogel's Cinema 16 is from Scott MacDonald's November 30, 1996, conversation with Brakhage in *Cinema 16: Documents Towards a History of the Film Society*, ed. Scott MacDonald (Philadelphia: Temple University Press, 2002), 298.
37. Brian O'Doherty, *New York Times*, April 26, 1964. See also Paul Cummings, "Oral History Interview with Charles Alan, 1970 Aug. 20–25," Archives of American Art, Smithsonian Institution, http://www.aaa.si.edu/collections/oralhistories/transcripts/Alan70.htm (accessed 2007).
38. Stan VanDerBeek, "If the Actor Is the Audience," *Film Culture* 24 (1962): 92. VanDerBeek first raised the idea of the "Gallery Theatre" in "The Cinema Delimina: Films from the Underground," *Film Quarterly* 14 (Summer 1961): 5–15.
39. Some of the boxes Cornell constructed literally did glow from within, having either a tiny electric light built into the box itself or a translucent backing such that illumination from behind would provide something like the effect of rear-screen projection in cinema.
40. The abstract expressionist canvases of Jackson Pollock were thus sometimes presented in the "surrealist" mode due to the early critical reception of that movement. See Charlotte Klonk, *Spaces of Experience: Art Gallery Interiors from 1800 to 2000* (New Haven, CT: Yale University Press, 2009), 144.
41. See Joseph Cornell, *Joseph Cornell's Theatre of the Mind: Selected Diaries, Letters, and Files*, ed. with an introduction by Mary Ann Caws (New York: Thames & Hudson, 2000).
42. André Breton, "As in a Wood," in Hammond, *The Shadow and Its Shadow*, 73 (see chap. 1, n. 28).
43. Robert Morris, "Notes on Sculpture, Part 1," *Artforum* 4, no. 6 (February 1966): 44–46, and Morris, "Notes on Sculpture, Part 2," (see introduction, n. 16).
44. According to Harry Flynt, the sculpture was first publically shown at a concert of La Monte Young and Richard Maxfield at the Harvard-Radcliffe Club in Boston on March 31, 1961. Cited in Brandon LaBelle, *Background Noise: Perspectives on Sound Art* (New York: Continuum, 2006), 86, n. 38.

45. Annette Michelson, "Robert Morris: An Aesthetics of Transgression," in *Robert Morris* (Washington, DC: Corcoran Gallery of Art, 1969), 49.

46. Kimberly Paice, *Robert Morris: The Mind/Body Problem* (New York: Guggenheim Foundation, 1994), 104.

47. See Kimberly Paice, "The Duchamp Connection," in Paice, *Robert Morris*, 112–16.

48. By contrast, Rosalind Krauss has called attention to the very incompleteness that the work's structure seems to model: "The presumed self-containment and autoreferentiality of the work ... is exploded by the cord connecting the work to the plug in the wall, that in turn connects to the circuitry in the building, that in turn connects to the current in the ground ... The mockery of this electrical dependence had, of course, been wired into the very possibility of *Box with the Sound of Its Own Making*'s ability to 'think.'" Rosalind Krauss, "The Mind/Body Problem: Robert Morris in Series," in Paice, *Robert Morris*, 4.

49. Morris later clarified that the playback mechanism was too large to place within the box and was usually placed away from the box, behind a curtain or other partition.

50. Caleb Kelly uses the term "demechanization" in *Cracked Media: The Sound of Malfunction* (Cambridge, MA: MIT Press, 2009), 139.

51. The classic account of this psychic transaction is provided in Christian Metz, *The Imaginary Signifier*, trans. Celia Britton et al. (Bloomington: Indiana University Press, 1982).

52. Michael Kirby states that "water could be heard inside and seen on a closed translucent curtain on which was projected the life-sized images of a girl taking a shower." Kirby, "The Uses of Film in the New Theater," *Tulane Drama Review* 11, no. 1 (1966): 52. Adrian Henri describes "a real shower with a film of a girl taking a shower projected on to the curtain." Henri, *Total Art: Environments, Happenings, and Performance* (New York: Oxford University Press, 1974), 106. Chrissie Iles states that "a film of a woman taking a shower is projected in a continuous loop onto a curtain, behind which water cascades inside a metal shower stall." Iles, *Into The Light: The Projected Image in American Art, 1964–1977* (New York: Whitney Museum of American Art, 2001), 86. The only accurate historical description of the work was provided by Jonas Mekas, who wrote that the "effect was achieved by projecting a color film of the girl taking a shower onto the back of the shower box which was made of plastic glass, on the other side of which water was running down ... getting the amazing tridimensional effect (probably because of the haziness and thickness of the glass)." Mekas, "The Expanded Cinema of Robert Whitman," in *Movie Journal*, 189 (see chap. 1, n. 11).

53. Whitman, as quoted in Michael Kirby, *Happenings: An Illustrated Anthology* (New York: E. P. Dutton, 1965), 136.

54. Iles, *Into the Light*, 86.

55. See n. 51 above for examples of *Shower*'s historical reception. Neither of the two major exhibition catalogs featuring Whitman's *Cinema Pieces*—Iles's *Into the Light* (2001) and *Robert Whitman: Playback*, ed. Lynne Cooke, Karen Kelly, and Bettina Funcke (New York: Dia Art Foundation, 2003)—feature any documentation of this "disruptive" imagery.

56. Crary, *Techniques of the Observer*, 110.

Chapter 4

1. Given Whitman's interest in silent comedy, his first image of the projector may have been an homage to Buster Keaton's 1924 classic *Sherlock, Jr.*, whose projectionist/

protagonist falls asleep on his machine and is carried into the world of the projected image.

2. Robert Smithson, "The Museum World," *Arts Yearbook* (1967), reprinted under the title "What Is a Museum? A Dialogue between Allan Kaprow and Robert Smithson," in Smithson, *Collected Writings*, 43–51 (see introduction, n. 5).
3. Michael Kirby, "The New Theatre," *Tulane Drama Review* 10, no. 2 (1965): 26.
4. Barbara Rose, "Considering Robert Whitman," in *Projected Images* (Minneapolis: Walker Art Center, 1974), 41.
5. Kirby, "Uses of Film in the New Theatre," 52 (see chap. 3, n. 51).
6. Forti studied with Anna Halprin in San Francisco before coming to New York. Simone Forti, "Commentary for *American Moon*," in *Robert Whitman: Performances of the 1960s*, DVD (Houston: Artpix Notebooks, 2003), included in Cooke, Kelly, and Funcke, *Robert Whitman: Playback* (see chap. 3, n. 54).
7. Toby Mussman, "The Images of Robert Whitman," in Battcock, *New American Cinema* (see chap. 1, n. 65).
8. Kostelanetz, *Theatre of Mixed Means*, 224 (see chap. 1, n. 31).
9. Sontag, "Against Interpretation," in *Against Interpretation and Other Essays* (New York: Picador, 2001), 14.
10. "Artpix interview on *Prune.Flat.*," in *Robert Whitman: Performances of the 1960s*.
11. See David Joselit's "Eating and Dreaming: Robert Whitman's 1960s Happenings," in Cooke, Kelly, and Funcke, *Robert Whitman: Playback*. My captions for figures 4.3 and 4.4 are citations from Joselit's description on page 52, where he importantly remarks on the "ethically ambiguous violence" within the sequence.
12. As can be seen from Peter Moore's photodocumentation of the 1965 performance at the Film-Maker's Cooperative theater, *Prune.Flat.* was originally projected against a thin paper screen unfurling at the edges, whose inevitable oscillation during the performance would have emphasized both its materiality and its ephemerality—heightening the complexity of the spatial projection.
13. This is Slavoj Žižek's formulation of the Freudian fetishistic split that fantasy provokes in the field of vision. See *The Sublime Object of Ideology* (London: Verso, 1989).
14. Kostelanetz, *Theatre of Mixed Means*, 228.
15. Kostelanetz continues, "Even though Whitman himself told me in conversation that he didn't care how precise the visual match was, the difference in *effectiveness* is enormous. Sometimes I wonder how well he knows what he is doing." Kostelanetz, 1965 notes on *Prune.Flat.* published in "Discovery of Alternative Theatre," 128–72 (see chap. 1, n. 30).
16. Kostelanetz, *Theatre of Mixed Means*, 229.
17. Kostelanetz, *Theatre of Mixed Means*, 225; Cooke, Kelly, and Funcke, *Robert Whitman: Playback*, 209.
18. Cooke, Kelly, and Funcke, *Robert Whitman: Playback*, 209.
19. Original lecture given at New York Film Festival, 1966, published as Annette Michelson, "Film and the Radical Aspiration," *Film Culture* 42 (1966): 34–42.
20. As one of the most influential early advisors for the PhD in cinema studies, Michelson has exerted an incredible influence on the development of academic film studies, above all in the realm of experimental film. For an example of this intertextual engagement, see Eric de Bruyn, "Alfaville, or the Utopics of Mel Bochner," *Grey Room* 10 (2003): 76–111.

21. Carrie Lambert-Beatty's work is here indispensable in illustrating that Rainer's complex critique of aesthetic spectatorship—usually traced to her experimental filmmaking of the 1970s—was already well developed in her choreographic work of the mid-1960s. Like the contemporaneous experiments in expanded cinema, Rainer's work would seem to have important historiographic implications for the development of film theory in the next decade. Lambert-Beatty, *Being Watched: Yvonne Rainer and the 1960s* (Cambridge, MA: MIT Press, 2008).
22. Robert Ellis Dunn, unpublished notes, March 30, 1980, cited in Sally Banes, *Democracy's Body: Judson Dance Theater, 1962–1964* (Durham, NC: Duke University Press, 2002), 5.
23. Banes, *Democracy's Body*, 40.
24. John Herbert McDowell, interview by Michael Rowe and Amanda Degener, New York, February 19, 1980, cited in Banes, *Democracy's Body*, 40. Summers's own intermedia presentation *Fantastic Gardens* of 1964 used the entire performance space, located the audience in several settings, bathed the whole space in film and slide projections, and combined many works of music and sculpture with her own dances, many of them improvisational scores realized by the dancers.
25. James Waring, John Herbert McDowell, Judith Dunn, Arlene Croce, and Don McDonagh, "Judson: A Discussion," *Ballet Review* 1, no. 6 (1967): 37; McDowell, interview by Rowe and Deneger, 40.
26. Allen Hughes, "Dance Program Seen at Church," *New York Times*, July 7, 1962, cited in Banes, *Democracy's Body*, 40.
27. Frederick A. Talbot, *Moving Pictures: How They Are Made and Worked* (London: William Heinemann, 1912), 7.
28. Henri Bergson, *Creative Evolution*, trans. Arthur Mitchell (1907; New York: Henry Holt, 1911), 332.
29. Allen Hughes, "Leaps and Credenzas," *New York Times*, August 1, 1965. Gordon Mumma had previously worked with Robert Ashley to construct a range of similar electronic triggers for Milton Cohen's "Space Theatre" in Ann Arbor, Michigan, several years before. See Leta Miller, "ONCE and Again: The Evolution of a Legendary Festival," liner notes to *Music from the ONCE Festival 1961–1966*, New World Records, 80567–2, 2003.
30. James Klosty, *Merce Cunningham* (New York: E. P. Dutton, 1975). This fundamental problem recurred in the work of Yvonne Rainer as she vacillated between giving over all directorial authority to her dancers, even dissolving herself within the Grand Union collective, and insisting on a more authoritative direction in her filmmaking of the 1970s and 1980s.
31. John Cage, *I–VI*, The Charles Eliot Norton Lectures (Cambridge, MA: Harvard University Press, 1990), 177.
32. Retallack, *Musicage*, preface, xxx (see chap. 1, n. 21).
33. Trevor Pinch and Frank Trocco, *Analog Days: The Invention and Impact of the Moog Synthesizer* (Cambridge, MA: Harvard University Press, 2002), 76.
34. Laura Kuhn, "Interview by Laura Kuhn," in *Art Performs Life: Merce Cunningham/Meredith Monk/Bill T. Jones* (Minneapolis: Walker Art Center, 1998), 26.
35. Carolyn Brown, *Chance and Circumstance: Twenty Years with Cage and Cunningham* (New York: Knopf, 2007), 459.
36. Walter Terry, "Parting Shot Applause," *New York Herald Tribune*, July 24, 1965, 4.
37. David Revill, *The Roaring Silence: John Cage, A Life* (New York: Arcade, 1993), 212.
38. Gruen, "New Bohemia" (see chap. 1, n. 68).

39. Leo Steinberg, "Reflections on the State of Criticism," *Artforum* 10, no. 7 (1972): 37–49.
40. Cage, *Silence*, 102 (see chap. 1, n. 17).
41. Hector Currie and Michael Porte, eds., *Cinema Now: Stan Brakhage, Stan VanDerBeek, John Cage, Jonas Mekas*, Perspectives on Underground Film, no. 1 (Cincinnati, OH: University of Cincinnati Press, 1968), 9.
42. Ibid., 16.
43. Stan VanDerBeek, "Move-Movies," *Film Culture* 43 (1966): 10; Stan VanDerBeek, "Letter to Lenny Lipton," *Film Culture* 48–49 (1970): 37–40.
44. VanDerBeek, "Move-Movies"; Renan, *Introduction*, 229–34 (see introduction, n. 23).
45. Colomina, "Enclosed by Images" (see chap. 1, n. 10). The American National Exhibition in Sokolniki Park, Moscow, was site of the famous "Kitchen Debate," in which Richard Nixon and Nikita Khrushchev argued the relative merits of their respective political systems through the proxy of household appliances.
46. *Your World of Tomorrow: Democracity Guidebook* (New York: Rogers-Kellogg-Stillson, Inc., 1939), 20.
47. "All in all, the creative act is not performed by the artist alone; the spectator brings the work in contact with the external world." Marcel Duchamp, "The Creative Act," Session on the Creative Act, Convention of the American Federation of Arts, Houston, Texas, 1957 (Marcel Duchamp in conversation with William Seitz, Rudolf Arnheim, and Gregory Bateson) *ART-News* 56, no. 4 (1957).

Chapter 5

1. On the event, see Robert Christgau, "When VanDerBeek a Movie-Drome Decreed," *New York World Journal Tribune*, March 5, 1967; Fran Heller, "Masters and Mavericks," *Newsweek*, October 3, 1966; and the pictorial "Filmmakers Take a Trip," *Village Voice*, September 22, 1966, 22.
2. The VanDerBeek archive at MoMA lists "The Underground Takes to the Air: VanDerBeek tells what your in for, he's up to, the why for? flics—flims-fill'ums on homey tv!!!!" (Channel 4: October 23, 1965) and "The Underground Comes up for Air ... an Electric Collage ... by Stan VanDerBeek" (Channel 2: February 27, 1966).
3. See Gloria Sutton, "Stan VanDerBeek's Movie-Drome: Networking the Subject," in *Future Cinema: The Cinematic Imaginary after Film*, ed. Jeffrey Shaw and Peter Weibel (Cambridge, MA: MIT Press, 2003), 136–43.
4. Richard Roud, "Cinderella Status," and Amos Vogel, "What Is and What Will Be," in *Fourth New York Film Festival Program* (1966), 16.
5. Mekas, *Movie Journal*, 252–54 (see chap. 1, n. 11).
6. See Lee Grieveson and Haidee Wasson, eds., *Inventing Film Studies* (Durham, NC: Duke University Press, 2008).
7. Robert Breer, whose animated shorts were exhibited regularly over the course of thirty-five years, is the exception that proves the rule. His *Breathing* had been shown already in 1964, then *Fist Fight* in 1965, *69* in 1969, *PBL #2* in 1970, *70* in 1971, *FUJI* in 1975, *LMNO* in 1979; *TZ* in 1980; *Swiss Army Knife with Rats and Pigeons* in 1982; *Trial Balloons* in 1983; and *Time Flies* in 1999. Nevertheless, all eleven of these films together total barely over an hour.
8. Pat Hackett and Andy Warhol, *Popism: The Warhol '60s* (New York: Harper & Row, 1980), 211–12. The installation was shut down prematurely in any case, when a single-note soundtrack La Monte Young was to provide proved too loud for the festival manage-

ment to be able to accept. Branden Joseph describes this ill-fated collaboration in "'My Mind Split Open': Andy Warhol's 'Exploding Plastic Inevitable,'" *Grey Room* 8 (Summer 2002): 80–107, claiming that it sought "to negate, rather than embrace, the realm of commercial culture, allowing for a consciousness of individual perception and an experience of bodily depth against the expropriating alienation of spectacle" (86). I would only stress that "expropriating alienation of spectacle" reads as a critique of the festival as such, but many of the works screened there—from Luis Buñuel's absurdist *Golden Age* (1931) and Jean-Luc Godard's Brechtian antiwar film *Band of Outsiders* (1963) to Robert Breer's handmade animation *Breathing* (1963) and Jonas Mekas's personal document of the Living Theater in *The Brig* (1964)—were entirely opposed to both mainstream commercial culture and industrial cinematic spectacle, even if their means do not correspond to the aesthetics of minimalism. Lest it not be clear, my critique of the festival is not intended to denigrate it, but merely to underline the effect that its rather limited conception of cinematic art would have on the emergence of expanded cinema in this time.

9. Caroline Jones has written a detailed account of the Factory as a cultural and rhetorical trope for Warhol's production, exploring not only the specific importance of Warhol's working-class background in the evolution of his thinking about production and management, but also the more general aesthetic trajectory in this period, leading out of the isolated authorial expression of the artist's studio toward the collective or corporate model of production embodied by the industrial film studio. See Jones, *Machine in the Studio: Constructing the Postwar American Artist* (Chicago: University of Chicago Press, 1996), 189–267.
10. Annette Michelson, "'Where Is Your Rupture?': Mass Culture and the *Gesamtkunstwerk*," *October* 56 (1991): 54–55. In Michelson's influential reading, the Factory represented an upending of the nineteenth-century "total work of art" in a Bakhtinian carnival of exaggerated performance and ritualistic reversal.
11. "Pop Goes the Videotape," and "What Is a Video Tape Recorder?," *Tape Recording* 12, no. 5 (September/October 1965): 14–19; 64–65.
12. Andy Warhol, *Philosophy of Andy Warhol: From A to B and Back Again* (New York: Harcourt Brace Jovanovich, 1975), 26–27.
13. Andy Warhol, *a: a novel* (New York: Grove Press, 1968). The tape recordings were made on three separate occasions from 1965 to 1967 and later transcribed for publication.
14. Warhol, *a*, 56. All typos in original manuscript.
15. This was not technically true, because Burton was given a copy of his own, and after his death, his widow allowed this copy to be remastered and rereleased on VHS in 1995 and on DVD in 1999. Russ Alsobrook, "Back to the Future: Reflections on the Brief History of Video Moviemaking," *International Cinematographers Guild Magazine*, September 2001.
16. Sam Lucchese, "Fox to Show Burton's *Hamlet*," announcement in the *Atlanta Journal-Constitution*, undated file.
17. See "USA Artists: Andy Warhol and Roy Lichtenstein," in Goldsmith, *I'll Be Your Mirror*, 80 (see chap. 1, n. 59).
18. Warhol may have gotten his title from Robert Breer's 1960 film *Inner and Outer Space*, which he had probably seen at the Film-Makers' Cinematheque.
19. The *Screen Tests*, originally called "Film Portraits" or "Stillies," were recorded on one-hundred-foot reels at twenty-four frames per second for two minutes and forty-six seconds and then projected at sixteen frames per second for four minutes and twelve seconds. See Callie Angell, *Andy Warhol Screen Tests: The Films of Andy Warhol: Catalogue*

Raisonné (New York: Abrams, 2006). According to Howard Junker, Warhol had considered making film loops out of them and selling them as *Living Portrait Boxes*. Howard Junker, "Andy Warhol: Movie Maker," *Nation*, February 22, 1965.

20. The story of Edie's background, brief relationship with Warhol, and tragic early death at 28 is far too complex to recount in the present context. The classic account is Jean Stein and George Plimpton, ed., *Edie: An American Girl* (New York: Knopf, 1982).
21. Warhol, *Philosophy of Andy Warhol*, 33.
22. "What Edie Said in *Outer and Inner Space*," transcribed by Lisa Dillon Edgett, in Bill Jeffries, ed., *From Stills to Motion & Back Again: Texts on Andy Warhol's "Screen Tests" & "Outer and Inner Space"* (Vancouver, BC: Presentation House Gallery, 2003), 31.
23. Mladen Dolar, *A Voice and Nothing More* (Cambridge, MA: MIT Press, 2006), 41.
24. I can only gesture here toward this rich and still underdeveloped theoretical topos. The classic elaborations can be found in Michel Chion's 1984 text *The Voice in Cinema* (New York: Columbia University Press, 1999) and in Kaja Silverman's *The Acoustic Mirror: The Female Voice in Psychoanalysis and Cinema* (Bloomington: Indiana University Press, 1988).
25. Stephan Koch, *Stargazer: Andy Warhol's World and His Films* (New York: Praeger, 1973).
26. Branden Joseph provides the definitive account of the EPI in "'My Mind Split Open.'"
27. "Expanded Cinema Symposium," *Film Culture* 43 (1966): 2.
28. Michelson, "Film and the Radical Aspiration" (see chap. 4, n. 19).
29. Ken Dewey, "An Odyssey out of Theatre," *Theatre Papers* #11, ed. Peter Hulton, 1977 (Dartington College, Devonshire, Great Britain, 1977), unpaginated, "a verbatim record of interviews with Ken Dewey during the winter of 1968" by Peter Hulton. On Kaprow's complex relationship to performance and radical theater, see Judith Rodenbeck, *Radical Prototypes: Allan Kaprow and the Invention of Happenings* (Cambridge, MA: MIT Press, 2011). On the complexities of navigating between and across the disciplinary paradigms of theater and the visual arts in contemporary art practice and criticism, see Shannon Jackson, *Social Works: Performing Art, Supporting Publics* (New York: Routledge, 2011).
30. Riley worked entertaining GIs at a base until the assassination of JFK changed the base policies, making it hard for him to find work.
31. According to Keith Potter, it was Dewey who secured Riley's access to the ORTF radio studios in Paris where *The Gift* was recorded. Potter, *Four Musical Minimalists: La Monte Young, Terry Riley, Steve Reich, Philip Glass* (Cambridge: Cambridge University Press, 2000), 105.
32. Kyle Gann, *Music Downtown: Writings from the Village Voice* (Berkeley: University of California Press, 2006), 194.
33. "Interview with Ken Dewey by Fred Wellington," *Film Culture* 43 (1966): 2–3; Dewey, "Odyssey out of Theatre."
34. Mekas, *Movie Journal*, 216 (see chap. 1, n. 11).
35. Ibid.
36. *I (with John Graham)* was first presented as a tape piece alongside *Music from "The Gift" (with Chet Baker)* in the "oneyoungamerican" concert of November 1, 1964, produced by Morton Subotnick at the San Francisco Tape Music Center. See Edward Strickland, *Minimalism: Origins* (Bloomington: Indiana University Press, 1993), 173–74.
37. Strickland, *Minimalism*, 185.
38. Steve Reich, liner notes to *Early Works*, CD, Nonesuch Records (1987). This section is indebted to Sumanth Gopinath's acute analysis in "The Problem of the Political in Steve

Reich's *Come Out*," in *Sound Commitments: Avant-Garde Music and the Sixties*, ed. Robert Adlington (Cambridge: Oxford University Press, 2009), 121–44.

39. Interview with Ev Grimes, December 15–16, 1987, New York, #186 a-1 OH V, tape and transcript, Oral History of American Music, Yale University, tape 186b, cited in Gopinath, "Problem of the Political," 142, n. 24.
40. In an introduction to Davidson's work, Congressman John Lewis has written, "Without the media and without these powerful images, I don't know where we'd be today; I don't know how the movement would have succeeded . . . it was the unbelievable photographs published in newspapers and magazines that literally brought people from around the globe to small Southern towns to join the movement." Foreword to Bruce Davidson, *Time of Change: Civil Rights Photographs, 1961–1965* (Los Angeles: St. Ann's Press, 2002), unpaginated.
41. *Eyes on the Prize: America's Civil Rights Years*, episode 6, "Bridge to Freedom (1965)," produced, written, and directed by Callie Crossley and James A. Devinney, edited by Charles Scott (Blackside, Inc., 1986/2010).
42. Ken Dewey, "5 November 1966 Statement by Ken Dewey on His Own Piece, a 'Continuous Environment' called *Selma Last Year*," *Film Culture* 43 (1966): 3.
43. Anne Wagner, "Warhol Paints History, or Race in America," *Representations* 55 (Summer/ Winter 1996): 98–119. Moore's imagery appeared in "Ominous Spectacle of Birmingham," *Life*, May 17, 1963, 26–36.
44. Dewey, "5 November 1966 Statement," 3.
45. *Bruce Davidson: Photographs*, exhibit at MoMA, July 7–October 2, 1966.
46. Christopher Philips, "The Judgment Seat of Photography," *October* 22 (Fall 1982): 27–63.
47. 1966 New York Film Festival press release, "Selma Last Year" file, Schomburg Center for Research in Black Culture, New York Public Library.
48. Dewey, "5 November 1966 Statement," 3.
49. On the problems of translating the SCLC's successful Southern strategies to the North, see James R. Ralph Jr., *Northern Protest: Martin Luther King, Jr., Chicago, and the Civil Rights Movement* (Cambridge, MA: Harvard University Press, 1993).
50. Despite the turmoil of the 1950s and 1960s, Hyde Park has managed to retain an uncommon degree of racial and socioeconomic diversity. Nevertheless, it follows the income distribution of most major urban areas, with a relatively stable number of poor, but growing numbers of rich crowding out a rapidly shrinking middle class.
51. Dewey's work was titled *Last Year at Selma* for its one-day exhibition at the Unitarian Church in Hinsdale, IL, on Sunday, April 17, 1966. It was presented on April 18 at the NAACP branch in LaGrange and from April 19 to 23 at the Friendship House (a Catholic Interracial Council affiliate), according to a press release dated April 15, 1966, in the Schomburg Center, NYPL.
52. Martin Luther King Jr., as quoted in "Dr. King Is Felled by Rock," *Chicago Tribune*, August 6, 1966.
53. See Arnold R. Hirsch, *Making the Second Ghetto: Race and Housing in Chicago, 1940–1960* (Chicago: University of Chicago Press, 1998), 265.
54. *Report of the National Advisory Commission on Civil Disorders* (Washington, DC: US Government Printing Office, 1968).
55. Dewey, "Odyssey out of Theatre."
56. Dewey, "5 November 1966 Statement," 3.
57. Dewey, "Odyssey out of Theatre." Italics mine.

58. Ibid.
59. Ibid.
60. Dewey, "5 November 1966 Statement," 3.
61. Roy Reed, "Alabama Police Uses Gas and Clubs to Rout Negroes," *New York Times*, March 8, 1965.
62. Sony provided Dewey with two VCK-2000 video cameras, two TCV-2010 transportable video recording units with built-in 8-inch monitors, and one CV-2000D home video recording unit to drive a CVM-2300U 23-inch video monitor.
63. "Interview with Ken Dewey by Fred Wellington."
64. "Selma Last Year" file, Schomburg Center, NYPL.
65. Marshall McLuhan, "Art as Anti-Environment," *Arts News Annual* 31 (February 1965): 55–57. All further quotes in this paragraph are from this source.
66. "Interview with Ken Dewey by Fred Wellington," 2.
67. Dewey, "Odyssey out of Theatre."
68. The bulk of the Ken Dewey archive remained inaccessible in the New York Public Library's storage rooms for almost twenty years, before finally being made available in 2013.
69. Judith Rodenbeck has detailed how art criticism would use a "differentiation between a Brechtian analytic secularism and an Artaudian mythopoeic expressionism as a heuristic wedge to isolate minimalism from other time-based work," claiming that such a tidy opposition is a "structural simplification of the historical record" that "has created an aporia in our understanding of American postwar practices." Rodenbeck, "Madness and Method: Before Theatricality," *Grey Room* 13 (Fall 2003): 54–79 (60).

Epilogue

1. Krauss, *Passages in Modern Sculpture* (see chap. 1, n. 22).
2. Krauss, *Voyage on the North Sea*, 30 (see introduction, n. 10).
3. Rodowick, "Dr. Strange Media," 1400 (see introduction, n. 9). Rodowick gives a fuller elaboration in his *Reading the Figural* (see introduction, n. 9) and traces the early film-theoretical debates around the founding of the discipline in his *Crisis of Political Modernism* (see introduction, n. 8).
4. Michelson, "Film and the Radical Aspiration" (see chap. 4, n. 19).
5. Rodowick, "Dr. Strange Media"; Rodowick, *Virtual Life of Film* (see introduction, n. 9).
6. Rancière's conception of the aesthetic regime and its relationship to cinema has been most fully articulated to date in his *Les écarts du cinema* (Paris: La Fabrique, 2011) and *Aisthesis: Scènes du régime esthétique de l'art* (Paris: Galilée, 2011).
7. Rancière, "Thinking between Disciplines," trans. Jon Roffe, *Parrhesia*, no. 1 (2006), 6.

Illustration Credits

Figures I.1 and I.2: Courtesy of the artist, Luhring Augustine, New York, and Galerie Barbara Weiss, Berlin

Figure I.4: Krauss, Rosalind E., *The Originality of the Avant-Garde and Other Modernist Myths*, figure, page 283, © 1985 Massachusetts Institute of Technology, by permission of The MIT Press

Figure 1.1: © Estate of Roy Lichtenstein

Figure 1.5: Author illustration based on graphics from Wikimedia Commons

Figure 1.6: Digital image © The Museum of Modern Art / Licensed by SCALA / Licensed by Art Resource, NY. © 2012 Artists Rights Society (ARS), New York / ADAGP, Paris

Figure 1.7: Photograph by Brad Iverson

Figure 1.8: Photo by Peter Moore © Estate of Peter Moore / VAGA, New York, NY

Figure 1.9: Photo © Estate of Robert R. McElroy / Licensed by VAGA, New York, NY

Figure 1.10: © 1965 Claes Oldenburg, courtesy of the Oldenburg van Bruggen Studio

Figure 1.11: Photograph courtesy of Ronald Beasley

Figure 1.12: Photograph by Michael Chikiris, courtesy of Anthology Film Archives

Figure 2.11: © Gil J Wolman Archives, Paris, 2012; courtesy of Hedy Laure and Barbara Wolman

Figure 2.12: © Gil J Wolman Archives, Paris, 2012; courtesy of Hedy Laure and Barbara Wolman; photograph by Vanessa Miralles

Figure 3.1: © Galerie Denise René, Paris

Figures 3.3–3.5: Images courtesy of the artist, Kate Flax, and gb agency, Paris

Figures 3.6 and 3.7: © Galerie Denise René, Paris; © 2012 Calder Foundation, NY / Artists Rights Society (ARS), NY

Figure 3.8: © Galerie Denise René, Paris; © 2012 Artists Rights Society (ARS), New York / ADAGP, Paris

Figure 3.9: © Galerie Denise René, Paris, and Robert David; © 2012 Artists Rights Society (ARS), NY / ADAGP, Paris

Figure 3.10: © 2012 Artists Rights Society (ARS), New York / ADAGP, Paris / Succession Marcel Duchamp

Figures 3.11, 4.5, and 4.11: Images courtesy of the Estate of Stan VanDerBeek

Figure 3.13: Courtesy of the artist, Kate Flax, and gb agency, Paris

Figures 3.14 and 3.16–3.18: Courtesy of the artist, Kate Flax, and gb agency, Paris, photograph by Marc Domage

Figure 3.15: Courtesy of the artist, Kate Flax, and gb agency, Paris, photograph by Yoann Gourmel

Figures 3.19 and 3.20: Art © The Joseph and Robert Cornell Memorial Foundation/Licensed by VAGA, New York, NY.Digital image © The Museum of Modern Art / Licensed by SCALA / Art

Resource, NY; photograph by Soichi Sunami

Figure 3.21: Art © The Joseph and Robert Cornell Memorial Foundation/Licensed by VAGA, New York, NY.

Figure 3.22: © 2012 Estate of Rudy Burckhardt / Artists Rights Society (ARS), New York. Image courtesy of Sonnabend Gallery, New York

Figure 3.23: © 2012 Robert Morris / Artists Rights Society (ARS), NY. Image courtesy of Sonnabend Gallery, New York

Figure 3.24: © 2012 Artists Rights Society (ARS), New York / ADAGP, Paris / Succession Marcel Duchamp; CNAC/MNAM/ Dist. Réunion des Musées Nationaux–Grand Palais / Art Resource, NY

Figures 3.25 and 3.26: Photograph © Manfred Montwé

Figure 3.27: © Robert Whitman, courtesy of The Pace Gallery; photograph by Nic Tenwiggenhorn; image courtesy of Dia Art Foundation

Figure 3.28: © Robert Whitman, courtesy of The Pace Gallery; photograph by Howard Agriesti, Cleveland Museum of Art; image courtesy of Dia Art Foundation

Figure 4.1: © Babette Mangolte, all rights of reporduction reserved

Figure 4.2: © Robert Whitman, courtesy of The Pace Gallery, photograph by Robert R. McElroy, courtesy of The Pace Gallery; Photo © Estate of Robert R. McElroy / Licensed by VAGA, New York, NY

Figures 4.3 and 4.4: Robert Whitman: Performances from the 1960s © 2003 Artpix

Figure 4.6: Photograph by S. Greenberg

Figure 4.10 and 4.15: Image courtesy of the Estate of Stan VanDerBeek, photograph by Bob Hanson

Figure 4.11: Photo by Peter Moore © Estate of Peter Moore/VAGA, New York, NY

Figures 4.12 and 4.13: © 2012 Eames Office, LLC (eamesoffice.com)

Figure 4.14: Image courtesy of *Popular Mechanics*, originally published in the March 1939 issue

Figures 5.1 and 5.3: © Elliott Landy

Figure 5.2: *The New York Times*/Redux

Figure 5.7: © The Andy Warhol Foundation for the Visual Arts, Inc. / Artists Rights Society (ARS), New York

Figure 5.8: *New York Daily News* Archive / Getty Images

Figure 5.9: Photographs by Wayne E. Bretl

Figure 5.10 and 5.11a–b: Film still courtesy of The Andy Warhol Museum © 2012 The Andy Warhol Museum, Pittsburgh, PA, a museum of Carnegie Institute. All rights reserved

Figure 5.14: Photo by Peter Moore © Estate of Peter Moore/VAGA, New York, NY

Figures 5.16 and 5.17: The Museum of Modern Art Archives, NY, photograph by Rolf Peterson. Digital Image © The Museum of Modern Art / Licensed by SCALA / Art Resource, NY

Figures 5.18 and 5.25: © Bruce Davidson/ Magnum Photos

Figures 5.19 and 5.20: Photograph by James Marchael

Figures 5.19–5.29: Kenneth G. Dewey / Selma, Last Year Photograph Collection, Photographs and Prints Division, Schomburg Center for Research in Black Culture, The New York Public Library, Astor, Lenox and Tilden Foundations and the Estate of Kenneth G. Dewey

Index

Page numbers followed by "f" refer to figures.

www.ingramcontent.com/pod-product-compliance
Lightning Source LLC
LaVergne TN
LVHW081258100826
845148LV00005B/904
* 9 7 8 0 2 2 6 8 4 2 9 9 8 *

IMAGES
of America

LEBANON

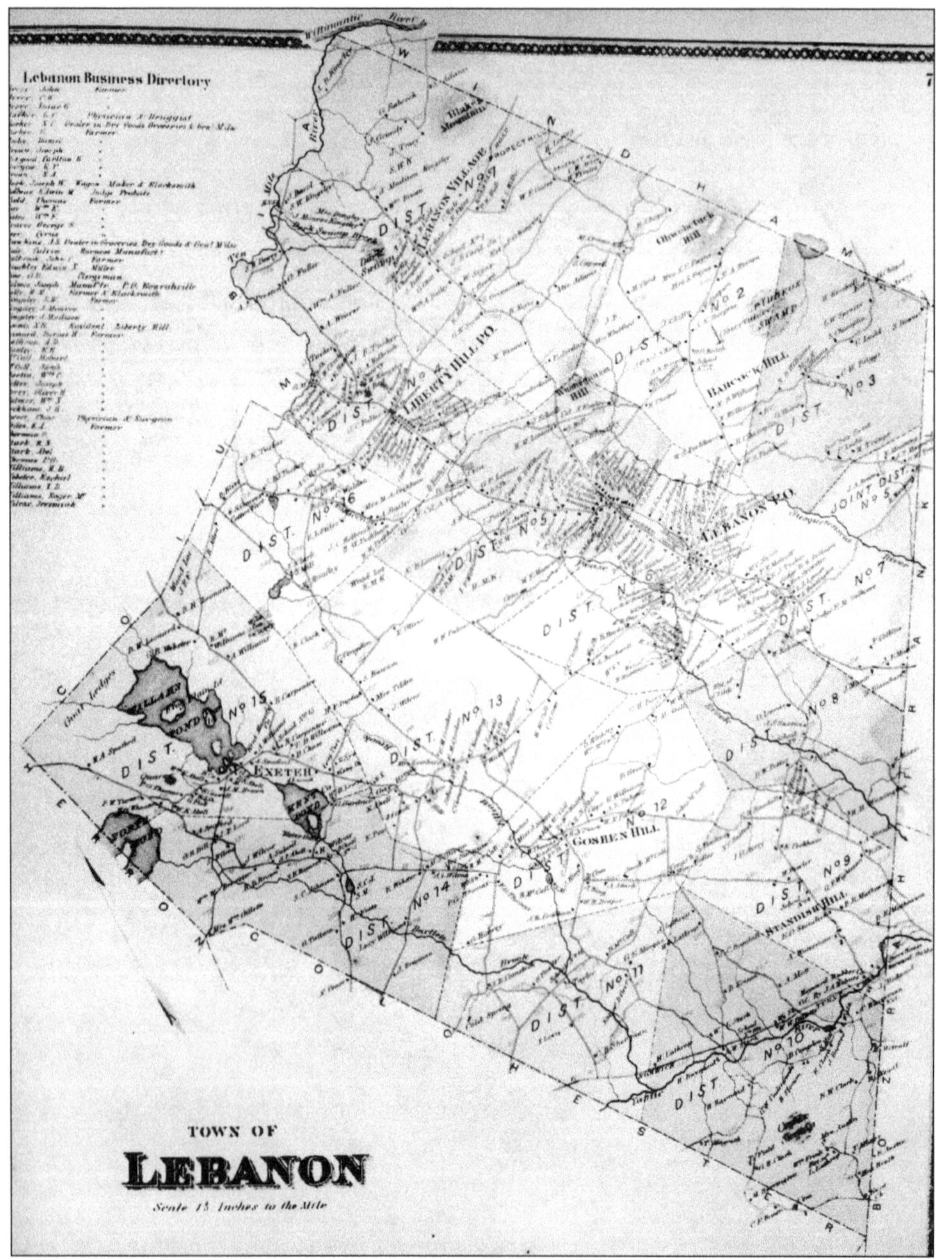

A Map of Lebanon, 1868. This map outlines the 16 school districts and includes a local business directory. It was published by F. W. Beers & Company of New York City.

On the cover: **The Lebanon Creamery.** Once the largest creamery in the state, the Lebanon Creamery opened for business in 1885 in a converted building on Susquetonscut Brook, below the present elementary school on Route 207. Butter from the creamery was shipped by rail to city markets. When markets changed, business gradually fell off. The creamery assets were finally sold at auction in 1933. (Courtesy LHS.)

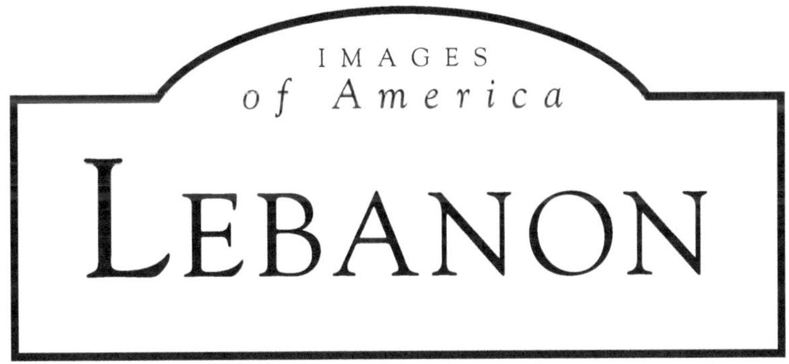

Alicia Wayland, Ed Tollmann, and Claire S. Krause
for the Lebanon Historical Society

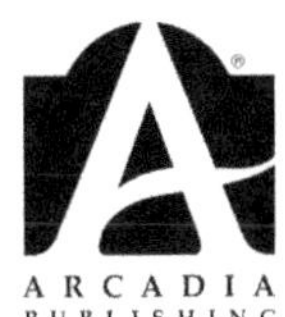

ISBN 978-1-5316-2080-6

Published by Arcadia Publishing,
Charleston, South Carolina

Library of Congress Catalog Card Number: 2004101194

For all general information, contact Arcadia Publishing:
Telephone 843-853-2070
Fax 843-853-0044
E-mail sales@arcadiapublishing.com
For customer service and orders:
Toll-free 1-888-313-2665

Visit us on the Internet at www.arcadiapublishing.com

To the men and women of Lebanon who served in the armed forces throughout our nation's history.

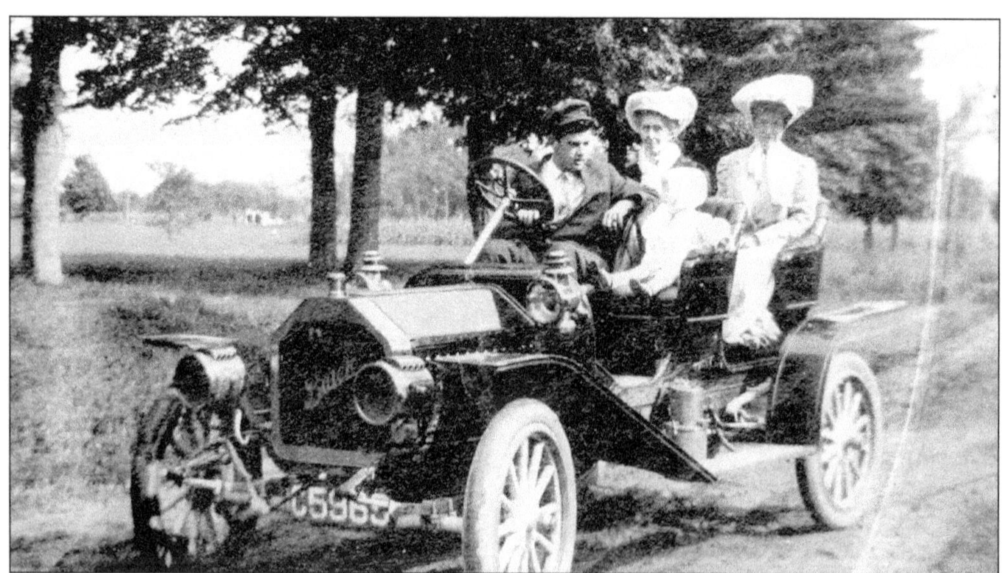

Driving 'Round the Green. Mercy Tucker Gillette, who lived on West Town Street, owned one of the first automobiles in Lebanon and loved to drive around the town green to show off. In this early 1900s photograph, she appears on the far right; her sister Phebe Tucker Irish is in the center. The driver and the child are unidentified. Mercy was the wife of Isaac Gillette, judge of probate from 1885 to 1906. (Courtesy Arlene McCaw.)

Contents

ACKNOWLEDGMENTS

This book would not have been possible without the support of the board of directors of the Lebanon Historical Society, who graciously agreed to make the historical society's archival material available to the authors for use in the book. Photographs, postcards, and maps from these collections are credited as LHS, whether the item was received through gift or purchase. As we examined these records, we realized the debt owed to the people who contributed material to the LHS archives over the years. We extend our thanks and appreciation for their contributions to the preservation of Lebanon's history. Photographs and postcards that are privately owned are credited by the name of the contributor. We are grateful for their permission to use these items.

Special thanks are due Grace Sayles, who scanned all the materials produced in this book with her customary professionalism and good advice. She was indispensable to our efforts.

The idea for the book arose from the desire of Ed Tollmann to share his extensive collection of Lebanon memorabilia with a larger audience. Alicia Wayland and Claire S. Krause share his passion for our town's history. All three authors joined forces to bring together some of the stories of Lebanon people and places for your enjoyment. Alicia Wayland compiled the introduction and chapters 1, 2, 4, 6, 7, and 8. Ed Tollmann compiled chapter 3. All images in that chapter are from his personal collection. Claire S. Krause compiled chapter 5.

—Alicia Wayland, Ed Tollmann, and Claire S. Krause

INTRODUCTION

Lebanon was called Poquechaneed by the Mohegan Indians, who hunted the hills and valleys before the arrival of the first English settlers in the 1690s. In 1692, four proprietors from Norwich and Stonington purchased the first land tract in Lebanon from Oweneco, sachem of the Mohegans. The tract was called the Five Mile Purchase and encompassed most of present-day Lebanon.

Settlement of the town began in 1695 on land granted by the proprietors to settlers from Connecticut and Massachusetts. Earlier land grants by the General Assembly and other purchases from the Mohegans adjacent to the Five Mile Purchase, including the Clarke and Dewey Purchase to the north, were also being settled.

On October 10, 1700, these tracts of land were incorporated by the General Assembly as the town of Lebanon, an area covering 80 square miles. Boundaries were established and permission to gather a church was given. The First Congregational Church was organized shortly thereafter. In 1804, the northern section of town, called the North Society or Lebanon Crank, was set off as the town of Columbia. Columbia shared equally in Lebanon's history until that date.

By 1725, Lebanon was a thriving agricultural town with sawmills, gristmills, tanneries, and other trades connected with farming. Much of the prosperity of the early years was based on stock raising. Cattle were driven to market in Boston and Norwich, and later the town was the center of the colony's meat-packing industry. The census of 1774 indicates Lebanon was one of the largest and most prosperous towns in the colony.

Lebanon is best known for its role in the American Revolution. Among its patriots were William Williams, signer of the Declaration of Independence, and the rebel Gov. Jonathan Trumbull, the only colonial governor to become the governor of a state when independence was declared. Trumbull directed Connecticut's great contributions to the patriot cause, primarily from his War Office across from the town green, giving Lebanon its nickname of "the Heartbeat of the American Revolution."

During the 19th century, Lebanon farmers concentrated on dairying, first in butter and cheese and then in the production of whole milk. The Yankee population dwindled as many residents left town for jobs in the cities or to take up new western lands. Many of the Irish, Jewish, Slavic, and German settlers from Ukraine who migrated to Lebanon during this period continued farming the land.

In the mid–20th century, improved roads made Lebanon attractive to city dwellers, spurring a growth in suburban development. Agriculture is still the major economic activity, preserving the rural landscape, but now 90 percent of the residents commute out of town to work.

Lebanon is the birthplace of five of the state's governors, more than any other town. They are, with terms of office, as follows: Jonathan Trumbull, 1769–1784; Jonathan Trumbull Jr., 1797–1809; Clark Bissell, 1847–1849; Joseph Trumbull, 1849–1850; and William A. Buckingham, 1858–1866. Lebanon is also the birthplace of Dr. William Beaumont, a U.S. Army surgeon who discovered the secret of human digestion.

The town's most distinctive feature is the mile-long town green, listed on the National Register of Historic Places. The northern section of the green is a vast, open meadow of 27 acres where neighboring farmers make hay. It is the only town green still in agricultural use. The southern end of the green is the site for many civic, cultural, and recreational activities that take place throughout the year. A favorite event is the Lebanon Historical Society's annual outdoor antiques show, held on the green on the last Saturday in September.

Museums and other historic sites around the town green tell the story of Connecticut's significant role in national history during the Revolutionary period, as well as Dr. Beaumont's unique place in medical history. The Lebanon Historical Society Museum and Visitor Center features local history exhibitions, a research and genealogy library, and visitor amenities.

Each generation has made its mark on the town throughout more than 300 years of town history. This pictorial history provides glimpses of some of the people, places, and events that make Lebanon a town to remember from past to present.

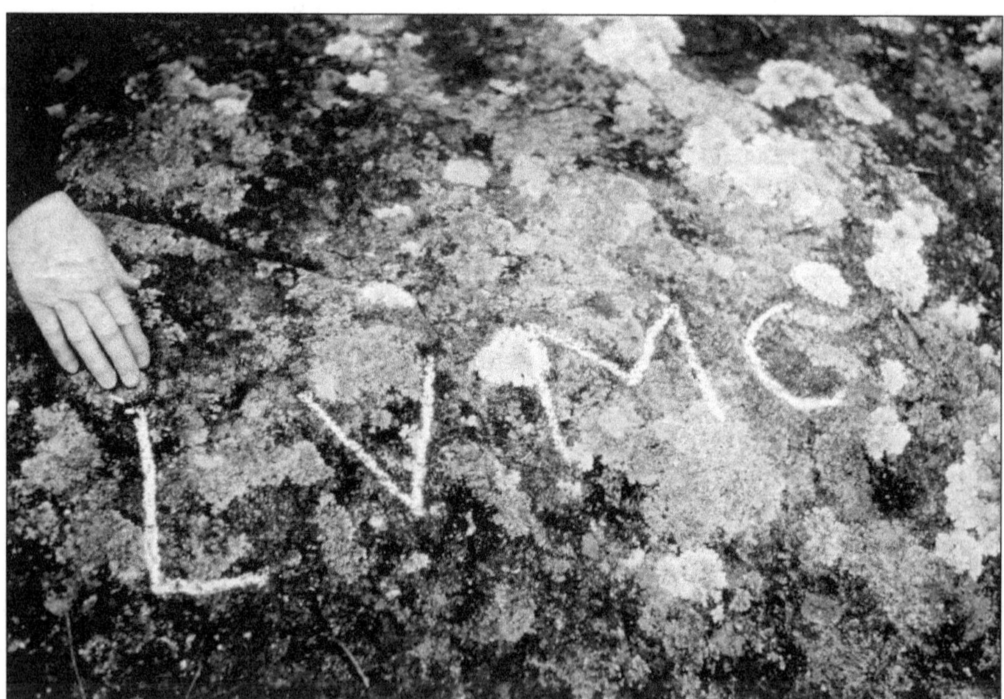

Five Mile Rock. This rock marks the southwest corner of the Five Mile Purchase. The chiseled letters LVMC stand for "Lebanon Five Mile Corner." In 1705, the General Assembly finally confirmed Oweneco's 1692 sale to the four original proprietors and all subsequent land transfers, then ordered a survey of the tract with marked rocks to be set in all corners. This corner rock is located off Randall Road on private property. (Courtesy LHS.)

One

Notable People and Places

During the early settlement period, land was cleared, crops sown, buildings erected, and primitive roads constructed. After the initial hardships of settlement, the town grew rapidly. The colony census of 1756 counted a population of 3,274, making Lebanon the sixth-largest town in terms of population, greater even than Hartford.

Much of the prosperity of the early years was due to Joseph Trumbull, who moved to Lebanon from Simsbury in 1704. He drove local cattle to city markets, where he exchanged the herds for manufactured goods to sell in his store. He was also involved in the West Indies trade, the largest outlet for colonial provisions.

Jonathan Trumbull (1710–1785), Joseph's son, greatly expanded the family business, carrying on an extensive overseas trade. He was increasingly influential in colony affairs as a member of the General Assembly, and he was elected lieutenant governor in 1767. In 1769, Jonathan Trumbull became governor, a post he would hold for nearly 15 years during one of the most tumultuous periods in the nation's history.

When news of the April 1775 Lexington-Concord alarm reached the area, Governor Trumbull turned his former store into his headquarters. During the American Revolution, more than 500 meetings of the Council of Safety were held in this building, known as the War Office.

Throughout the entire war, at least 677 Lebanon men served in the militia and the Continental Army at some time. This figure represents more than 50 percent of the adult male population.

William Williams was one of the most ardent supporters of independence. As a delegate to the Continental Congress in 1776, he was one of Connecticut's four signers of the Declaration of Independence. Williams was also married to the governor's daughter Mary Trumbull.

Governor Trumbull's office was the command post for Connecticut's outpouring of provisions to the war effort. He responded repeatedly to Gen. George Washington's urgent pleas for provisions for the Continental Army. The cattle drives from Connecticut saved the starving soldiers at Valley Forge and Morristown. Connecticut is called the Provisions State for these efforts.

Washington also called on the governor to supply the French army, led by the comte de Rochambeau. Two years after France entered into an alliance with the United States, transport ships landed 5,000 French soldiers at Newport, Rhode Island, in July 1780. In November of that same year, Rochambeau sent about 220 hussars from the duc de Lauzun's Legion, the cavalry unit of his army, to Lebanon, where forage for horses was more plentiful.

Washington stayed in Lebanon the night of March 4, 1781, on his way to Newport to meet with General Rochambeau. Here, he reviewed the French legionnaires before continuing his journey. Shortly after the visit, Jonathan Trumbull Jr. accepted Washington's invitation to become his military secretary. He remained by Washington's side until the army was disbanded in 1783.

After a seven-month encampment, Lauzun's Legion left Lebanon in June 1781, as the French army marched from Newport through Connecticut to meet Washington on the Hudson River. Four months later, the allied armies crushed Lord Cornwallis and the British at the Battle of Yorktown in Virginia. The surrender of Cornwallis on October 19, 1781, virtually ended military operations, although New York City remained occupied until 1783.

Throughout the war, the fidelity of Connecticut's patriots was upheld through military defeats, financial chaos, and wartime shortages by the leaders who organized the state's contributions to the patriot cause from their modest buildings around the town green.

The preservation of these historic buildings and the role of these leaders in securing the nation's independence led to the establishment of the Lebanon Green National Register District in 1979. The town green is still the heart of the community and continues to inspire visitors as they walk in the footsteps of patriots.

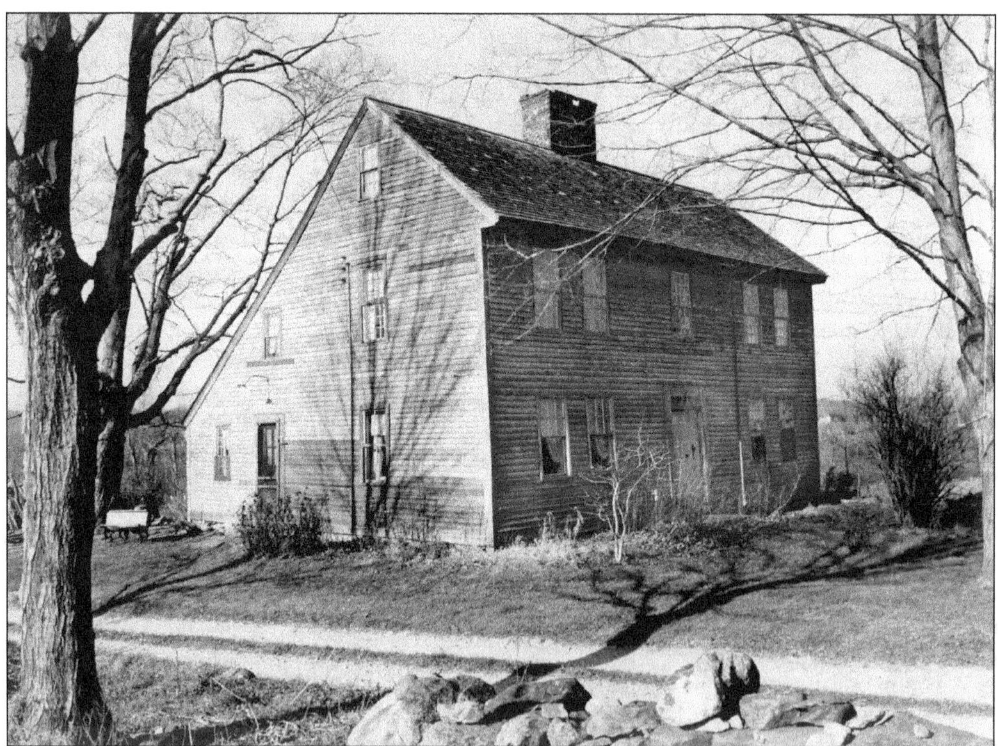

THE CLARK HOUSE, C. 1708. The oldest known surviving house in Lebanon was built by Moses Clark on Madley Road. It is the birthplace of Col. James Clark (1730–1826), who led the Lebanon militia to Cambridge in 1775, then fought at Bunker Hill. Clark also fought at the battles of Harlem Heights and White Plains. This early 1900s photograph shows the house before it was restored. (Courtesy LHS.)

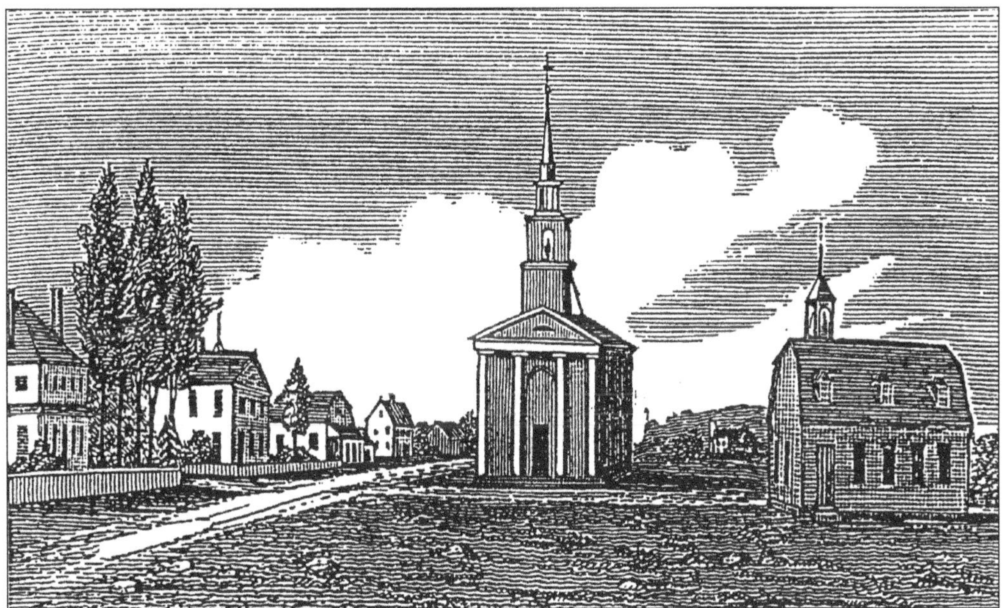

The Tisdale School. Jonathan Trumbull and several townspeople founded the Tisdale School as a subscription school in 1743. In 1762, the original frame structure was replaced by the two-story brick building shown on the right. The school was named after Nathan Tisdale (1732–1787), a brilliant teacher who drew students from as far away as the West Indies. The building was torn down sometime before 1844. (Courtesy John Warner Barber, *Connecticut Historical Collections*, 1836.)

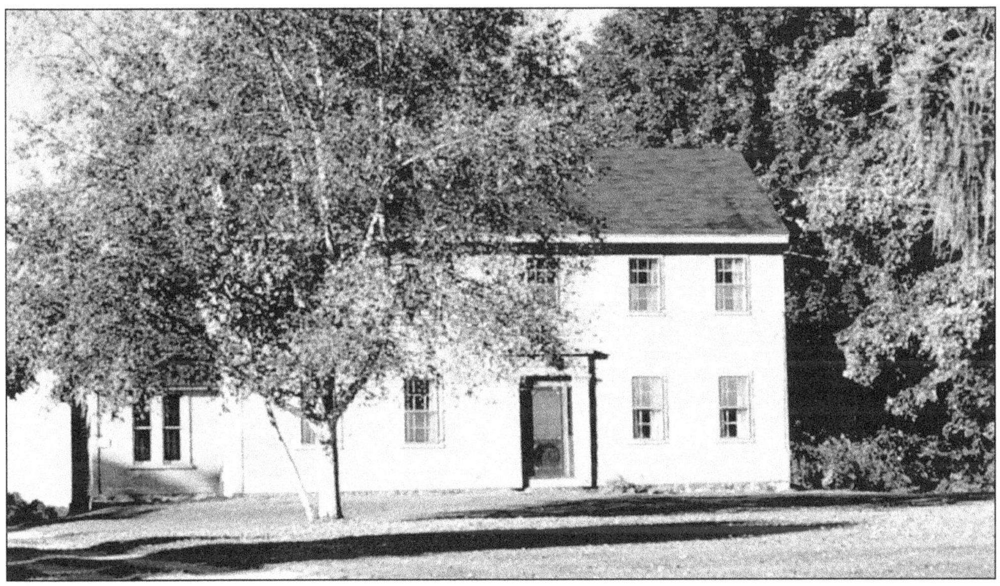

The Welles House, 1712. Solomon Williams, the third pastor of the First Congregational Church, purchased this house in 1722. His eight children, including William, signer of the Declaration of Independence, were born here. Solomon was a leader in the founding of the Philogrammatican Library in 1738 and kept the library books in this house. Only the third library in the colony, it was dissolved in 1792. (Photograph by Grant Huntington; courtesy town of Lebanon.)

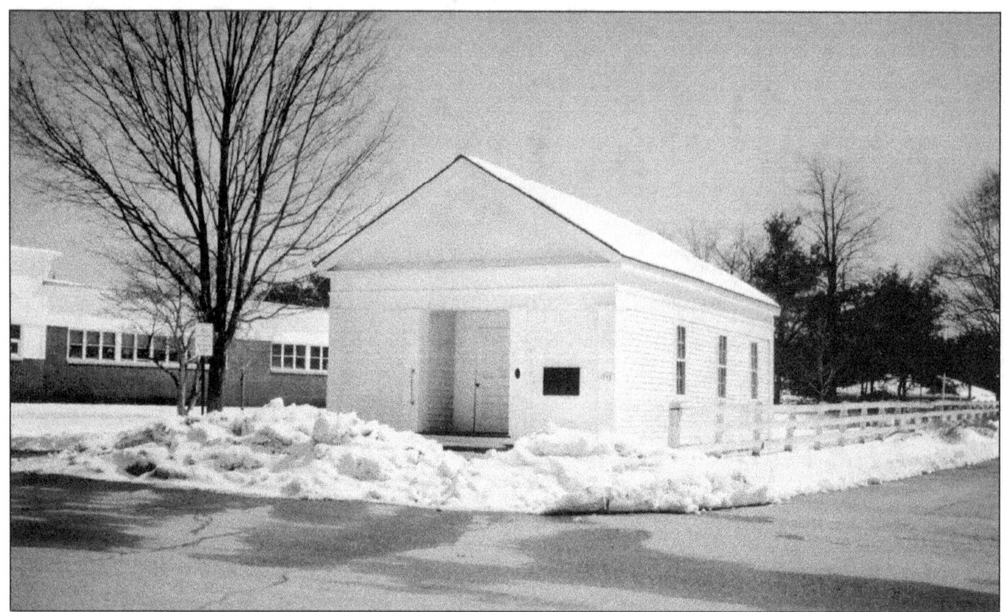

Moor's Indian Charity School. In the North Society (now Columbia), Pastor Eleazar Wheelock opened a school for American Indian children in 1754, where he trained both whites and American Indians as missionaries. In 1769, Wheelock moved his school to Hanover, New Hampshire, and also founded a new college named after the Earl of Dartmouth. This school building, considered the forerunner of Dartmouth College, is a historic landmark in the center of Columbia. (Courtesy LHS.)

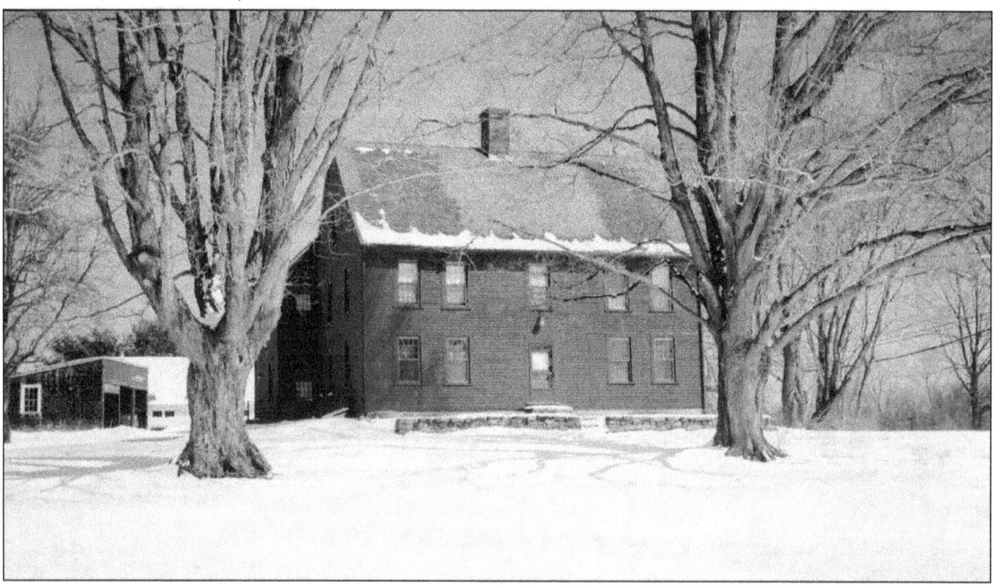

The Wheelock House, c. 1735. Eleazar Wheelock served as the Congregational minister of the North Society from 1735 to 1769. During this time, he also conducted a school for college-bound boys in his home. His most famous pupil was Samson Occom, a Mohegan Indian who studied there from 1743 to 1748. Occom was the first Mohegan to become an ordained minister, and his success led Wheelock to open the school for American Indian children in 1754. (Courtesy LHS.)

The Rebel Governor. Jonathan Trumbull was the only colonial governor to become governor of a state when independence was declared in 1776. He served from 1769 to 1784. During the Revolution, he mobilized the state to provide men and supplies for the patriot cause. His leadership was critical to the final victory. When Trumbull died, Gen. George Washington wrote that his service placed him "among the first of patriots." (Courtesy town of Lebanon, special collection.)

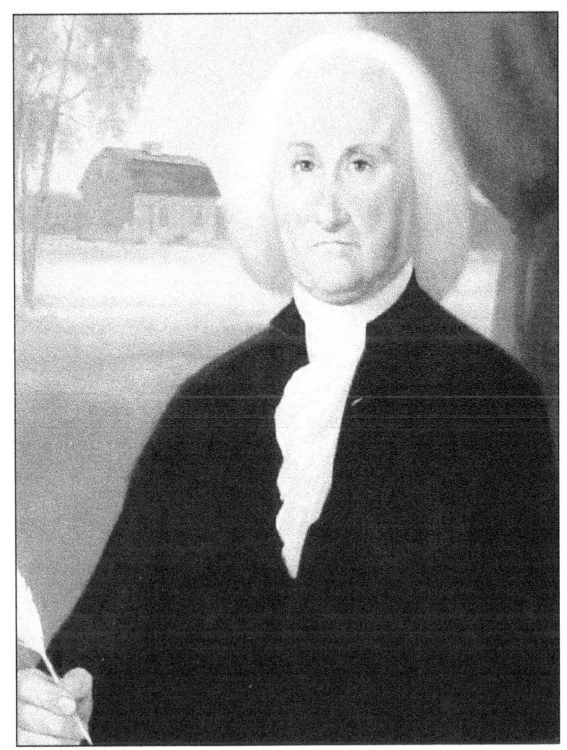

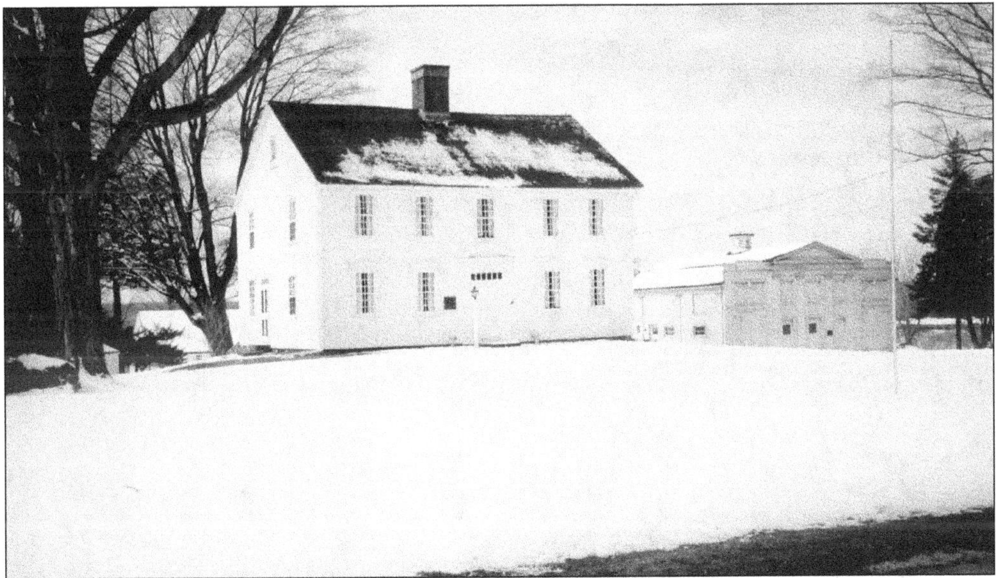

The Governor Trumbull House, c. 1740. Jonathan Trumbull moved his family into this house when he inherited it from his father in 1755. His youngest child, John Trumbull, a patriot and artist of the Revolution, was born here in 1756. The Wadsworth Stable, originally located on the estate of Col. Jeremiah Wadsworth in Hartford, was moved here in 1954. Both buildings are now museums owned by the Connecticut Daughters of the American Revolution. (Courtesy LHS.)

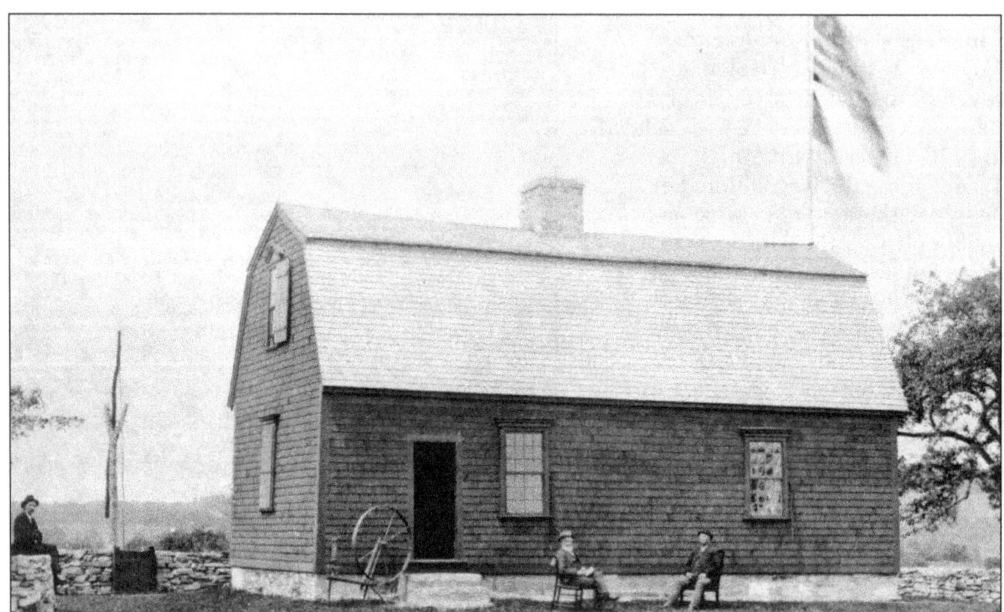

The Revolutionary War Office. At the outbreak of hostilities, Gov. Jonathan Trumbull turned his former store into his headquarters, leading to Lebanon's nickname, "the Heartbeat of the American Revolution." More than 500 meetings of the Council of Safety were held in this building, which is now a museum owned by the Connecticut Society, Sons of the American Revolution. The photograph was taken in 1892, shortly after the society had acquired and restored the building. (Courtesy Virginia Mullaly.)

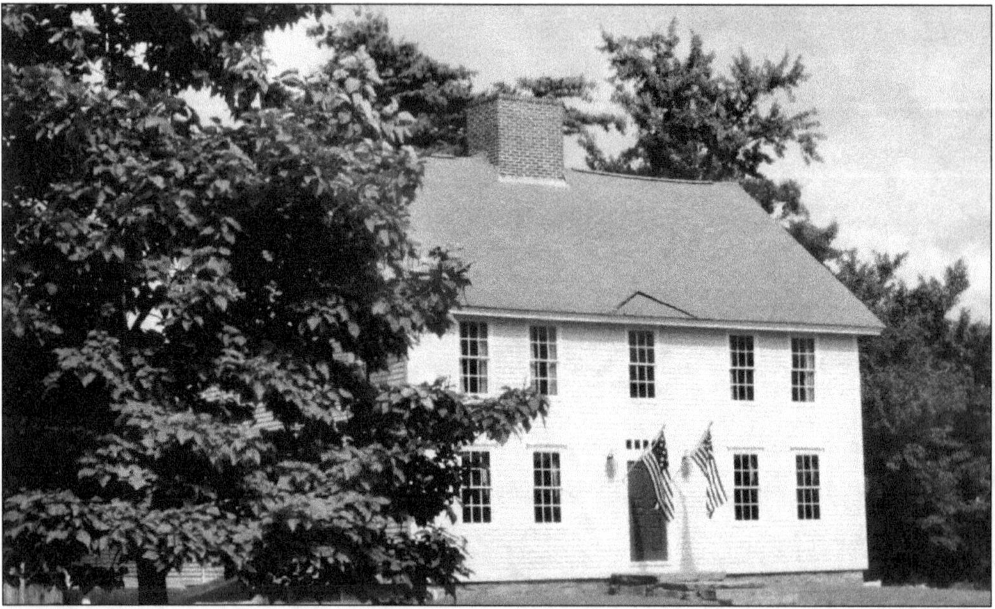

The Jonathan Trumbull Jr. House, c. 1769. Governor Trumbull's four sons—Joseph, Jonathan Jr., David, and John—all served in the Revolution. Jonathan Jr. was military secretary to Gen. George Washington and later served in the first Congress elected under the Constitution in 1789. Like his father before him, Jonathan Trumbull Jr. served as governor, from 1797–1809. His house is now a museum owned by the town of Lebanon. (Courtesy LHS.)

A Bold Patriot. William Williams (1731–1811) was one of Connecticut's four signers of the Declaration of Independence. He was a fiery orator and eloquent pamphleteer who tirelessly toured the state to urge support for the war and to enlist recruits. Williams served in the Continental Congress for a short period, then returned home to provide indispensable service on the Council of Safety throughout the war. (Courtesy First Congregational Church of Lebanon, special collection.)

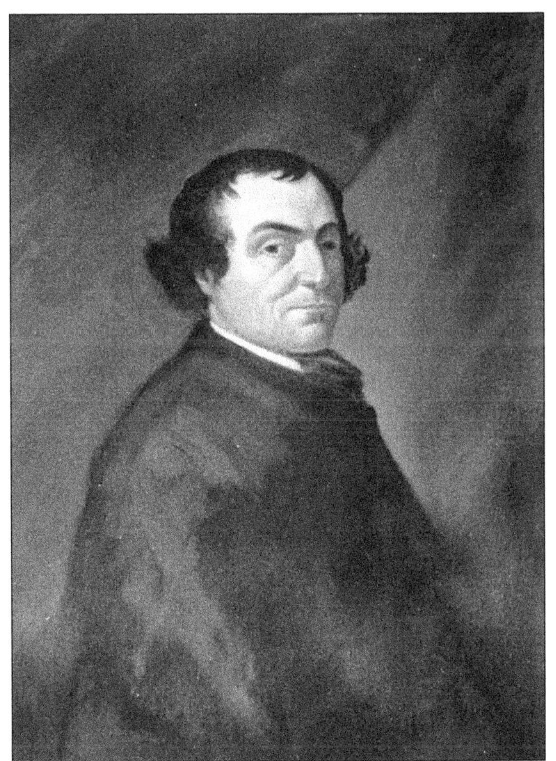

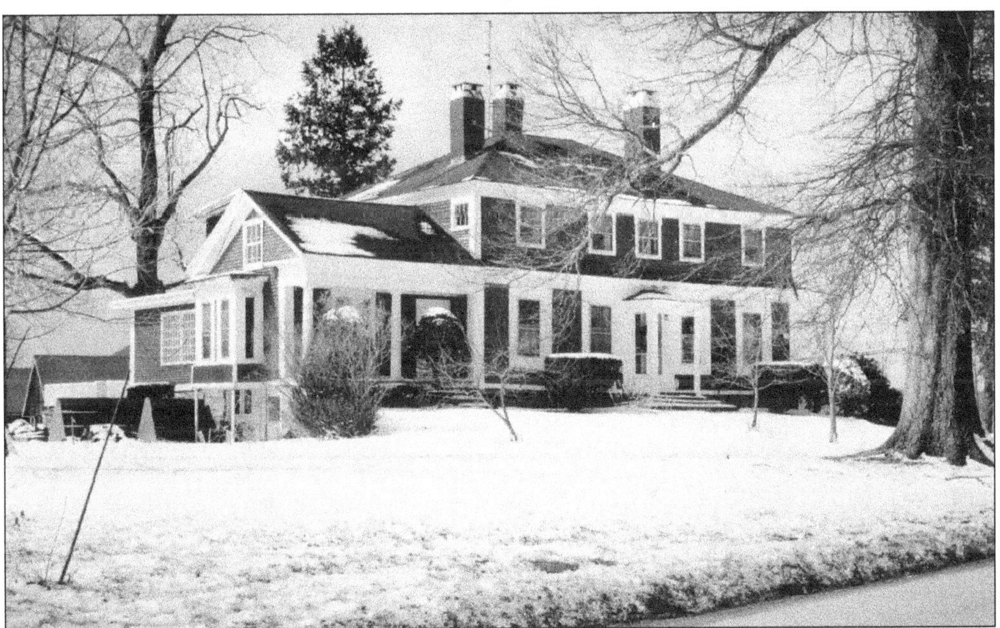

Redwood, 1778–1779. David Trumbull, son of the governor, commissioned Isaac Fitch of Lebanon to design and build this house. During the encampment of the French army's cavalry unit in Lebanon from 1780 to 1781, David turned over his house to their commander, the duc de Lauzun, to use as his headquarters. David's son Joseph, born here in 1782, served as governor from 1849 to 1850, the third generation of Trumbulls to head the state. (Courtesy LHS.)

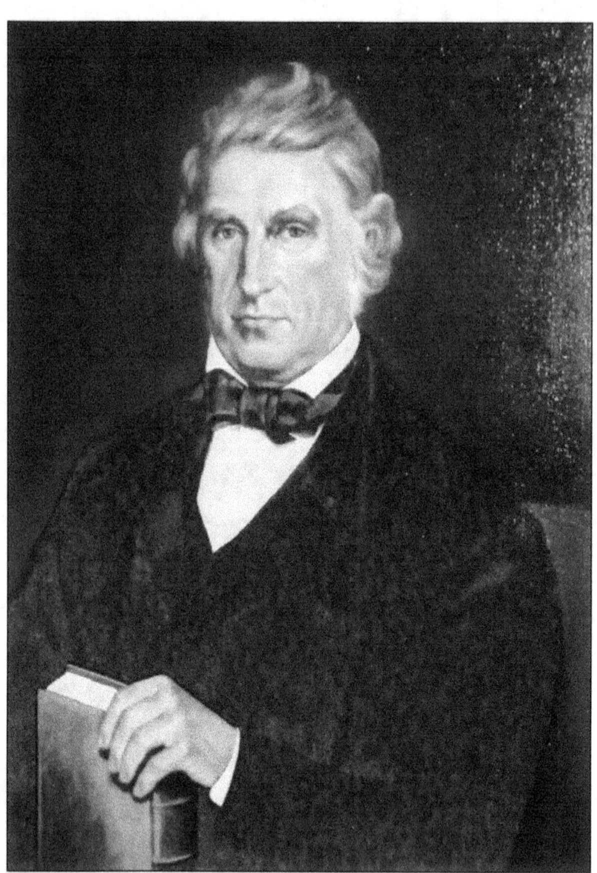

A Frontier Doctor. Dr. William Beaumont, born in Lebanon in 1785, was a pioneer medical researcher. As a U.S. Army surgeon, Beaumont was assigned to Fort Mackinac, a wilderness outpost in northern Michigan. There he conducted experiments on a wounded fur trapper that established for the first time the complex nature of digestion. He published his research in 1833 to worldwide acclaim. Nearly all of his conclusions are still studied today. (Courtesy LHS.)

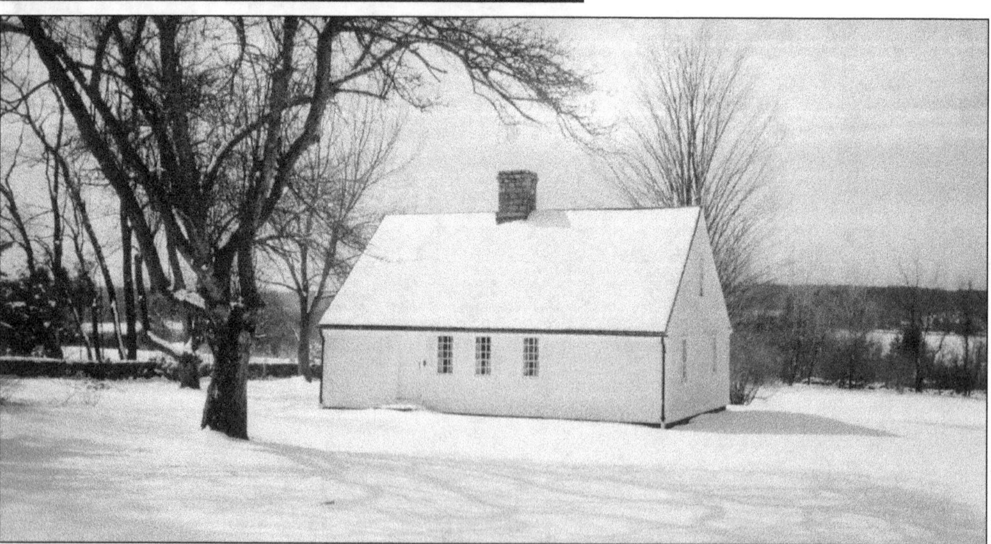

The Beaumont Homestead. Dr. Beaumont's childhood home was built by his father, Samuel, c. 1750. The Beaumont Medical Club of Yale University moved the house from its original location on Village Hill Road to a site behind the Governor Trumbull House. The house was restored, and one room was re-created as an early 19th-century doctor's office. It is now a museum owned by the Lebanon Historical Society. (Courtesy LHS.)

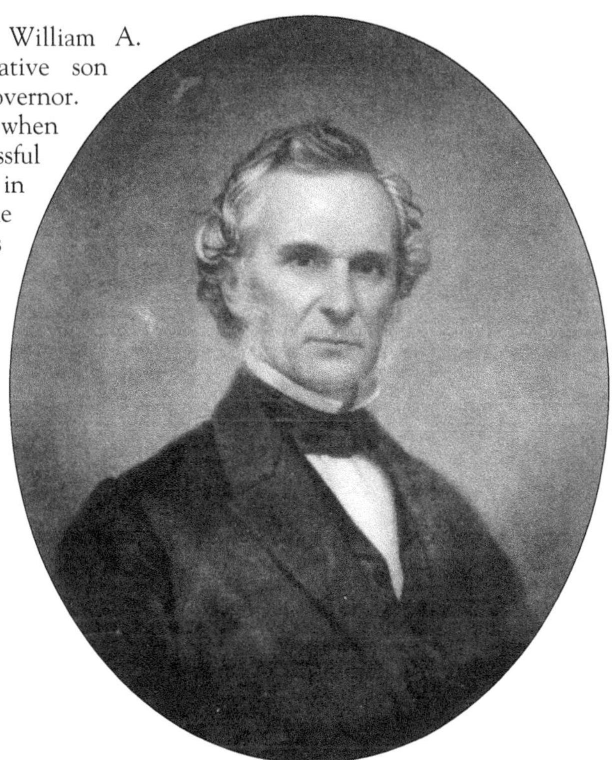

THE CIVIL WAR GOVERNOR. William A. Buckingham was the fifth native son of Lebanon to serve as governor. Buckingham moved to Norwich when he was 19 and became a successful merchant. Elected governor in 1858, he served through the Civil War to 1866. Under his leadership, Connecticut once again became the "Provisions State," producing food, textiles, machine tools, and armaments for the Union army. (Courtesy First Congregational Church of Lebanon, special collection.)

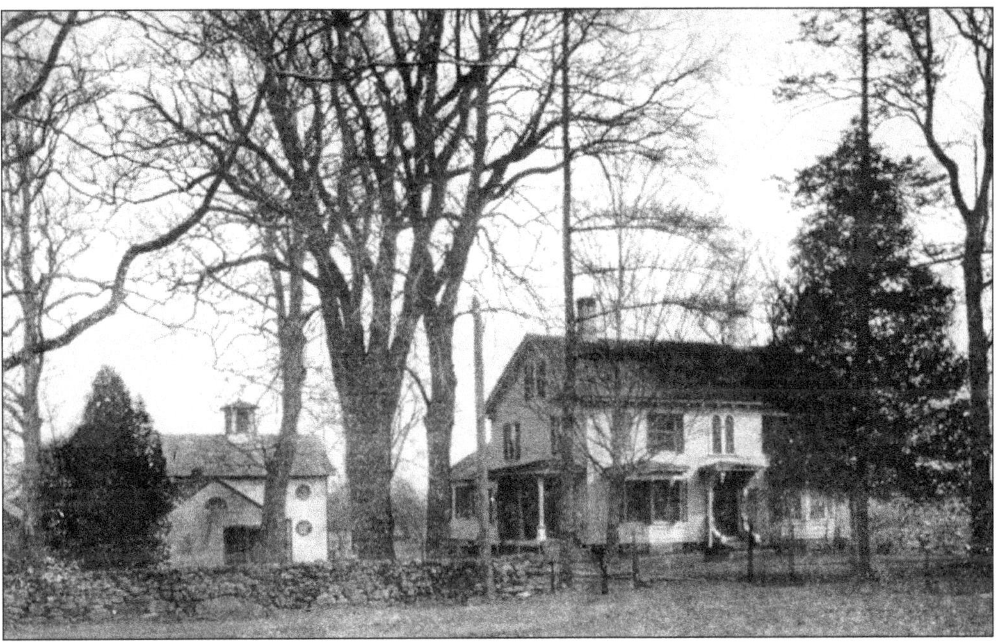

THE SECOND BUCKINGHAM HOUSE. Governor Buckingham, born in Lebanon in 1804, grew up in this house, built by his father, Samuel, sometime after 1808. That year, the proprietors of the still-undivided land sold Samuel a strip from the highway on which to build a new house. This 1907 photograph shows the mid–19th century dairy barn with its circular windows and cupola. The building now houses a veterinary clinic. (Courtesy Charles H. Baldwin, D.V.M.)

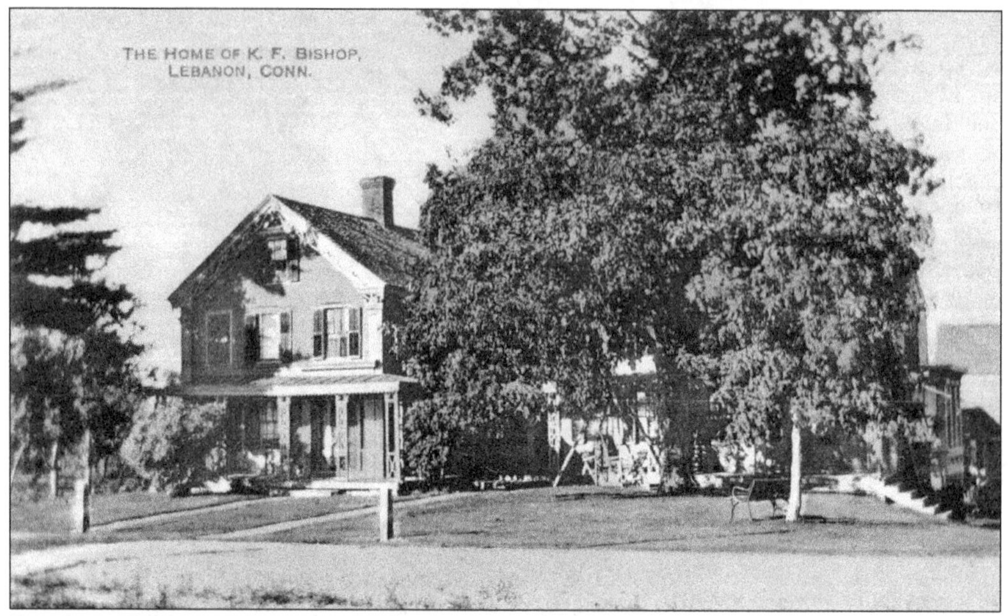

Dr. Sweet's House, c. 1850. Charles Sweet (1810–1896) was known as "Bonesetter Sweet," famous for his ability to set broken or dislocated bones. His office was located on the green where the library now stands. Patients boarded at his "remedial institution" (on the site of the present community center) for treatment of various diseases. Selectman Karl Bishop lived in the house when this early 20th century postcard was made. (Courtesy Ed Tollmann.)

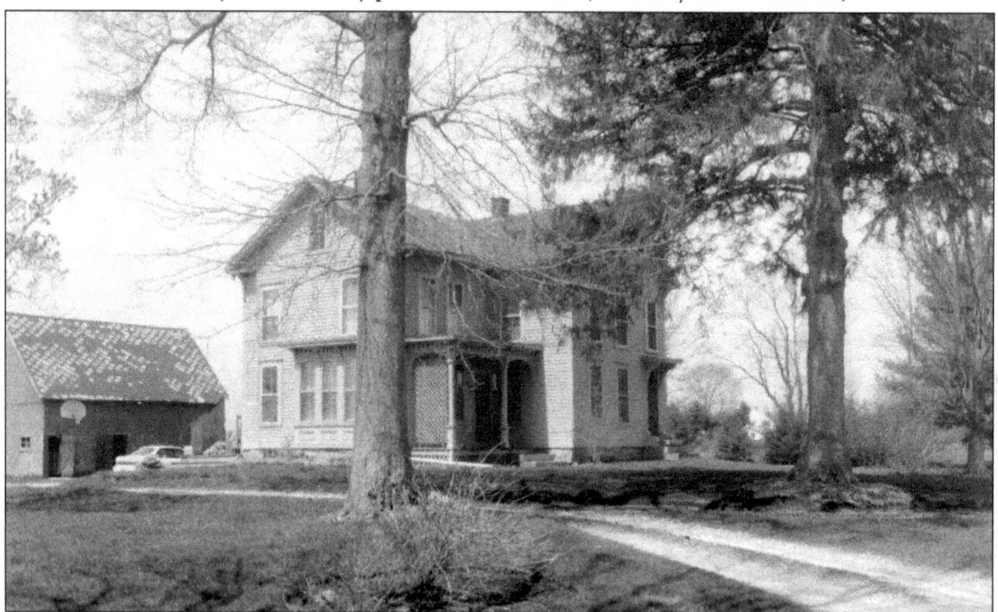

The Constitution Oak. This Eastlake-style house on West Town Street was built by Isaac Gillette *c.* 1880. Gillette was Lebanon's delegate to the state's 1902 Constitutional Convention. Each delegate received a pin oak sapling as a memento. The saplings were planted statewide, in both public and private locations, the first mass commemorative tree planting in the state. Gillette planted his sapling on his front lawn, where it still flourishes. (Courtesy LHS.)

Two

Houses of Worship

Lebanon's houses of worship have evolved from the single established Congregational church of the Connecticut colony to a diversity of denominations to meet the spiritual needs of the town's residents. The First Congregational Church of Lebanon was organized on November 27, 1700. In 1706, the first meetinghouse was erected, at the intersection of the two main roads in the town center. A new meetinghouse was built on the site of the present church in 1732.

The meetinghouse was the focal point of the community. Town meetings, elections, and Sabbath services took place in the same building. Here, too, the stirring events of independence and the Revolution were debated.

The Rev. Solomon Williams, the third minister, served the society for 54 years, from 1722 to 1776. He was a strong influence during the formative years of the town and left money in his will for the support of the Revolution. He was the father of William Williams, signer of the Declaration of Independence.

The brick meetinghouse was designed by John Trumbull, son of Governor Jonathan Trumbull. Built from 1804 to 1809, it is the only surviving example of the artist's architectural work.

The town was soon divided into several ecclesiastical societies because of the difficulties of traveling by foot or horseback to the town center. In 1715, the inhabitants of the northern section of town were granted permission to form the Second, or North, Society, now the town of Columbia. The North Society's best-known pastor was its third, Eleazar Wheelock, who served from 1735 to 1769.

The third society was organized as the Goshen Congregational Church in 1729. It originally served the neighborhoods of Goshen and Exeter, but Exeter was split off as a separate society in 1773. The Goshen church has served the community for 275 years, making it the second-oldest extant church in Lebanon.

The Lebanon Baptist Church, at the north end of the town green, was organized in 1805, the result of a long-simmering controversy over the location of the Congregational meetinghouse, a mile distant at the south end of the green. After much thought and study, many parishioners left the Congregational church to unite with the Baptist church. Their first meetinghouse was built in 1805. Hard feelings over the split must have died down early, because both meetinghouses were used as sites for town meetings until the town hall was built in 1848.

The Lebanon Jewish Congregation was formed in 1903, meeting in the homes of members. By 1920, Lebanon had nearly 100 Jewish families. The congregation purchased the vacant Levita Street Schoolhouse in 1933 to use as a synagogue. When this burned in 1955, the congregation built a new synagogue on Goshen Hill Road. After World War II, the congregation dwindled, and the synagogue was sold to the Lebanon Bible Church in 1995.

The German people of Lebanon arrived from the Ukrainian village of Karlswalde, where their parents and grandparents had settled as farmers. Karlswalder immigrants, arriving between 1911 and 1928, settled in the Village Hill area. The Redeemer Lutheran Church, built entirely by the volunteer labor of members, was completed in 1944. The intricate woodwork was carved by Godfrey Laibrandt, who also carved the woodwork in the First Congregational Church when it was restored after the 1938 hurricane.

The St. Francis of Assisi R.C. Church began as a mission church in a converted residence on the east side of the green in 1943. Expanded membership led to the need for a larger building. In 1965, the church purchased a large parcel on West Town Street as the site for a new building and set about raising money for construction. Construction finally began in 1979 and was completed the following spring. St. Francis became a parish in its own right in December 1980.

The Andover, North, and Exeter Ecclesiastical Societies, the Scott Hill Baptist Church, the Methodist Episcopal Church, the St. Mary Mission Chapel, the Liberty Hill Church, and the Jewish synagogue are no longer with us. They were among the spiritual roots of the community that provided the moral foundation that sustains us today.

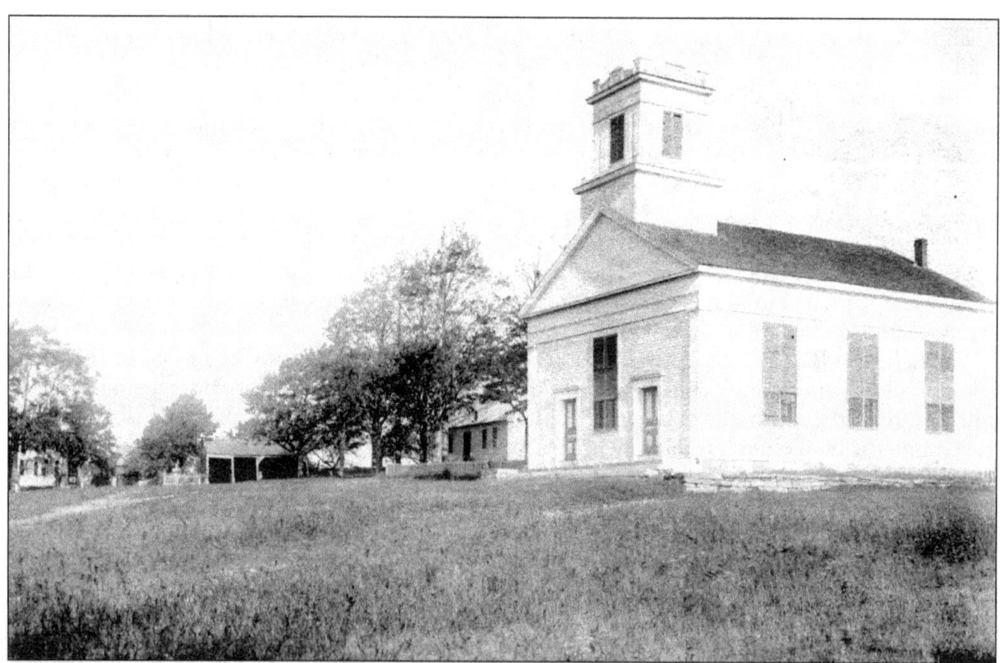

The Exeter Congregational Church. The Exeter section of Lebanon was served by the Goshen church until it was set off as a separate society in 1773. In 1844, Exeter's meetinghouse was replaced by this new church on Olenick Road. Because of declining membership, the church merged with Liberty Hill in 1919 and finally dissolved in 1945. The vacant building deteriorated over the years and was demolished in the early 1960s. (Courtesy LHS.)

The Brick Meetinghouse. The First Congregational Church of Lebanon was formally organized in November 1700. The first meetinghouse, used for both town meetings and religious services, was built in 1706, and the second was built in 1732. The third meetinghouse was designed by John Trumbull, an artist of the Revolutionary War period, and was constructed between 1804 and 1809. Its graceful spire rising over the hilltop is a local landmark. It is the only surviving example of Trumbull's architectural work. (Photograph by Grant Huntington; courtesy town of Lebanon.)

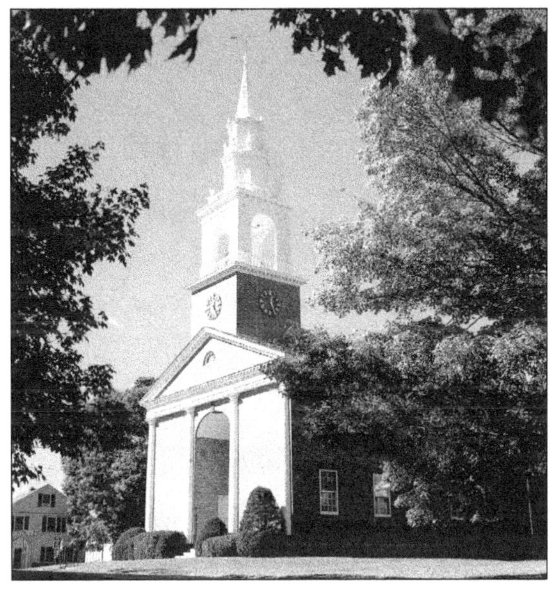

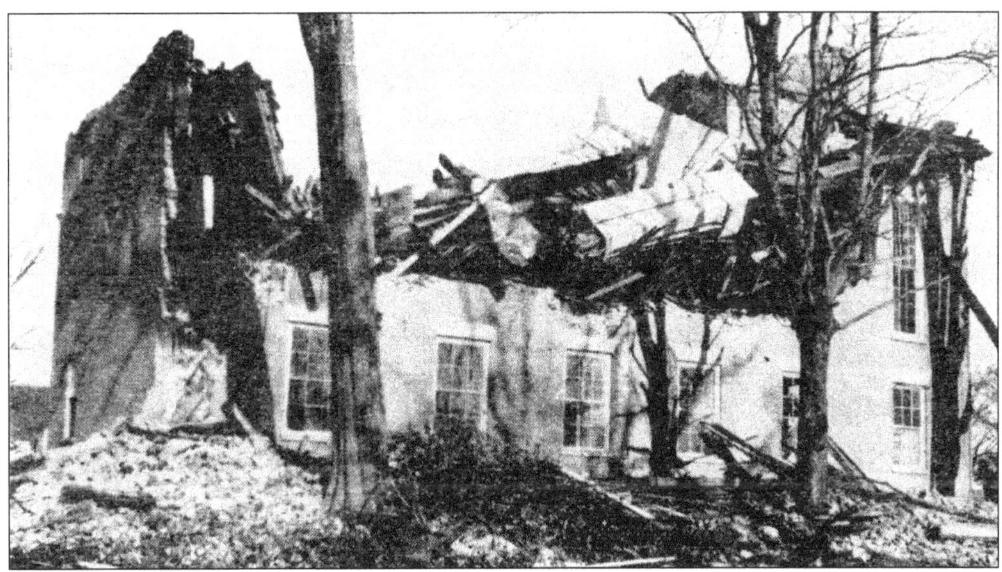

Devastation. The church stood directly in the path of the 1938 hurricane. High winds toppled the steeple, sending it crashing into the nave. The interior lay in ruins. Rebuilding, interrupted by World War II, was completed in 1950, except the steeple. In 1954, the finished steeple was dedicated to the memory of William Williams. The church was restored to John Trumbull's original design. (Courtesy Virginia Mullaly.)

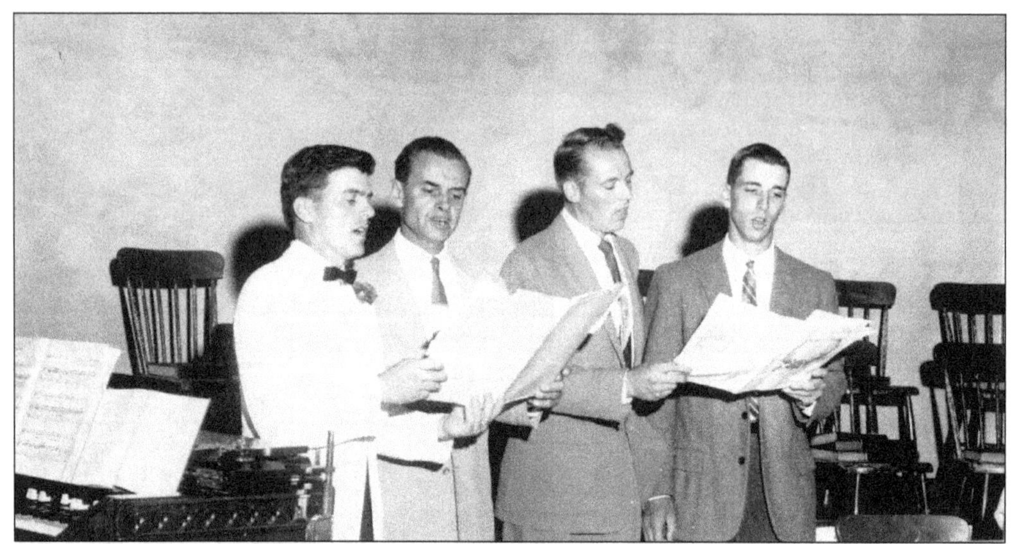

WEDDING SONGS. Henry Grabber, Walter Jakoboski, Russell Blakeslee, and Robert McCaw, shown from left to right, sang at the wedding of Kenneth Lathrop and Gretchen Grabber in 1955. The wedding was performed at the First Congregational Church. (Courtesy Russell Blakeslee.)

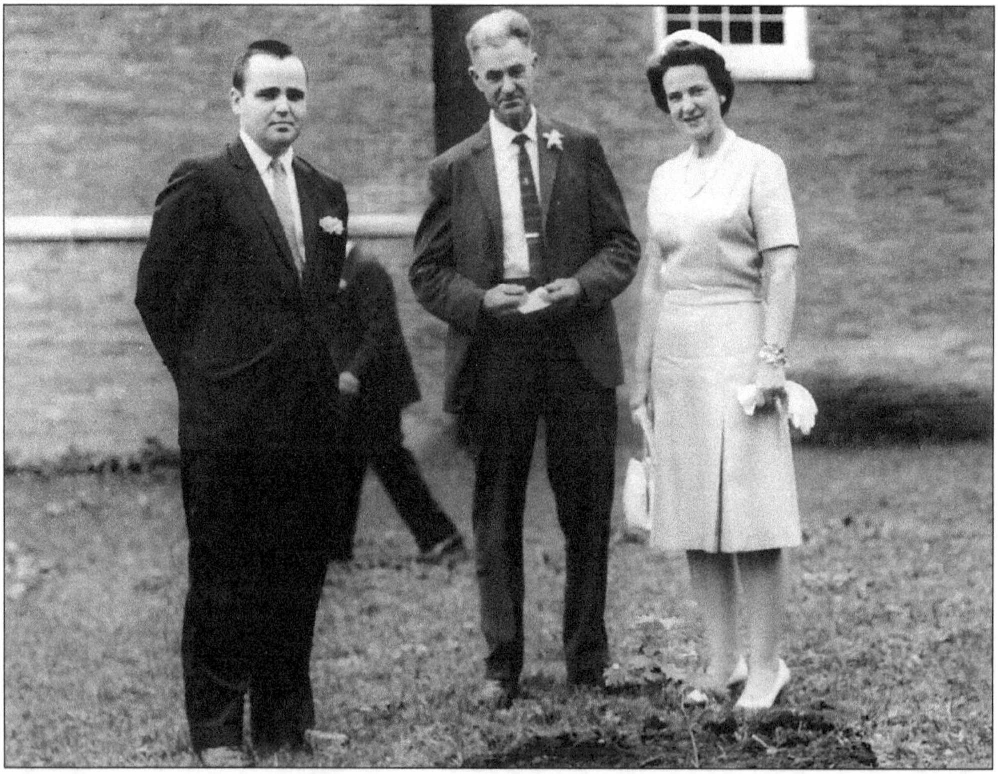

TREE PLANTING. A Charter Oak sapling was planted at the dedication of the new fellowship hall at the First Congregational Church in June 1962. Admiring the sapling donated by Dr. William Jahoda are, from left to right, Rev. Richard L. Rush, Leslie Clarke Sr., and Alison McBride. The tree, a direct descendant of Connecticut's famed Charter Oak, now towers over the lawn behind the hall, providing welcome shade during outdoor events. (Courtesy William Jahoda.)

The 300th Anniversary Cake. A Colonial worship service on November 26, 2000, concluded a year of activities celebrating the 300th anniversary of the First Congregational Church. Attending the reception afterward were Art Wallace (in period clothing at the far left), Neil Whitehead, and Ellen Lathrop. Rose Pogmore made the anniversary cakes, which were decorated with replicas of the brick meetinghouse. (Courtesy William Jahoda.)

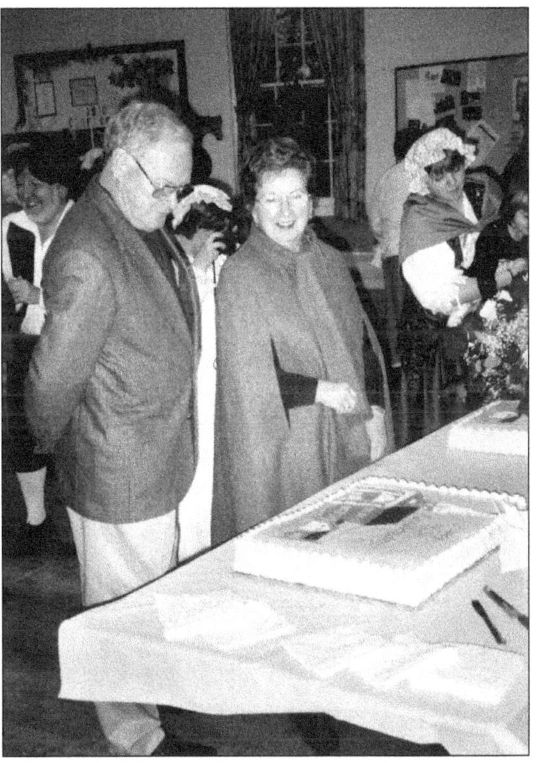

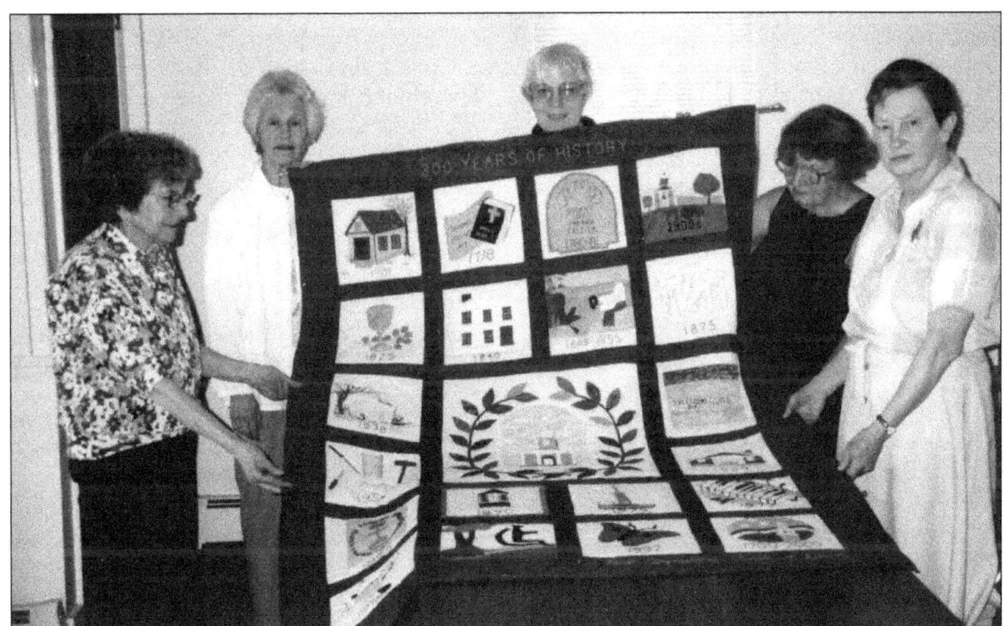

A Gift of Faith. Displaying the wall hanging made in 2000 for the tercentennial of the First Congregational Church are, from left to right, Phyllis Bartizek, Margery Jahoda, Sylvia Ryan, Helen Szajda, and Evelyn Lathrop. A committee designed the quilt and organized 21 people to make the squares. Members were chairwoman Margery Jahoda, Helen Szajda, Sylvia Ryan, Iola Jakoboski, Lucia Day, Evelyn Grabber, and Beverly York. (Courtesy William Jahoda.)

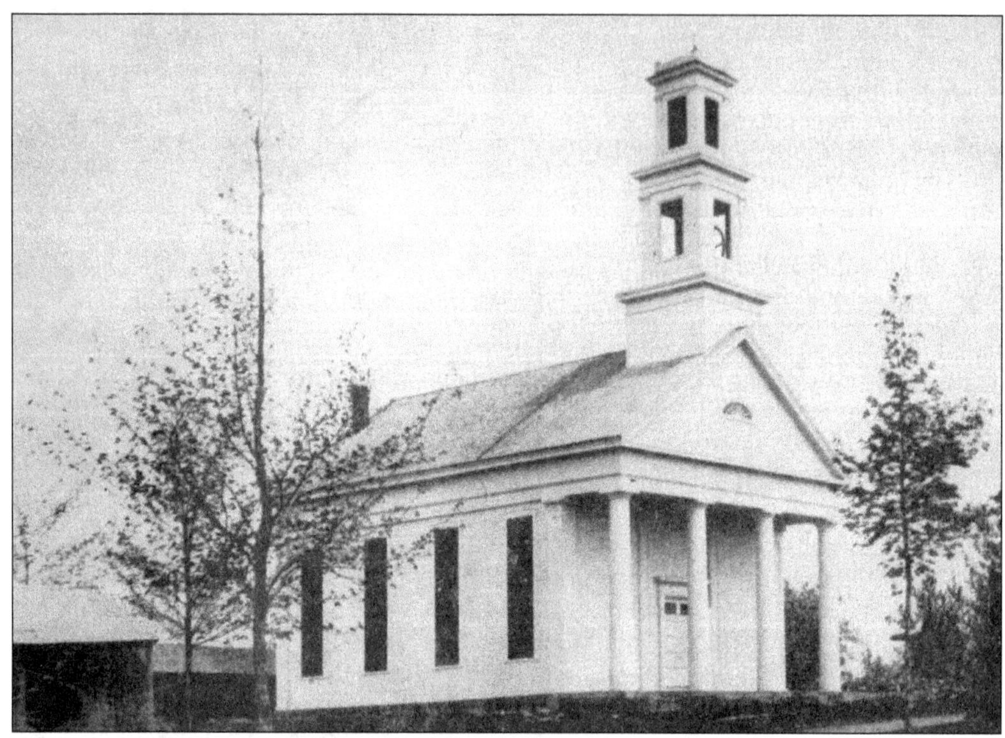

The Old Goshen Congregational Church. The Goshen church was organized in 1729 to serve the Goshen Hill and Exeter neighborhoods. The original site was on Goshen Hill Road near the McCall Road intersection. After the Exeter members separated in 1773, the Goshen congregation built a new meetinghouse on Church Road in 1801. It was significantly remodeled in the Greek Revival style in 1852. The church burned to the ground in 1898. (Courtesy LHS.)

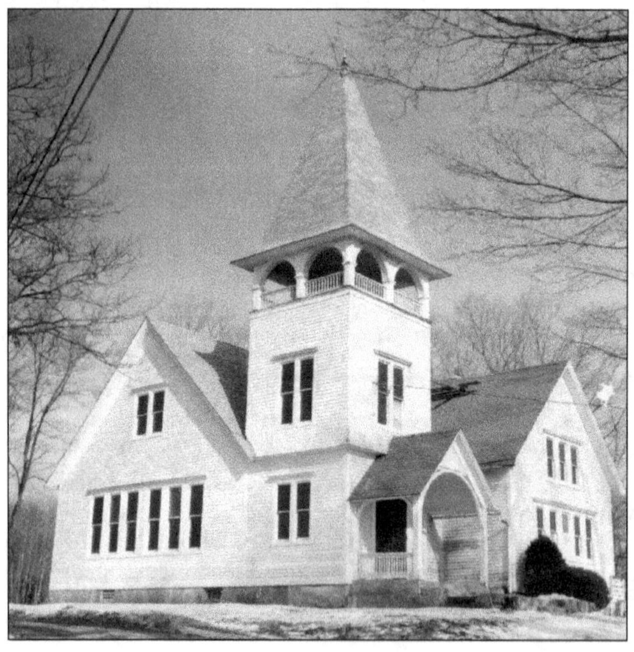

A Victorian Gem. After the fire, the Goshen congregation built a new church in the Victorian style. The kerosene chandelier saved from the fire hangs in the sanctuary, and the church bell was recast from the melted remains of the bell hanging in the old church. A fellowship hall was added in 1997. The Goshen Congregational Church has been a central part of the surrounding community for nearly three centuries. (Courtesy LHS.)

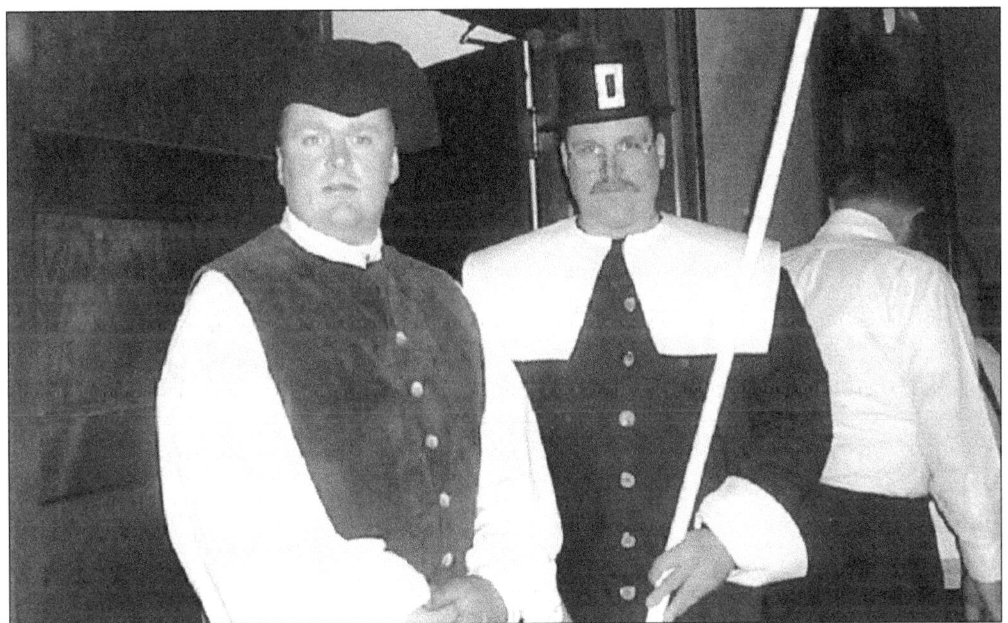

A Puritan Worship Service. The Goshen Congregational Church celebrated its 275th anniversary in 2004. A Puritan worship service on January 11 was the first of many events held throughout the yearlong celebration of the church's rich history in the community. Brothers Frank (left) and Kevin Blakeslee were among the many parishioners who attended the service in period attire. (Courtesy Russell Blakeslee.)

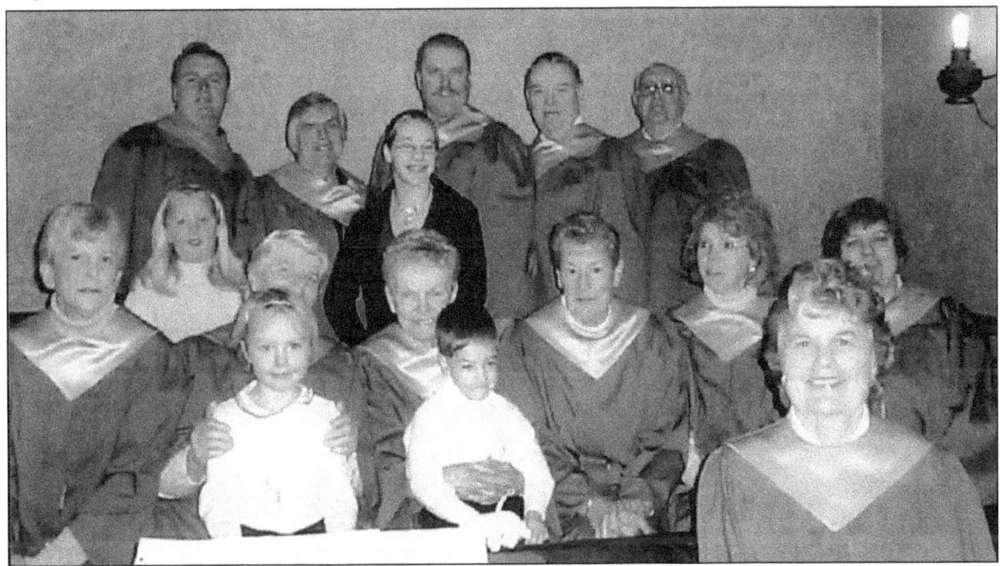

The Goshen Church Children's and Senior Choirs. Gathered here, from left to right, are the following: (first row) Alicia Watson, Gretchen Lathrop (holding Emelia Blakeslee), Gloria Corbett (holding Charlie Weinsteiger), Ann Dorflinger, Alison Palshaw, and Maureen McCall; (second row) Lillian Blakeslee and Heather Weinsteiger; (third row) Frank Blakeslee, Henry Grabber, Kevin Blakeslee, Russell Blakeslee, and Kenneth Lathrop. Missing are Diane Gray and children Mae and Tony Santillo and Joelle Tomick. Organist and choir director Jonica Blakeslee appears in front, at the far right. (Courtesy Russell Blakeslee.)

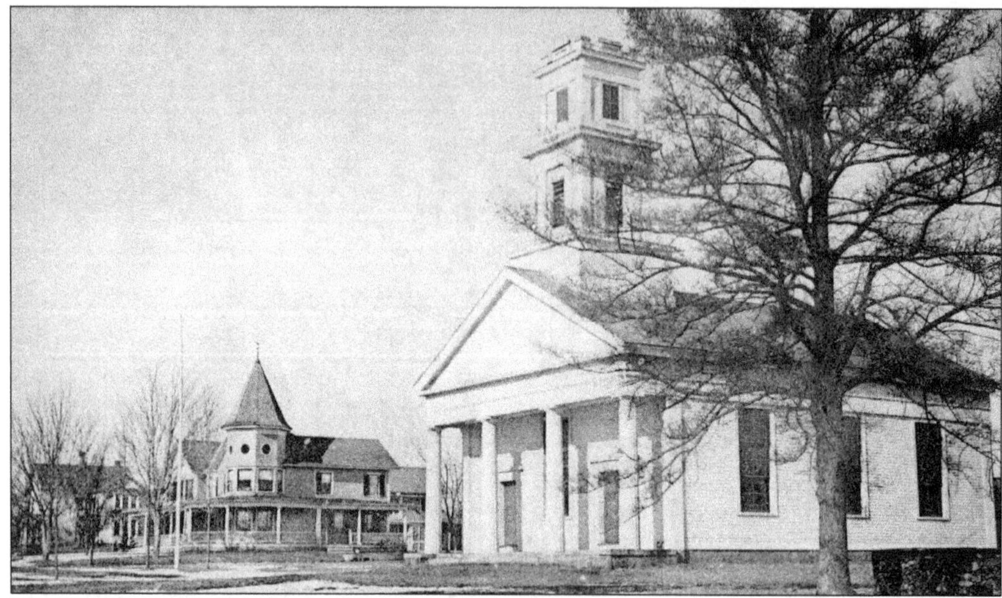

The First Baptist Church. The first meetinghouse of the Lebanon Baptists dates from the founding of the church in 1805. This Greek Revival church replaced it in 1841. A chapel, built from lumber from an old cheese factory, was added in 1907. The deteriorated second stage of the steeple was removed in the 1930s. This photograph, taken before 1900, shows the Joseph Abel house next door, which burned in 1910. (Courtesy LHS.)

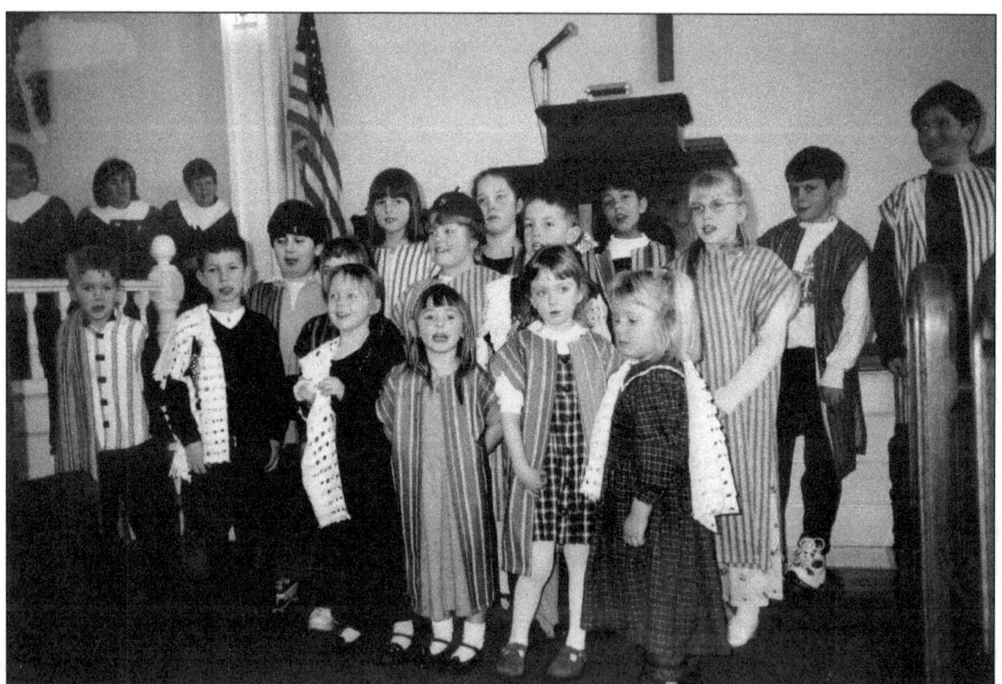

Sunday School. Sunday school children at the First Baptist Church take part in the regular Sunday worship services on a monthly basis. Here, the children are dressed in Biblical costumes as they present a Bible story to the congregation in March 2000. (Courtesy Beverly Duntz.)

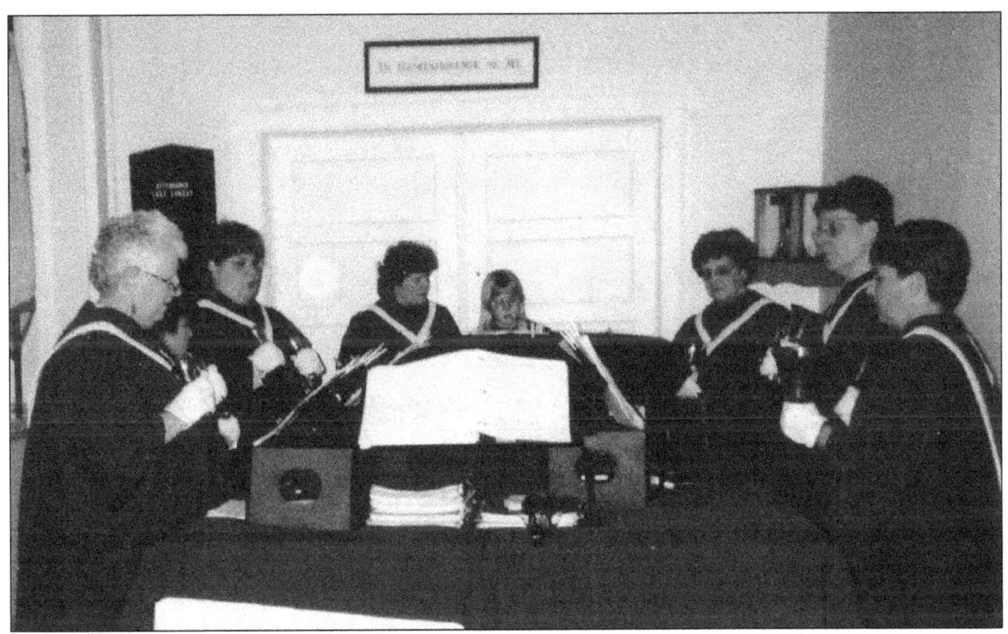

The Bell Choir. The bell choir of the First Baptist Church plays at almost every Sunday worship service. Members seen here are, from left to right, Joyce Kelly, Shirley Deflaviis, Sue Lyon, Molly Lathrop, Bonnie Lathrop, Beverly Duntz, Deborah Martin, and Lynn Littlefield. Their musicianship is highly regarded, and the bell choir also performs at many community events. (Courtesy Beverly Duntz.)

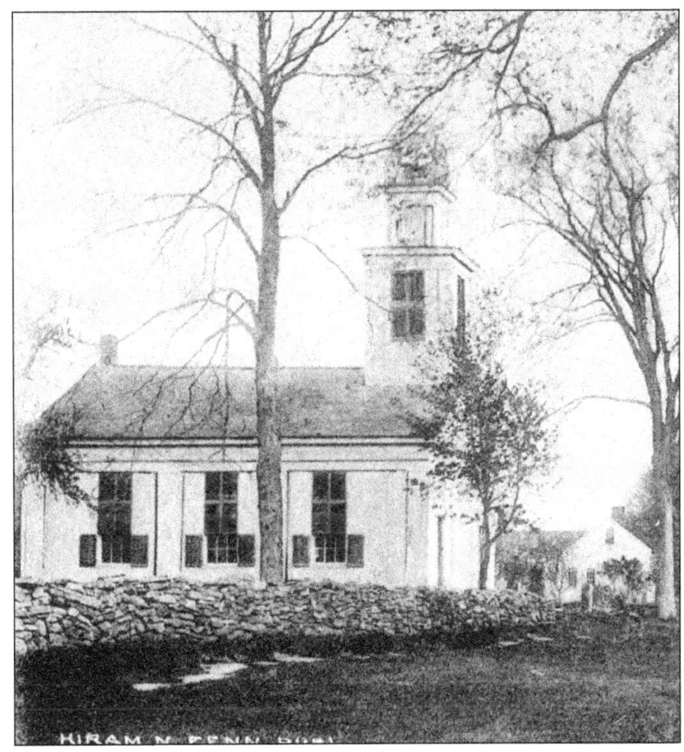

The Liberty Hill Church. Built in 1838, this building became a Congregational mission in 1892 and a full church in 1912. In 1919, the Exeter church was joined to Liberty Hill. In 1945, its assets were transferred to the First Congregational Church. The building was used by the Liberty Hill Men's Club and the Lebanon Guild of Arts and Crafts for many years before being sold to a private party in the 1970s. Once a vital part of the Liberty Hill community, it has now collapsed. (Courtesy Ed Tollmann.)

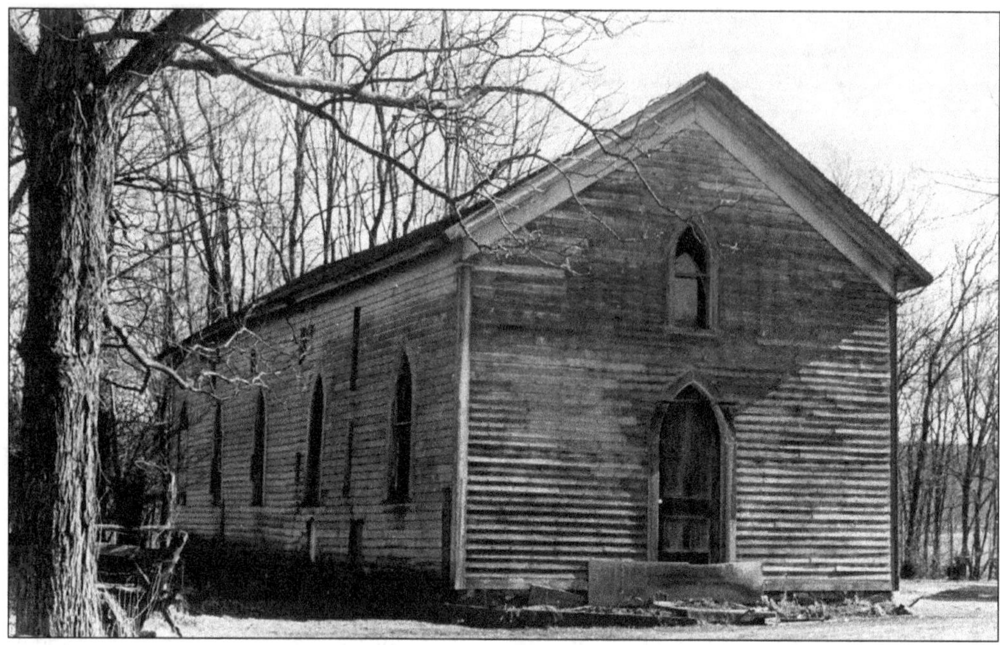

The St. Mary Mission Chapel. Sometime between 1860 and 1870, Irish Catholic immigrants built this chapel on McGrath Lane as a mission church under the Colchester parish. The Irish settlers worked in the rubber and paper mills on the Yantic River. When the mills failed, many moved to the cities to find work, and the congregation dwindled. The church was finally closed in 1921. The old building is now used for storage. (Courtesy Barbara Wengloski.)

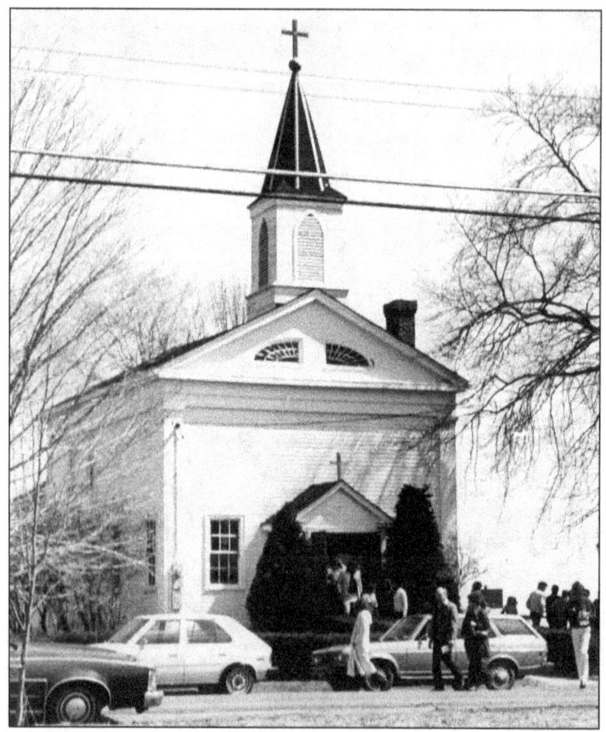

The Former St. Francis of Assisi Church. This house, located at 812 Trumbull Highway, was built by Leonard Hebard c. 1840. It was purchased and converted for use as a mission church for Lebanon Catholics in 1943. A steeple was installed on the roof. When the new St. Francis church opened in 1980, the house was sold and converted back to a residence. (Courtesy Barbara Wengloski.)

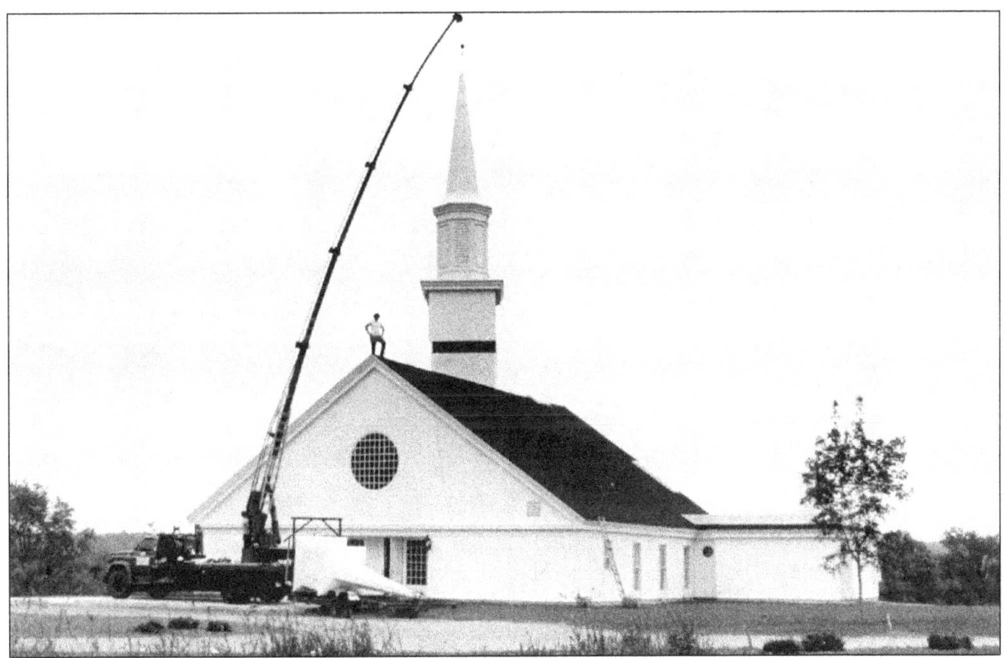

The St. Francis of Assisi Church. Expanding membership led to the need for a new church building for local Roman Catholics. In 1965, the church purchased a large parcel on West Town Street, and parishioners began raising funds for a building. Construction finally began in 1979 and was completed the next spring, when the steeple was set in place. In 1985, St. Francis added a parish hall and rectory. (Courtesy Barbara Wengloski.)

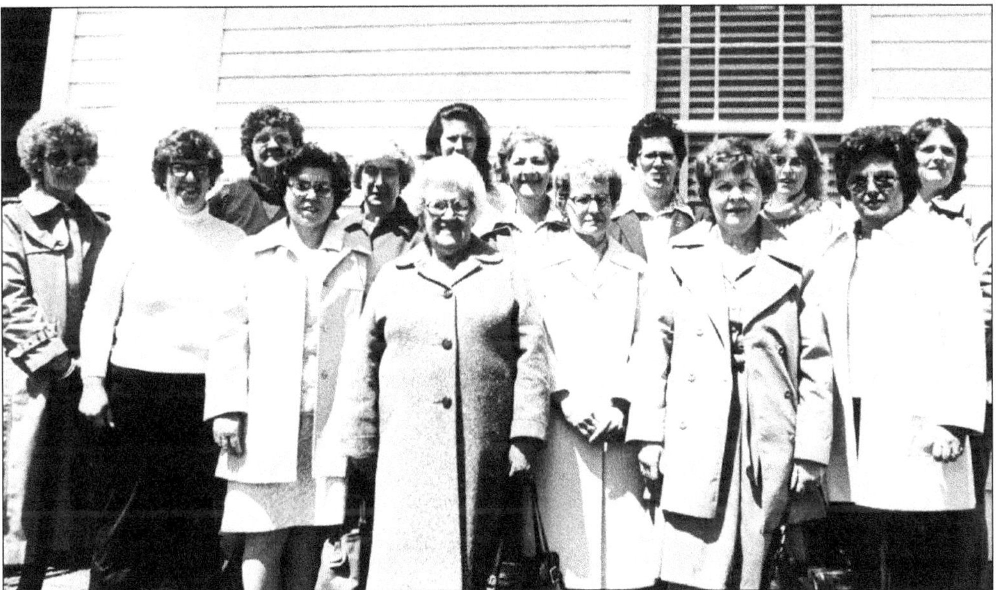

The Ladies Guild. The St. Francis Ladies Guild was organized in 1949 and celebrated its 50th anniversary in 1999. For over half a century, the members have carried out a large number of service activities and projects to benefit both their church and the community. They also participate in events that foster the ecumenical movement. This photograph was taken in 1980; the guild members are unidentified. (Courtesy Barbara Wengloski.)

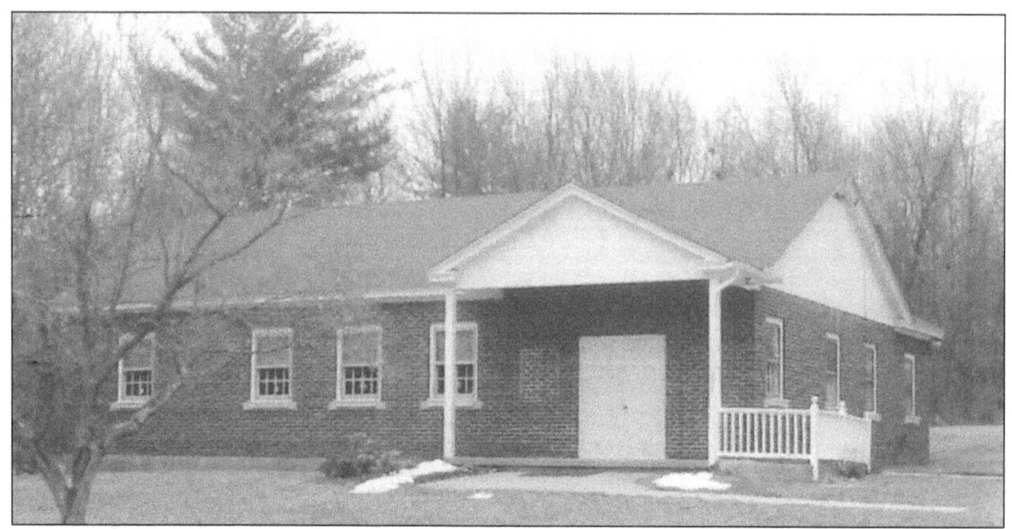

The Lebanon Bible Church. This church began as a mission of the Scotland Christian Fellowship Church in 1987, with the members meeting in each other's homes in Lebanon. In 1991, it was incorporated as the Lebanon Bible Church and began renting the Jewish synagogue on Goshen Hill Road. The Lebanon Jewish community no longer had the necessary quorum for services and did not need the building. The church purchased the building in 1995. (Courtesy LHS.)

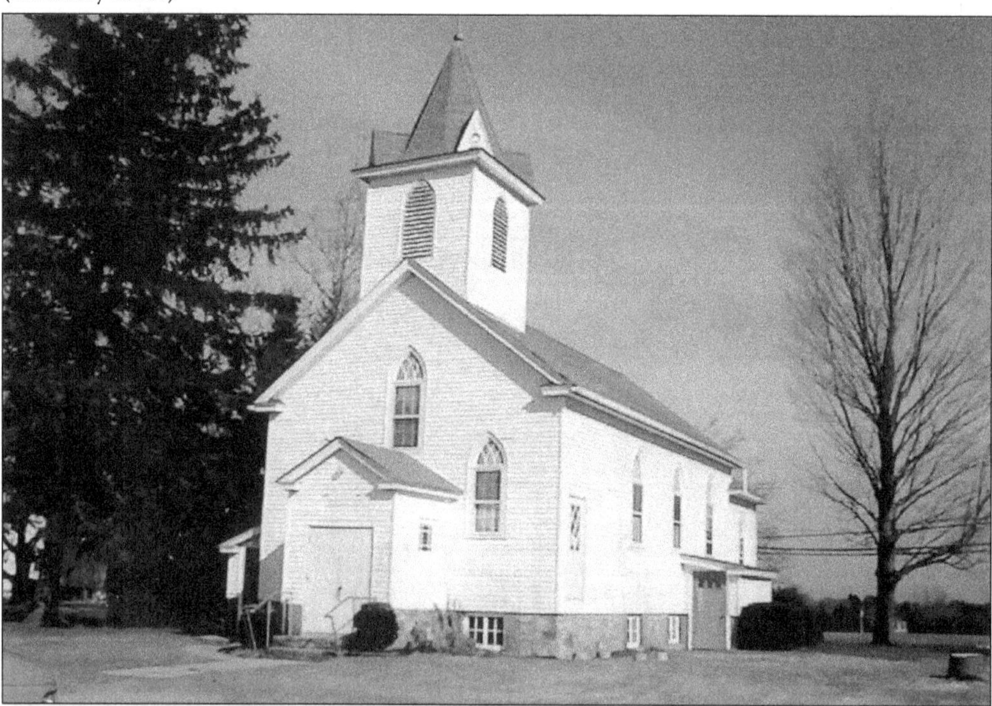

The Redeemer Lutheran Church. German immigrants began arriving in Lebanon from Ukraine in 1911. At first, they traveled to Willimantic to attend church services. In 1937, they purchased the vacant Village Hill Schoolhouse for a church, but the 1938 hurricane weakened the building. The salvaged lumber was used in the construction of this church, designed by Gottlieb Laibrandt and built entirely by volunteer labor. (Courtesy Claire Krause.)

Three

The Liberty Hill Neighborhood

The road leading into Liberty Hill from Chestnut Hill (Columbia) was known as the Hartford to New London Stage Coach Road. Horse-drawn coaches traveled the highway carrying passengers, freight, and mail. Liberty Hill had its own post office and received mail three times a week. The post office was housed in a general store, the second building south of the present Swyden's Store. Until a fire in 1906, Liberty Hill contained two general stores. Liberty Hill was a regular stop, with the general store on the west and Gay's Tavern on the east side of the highway. Passengers were able to secure lodging, food, and supplies in Liberty Hill. Locals would also gather at the tavern and discuss the happenings of the day. The organization papers for the Liberty Hill Church were written in Gay's Tavern, with George Gay as clerk, in 1837.

A gristmill situated on the west side of the highway was the first building on Liberty Hill's boundary with Columbia. This mill was operated with waterpower from a millpond fed by the Ten Mile River, which served as the boundary line between Lebanon and Columbia. Local farmers brought their grain to the mill to be ground. Across the street was a blacksmith shop.

In 1873, with the arrival of the Boston & New York Air Line Railroad, Liberty Hill changed. The mail was now delivered by rail. A train station and store were built just over the town line in Chestnut Hill to accommodate passengers and freight. The station served as the post office for Chestnut Hill, with Liberty Hill's post office still at the general store in the village. When Eva Dimon was appointed Chestnut Hill postmistress in 1905, she moved the post office into her house in Liberty Hill. The residents of Chestnut Hill complained bitterly that they would now have to enter another town to get their mail. Worse yet, they would be crossing from Tolland County to New London County. The complaints fell on deaf ears. Instead of moving the post office back or combining it with Liberty Hill's, the postal service left it named the Chestnut Hill Post Office even though Chestnut Hill was not in the town of Lebanon. In 1907, the Liberty Hill Post Office was eliminated, leaving the Chestnut Hill Post Office to serve both Chestnut Hill and part of Liberty Hill. This change caused considerable confusion, for everyone who lived in Lebanon from the town border south to the Route 87 and 207 intersection had a Chestnut Hill address. Remember that Chestnut Hill is in the town of Columbia. The village of Liberty Hill runs from the Ten Mile River to Pease Brook.

School No. 4 was at the corner of Cook Hill Road and Trumbull Highway. This school served Cook Hill and Liberty Hill students. Across from the school to the west was a magnificent granite quarry where foundation stones and large step stones were cut and sold. Before you entered the village, a peat moss bed could be observed to the left of the highway. As you entered the village, the stately homes of such families as Loomis, Gay, Babcock, Clarke, Kingsley, and Fuller dotted both sides of the highway.

The Liberty Hill Church served as the center of activity, with a very active congregation until the 1940s. Leaving the village, the last home on the left was known as the Chestnut Hill House. There, water from a mineral spring was advertised as a life-extending elixir. Folks would come and stay to relax and partake of the mineral water.

Liberty Hill was once a vibrant, active community with beautiful homes, granite sidewalks, two general stores, a gristmill, a blacksmith shop, a school, and its own house of worship. But the 1940s witnessed the decline of the village. The church was consolidated with the First Congregational Church in Lebanon Center, and the schoolhouse was sold to the Liberty Hill Men's Club in 1936, when the new elementary school was opened. All photographs in this chapter are from Ed Tollmann's personal collection.

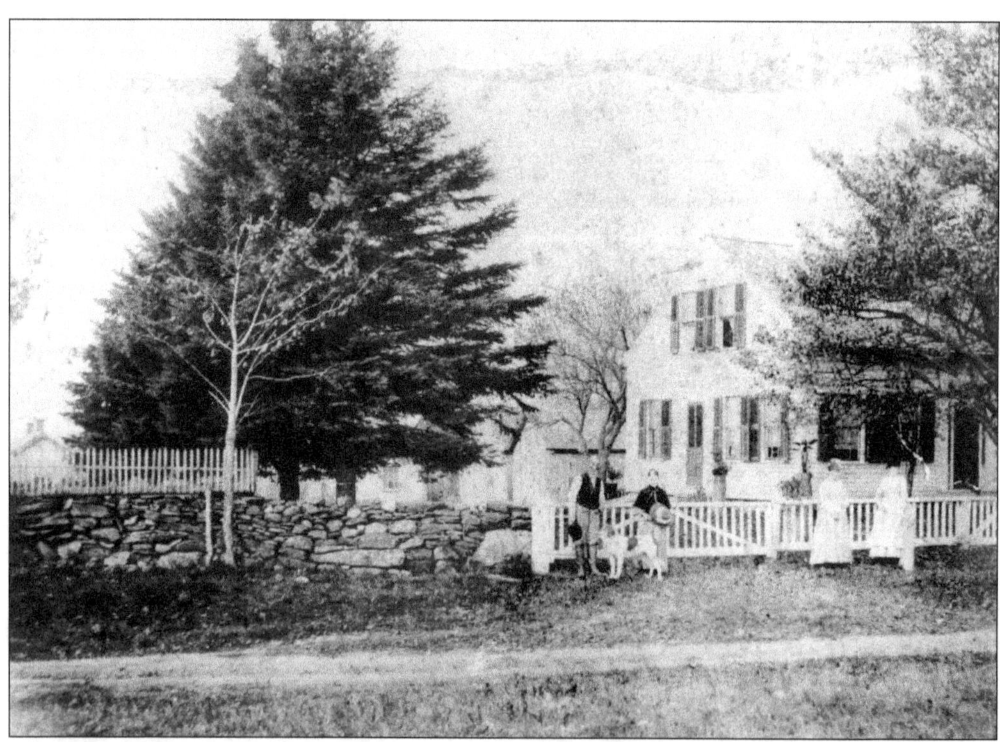

The White Feather Farm. When this photograph was taken, the White Feather Farm, on Cook Hill Road, was the first farm on the left from Trumbull Highway. A white feather weathervane identified the farm for many years. There, the Goodrich family hatched and sold chicks. Charles and Nancy Goodrich (left) and their daughters Abbie and Flora were photographed in front of their farmhouse in 1889.

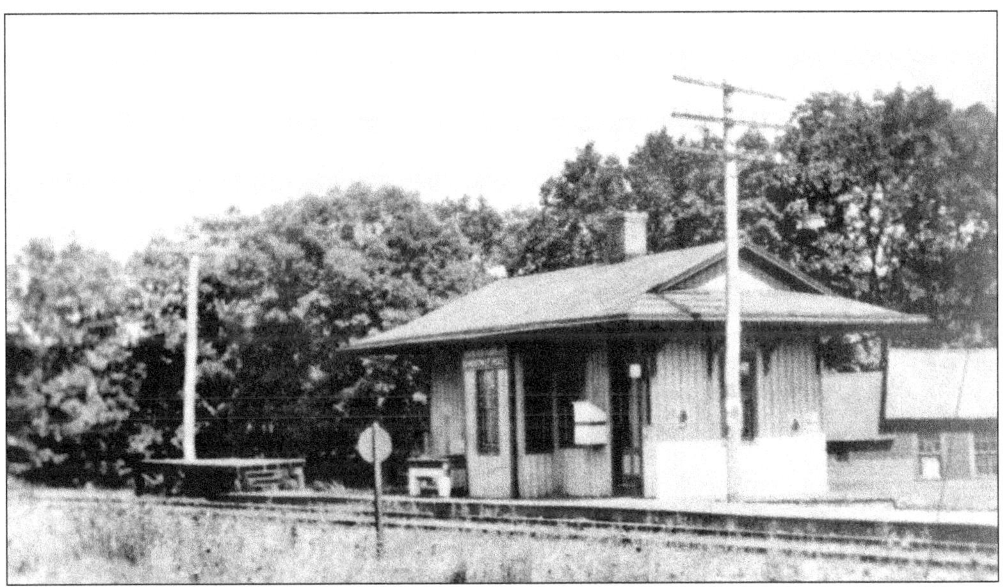

The Chestnut Hill Station. This railroad station was located just before the Lebanon town line in Columbia, and served the village of Liberty Hill. Students rode the "airline" to and from Windham High School, and families took it to Willimantic and other cities. Special reduced-price tickets, as seen at the right, were provided for high school students.

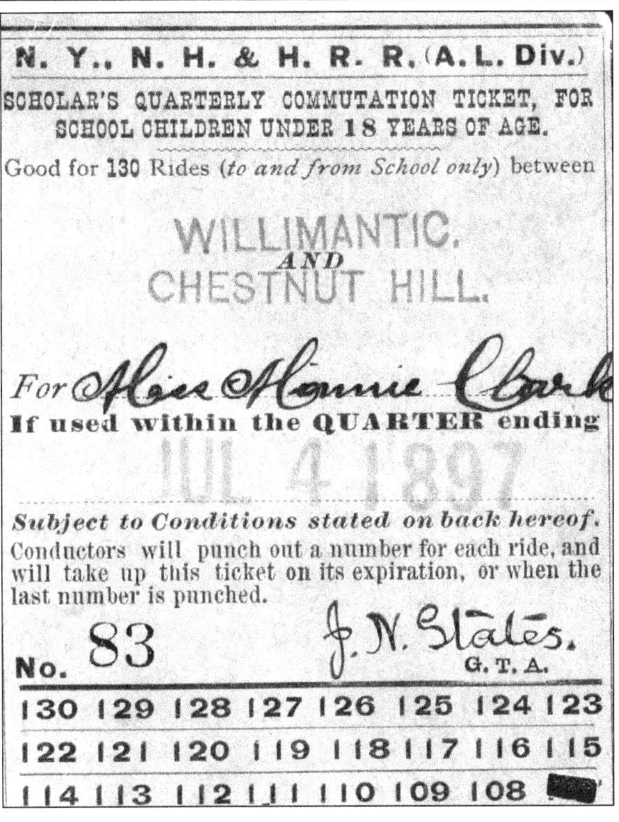

N. Y., N. H. & H. R. R. (A. L. Div.)

SCHOLAR'S QUARTERLY COMMUTATION TICKET, FOR SCHOOL CHILDREN UNDER 18 YEARS OF AGE.

Good for 130 Rides (*to and from School only*) between

WILLIMANTIC,
AND
CHESTNUT HILL.

For Miss Minnie Clark

If used within the QUARTER ending

JUL 4 1897

Subject to Conditions stated on back hereof.

Conductors will punch out a number for each ride, and will take up this ticket on its expiration, or when the last number is punched.

No. 83

J. N. States.
G. T. A.

130 129 128 127 126 125 124 123
122 121 120 119 118 117 116 115
114 113 112 111 110 109 108

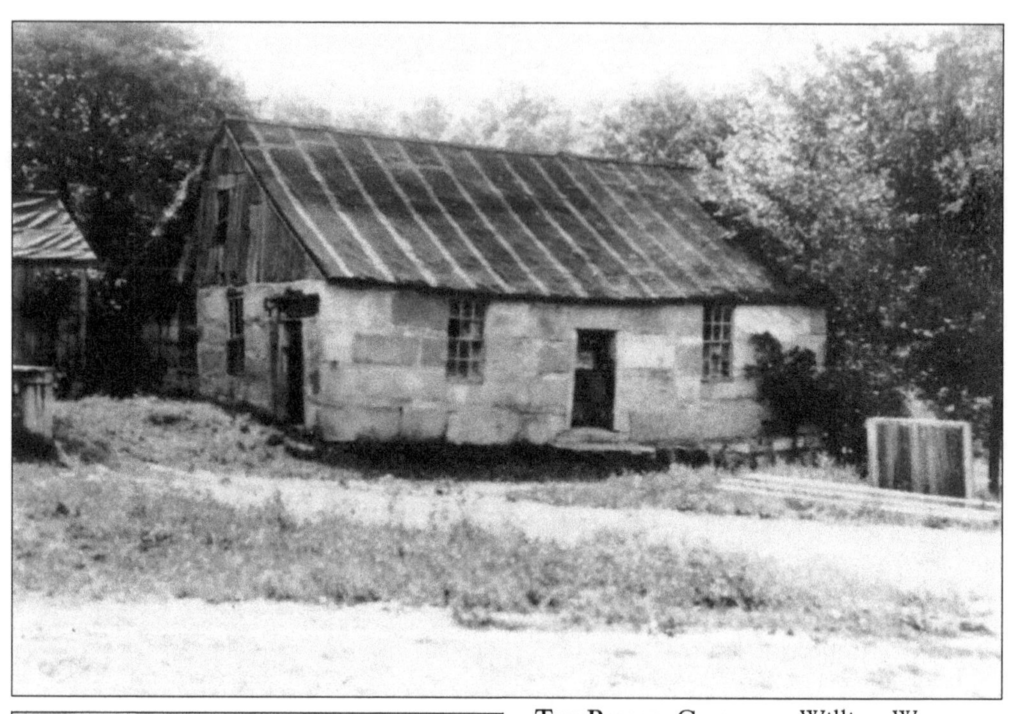

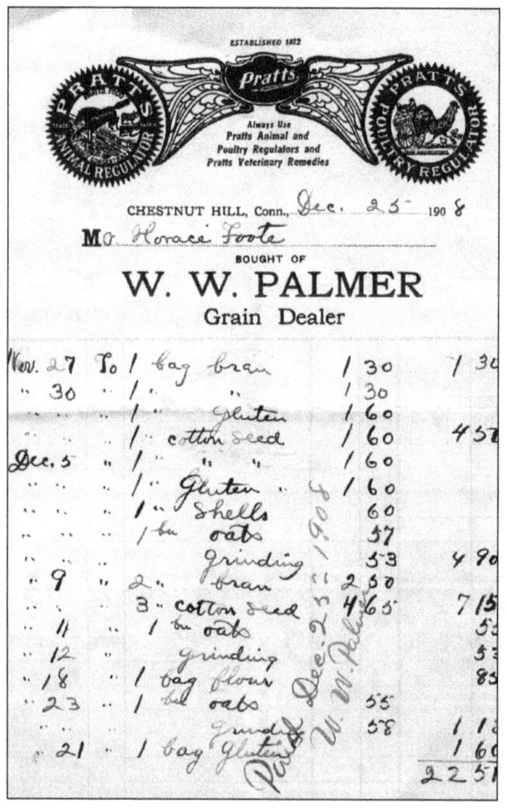

Pratts

PRATTS ANIMAL REGULATOR

PRATTS POULTRY REGULATOR

Always Use Pratts Animal and Poultry Regulators and Pratts Veterinary Remedies

CHESTNUT HILL, Conn., Dec. 25 1908

Mr. Horace Foote

BOUGHT OF

W. W. PALMER

Grain Dealer

Nov. 27	To	1 bag bran	1 30	1 3
" 30	"	1 " "	1 30	
" "	"	1 " gluten	1 60	
" "	"	1 " cotton seed	1 60	4 5
Dec. 5	"	1 " " "	1 60	
" "	"	1 " Gluten	1 60	
" "	"	1 " shells	60	
" "	"	1 bu oats	57	
" "	"	grinding	53	4 9
" 9	"	2 " bran	2 30	
" "	"	3 " cotton seed	4 65	7 1
" 11	"	1 bu oats		5
" 12	"	grinding		5
" 18	"	1 bag flour		8
" 23	"	1 bu oats	55	
" "		grinding	58	1 1
" 21	"	1 bag Gluten		1 6
				22 5

Paid Dec. 23 1908 W. W. Palmer

The Palmer Gristmill. William W. Palmer ran this gristmill for many years, grinding grain for local families. The mill was built in 1829 and was run by waterpower from an upstream millpond on the Ten Mile River. It was torn down in the 1950s, and a house was built on the site, the first on the right when coming into Liberty Hill.

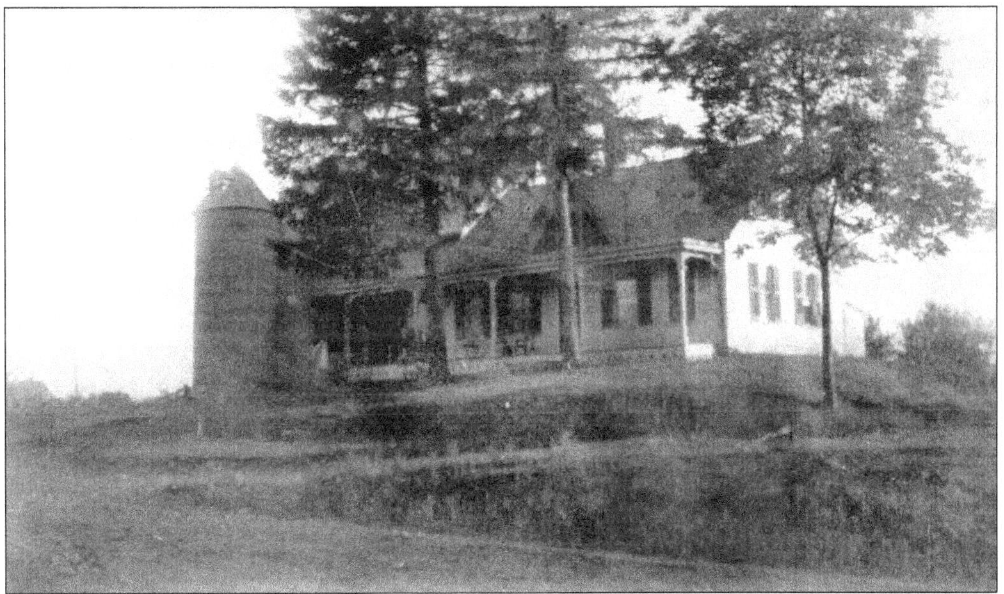

The Home of William W. Palmer. Located to the south of the gristmill, this house was electrified by the mill. In 1924, a fire originating in the attached barn destroyed the house as well.

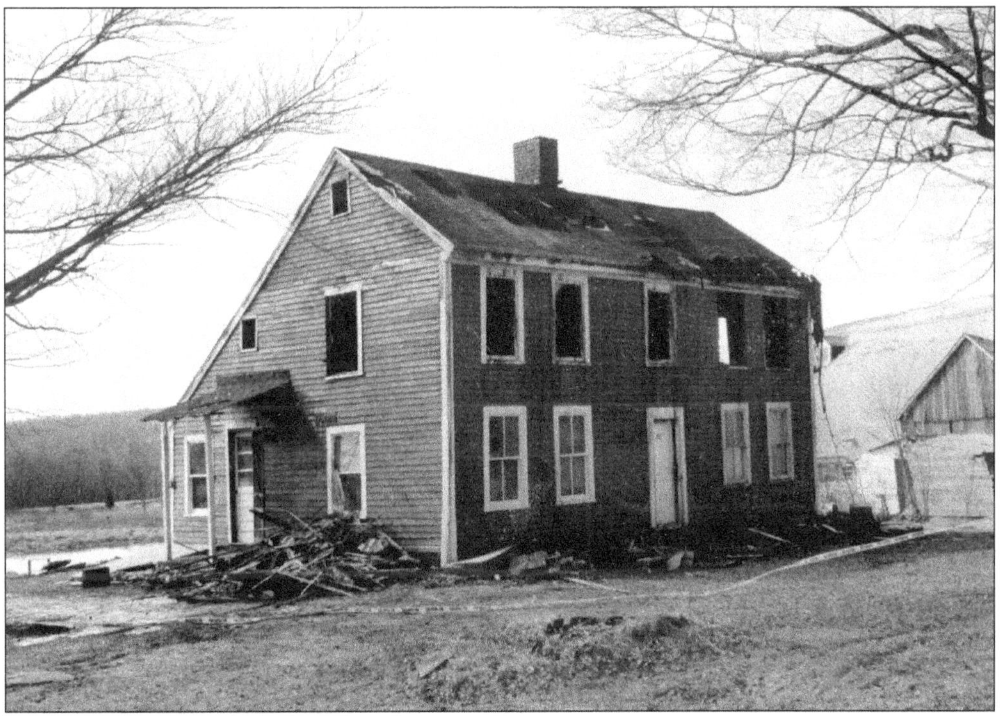

An Old Saltbox House. This house, one of the oldest saltbox homes in Lebanon, was located just south of the Ten Mile River on Trumbull Highway. It was torn down after being partially destroyed by fire in 1990.

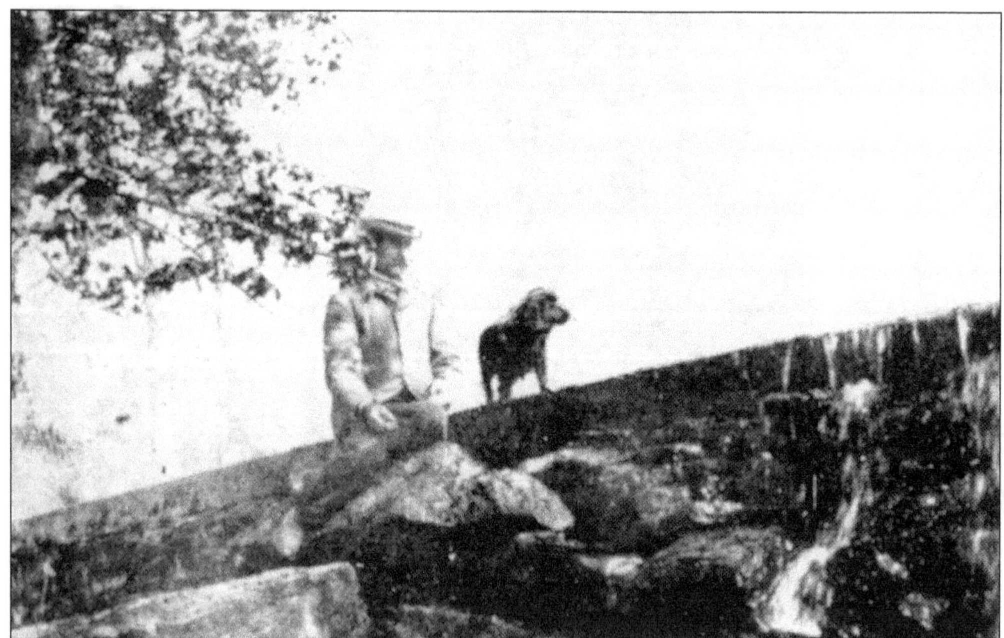

The Millpond. G. R. Dimon stands atop the millpond dam behind Palmer's gristmill with one of his cocker spaniels. Dimon ran Nomid Kennels, a clever backward spelling of his name.

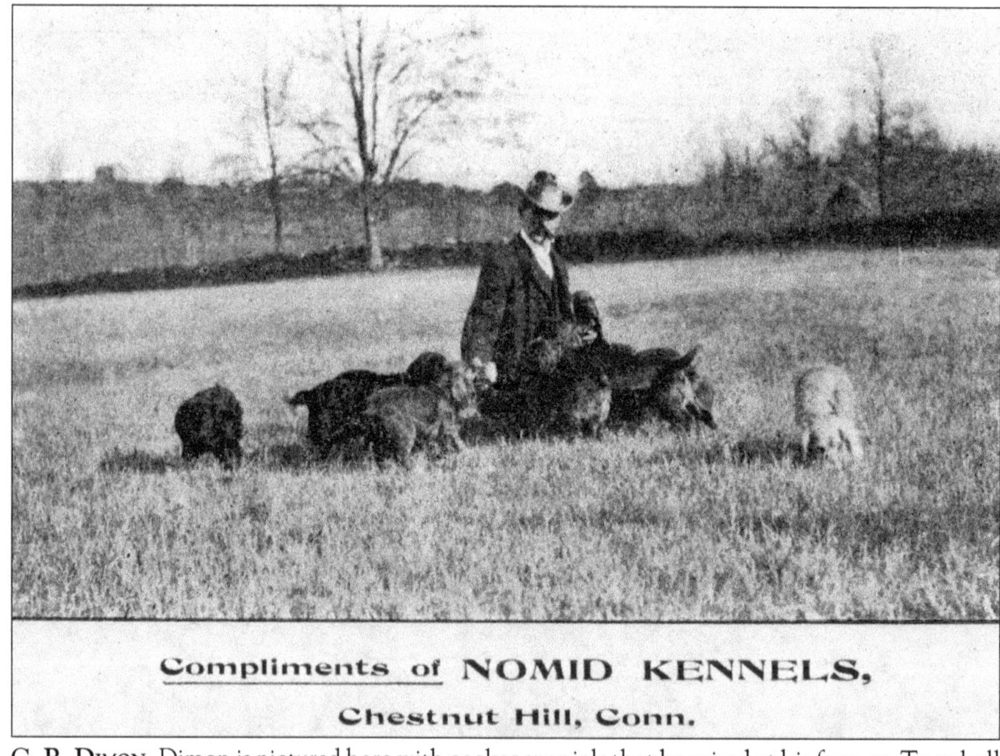

G. R. Dimon. Dimon is pictured here with cocker spaniels that he raised at his farm on Trumbull Highway. The cleared fields behind show an unobstructed view of the rural landscape all the way to Cook Hill Road.

The Liberty Hill School. Located on the corner of Cook Hill Road and Trumbull Highway, School No. 4, shown at the right, served Cook Hill Road and Liberty Hill. Teacher Flora (Bruce) Williams is pictured below in the middle of her students; the group is posing in front of a ledge north of the school. Williams taught first through eighth grades in one room.

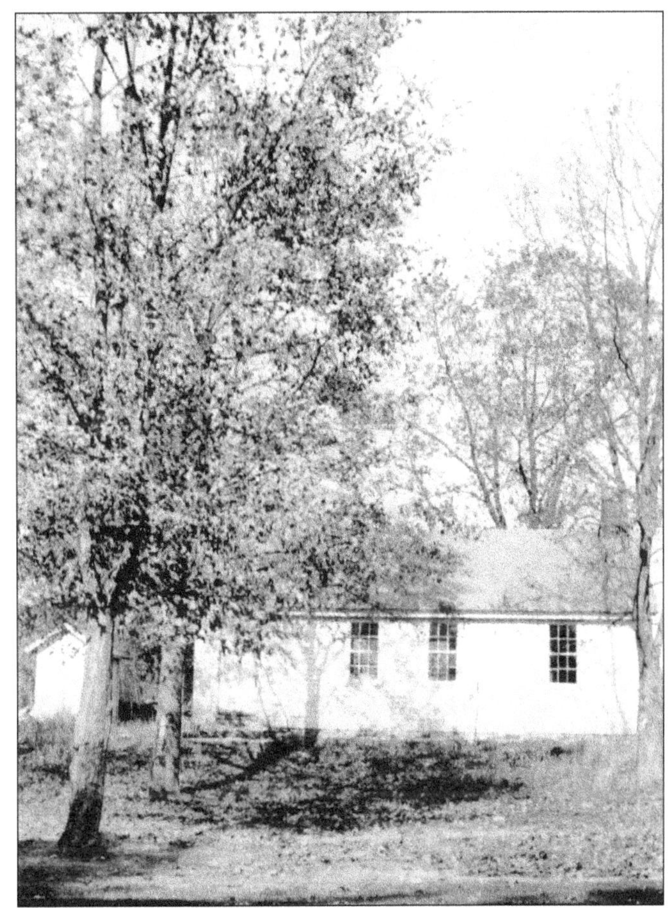

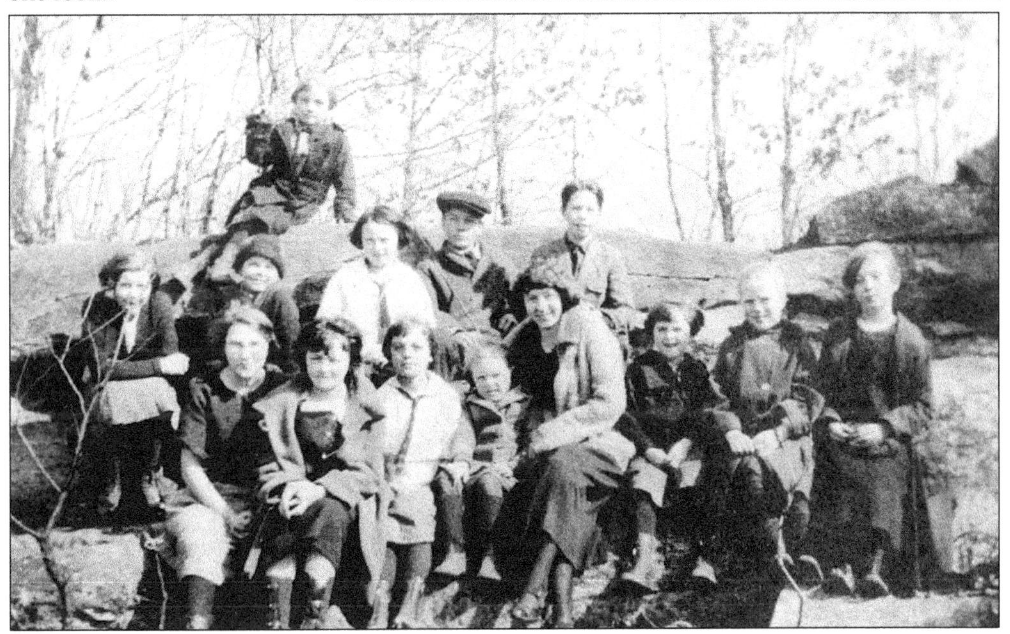

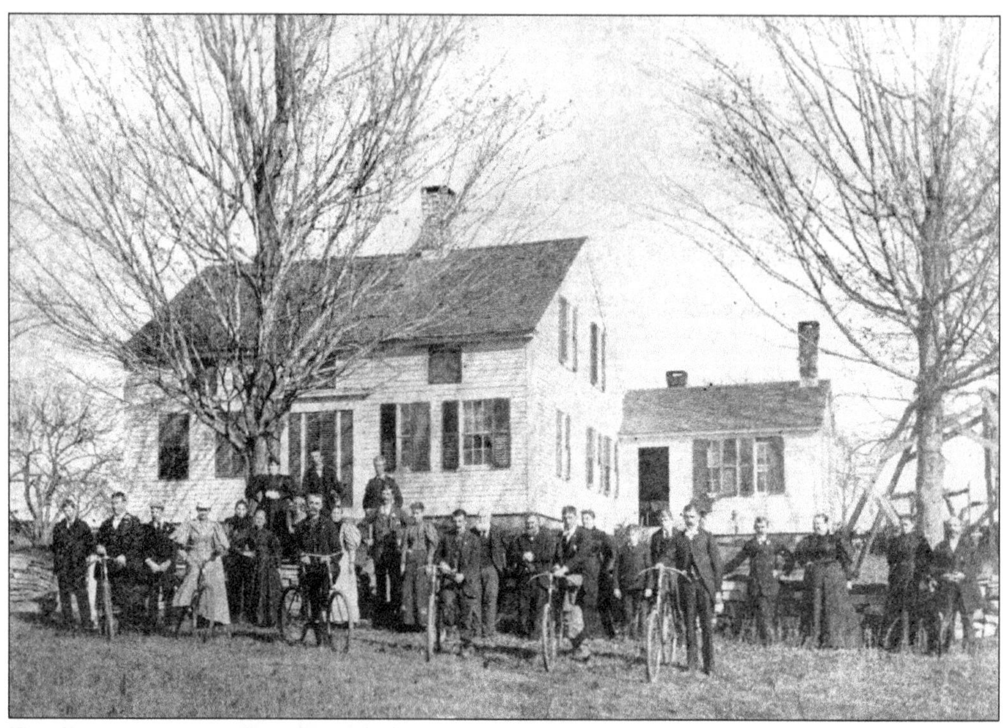

The Farm on Cook Hill. The Clark family enjoys a gathering *c.* 1880. This farm is on Cook Hill Road and has not changed much over the years. Everett Payson owned it from 1916 to 1947, when Russ Tollmann purchased the farm. Payson and Tollmann both served Lebanon as selectmen.

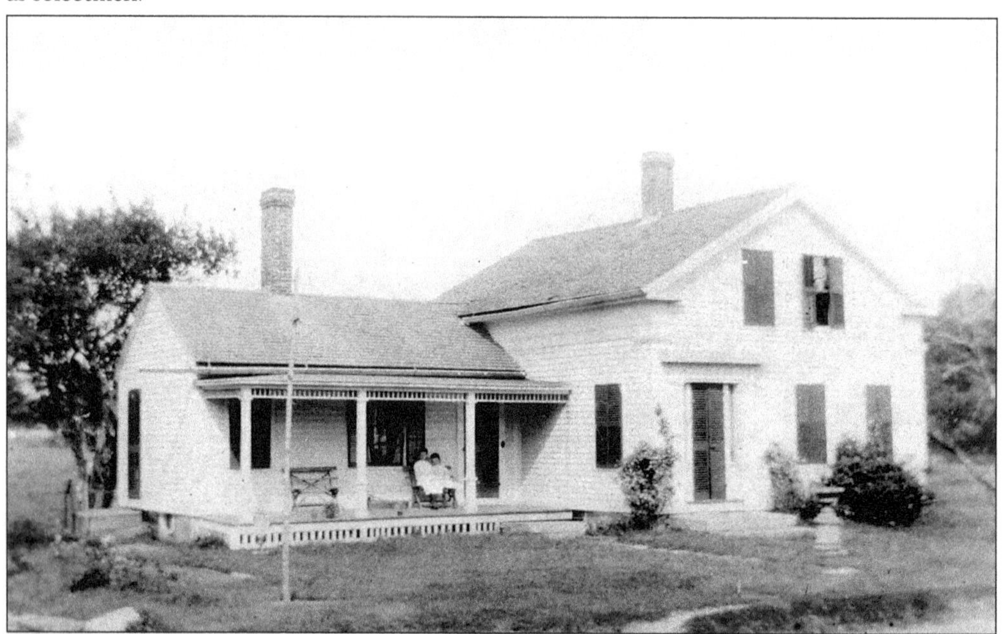

The Harvey House. This home is situated on the northern corner of Clarke Road and Trumbull Highway. It was owned by the Harvey family, which was very active in the Liberty Hill community.

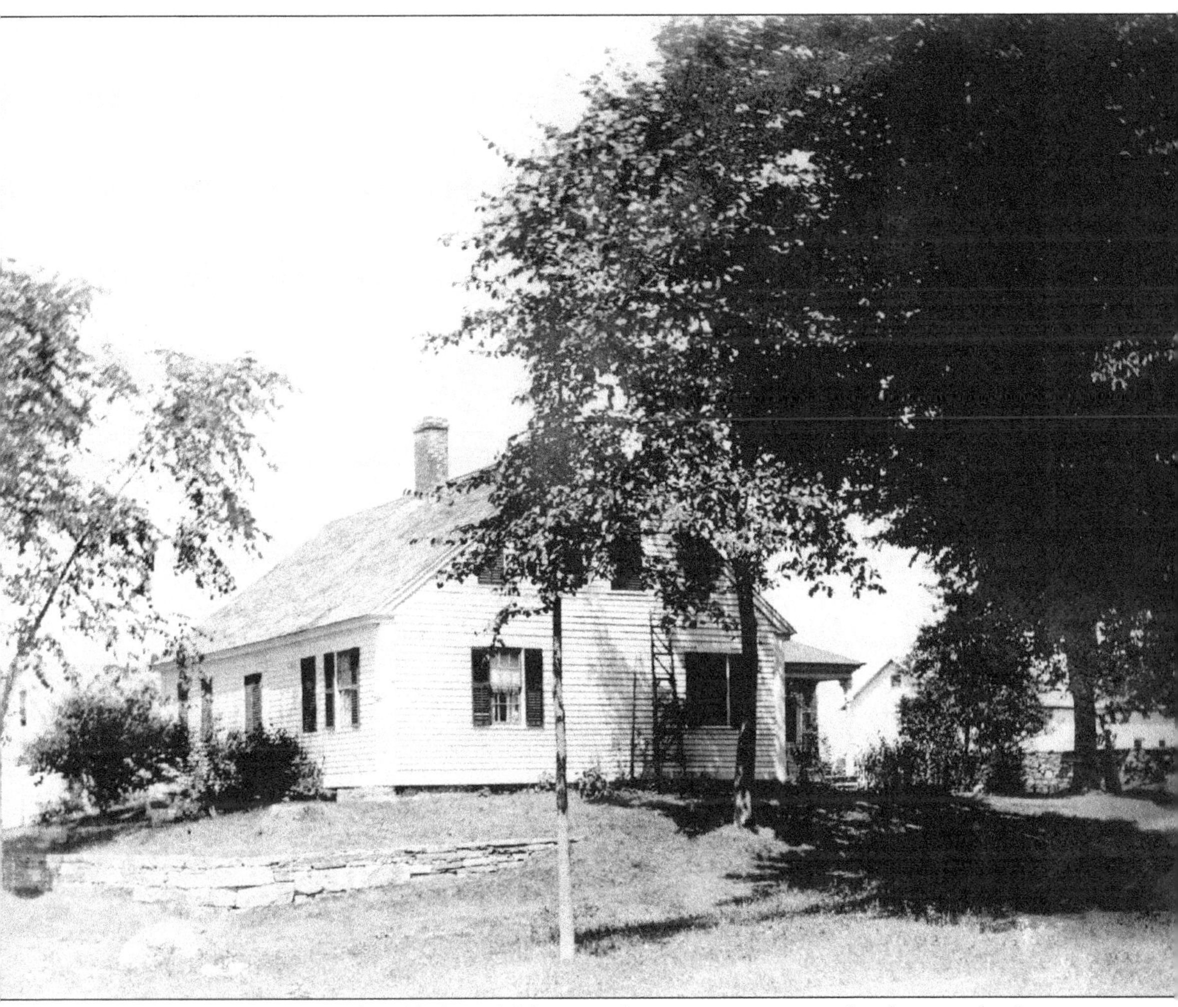

The John Clarke Home. John Clarke, a lifelong resident, was instrumental in bringing back to life the "village of Liberty Hill" in the early 1900s. His home stands on the northern corner of Burnham Road and Trumbull Highway.

ATTENTION!

If you want any Second-hand Goods come to Clarke's Great Auction Mart.

We can supply you with anything, it makes no difference what.

We have OX CARTS, OX WAGONS, PLOWS, HARROWS, and various kinds of Farming TOOLS, TWO-HORSE TEAM WAGONS, BUSINESS WAGONS, BUGGIES, CARRIAGES, ONE and TWO HORSE SLEDS and SLEIGHS, HARNESS, Heavy and Light, Single or Double, BLANKETS, ROBES, ETC., ETC.

Revolvers, Guns, Bicycles, Watches, Clocks, Furniture, Stoves, Crockery, Glass and Tin Ware, and a thousand and one things to numerous too mention.

If you have any articles of any kind that you wish to dispose of, bring them to me, or send me a discription of them, and I will sell them for you.

If you have any Old Fashioned Furniture or Crockery, let me know and I will make it worth your while.

AUCTION SALE

—OF—

Horses, Cattle, Etc., Every Month.

Articles sold at private sale every day except sundays.

If you have any work for an Auctioneer, let me do it, and I will guarantee you satisfaction.

Respectfully,

J. H. CLARKE,

LIBERTY HILL, CONN.

Baldwin Printing & Mfg. Co., 501 Main St., Willimantic, Conn.

JOHN CLARKE, AUCTIONEER AND ENTREPRENEUR. Pictured here is an advertisement for John Clarke's auction business. John, a shrewd businessman, was involved in many land and estate transactions.

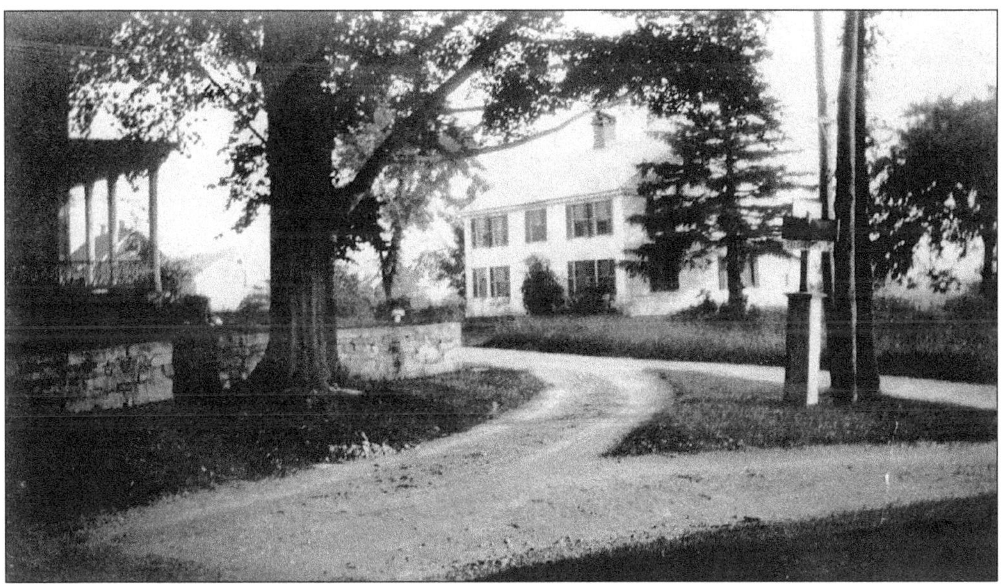

The Parsonage. This home was purchased by the Liberty Hill Church in 1918. The downstairs was used to house the pastor, and the upstairs was used for church meetings and dinners. The Liberty Hill Men's Club, formed in 1928, met upstairs for many years and was a very active civic group. The signpost at the intersection of Burnham Road and Trumbull Highway points the way to Colchester by way of Clarke Road.

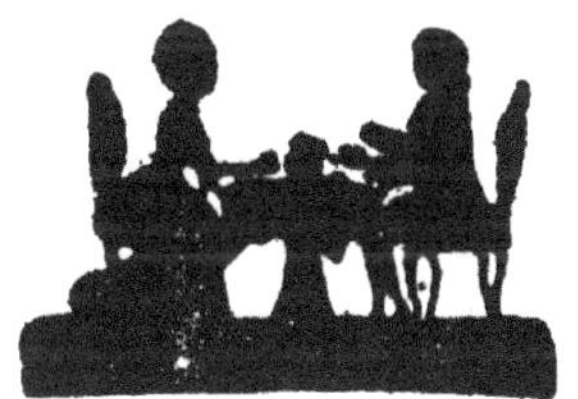

Liberty Hill Men's Club

Ladies' Night

Lebanon Baptist Chapel, Wed., Oct. 23, 1946

Supper at 7 o'clock

admits two — not transferable

Contribution $1.50

Frank Bartizek

Ladies' Night. Once a year, a ladies' night was held by the Liberty Hill Men's Club.

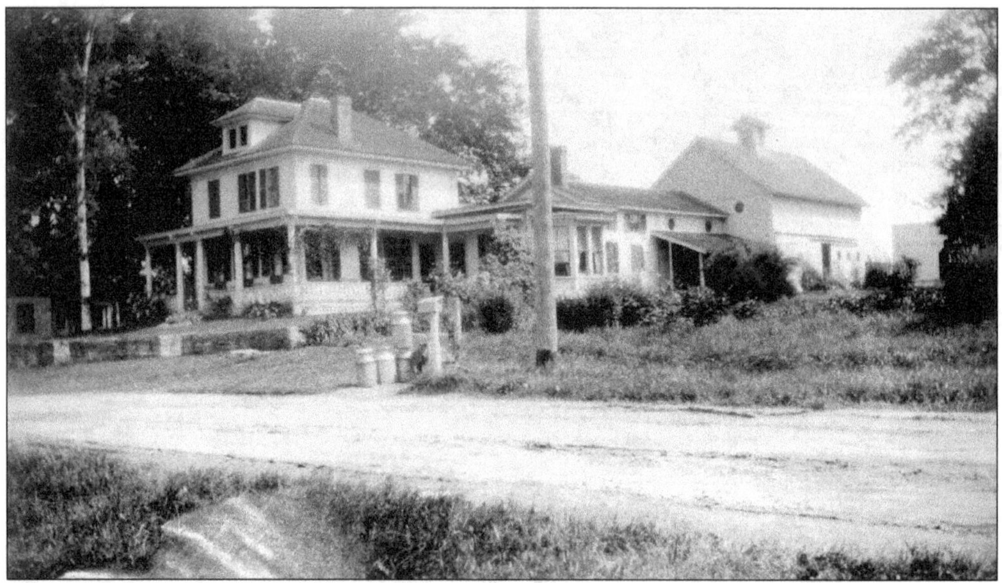

The Foote Farm. This beautiful farm is a great example of a "joined" New England farm where the farmhouse and outbuildings are all connected. Horace and Lizzie Foote operated it from 1889 until the 1940s. The house is still standing on the southern corner of Burnham Road and Trumbull Highway.

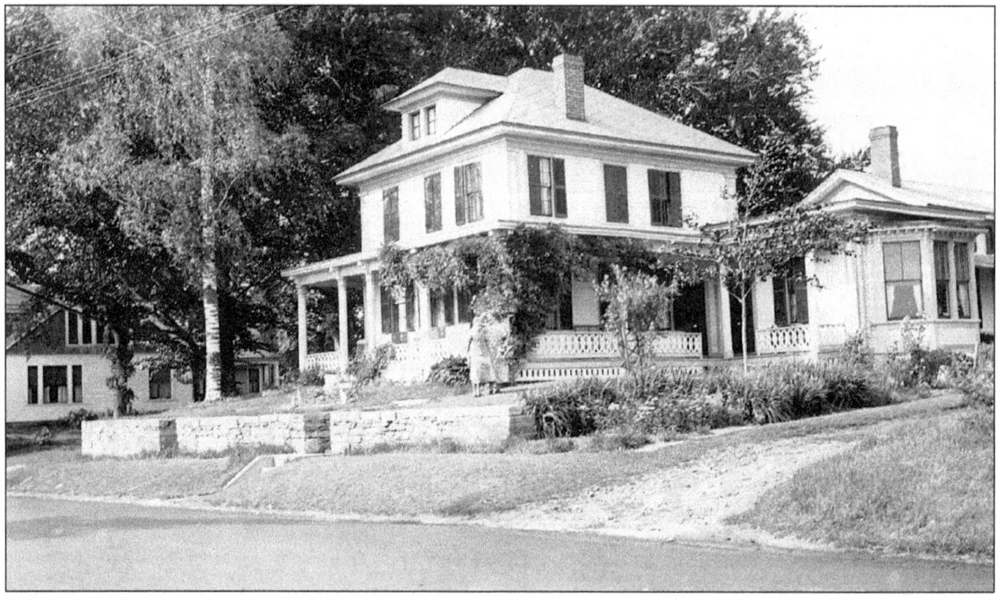

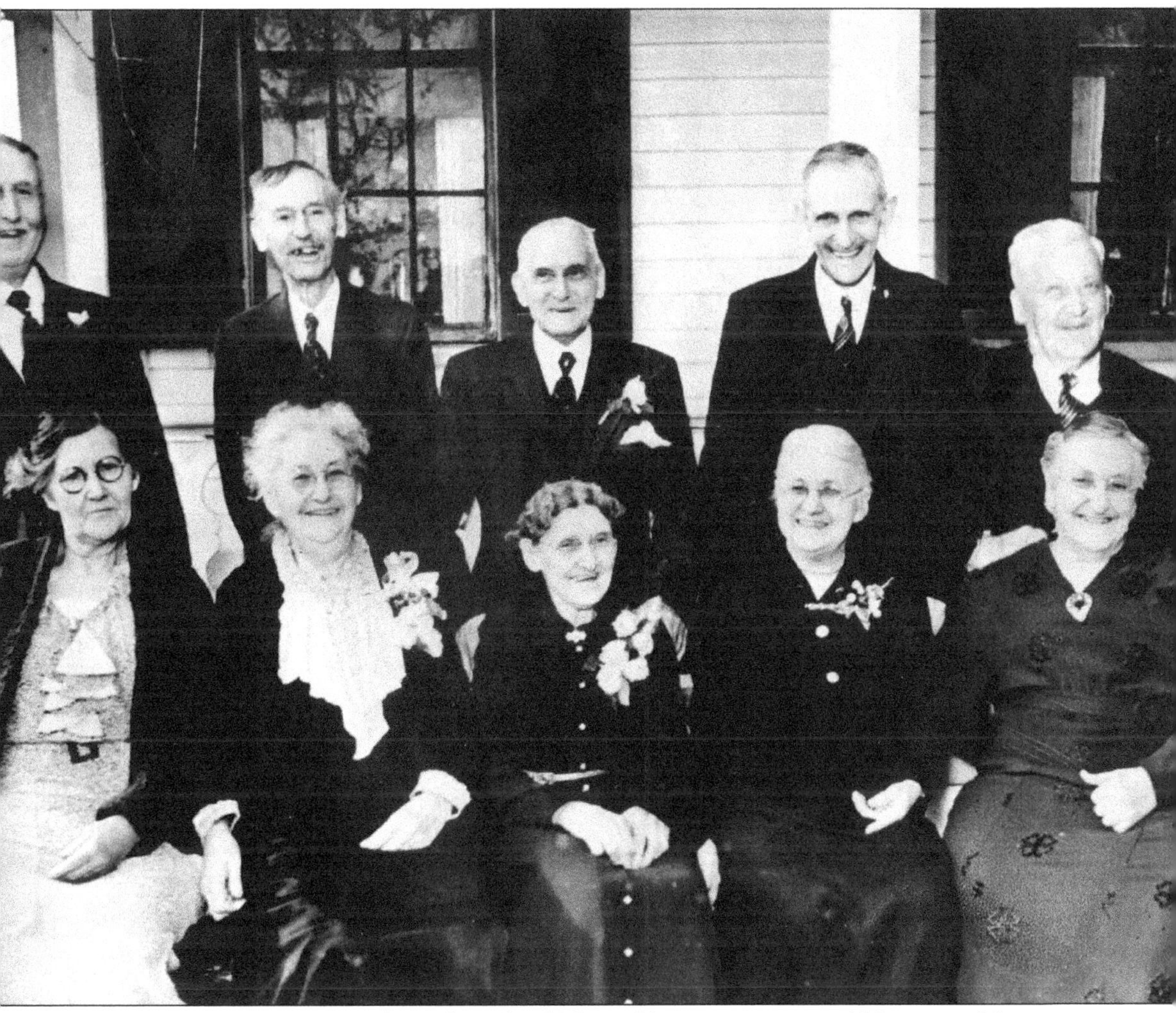

THE FOOTES' ANNIVERSARY. Attending the 50th wedding anniversary of Horace and Lizzie Foote in 1938 are, from left to right, Mr. and Mrs. Milo Davoll, Mr. and Mrs. Albert Peckham, Mr. and Mrs. Horace Foote, Mr. and Mrs. John Clarke, and Mr. and Mrs. James Choquette. The couples pictured here were the movers and shakers of the village. Mr. and Mrs. Choquette operated the general store.

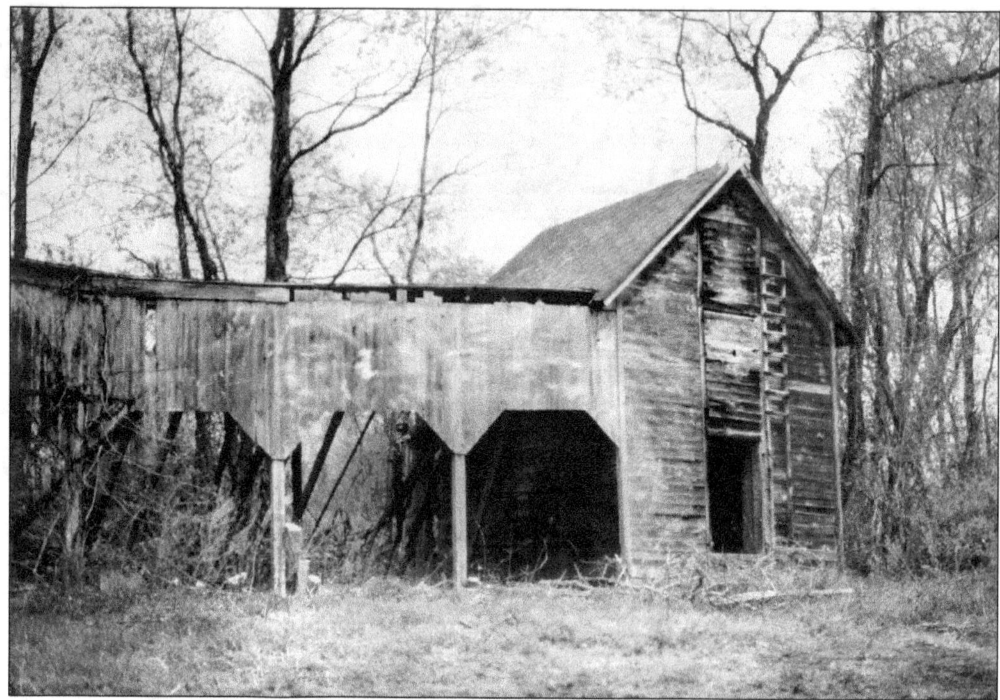

The Last Icehouse in Liberty Hill. This icehouse, part of the Foote farm, is a great example of one found in New England. Icehouses were a vital part of life before electricity.

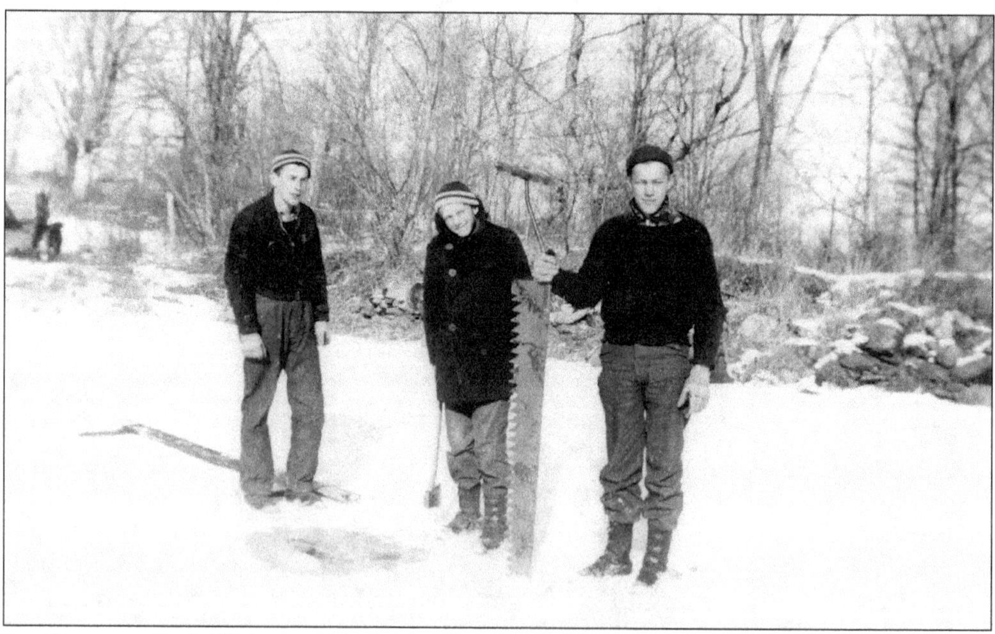

Ice Cutting. Fred, Walter, and Matt Arson, seen here from left to right, prepare to cut ice on Flumes Pond on Tobacco Street.

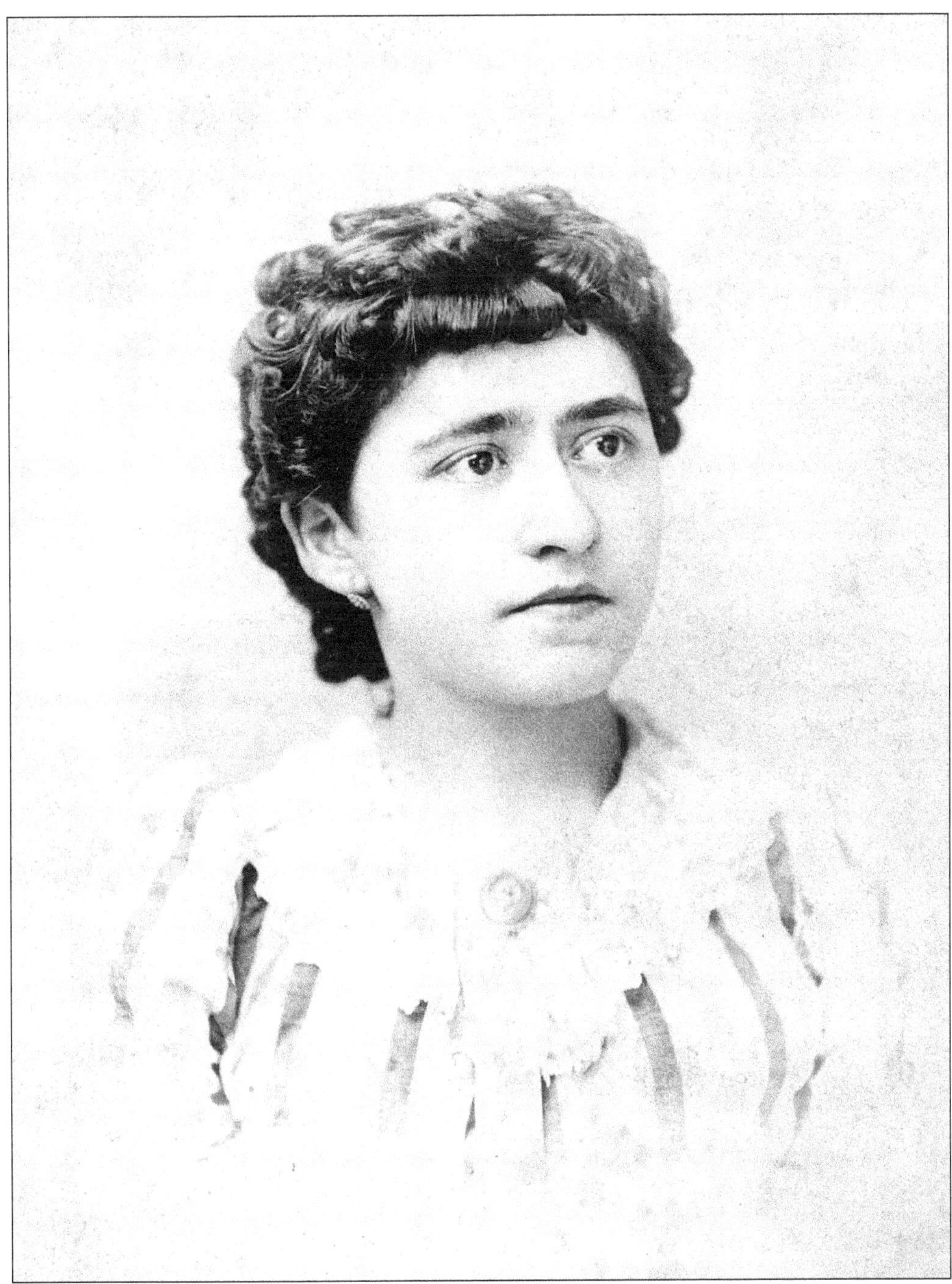

FLORA CAPLES. Flora Caples and her husband, Elmer, a carpenter by trade, came to Liberty Hill in the early 1900s. They purchased a piece of property that had been left vacant by a disastrous 1906 fire, which had destroyed three homes, a barn, and the Farnham Store, which also housed the Liberty Hill Post Office. Elmer and Flora built a house and soon became an integral part of the village. Elmer, known as a topnotch carpenter, built the upstairs addition to the local general store. Flora was postmistress and ran the post office out of her home for many years in the 1940s.

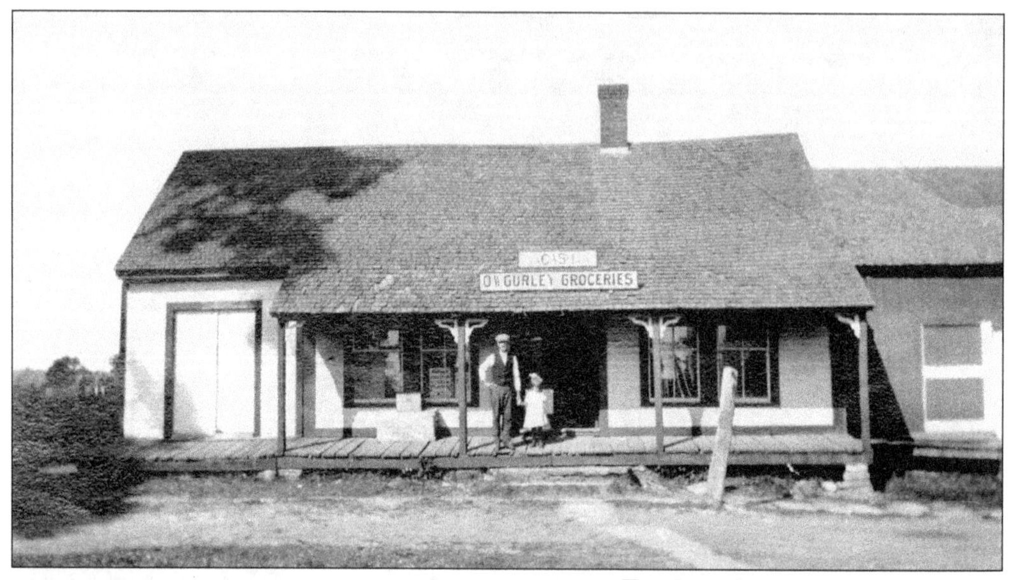

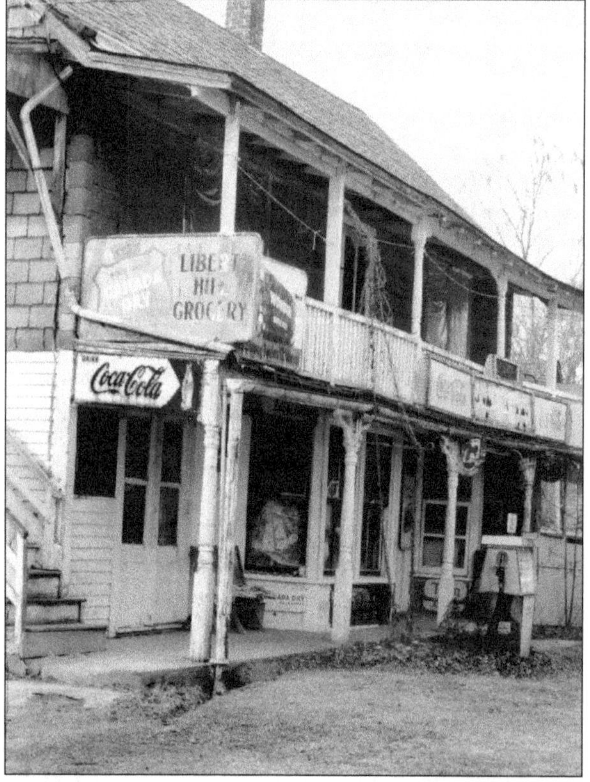

The Liberty Hill Store. Orville Gurley owned the Liberty Hill Store, shown above, from 1918 to 1925. He is seen above with his daughter Mildred. In 1925, James and Lena Choquette purchased the store and hired Elmer Caples to add a second story, shown at the left, where they then lived. In 1943, the property was sold to the Assad Swyden family, which ran the store and service station into the late 1980s.

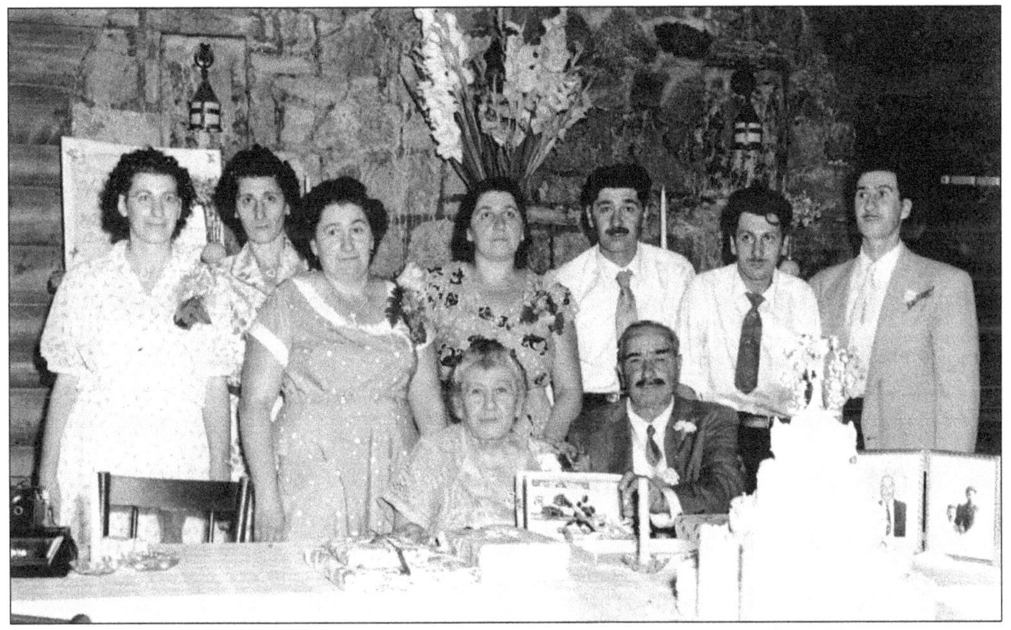

The Swydens' Anniversary Party, 1955. Assad and Mary Swyden's 50th wedding anniversary party was held at the Log Cabin Restaurant. The couple is seated at the table. Pictured behind them, from left to right, are their children, Julia, Olga, Minerva, Sophie, David, Sammy, and Louis. The Swyden family ran the general store and owned numerous pieces of property in Liberty Hill.

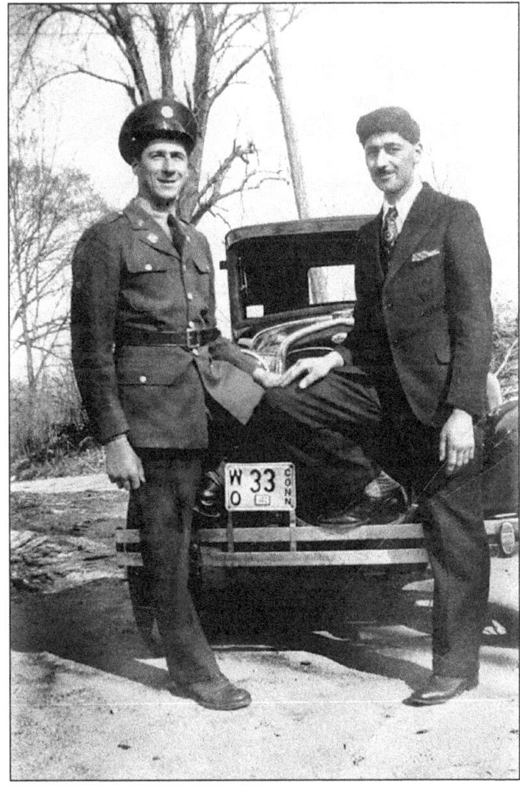

Home during World War II. While home, Louis Swyden enjoys a visit with his brother David Swyden.

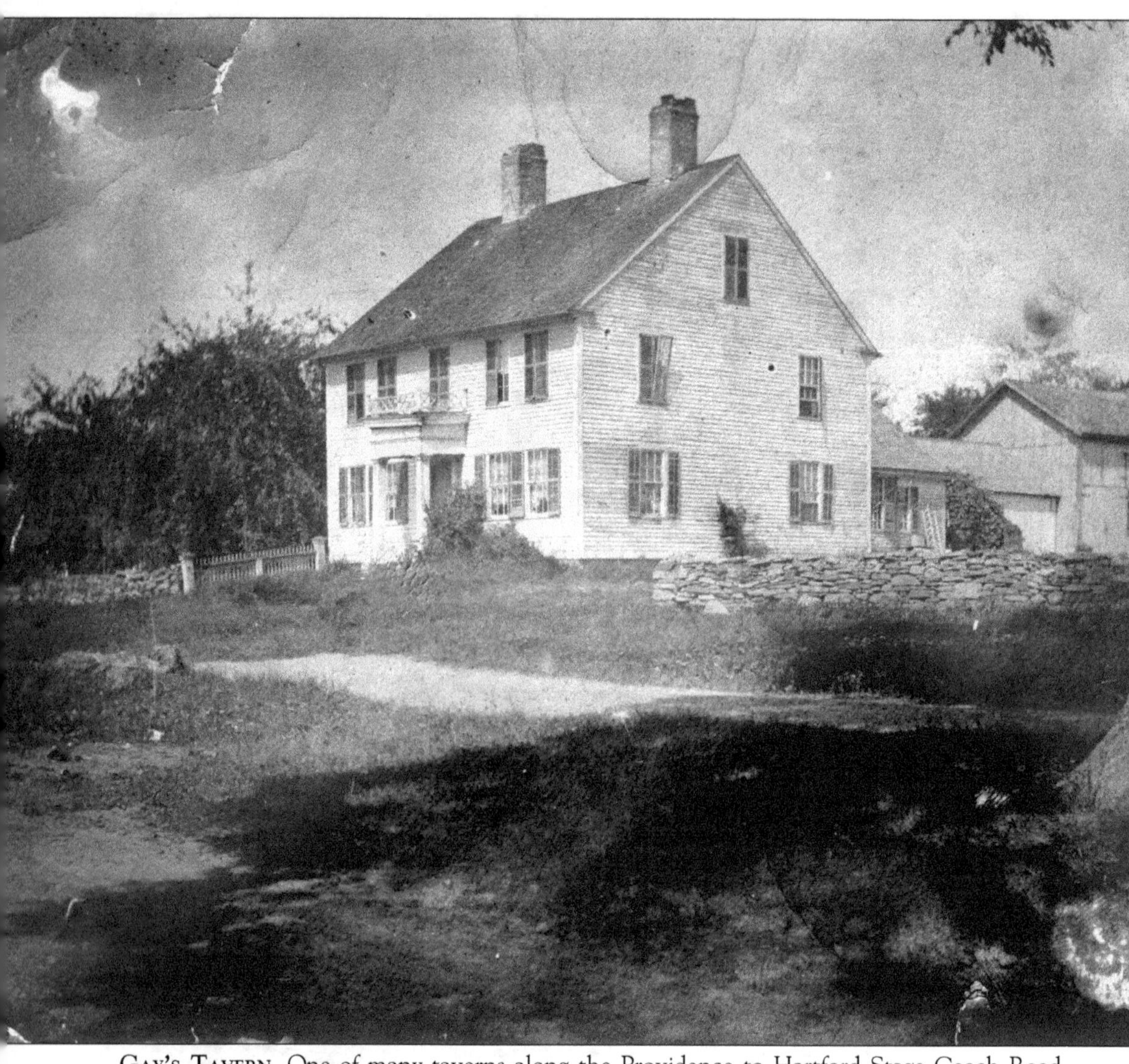

Gay's Tavern. One of many taverns along the Providence to Hartford Stage Coach Road, Gay's Tavern was named for George Gay, who owned it while the stagecoaches were running. The tavern was purchased by the Loomis family. After the roof blew off in the 1938 hurricane, the building was bought by the Schweitzer family and turned into a Cape-style house.

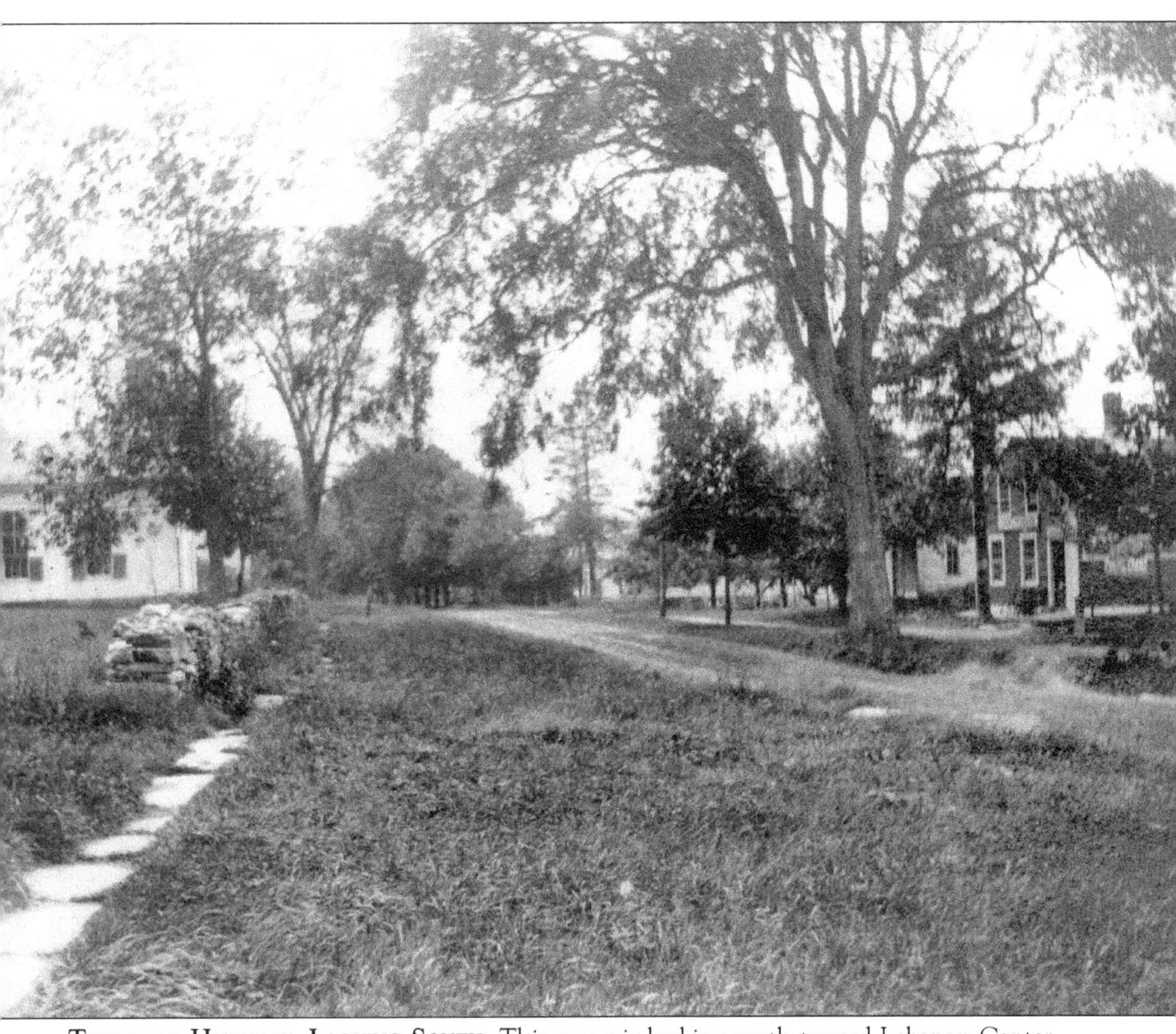

TRUMBULL HIGHWAY, LOOKING SOUTH. This scene is looking south toward Lebanon Center. On the left is the Liberty Hill Church. To the right is the Farnham General Store, which was owned by John Farnham and housed the Liberty Hill Post Office for many years. The house, store, barn, and woodshed owned by John Farnham all burned to the ground in an early morning fire on November 12, 1906.

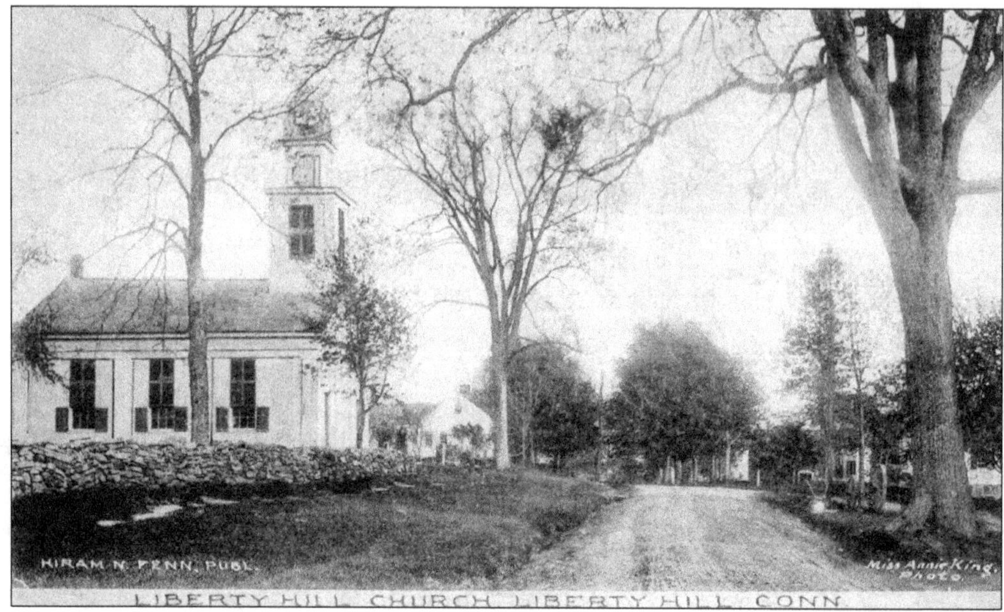

The Liberty Hill Church. This church was built in 1838 and was a First Christian Church for many years. It became a Congregational mission church in 1892 and a full church organized as the Liberty Hill Church in 1912. The congregation bought and maintained a parsonage and was very active until the early 1940s, when, due to a dwindling membership, the church was deeded over to the Lebanon First Congregational Church in 1945.

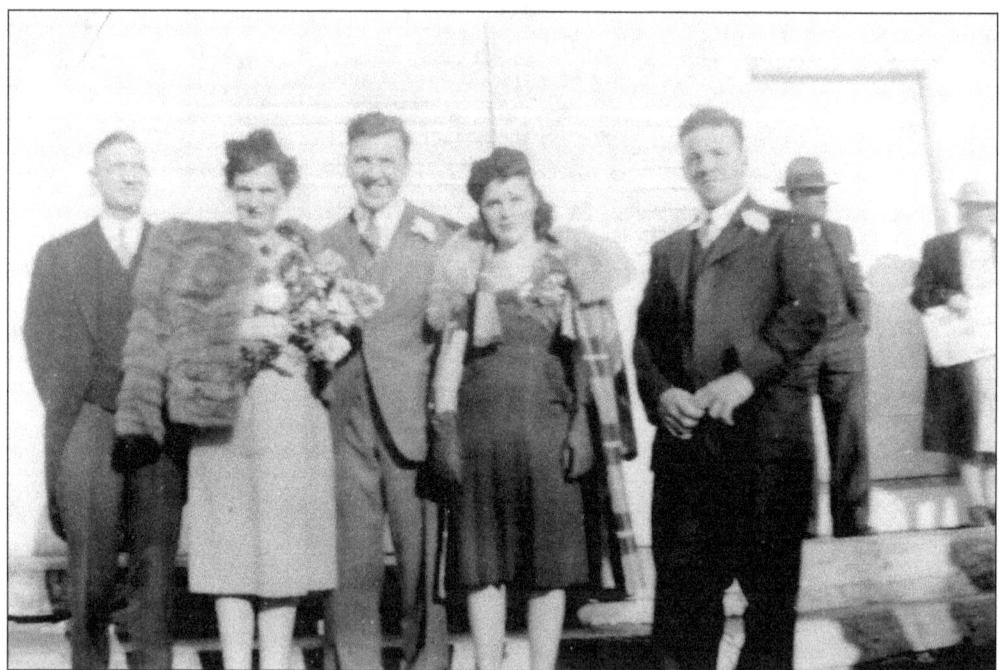

A Wedding at Liberty Hill. Isabelle and Henry Haddad married in 1942. Pictured from left to right are Pastor Howard C. Champe; Isabelle; Henry; Hazel Wood, sister of the bride; and Fred Haddad, brother of the groom.

The Home of James and Mary Clarke. The Clarke family was a very active and a vital part of Liberty Hill.

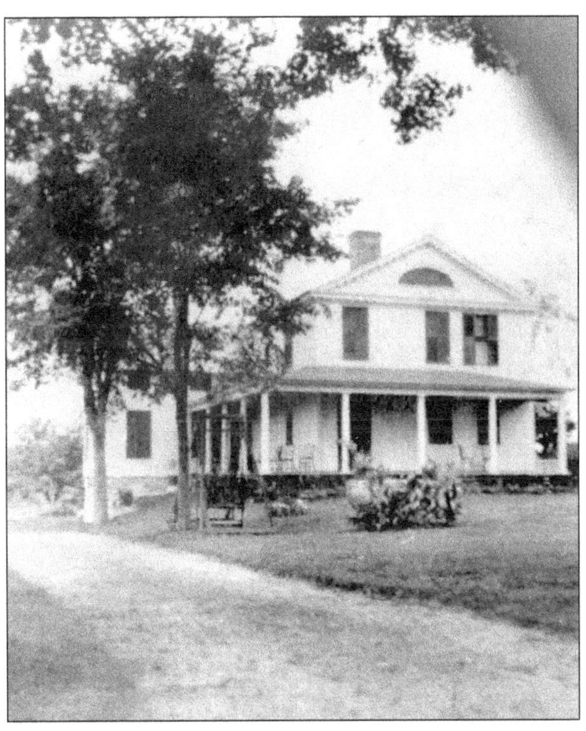

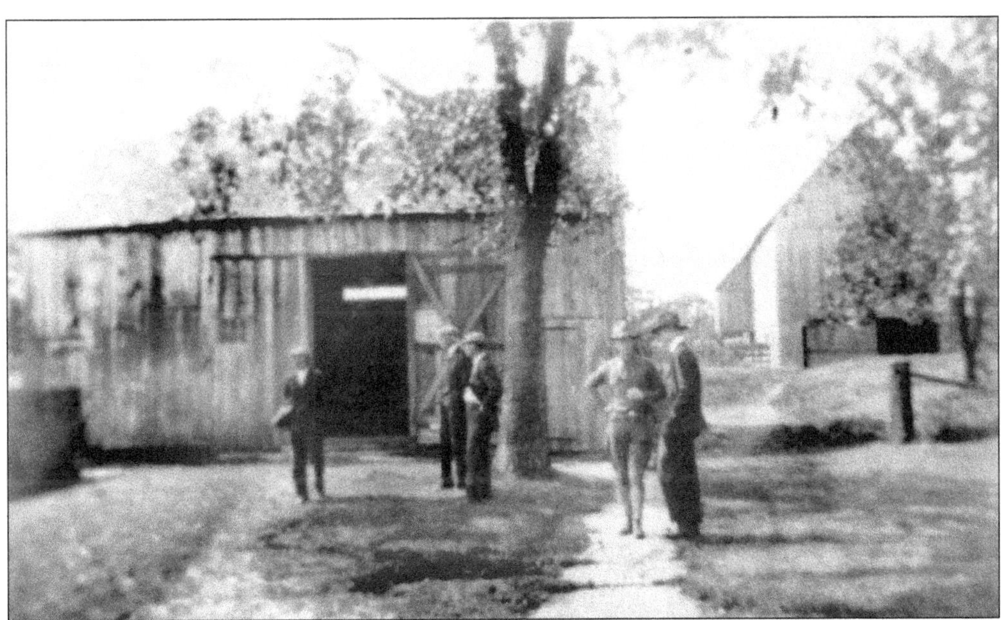

A Clarke Family Gathering. This photograph was taken during World War I, probably at a gathering for an unidentified family soldier (second from the right). The barn to the right was destroyed by the 1938 hurricane and was rebuilt by Leslie Clarke Sr. It is now an antique shop.

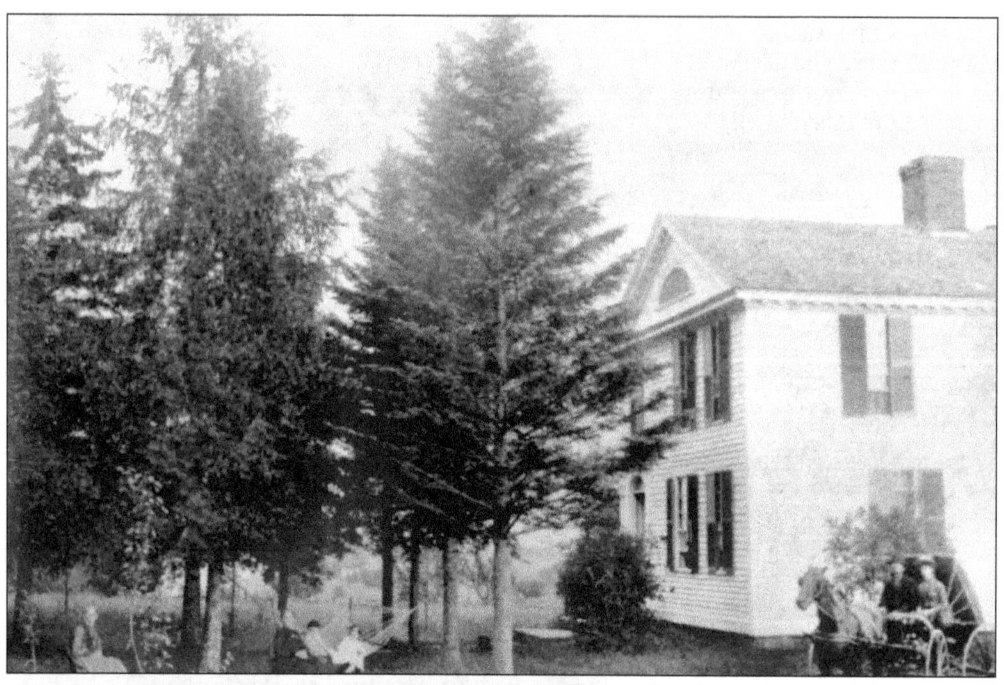

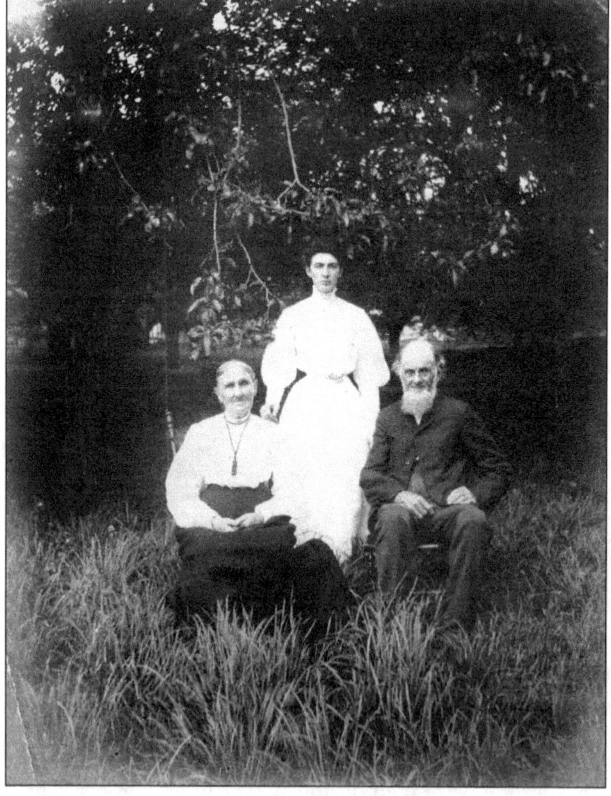

The James Clarke House. In the above photograph, the Clarke house is shown before the Victorian porch was added. The structure still stands on Route 87, just north of the Liberty Hill Farm greenhouses. At the left, James and Mary Clarke and their daughter Minnie are shown at the house in the mid-1880s.

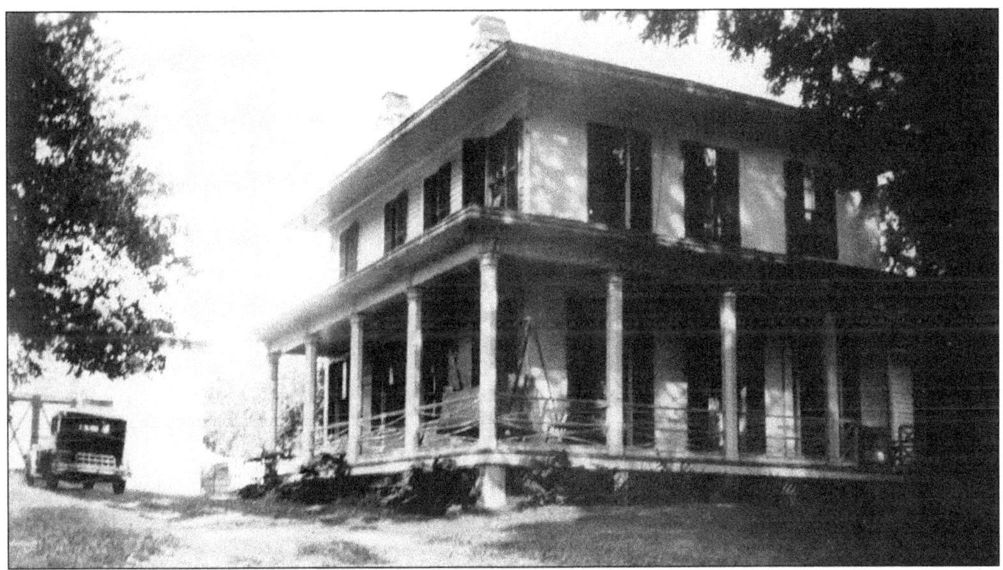

The Home of Capt. Sluman Gray. Captain Gray, skipper of a whaling vessel, died at sea. His wife, Sarah, was aboard the *James Maury* when he passed away. She demanded that he be brought back to Liberty Hill to be interred. In order to preserve his body, she had it placed in a barrel of rum until he could be laid to rest. He was buried in the Liberty Hill Cemetery. His gravestone is shown at the right. Some of the names are misspelled on the gravestone

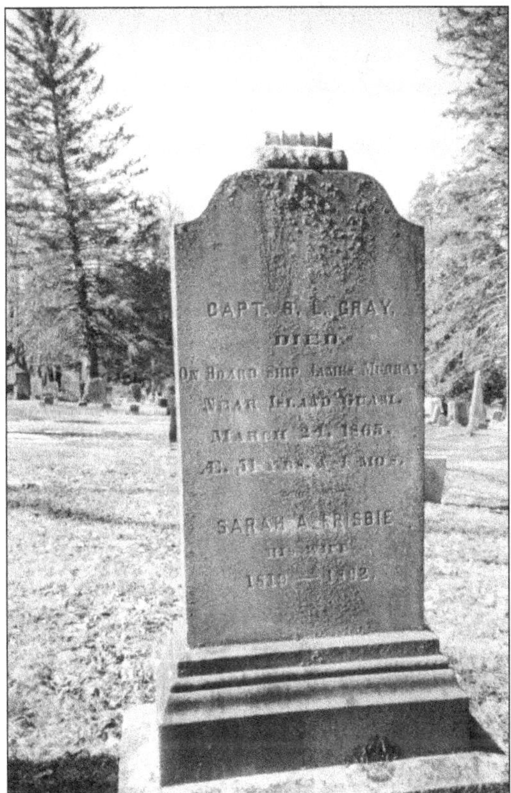

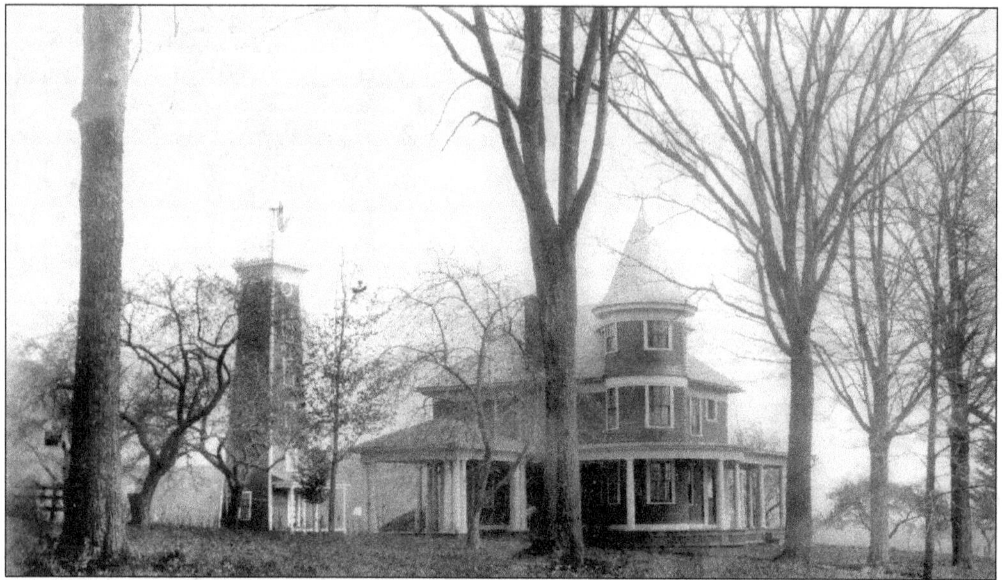

The Home of Henry and Minnie Ohlers. This home was remodeled in Victorian fashion by Paul McCormac. Mr. and Mrs. McCormac were killed in an automobile accident on Boston Post Road on December 7, 1907, in Norwalk. In 1908, Henry and Minnie Ohlers purchased the home from the McCormac estate. The property stayed in the Ohlers family until the 1990s. Note the windmill next to the house; it was said that Long Island Sound could be seen from the top. The windmill was destroyed by the 1938 hurricane, leaving just the first two stories.

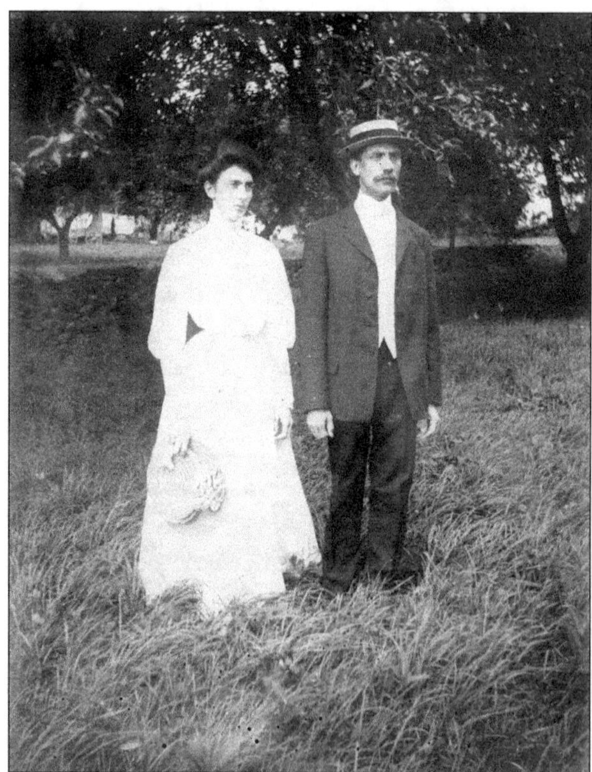

Henry and Minnie Clarke Ohlers. Henry and Minnie were married in 1902. Many people still remember their son Homer, who delivered mail from the Chestnut Hill Post Office until it closed. He then delivered mail from the Lebanon Post Office.

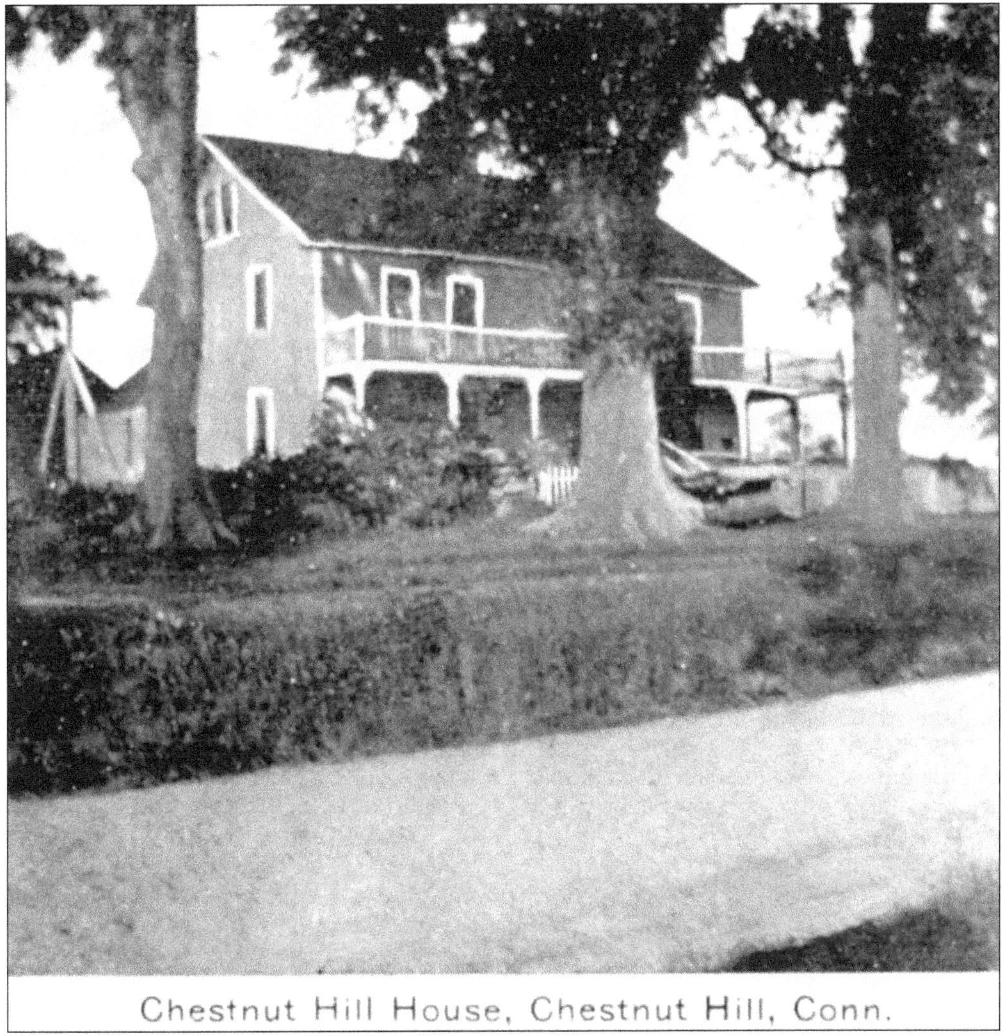

Chestnut Hill House, Chestnut Hill, Conn.

The Chestnut Hill House. This home, situated on the east side of Trumbull Highway across from the Liberty Hill Plant Farm, was a bed-and-breakfast and spa of its day. Water was bottled from the mineral spring on the property and sold as a youth elixir. People would travel to Liberty Hill to partake of the water and stay at the Chestnut Hill House.

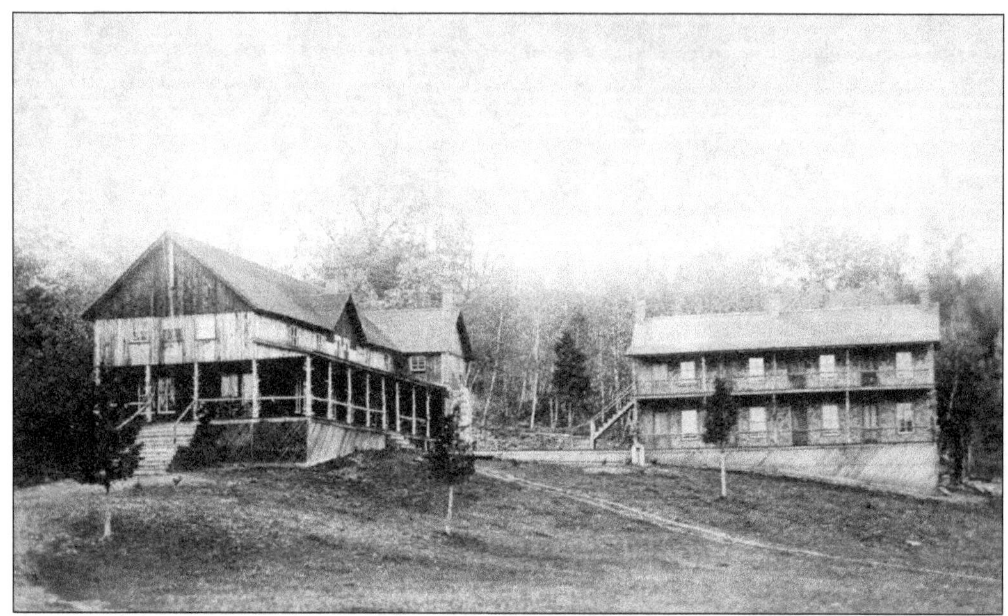

The Liberty Club. In 1888, a group of Boston sportsmen formed the Liberty Club for the purpose of hunting and fishing. Frank Barnes and Joseph Scott had been staying in Lebanon off and on with E. A. Stiles to enjoy the hunting in the area. It was their idea to form the club. From Stiles, they bought the property on Clubhouse Road where the present-day Camp Laurel Girl Scout camp is located. The clubhouse, pictured here, was erected by Barnes, Scott, and 13 other men from Boston. It burned on June 2, 1925. The only part of the building that is still intact is the stone fireplace, around which a new structure was constructed.

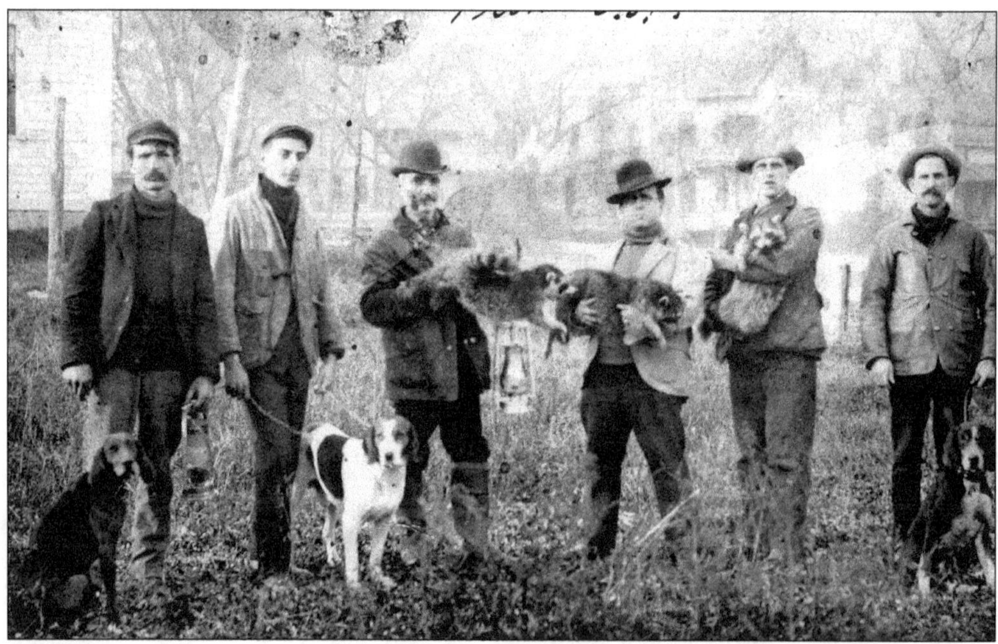

A Successful Hunt. Liberty Club members return from a coon hunt in 1912.

Four

The Farming Community

Livestock raising brought early prosperity to Lebanon. Joseph Trumbull, who moved here from Simsbury in 1704, was a merchant who bought cattle from farmers in Lebanon and neighboring towns. The cattle were driven to markets in Boston and Norwich, where Trumbull exchanged the herds for manufactured goods to sell in his store.

The trades that developed were necessary adjuncts to agriculture. Tradesmen made boots, saddles, harnesses, furniture, axes, hoes, knives, and other tools for farmers. Millers ground the grain, and fulling mills processed wool. But these were for local use and were not part of the export trade.

Lebanon gradually evolved into a major stock-raising center. This growth was largely due to Joseph's son Jonathan Trumbull, the future governor, who greatly expanded the business when he joined his father, probably in 1730. Jonathan soon took over as the principal operator of the business, which became the largest meat-packing business in the colony.

Local farmers produced livestock, lumber, barrel staves, barreled meat, butter, and cheese for the export market. Live animals could be driven to distant cities, but barreled staples and lumber products were carted to Norwich because of the poor roads. These products were shipped overseas, to larger towns along the coast, and to the West Indies.

The growth in livestock production meant that farmers needed to keep large acreage for pasture. The population was expanding rapidly, and there was less land available for sons to inherit or purchase; all public land in the colony was taken by 1750. In the 1760s, many young families moved to western Massachusetts, New Hampshire, and Vermont, where land was available. By 1797, more than 13,000 acres were listed as pastureland on Lebanon tax lists.

In the early 19th century, stock raising declined with the growth of cheaper imports from the Midwest. Lebanon farmers concentrated on dairying, first in butter and cheese and then in whole milk. The increase in dairy production also brought changes to the landscape. Because dairy cattle have to be confined, fencing increased dramatically to enclose pastures. Where the farmer's product—primarily livestock—had formerly "walked out" to market, now the product had to be carried out. This necessitated the construction of new roads for horses and wagons to carry dairy products to market, further changing the landscape.

Barn designs also changed from the English style, with openings on the broad side, to the New England style, with openings on the gable end. Dairying also called for new businesses to handle these products. The opening of the Lebanon Creamery on Exeter Road in 1885 reflects the new trend in agriculture. The cream for the butter was furnished by local farmers, who installed cooling tanks chilled by ice stored in icehouses.

The railroads expanded the market for dairy farmers, providing quick transport to the cities. Refrigeration using block ice in the cars allowed the creamery to send its butter far and wide.

The new markets helped keep farmers in business. In the 20th century, dairy farmers switched to whole-milk production, and the Lebanon Creamery, once the largest in the state, closed in 1933. Farmers now send their milk by trucks to large cooperative milk plants, but the railroad still brings fertilizer and feed to dairy and egg farmers.

In the 20th century, gasoline-powered mechanical equipment and the advent of electricity revolutionized agriculture. While easing the burden of manual labor, these developments also changed the face of agriculture in Lebanon. Many of the smaller dairy farms have gone out of business, while the dairies that do remain are run on a larger and more intensive scale. Modern agribusinesses include a major egg-production factory, a large nursery-stock operation, and a compost business. There are also a number of small farms providing maple syrup, fresh produce, fruit, beef cattle, horses, and llamas.

Today, the economy of Lebanon is still primarily agricultural, although it faces increasing pressures from suburban development. Only time will tell if the ancient roots of agriculture will vanish into history as town life continues to unfold in the 21st century.

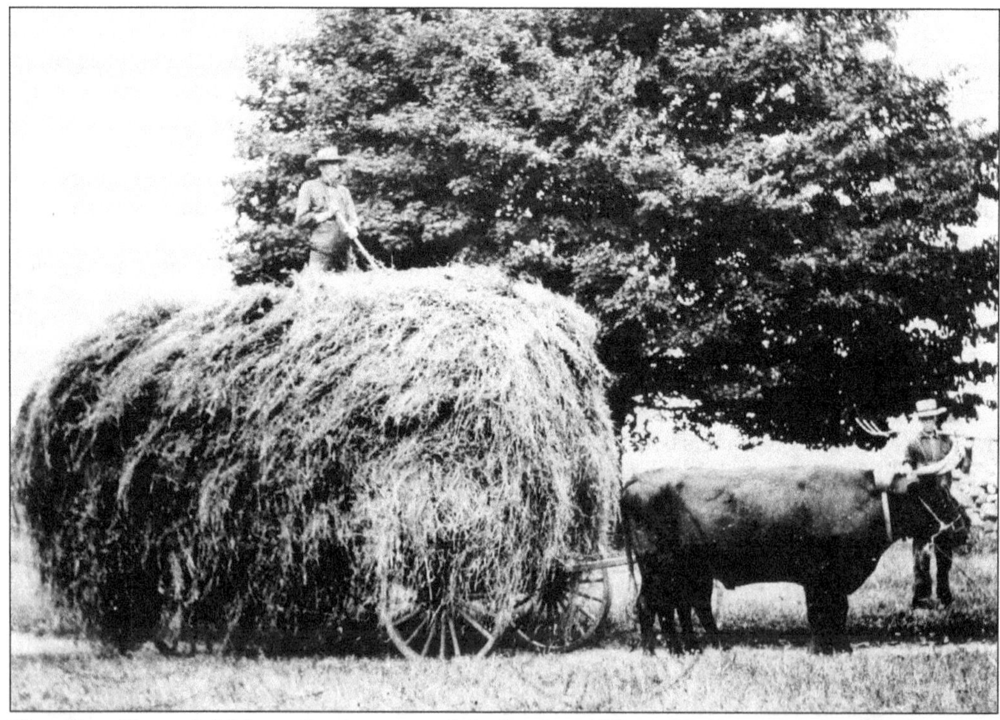

The Geer Farm. J. Nelson Geer, on top of the load, and Elmer N. Geer, standing by the oxen, have just completed loading a wagon with hay *c.* 1905. The Geer farm was located on Exeter Road, near the present high school. (Courtesy Harold Geer.)

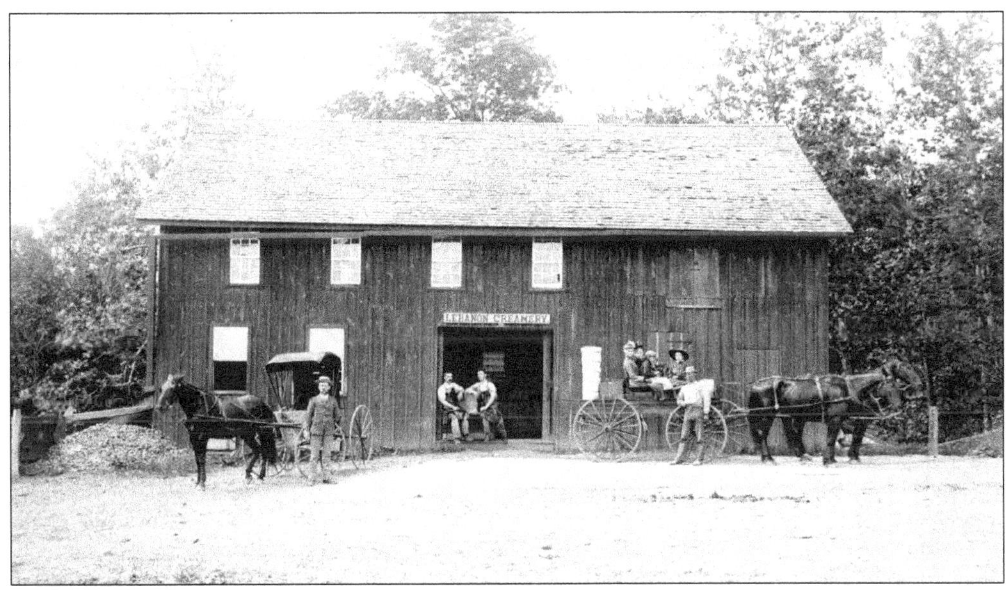

THE LEBANON CREAMERY. The Lebanon Creamery opened for business in 1885 on Susquetonscut Brook, below the present elementary school on Route 207. Cream was gathered from local farmers and brought here to be churned into high-quality butter. Creamery butter won a gold medal at the 1893 World's Fair in Chicago. Although the Lebanon Creamery was once the largest creamery in the state, business fell off as markets changed. The assets were sold at auction in 1933. (Courtesy LHS.)

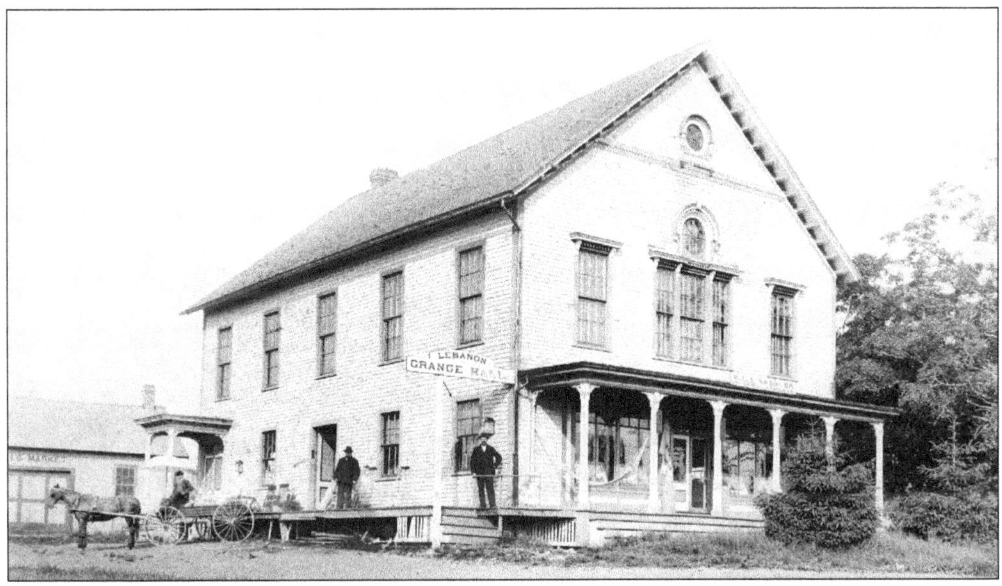

THE LEBANON GRANGE HALL. The Granger Movement began after the Civil War as a national association to advocate for issues important to farmers. It also became a strong social force wherever local Granges were established. The Lebanon chapter, organized in 1884, built this meeting hall and store in 1885. The center of community activities for many years, it is now the Lebanon Green Market. (Courtesy LHS.)

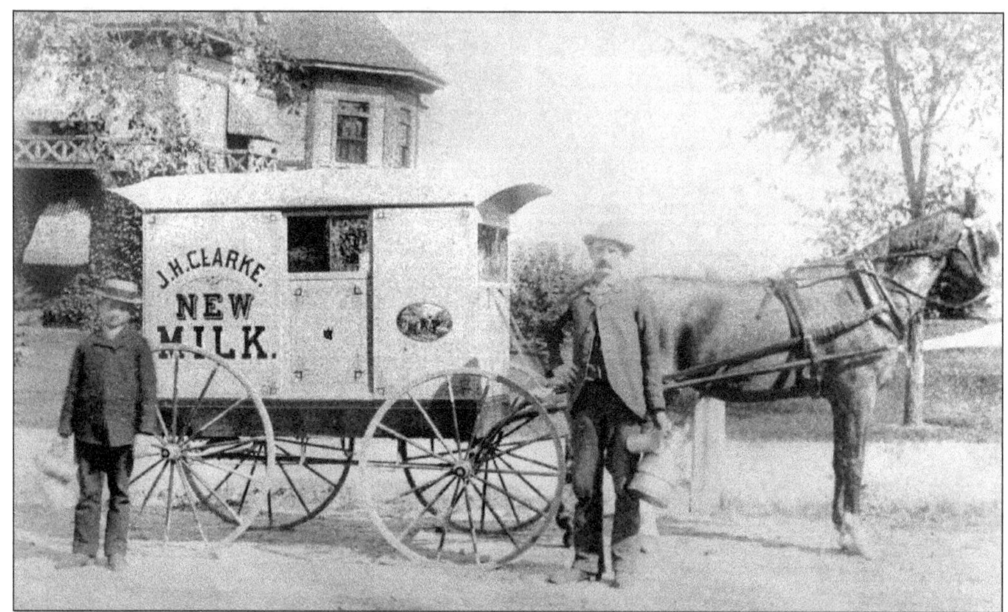

The Milk Route. John Clarke is shown here with his milk wagon sometime in the early 1880s. He sold his milk route in 1892 but continued operating his farm in the Liberty Hill section of town for many years. The area covered by his milk route is not known but was probably in the nearby city of Willimantic, since local people normally had ready access to fresh milk. (Courtesy Ed Tollmann.)

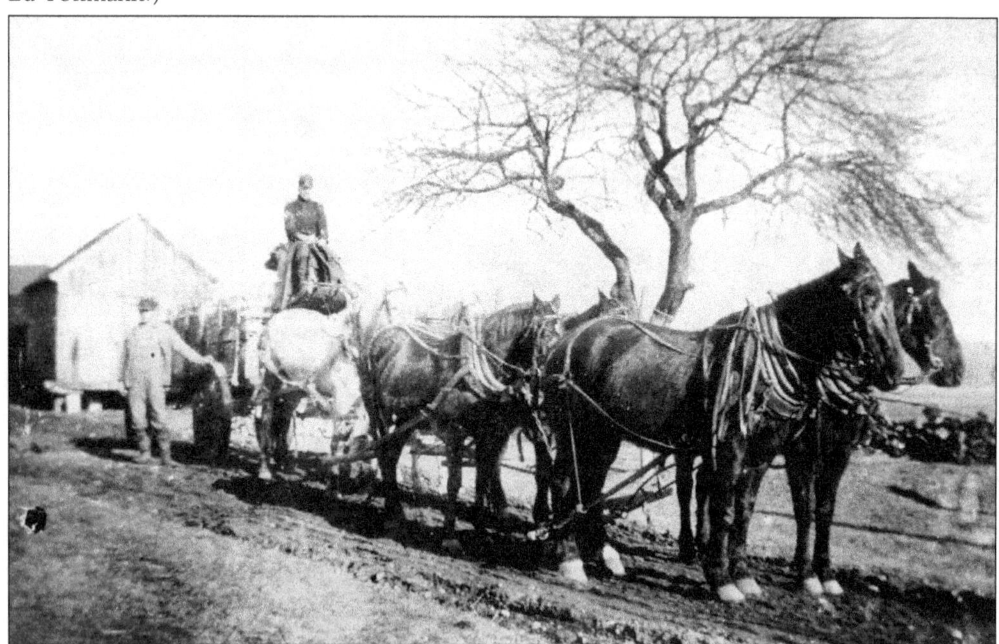

A Six-Horse Team. In this early 1900s photograph, Reuben Manning drives a six-horse team, with a load of milk cans, to the train station in South Windham. Each pair of horses—the pole horses, the middle pair, and the lead pair—had to have a pair of heavy leather reins. The weight of all those long reins equaled 25 to 30 pounds pulling on each arm throughout a drive. (Courtesy Harold Geer.)

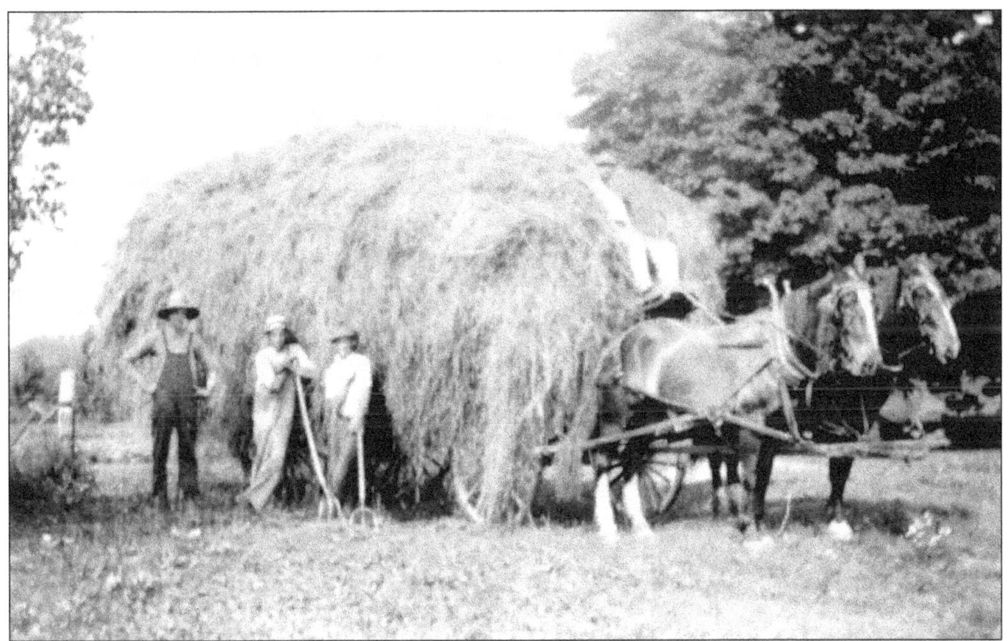

The Hoxie Farm. Everett Hoxie had a large farm on Waterman Road. This photograph, taken *c.* 1913, shows Everett atop the hay load, driving the horses. His three sons stand next to the wagon. Everett Hoxie also owned oxen but preferred to use the faster horses for haying. (Courtesy Phyllis Bartizek.)

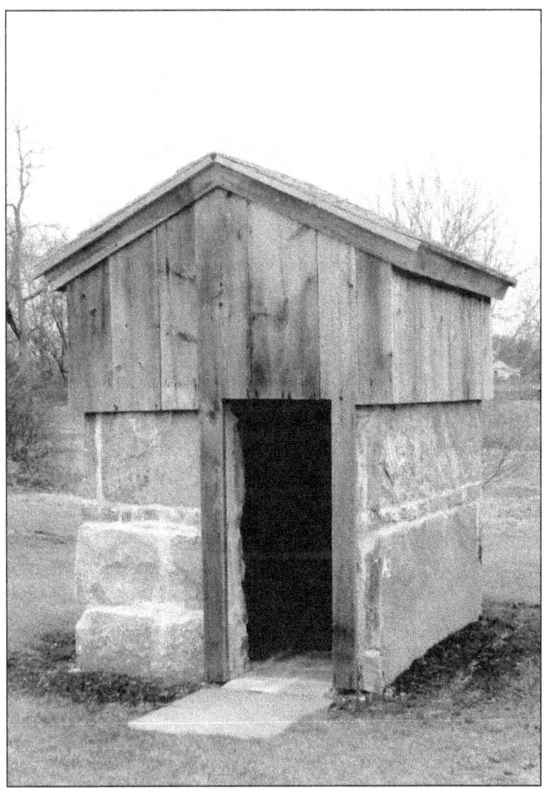

A Smokehouse. Dating from *c.* 1820, this stone smokehouse was located on a farm on Tobacco Street. Most farms had smokehouses to preserve food before the advent of modern canning methods and refrigeration. This smokehouse is one of the few surviving examples in New England. Although it was missing its roof, the smokehouse was purchased by the Lebanon Historical Society and was moved to the museum grounds. It was restored by Glenn Pianka. (Courtesy LHS.)

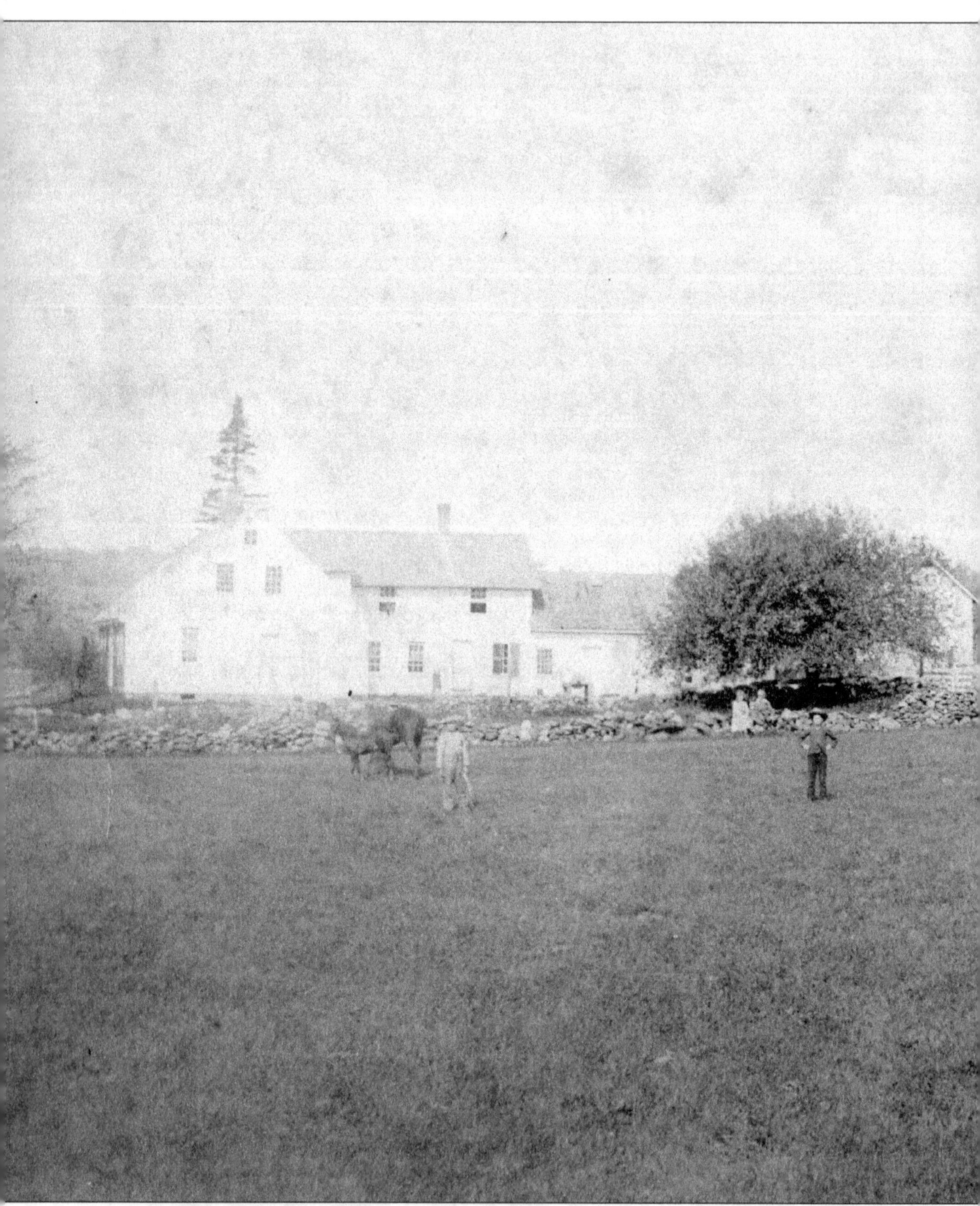

THE MANNING HOMESTEAD. Nathaniel Manning and his family pose for an itinerant photographer in the late 1880s. The Manning farm was located on Exeter Road (Route 207), just north of the intersection with the present Industrial Park Road near the Franklin town line. Families often posed with their prized possessions when the photographers came around. In this

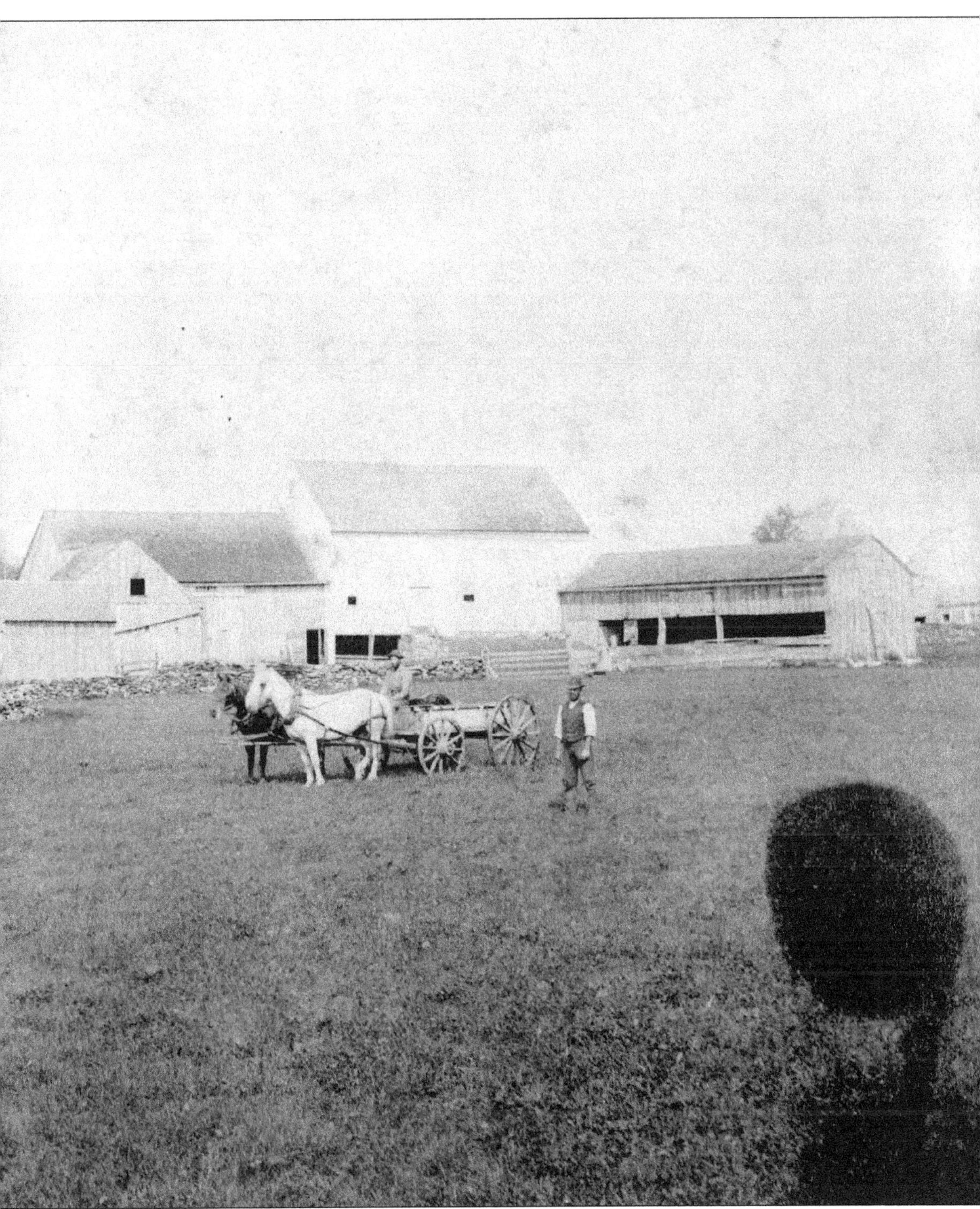

case, Nathaniel shows off his horses. This photograph is unusual for its time, however, because it shows the entire layout of a 19th-century farm, including the house, barns, and numerous outbuildings. Only the house stands today. (Courtesy Harold Geer.)

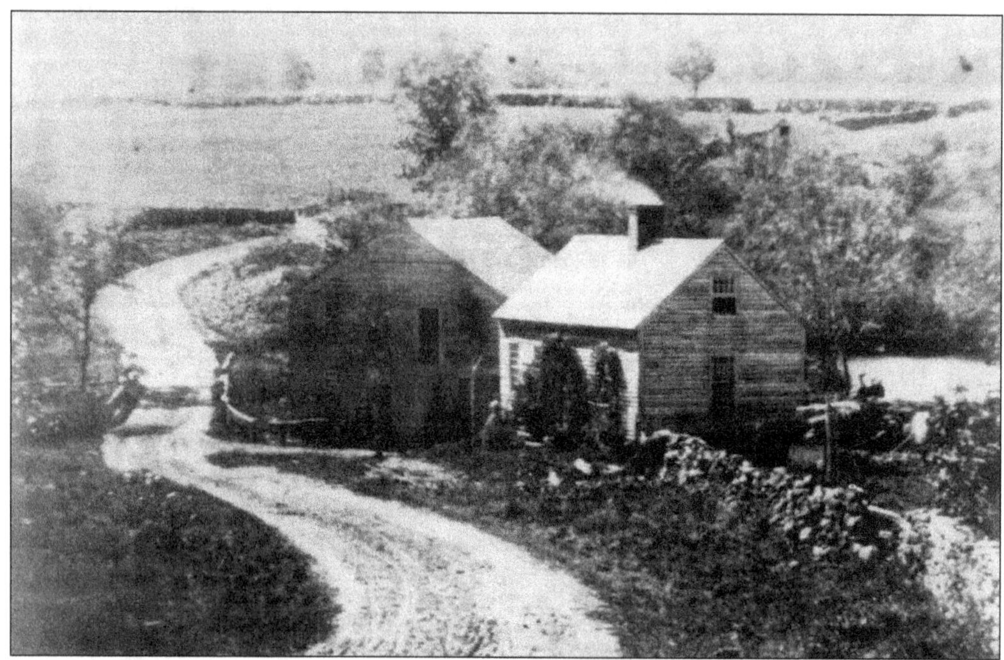

The Old Gristmill. This pre-1880 view of the old gristmill looks west over Exeter Road (Route 207) down to the bridge over Pease Brook. A gristmill was first located on this site in early settlement days. The miller's house is in the foreground, and the mill is behind it. Besides providing power to grind grain for farmers, the millpond was a source of ice. (Courtesy LHS.)

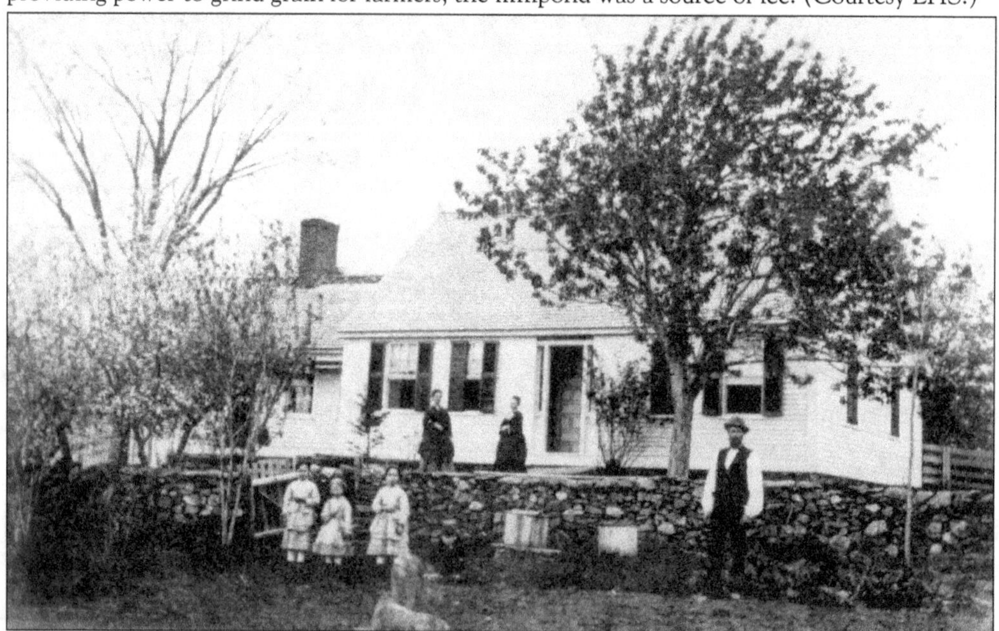

The Peckham-Blakeslee Farm. The Peckham and Blakeslee families have lived in this farmhouse at 453 Kick Hill Road since it was built *c.* 1790. Here, William Peckham, at the right, poses with his family *c.* 1874. At the left, his twin daughters stand on either side of their cousin Lillian (Peckham) Blakeslee, Russell Blakeslee's grandmother. In front of the doorway are William's wife (left) and Mrs. Asa Peckham. (Courtesy Russell Blakeslee.)

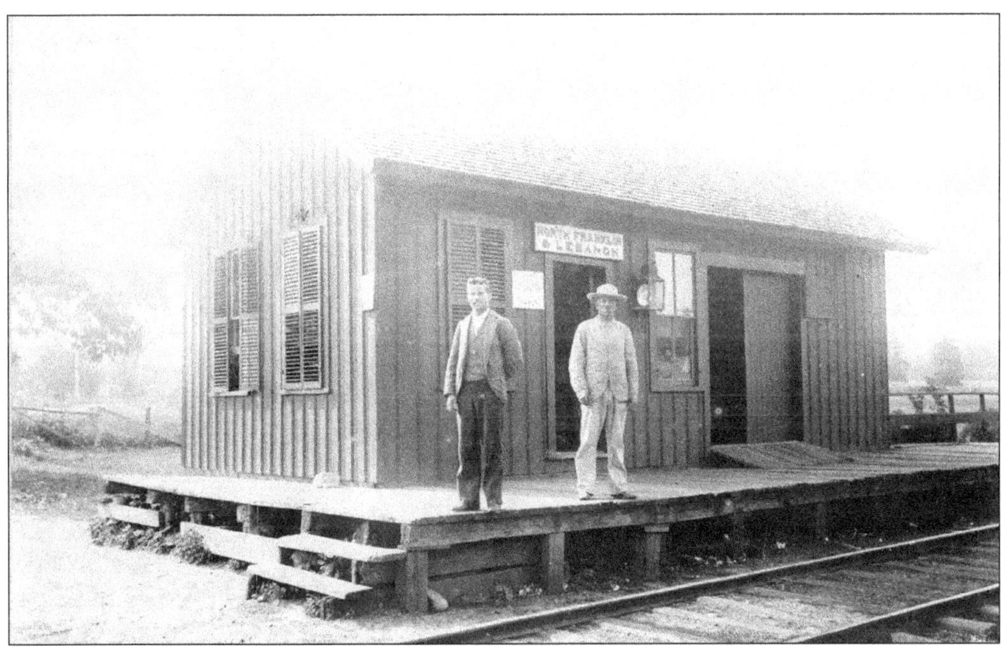

The Railroad Arrives. The first railroad to serve Lebanon was the New London, Willimantic & Palmer Railroad, which began operations in 1849. This undated photograph shows the Lebanon–North Franklin freight house at the local station. The railroad was a boon to travelers but especially to Lebanon dairy farmers, who found a much larger market for their products in the big cities. (Courtesy LHS.)

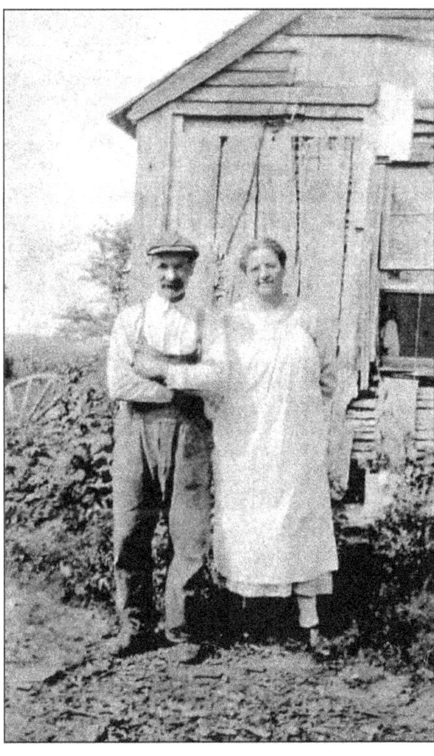

Jewish Settlers. Morris Valinsky, who bought a farm in 1890 on what is now Valinsky Road, was the first Jewish settler in Lebanon. Thus began a wave of Jewish immigrants to Lebanon, people who transformed their worn-out farms into productive dairy and egg farms and laid the foundation of the large poultry industry in New London County. Morris and his wife, Anna, appear here in 1919. (Courtesy LHS.)

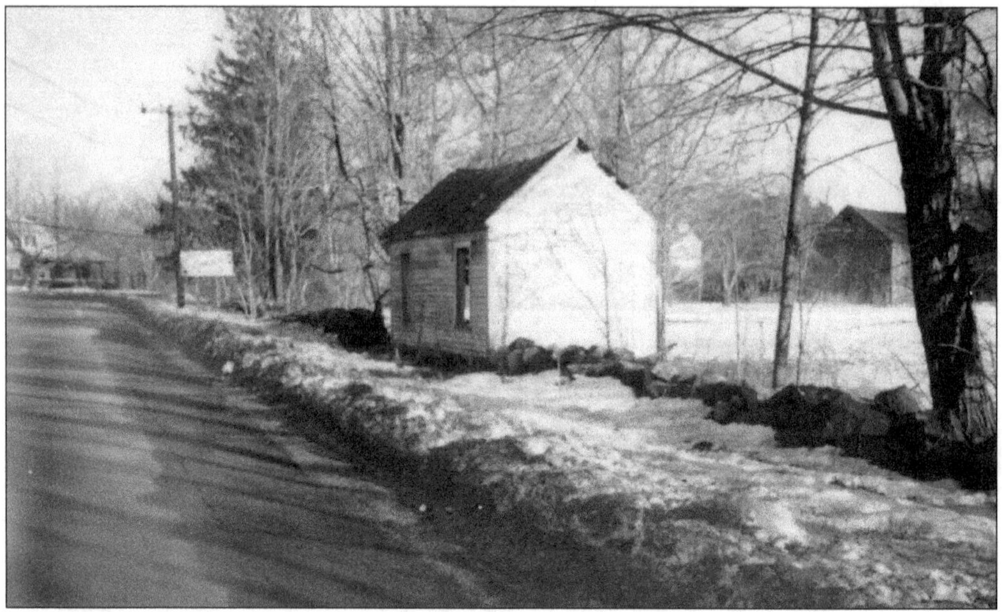

The Broom Shop. From his broom shop at the north end of the town green on Route 87, Eugene Lyman provided farm families a wide variety of brooms—from small whisk brooms to large, sturdy barn-cleaning brooms. The broomcorn was raised by local farmers from seed supplied by Lyman. Members of the Lebanon Historical Society restored the dilapidated building in 1974 and furnished it with broom-making equipment. It was later moved to the museum grounds. (Courtesy LHS.)

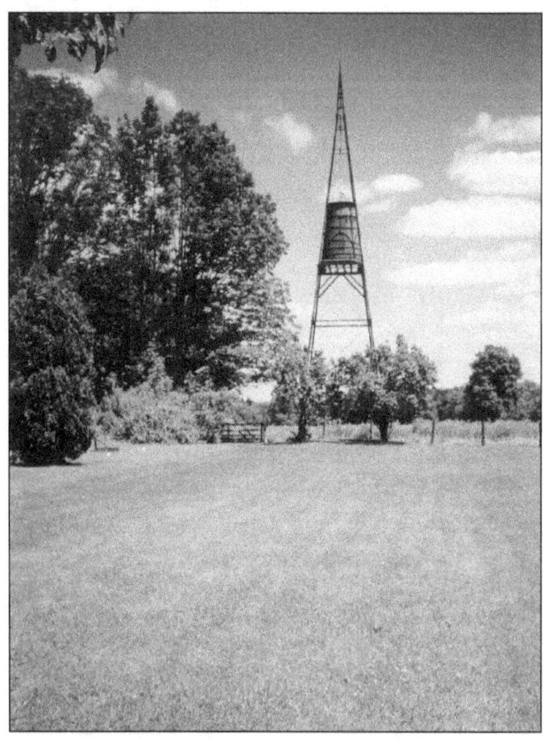

A Water Tower. Although the blades are missing, the tower of an old windmill water system still stands on the McCaw farm, on the east side of the town green. Many Lebanon farms, including five farms around the green, had windmills before electricity came into use. Water piped from a well was stored in a tank halfway up the tower. Gravity fed the water to the barns and the house when spigots were opened. (Courtesy LHS.)

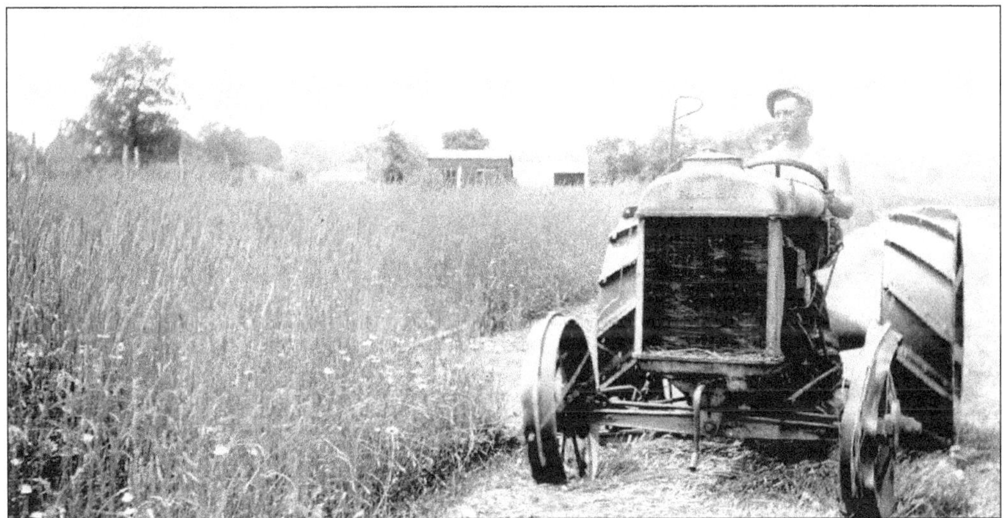

Farm Equipment. In this 1935 photograph, Pete Taylor drives a very early Fordson tractor, which did not have pneumatic tires. Tractors gradually replaced the horses, oxen, and mules that had served farmers for centuries. (Courtesy Robert Slate.)

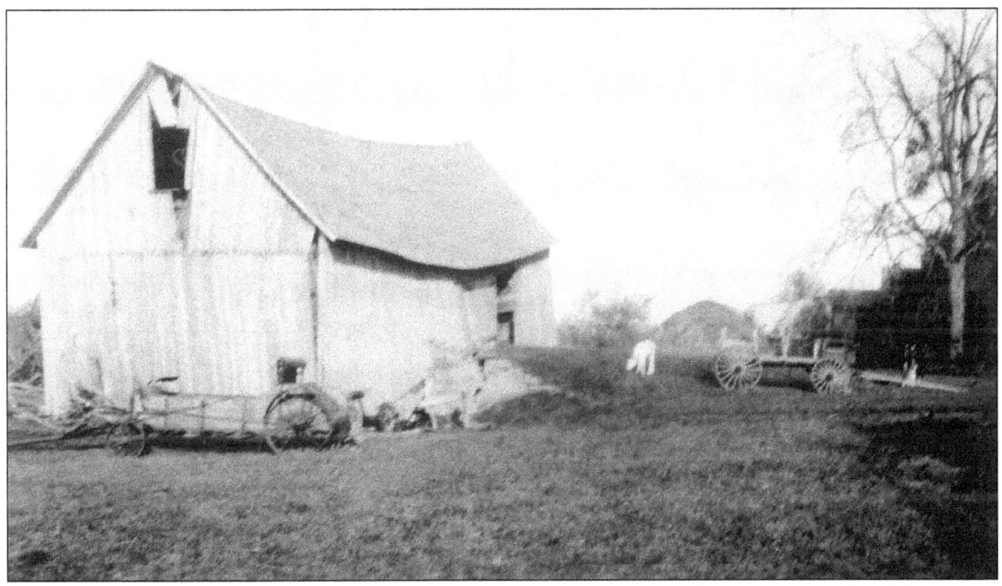

Storm Damage. The destructive force of the 1938 hurricane laid waste to much of the town, which stood in the direct path of the storm. Farmers suffered the most, for many lost the barns, outbuildings, orchards, and animals that had provided them with their livelihood. This barn, owned by Leslie Clark Sr., had to be torn down and replaced with a new barn. That barn is now the antiques shop on Route 87. (Courtesy Ed Tollmann.)

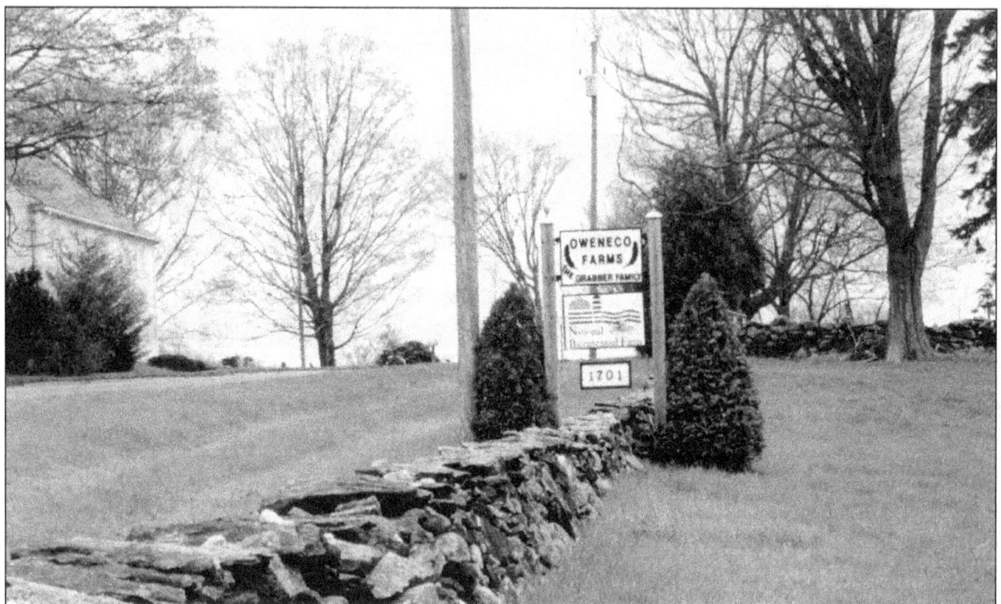

The Oweneco Farm. The Oweneco Farm has been farmed by the same family for over 300 years. Brothers Henry and Spafford Grabber operate the farm their ancestor Thomas Spafford bought from the son of Uncas, the Mohegan chief, 10 generations ago in 1701. The original 120-acre parcel has expanded to over 300 acres through purchases of contiguous land. The Grabbers concentrate on raising corn and hay. (Courtesy LHS.)

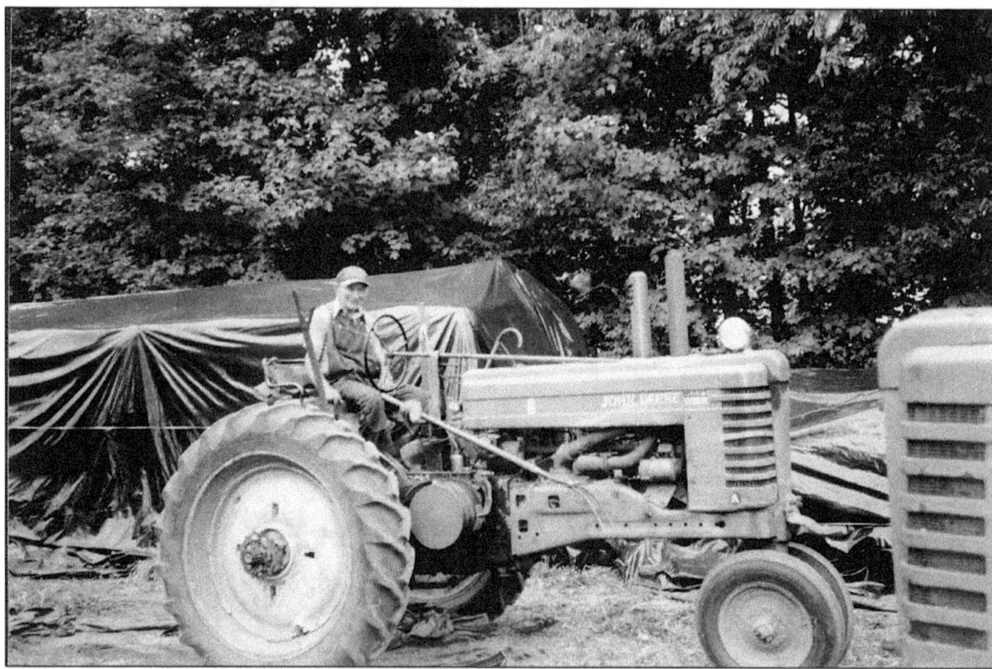

Still Working. Meyer Himmelstein, born in 1919, bought a used John Deere tractor in 1948 to pull the hay baler he had bought the same year. The hay baler Meyer purchased was one of the first in Lebanon. Both machines, still in working condition, are used on the farm today. The Himmelstein farm is located on Exeter Road and North Street. (Courtesy Eva Himmelstein.)

Five

The Village Hill Neighborhood

The history of the Village Hill German population of Lebanon is a story of faith, family, and farming. Bonded by common culture and traditions, the Germans made their pilgrimage to America in the early 20th century in search of freedom and opportunity. Their ancestors before them had emigrated from Germany to Poland and Russia in their search for a better life, free of religious and ethnic persecution.

Karlswalde, their last home in Europe before their voyage to America, was a beautiful village in the western part of Ukraine, near the Polish border. Formerly a Mennonite village, it contained large homes and well-kept farms. The new German settlers who had migrated from Poland prospered there for 50 years. They built their own school and church and kept up their German language and traditions. Forced to flee because of the unrest and upheaval prior to World War I and the Russian Revolution, many of them came to the United States.

Upon their arrival, they were met by family members who provided shelter and job opportunities. They settled in Poughkeepsie, New York; Boston, Massachusetts; and Long Island. They found jobs as gardeners, railroad workers, factory laborers, domestics, and tradespeople. They learned English and became part of the American mainstream. But some of them never gave up the dream of owning land and farming again in the old tradition. Spurred on by Philip Krause, who had recently moved to Village Hill, relatives moved to Lebanon as land became available. The farms were run down and abandoned, a far cry from the fertile farmland of Ukraine. By 1928, 12 families, former residents of Karlswalde, had moved into the Village Hill area, in close proximity to each other. It reminded many of Karlswalde. Each farm had about 100 to 150 acres of land, as well as a house and barns.

The people survived because of their community spirit, or *Gemeinschaft*. Still mindful of the old traditions, they worked together during labor-intense seasons, sharing tools, horses, and machinery and cooperating during harvesting, ice-cutting, and animal-husbandry chores. They harvested corn and hay and raised cows, pigs, chickens, and other fowl. They sold milk, eggs, vegetables, and fruit directly into the marketplace. Women and children worked alongside the men as they became small farm-family entrepreneurs. They had to struggle to make ends meet, but the land provided them sustenance. Industrious and hardworking, they added to the Lebanon economy.

Of paramount concern to the new settlers were their spiritual needs. The first families to arrive in Connecticut found a German-speaking minister from the New London mission for the Lutheran church. The small congregation, consisting of German-speaking communicants from Lebanon, Coventry, and Willimantic, was founded in 1916 and held services at the Ebenezer Lutheran Church in Willimantic each Sunday afternoon. In 1937, the congregation purchased the Village Hill Schoolhouse for the purpose of conversion into a church for the Redeemer congregation. It took seven years to build and was completed in 1944. The simple charm of the church design is enhanced by original woodcarvings rendered by Gottlieb Laibrandt, a master craftsman, on the altar, pulpit, and windows. The church has been designated a historic site and has been placed on the Connecticut State Register of Historic Places. It has become a landmark of the Village Hill section of Lebanon.

The "Karlswalders" had finally found their home in a country where their way of life was not threatened. Many of the descendants of these immigrants still live in the area and are actively involved in community activities. The Village Hill area was often called the "other Karlswalde." This unique neighborhood is an excellent example of a transplanted European culture existing in a traditional New England town.

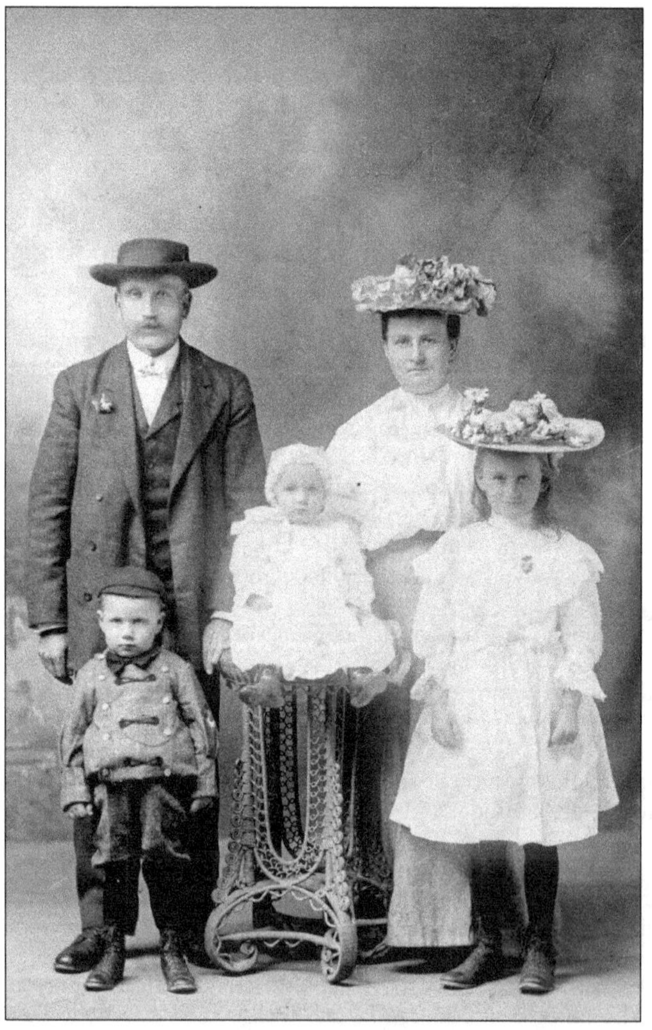

THE FRED KRAUSE FAMILY, C. 1906. Entering Ellis Island on February 22, 1905, the Krause family made its way to Poughkeepsie, New York, where Fred worked as a gardener for eight years before moving to Village Hill in Lebanon to join his brother Philip and purchase a nearby farm. This photograph shows Fred and Elizabeth Krause with their children, son Edmund (left) and daughters Frieda (center) and Caroline (right). (Courtesy Claire Krause.)

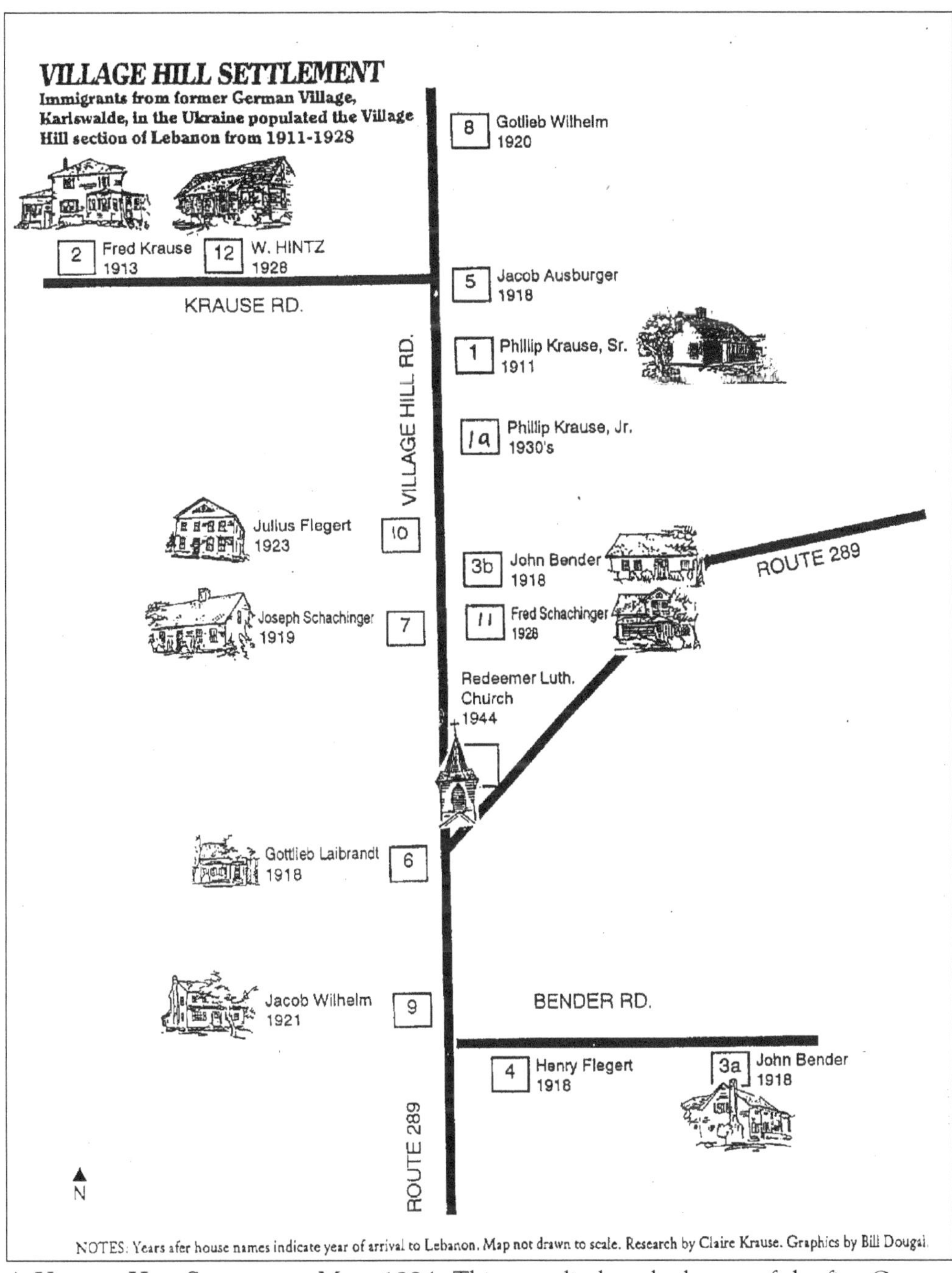

A Village Hill Settlement Map, 1994. This map displays the homes of the first German Village Hill settlers (1914–1928) and includes the settlers' names, the years of their arrival, and the locations of their homes. (Research by Claire Krause, graphics by Bill Dougal; courtesy Claire Krause.)

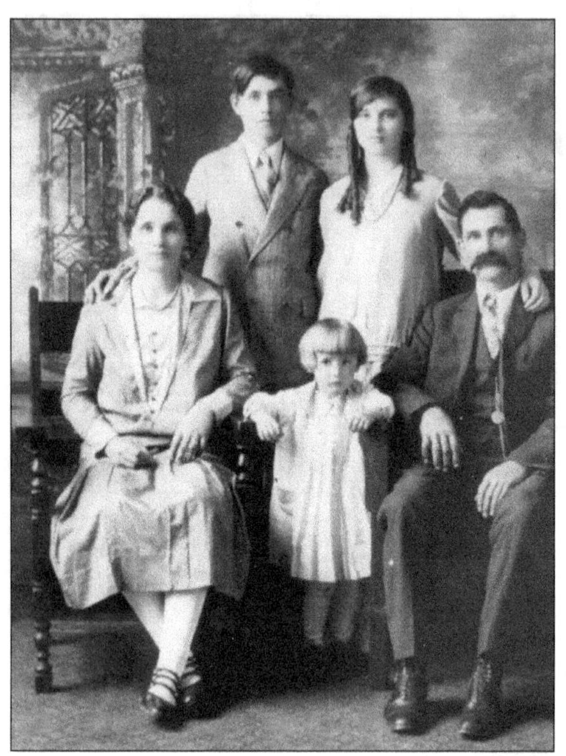

The Gottlieb Laibrandt Family, c. 1927. Gottlieb and Agatha Laibrandt emigrated from Ukraine in 1913. They first came to Boston, where Gottlieb worked as a cabinetmaker, building showcases for the F. W. Woolworth Company. They then moved to Village Hill in 1918 and purchased a farm near family and friends. Shown here, from left to right, are the following: (first row) Agatha, daughter Helen, and Gottlieb; (second row) son John and daughter Martha. (Courtesy Claire Krause.)

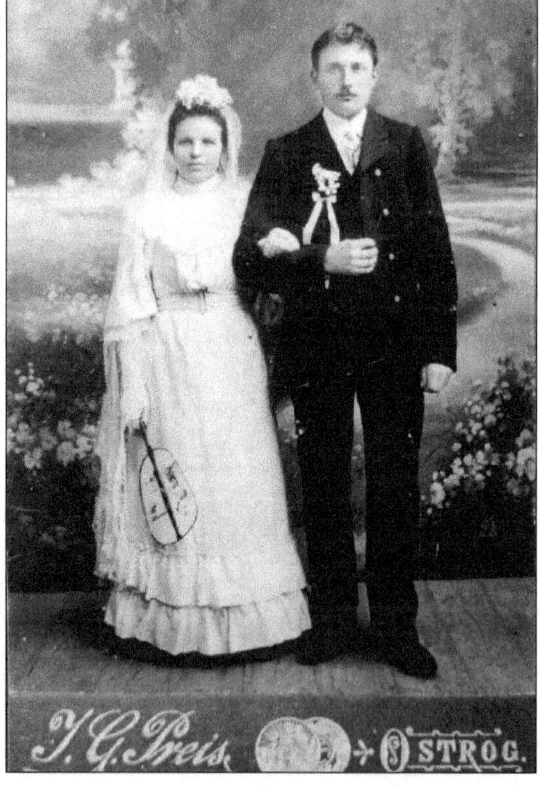

The John and Justina Bender Wedding, 1908. This wedding photograph of John and Justina (Schachinger) Bender was taken in Ostrog, Russia, near Karlswalde. The Benders came to the United States in 1909, settling in Jamaica, New York, where John worked for the Long Island Railroad. They arrived in Lebanon in 1918 and purchased a farm in Village Hill. (Courtesy Claire Krause.)

THE SCHACHINGER BROTHERS, C. 1908. Fred (left) and Joseph Schachinger sent this photograph to their family in Karlswalde shortly after arriving in the United States. Fred worked as a baker in Jamaica, New York, while Joseph worked for the Long Island Railroad. Their two sisters, Justina and Lydia, followed them, and they all moved to Village Hill and bought land on Village Hill Road. (Courtesy Claire Krause.)

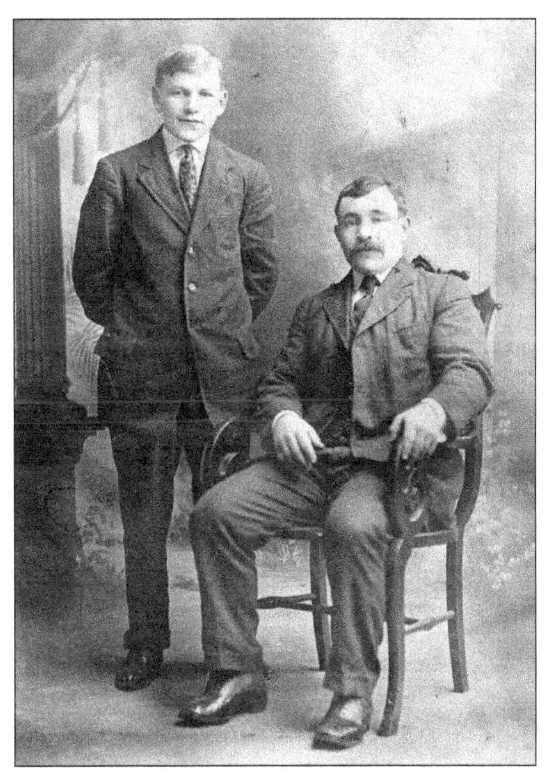

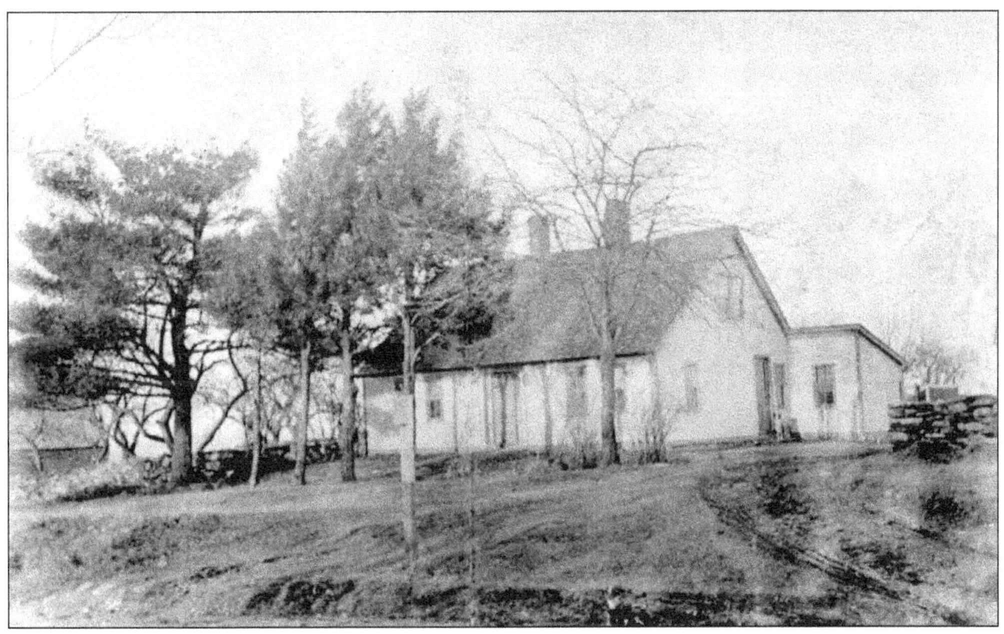

THE BEAUMONT HOMESTEAD, C. 1920. The first German settler to purchase land in Village Hill was Philip Krause in 1911. It was later discovered that his home on Village Hill Road was the birthplace of Dr. William Beaumont, the world-famous pioneer physiologist. After the house was moved to the Lebanon Green in 1976, the vacant lot was donated to the town for a park. (Courtesy Claire Krause.)

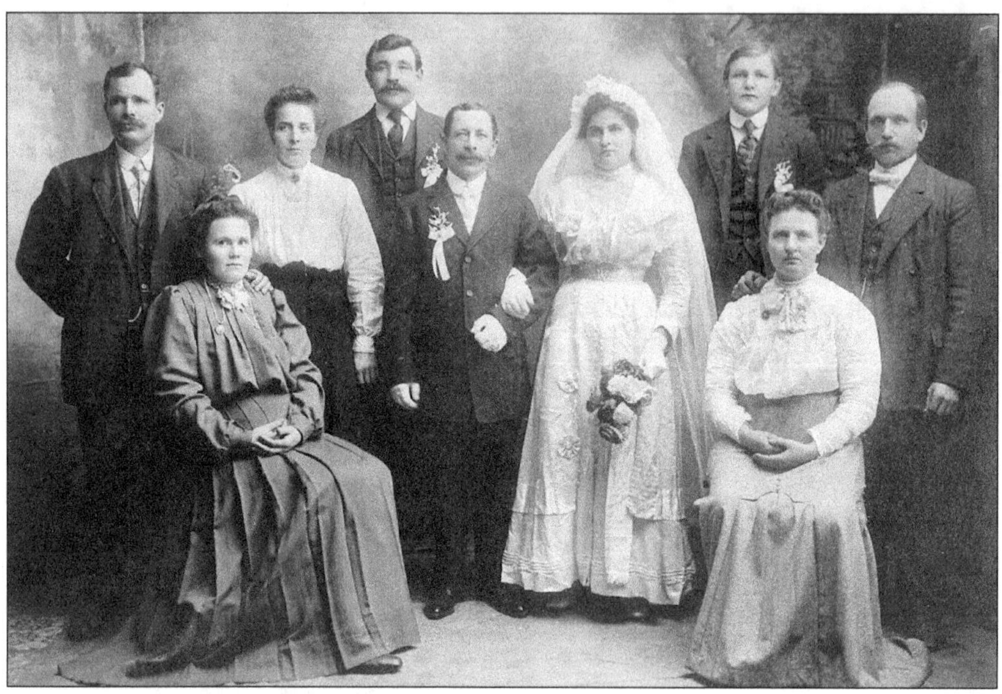

The Jacob and Justina Wilhelm Wedding, c. 1908. One of the first weddings of the newly arrived Karlswalde immigrants took place in Jamaica, New York. Pictured, from left to right, are the following: Philip Wilhelm; his wife, Elizabeth (seated); Anna Bender; Joseph Schachinger; Jacob and Justina Wilhelm; Fred Schachinger; Fred Krause; and his wife, Elizabeth (seated). With the exception of Philip and Elizabeth Wilhelm, they all moved to Village Hill as land became available. (Courtesy Claire Krause.)

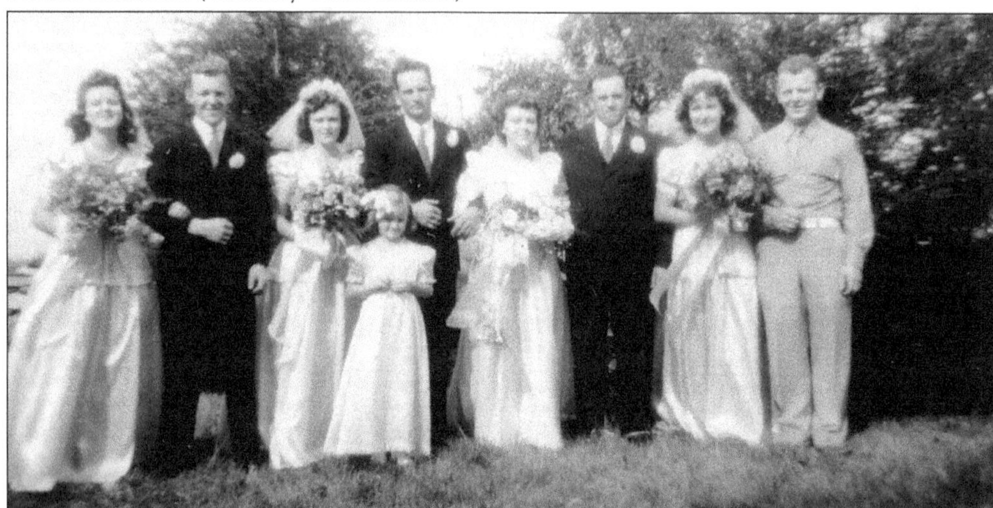

Wedding Bells, Village Hill, September 1944. The first wedding held in the newly built Redeemer Lutheran Church on Village Hill Road in Lebanon was that of Arnold Krause and Helen Flegert. Seen here, from left to right, are Claire Schachinger, Harry Flegert, Helen Bender, Barbara Bender (flower girl), Harold Krause, Helen (Flegert) Krause, Arnold Krause, Mildred Schachinger, and Arthur Flegert, all first-generation descendants of the Karlswalde Germans. (Courtesy Claire Krause.)

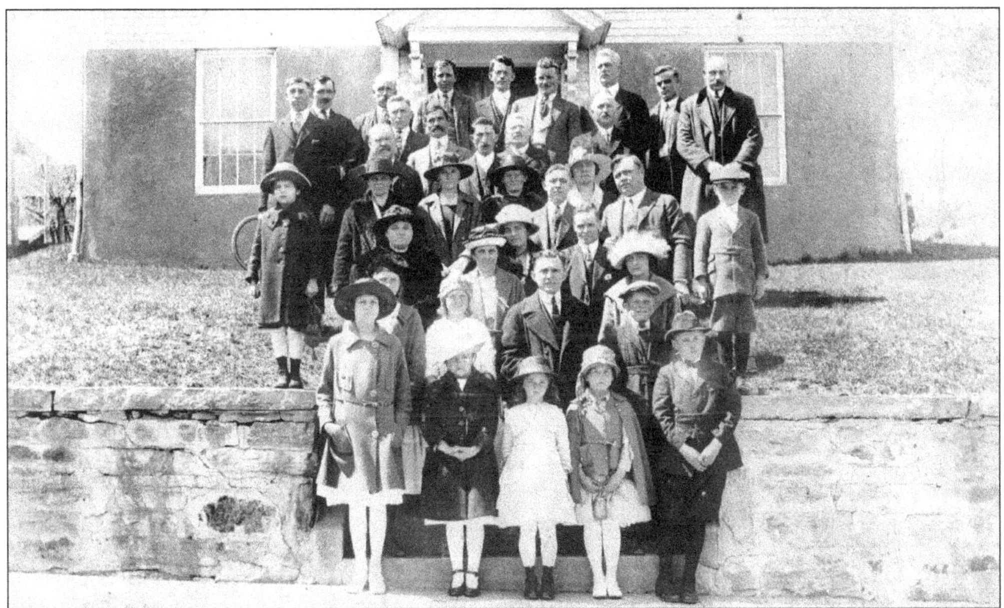

THE EBENEZER LUTHERAN CHURCH, WILLIMANTIC, C. 1919. Services for the Redeemer Lutheran Church, organized in 1916, were first held in the Ebenezer Church until the new Lebanon sanctuary was built. Here, the congregation appears on the steps of the Ebenezer Church; members of the Bender, Krause, Laibrandt, Schachinger, and Ausburger families can be seen. (Courtesy Claire Krause.)

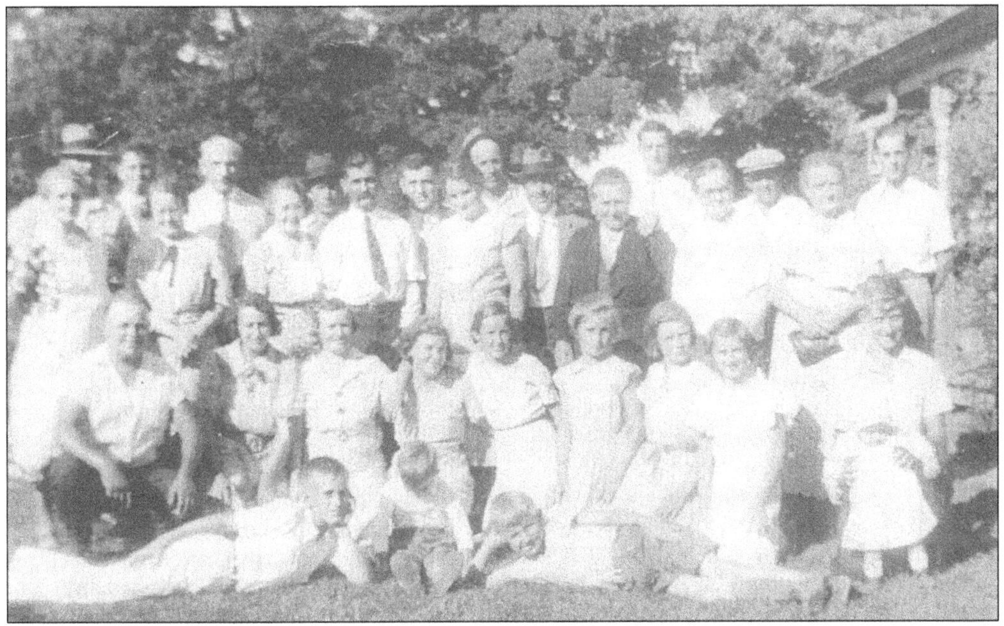

THE VILLAGE HILL KAFFEE KLATCH, C. 1936. Originally started by the Ladies Aid organization of the church, the Kaffee Klatch quickly became family oriented, as evidenced by this photograph taken at the John Bender farm. "Gossip over a cup of coffee" also included home-baked goods made by the hostess of the day, camaraderie, and games for the children. Held monthly, these get-togethers were a popular pastime. (Courtesy Claire Krause.)

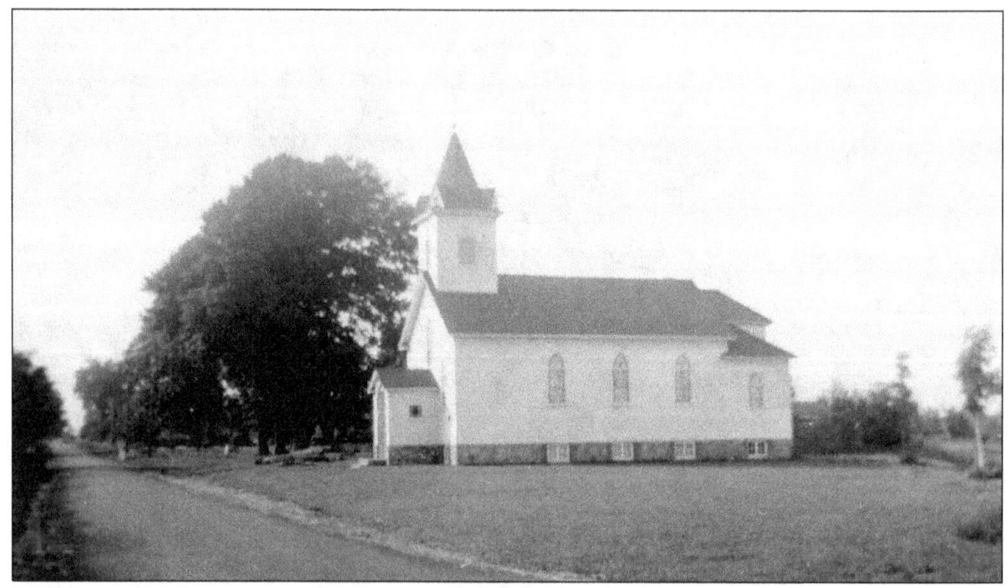

The Redeemer Lutheran Church, 1944. The newly built church was situated on a rise at the junction of Village Hill Road and Beaumont Highway, about five miles north of Lebanon Center. The congregation was comprised of parishioners from Lebanon, Willimantic, and Coventry. Redeemer has become a landmark of Village Hill and is listed on the Connecticut State Register of Historic Places. (Courtesy Helen Bender.)

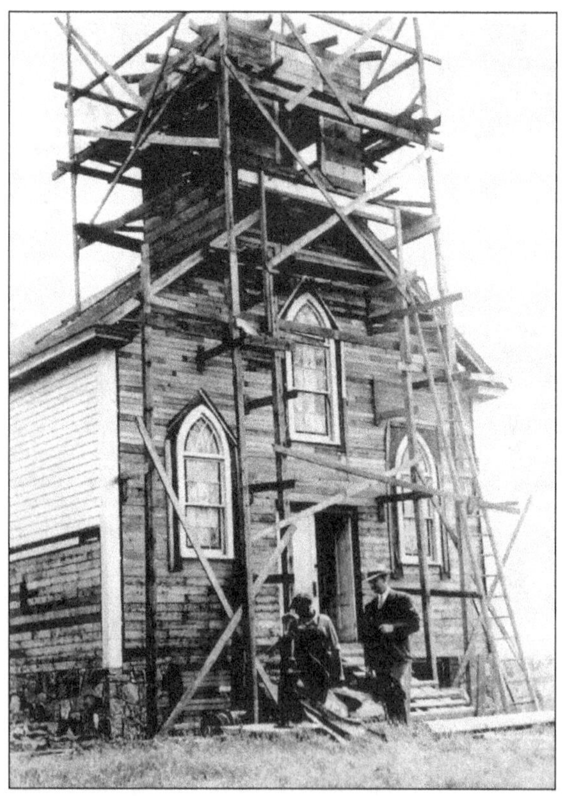

The Redeemer Church Steeple, c. 1940. Entertaining a visitor from Detroit, Michigan, Gottlieb Laibrandt pauses in his work on the church steeple. Laibrandt, a master craftsman, received his early training in Karlswalde, Ukraine. The Lebanon church was designed after the Karlswalde Lutheran Church, which he helped to build there. The church took seven years to build and was completed entirely with the parishioners' volunteer labor. (Courtesy Helen Bender.)

THE REDEEMER CHURCH SACRISTY, C. 2002. The central point of the altar is a large canvas painting of Christ entitled *Come Unto Me*. It was set into the paneling of the altar and framed in native oak by Gottlieb Laibrandt. Intricate carvings rendered by Laibrandt are evident throughout the church—on the altar, in the oak chairs, on the baptismal font, and in the pulpit. (Courtesy Claire Krause.)

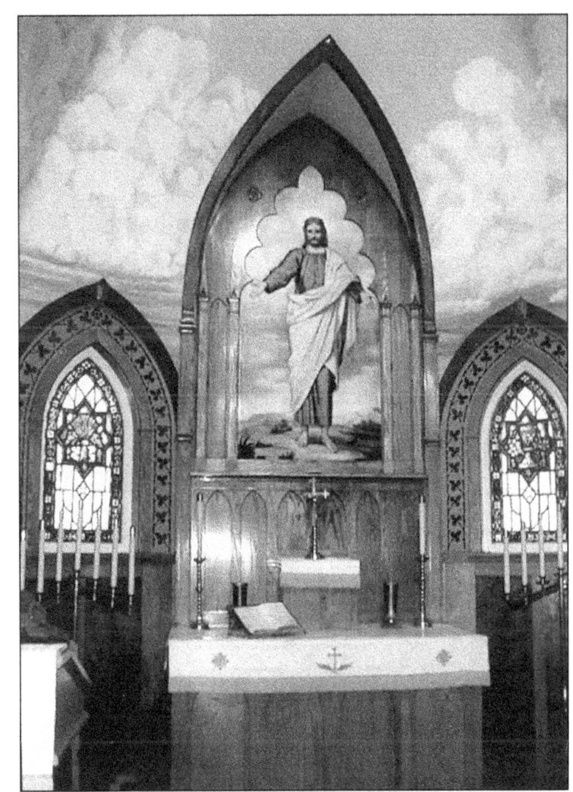

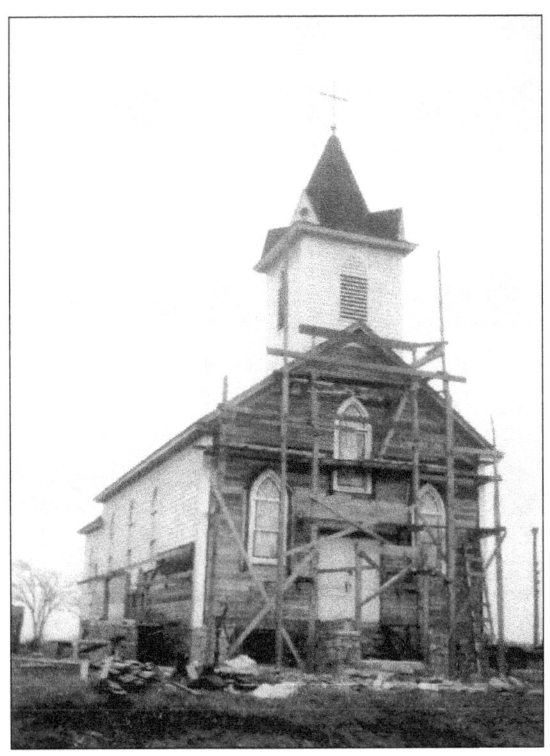

THE REDEEMER BELL TOWER, C. 1940. The church exterior nearly completed, work on the interior began, taking several years to finish. The church is located on the original foundation of a one-room schoolhouse—School District No. 1, dating back to 1850—that had been destroyed in the hurricane of 1938. The men in the congregation used as much lumber from the old schoolhouse as possible to build the church. (Courtesy Helen Bender.)

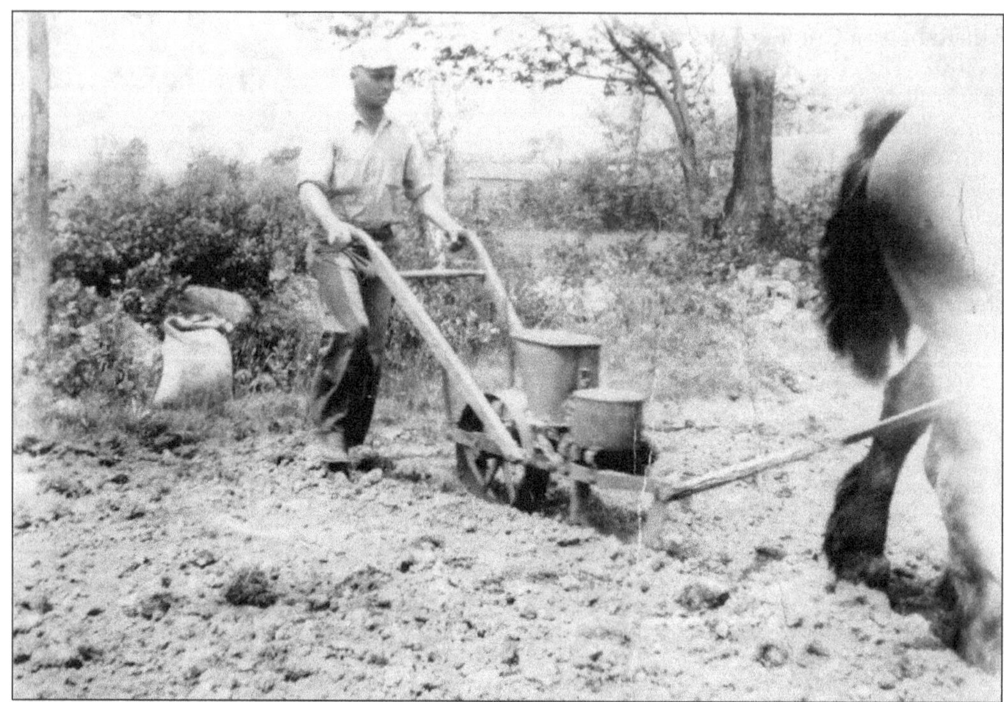

PLANTING CORN, THE LAIBRANDT FARM, C. 1939. Mid-May, when the weather was warm, the fields were marked and prepared for planting corn. Hand-planters were used in the smaller fields, and horse-drawn planters were used for the larger fields. Here, John Laibrandt guides the horse-drawn planter as a helper leads the horse up and down the rows. (Courtesy Helen Bender.)

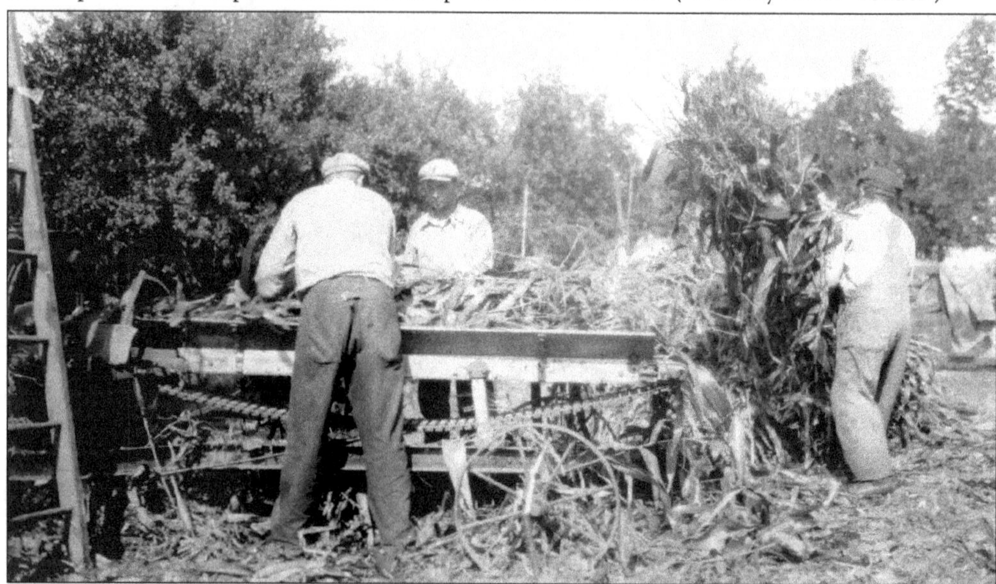

BRINGING IN THE SHEAVES, C. 1930. Corn was harvested in the fall, when it was ripe. Hand-cut in the fields, it was loaded onto a wagon, taken to the barn, and blown into the silo. In this photograph, from left to right, Village Hill farmers Edmund Krause, John Laibrandt, and Gottlieb Wilhelm load corn through the blower into the silo at the Fred Krause farm. (Courtesy Claire Krause.)

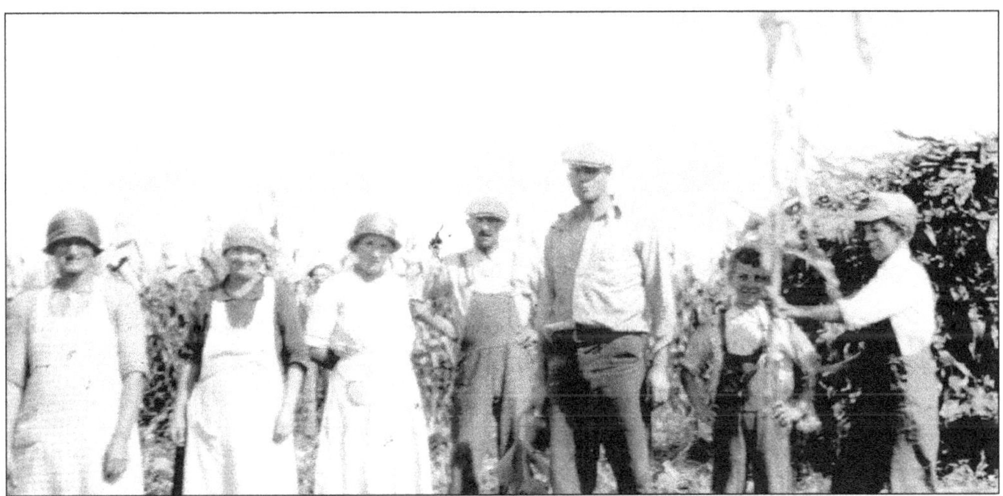

HARVESTING CORN, THE FRED KRAUSE FARM, C. 1930. Stopping only to have its photograph taken, this team of men, women, and children labored to harvest the corn before the fall frost. Families went from farm to farm, sharing machinery and labor. The women at each home prepared meals for the crew. This photograph shows, from left to right, Christine Wilhelm, Caroline Ausburger, Agatha Laibrandt, Jacob Ausburger, Edmund Krause, Harold Krause, and Ewald Wilhelm. (Courtesy Claire Krause.)

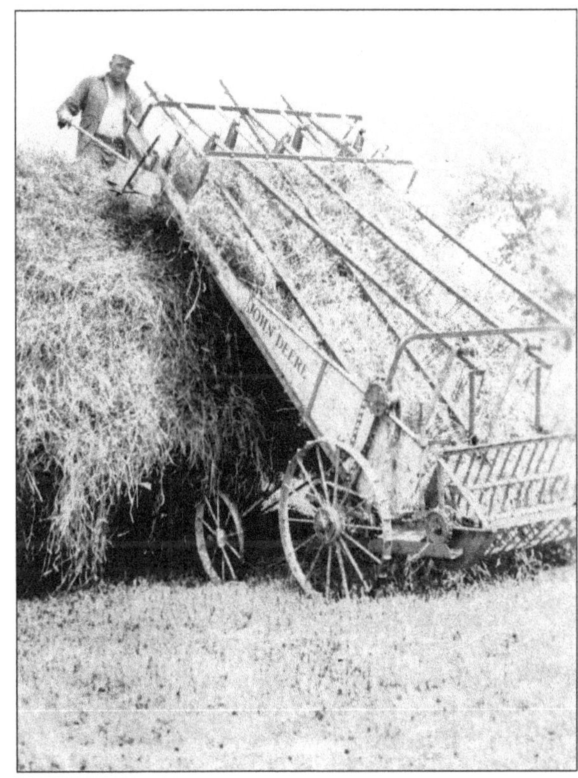

A HAY-LOADER, C. 1930. Finding an easier way to load hay on a wagon, the Krause farm purchased this John Deere hay loader for $175. Hay was mowed in the field, raked, and then put on the wagon using the loader. The wagon was taken to the barn, where it was unloaded using a large hayfork and horsepower, making the process less labor intensive. (Courtesy Claire Krause.)

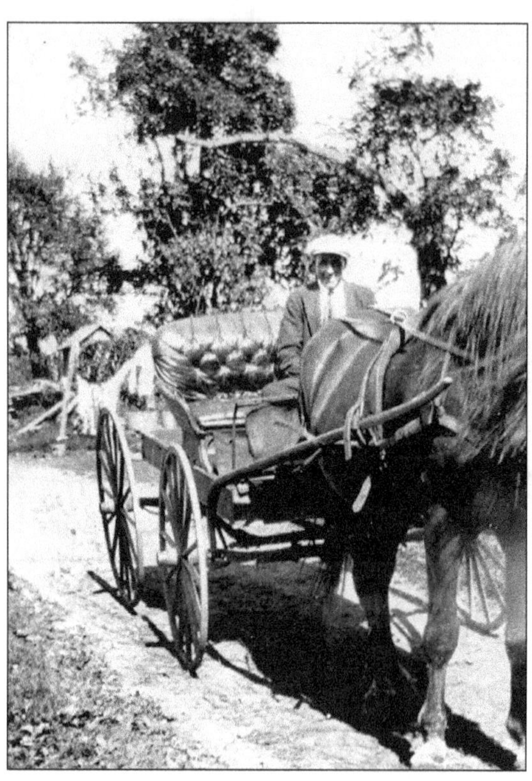

"Peas, Corn, Potatoes!" c. 1920. During the summer, Village Hill farmers sold their produce in the streets of Willimantic. Going door-to-door, hawking or "peddling" their wares, they sold homegrown fruits and vegetables by the quart for "5 cents, 10 cents, 25 cents," until all the items were sold. Here, Fred Krause goes to market on his special wagon led by Pete, his trusted horse. (Courtesy Claire Krause.)

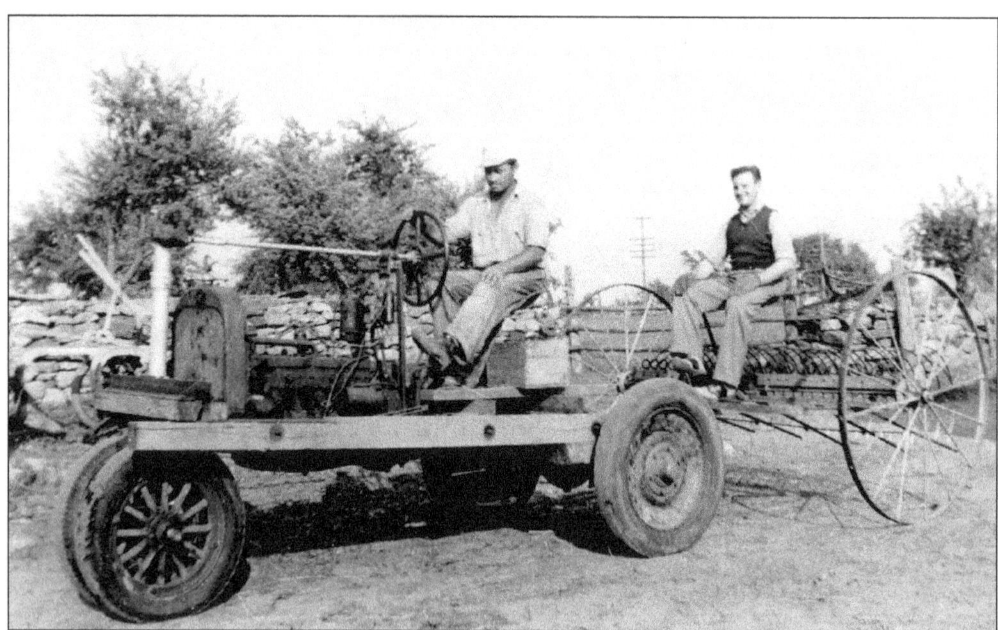

The Horseless Farm Machine, c. 1941. This homemade tractor, made up of spare car and truck parts on a three- by six-foot wooden frame, was used for pulling farm equipment. John Laibrandt, the driver, and Edward McSweeney, the hay-rake operator, prepare to rake the hay fields on the Laibrandt farm. These machines, sometimes called "Doodle Bugs," provided much pleasure for the farm family. (Courtesy Helen Bender.)

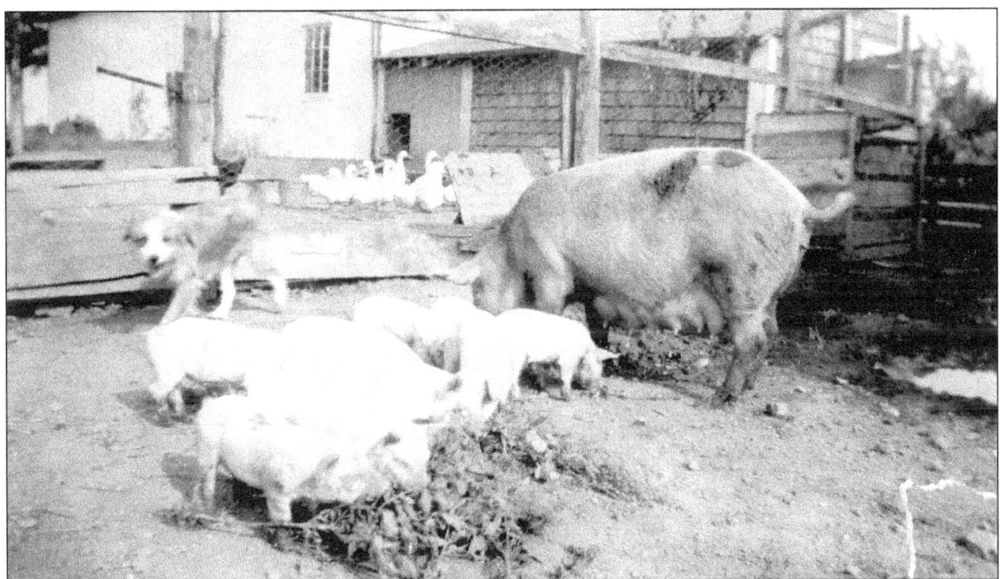

"And on This Farm There Was . . . " the Laibrandt Farm, c. 1940. A typical farm in Village Hill had cows, horses, pigs, ducks, chickens, and geese, which provided milk, eggs, meat, and fowl for the table. The farm dog helped to herd and guard the animals. Every household had a vegetable garden for personal consumption, and enterprising homemakers preserved enough food to last the family through the year. (Courtesy Helen Bender.)

A Pork Fest, the Laibrandt Farm, c. 1940. Every fall, when the weather turned cold, it was time to butcher the pigs for the family's winter food. In another cooperative effort with other "Village Hillers," the pigs were cut up into serving size (ham, bacon, and chops). Smaller pieces were ground up to make sausages, which were then smoked in the smokehouse; the fat was rendered to make lard. (Courtesy Helen Bender.)

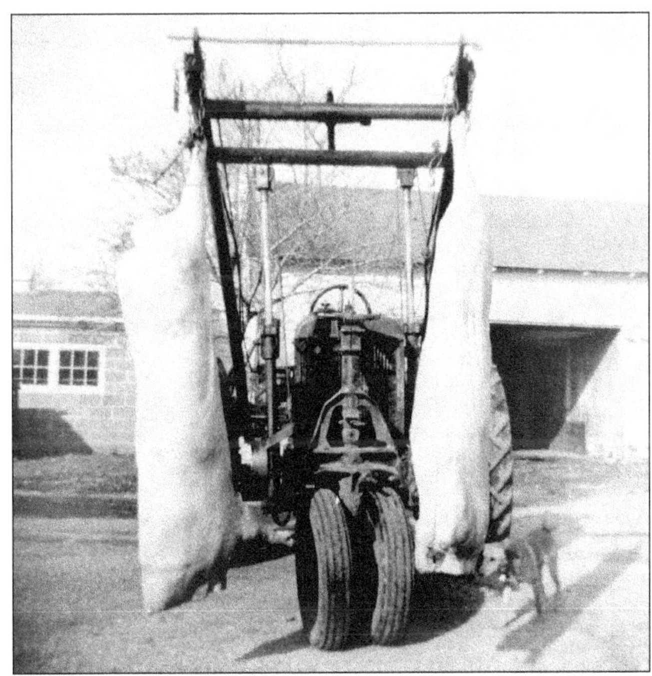

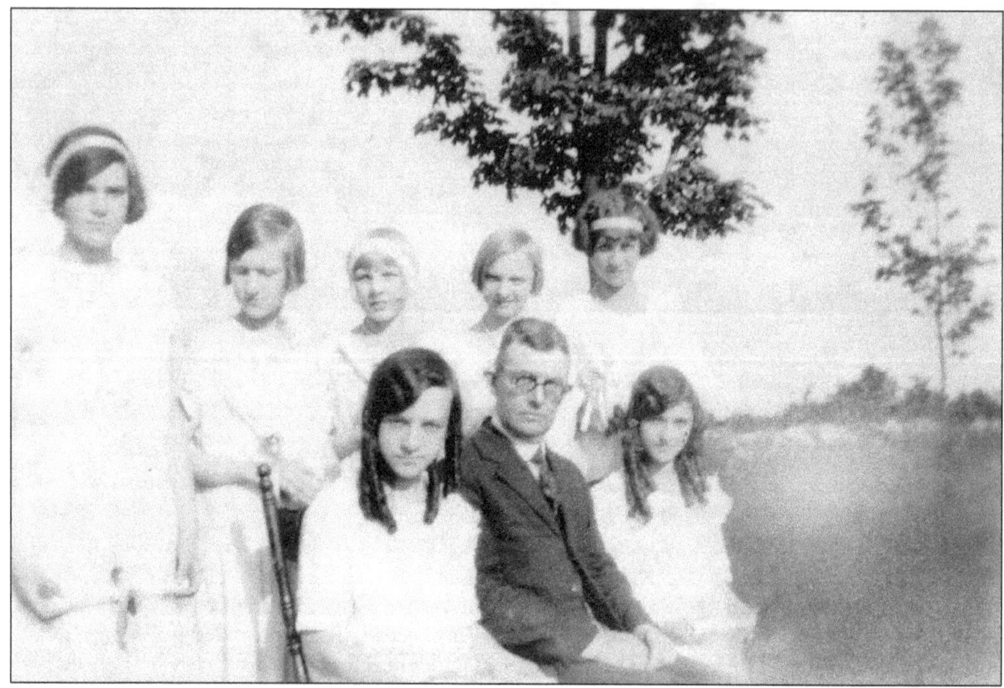

Grammar School Graduation, 1927. Graduations from the one-room schoolhouses were held at the Lyman Memorial High School in Lebanon. This photograph shows the eighth-grade girl graduates from the Village Hill School. Pictured, from left to right, are the following: (first row) Eleanor Schachinger, teacher George Briggs, and Martha Laibrandt; (second row) Lillian Fishbein, Florence Oden, Agnes Bergeson, Lillian Bergeson, and Wilma Krause. (Courtesy Claire Krause.)

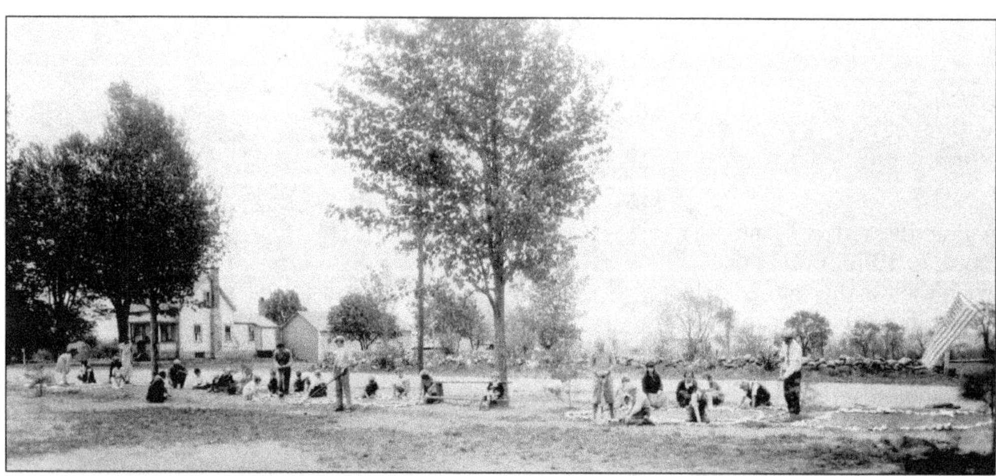

Arbor Day, the Village Hill School, 1935. Celebrating Arbor Day, students at the Village Hill School planted small flower gardens from seeds at the site of Village Hill Road. Seen here, from left to right, are Mildred Segal, Helen Wilhelm, Eleanor Wilhelm, Helen Bender, Lawrence Flegert, Eugene Brisson, Arthur Flegert, Helen Laibrandt, Arthur Ausburger, unidentified, Irene Carney, Edward Bender, Harry Flegert, Edward Bender, Edith Carney, Harriet Hinckley, Harold Wilhelm, and Armand Brisson. (Courtesy Helen Krause.)

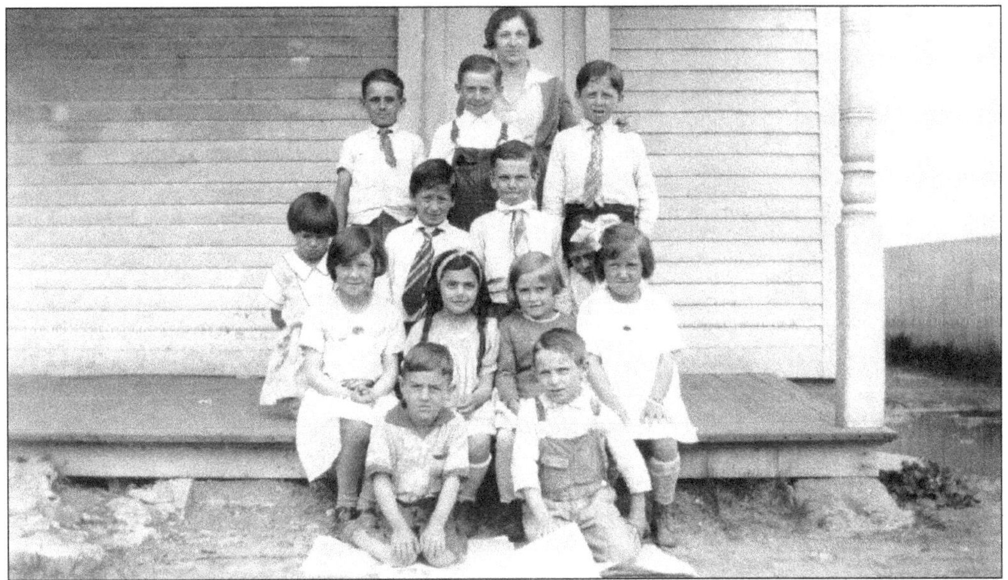

"School Days, School Days," 1931. Lower-grade students from Village Hill pose in front of the one-room schoolhouse with their teacher, Rose Gold (standing in the back row). Pictured, from left to right, are the following: (first row) Arthur Tanner and Otto Ausburger; (second row) Martha Stebner, Mildred Segal, Helen Laibrandt, and Mildred Schachinger; (third row) Pearl Wallace, Harold Wilhelm, Harold Krause, and George Wilhelm (behind Mildred); (fourth row) Ernest Brisson, Arthur Ausburger, and Philip Flegert. (Courtesy Helen Krause.)

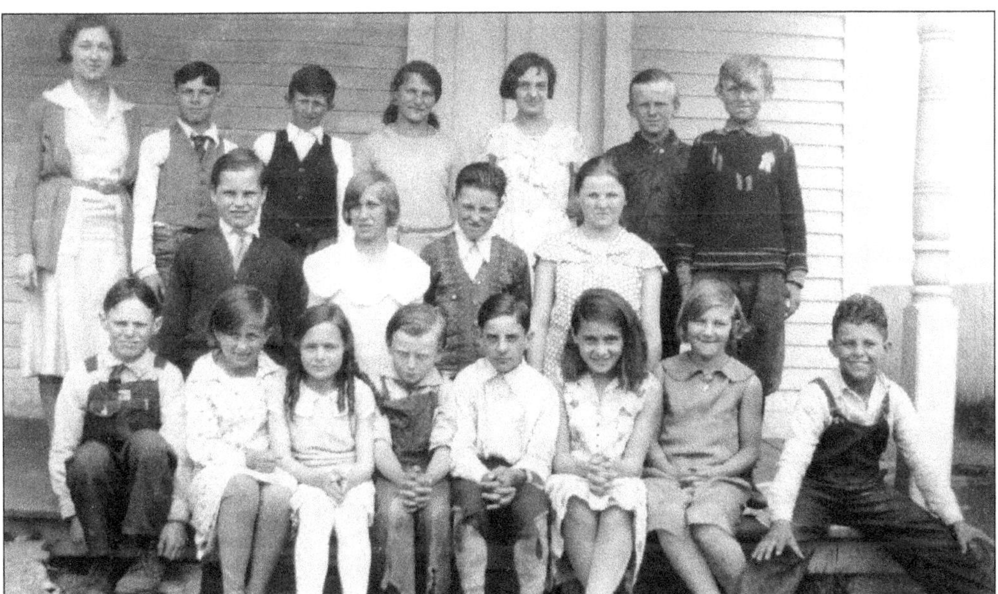

"The Three Rs," 1931. Upper-grade students from the Village Hill School appear with their teacher, Rose Gold. Shown, from left to right, are the following: (first row) Jacob Segal, Helen Wilhelm, Lena Segal, Arthur Flegert, Armand Brisson, Rose Kadupski, Helen Flegert, and Edward Wilhelm; (second row) Lawrence Flegert, Elsie Wilhelm, Arthur Stebner, and Edna Flegert; (third row) teacher Rose Gold, Philip Segal, Ewald Wilhelm, Jeanette Segal, Anna Brisson, Julius Flegert, and Arthur Bender. (Courtesy Helen Krause.)

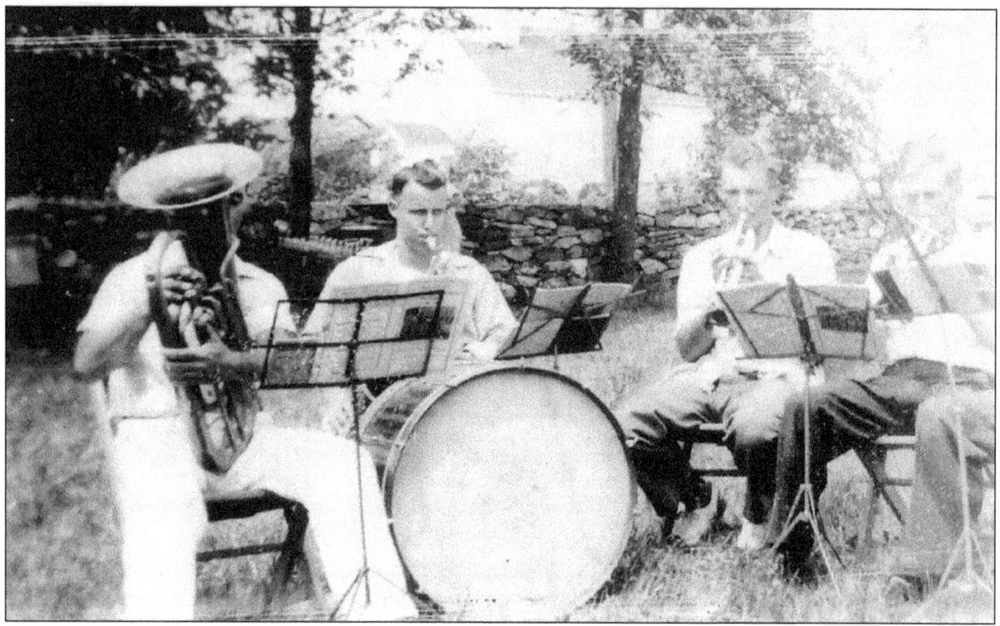

The Village Hill Band, c. 1945. The Village Hill Band played lively music for special occasions. Here, the band plays for the Fourth of July musical chairs game. Band members seen here are, from left to right, John Laibrandt (tuba and drums), R. Clinton Card (saxophone), Harry Cadow (trumpet), and Arthur Ausburger (trumpet). Absent is Arthur Bender (clarinet). (Courtesy Helen Bender.)

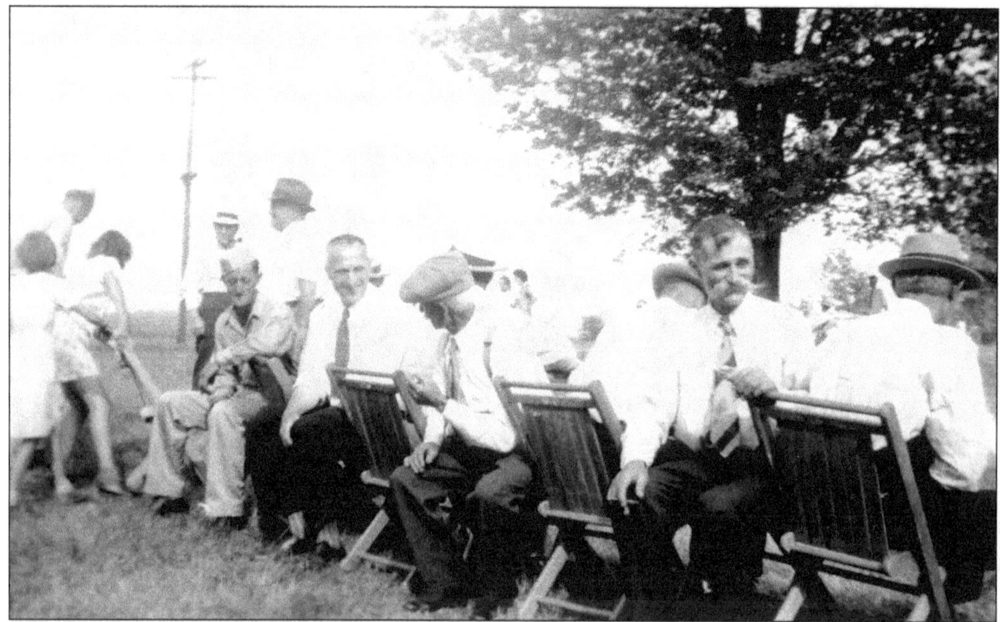

Music, Music, Music, c. 1945. The church picnic, initiated by the Ladies Aid Society, attracted many church members with delicious food offerings, including the all-time favorites—grinders and strawberry shortcake. Activities included children's games and races, musical chairs, an adult shoe-kick, and an afternoon softball game for all ages. This photograph shows the men of the church testing their skill in a game of musical chairs. (Courtesy Helen Bender.)

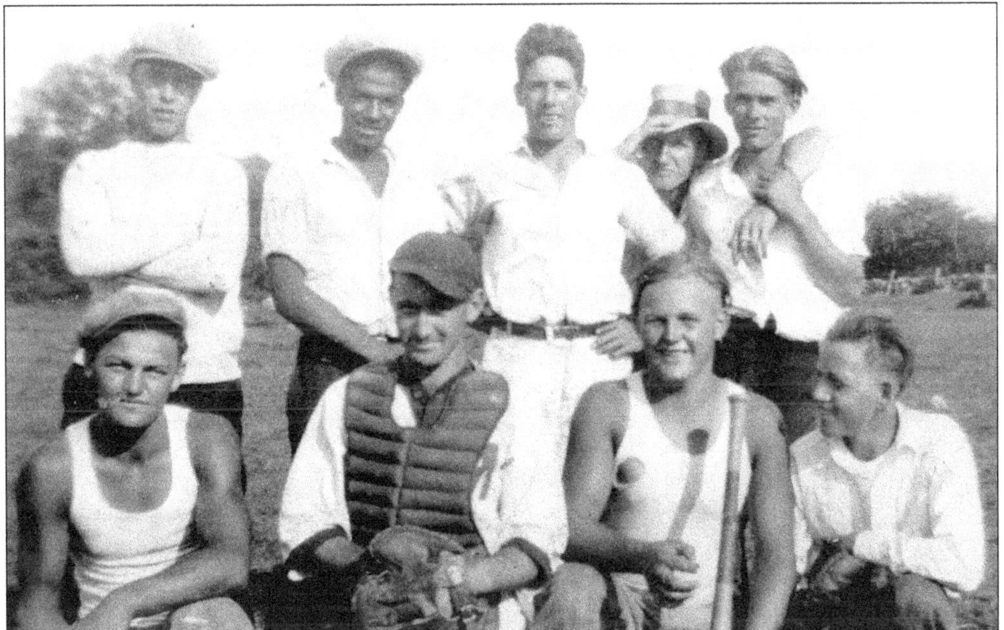

PLAY BALL, C. 1930. The Village Hill baseball team played teams from Eagleville, South Windham, Chestnut Hill, Columbia, and Lebanon. Playing each summer for about seven years, the team won many games and had a loyal following. Members pictured here, from left to right, are the following: (first row) Walter Bender, Frank Kadupski, Arnold Bender, and Arnold Krause; (second row) Leo Dubriel, Oscar Flippen, Ruby Segal, Edmund Krause, and John Kadupski. (Courtesy Marion Russo.)

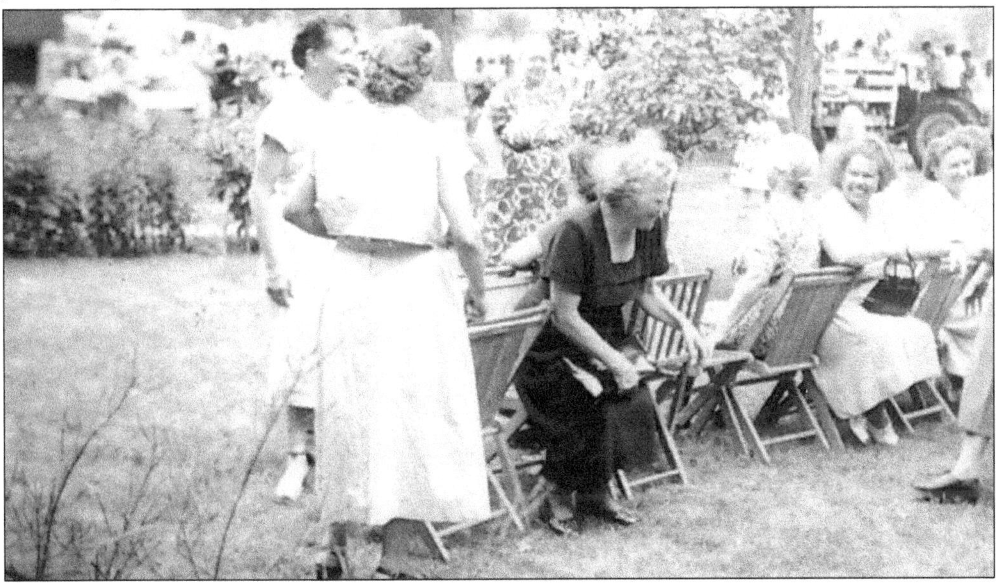

FUN ON THE FOURTH, C. 1940. The Fourth of July picnic was held on the Redeemer Lutheran Church lawn each year. Visitors and guests came annually from Boston and New York and occasionally from Michigan, Kansas, and Canada to enjoy the reunion of families and friends. Here, women enjoy a game of musical chairs. The tractor-driven hayride is visible in the background. (Courtesy Claire Krause.)

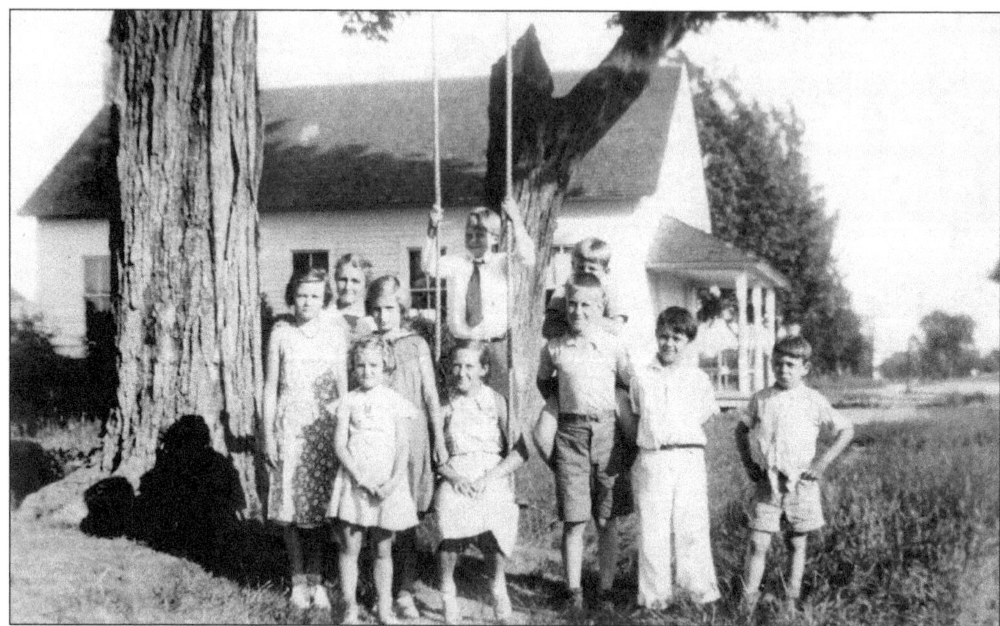

In the Good Old Summertime, c. 1935. The hanging of the rope swing on the maple tree near the school coincided with the New York City and Boston relatives' annual visit to Village Hill. Standing on the left of the swing are, from left to right, Helen Bender, Justina Bender, Irma Engelbrecht, and Claire Schachinger. On the swing are Edward Bender and Mildred Schachinger. To the right of the swing are Fred Schachinger, Arthur Engelbrecht, Harold Wilhelm, and Albert Wilhelm. (Courtesy Claire Krause.)

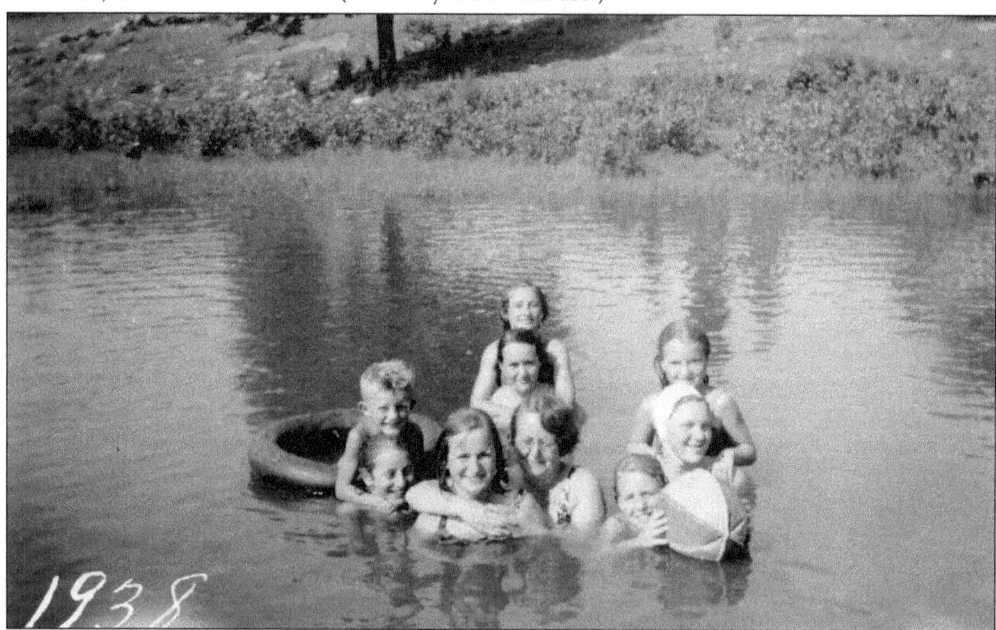

The Ol' Swimming Hole, Flegert's Pond, c. 1938. Every summer afternoon after chores, Village Hill children and their friends would have a refreshing swim in the pond. The younger swimmers used tire inner tubes to keep afloat. There was a diving board for the more adventurous. No summer day was complete without this dip in the water. (Courtesy Helen Krause.)

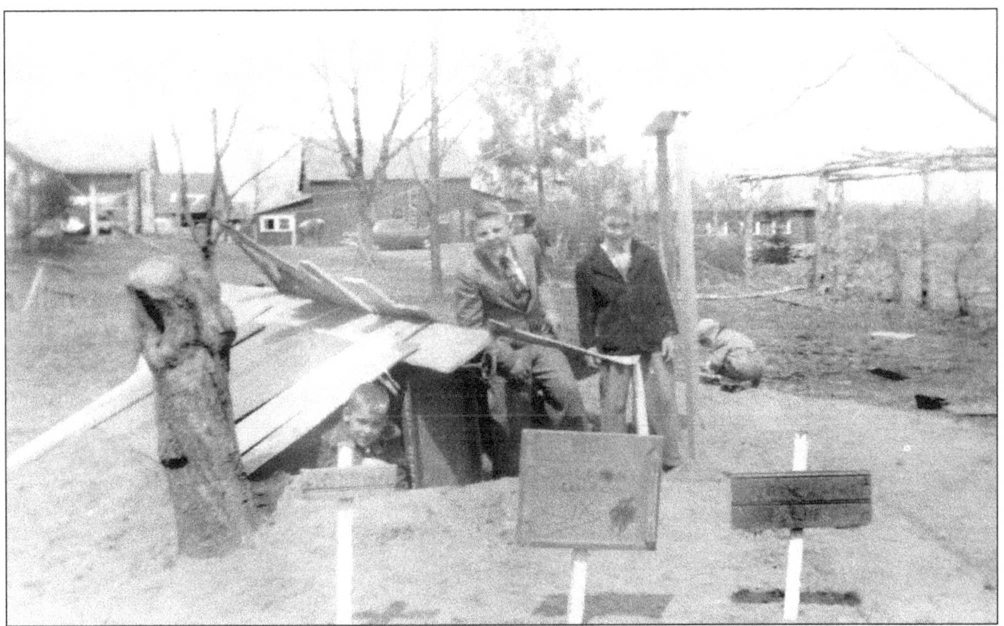

Farm Fun, c. 1950. Charles Bender, Billy Scar, Ronald Bender, and James Bender, seen here from left to right, play in a sand pile in Arthur Bender's backyard. In the background is the John Bender farm with its variety of buildings: barn, milk house, chicken house, smokehouse, pig house, icehouse, tool shed, and woodshed. (Courtesy Helen Bender.)

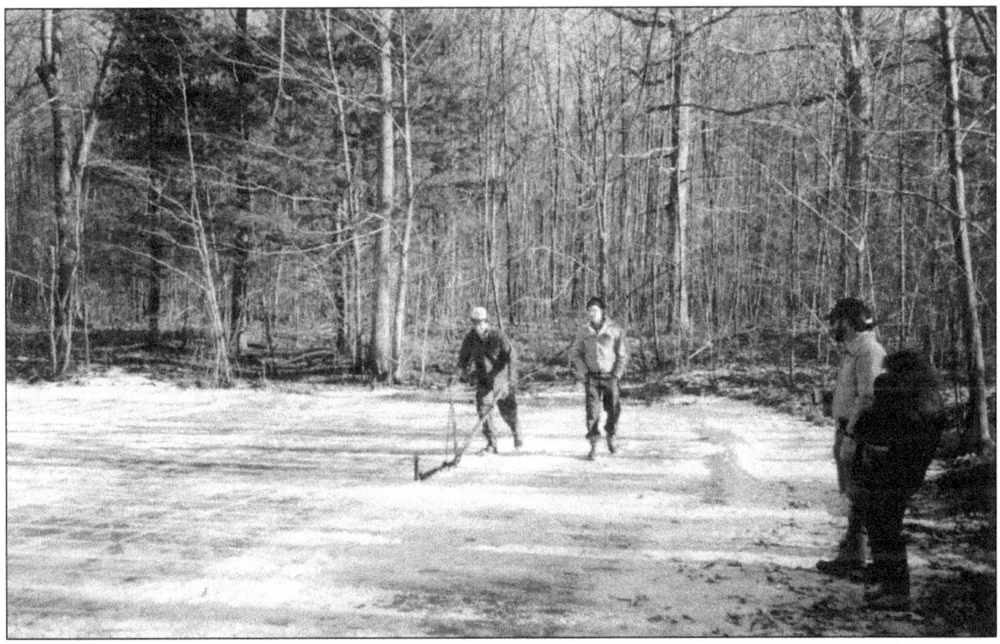

Marking Ice, the Laibrandt Farm, 1978. Ice cutting, a necessity for farms before the advent of refrigeration, was usually scheduled at the end of January, when the ice was thickest (about 8–10 inches). The ice had to be squared off using a special marker that scraped lines across the ice, as shown in this photograph. The Bender family organized this ice-cutting reenactment. (Courtesy Helen Bender.)

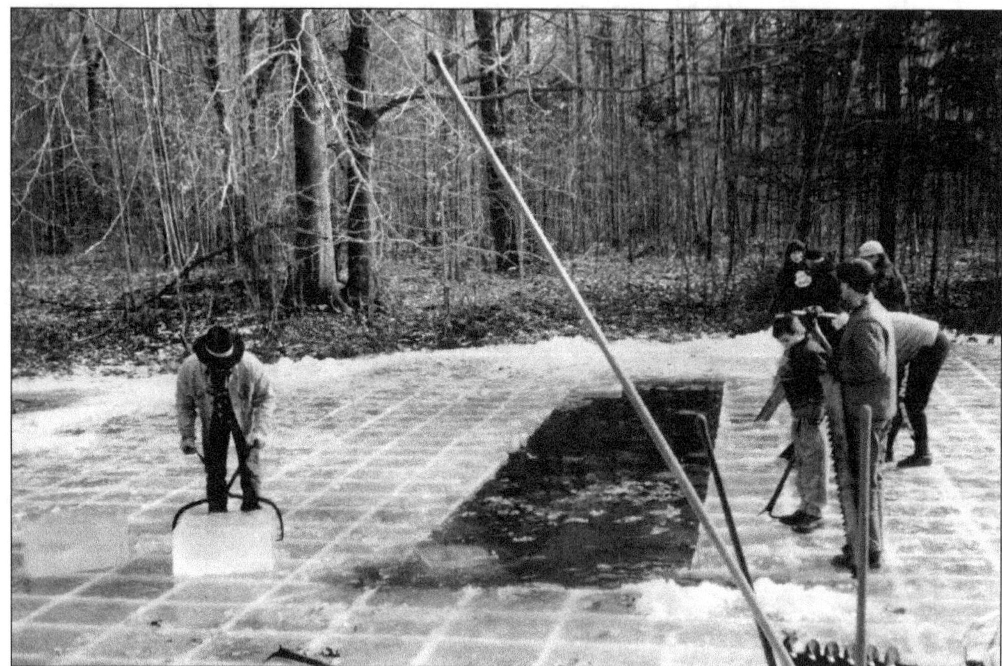

Cutting Ice, the Laibrandt Farm, 1978. Ice was cut about 6 to 12 inches deep and sawed into square blocks. Ice tongs and ice picks were used to pick up the blocks and load them onto a wagon. The blocks were then unloaded in the ice house, where they were covered with sawdust and stacked carefully in order to last through the summer months. (Courtesy Helen Bender.)

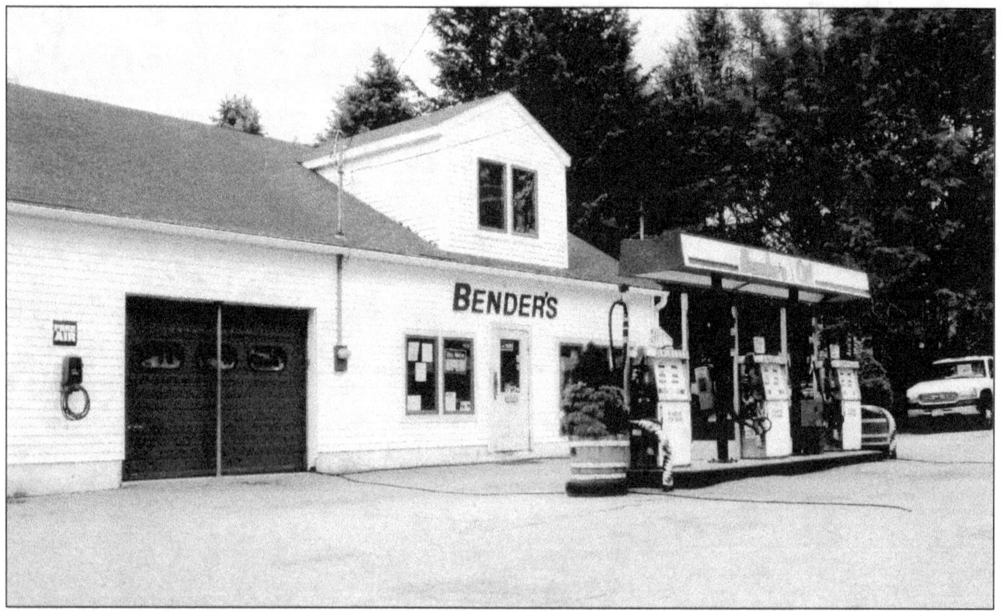

Bender's Oil Service, 2004. In 1947, Arnold Bender opened the first locally owned and operated fuel-oil business. Starting with one truck, he gradually built up the business. At first, the gas station included a small convenience store. Later, it was a used-car business as well as an automobile parts and repair shop. In 1959, Arnold's brother Arthur joined him, and the partnership became mainly a fuel-oil business, as it is now. (Courtesy Helen Bender.)

Six

School Bells

The Puritan ethic of early town settlers placed a strong emphasis on education and learning. Children were taught at home and then at local primary schools. Ministers usually tutored the boys who wanted to go on to higher education.

The earliest record found of a school dates from 1717, when the town voted to set up two schools. The following year, the town approved several more schools in outlying districts. There is no record of where these schools were located, but they would have been primary schools. Jeremiah Mason, born in 1768, grew up in the Goshen neighborhood and recalled in his memoirs that there was no school building in his district when he was a child. School was held in a room in a private home in the winter months.

The "country money," the contribution the Colonial legislature made to operate the schools, supplied most of the money for their operation. Local school taxes were negligible for much of the 18th century. The ecclesiastical societies were in charge of the schools from 1712 to 1795.

The Tisdale School, founded by Jonathan Trumbull and several townspeople, was built on the site of the present town hall in 1743. It provided a quality education for tuition-paying students. The school became known by the name of its master, Nathan Tisdale, who started teaching at the school in 1749. Tisdale taught the standard classical curriculum and added courses in surveying and navigation. Most of the students were boys.

In the North Society, Eleazar Wheelock conducted a school for college-bound boys in his home. In 1754, he opened a school for American Indian children, whom he hoped to train as missionaries. It was called Moor's Indian Charity School, named after the benefactor who donated land and a building. Joseph Brant, the celebrated Mohawk Indian chief, attended the school as a youth.

Towns were allowed to establish local school districts within the societies beginning in the late 1790s. Neighboring families could join together, agree to build a school, hire a teacher, and tax themselves to pay the cost. District committees were set up to oversee the schools, prompting the beginning of the 16 school districts in Lebanon during the early 19th century.

The one-room schools each had a wood stove and an outdoor privy. There was no standard curriculum and no standard term calendar. Students ranged in age from 4 to 20 years old. Teachers boarded with families in the district and displayed wide variations in teaching quality. There was never enough money, either from district taxes or the state school fund, to properly fund teacher salaries and provide adequate supplies. In spite of these deficiencies, the one-room schools provided basic skills in reading, writing, and arithmetic, which served their students well.

It was not until 1909 that the state abolished the independent school districts and set them under a town school committee. In 1910, the local districts deeded their properties to the town. A few schools were closed for economy. In 1919, the number of schools was reduced from 14 to 9. Final consolidation of the one-room schools had to wait until 1936, when a federal grant enabled the town to build the central elementary school on Route 207.

In the meantime, Lebanon finally opened its first high school in 1922. Prior to that time, students wanting a high-school education had to travel to Colchester, Norwich, or Willimantic.

In 1920, the town received a large bequest to build a high school from the estate of George W. Lyman, who had no children. The construction fund was augmented by town appropriations, and the first high school was opened in 1922. In accordance with a clause in Lyman's will, the school was named after him. Now at its third location, the Lyman Memorial High School still carries the name of the man who left his fortune to benefit the town's children.

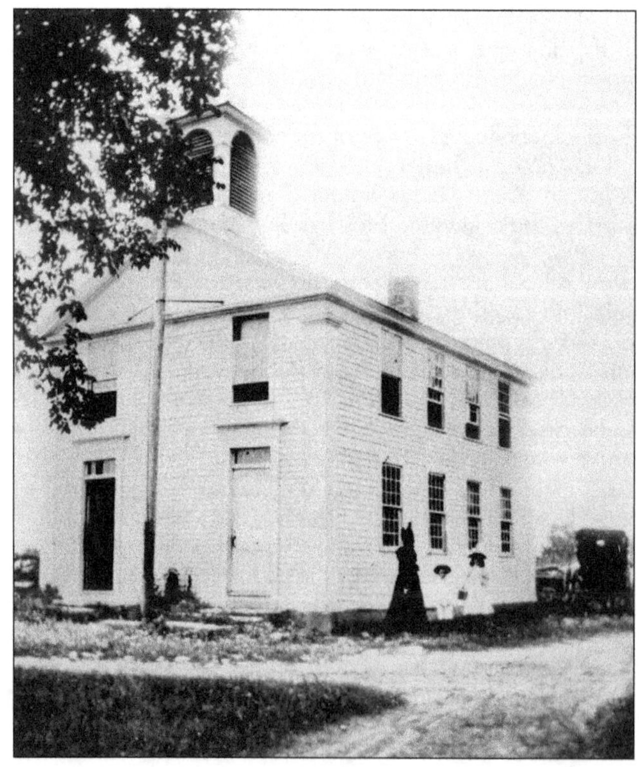

The Old Goshen School. The Goshen Hill Schoolhouse, shown here in 1898, at one time housed a "select school" called the Goshen Academy in an upper room. Students paid private tuition to attend and took coursework beyond the elementary-school level, but it was not a true high school. The Goshen School was torn down after years of abandonment. (Courtesy LHS.)

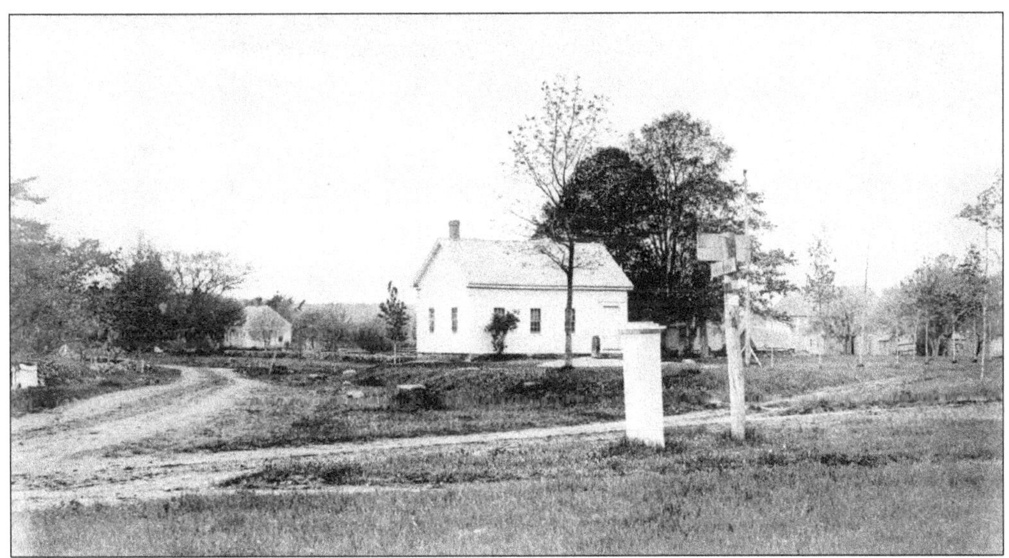

School No. 5. This school was located at the junction of Routes 87 and 289, on a small triangle of land with dirt roads around all sides. In the 1930s, the state rebuilt the corner, closing the road behind the school and reducing the frontage. The school has been moved, but the town still owns the small parcel in front of the house. This photograph was taken *c.* 1904. (Courtesy Robert Slate.)

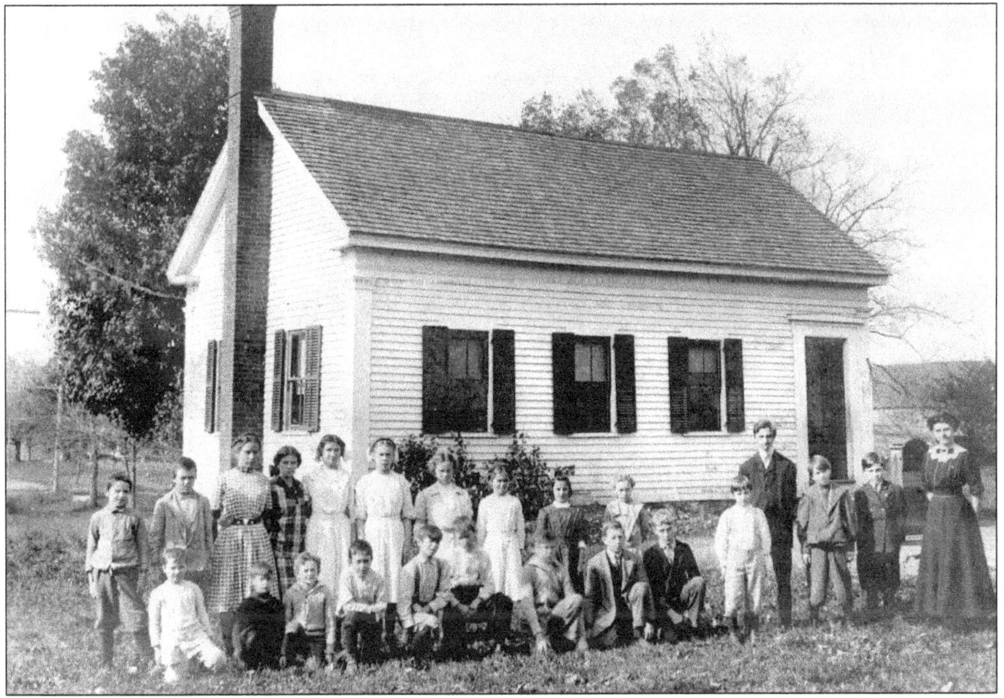

The Children of School No. 5. This photograph, taken after 1904, displays how the chimney was moved to the side of the building. When the one-room schools were consolidated in 1936, the building was sold to the adjacent landowner. The land under the school, however, was owned by the town, and no improvements could be made. The building was eventually moved to Chappell Road, where it is now a residence. (Courtesy LHS.)

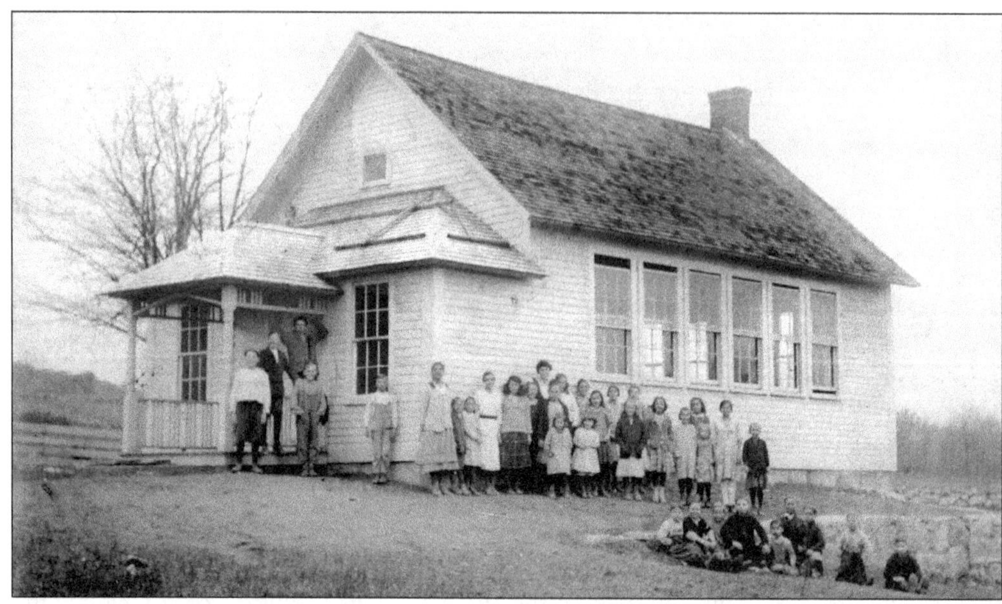

SCHOOL NO. 9. Located along a curve on Waterman Road, this school was near the Hayward Rubber Company's mill on the Yantic River. Many of the children of the Irish immigrants who worked in the mill attended this school. When the state reconstructed Route 2, a new section of Waterman Road was built to form a straighter intersection at the highway bridge approach. The old street is now an extension of McGrath Lane, where the school was converted to a residence. (Courtesy LHS.)

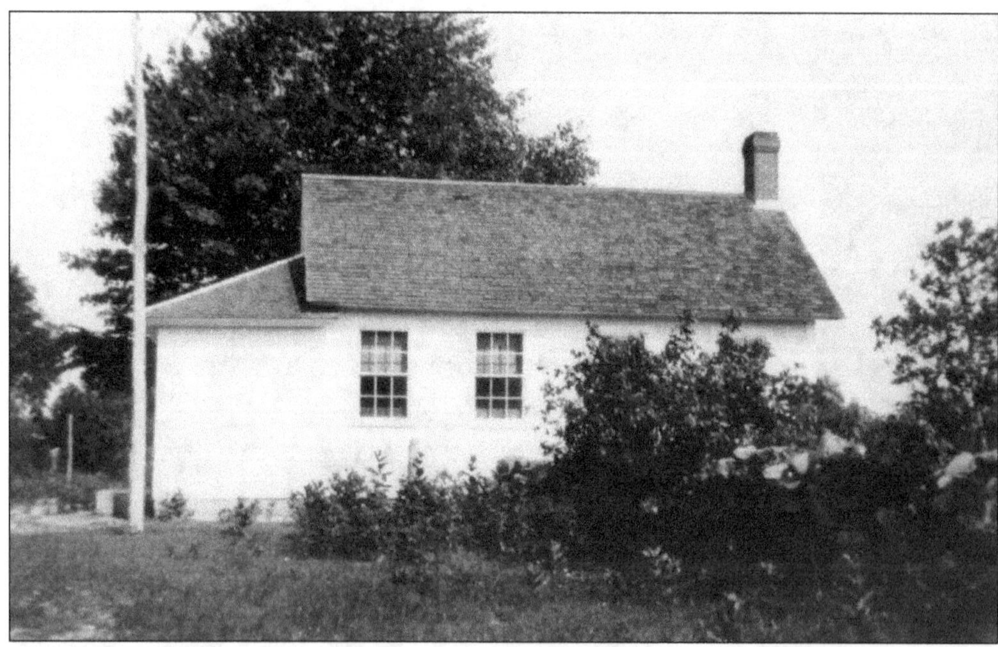

SCHOOL NO. 16. This school was located on Tobacco Street at the corner of Clarke Road. This 1914 photograph, taken by teacher Georgia Robinson, shows a side view of the building and includes the flagpole. (Courtesy LHS.)

THE CENTER SCHOOL. School No. 6 was in the town center, between the First Congregational Church and the corner store. In 1937, after the new elementary school had opened, it became the town library. The town purchased the parcel in 1966 and demolished the store to build a new library. When the new library was completed, the old school was torn down and the brick walkway and the Trumbull monument were installed. (Courtesy Ed Tollmann.)

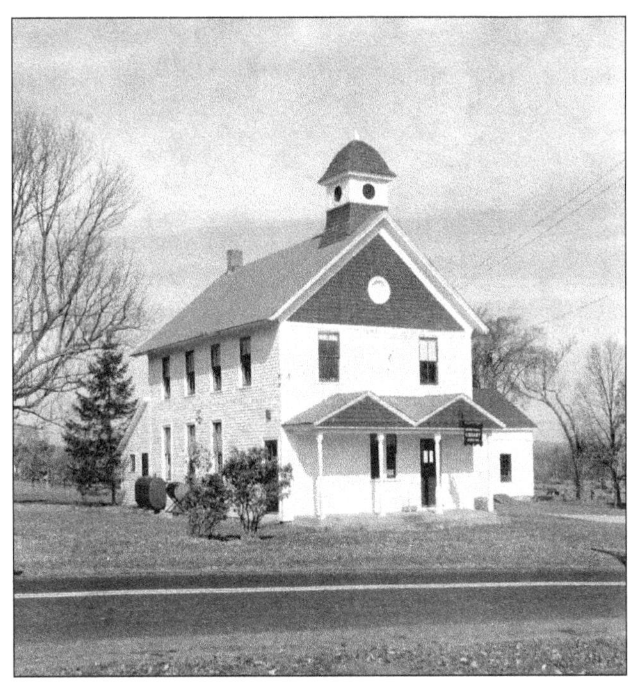

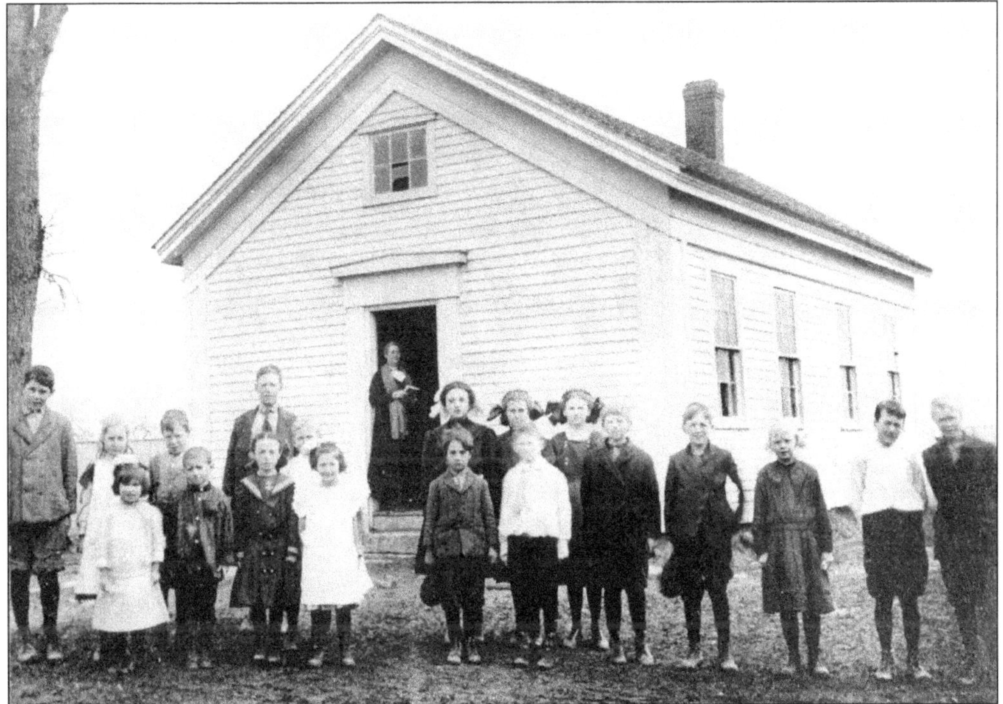

THE OLD VILLAGE HILL SCHOOL. This photograph of School No. 1 was taken *c.* 1900. Nineteen students appear in front of the school; the teacher is in the doorway. The school burned in 1918 and was replaced in 1919. That building, later sold to the Lutheran Church, was severely damaged in the 1938 hurricane. The scrap wood was saved and used in constructing the church. (Courtesy Helen Krause.)

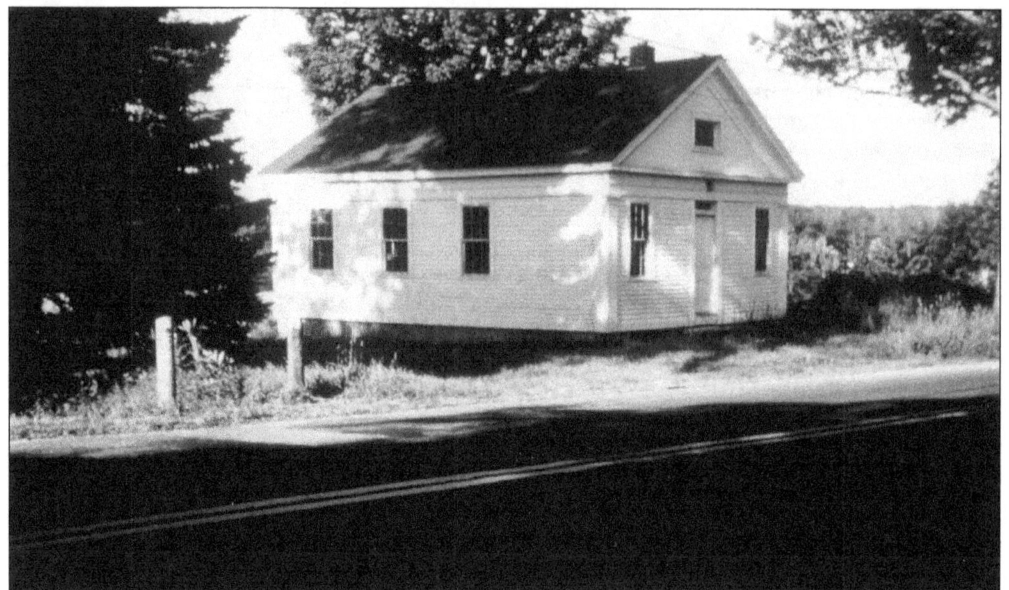

School No. 13. Located on Route 207 across from the intersection with Clubhouse Road, this building is now a private residence. When the schools were consolidated in 1936, a number of the old schoolhouses were sold and converted into dwellings. (Courtesy LHS.)

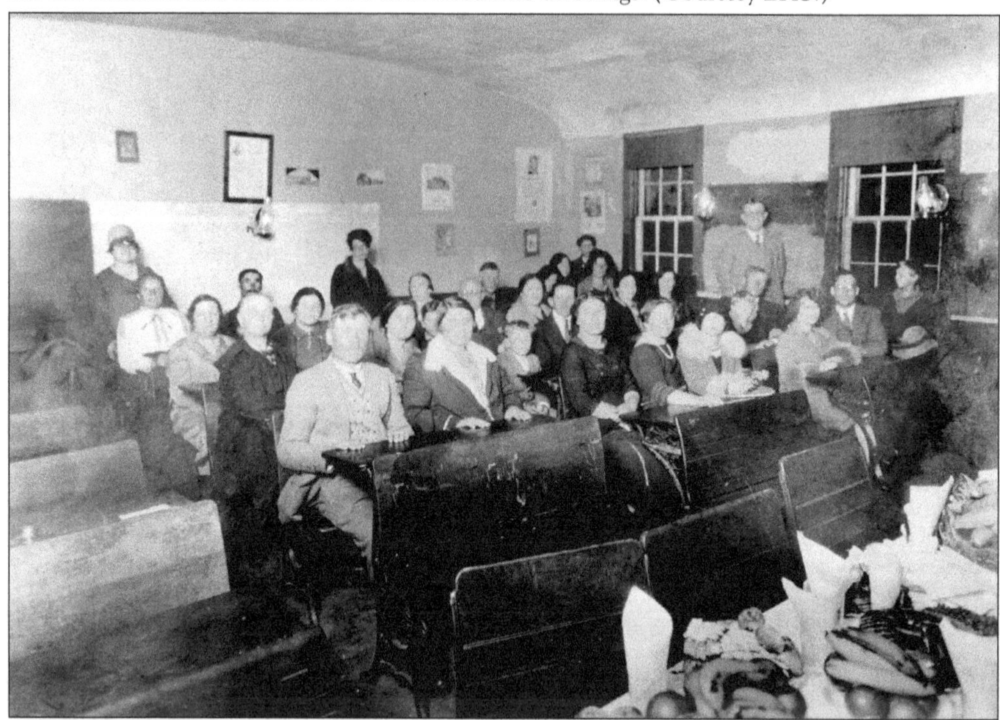

An Adult Class. In 1928, 22 immigrants who had moved to Lebanon to farm petitioned for a night school, where they could learn more about farming and where those who were foreign-born could study the English language. Many had heavy mortgages and needed to learn modern farming techniques in order to prosper. The adult school was set up in School No. 13 and proved very successful. Here, a night school class graduates, probably in 1929. (Courtesy LHS.)

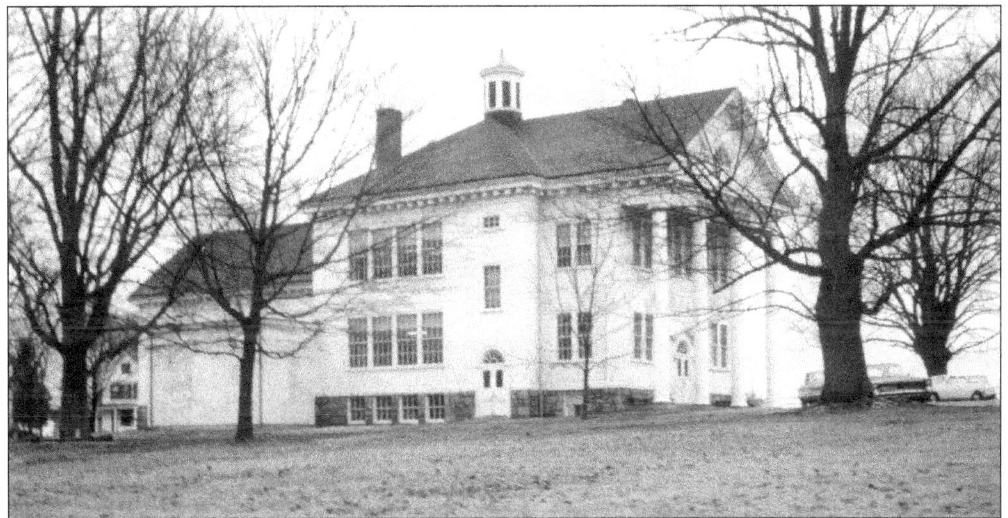

The First Lyman Memorial High School. In 1920, George W. Lyman left the town a generous bequest toward a high school; town appropriations supplemented those funds. To make room for the school, the old town hall was moved across Route 207 to a site north of the present library. The school opened in September 1922. After a combined junior-senior high school was built in 1958–1959, town offices were eventually moved into this building. (Courtesy LHS.)

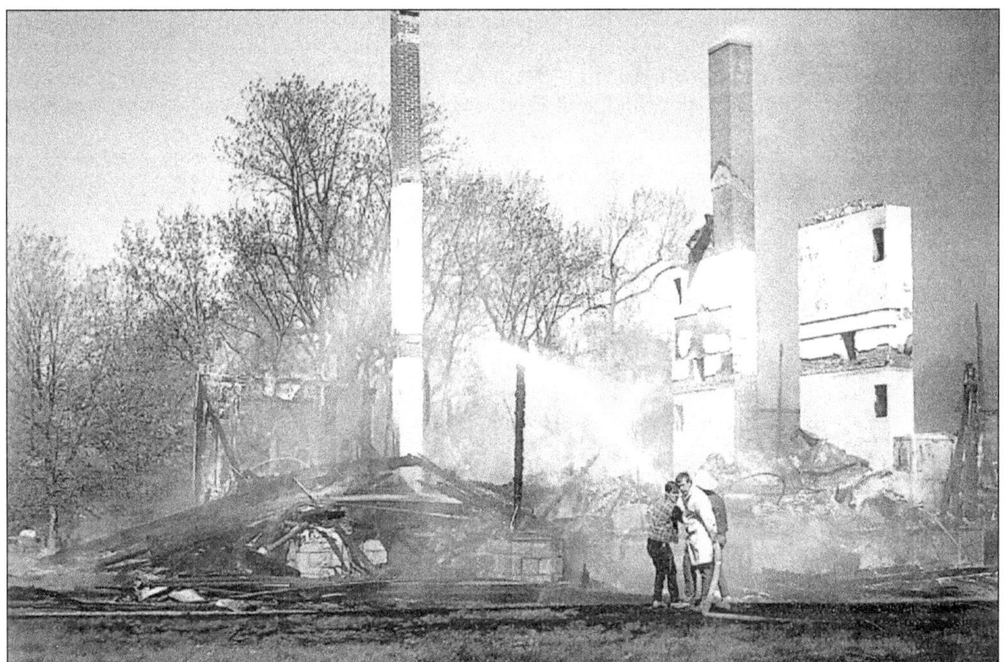

Town Hall Destroyed. For a time, the old high school housed an overflow of elementary school children until a new addition to the elementary school was built. A fire-proof vault was then installed in the high school, and town offices were moved from officials' homes to the high school building. On May 7, 1968, a spectacular fire leveled the structure. Many records were lost, but the town's land records and the town clerk's records were saved, as they were in the vault. (Courtesy LHS.)

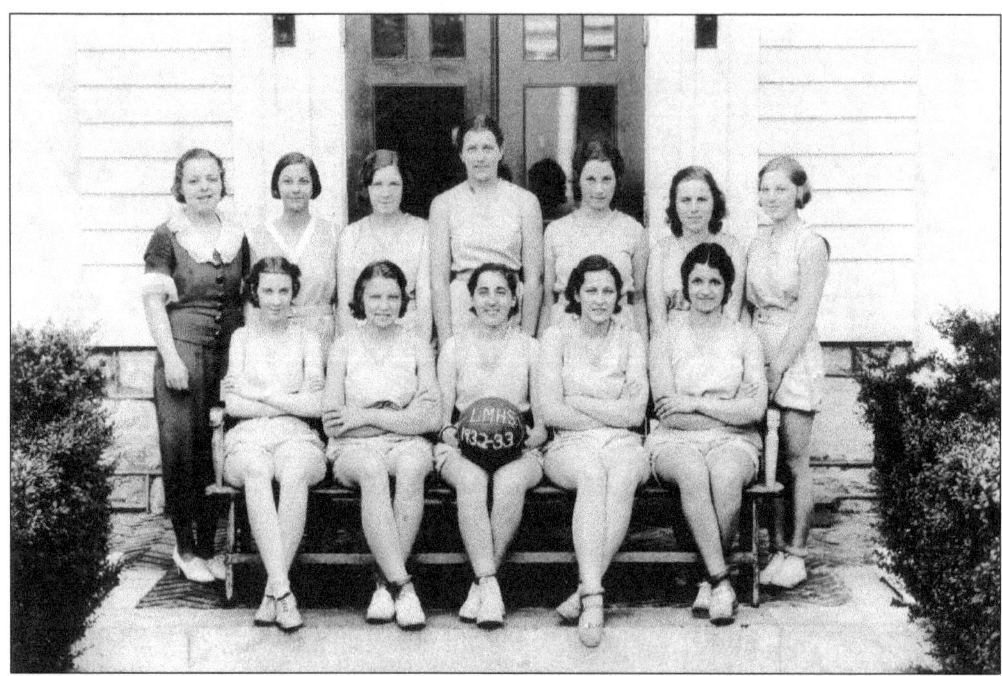

The First Girls' Basketball Team. Girls were able to participate in a formerly all-male sport when they organized a basketball team in 1931. Teacher Rima Campo was their coach. Pictured, from left to right, are the following: (first row) Edith (Jones) Burgess, Elsie (Lamonte) Ferry, Hazel (Cummings) Sweet, Fannie Weronik, and Mary (Marasculo) Brewster; (second row) Coach Rima Campo, Delphine Ladd, Phyllis (Hoxie) Bartizek, Olive (Cox) Brown, Rose Cohen, Olga Schweitzer, and Sophia (Horiska) Dziadul. (Courtesy LHS.)

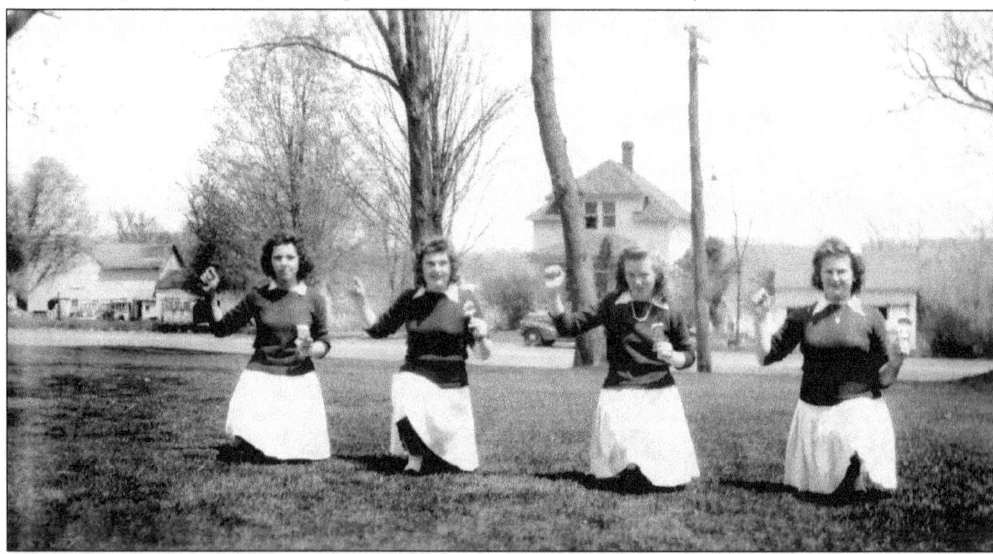

The First Cheerleaders. These four young women were the first cheerleaders at the Lyman Memorial High School. Organized in 1946, the cheerleaders were, from left to right, Burtis Blakeslee, Jonica Grabber, Cynthia Clarke, and Gloria Petrofsky. They wore red sweaters and white skirts. This photograph was taken on the lawn on the east side of the old high school. (Courtesy Gloria Bigenski.)

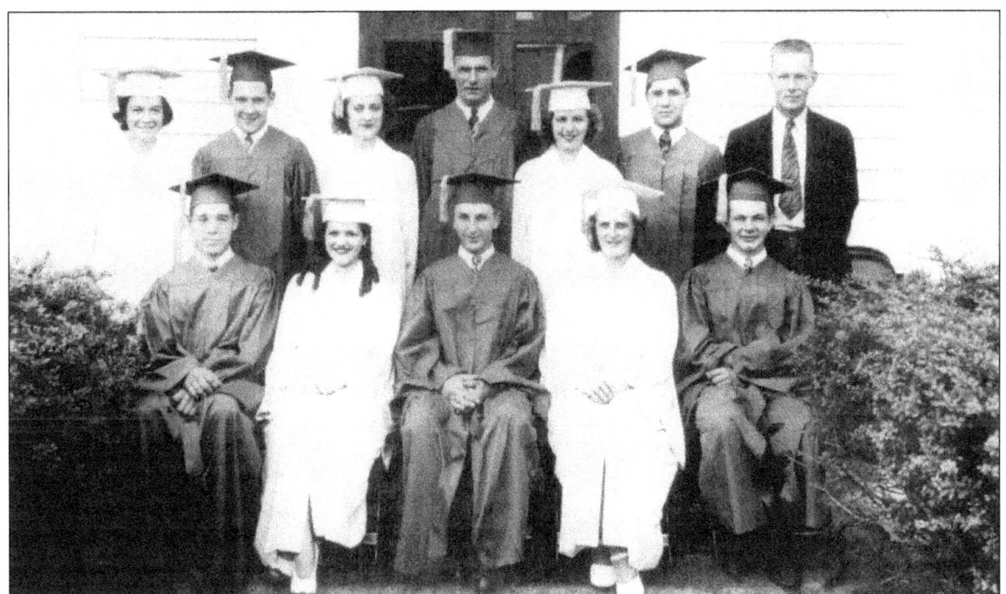

The Smallest Graduating Class. With only 11 members, the Lyman Memorial High School Class of 1944 was the school's smallest. Pictured, from left to right, are the following: (first row) Wallace Blakeslee Jr., Ethel (Chalifoux) Fontaine, Walter Dziadul, Michaeline Watras, and Lyndon Briggs; (second row) Gladys (Kneeland) Wright, Oliver Manning, Katherine (Kelley) Malone, William Wasylishyn, Helen (Plonowsky) Walsh, Joseph Sanzone, and Principal E. Fenn Nourse. (Courtesy LHS.)

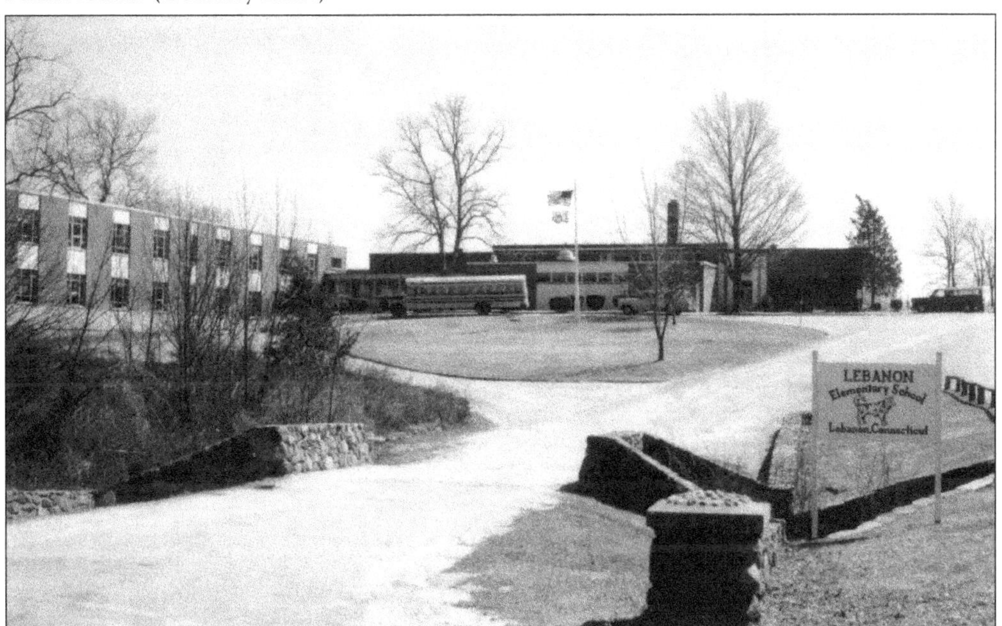

The Lebanon Elementary School. In 1936, the one-room schools were consolidated into a central elementary school on Route 207 with the aid of a federal grant. A 1937 report noted that the children no longer had to go outside to use toilet facilities or to get water from wells! This 1980s photograph shows some of the additions necessitated by the growing population. Voters approved yet another expansion in February 2004. (Courtesy LHS.)

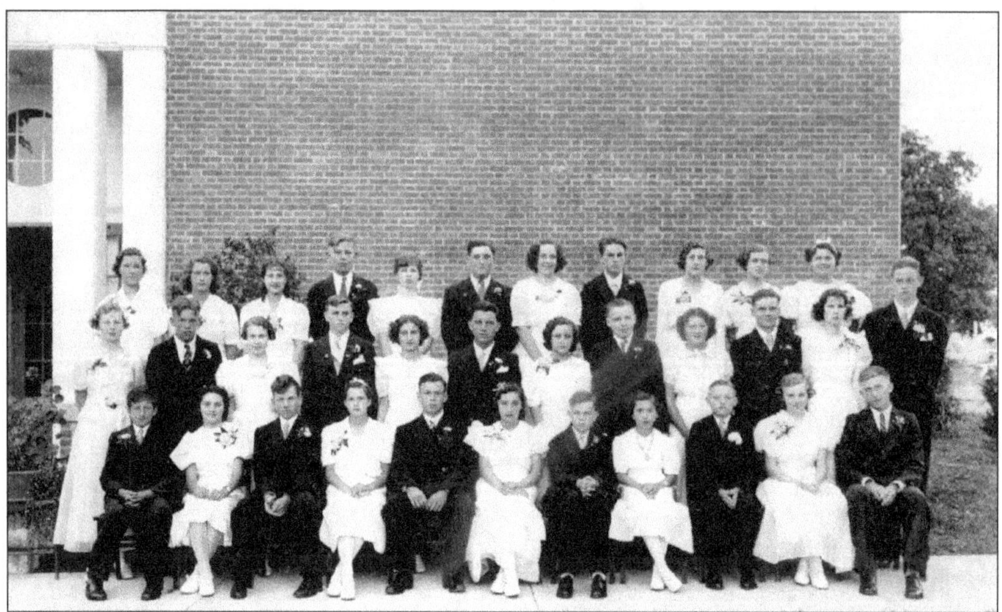

The First Graduates. In June 1937, 34 children graduated from the eighth grade in the new Lebanon Elementary School. The graduates ranged in age from 12 to 16 years—remember, they were coming from the one-room school system, which had a wide variation in grade levels. On the list of occupations for their fathers, all but two are recorded as farmers, an indication of how rural Lebanon was at that time. (Courtesy Harold Krause.)

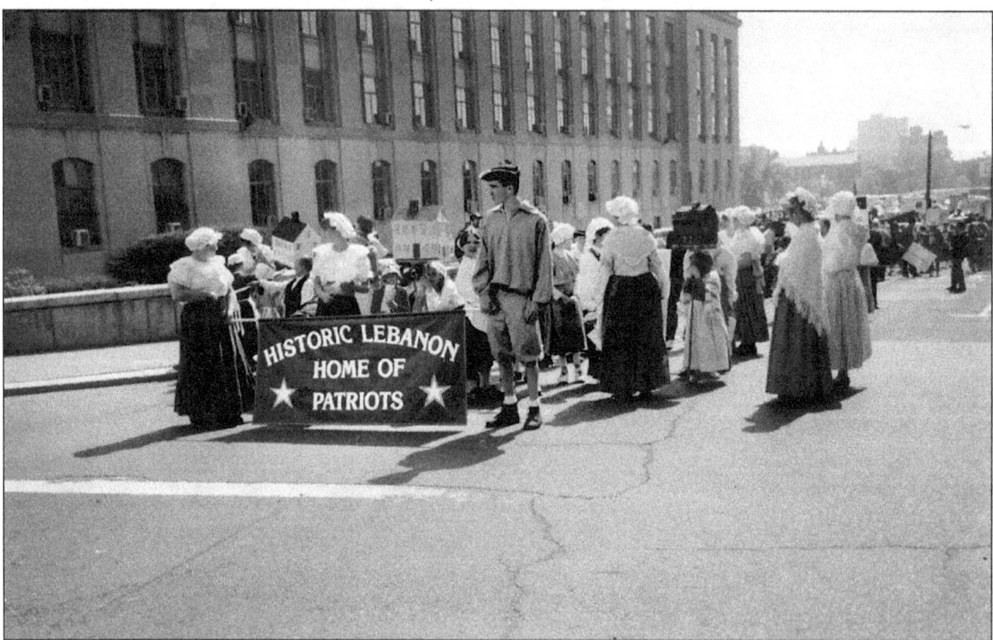

A Hartford Parade. Teachers and students from Lebanon public schools marched in the state parade celebrating the New Old State House on May 11, 1996. The theme was "Historic Lebanon, Home of Patriots." Fourth-graders designed models of five historic buildings to carry. They were backed up by high school band and chorus members as they marched to the song *We're Proud to Come from Lebanon*. (Courtesy LHS.)

Seven

Lebanon in World War II

On December 7, 1941, the Japanese bombed Pearl Harbor. Germany and Italy declared war on the United States on December 11. Our country was at war and quickly mobilized. In Lebanon, a farming town of only 1,467 residents, at least 146 young men and women served in the armed forces. They served on land and sea and in the air, from Europe to Africa to the Pacific Islands and China. Seven lost their lives. Many were wounded or missing in action until located in prisoner-of-war camps.

Those who remained at home served the war effort in other ways. Many residents held defense jobs, labored to increase farm output without extra hands, and volunteered as air-raid wardens and aircraft spotters.

To tell their story, Ed Tollmann planned a small exhibit of his World War II memorabilia with the Lebanon Historical Society. The idea grew, as families and veterans added enough material to fill an entire exhibition room.

The exhibit, From Home Front to Battlefield: Lebanon in World War II, opened after the town's annual Memorial Day parade in 2001. Originally scheduled to be open for a year, the exhibit was not closed until December 7, 2003. It touched the hearts of all who saw it. The walls were covered with photographs of young Lebanon soldiers, fresh-faced in their uniforms. Their going-away parties, wartime weddings, and visits home were all chronicled. Their medals, Purple Hearts, Bronze Stars—even their old uniforms—were there. The flag presented to the family of Anthony Musial, who lost his life, was there. So was the bullet-holed helmet worn by Ewald Wilhelm when he was wounded in Italy

The home-front story was told, too. Ration books, civil defense identification cards, photographs, faded newspaper clippings, and artifacts such as a "victory" bike were found. Most touching were the letters from loved ones in the service.

All these things had been put away and saved for over 50 years. The story of how the war affected all of Lebanon was there.

This chapter provides an overview of the World War II exhibit. It also highlights how Lebanon has remembered and paid tribute to all her veterans over the years.

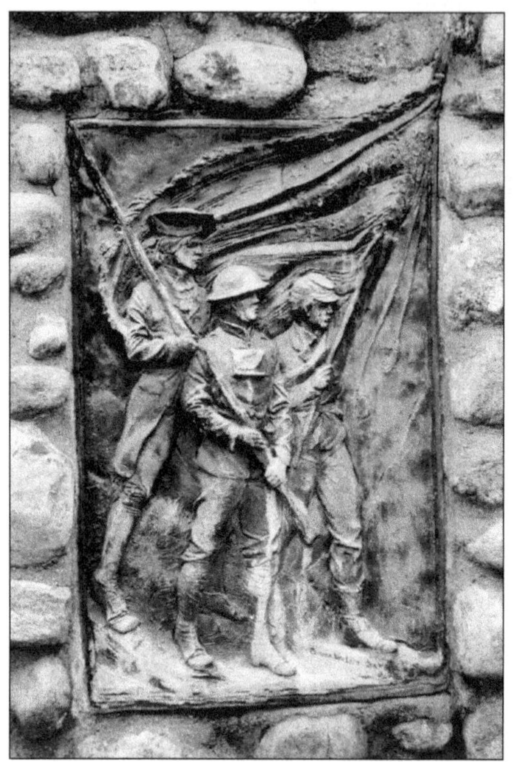

The Flagpole Monument. The flagpole in front of town hall was erected in 1923 and was the first war memorial in town. On a bronze plaque is a composite of three soldiers, each one representing a different war: the American Revolution, the Civil War, and World War I. The plaque was created by Bruce Wilder Saville, a famous sculptor of that period. The monument symbolizes Lebanon's honor and respect for those who had served up to that time. (Courtesy LHS.)

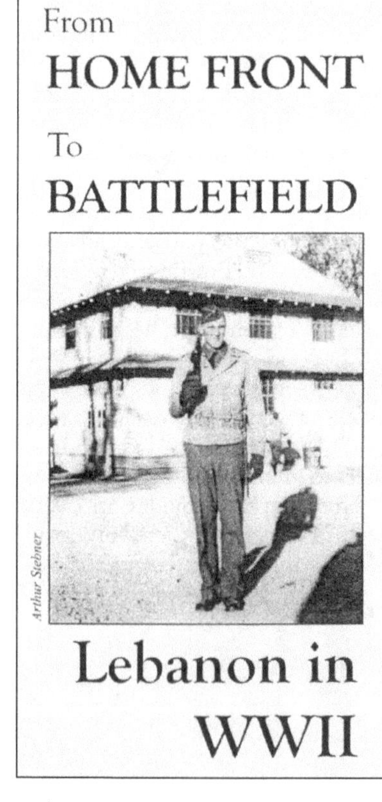

The Exhibition Opens. All Lebanon veterans and their families were invited to a special reception and preview before the public opening of the exhibition From Home Front to Battlefield: Lebanon in World War II. Members of American Legion Post 180 of Lebanon were the color guard. The cover of the program featured a photograph of Arthur Stebner during World War II. Stebner was a past commander of the post. (Courtesy LHS.)

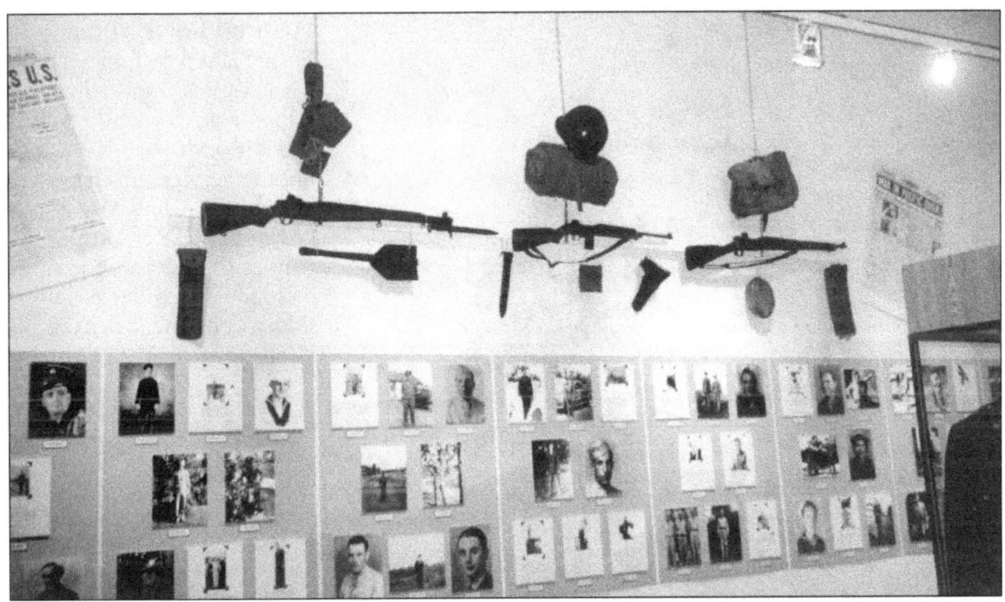

The Wall of Honor. Photographs of young Lebanon servicemen and servicewomen in uniform lined one wall of the exhibition. Of the more than 146 people who served, 77 left wartime photographs that were located. Above the photographs were some of the many artifacts collected. The front pages of local newspapers featuring war news were enlarged and added to the wall display. (Courtesy LHS.)

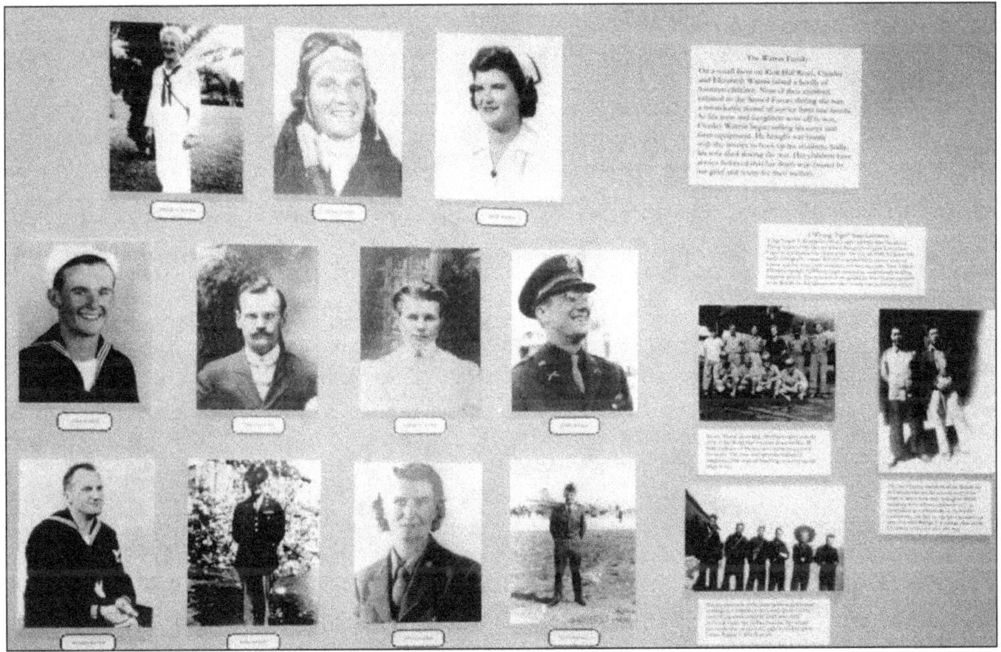

The Watras Family. On a small farm on Kick Hill Road, Charles and Elizabeth Watras raised a family of 14 children. Nine of their children—Edward, Ernest, Helen, John, Joseph, Michael, Peter, Stella, and Henry—enlisted in the armed forces during World War II, a remarkable record of service from one family. Photographs of Charles and Elizabeth, in the center, are surrounded by those of their uniformed children. (Courtesy LHS,)

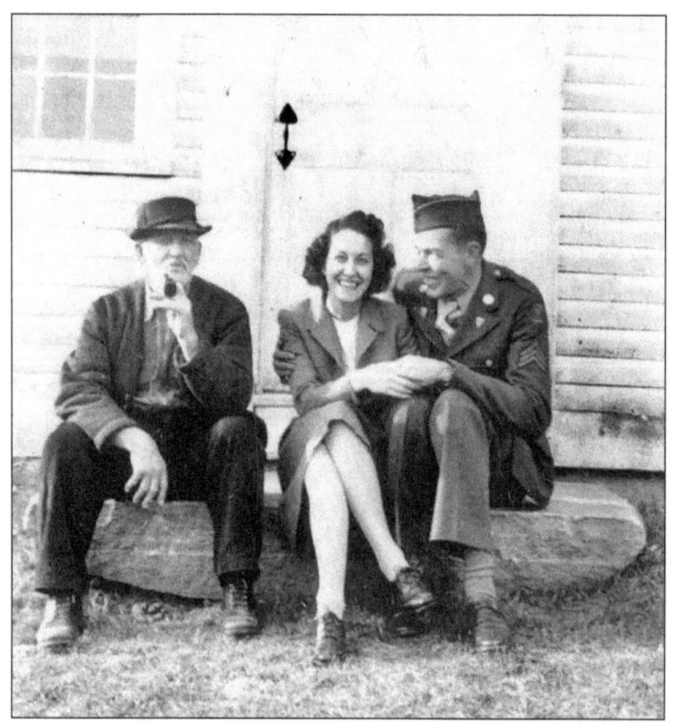

Home on Leave. Alton and Susie Slate pose for a picture with Alton's grandfather Albert Kingsley while Alton is home on leave. The photographs on this page and the following page are only four of dozens in the exhibit that reveal touching reunions of families and their soldier sons and daughters. (Courtesy Robert Slate.)

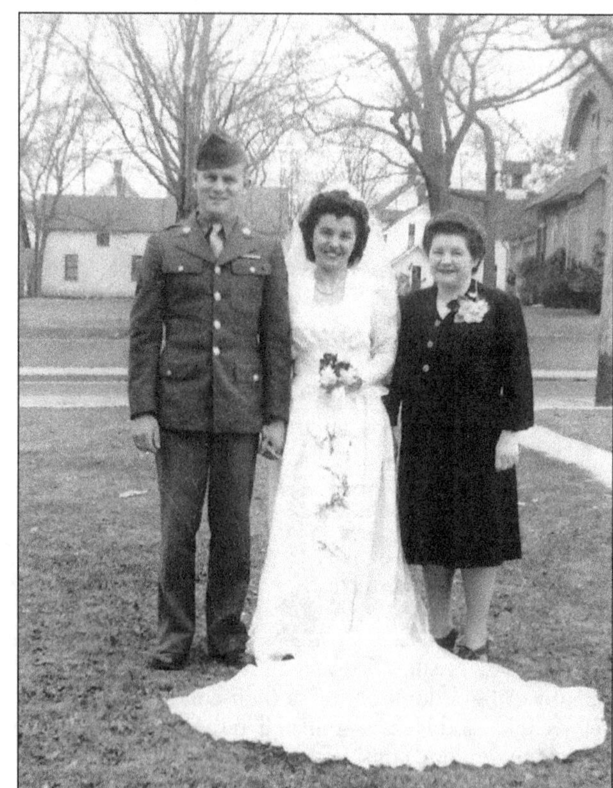

A Wartime Wedding. Edmund Szczurek married his sweetheart, Claire Lacouture, in one of several wartime weddings of Lebanon soldiers. Claire's mother, Rose, stands beside the bride. (Courtesy Edmund Szczurek.)

A FAMILY PORTRAIT. Albert and Phyllis (Hoxie) Bartizek had this portrait taken with their infant son Brian because Albert knew he would be shipped out to the Pacific when he returned to his base. (Courtesy Phyllis Bartizek.)

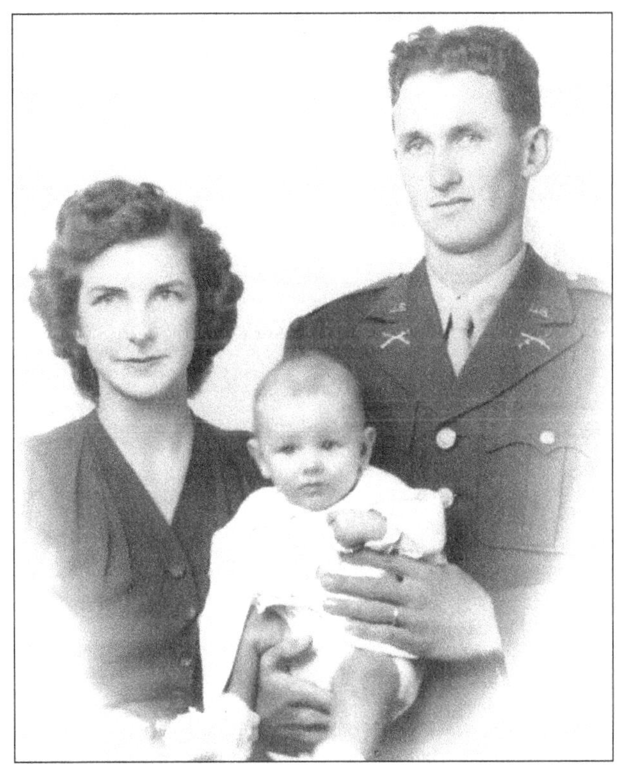

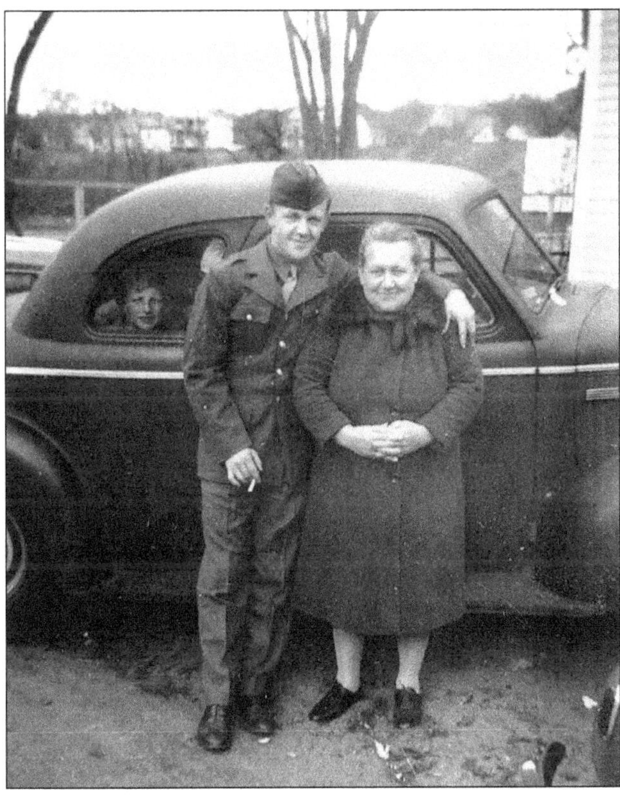

A TENDER GOODBYE. In this photograph, Harry Flegert hugs his mother, Lydia Flegert Ausburger, as he prepares to return to his base. (Courtesy Helen Krause.)

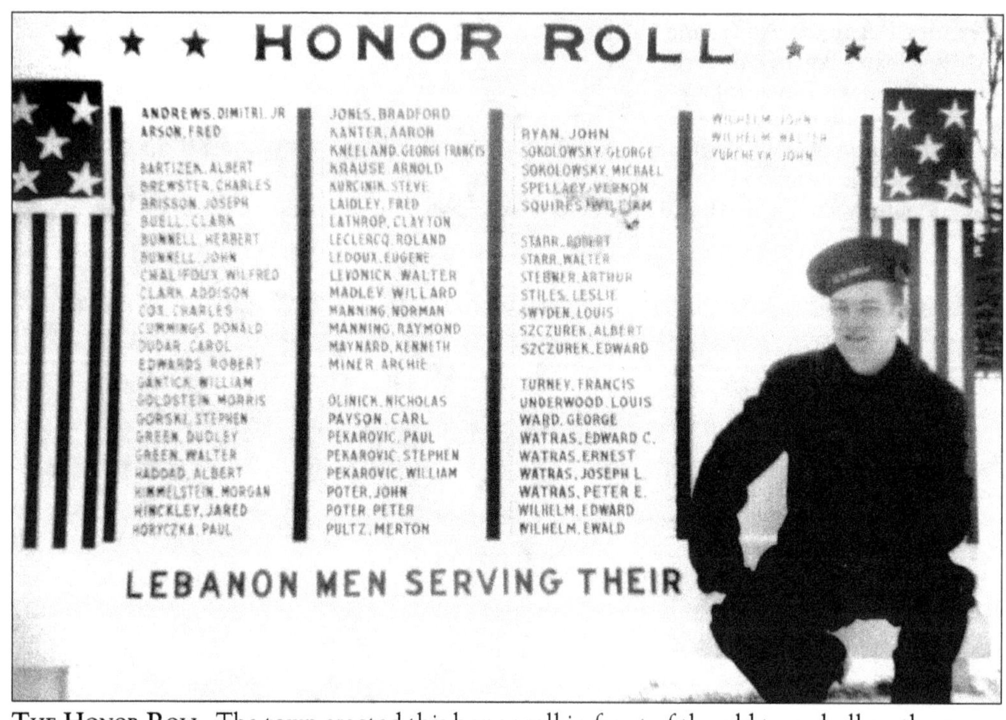

The Honor Roll. The town erected this honor roll in front of the old town hall on the upper green in September 1942. Only the names of the soldiers from the first draft are listed. The names of all the soldiers who served are listed on the monument erected after the war, at the east end of the driveway into town hall. The young sailor is Wilfred Chalifoux. (Courtesy Helen Krause.)

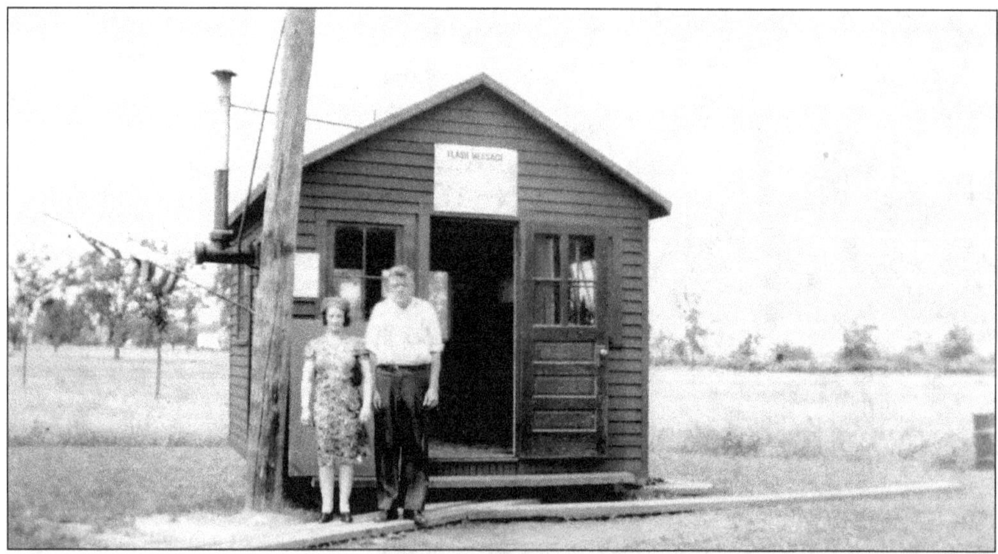

A Plane Spotter's Cabin. A civilian plane-spotting post was set up on the town green opposite the War Office. The post was built by volunteers from timber salvaged from an old mill in Willimantic. The chimney pipe vented a small stove used in cold weather. Civilian defense volunteers manned the post 24 hours a day. Mr. and Mrs. William Congdon manned the post on Sundays from 12 noon to 2 p.m. (Courtesy LHS.)

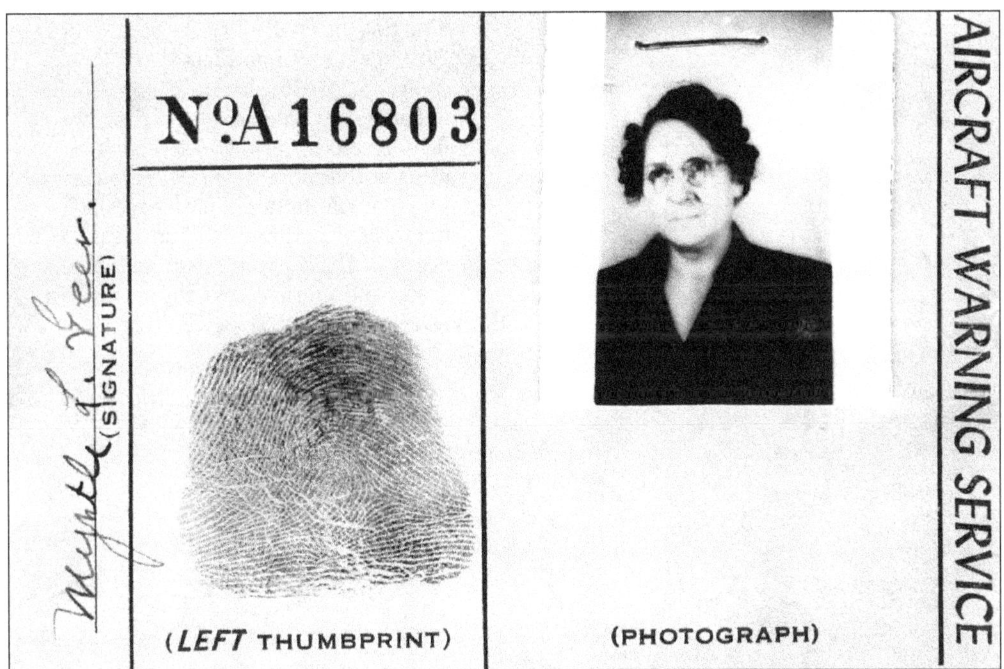

AN IDENTIFICATION CARD. The Lebanon post was one of an elaborate system of civilian plane-spotting stations organized along the Atlantic seaboard. Nearly 300 Lebanon residents volunteered to be spotters. They were issued official identification cards by the Aircraft Warning Service, which was part of the Army Air Forces. The photographs were taken by members of a high school camera club. The pictured card was issued to Myrtle L. Geer. (Courtesy Harold Geer.)

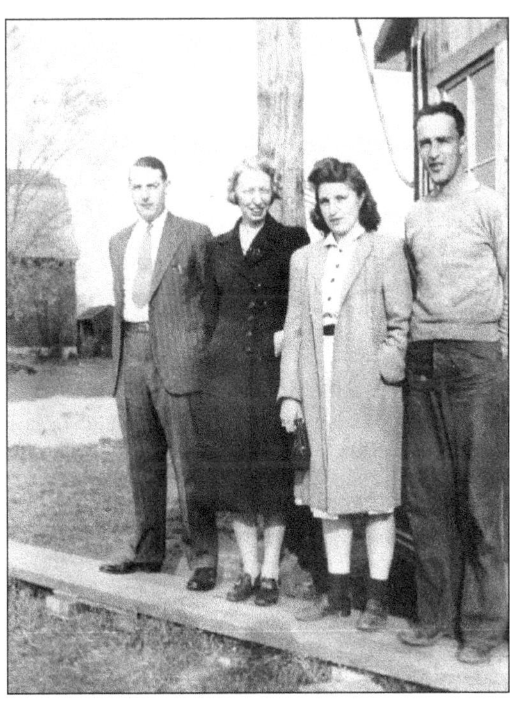

WORKING IN SHIFTS. The aircraft spotter's post had to be manned 24 hours a day, seven days a week. The town was divided into seven sections. Each section was assigned one day of the week to cover. Shifts were limited to two hours so as not to be a burden. On Mondays, Mr. and Mrs. Jared Hinckley (left) served from 6 to 8 a.m., followed by Mr. and Mrs. Karl Phillips (right) from 8 to 10 a.m. (Courtesy LHS.)

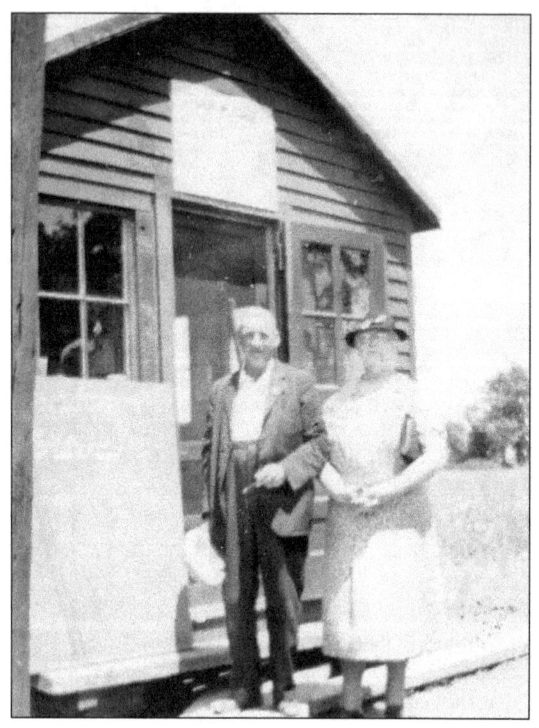

The Saturday Shift. On Saturdays, William Connor and Sarah Abell showed up early at 6 a.m. Sarah Abell, Lebanon's town clerk at the time, was first elected in 1930 and served 35 years in that post until her retirement in 1965. Her father, Charles J. Abell, held the office from 1892 until his death in 1930. Sarah Abell had served as his assistant from 1918 until her own election in 1930. (Courtesy LHS.)

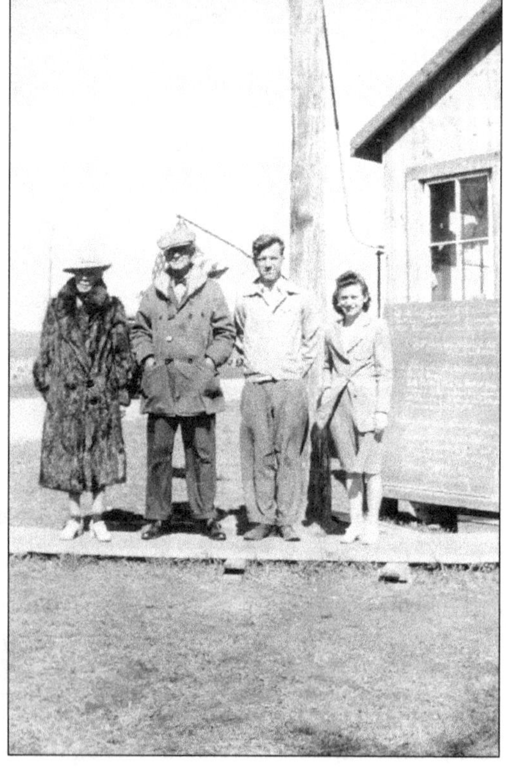

Changing Shifts. Mr. and Mrs. Vernon Boothby (left) change shifts with John and Helen Musial (right). Spotters were trained to identify the different types of aircraft. They listened for the sounds of planes, and when one flew near, they identified it and called in its location. In October 1943, as the threat of attacks decreased, plane spotting was reduced to an alert status. The service was officially terminated in May 1944. (Courtesy LHS.)

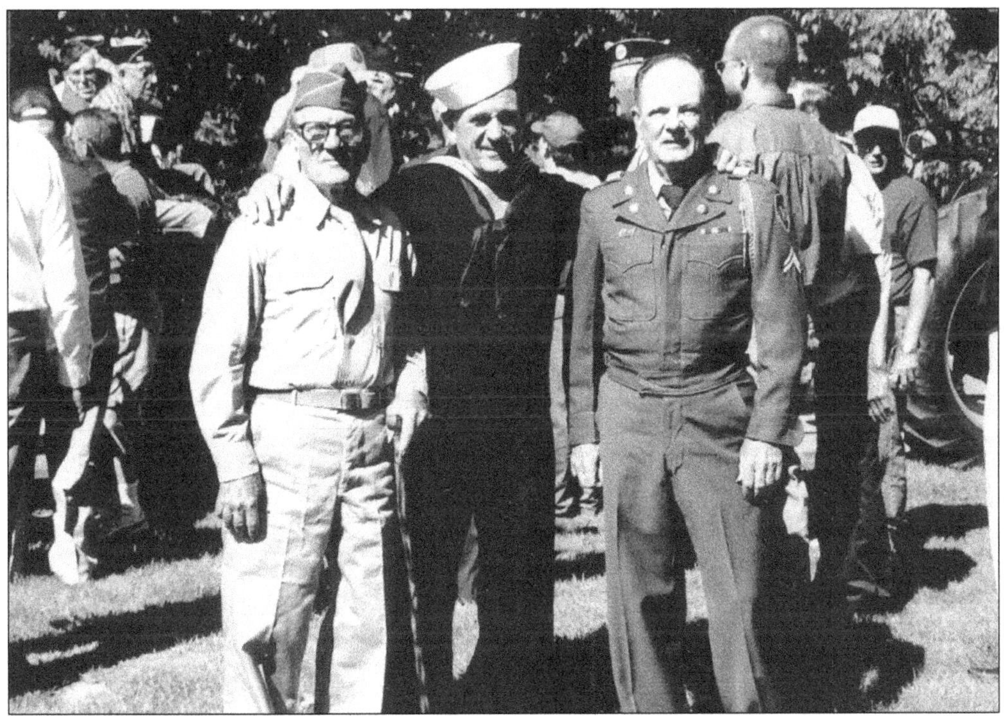

At the Parade. Veterans attending the 2000 Memorial Day parade included, from left to right, brothers Joseph, Ernest, and Eugene Brisson. Many Lebanon families had two or three sons and daughters in the service at the same time during World War II. (Courtesy LHS.)

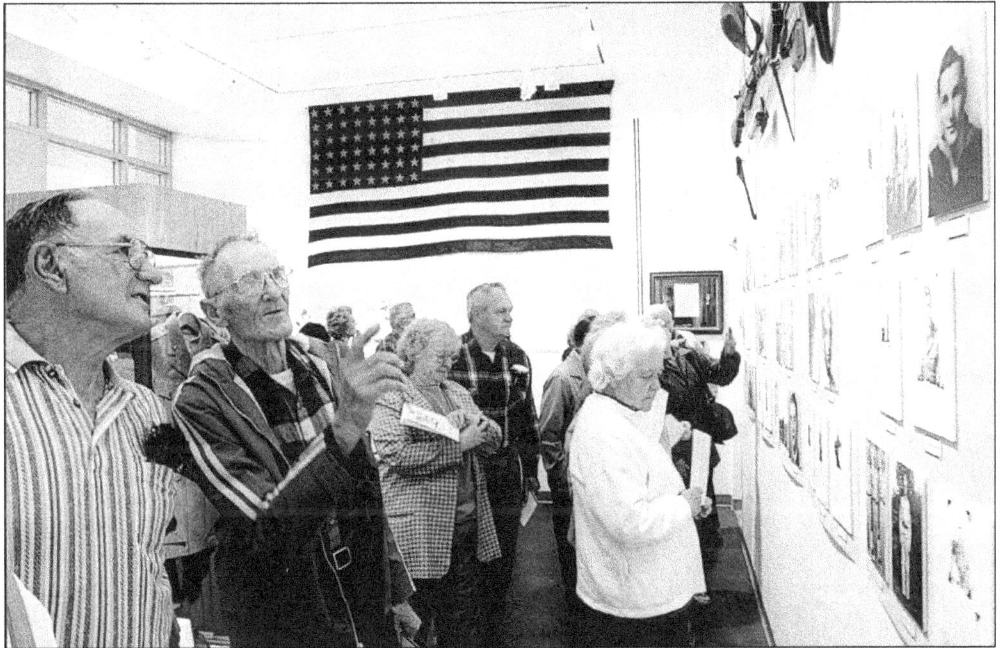

At the Exhibition. The World War II exhibit opened May 25, 2001, at the Lebanon Historical Society Museum. Locating their photographs on the Wall of Honor are brothers Stephen (left) and Nicholas Olenick. (Courtesy of the *Chronicle*, Willimantic, CT.)

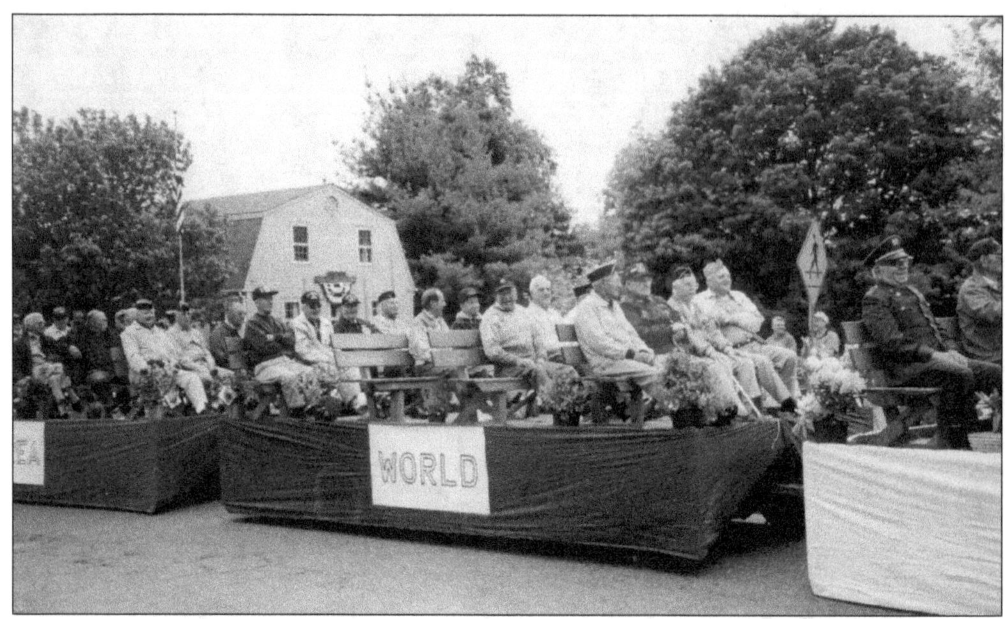

Honoring Veterans. Charles Bender, remembering how veterans of World War I were honored when he was a boy, was determined to do something for veterans of World War II and other conflicts. Since older veterans were not able to march the length of the parade route, he provided decorated wagons for the 2000 Memorial Day parade. The wagons are now provided each year. (Courtesy LHS.)

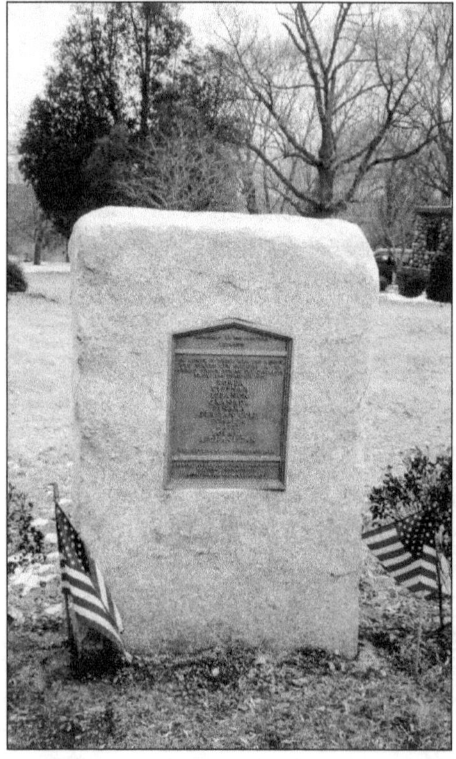

Lebanon Remembers. On November 11, 2002, American Legion Post 180 dedicated a new war memorial at its headquarters to honor veterans of other conflicts since World War II, from 1946 through 2002: Korea, Vietnam, Lebanon, Granada, Panama, the Persian Gulf, Somalia, Haiti, Bosnia, and Afghanistan. It was moved to the town green in May 2003. The monument is made from the same stone as the base of the Statue of Liberty. (Courtesy LHS.)

Eight

Lebanon Then and Now

Throughout more than 300 years of town history, thousands of families have lived in Lebanon. Some were here for a brief period; others stayed for many generations. Descendants of several families who settled the town in the 1690s still call Lebanon their home. No matter how recent or long ago their arrival, all of these families had an effect on the town. Their stories are the main fabric of our community.

In a sense, all of them were immigrants. The Clarke, Lyman, and Dewey families came to the frontier town of Lebanon from Massachusetts towns, primarily in the Northampton area; the Brewsters and Huntingtons arrived from Norwich, the Trumbulls from Simsbury. These are just a few of the more familiar names of those arriving in the early settlement period.

Over the years, other immigrant groups have arrived. Many took up the farms abandoned by Yankee settlers who were moving on to farmland in the upper New England states and the Midwest or to the cities to take urban jobs. Lebanon's population declined significantly in the 19th century. The first United States census, in 1790, showed a high of 4,166 people. It would not reach this figure again until 1980! In the early 20th century, the population averaged about 1,400 people. Only the arrival of new immigrants helped to sustain the town.

An influx of Rhode Islanders, leaving the poorer, sandy soils of that state, helped stem the population loss in the 19th century. These Rhode Island families—the Chappell, Tucker, Peckham, Browning, Briggs, Champlin, Nye, Larkin, and Sherman families, and many others—still have descendants in town.

Lebanon's closest brush with the Industrial Revolution came from the Hayward Rubber Company and two paper mills on the Yantic River. The rubber company, established in Colchester in 1847, opened a satellite mill in Lebanon in 1850 to process raw rubber. Large numbers of Irish immigrants, escaping the famine in their homeland, came to Colchester and Lebanon to work at the Hayward plants. There were about 200 Irish families in Lebanon alone by 1860. Some of the Irish worked on farms, but most worked at the rubber company.

When the rubber company closed in 1886, many of the Irish stayed on to work in the two paper mills on the Yantic. Both paper mills burned—the Browning Mill in 1893 and the Yantic River Paper Mill in 1913. Large numbers of Irish settlers left to find jobs in the cities. But the legacy of these immigrants remains in the first Catholic mission church established in Lebanon and in the family names—such as Lynch, Murphy, Dixon, Clifford, Duffy, McGrath, and O'Sullivan (now Sullivan)— that are an important part of town history.

The first Jewish immigrant arrived in 1890. As the 20th century dawned, many Jewish immigrants from Eastern Europe settled in the Goshen and Exeter areas, turning their poor land into thriving dairy and poultry farms.

A group of German immigrants from the Ukrainian village of Karlswalde settled as a close-knit community in the Village Hill area beginning in 1911. They built up the old farms into highly productive dairy farms.

Many Slavic people also found their way to Lebanon from 1900 to World War I. Coming from Czechoslovakia, Austria-Hungary, Poland, and part of Ukraine, they, too, bought old farms, but theirs were in scattered locations around town. After World War II, they were joined by a second group of Slavic immigrants.

During the 1950s, improved roads and the growth of jobs in surrounding towns made Lebanon attractive to different immigrants: city dwellers attracted by the rural landscape. The last interim census showed the population approaching 7,000.

Once everyone farmed. Now 90 percent of the population commutes out of town to work. In response to this shift, the town has developed a diversity of volunteer organizations to meet the needs and interests of both children and adults. Hundreds of residents give countless hours to the town commissions and boards and to numerous community and religious organizations. They provide the same connection to their community that the Grange and the Farm Bureau still nourish in their members.

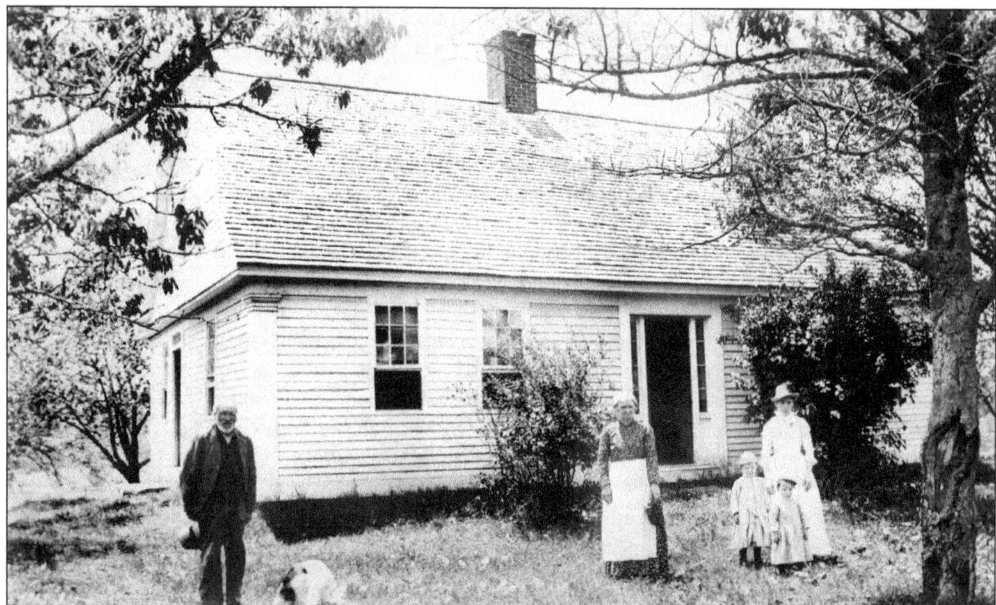

THE LYMAN HOUSE. Built in the very early 1700s, this house at 595 Trumbull Highway belonged to the Lyman family. Richard Lyman was a proprietor of the Five Mile Purchase. Shown *c.* 1890 are Thomas Lyman (left), his wife Harriet (center), and their daughter Mary Jane Lyman Kingsley (right). Mary Jane's daughters, Mary Matilda Kingsley (left) and Minnie Morgan Kingsley, stand in front of her. Mary Matilda Kingsley was Alton Slate's mother. The Jon Slate family now lives in the house, continuing the family tradition. (Courtesy Robert Slate.)

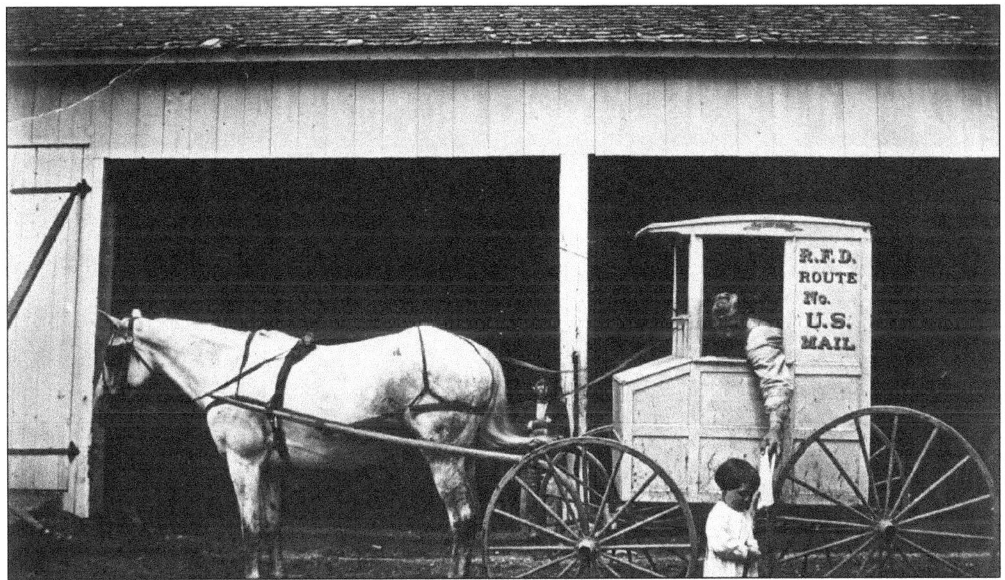

The Mail Service. Rural free delivery was established in Lebanon in 1901, bringing mail service to outlying farms and homes. Burnette Cummings, one of the first carriers, is pictured here in the early 1900s. Even after automobiles became available, carriers had to use horses when the dirt roads turned to mud in the spring. (Courtesy Arlene McCaw.)

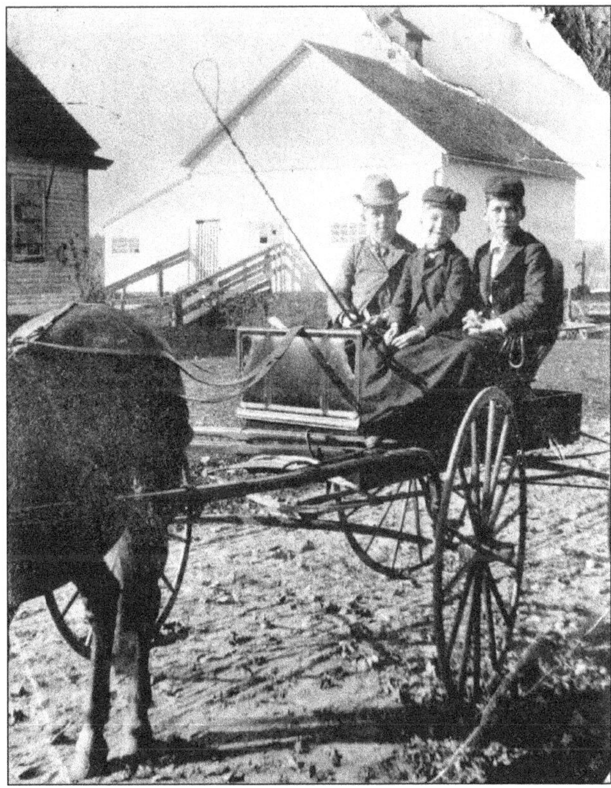

Going for a Ride. Three of the Cummings brothers—Leo, Carlton, and Rexford, shown from left to right—sit in a carriage at an unidentified farm sometime in the 1880s. They were three of nine children, only one of whom was a girl. Of the eight brothers, Carlton, known as "Chappie," and Rexford also became mail carriers like their brother Burnette. Rexford was a carrier for more than 30 years. (Courtesy LHS.)

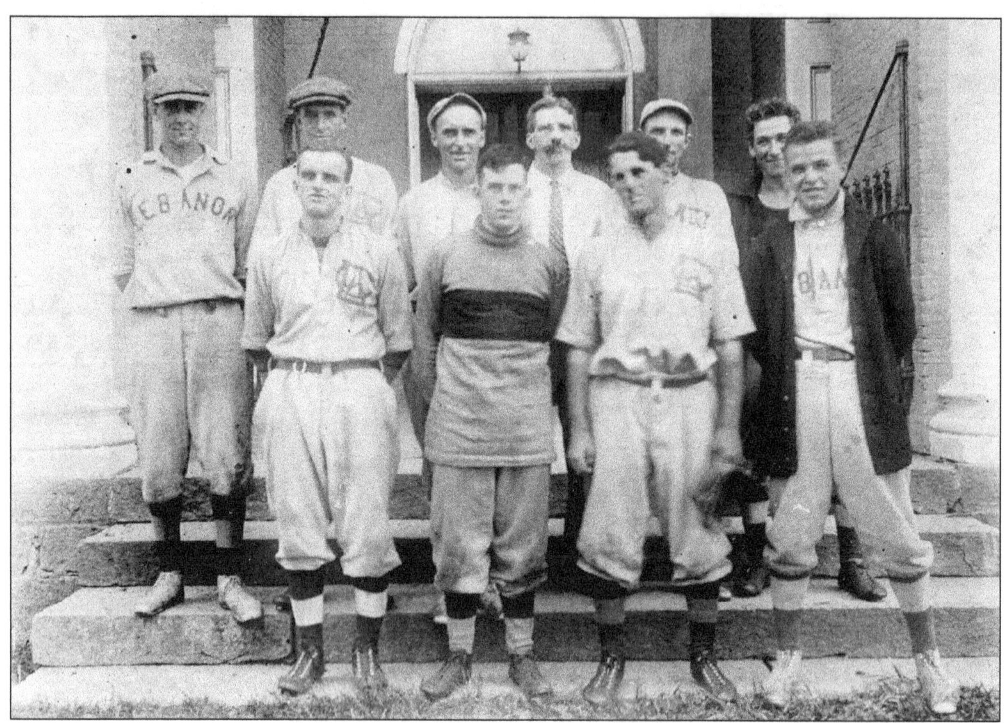

Teammates. Baseball was a popular sport in Lebanon in the early 20th century. These young men, several of whom wear "Lebanon" shirts, were part of an inter-town league with intense rivalries. Appearing in this 1915 photograph, from left to right, are the following: (first row) Monroe Pultz, Harold Mason, Chauncey Williams, and Dick Brown; (second row) Elmer Geer, Myron Hoxie, Norman Pultz, Otto Pultz, Ed Jones, and Rex Cummings. (Courtesy Harold Geer.)

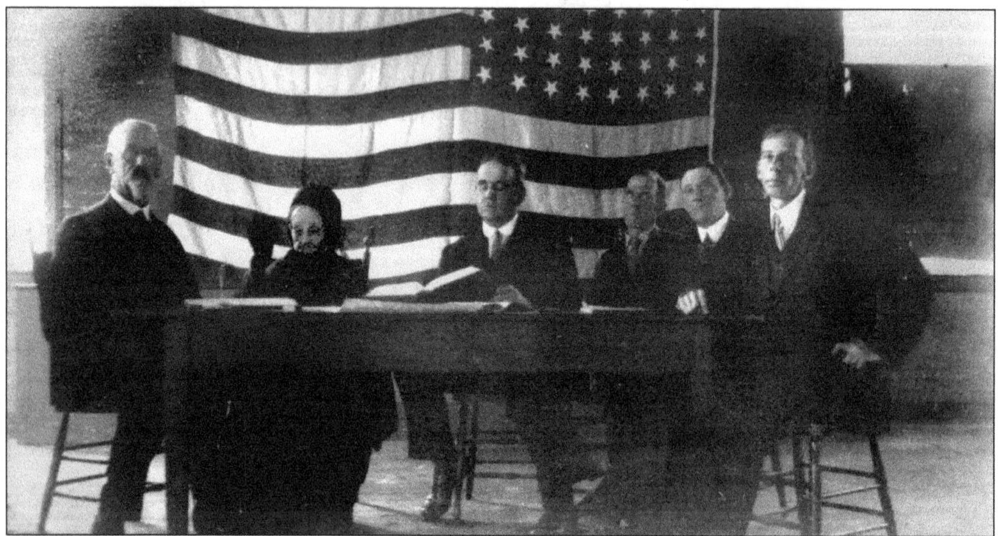

Women Get the Vote. Elizabeth Clark Perry Lillie, aged 99 and three-quarters, was one of the first Lebanon women to register to vote in 1920. With her are, from left to right, Charles J. Abell, town clerk; Karl F. Bishop, first selectman; James Randall and Fred N. Taylor, registrars; and William B. Clark, selectman. Sadly, Lillie died just before she was to cast her first ballot. (Courtesy LHS.)

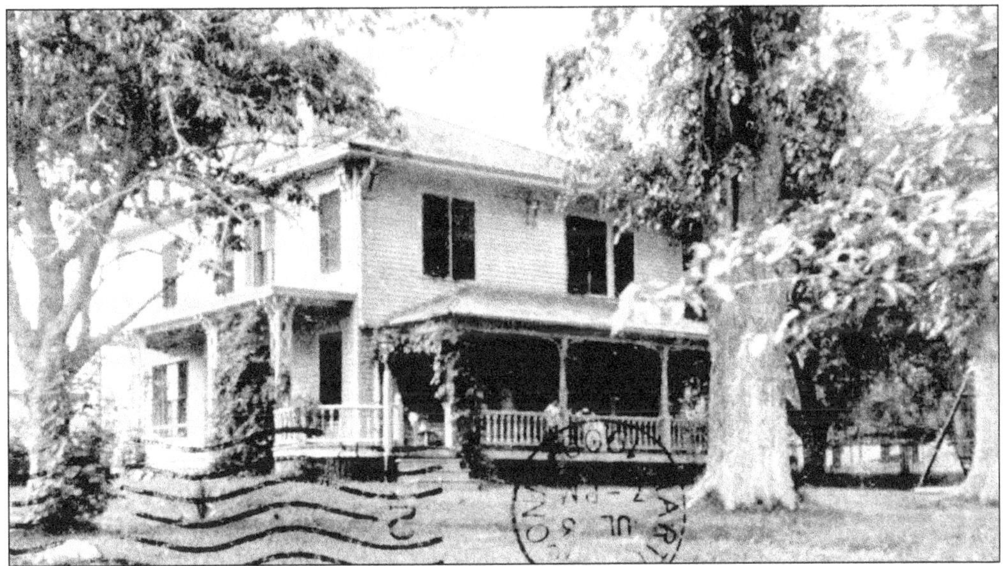

The Dr. Danielson House. Jesse Wright built this house at 927 Trumbull Highway *c.* 1860. His son Arthur Wright earned the first Ph.D. in science awarded in America. He was a pioneer researcher in physics and astronomy at Yale University. The Wright Nuclear Structure Laboratory at Yale is named for him. Dr. Edwin L. Danielson opened a medical office in the house in 1887 and practiced here until his death in 1918. (Courtesy LHS.)

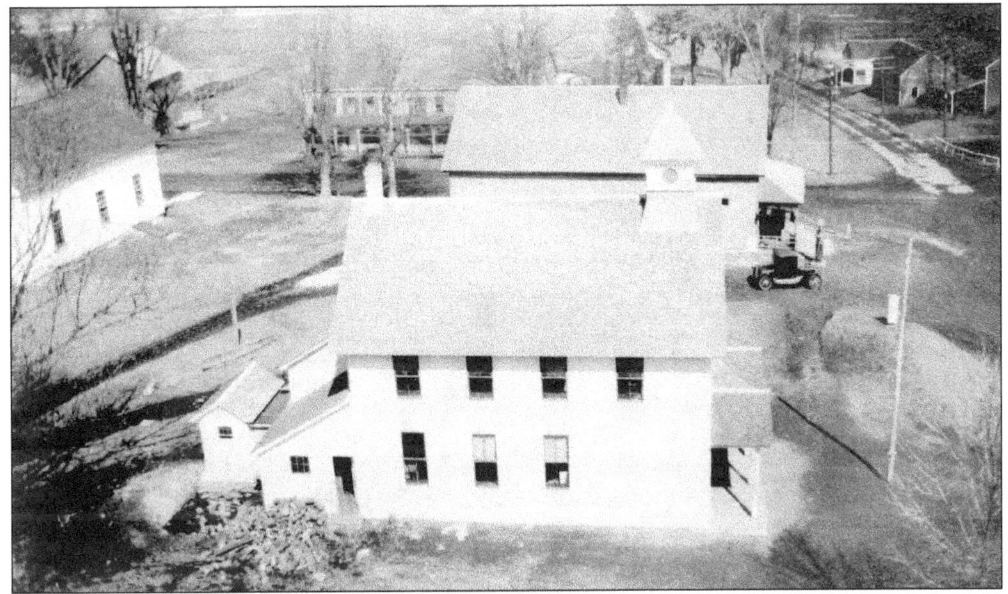

A Bird's-Eye View of the Town Center. This photograph was taken from the steeple of the First Congregational Church in the 1920s. The Center School and the general store are in front. The library is now located on this corner. To the left is the old town hall. Across the street is the old boardinghouse, now the community center. The site of the present American Legion hall was occupied by a restaurant. (Courtesy Russell Blakeslee.)

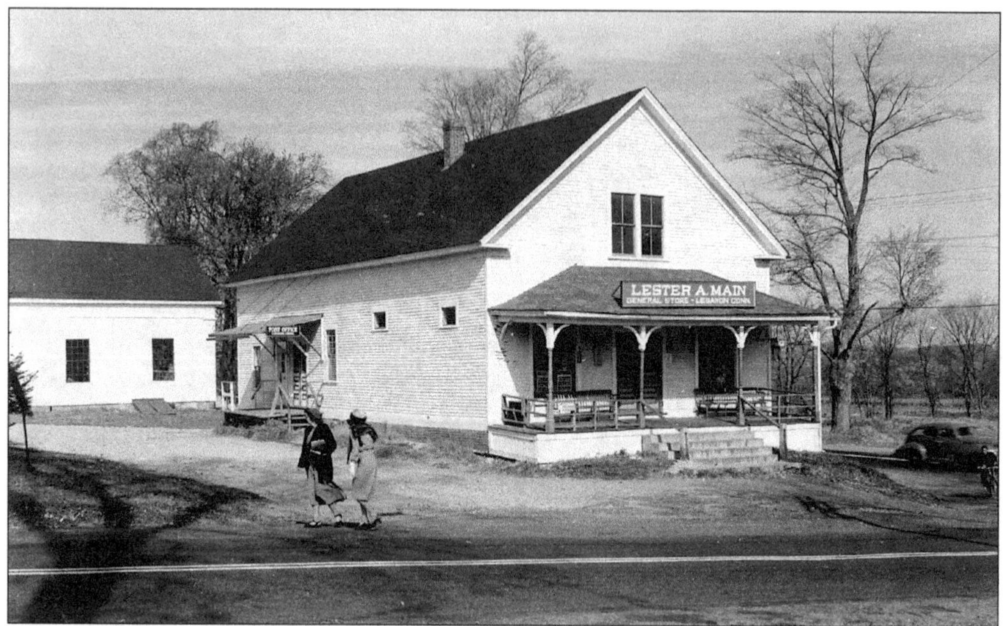

Main's Store in the 1950s. Lester A. Main operated this general store from 1929 until he retired in the 1960s. The town purchased the store and lot from the next owner in 1966 and razed the building to construct the new library building. Main sold everything from meat to work boots, and there were gasoline pumps on the highway side. The post office operated from the back of the store. (Courtesy Ed Tollmann.)

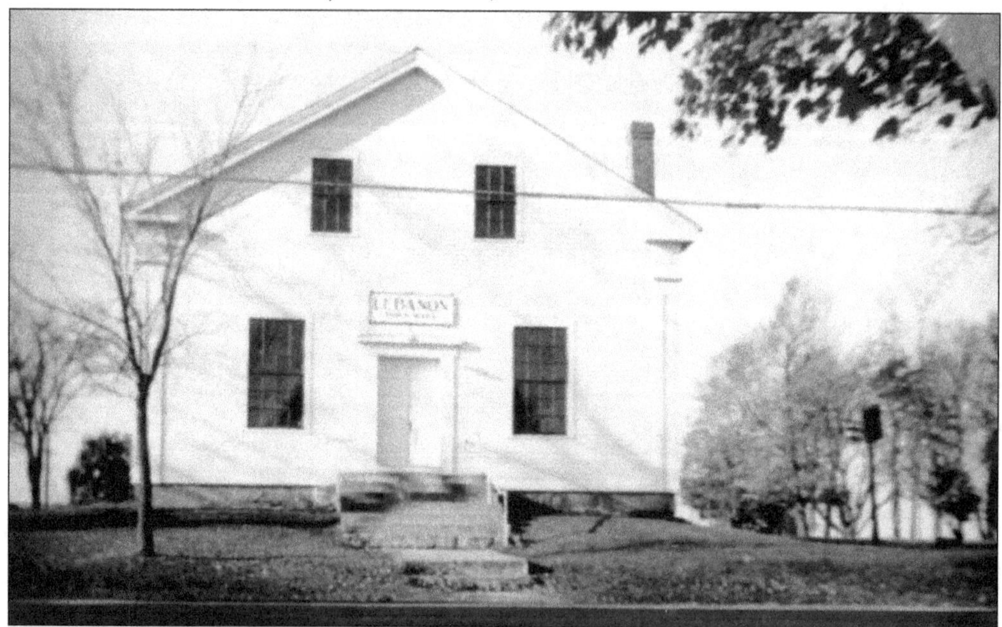

The Old Town Hall in the 1950s. Lebanon's first town hall was built in 1848 on the green, where the present town hall stands. In 1921, when the town decided to build its first high school on the site, the town hall was moved to the northern green, behind the store. The building was dismantled in 1968, and some of the lumber was used to panel a room in the community center. (Courtesy Ed Tollmann.)

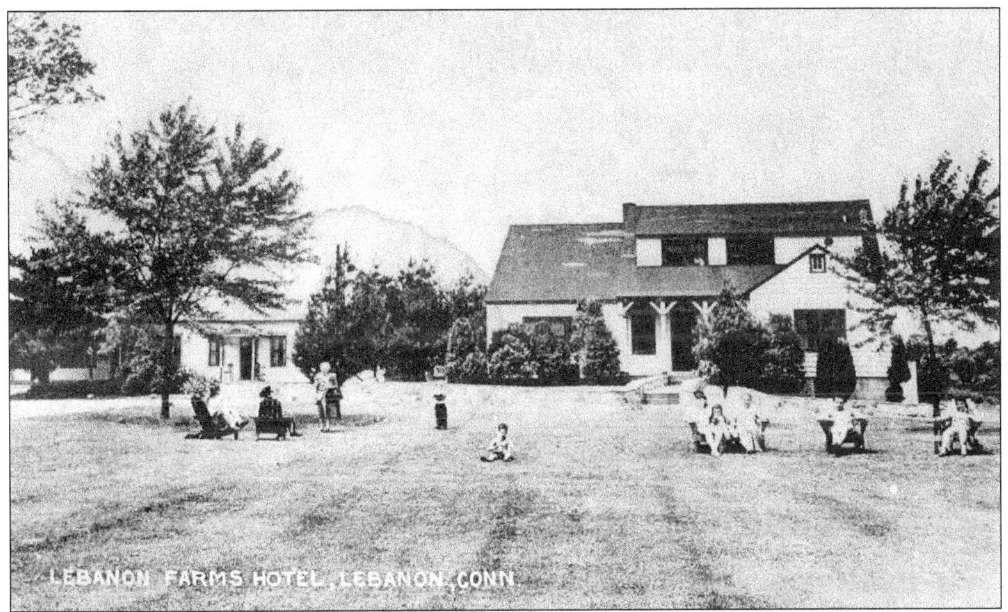

A Summer Resort. The Lebanon Farms Hotel, on Camp Mooween Road on the Yantic River, was a popular place for city people to vacation. The big attraction was a beautiful nine-hole golf course. In the 1960s, the state acquired the golf course land in order to relocate Route 2, and the hotel went out of business. The site is now occupied by the Southeastern Council on Alcoholism and Drug Dependence facility. (Courtesy LHS.)

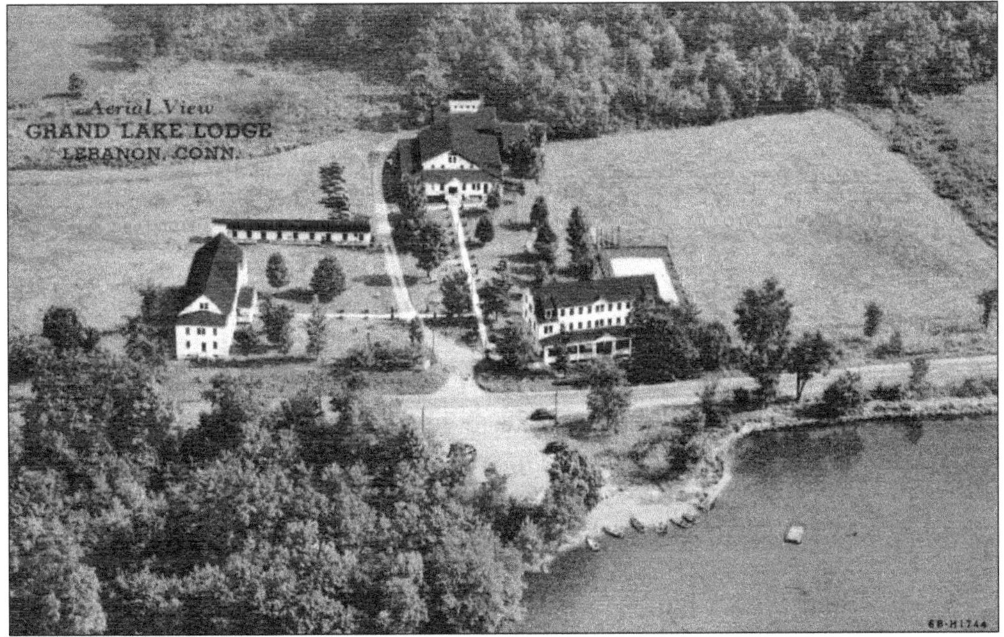

The Resort on Lake Williams. In the early 1900s, a small hotel was built across from Lake Williams. The hotel was greatly expanded in the late 1920s, when the Liebman family owned it. Called Grand Lake Lodge, the complex could serve 250 people a day. It was sold in 1957, then closed after a fire in 1976. In the 1990s, it was renovated and reopened as the Spa at Grand Lake. (Courtesy LHS.)

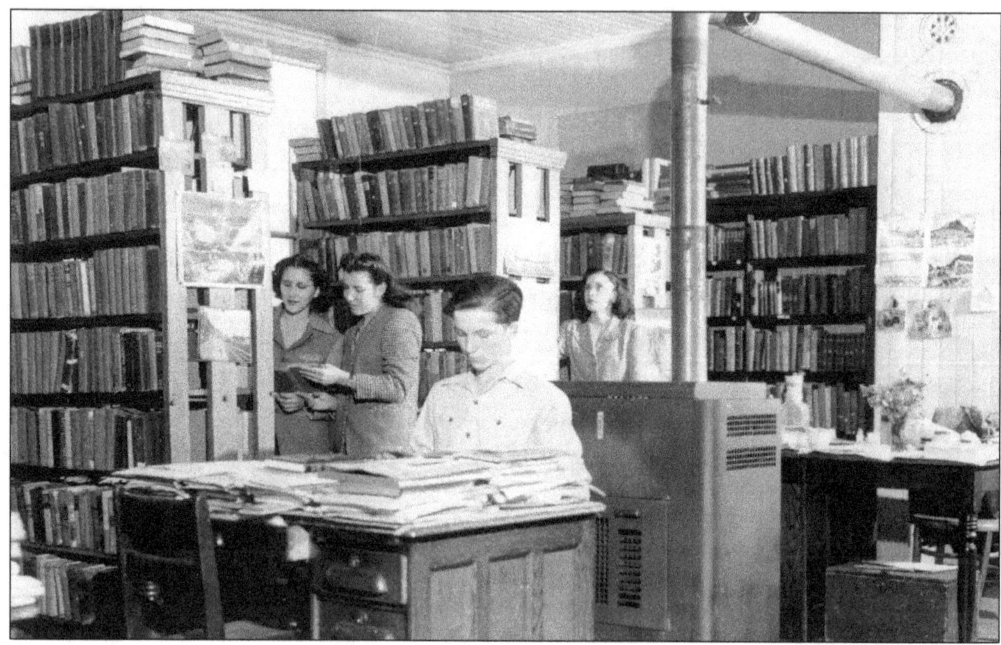

The Town Library in Center School. The Jonathan Trumbull Library has had four different locations since it was established as the town's first public library in 1896. It was first located in the War Office, and it was then moved to the new high school on the lower green in 1922. In 1937, it was moved to the Center School, which had been vacated by the consolidation of elementary schools. The fourth location is the present library building. (Courtesy LHS.)

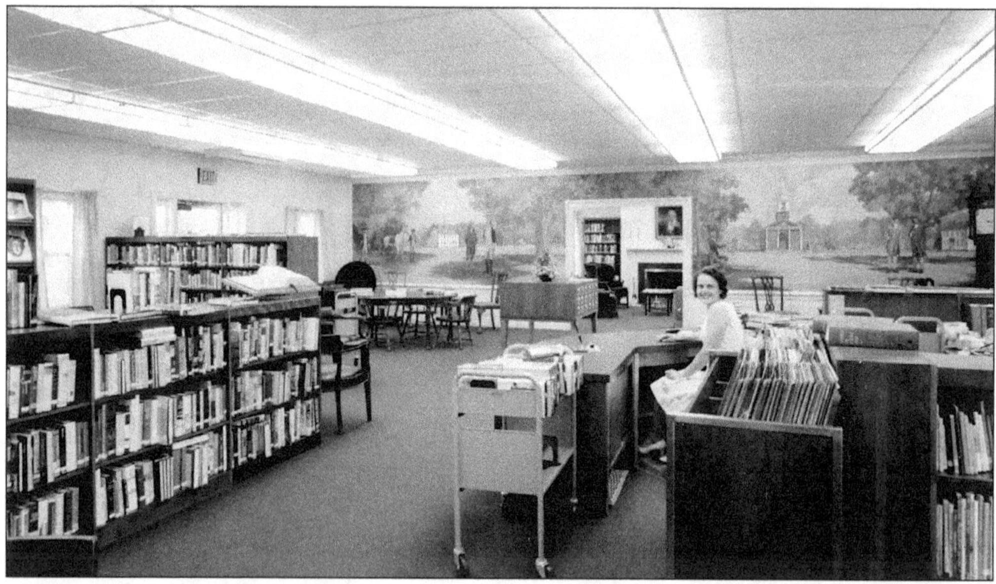

The New Jonathan Trumbull Library. Dolly Randall, library director, is all smiles as she surveys her beautiful surroundings in the new library building at the opening in 1968. The library was built next to the Center School, on the site of the former Main's store. The library and 1974 addition are gifts of the town's benefactor. The Center School was demolished after the new library opened. (Courtesy Barbara Wengloski.)

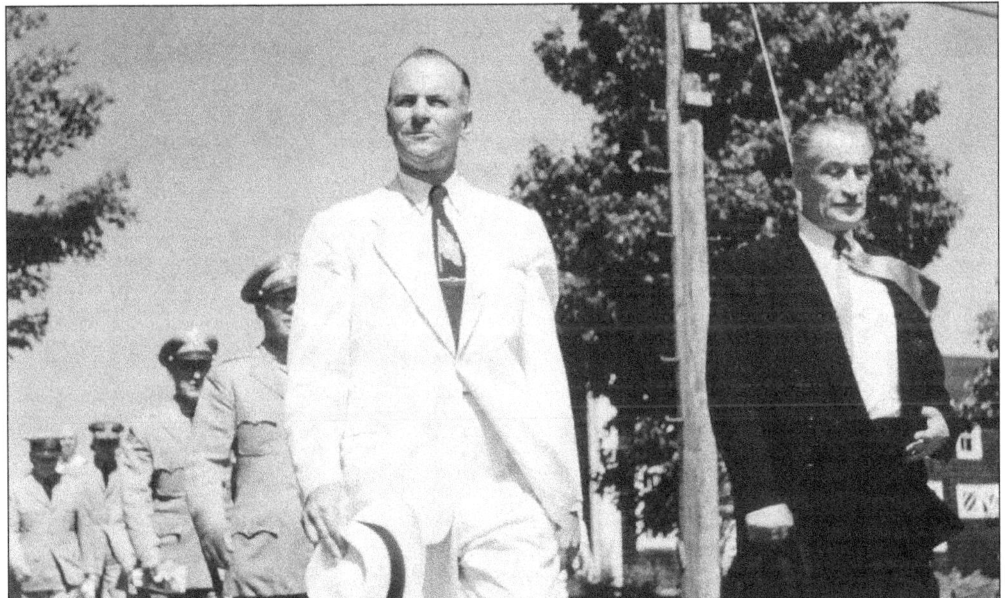

The Pageants. A series of historical pageants on the town green, beginning in 1949, enlisted hundreds of town residents in their production. Dramatic productions of Colonial and Revolutionary War events, they drew huge audiences. They were enlivened by periodic Boy Scout camporees on the green on the same weekends. Gov. John Lodge, left, marched in the 1952 pageant parade, and his wife performed in a skit. (Courtesy LHS.)

Camping at the Pageant. Posing in the front row are, from left to right, Jeanie Bender, Claire Kelley, Roberta Greenberg, and Jean (King) Reichard. They were among the Lebanon Girl Scouts camping on the town green during an early 1950s pageant. There are now 162 Lebanon girls registered in the 15 Lebanon troops. Both the Girl Scouts and Boy Scouts are active programs for Lebanon youth. (Courtesy Barbara Wengloski.)

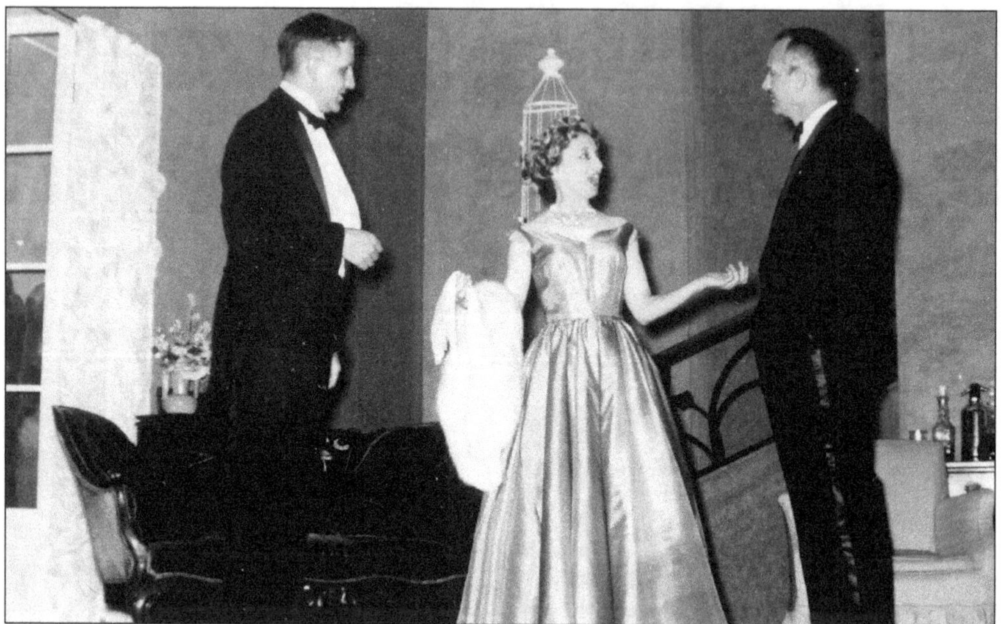

The Play's the Thing. Grant Tuttle, Arlene McCaw, and David Day, seen here from left to right, perform in a production of *Jane* put on by the Lebanon Guild of Arts and Crafts. The guild, formed in 1951 to encourage the arts and crafts in Lebanon, had more than 100 members at its peak. Many were involved in the play productions, which included 25 full-length plays. The last production was in 1966. (Courtesy Harold Geer.)

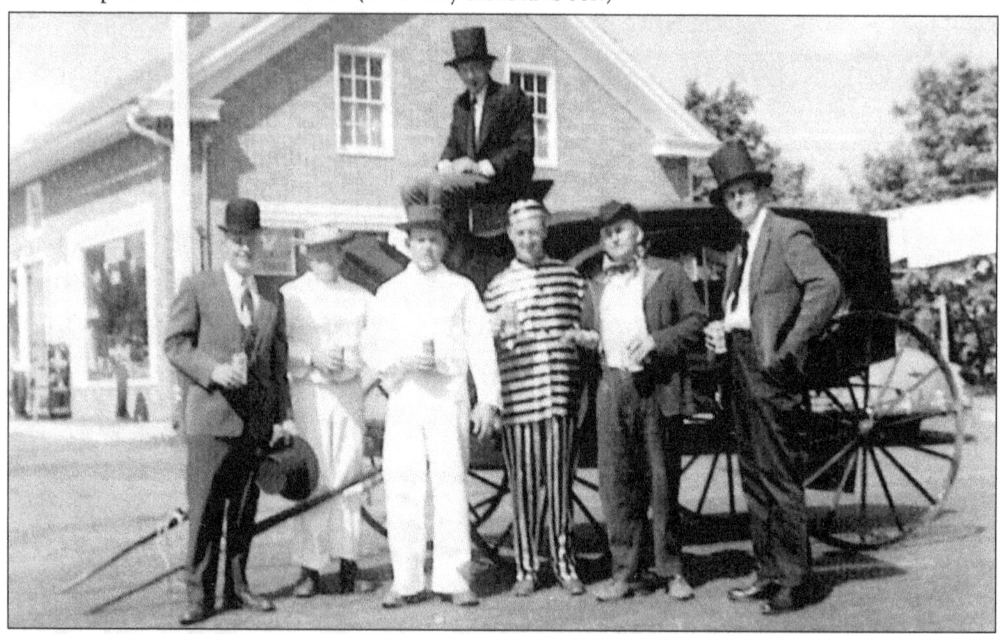

Hidden Away. In the 1950s, a group of townspeople spirited away an old hearse that the town was going to discard. They kept it hidden except for appearances at special events. In 1959, driver Harold Geer took the hearse to a parade in Willimantic. Accompanying him are, from left to right, Delton Briggs, Russ Clapp, Tom Wentworth, Tom Flannagan, Russ Tollmann, and Leslie Clarke Jr. The hearse is now owned by the Lebanon Historical Society. (Courtesy Harold Geer.)

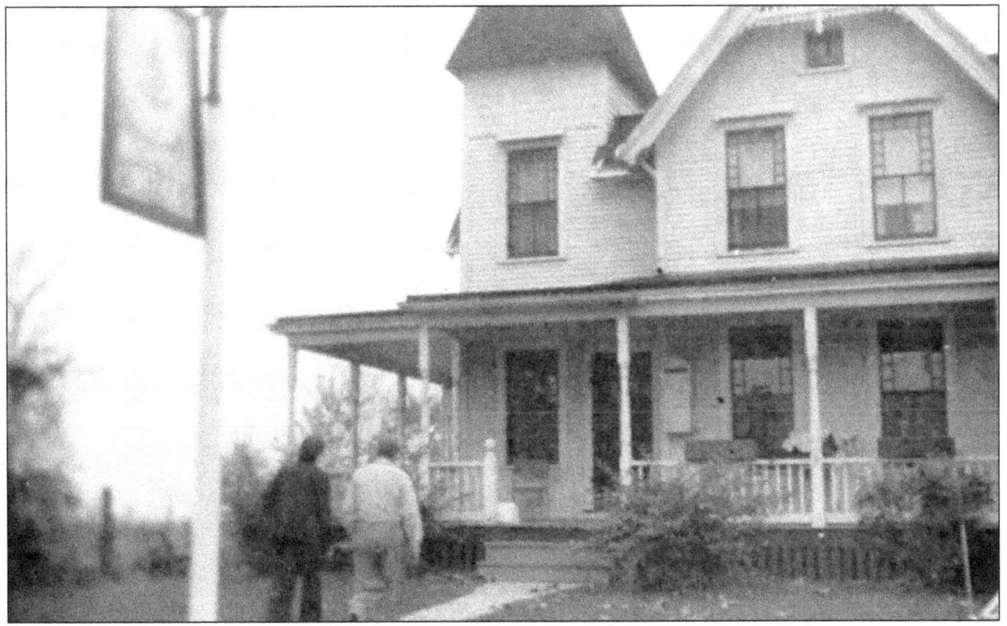

The Telephone Service. This 1898 house, at 798 Trumbull Highway, was purchased by Southern New England Telephone in 1913 for the local telephone exchange. Elizabeth Troland lived here as the chief operator from 1915 to 1950. In 1950, SNET built a modern building on the lot to begin the switch to direct dialing. George Randall then bought the house and moved it to the lot next door. (Courtesy Ed Tollmann.)

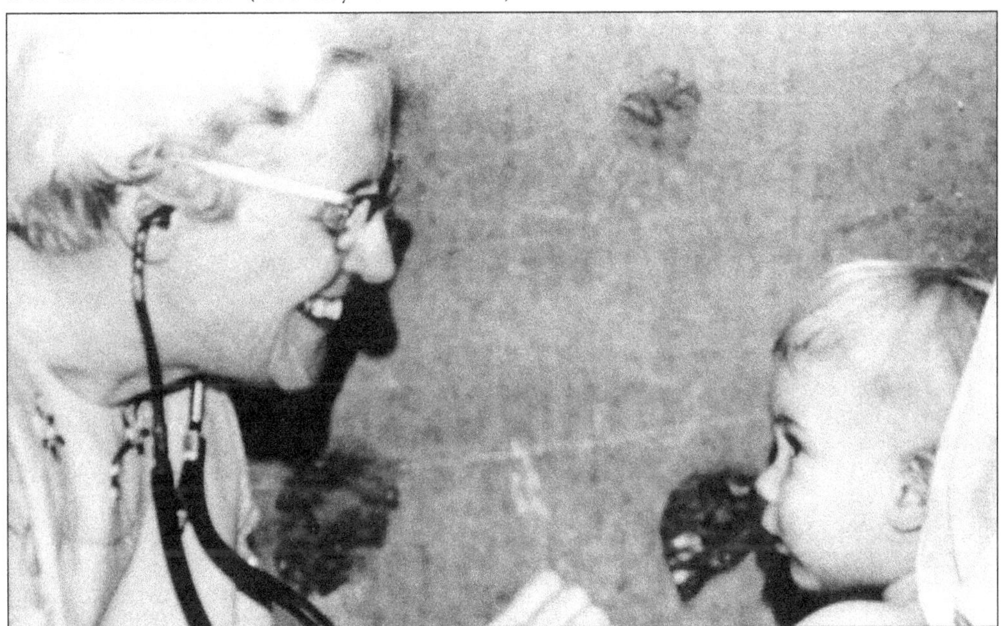

A Beloved Physician. Dr. Imogene Manning checks a baby at the Lebanon Well-Child Clinic in 1974. In addition to her regular practice, Dr. Manning served as the town's school medical adviser for 20 years. Although she was a pediatrician, townspeople felt they could call on her day or night for any type of medical advice. She also served as historical society president from 1975 to 1979. She died in 1982. (Courtesy LHS.)

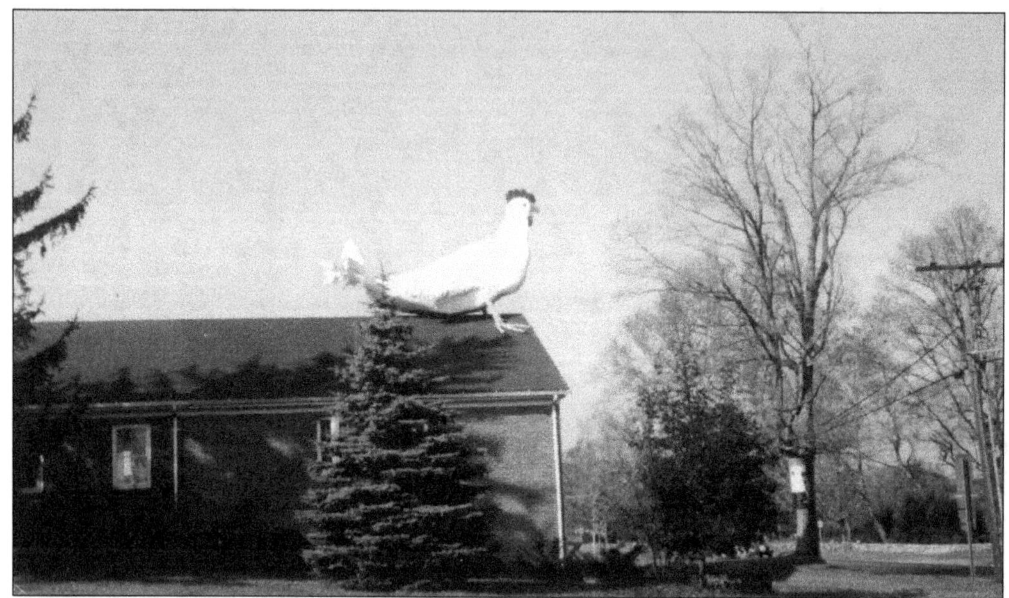

A Halloween Chicken. An anonymous group of residents known as the Pranksters delights in poking fun at current political and social issues in town. The morning after Halloween, residents head for the green to see what the Pranksters put up during the night. The most famous was the huge chicken that appeared on top of the library when a large egg-production facility was proposed in Lebanon. (Courtesy Barbara Wengloski.)

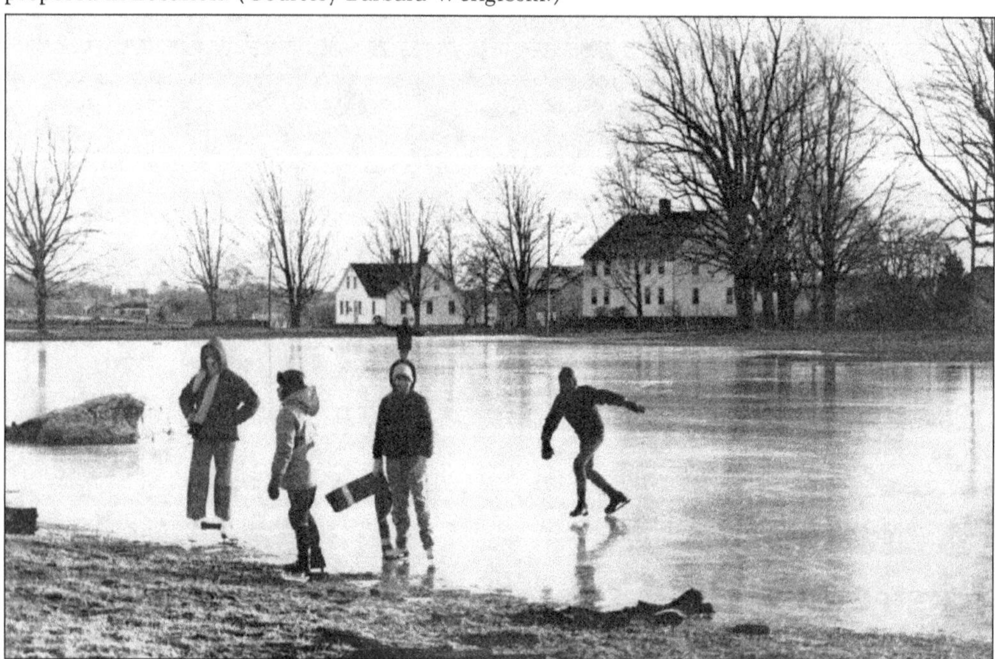

The Skating Pond. Ice-skaters enjoy the pond created on the town green each year when water collects behind a small dam that is closed in early winter. The early 19th-century house on the left in the background was moved in 1990 to another lot on the street. The Colonial house on the right dates from *c.* 1740. The old barn in the center has been converted to a farm stand. (Courtesy LHS.)

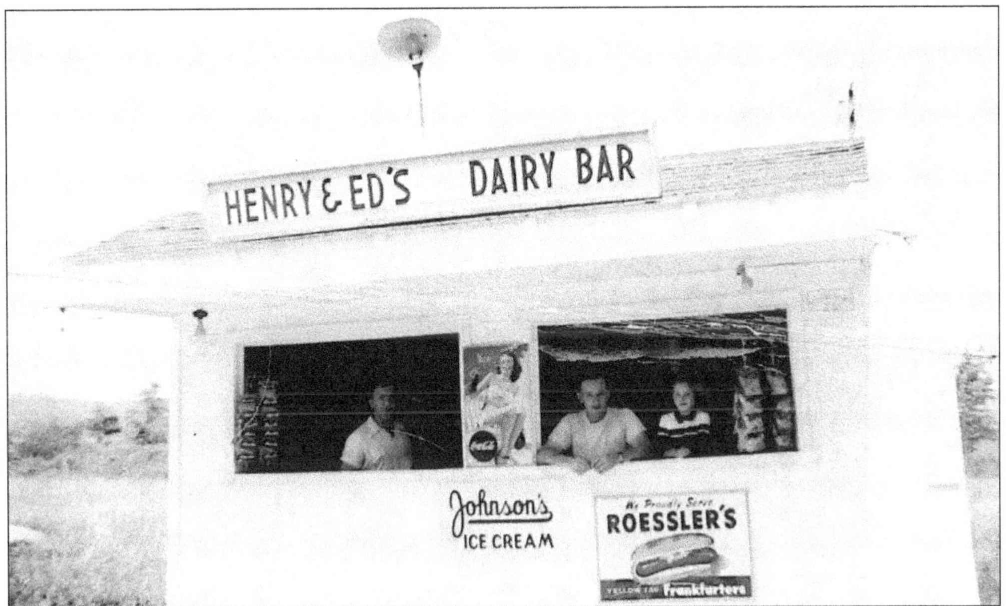

Ice Cream, Anyone? In the 1950s, Henry Haddad and Ed Clark opened a dairy bar on Route 87, south of the Oliver Road intersection. Ed's daughter Susan Coutu helped out. Ed Clark served 35 years as superintendent of the Lebanon Country Fair. He also opened the first horse ring in the region and was a former owner of the Lebanon Green Store. He was first selectman from 1979 to 1987. (Courtesy Ed Tollmann.)

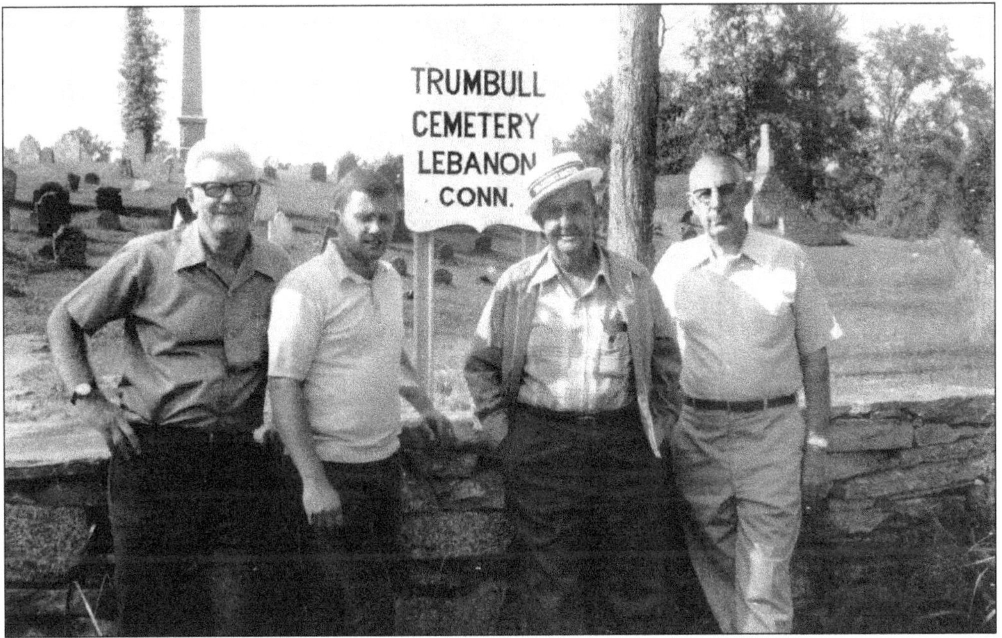

A Caring Commission. The Lebanon Cemetery Commission was established in 1972 to provide better care for all town cemeteries, some of which suffered from neglect. Here, from left to right, Phillip Kohler, Ed Tollmann, Henry Aspinall, and Jared Hinckley, all members of the new commission, stand in front of their new sign at the Trumbull Cemetery. This cemetery has fine examples of early Colonial stone carving. (Courtesy Ed Tollmann.)

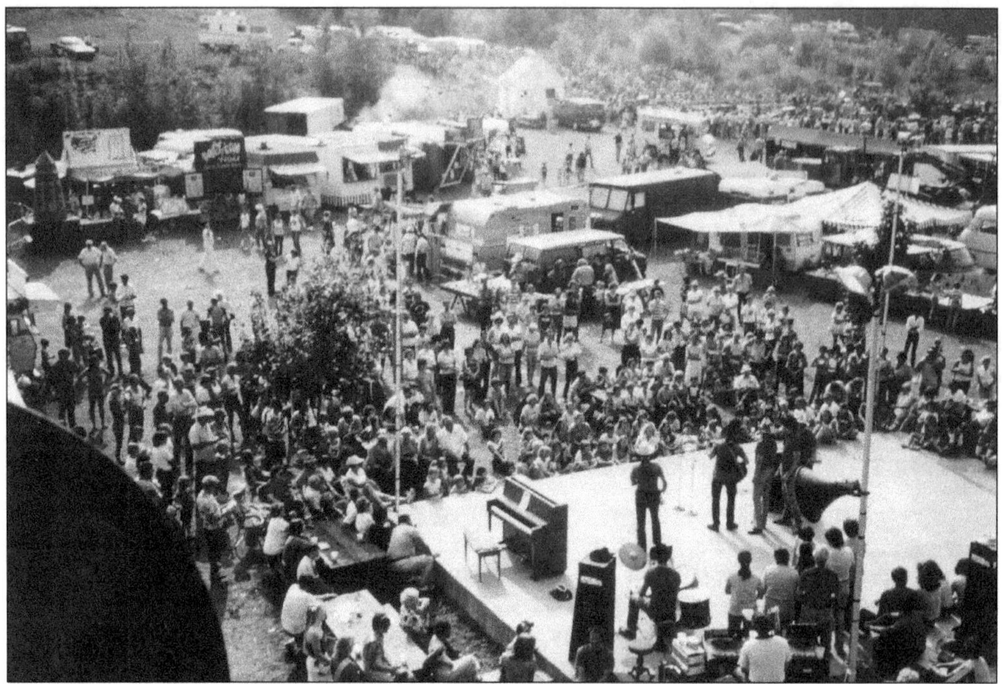

The Country Fair. The Lebanon Lions Club, chartered in 1952, sponsors the Lebanon Country Fair. It has grown from a small fair held on the town green to a major state fair attracting more than 30,000 visitors to the club's fairgrounds on Mack Road. The fair is a major fund-raiser for the club's charitable work. It is a showcase of agricultural exhibits, home arts, commercial exhibits, entertainment, and midway attractions. (Courtesy Ed Tollmann.)

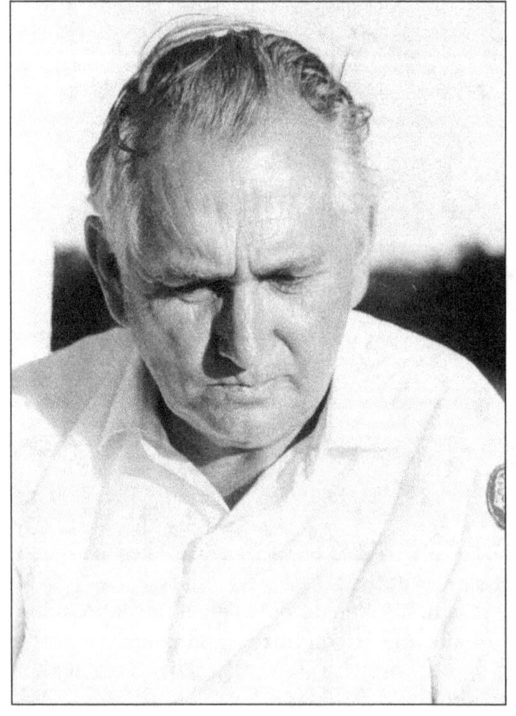

The Voice of the Fair. Russell Tollmann, former first selectman, is shown in the tower on the Lions Club fairgrounds, where he announced events on the microphone just below. For years, he was known as the voice of the Lebanon Country Fair. From his high vantage point, he would spot people he knew and call out their names and a greeting. His friendly chatter made everyone feel welcome. (Courtesy Ed Tollmann.)

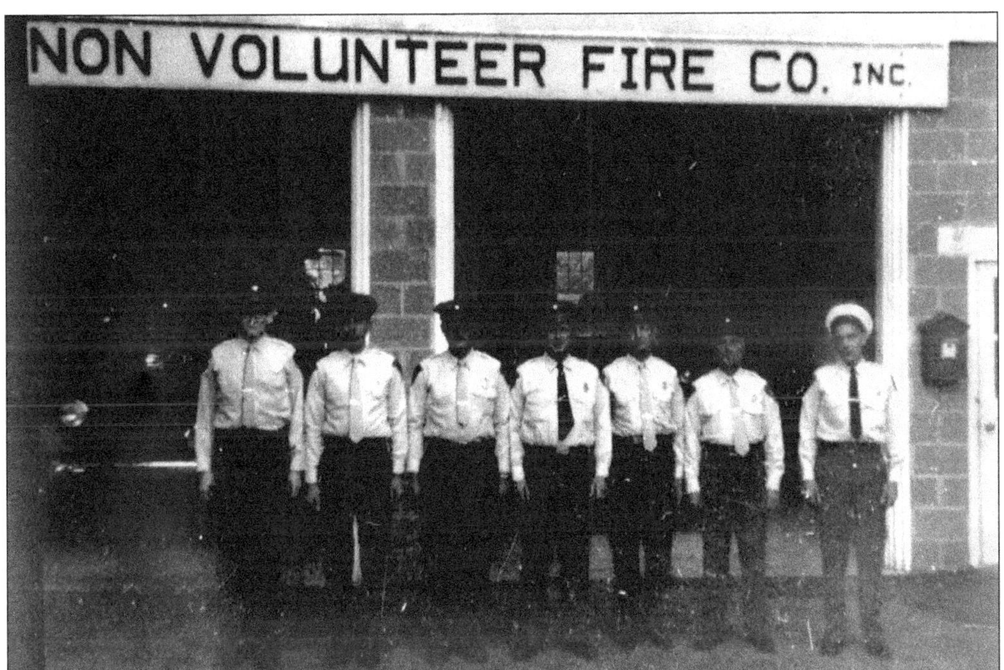

VOLUNTEER FIREFIGHTERS. The Lebanon Volunteer Fire Department was organized in 1943. The first firehouse was built across from the town hall in 1946. The volunteers did much of the construction work. Standing in front of the building in 1963 are, from left to right, members Robert Cady Sr., Jim McCaw, Doug Black, Adam Gantic, Don Jones, John Laibrandt, and Bill Brewster Sr. (Courtesy Jennie Brewster.)

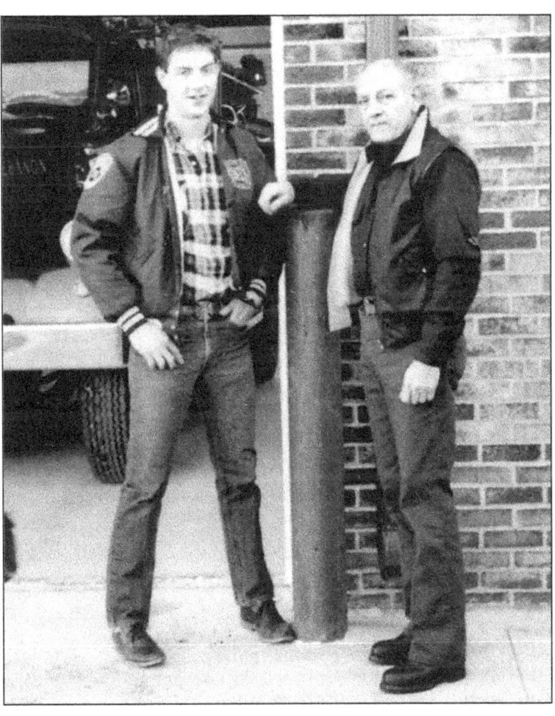

THE FIREFIGHTING TRADITION. William Brewster Sr., a charter member of the Lebanon Volunteer Fire Department, served as assistant chief for 12 years, as chief for 6 years, and as treasurer for 35 years. His son William Brewster Jr., appearing with his father at the dedication of the new fire safety complex in 1987, is also a firefighter. He designed the firefighters' memorial in front of the complex. (Courtesy Jennie Brewster.)

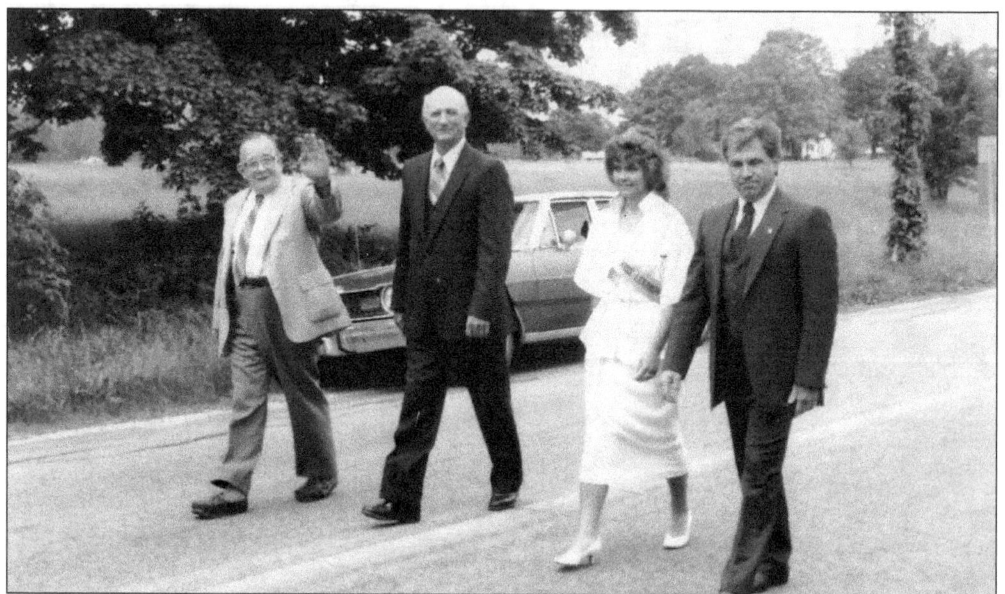

Parade Marchers. Leading the annual Memorial Day parade in 1986 are, from left to right, first selectman Ed Clark, selectman Ed Bender, unidentified, and selectman Robert Leone. Now retired, Ed Bender managed the family farm on Rafferty Road for many years. A former dairy farmer, Robert Leone held the post of second selectman for 28 years, retiring from politics in 2001. He is a popular local auctioneer. (Courtesy LHS.)

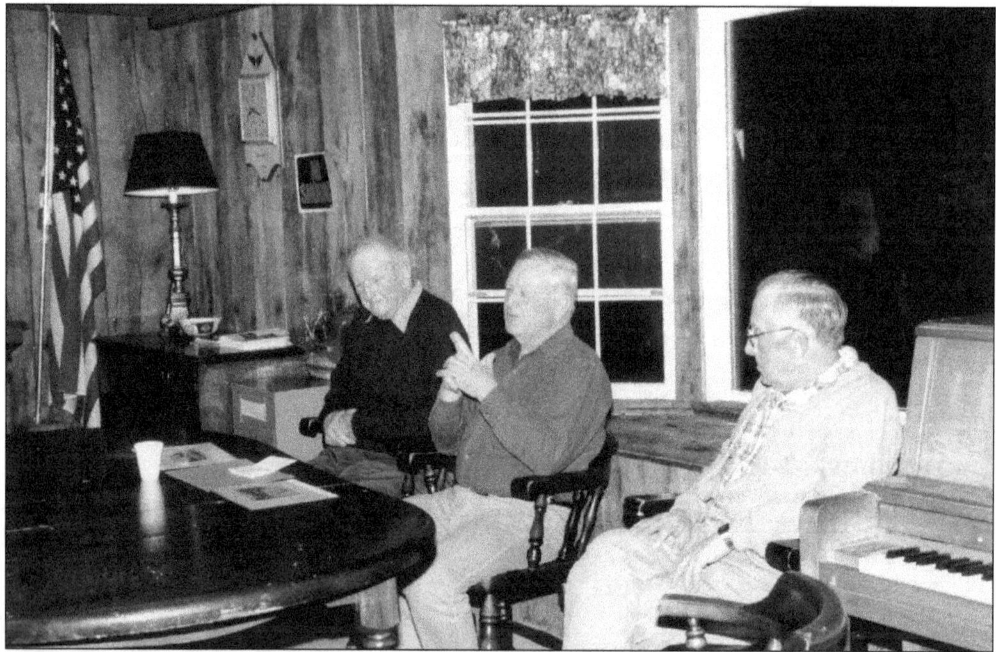

Reminiscing. At a meeting of the historical society in 1996, Frank Bartizek, Delton Briggs, and Ted Littlefield, seen here from left to right, drew on their memories of the "good old days" to entertain the audience with stories about Lester Main's General Store. The store, located where the library now stands, was the place to buy "everything," meet friends, catch the latest gossip, and lounge on the porch in summer or around the potbelly stove in winter. (Courtesy LHS.)

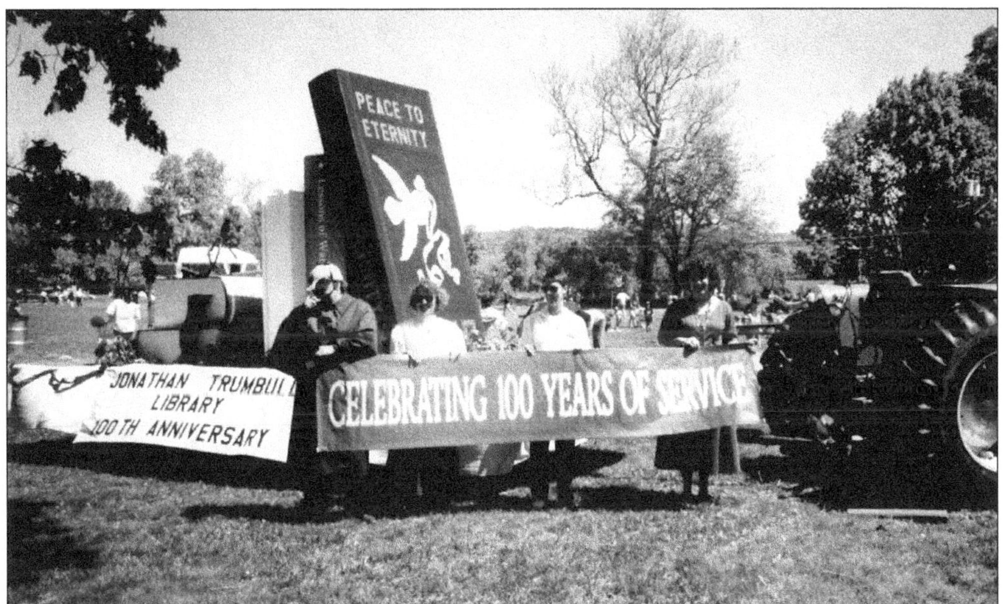

The Library Centennial. The Jonathan Trumbull Library turned 100 years old in 1996, and many special activities took place during the year to celebrate. The library's float in the Memorial Day parade featured giant replicas of books. Marching with the banner are, from left to right, Mary Beth Yarmac, Sue Kane, Barbara Wengloski, and Linda Slate. (Courtesy Barbara Wengloski.)

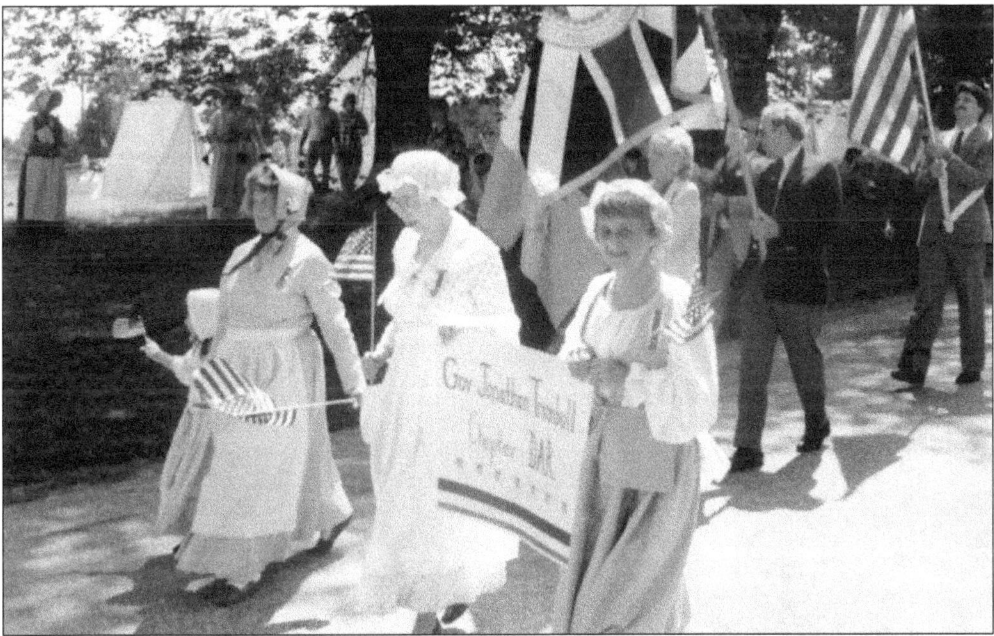

DAR Marchers. Every year, a contingent from the local chapter of the Connecticut Daughters of the American Revolution marches in the Memorial Day parade. In this undated parade photograph, Nancy Lyon (left) walks with her granddaughter. Jean McArthur (center) and Virginia Mullaly (right) carry the chapter banner. The chapter is named, of course, after Gov. Jonathan Trumbull of Lebanon. (Courtesy Virginia Mullaly.)

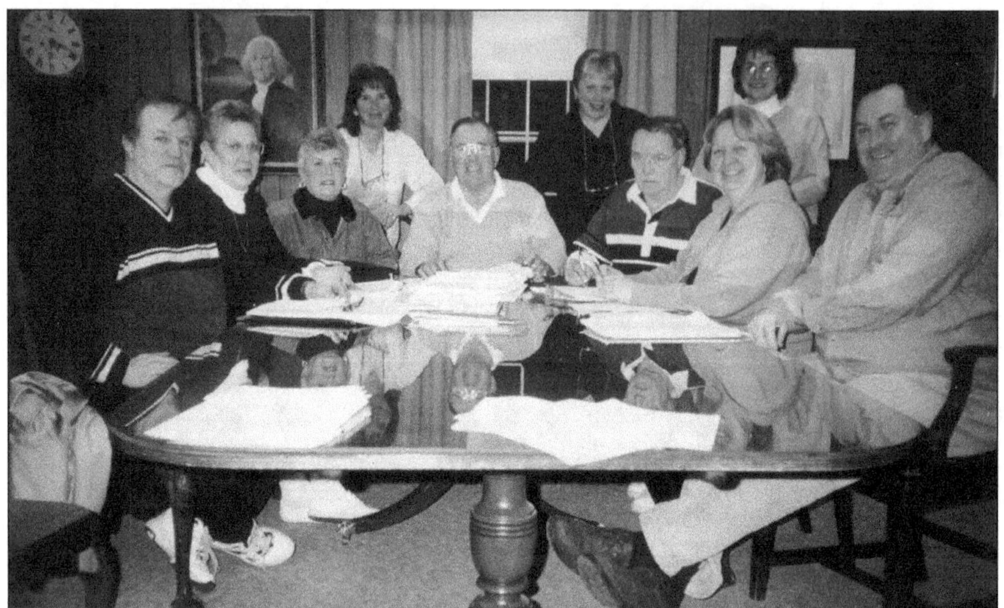

THE TERCENTENNIAL COMMITTEE. This committee was appointed by the selectmen in 1998 to organize the town's official tercentennial celebration in 2000. Members, seen here from left to right, are as follows: (sitting) Robert Leone, treasurer Jennie Brewster, Sandra Chalifoux, chairman Robert Wentworth, secretary Russell Blakeslee, Marion Russo, and Tom Hinsch; (standing) committee member Leah Tanger, parade subcommittee chairman Glenda Murphy, and fund-raising subcommittee chairman Joyce Okonuk. The subcommittees were set up by the tercentennial committee to organize various activities. (Courtesy LHS.)

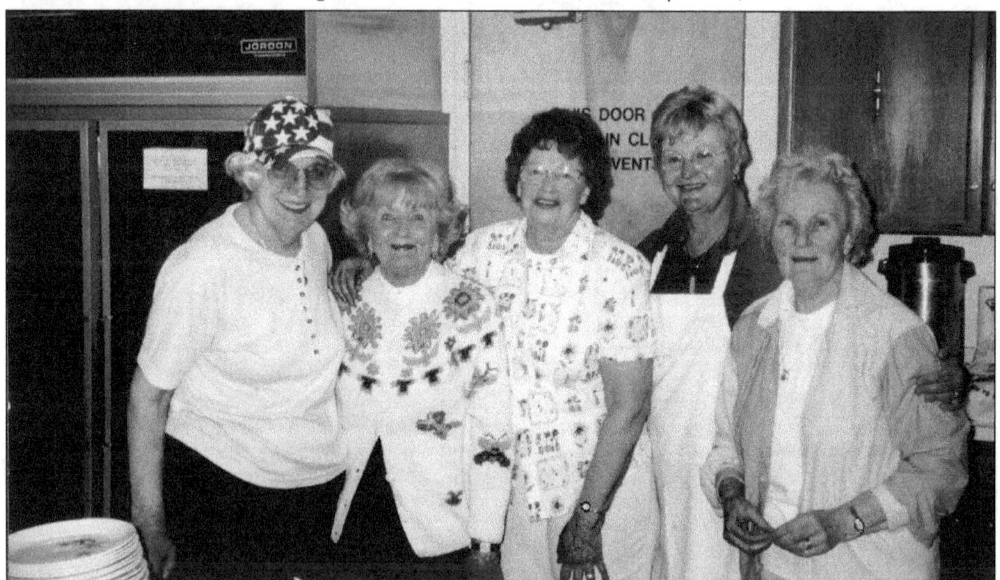

GOOD COOKS. The Commission on the Aging has been serving the needs of elderly residents since it was formed in 1976. Recently, the commission started a monthly luncheon and program for a large group of more active retirees dubbed the "Junior Seniors." Preparing one of the lunches, held at the fire safety complex, are, from left to right, Sylvia Ryan, Dee Kruppa, Priscilla Donnelly, Sandra Morin, and Evelyn Buckley. (Courtesy William Jahoda.)

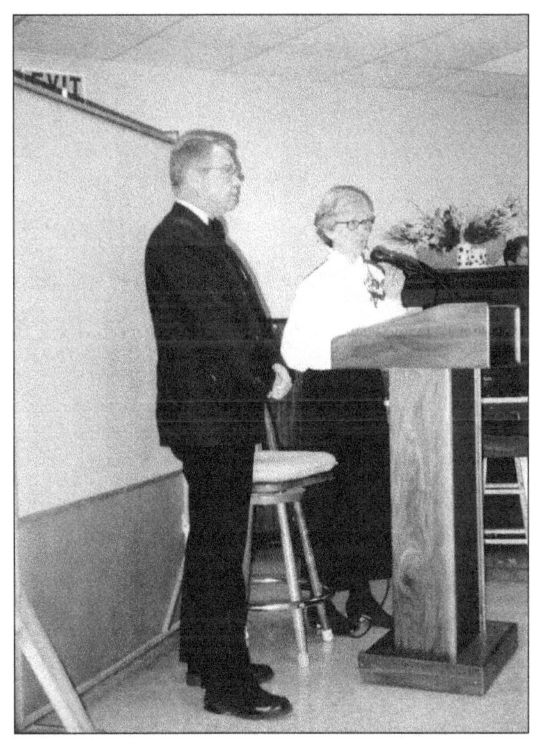

The Sound of Music. Alberta "Bertie" Hawkins is the founding director of the Lebanon Community Chorus, organized in 1972. A devoted volunteer, Bertie had built up the original 12-member group to one totaling more than 60 members when she retired in 1993. The chorus performs only occasionally now, when Bertie comes out of retirement to lead them for a special event. Cal Lord, program master of ceremonies, stands next to her. (Courtesy William Jahoda.)

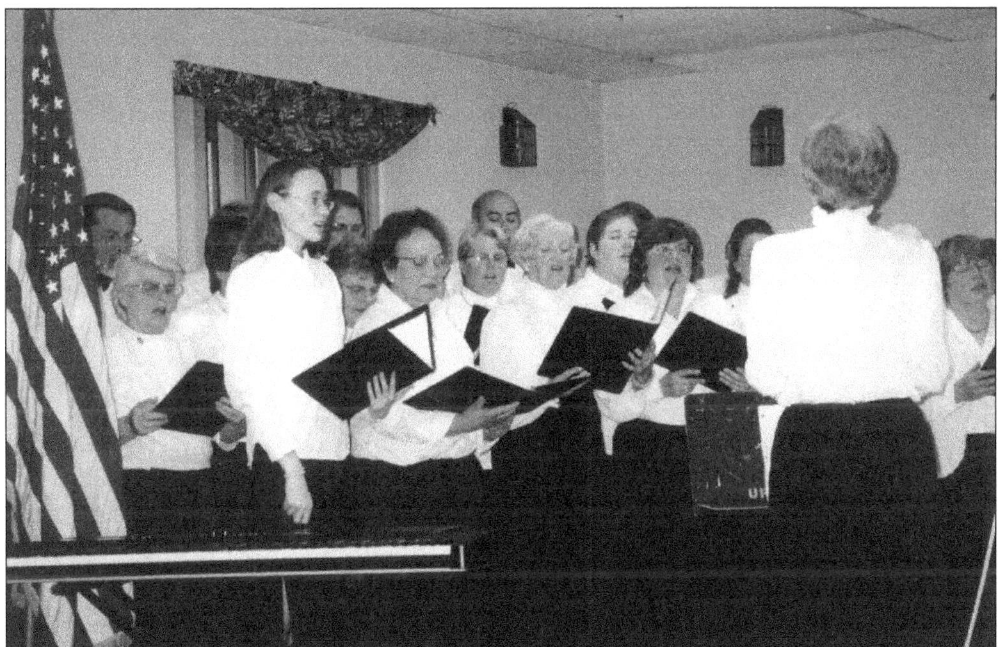

Performance Time. Members of the Lebanon Community Chorus reunited for a special performance at the historical society's 2003 annual meeting. Pictured in front are, from left to right, Gretchen Lathrop, Jacquie Proulx, Rose Miller, Jean Souter, Ellen Gillon, and Dot Davis (at the far right). The chorus was known for its professional performances of sacred and secular music. (Courtesy William Jahoda.)

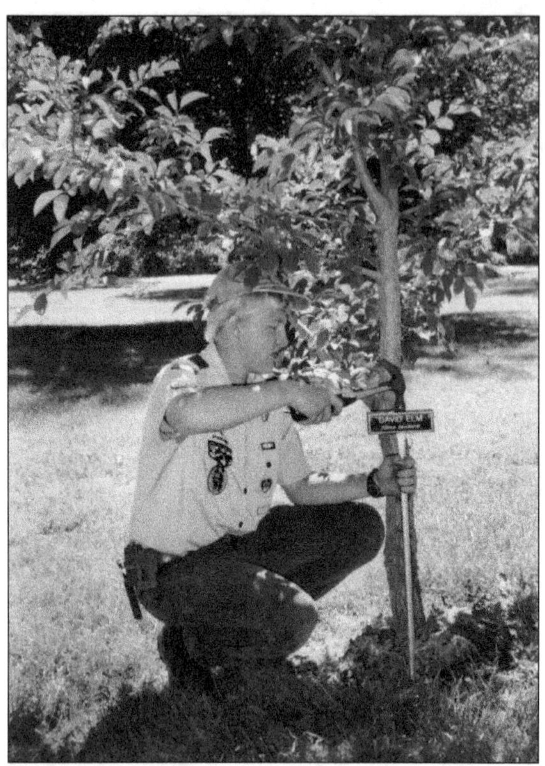

An Eagle Scout Project. For his 2000 Eagle Scout project, Rob Miles worked with mentor Dr. William J. Jahoda to make identification signs for trees around the town green. The David elm, planted by Dr. Jahoda in 1999, is resistant to Dutch elm disease, which devastated the American elm. It is the first one planted in Connecticut. Dr. Jahoda is raising more seedlings for distribution around town. (Courtesy William Jahoda.)

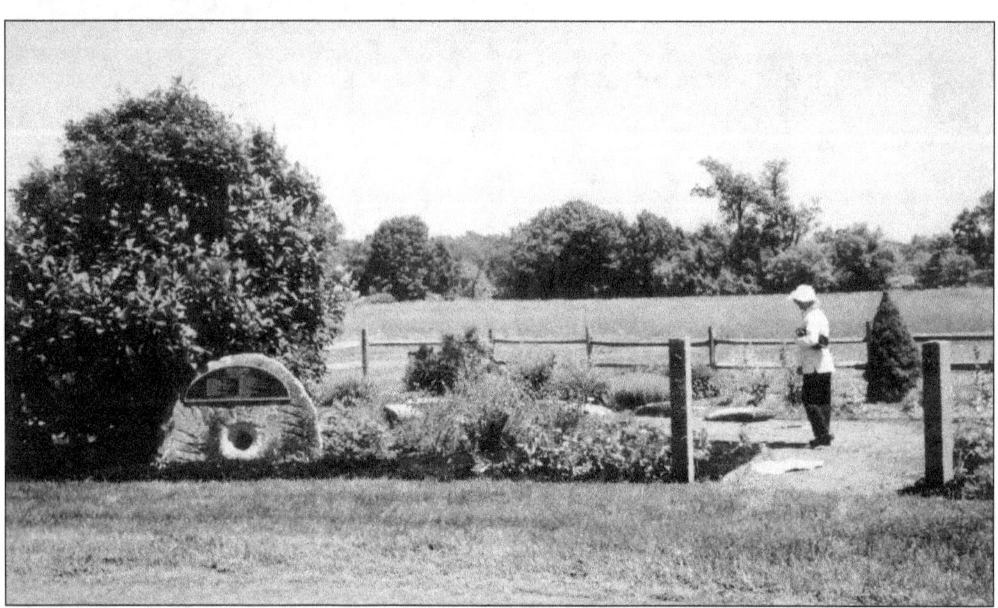

The Heritage Garden. Marge Jahoda wanders through the Heritage Garden, created by the Lebanon Garden Club on the grounds of the Jonathan Trumbull Jr. House, the town-owned museum. Beginning in 1998, club members designed and planted a three-section garden displaying various types of plants from the Colonial, Victorian, and contemporary periods. Every spring, the club beautifies the town center with annual plants around public buildings. (Courtesy William Jahoda.)

www.ingramcontent.com/pod-product-compliance
Lightning Source LLC
LaVergne TN
LVHW081546100826
845153LV00004B/323